100 GREAT WELSHMEN

– EMINENT BRITONS VOLUME 1 –

Terry Breverton

Wales Books
Glyndŵr Publishing
2001
ISBN 1-9903529-03-4

Terry Breverton studied in the universities of Manchester, Birmingham and Lancaster, has had a career in international management consultancy, and has been a board level director of multinational companies. Upon returning to live in Wales, and take up a post in academia, he founded Wales Books (Glyndŵr Publishing), to counter-balance existing material upon Wales, and to promote Welsh heritage and culture to the Welsh people and potential tourists. He is also the chairman of www.cysgod.com, a web-based organisation initially set up as a part of www.walesbooks.com The purposes of Cysgod are two-fold: to link Welsh societies across the globe; and to encourage further research and publications upon 'forgotten' Welshmen such as Dr Richard Price and Owain Llawgoch. It is hoped that such work will also rehabilitate Iolo Morganwg in the eyes of academics and force them to reassess history from original sources, rather than from the opinion of their teachers' teachers.

Breverton has in the past published research papers upon multinational tax avoidance, children's books and is the author of the acclaimed 'An A-Z of Wales and the Welsh', 'The Secret Vale of Glamorgan' and 'The Book of Welsh Saints', all published in 2000. This present volume will be followed by a book upon '100 Great Welsh Women' later in 2001, and there will be future volumes upon other 'Great Welshmen' published in 2002. Unlike most other books published upon Wales and the Welsh, this book has received neither Arts Council nor lottery funding. It has, like all other Wales Books publications, been priced to break even and to cover the costs of publishing more books upon Wales. Forthcoming publications are detailed in the back of this book. We welcome submissions of manuscripts, by which method we will be publishing both a rational reassessment of Prince Madoc, and a life of the great warrior Owain Llawgoch in 2002.

Also by Terry Breverton:

An A-Z of Wales and the Welsh (publisher Christopher Davies 2000)
300pp ISBN 0 715407 341

The Secret Vale of Glamorgan (publisher Wales Books 2000)
228pp, illustrated 1 903529 00

The Book of Welsh Saints (publisher Wales Books 2000)
614pp hardback, illustrated ISBN 1 903529 018

Also published by Wales Books (Glyndŵr Publishing)

The Dragon Entertains - 100 Welsh Stars, by Alan Roderick 2000
ISBN 1 903529 026

For Alexander Lewis Breverton

Copyright 2001 Terry Breverton

Published in 2001 by Wales Books (Glyndŵr Publishing),
Porth Glyndŵr, Sain Tathan, Bro Morgannwg CF62 4LW
www.walesbooks.com

ISBN 1 903529 034

Front cover: *Dylan Thomas' bedroom in Swansea.*
Back cover: *R. S. Thomas.*

Both photographs by Bernard Mitchell
(available from bernardmitchell@supanet.com or Tel: 01974 831366)

Printed and bound in Wales by
J & P Davison, 3 James Place,
Trefforest, Pontypridd

CONTENTS

APPENDICES

100 GREAT WELSHMEN

Eminent Britons Part I

INTRODUCTION

'The scrupulous and the just, the noble, humane, and devoted natures; the unselfish and the intelligent may begin a movement – but it passes away from them. They are not the leaders of a revolution. They are its victims.' Joseph Conrad 'Under Western Eyes' 1911

There is an inherent danger in nationalism, but only when used by politicians and proponents of military force. However, nationalism, in the sense of patriotism, must be encouraged across Wales, as it is losing the knowledge of its past. Nationalism is about showing the English Government, the government of the south-east of Britain, that Cymru has not yet been killed, that the British people and its culture, language, heritage and history, is not extinct. It has survived every attempt to kill it as the premier nation of the British Isles since the Germanic invasions of the 6th century and since the Act of Union of 1573. The spirit of Cymru still lives, but is in as critical condition as its economy. The problem is that the British people do not realise that to be British is to be Cymraeg. Cymru needs desperately to re-find itself. It has always been a nation of literacy, poetry, pacifism and socialism, with a deep undercurrent of Christianity, in the sense of brotherhood and antagonism to violence. This book is meant to be the start of a series on the British men and women who have featured in history, and hopefully shows how important Wales and its people have been in the development of the modern world. Readers may note that the country has massively influenced the course of American, and therefore, world history. The Christian, pacifist nature of the British-Welsh shines through the pages of this and successive books. The country has no known record of torture, nor of aggression against other nations except in defence of its remnant of Britain.

One entry has not been fully written by the author. The appendix entry on Llywelyn the Last is by Anthony Edwards, a man who has spent a great part of his life digging for the truth behind the treachery that led to Llywelyn ap Gruffudd's murder and the consequent genocide of his forces (-there were no English casualties noted against at least 3000 Welsh deaths). The rumours of widespread killings after these events has enabled me to add in that most famous Hungarian poem, 'The Massacre of the Bards'. Work by Bryan Davies upon Owain Llawgoch is also of major importance to this volume. Owain's assassination on the orders of the

English king affected the line of succession in Wales, and ultimately led to Henry Tudor taking the English crown. It is hoped that as many Welsh people as possible visit Mortagne-sur-Gironde in August 2003 to see the unveiling of his monument there, and partake in the celebrations. The line of of the last Prince of Wales and Gwynedd may still exist in France. There is also a relevant appendix entry upon the coal-miner, a strong poem entitled 'Chalice', by David Jervis. Ted Hughes called this unknown poem 'a fascinating assemblage'.

This book is not meant as an academic tome, as its purpose is to show tourists the type of people the Welsh are, and also to tell the Welsh themselves what they are not taught in schools. They may know about Dr Livingstone, but not about Stanley; about Shakespeare but not about Dafydd ap Gwilym; about Tony Blair but not about David Lloyd George; about the illiterate butcher Edward 1 but not Owain Glyndŵr, and so on, ad infinitum. Again, apologies to anyone whose 'hero' (or favourite 'villain') is not included on this first listing of great Welshmen - this is, like my 'A-Z', an eclectic listing based on the knowledge of someone who spent his years between 18 and 50 living outside Wales. Like 'The Book of Welsh Saints', this publication is part of an ongoing attempt by the author to promote Wales and its people, in the face of the continuous onslaught of Anglicisation by settlement and the media. The utter ineptitude of Welsh political organisations, placemen quangos and a remote, uncaring London government, over the last five decades, has depressingly failed to secure a reasonable future for Wales. There are no prospects for its young people, the best of whom are forced to emigrate for work, with no sign of any change in this scenario. Wales is the most under-privileged region of the British Isles, and one of the most economically-depressed in the European Union. There is no economic regeneration, yet the city of Liverpool (population 700,000) will eventually have received more Objective One Funding than the whole of Wales (population 3,000,000). When Eastern Europe joins the EU, even that potential source of funding will dry up. The future is not bleak, but black, for one of the countries which has contributed most to civilisation in the true (non-violent) sense of the word. The corruption of authority and the abuse of power has seemingly affected Wales more than any other part of the UK economy, itself in relative terminal decline. More money is spent on 'defence' of this tiny set of islands by the British government than upon education - one of the greatest PR con-tricks of all time was the decision by the Ministry of War to rename itself the Ministry of Defence. Military expenditure has very little place in the modern world - it appears that no London government realises that no-one wishes to invade Britain. And with all this spending, it cannot even halt the war in Ireland.

The author was extremely tempted to add Elvis Presley to this first book, because of the massive international publicity engendered by the author's 'An A-Z of Wales and the Welsh', and 'The Book of Welsh Saints'. (Publicity often seems easier to achieve overseas than in the foreign-owned Welsh media.) Likewise, Tennessee Williams, Howard Hughes, Jerry Lee Lewis, Hank Williams, Daniel Boone and Harold Lloyd could probably be included to increase American sales. However, I hope that the following personalities, all of Welsh stock, stimulate further research and books upon them. Hopefully, another three books in the series of eminent Britons will follow soon, and suggestions for inclusion will be most welcome.

As this book, like all others from Wales Books (Glyndŵr Publishing), receives no financial support from the various subsidising authorities, it is easy for the author/publisher to comment upon the deep discontent felt by many Welshmen today. The story of Wales is one of continuous external aggression for the last two-thousand years, of constant denigration by those who know nothing of its past, of the systematic stripping of its resources, of the non-representation of its people, and of a cultural settlement into England's oldest colony. Wales needs a 'great Welshman' today, to lead the country out of its past, to stimulate investment in real work, not in 'inward investment' part-time assembly jobs or in the tyranny of short-term 'call centres'. Wales deserves better from its decision-makers, but they will have to realise that the lack of any ethics of the 'free market-place' means that right-wing demagogic free-tradery has no place in Wales' future prospects. The problem is that politicians do not understand economics - and neither do their economic advisers. Just like academics teaching business, less than one in a hundred has ever had any type of position in the business community.

More publications from Wales Books (Glyndŵr Publishing) will be featured on our website www.walesbooks.com. As mentioned, we have also founded cysgod.com, a shelter organisation to stimulate new research upon Wales, its heroes and its land, and to link Welsh societies across the world. One of the joys of independent publishing is that Wales Books is free from the constraints of political correctness, as it receives funding from nowhere. Thus we can act as a counter-balance to those who state categorically that Iolo Morganwg was a forger. We believe that he was a truly great man (see the author's 'The Secret Vale of Glamorgan' for more details) and would welcome publishing more research on his mass of writings. A 'fraudster' would surely have claimed Arthur for his beloved Glamorgan and Gwent. Similarly Lloyd George has been pilloried over the years, but he was possibly the outstanding world statesman of the 20th century. John Charles should surely have been knighted - a player to stand alongside or above Pele. We believe that the Madoc legend contains far more than a germ of truth in it. The stories were denigrated, one reason being that the Mandan Indians called a bird a 'pen-gwyn' or 'white head'. Critics asked whoever heard of penguins in North America, but the bird the Indians were referring to is America's emblem, the bald eagle, with its distinctive white head. We think that there may be descendants of the great warlord Owain Llawgoch still alive in France, so that the royal House of Gwynedd may still be extant, despite the exterminatory efforts of the English crown. This would give us a real Prince of Wales, not someone whose real name is Charles Albert Glucksburg-Sonderburg-Schelswig-Holstein-Saxe-Coburg-Gotha, and who has absolutely no interest in the nation. The man is not the Prince of Wales and should drop the title, which was never given by the Welsh people, but announced by a French king for his son, after the murder of the last true Prince of Wales, Llywelyn ap Gruffydd. These comments may offend some people, but every British person reading this book has more genealogical right to the English throne than the present incumbents. We tend to accept people in positions of authority unthinkingly - the problem is that most of those people in power are also unthinking and unworthy, as well as uncaring.

This is a nationalist book by a nationalist book company, but nationalist in the interest of truth rather than revenge; in the interest of research rather than the acceptance of adulterated histories; and in the interest of educative literacy rather than popularity with the 'crachach', Welsh media, critics and politicians. We want people not just to be proud of Wales, but to know why they should feel pride. Pride without knowledge is jingoism. Hopefully, when true Welshmen read this publication, they will want to help put something back into Wales - help with the process of rediscovering our hidden past and safeguarding our future. This is crucially important for our country. If nationalism dies, we have nothing left, and the paradigm of what has happened to the national game in its national stadium will haunt future generations. We can see what is happening to Wales if we attend a rugby match like Wales-Samoa or Wales-USA - the concept of national difference is crumbling before our eyes - we are not turning European, but English. Painting one's face red, Mexican-waving, interminably singing 'oggy-oggy-oggy' and waving madly at the TV cameras is not being Welsh - it is not knowing what Cymru is or what it means to be Cymraeg. A nation cannot exist without knowledge and renewal - it will otherwise fade away - we owe it to these '100 Great Welshmen' to build upon their achievement. Cymru am Byth!

100 GREAT WELSHMEN

EMINENT BRITONS VOLUME 1

PRESIDENT JOHN ADAMS   October 30 1735 - July 4 1826
'FIRST OCCUPANT OF THE WHITE HOUSE'

Penybanc farm, near Llanboidy in Carmarthenshire, is the ancestral home of the second and sixth Presidents of the United States, John Adams and his son, giving Wales *five of the USA's first six Presidents.* (America has had eleven Presidents of Welsh origin, including the two Adams, the two Harrisons, Monroe, Jefferson, Madison, Lincoln, Garfield and Coolidge). In 1422, John Adams of Buck's Poole in Pembroke was born, and he married the only daughter of Mr John, a yeoman

John Adams

farmer who owned Penybanc Farm. John Adams took over the farm, and of his three sons, two joined the forces of Rhys ap Thomas. Rhys ap Thomas' support was crucial in the march across Wales of Henry VII to fight Richard III at Bosworth Field. The young men never returned, so they either died at Bosworth, or followed Henry to London to serve the Tudors. Of the line of the remaining son, David Adams went to Queen Elizabeth Grammar School in Carmarthen, was ordained in 1661 by the Archbishop of St David's, and emigrated to America in 1675. Two generations later, John Adams was born.

John Adams (second President 1797-1801) had been a member of the Continental Congress and signed the Declaration of Independence, during which he was *'the colossus of the debate'.* He proposed Washington as commander-in-chief of the armed forces. In 1779 he went to France and negotiated the treaty with England which ended the American War of Independence.

A letter by John Adams was sold in 1999 at Sotheby's for £400,000, a sum only exceeded in a manuscript valuation, by letters from the presidents Lincoln and Washington. Written just three days before the signing of the Declaration of Independence, it foretold the bloodshed which would accompany the break with Britain. He wrote to Archibald Bullock of Georgia *'The object is great which We have in our View, and We must expect a great expense of blood to obtain it. But We Should always remember that a free Constitution of civil Government cannot be purchased at too dear a rate as there is nothing, on this side (of) the New Jerusalem, of equal importance to mankind.'* With Jefferson and three others, he was part of the committee that had drafted the Declaration. In the three-page letter, Adams said that the deliberations of Congress on the declaration would be the greatest debate of its life, and added *'May Heaven help the new-born Republic, and make it more glorious than any former Republics have been.'* The letter was signed July 1st, and after intensive debate, the Declaration of Independence was ratified on July 4th, 1776, breaking the original 13 colonies away from Great Britain, and ensuring the American Revolution.

Even more remarkable as a political philosopher than as a politician, he noted that *'People and nations are forged in the fires of adversity.'* Born in the colony at Massachusetts Bay, like his cousin Samuel Adams, he was educated as a lawyer at Harvard, and soon became identified with the patriot cause. In 1758 John Adams began to practise as a lawyer, after teaching at school for a short time. In 1765 the English Government passed the Stamp Act, a tax on documents, newspapers, licences, insurance policies and even playing cards. Adams wrote important articles against the Act in the Boston Gazette. He was now established as a political thinker, an opponent of England's colonial policies and as a champion of individual liberties. Adams moved to Boston in 1768 to become a leading attorney there. He led in the movement for independence, being a delegate to the First and Second Continental Congresses. During the Revolution, he served in France and Holland in diplomatic roles, helping to negotiate the final peace treaty with England. In 1778 he was in Paris helping Benjamin Franklin to strengthen ties with France and other European nations. In 1780 Adams wrote the Massachusetts Bill of Rights, and in 1782 with Benjamin Franklin arranged a peace treaty with France.

From 1785 to 1788 he was the first American Minister to the Court of St James, in effect America's first ambassador to England, before returning to be elected as Vice-President under George Washington in 1789. However, like many later able vice-presidents, he felt that there was not enough in the job for his capabilities and complained to his wife, Abigail, *'My country has in its wisdom contrived for me the most insignificant office that ever the invention of man contrived or his imagination conceived.'* Probably as a result, Adams never attended any of Washington's birthday celebrations when he succeeded him as President, 1797-1801.

Adams just edged out Thomas Jefferson, the leader of the Democratic-Republicans, in the 1796 election for President. According to the law of the time, Jefferson became his vice-president, although belonging to a different party to Adams' Federalists. England and France were at war, and under Adams, the USA stayed neutral.

However, Adams' new administration had major problems with France, which refused to receive its envoy, and suspended commercial relations. He sent three commissioners there, but Talleyrand refused to negotiate with them unless they made a $10 million loan and paid a huge bribe of $250,000. (This was known as the XYZ Affair). Adams reported this to Congress, and he and his Federalist party became hugely popular for their honesty and openness. Congress gave money for three new frigates and authorised the training of a provisional army. Adams did not formally declare war, but built up a navy capable of clearing French privateers out of American sea-lanes. He created the US Navy Department in 1798, to discourage French pirates in the West Indies and Moorish privateers along the Barbary Coast of Africa. Also in 1798 the USA stopped all French trade after the seizure of the Retaliation, an American schooner, off Guadaloupe. The French did not have the financial strength for war, and long negotiations eventually brought peace in 1800, and free traffic for American merchant ships. The bloody but undeclared war also saw the formation of the US Marines, and the passing of the Sedition and Naturalisation Acts, both of which are still in force today. However, Adams' peace treaty infuriated the mass of Americans, and divided his Federalist party, leaving Thomas Jefferson to squeeze in at the 1800 election with a small majority.

Just before the election, on November 1st, 1800, Adams took up residence in the unfinished White House, still littered with debris. It was then known as the President's House, and later as The President's Palace. Not until Teddy Roosevelt was president was the name 'White House' used officially for the building. (Adams had been unexpectedly and unofficially beaten as 'first occupant' by the Welsh-American Secretary of State, John Marshall. He needed a temporary place to stay in the new capital city of Washington, rising by the Potomac River in the summer 1800). On Adam's second evening in its damp, unfinished rooms, he wrote to his wife Abigail *'Before I end my letter, I pray to Heaven to bestow the best of Blessings on this House and all that shall hereafter inhabit it. May none but honest and wise Men ever rule under this roof.'* In early December Abigail joined Adams, with just six rooms available, all in poor condition. She hung out the presidential laundry in the *'large unfinished room'*, the future East Room. John Adams retired to his farm in Braintree (now Quincy) in Massachusetts on March 4th, 1801, and wrote almost weekly to his fellow-Welshman Thomas Jefferson. His last words were *'Thomas Jefferson survives'*, not knowing that his great friend had died at Monticello just a few hours earlier. In 1818, Adams wrote: *'The Revolution was effected before the war commenced. The Revolution was in the hearts and minds of the people'*.

Adams and Jefferson were the only two presidents to sign the Declaration of Independence, and they both died on its 50th anniversary, July 4th, 1826. Adams, a man of poor health throughout his life, lived for 90 years and 247 days, longer than any other President. (His son lived to 80, and his cousin Samuel to 82). This remarkable man contributed greatly to the formation of the USA both during the American Revolution and in its formative years.

PRESIDENT JOHN QUINCY ADAMS July 11 1767 - February 23 1848
'THE DIPLOMAT PRESIDENT'

The son of President John Adams and Abigail Smith, John Quincy Adams was born on the family farm at Braintree (Quincy) Massachusetts. Until the recent accession of George W. Bush (by a minority popular vote), Adams was the only son of a President to become President, and indeed his mother had told him that *'one day the state would rest upon your shoulders'*. His lifetime consisted of two notable careers, separated by *'a strange interlude'*. The first career was as a superb diplomat who rose to become Secretary of State, the second as a member of the House of Representatives and an opponent of slavery. The strange interlude was the Presidency.

During the years of the Revolution, Adams was primarily taught by his gifted and distinguished parents, and accompanied his father on diplomatic missions to

Europe, from the age of ten onwards. A 1774 letter from little 'Johnny' to his father at the Continental Congress of Philadelphia, written when he was just 7 years old, survives: '*Mamma says you will accept my endeavours to write and that my duty to you may be expressed in poor writing as well as good. I hope that I will grow a better boy and that you will have no occasion to be ashamed of me when you return...We all long to see you. I am sir, your dutiful son.*' John Quincy learned fluent French in Paris and later studied at the University of Leiden. In 1782-83, he acted as an interpreter and secretary on a diplomatic mission to the Russian Court at St Petersburg (French was the language of court), returning to Holland via Scandinavia and Hanover. Educated in classical languages, history and mathematics, he returned to America in 1785 and graduated from Harvard in 1767, studied law at Newburyport, Massachusetts, then began practising law at Boston in 1790. Adams defended George Washington's policy of neutrality towards France, in a series of articles in Boston newspapers, and was rewarded with the appointment of Ambassador to Holland, 1793-1797. He spoke Dutch fluently.

Adams then became Minister to Berlin from 1797-1801, also working on diplomatic missions to England. Upon John Adams' ascendancy to the Presidency in 1801, he relieved his son of the German post, and John Quincy Adams returned to practise law once again in Boston. By 1803 he had been elected as a Federalist to the Senate, but incurred the enmity of his fellow party members by voting for Thomas Jefferson's embargo bill. He was also the only Federalist to back Jefferson's bill to purchase the Louisiana Territory from France. He knew that it would weaken the voting power of New England but strengthen the infant USA incredibly. His peeved party colleagues recalled the independent-thinking Adams from the Senate, by nominating his successor two years early.

However, John Quincy Adams was now also Boyleston Professor of Oratory and Rhetoric at Harvard from 1806-1809, and also practising law, when President James Madison appointed him to the crucial post of First Minister of the United States to Russia. At the court of Czar Alexander I, Adams reported on Napoleon's movements across Europe and upon the invasion of Russia. Also, in 1812 war broke out between the USA and England. Czar Alexander tried to arrange peace between the two countries, but not until his friend Adams was called to the Ghent negotiations was there any progress towards a treaty. John Quincy Adams then became Minister of the United States to England from 1809-1814. Thus he had served as Ambassador to Holland, and also to the super-powers of Germany, Russia and England over a 20-year period. Only France, the country he

John Quincy Adams

probably knew best, was 'missing' from his portfolio. President James Monroe (like former President Madison, also of Welsh ancestry) called Adams back home as Secretary of State in 1817, a post he held for both of Monroe's administrations, until 1825. '*More than any other man he helped to crystallise and perfect the foundations of American foreign policy, including the Monroe Doctrine, which, however, appropriately bears the name of the president who assumed responsibility for it and proclaimed it to the world.*' As mentioned, Adams had previously negotiated the famous Treaty of Ghent, to end the War of 1812 between England and America. This treaty had warned off any further European colonisation in the Western Hemisphere, in return for US non-interference in Europe. He was the real author of this 'Monroe Doctrine', which has been a recurring strategic theme in American policy ever since.

His greatest diplomatic triumph in this time was the Transcontinental Treaty with Spain, signed in 1819 and ratified in 1821. Taking advantage of Andrew Jackson's military incursions into Florida, and of Spanish weakness in dealing with revolutions in its South American colonies, a new frontier line was drawn from the Gulf of Mexico along the 42 degree parallel to the Pacific Ocean. (Adams was the only member of Monroe's cabinet who backed Jackson in the First Seminole War, and it was he who persuaded Monroe to push for acquiring Florida from Spain.) This treaty has been called *'the greatest diplomatic victory ever won by a single individual in the history of the United States.'* Thus Welshmen were responsible for peaceably taking both Spanish and French territories for the new country of America, as Jefferson (q.v.) had bought the vast French possessions. At this same time, Secretary of State Adams was defending the north-east frontier line against proposed British changes, holding the line at 49 degrees in Oregon. He was almost definitely the greatest Secretary of State in American history, helped by his accumulated experience of diplomacy across Europe and Russia.

Adams was inaugurated as sixth President from on March 4th, 1825, serving until 1829. He was a minority President, chosen by the House of Representatives. In 1824 there had been an inconclusive contest, with Jackson and Crawford leading. Another candidate, Henry Clay, a former opponent of Adams, suddenly threw his support behind him, and this *'corrupt bargain'* gave Clay the Secretary of State's post under President Adams, with the supposition that he became Adams' natural successor.

Adams' inaugural address included the words *'Knowing that "except the Lord keep the city, the watchman waketh but in vain", with fervent supplications for His favour, to His over-ruling providence I commit, with humble, but fearless confidence, my own fate, and the future destinies of my country.'*

'The Encyclopaedia Americana' calls John Quincy Adams *'a President too far in advance of his times. The loose democracy of his day wanted the least government possible. And the South feared that his programme of national power for internal improvements, physical and moral, under a consolidated federal government might pave the way for the abolition of slavery.'* Adams believed that freedom had been won, and it was his duty to exert national power to make that freedom more fruitful for the people. He wanted strong national policies under the President's executive leadership: the Bank of the United States as an instrument of the national fiscal authority; a national tariff to protect domestic industries; national administration of public lands for their controlled and methodical disposal and settlement; a broad programme of national physical improvements to roads, canals and railways; national direction in education, and the development of science. However, this was alienating all those in economic power, and he had no real party to back him up. Andrew Jackson easily defeated Adams in the 1828 re-election campaign. Adams was guilty of appointing men of competence to office, sometimes political opponents, rather than politicians of influence. A man of unswerving principles and with a tremendous sense of duty to his nation and its people, he stands as an example to all current politicians.

A great orator, he was the only President elected to serve as a Congressman after his term of presidency. John Quincy Adams was elected in November 1830, for the Plymouth District of Massachusetts. He stated *'Not in my opinion would an ex-President of the United States be degraded by serving as a selectman of his town, if elevated thereto by the people.'* Again according to the Encyclopaedia Americana, he saw himself not as an ex-President, but as the *'representative of the whole nation. As a member of Congress the elderly Adams displayed the most spectacular phase of his life-long career in public service. He preached a strong nationalism against the states' rights and pro-slavery dialectics of John C. Calhoun'.* Adams wrote *'Individual liberty is individual power, and as the power of a community is a mass compounded of individual powers, the nation which enjoys the most freedom must necessarily be in proportion to its numbers the most powerful nation.'* In 1839 Adams tried to introduce Congress resolutions so that no-one could be born a slave after 1845. He said *'Slavery is the great and foul stain upon the North American Union, and it is a contemplation worthy of the most exalted soul whether its total abolition is or is not practicable.'*

Also as a Representative, Adams single-handedly fought and petitioned against the annexation of Texas as a slave state, the petition being signed by several women. When these women were rebuked by the Representative from Maryland for not attending properly to their domestic duties, Adams said *'Are women to have no opinions or actions on subjects relating to the general welfare? Where did the gentleman get this principle? Did he find it in the sacred history (the Bible) - in the language of Miriam the prophetess, in one of the noblest and most sublime songs of triumph that ever met the human eye or ear? Did the gentleman never hear of Deborah, to whom the children of Israel came up for judgement? Has he forgotten the deed of Jael, who slew the dreaded enemy of her country? Has he forgotten Esther, who by her petition saved her people and her country?* Unusually pro-feminist for the time, Adams also said *'Why does it follow that women are fitted for nothing but the cares of domestic life, for bearing children and cooking the food of the family? ... I say women exhibit the most exalted virtue when they depart from their domestic circle and enter on the concerns of their country, of humanity, and of their God!'*

Adams died in the Speaker's Room in Washington on in 1848, while serving his last term as representative. On his deathbed he murmured *'Independence forever!'* and his dying words were *'This is the last of earth. I am content.'*

FOOTNOTE:
Incidentally, the grandson of John Quincy Adams, and great-grandson of John Adams, was Henry Brooks Adams (1838-1918), the famous American man of letters and novelist. In 1807 he described the complexity of the *'multiverse'* of modern society, and the predicament of modern man in an increasingly technological world. Henry Adams was posthumously awarded the Pulitzer Prize for his autobiography that had been published in 1907. His brother Brooks Adams (1848-1927) was a noted geopolitical historian. Their father Charles Francis Adams (1807-1886), the son of John Quincy, was a diplomat and author and minister to Britain during Lincoln's presidency in The Civil War.

SAMUEL ADAMS September 27 1722 - October 2 1803
'FATHER OF THE AMERICAN REVOLUTION'

Samuel Adams may seem a name peripheral to history, but the author was sipping a pint of Samuel Adams draught porter at the Moultrie Tavern in Charleston, South Carolina a few years back. The heat was intense, there were pelicans diving in the harbour, parrots in the palm trees, flowering azalea and bougainvillaea everywhere, and I was drinking something suspiciously non-gassy and delicious like Brains Dark Ale from Cardiff. This excellent Boston beer had been named after Samuel Adams, the Welsh second cousin of John Adams, and **the chief instigator of The Boston Tea Party** in 1773. He had organised opposition to The Stamp Act in 1765, and organised the Non-Importation Association in 1798, and the Boston Committee of Correspondence in 1722. After the Tea Party he was a delegate to the International Congresses of 1774 and 1775, before being one of the signatories to The Declaration of Independence in 1776. Samuel Adams called the English '*a nation of shopkeepers*' long before Napoleon.

Thus the main flash-point in the independence of America, the Boston Tea Party, was caused by a Welshman. Both the duty imposed by the Sugar Act and the measures to enforce it caused consternation among New England merchants. They contended that payment of even the small duty imposed would be ruinous to their businesses. Merchants, legislatures and town meetings protested against the law, and colonial lawyers found in the preamble of the Sugar Act the first tendencies towards '*taxation without representation*', the slogan that was to draw many to the American cause against the mother country.

Adams was the son of a brewer, a cousin of John Adams, and was the great political leader of Boston. Boston was then a town of around 15,000 people, the most important urban conurbation in America, but was rapidly being overtaken by New York and Philadelphia. He graduated with a Master of Arts from Harvard in 1743, began to study law, then failed in business before turning full-time to political life. In 1765 Samuel Adams was chosen as 'Moderator' by the town meeting, and also as a delegate to Boston's General Court. He formed an alliance with Ebenezer Mackintosh, which became the famous '*Sons of Liberty*'. Under Adams' Puritan lead, Boston acquired a reputation for radicalism in the 1860's, with violent Stamp Act riots in 1766, where the perpetrators escaped prosecution.

In 1764, the English Parliament had enacted a Currency Act '*to prevent paper bills of credit hereafter issued in any of His Majesty's colonies from being made legal tender*'. Since the colonies were a deficit trade area and were constantly short of hard currency, this measure added a serious burden to the colonial economy. Equally objectionable from the colonial viewpoint was the Quartering Act, passed in 1765, which required colonies to provide royal troops with provisions and barracks. The last of the measures inaugurating the new colonial system sparked the greatest organised resistance. Known as the 'Stamp Act', it provided that revenue stamps be affixed to all newspapers, broadsides, pamphlets, licenses, leases or other legal documents, the revenue to be used for '*defending, protecting and securing*' the colonies. The Stamp Act hurt all people who did any kind of business. Thus it aroused the hostility of the most powerful and articulate groups in the American population: journalists, lawyers, clergymen, merchants and businessmen, North and South, East and West. Soon leading merchants across the Eastern seaboard organised for resistance and formed non-importation associations based upon Adams' example in Boston.

Trade with the mother country fell off sharply in the summer of 1765, as prominent men followed Adams' lead and organised themselves into the 'Sons of Liberty', secret organisations formed to protest against the Stamp Act, often through violent means. From Massachusetts to South Carolina, the act was nullified, and mobs, forcing luckless customs agents to resign their offices, destroyed the hated stamps. The British Parliament was unwilling to accept the colonial arguments. British merchants, however, feeling the effects of the American boycott, threw their weight behind a repeal movement, and in 1766 Parliament yielded, repealing the Stamp Act and modifying the Sugar Act. However, to mollify the supporters of central control over the colonies, Parliament followed these actions with passage of the Declaratory Act. This act asserted the authority of Parliament to make laws binding the colonies *'in all cases whatsoever'*.

The year 1767 brought another series of measures that the colonists hated. Charles Townshend, British Chancellor of the Exchequer, was called upon to draft a new fiscal program. Intent upon reducing British taxes by making more efficient the collection of duties levied on American trade, he tightened customs administration, at the same time sponsoring duties on colonial imports of paper, glass, lead and tea exported from Britain to the colonies. The so-called Townshend Acts were based on the premise that taxes imposed on goods imported by the colonies were legal while internal taxes (like the Stamp Act) were not.

The agitation following enactment of the Townshend duties was less violent than that stirred by the Stamp Act, but it was nevertheless strong, particularly in the cities of the Eastern seaboard. Merchants once again resorted to non-importation agreements, and people made do with local products. Colonists, for example, dressed in homespun clothing and found substitutes for tea. They used home-made paper and their houses went unpainted. In Boston, enforcement of the new regulations provoked violence. When customs officials sought to collect duties, they were set upon by the populace and roughly handled. For this infraction, two British regiments were sent to protect the customs commissioners. The presence of British troops in Boston was a standing invitation to disorder. On May 9, 1768, customs officials in Boston checked John Hancock's shop, the Liberty, which had just returned from Madeira. It reported in with just 25 pipes of wine (3150 gallons), far below its capacity, and it was discovered that the bulk of its cargo had been illicitly landed. The British warship Romney seized the ship for smuggling, and the Sons of Liberty rioted in Boston. Throughout 1769 and 1770 there were constant flare-ups between the 'redcoats' and the citizens of Boston. Adams, as the most influential member of the lower house of Massachusetts, drafted most of the colony's protest letters against the British, including the Circular Letter in 1768 against the Townshend Acts. From 1770, Adams was the focal point in the creation of inter-colonial committees of correspondence to sustain the spirit of resistance.

On March 5, 1770, antagonism between Boston citizens and British soldiers again flared into violence. What began as a harmless snowballing of British soldiers degenerated into a mob attack. Someone gave the order to fire. When the smoke had cleared, three Bostonians lay dead in the snow. Remembered as the *'Boston Massacre'*, the incident was dramatically propagandised by Adams' radicals as proof of British heartlessness and tyranny. Faced with such opposition, Parliament in 1770 opted for a strategic retreat and repealed all the Townshend duties except that on tea, which was a luxury item in the colonies, imbibed only by a very small minority. To most, the action of Parliament signified that the colonists had won a major concession, and the campaign against England was largely dropped. A colonial embargo on *'English tea'* continued but was not too scrupulously observed. Prosperity was increasing and most colonial leaders were willing to let the future take care of itself.

During a three-year interval of calm, a relatively small number of radicals strove energetically to keep the controversy alive, however. They contended that payment of the tax constituted an acceptance of the principle that Parliament had the right to rule over the colonies. They feared that at any time in the future, the principle of parliamentary rule might be applied with devastating effect on all colonial liberties. *The radicals' most effective leader was Samuel Adams,* who toiled tirelessly for a single end: independence. From the time he had graduated from Harvard College in 1740, Adams was a public servant in some capacity - inspector of chimneys, tax-collector and moderator of town meetings. A consistent failure in business, he was shrewd and able in politics, with the New England town meeting his theatre of action. Adams's goals were to free people from their awe of social and political superiors, make them aware of their own power and importance and thus arouse them to action. Toward these objectives, he published articles in newspapers and made speeches in town meetings, instigating resolutions that appealed to the colonists' democratic impulses.

In 1772 he induced the Boston town meeting to select a 'Committee of Correspondence' to state the rights and grievances of the colonists. The committee opposed a British decision to pay the salaries of judges from customs revenues; it feared that the judges would no longer be dependent on the legislature for their incomes and thus no longer accountable to it, thereby leading to the emergence of *'a despotic form of government'*. The committee communicated with other towns on this matter and requested them to draft replies. Committees were set up in virtually all the colonies, and out of them grew a base of effective revolutionary organisations. Still, Samuel Adams kept agitating for complete independence. President John Adams first coined the term *'working the*

Samuel Adams

political machine', and he believed that his cousin Sam was a master of this trade. Adams also described Samuel in action; *'Upon great occasions, when his deepest feelings were excited, nature seemed to erect him, without the smallest symbol of affectation, into an upright dignity of figure and gesture and gave a harmony to his voice which made a strong impression on spectators and auditors - the more lasting for the purity, correctness, and nervous elegance of his style.'* Samuel Adams plotted the Revolution with the young ship-owner John Hancock, who helped fund the Revolution with Welshman Francis Lewis, and with silversmith Paul Revere, who helped unite the colonies with his midnight ride.

In 1773, Britain at last furnished Adams and his allies with an incendiary issue to ignite the Revolution. The East India Company, finding itself in critical financial straits, appealed to the British government, which granted it a monopoly on all tea exported to the colonies. The government also permitted the East India Company to supply retailers directly, bypassing colonial wholesalers who had previously sold it. After 1770, such a flourishing illegal trade existed that most of the tea consumed in America was of foreign origin and imported, illegally and duty-free. By selling its tea through its own agents at a price well under the customary one, the East India Company made smuggling unprofitable and threatened to eliminate the independent colonial merchants at the same time. Aroused not only by the loss of their tea trade but also by the monopolistic practice involved, colonial traders joined Adams' radicals in agitating for independence.

In ports up and down the Atlantic coast, agents of the East India Company were forced to resign, and new shipments of tea were either returned to England or warehoused. In Boston, however, the agents defied the colonists and, with the support of the royal Governor Hutchinson, made preparations to land incoming cargoes regardless of opposition. Samuel Adams declared *'Fellow Countrymen, we cannot afford to give a single inch! If we retreat now, everything we have done becomes useless! If (Governor) Hutchinson will not send tea back to England, perhaps we can brew a pot of it especially for him!'* On that night of December 16, 1773, a band of 'Sons of Liberty' disguised as Naragansett (Mohawk) Indians, and led by Samuel Adams, boarded three British ships lying at anchor and dumped their 342 chests of tea cargo into Boston harbour. They took this step because they feared that if the tea were landed, colonists would actually comply with the tax and purchase the tea. Adams and his band of radicals doubted their countrymen's commitment to principle. A crisis now confronted Britain. The East India Company had carried out a parliamentary statute, and if the destruction of the tea went unpunished, Parliament would admit to the world that it had no control over the colonies. Governor Hutchinson of Massachusetts said *'This was the boldest stroke which had yet been struck in America....the body of people had gone too far to recede'.* The Prime Minister Lord North told King George III *'You will never meet with that proper obedience to the laws of this country until you have destroyed that next of locusts',* referring to Adams' followers in Boston. Official opinion in Britain almost unanimously condemned the Boston Tea Party as an act of vandalism and advocated legal measures to bring the insurgent colonists into line. Hutchinson described Samuel Adams as *'the greatest incendiary in the Empire'.* Adams himself confessed that *'Many persons wish, that as many dead Carcasses were floating in the Harbour as there are chests of Tea.'* Boston's actions were followed in other ports across the Eastern seaboard of America, unofficially destroying the East India Company's monopoly of trade with the colonies.

Parliament however responded with new laws in 1774 that the colonists called the *'Coercive or Intolerable Acts'.* The first, the Boston Port Bill, closed the port of Boston until the tea was paid for. This was an action that threatened the very life of the city, for to prevent Boston from having access to the sea meant economic disaster. Other acts restricted local authority and banned most town meetings held without the governor's consent. A Quartering Act required local authorities to find suitable quarters for British troops, in private homes if necessary. Instead of subduing and isolating Massachusetts as Parliament intended, these acts rallied its sister colonies to its aid. The Quebec Act, passed at nearly the same time, extended the boundaries of the province of Quebec and guaranteed the right of the French inhabitants to enjoy religious freedom and their own legal customs. The colonists opposed this act because, by disregarding old charter claims to western lands, it threatened to hem them in to the North and Northwest by a Roman Catholic-dominated province. Though the Quebec Act had not been passed as a punitive measure, it was classed by the Americans with the Coercive Acts, and all became known as the *'Five Intolerable Acts'*.

Colonial representatives met in Philadelphia on September 5, 1774, *'to consult upon the present unhappy state of the Colonies'*. Delegates to this meeting, known as the First Continental Congress, were chosen by provincial congresses or popular conventions. Every colony except Georgia sent at least one delegate, and the total number of 55 was large enough for diversity of opinion, but small enough for genuine debate and effective action. The division of opinion in the colonies posed a genuine dilemma for the delegates. They would have to give an appearance of firm unanimity to induce the British government to make concessions and, at the same time, they would have to avoid any show of radicalism or spirit of independence that would alarm more moderate Americans. A cautious keynote speech, followed by a *'resolve'* that no obedience was due the Coercive Acts, ended with adoption of a set of resolutions, among them, the right of the colonists to *'life, liberty and property'*, and the right of provincial legislatures to set *'all cases of taxation and internal polity'*. The most important action taken by the Congress, however, was the formation of a 'Continental Association', which provided for the renewal of the trade boycott and for a system of committees to inspect customs entries, publish the names of merchants who violated the agreements, confiscate their imports, and encourage frugality, economy and industry. Working closely with his cousin John Adams, Samuel's influence was crucial in rejecting a plan of union with England, and in boycotting English goods.

The Association immediately assumed the leadership in the colonies, spurring new local organisations to end what remained of royal authority. Led by the pro-independence leaders, they drew their support not only from the less well-to-do, but from many members of the professional class, especially lawyers, most of the planters of the Southern colonies and a number of merchants. They intimidated the hesitant into joining the popular movement and punished the hostile. They began the collection of military supplies and the mobilisation of troops. And they fanned public opinion into revolutionary ardour. Many Americans, opposed to British encroachment on American rights, nonetheless favoured discussion and compromise as the proper solution. This group included Crown-appointed officers, many Quakers and members of other religious sects opposed to the use of violence, many merchants, and some discontented farmers and frontiersmen from Southern colonies.

The king may have effected an alliance with these large numbers of moderates and, by timely concessions, so strengthened their position that the revolutionaries would have found it difficult to proceed with hostilities. But George III had no intention of making concessions. In September 1774, scorning a petition by Philadelphia Quakers, he wrote, *'The die is now cast, the Colonies must either submit or triumph.'* This action isolated the Loyalists, who were appalled and frightened by the course of events following the Coercive Acts.

General Thomas Gage commanded the garrison at Boston, where political activity had almost wholly replaced trade. Gage's main duty in the colonies had been to enforce the Coercive Acts. When news reached him that the Massachusetts colonists were collecting powder and military stores at the town of Concord, 32 kilometres away, Gage sent a strong detail from the garrison to confiscate these munitions. After a night of marching, the British troops reached the village of Lexington on April 19, 1775, and saw a grim band of 70 Minutemen (so named because they were said to be ready to fight in a minute) through the early morning mist. The Minutemen intended only a silent protest, but Major John Pitcairn, the leader of the British troops, yelled, *'Disperse, you damned rebels! You dogs, run!'* The leader of the Minutemen, Captain John Parker, told his troops not to fire unless fired at first. The Americans were withdrawing when someone fired a shot, which led the British troops to fire at the Minutemen. The British then charged with bayonets, leaving eight dead and 10 wounded. It was, in the words of Ralph Waldo Emerson, *'the shot heard 'round the world.'*

The British pushed on to Concord. The Americans had taken away most of the munitions, but the British destroyed whatever was left. In the meantime, American forces in the countryside mobilised, moved toward Concord and inflicted casualties on the British, who began the long return to Boston. All along the road, however, behind stone walls, hillocks and houses, militiamen from *'every Middlesex village and farm'* made targets of the bright red coats of the British soldiers. By the time the weary soldiers stumbled into Boston, they suffered more than 250 killed and wounded. The Americans lost 93 men. While the alarms of Lexington and Concord were still resounding, the Second Continental Congress met in Philadelphia, Pennsylvania, on May 10, 1775. By May 15, the **Congress voted to go to war**, inducting the colonial militias into continental service and appointing Colonel George Washington of Virginia as commander-in-chief of the American forces. In the meantime, the Americans would suffer high casualties at Bunker Hill just outside Boston. Congress also ordered American expeditions to march northward into Canada by fall. Although the Americans later captured Montreal, they failed in a winter assault on Quebec, and eventually retreated to New York.

Despite the outbreak of armed conflict, the idea of complete separation from England was still repugnant to some members of the Continental Congress. In July, John Dickinson had drafted a resolution, known as the Olive Branch Petition, begging the king to prevent further hostile actions until some sort of agreement could be worked out. The petition fell on deaf ears, however, and King George III issued a proclamation on August 23, 1775, declaring the colonies to be in a state of rebellion.

British warships continued down the coast to Charleston, South Carolina, and opened fire on the city in early June 1776. But South Carolinians had time to prepare, and repulsed the British by the end of the month. They would not return South for more than two years.

In January 1776, Thomas Paine, a political theorist and writer who had come to America from England in 1774, published a 50-page pamphlet, *Common Sense*. Within three months, 100,000 copies of the pamphlet were sold. Paine attacked the idea of hereditary monarchy, declaring that one honest man was worth more to society than *'all the crowned ruffians that ever lived'*. He presented the alternatives

-continued submission to a tyrannical king and an outworn government; or liberty and happiness as a self-sufficient, independent republic. Circulated throughout the colonies, *Common Sense* helped to crystallise the desire for separation.

There still remained the task, however, of gaining each colony's approval of a formal declaration. On May 10, 1776, a resolution was adopted calling for separation. Now only a formal declaration was needed. On June 7, Richard Henry Lee of Virginia introduced a resolution declaring *'That these United Colonies are, and of right ought to be, free and independent states...'* Immediately, a committee of five, headed by Thomas Jefferson of Virginia (q.v.), was appointed to prepare a formal declaration of independence for the Thirteen American colonies. Samuel Adams was a signatory, with other famous Welsh-Americans such as John Adams, Stephen Hopkins, William Williams, Francis Lewis, Lewis Morris, Robert Morris, Thomas Jefferson and Button Gwinnett. It may be that 18 of the 56 signatories were of Welsh stock.

Samuel Adams remained in the Continental Congress until 1781, helping draft the Articles of Confederation. After the Revolution his influence waned, although he was elected Lieutenant-Governor of Massachusetts 1789-1793, and elected Governor on the death of his friend John Hancock, serving from 1794-97. He retired in 1797, aged 75, and died aged 82 on October 2nd, 1803. In 1780 a publication in England by a Mr Galloway had reflected upon Adams' service to the former colonies: *'He eats little, drinks little, sleeps little, thinks much, and is most indefatigable in the pursuit of his object. It was this man, who by his superior application, managed at once the factions in the Congress at Philadelphia, and the factions of New England.'* More than any other man, Samuel Adams ignited the fire of American independence.

FOOTNOTE:
Upon November 17th, 1999, The Times reported 'The Dregs of the Boston Tea Party Found'. On the site of Griffin's Wharf, where the tea party ships were moored, has been found a section of wood, decorated with gold leaf and painted with an oil-based lacquer, which matches exactly the elaborate tea chests used in trade at the time. There may be more naturally-preserved artifacts preserved in the mud, of *'the most celebrated act of resistance before the American War of Independence.'*

YR ARGLWYDD RHYS 1132 - April 28 1197
THE LORD RHYS - RHYS AP GRUFFYDD AP RHYS AP TEWDWR

Gwenllian, sister of the great Owain Gwynedd (q.v.) and daughter of the warrior Gruffydd ap Cynan (q.v.), King of Gwynedd, was born in 1098, when Wales was under unceasing attack from the Normans. Owain Gwynedd had succeeded his father in leading the Welsh defence against the Marcher Lords, and Gwenllian married Gruffydd ap Rhys ap Tewdwr and lived in Dinefwr Castle, with her four sons, Morgan, Maelgwn, Mareddud and Rhys. On New Year's Day, 1136, her husband joined other Welsh forces in an attack upon the Norman invaders. Gruffydd ap Rhys was away in North Wales, trying to gain assistance from Gwenllian's father, Gruffydd ap Cynan. In his absence Maurice de Londres, the detested Norman Lord of Cydweli (Kidwelly) attacked the Welsh in South-West Wales. Gwenllian led the few defenders that were left in the area, although her youngest son, Rhys, was only four years old. Giraldus Cambrensis stated that *'she marched like the Queen of the Amazons and a second Penthesileia leading the army'*. In 1136, Gwenllian led her army against the Normans at Cydweli. A Norman army had landed in Glamorgan, and was marching to join the force of Maurice de Londres. Gwenllian stationed her rapidly assembled volunteers at the foot of Mynydd-y-Garreg, with the river Gwendraeth in front of her, and Cydweli Castle just two miles away. She sent some of her forces to delay the oncoming invasion force, but it evaded them and her remaining army was trapped between two Norman attacks.

One son, Morgan, was killed, another, Maelgwn, imprisoned, and towards the end of the fighting, Gwenllian ferch Gruffydd ap Cynan was captured and executed, over the body of her dead son. She had pleaded for mercy, but was beheaded upon de Londres' express order. The battlefield is still called Maes Gwenllian, a mile from the castle, and a stone marks the place of her death. She left an 8-year-old son Maredudd, and a 4-year-old son, Rhys ap Gruffudd, later to be known as The Lord Rhys. He was thus the grandson of Rhys ap Tewdwr who was slain by the Normans at Brycheiniog in 1093, and the nephew of the great Owain Gwynedd. Rhys ap Gruffydd's sister Nest married Ifor ap Meurig, the Welsh hero Ifor Bach who scaled the walls of Cardiff Castle to kidnap Earl William of Gloucester and regain his stolen lands. Against this troubled background, his father, Gruffydd, Prince of Deheubarth, also died within a year of Gwenllian in 1137. He had avenged his wife's death, defeating the Normans at the battle of Crug Mawr in 1136.

Leadership of the war against the invading Normans and Flemish settlers passed to the elder half-brothers of the infant Rhys, Anarawd and Cadell. In 1143,

Anarawd was treacherously murdered by his supposed ally, Cadwaladr of Gwynedd. Aged 13, we find Rhys and his elder full brother, Maredudd, fighting for their half-brother Cadell in 1146. Over the next decade, the kingdom of Deheubarth was bitterly reconstituted, with the expulsion of the de Clares from Ceredigion, and the Cliffords from Cantref Bychan and Llandovery. After defending the recently-captured Carmarthen Castle from a Norman counter-attack, the brothers also held off an attack by the men of Gwynedd on their weakened kingdom. In 1151 Cadell had been badly injured and left for dead by Norman knights and

Kidwelly Castle taken by Arglwydd Rhys
(photograph courtesy of WTB)

archers from Tenby while out hunting. He lingered on until 1175, being buried at Strata Florida, and Maredudd took over the kingship of Deheubarth from 1151. After Maredudd's early death, aged just 25, the 21-year-old Rhys took the throne. Already he had seen seventeen years of turbulence and death, which seems to have made him favour (given the choice) diplomatic negotiation rather than warfare.

The French King of England led another huge army into Wales, and the Welsh Chronicles state that Henry's intention was *'to exterminate all the Britons completely, so that the Brittanic name should never be remembered.'* However, Giraldus Cambrensis recorded an old Welshman telling Henry that Wales would never be conquered: *'No nation but this of the Welsh, not any other language, will answer for this corner of the earth on the Day of terrible Judgment before the almighty judge.'* Rhys reluctantly submitted to Henry II in 1158 (alsong with Owain Gwynedd and Malcolm IV of Scotland) to avoid more bloodshed across his shattered kingdom, ceding Ceredigion and much of Ystrad Tywi. As well as this act of homage, he was forced to give up the title of King of Deheubarth, and henceforth was known as 'The Lord Rhys'. When his kingdom was stronger, Rhys led a rising in 1164-65 to regain Ceredigion and Emlyn, taking the great castles of Cardigan and Cilgerran. From now until his death he retained this land, which stabilised Deheubarth as it had been on his accession in 1158. He also added parts of Dyfed after some of its Norman lords left to take part in the Irish Conquest. Around this time, Henry II was in disgrace following the murder of Thomas a'Beckett, and made friendly overtures to The Lord Rhys. He created Rhys Justice of South Wales, and from his main court at Dinefwr Castle he was the predominant magnate in Wales. A patron of religious orders, Whitland was under his protection, he took special care of Strata Florida and founded Talley Abbey.

The first authenticated eisteddfod was held in Cardigan Castle by The Lord Rhys, in 1176, but the present form of eisteddfod is an early nineteenth century recreation, thanks to Iolo Morgannwg. The mediaeval meeting of the bards called the Eisteddfod was revived as a means of attracting patronage for Welsh cultural activity. At first the competitions were confined to the traditional poetry composition (the strict Welsh form known as cynghanedd) and harp playing, but today choirs, bands, acting, recitation, fiction writing and painting can also be included. The 1176 date gives Wales the right to claim **the *oldest European festival,*** one with both poetic and political overtones.

Thomas Pennant described the eisteddfod of Lord Rhys: *'In 1176, the Lord Rhys, prince of South Wales, made a great feast at Christmas, on account of the finishing of his new castle at Aberteifi* (Cardigan), *of which he proclaimed notice through all Britain a year and a day before; great was the resort of strangers, who were nobly entertained, so that none departed unsatisfied. Among deeds of arms, and variety of spectacles, Rhys invited all the bards of Wales, and provided chairs for them, which were placed in his hall, where they sat and disputed and sang, to show their skill in their respective faculties: after which he bestowed great rewards and rich gifts on the victors. The bards of North Wales won the prizes; but the minstrels of Rhys's household excelled in their faculty. On this occasion the Brawdwr Llys, or judge of the court, an officer fifth in rank, declared aloud the victor, and he received from the bard, for his fee, a mighty drinking-horn, made of the horn of an ox, a golden ring, and the cushion on which he sat in his chair of dignity.'* Among the rivals for the bardic crown were Owain Cyfeiliog, Prince of Powys, and Hywel ap Owain Gwynedd, whose poems survive today. Hywel's more famous brother was Prince Madoc (q.v.), the legendary discoverer of America.

The last years of Yr Arglwydd Rhys were spent in dispute with some of his eight sons by Gwenllian ferch Madog ap Maredudd, and in fighting the Norman barons of Richard I, who did not care for Henry II's former special relationship with the Welshman. He was buried at St David's Cathedral, where his painted tomb effigy can be seen.

FOOTNOTES:

(i) In 2000 'The Sunday Times' ran an article upon the *'Richest of the Rich'* of the preceding millennium. Rhys ap Gruffyd, who made his fortune from *'land and war'* was rated 95th richest, with a fortune worth today £4.3 billion: *'Rhys was a marauding Welsh prince who lived - and prospered - by the sword. His*

Yr Arglwydd Rhys

military career began when he and his four brothers fought a long campaign to wrest much of their dominion of Deheubarth in southwest Wales back from Norman insurgency. By 1155 they had succeeded, but only at great cost, Rhys being the only one to survive the struggle. He extended his land in minor wars with rival Welsh nobles and later entered into an extraordinary alliance with his old enemy, Henry II, supporting the king's expedition to curb growing baronial power in Ireland in 1171. The deal made Rhys justiciar, effectively Henry's vice-roy, and established him as the predominant force in Wales. To cement his position, he bound himself to the most powerful local Anglo-Norman families through marriage and was probably responsible for the first compilation of Welsh law in book form....Rhys managed to hold onto most of his lands right up to his death, though in his final years rebellious sons challenged his authority and twice imprisoned him. Surprisingly for such a warlord, Rhys died peacefully and was worth about £5000. But over the years his territory was divided and re-divided among his ten sons and various nephews in often bloody struggles.'

(ii) From the medieval *'Book of Ystrad Fflur'*, written by the monks of Strata Florida Abbey, we find the following entries concerning the life of The Lord Rhys:

1136 In this year the lady Gwenllian died, (the mother of Rhys) brave as any of the sons of Gruffudd ap Cynan. And Morgan ab Owain slew Richard fitz Gilbert. And thereupon Owain and Cadwaladr, sons of Gruffudd ap Cynan, the splendour of all Britain and her defence and her strength and her freedom, held supremacy over all Wales and moved a mighty fierce host to Ceredigion. And they burned the castles of Aberystwyth, Dineirth and Caerwedros. Towards the close of the year they came again to Ceredigion with a numerous host and against them came Stephen, the constable, and all the Flemings and all the knights. And after fierce fighting Owain and Cadwaladr honourably won the victory at Crug Mawr. And the Normans and the Flemings returned home weak and despondent, having lost about 3000 men. And Geoffrey wrote the history of the kings of Britain.

1137 In this year died Gruffudd ap Rhys (the father of The Lord Rhys), the light of excellence and strength of South Wales. (Gruffudd ap Cynan also died) ... And for a third time the sons of Gruffudd ap Cynan came to Ceredigion and burned castles.

1156 In this year when Rhys ap Gruffudd heard that Owain, prince of Gwynedd, his uncle was coming with a great host to Ceredigion, he vigorously gathered a host and he came as far as Aberteifi (Cardigan) and there he raised a ditch to give battle.

1158 In this year after all the princes of Wales had made their peace with the king, Rhys on his own carried on war against the king. And after taking counsel of his leading men, and against his will he made peace with the king.

1159 In this year Rhys ap Gruffudd conquered the castles which the French had set up all over Dyfed. And then came the earl Reginald, son of King Henry, and a vast multitude of French and Saxons and Welsh with him. And without daring to attack Rhys where he was, they returned home after a bootless journey. And they offered Rhys a truce and he accepted it.

1163 In this year Henry, king of England, came to Deheubarth with a mighty host. And after Rhys ap Gruffudd had given him hostages, he returned again to England.

1164 In this year when Rhys ap Gruffudd saw that the king would not keep aught of his promise to him, he gained possession of all Ceredigion and inflicted repeated slaughters and despoilings upon the Flemings. And thereupon all the Welsh united together to throw off the rule of the French.

1165 In this year King Henry came to Oswestry, thinking to annihilate all Welshmen. And against him came Owain and Cadwaladr, sons of Gruffudd ap Cynan, and all the host of Gwynedd with them, and Rhys ap Gruffudd and with him the host of Deheubarth, and Owain Cyfeiliog and all the sons of Madog ap Maredudd and the host of all Powys with them, and the two sons of Madog ab Idnerth and their host. And both sides stayed in their tents until the king moved his host into Dyffryn Ceiriog and there he was defeated at Crogen. And in a rage he had the eyes of 22 hostages gouged out; and these included two sons of Owain ap Gruffudd (Owain Gwynedd) and two sons of Rhys. And Rhys took the castles of Cardigan and Cilgerran. And through the will of God and at the instigation of the Holy Spirit, and with the help of Rhys ap Gruffudd, a community of monks came to Ystrad Fflur...

1166 In this year the French and Flemings came to Cilgerran. And after many of them had been slain, they returned again empty-handed. And in this year Basingwerk was destroyed by Owain ap Gruffudd.

1167 In this year Owain and Cadwaladr and Rhys ap Gruffudd besieged and destroyed the castle of Rhuddlan.

1171 In this year Thomas, archbishop of Canterbury, a man of great piety and saintliness and righteousness, was slain by the counsel and at the instigation of Henry, king of England, before the altar of the Trinity in his own church in Canterbury. And Rhys ap Gruffudd forced Owain Cyfeiliog, his son-in-law, to submit to him, and took seven hostages from him. And Rhys made friends with the king (who had blinded two of his sons!) *and made peace with him.*

1172 In this year died Cadwaladr ap Gruffudd ap Cynan. And the king granted truce to Iorwerth ab Owain and his sons to come and discuss peace with him. And Owain ab Iorwerth was slain by the earl of Bristol's men. And after that Iorwerth and Hywel, his brother, placing no trust in the king, ravaged the lands around Gloucester and Hereford, pillaging and slaying without mercy. And the king left Rhys ap Gruffudd as justice on his behalf in all of Deheubarth and went to France.

1173 In this year many men and animals died, nor was it surprising: for there was born to Rhys a son by the daughter of Maredudd, his brother. And Iorwerth ab Owain took the castle of Caerleon by force.

1175...And Rhys ap Gruffudd took with him to the king's council at Gloucester all the princes of Wales who had incurred the king's displeasure. All those returned with Rhys, having obtained peace, to their own lands.

And immediately after that Seisyll ap Dyfnwal was slain through treachery in the castle of Abergafenni by Lord de Breos of Brecon. And along with him Geoffrey his son, and the best men of Gwent were slain. And the French made for Seisyll's court; and after seizing Gwladys, his wife, they slew Cadwaladr, his son. And from that day there befell a pitiful massacre in Gwent. And from that time forth, after treachery, none of the Welsh dared place trust in the French.

1176 In this year at Christmas Rhys ap Gruffudd, Yr Arglwydd Rhys, held court in splendour at Cardigan, in his castle. And he set two kinds of contest there: one between bards and poets, another between harpists and crowthers and pibgorn-players and various classes of music-craft. And he had two chairs set for the victors. And this was the second founding of the abbey at Cwm-hir.

1177... Rhys ap Gruffudd built the castle at Rhaeadr-Gwy.

1178 In this year the sons of Cynan waged war against Rhys ap Gruffudd.

1183 In this year died king Henry the Younger

1184...At Llansantffraid Rhys ap Gruffudd confined all his gifts to the community of Ystrad Fflur.

1186...Cadwaladr ap Rhys was slain in Dyfed

1187...Maelgwn ap Rhys, the shield and bulwark of Wales, ravaged the (Fleming-settled and Norman-held) *town of Tenby and burned it...the man who frequently slew the Flemings and who drove them to flight many a time.*

1188...Rhys ap Gruffudd accompanied Baldwin Archbishop of Canterbury, and Gerald of Wales as they preached the Crusade around Wales.

1189 In this year died Henry, king of England. And Rhys ap Gruffudd took the castles of St Clears and Abercorram and Llansteffan. And Maelgwn ap Rhys - a second Gawain - was seized and imprisoned by his father and his brother.

1190...Rhys ap Gruffudd built the castle of Cydweli and Gwenllian, daughter of Rhys, the flower and beauty of all Wales, died.

1191... Rhys ap Gruffudd took the castle of Nevern

1192 In this year Maelgwn ap Rhys escaped from the prison of the Lord of Brycheiniog. And Rhys ap Gruffudd took the castle of Llawhaden.

1193...And the warband of Melgwn ap Rhys manfully breached the castle of Ystrad Meurig. And Hywel Sais ap Rhys took Wizo's castle (Wiston) by treachery.

1194 In this year Rhys ap Gruffudd was seized by his sons and imprisoned; but Hywel Sais deceived Maelgwn and released his father from prison. And the sons of Cadwallon burned the castle of Rhaeadr-Gwy.

1195...the two sons of Rhys ap Gruffudd were a second time seized through treachery by their father and imprisoned.

1196 In this year Rhys ap Gruffudd gathered a mighty host, and he fell upon Carmarthen and destroyed it and burned it to the ground. And he took and burned the castles of Colwyn and Radnor. And Roger Mortimer and Hugh de Sai arrayed a mighty host against him. And Rhys armed himself like a lion with a strong hand and daring heart, and attacked his enemies and drove them to flight. And forthwith Rhys took Painscastle in Elfael.

1197 In this year there was an exceeding great mortality in all the islands of Britain. And, on the fourth day from the calends of May, died Rhys ap Gruffudd, prince of Deheubarth and unconquered head of all Wales. Alas for the glory of his battles and the shield of his knights, the defender of his land, the splendour of arms, the arm of prowess, the hand of generosity, the eye and lustre of worthiness, the summit of majesty, the light of reason, the magnanimity of Hercules!

ABBOT ARMEL d.c. 570 (d.552 according to Farmer)
ARTHMAEL, ARTHFAEL, ARZEL, ERMEL, HERMEL, ERMYN, ERVAN, THIARMAIL, ARMAGILLUS, THE REAL ARTHUR?

Feast Day 14-17 August, with August 16 being most popular in the Breton sources, and July 27 also noted in Vannes. June 13 is 'Le Passage' feast day in St Armel. He is invoked to cure headaches, fever, colic, gout and rheumatism, and was sometimes the patron of hospitals.

Saint Armel is included in this first volume of 'Eminent Britons' to stimulate discussion upon the Breton-Welsh Arthurian links. Princely Breton refugees fought for Arthur before some returned to Brittany to regain their lands. They married Arthur's sisters. It seems that their kinsman Arthur may have survived Camlan and returned to Armorica (Brittany) to plead their case at Childebert's court, and then with Samson dethrone the usurper king Conmire in Brittany.*

Abbot Armel was said to be the cousin of St Samson and St Cadfan, and from south-east Wales. He crossed to Brittany with many kinsfolk. Other relatives were the saints Maglorius, Malo, Padarn and Tudno. He was a member of Illtud's *'cor'* (college) of monks. He went to Brittany possibly to flee the 547 Yellow Plague, and one source says that he went with Abbot Carentmail who is probably Carannog. With the assistance of King Childebert, Armel founded monasteries at Plouarmel and Ploermel. Ploermel was formerly called Lann Arthmael. With Samson, he assisted in restoring the throne of Domnonia (Britanny) to King Iuthael in 555, and the famous 6th - 7th century Samson Cross in Llanilltud records the fact. There is St Armel south of Vannes, and another north-west of Bubry, near St Maurice (Meurig?). Plouarzel is west of St Renan, and another Plouarzel is near Lampaul. Ville Ermel is just north of Paimpont Forest, of Arthurian renown, as is Kersamson. Samson

Caerleon Roman Amphitheatre associated with Athur's Round Table
(photograph courtesy of WTB)

was a kinsman of Arthur, associated with helping Armel in Brittany.

Another source states that Armel was a native of Morgannwg, in the cantref of Penychen. King Arthur was said to have been born at Boverton in Penychen, and his uncle Pawl Penychen's Penllyn Court was just five miles north. There is a book of Breton names *'Tous les Prenoms Breton'* by Alain Stephan of Gissort University which states that Arzel/Armel was born in South Glamorgan, was connected to Childebert's court, and was a 'warrior-lord'. **There seem to be many links pointing that Armel and Arthur were the same person.** The Iolo mss. however record Armel as being the son of Hywel ab Emyr Llydaw, and the brother of Derfael Gardarn, Tudwal, Dwyfael and possibly Leonore, and cousin of Cadfan, Samson, Padarn, Maglorius and Malo. However, Breton mss. would surely record the fact that Armel was a grandson of Emyr Llydaw (Budic II). The Breton saints' lives are far better documented than those of Wales, and Armel would certainly have been recounted as a Breton rather than as a native of Glamorgan. Also Barber and Pykit believe that Arthmael ap Hywel Mawr was known as St Mael in Wales.

With Abbot Carentmail, Arthmael landed at Aber Benoit in Finistere and moved inland to found Plouarzel. Around 540, Jonas King of Domnonia had died and Conmore (Conmire, Conor, Marcus Conomorus, March) married his widow, forcing the rightful heir Prince Ithael (Judual, Iuthael**) to flee. Armel/Arthmael left Wales sometime after the battle of Camlan (537 or 539) and went to see King Childebert in Paris to plead Ithael's cause against Conmore. Samson's arrival compounded the religious pressure against Conmore, and together they organised an armed rising, and thus Conmore was killed in battle in 555. Arthmael was given a vast tract of land where he established a monastery, where the present St Armel's Church stands at Ploermel (Plouharzel) in Morbihan (seven miles south-east of Josselin). Intriguingly, Ploermel was the chosen place for the famous 'Combat of the Thirty' in 1351. Thirty knights from the English garrison at Ploermel met 30 knights from the French garrison at nearby Josselin. Described in vivid detail by Barbara Tuchman ('A Distant Mirror'), the slaughter only ended when the English leader Bemborough died.

Many Welsh princes handed on their territories or positions and retired in middle age to monasteries (even Maelgwn Gwynedd for a time). This may have been a mechanism to ensure the survival of the princedoms, rather than seeing them split up by cyfran (gavelkind) on the ruler's death. The strong legend that Arthur was 'unmanned' by a groin wound at Camlan may have had an effect upon his decision to seek the monastic life and hand his crown on to the son (Constans, Cystennin) of his ally Geraint ab Erbin, who had died at Llongborth. Arthur's surviving son Morgan may have been too young to take over.

In the valley of Loutehel, Armel struck the ground with his staff and supplied water for the valley. He founded the monastery at Ploermel, near a lake called l'Etang du Duc. Montsaint-Armel is also named after him, and his image appears in a stained glass window at St Saveur, Dinan, with a slain dragon (representing Conmore or the Saxons). He took the creature to the top of the mountain and ordered it to leap into the river below. Ergue-Armel outside Quimper was also formerly dedicated to him, as were churches at Langoet and Languedias, and four more chapels. In the Breviary of Leon, Arthmael is referred to as *'Miles fortissimus'* – *'the strongest of soldiers'*, and in the Rennes prose he is invoked as an 'armigere' against the enemies of salvation. He founded the monastery of St Armel-des-Bochaux near Rennes.

Henry VII's glorious chapel at Westminster Abbey features a gauntleted Armel, whom Henry Tudor believed saved him from shipwreck. Armel's mutilated statue also stands on Cardinal Morton's monument in the crypt of Canterbury Cathedral. Armel is commemorated on alabaster sculptures in Stonyhurst College and St Mary Brookfield church in London, and on the reredos at Romsey Abbey. In his Anglicised form, Ermyn, he was venerated at Westminster Abbey. St Ermyn's Hotel in Westminster stood on St Ermyn's Hill, first mentioned in records in 1496 as St Armille's Hill. Armel's chapel there is now represented by Christchurch in Westminster. Why would a Breton-Welsh Dark-Age warrior-monk, only celebrated in Brittany, be celebrated in London? St Erme in Cornwall appears to by Armel's only British foundation. Some historians state that the Roman Road, the Ermine way, was so-called because it was used by Ermyn's cavalry troops.

In the Middle Ages Armel was prayed to by people with gout and rheumatism. Sometimes a patron of hospitals, his invocation was said to cure headaches, fever, colic, gout and rheumatism. He is usually depicted in armour and a chasuble, leading a dragon with an ermine stole around its neck. He was said to have subdued a dragon – could this be the white dragon of the Anglo-Saxons rather than Conmore? As mentioned, recent researchers have placed Armel as King Arthur who went to Brittany after recovering from his wounds at Avalon (Enlli Island). If the grim Battle of Camlan happened in 539, then Arthur could have joined his Breton kinsmen to fight for them. The dragon, ermine and the placing of his saint's day in the Sarum Calendar in 1498, under the new Tudor dynasty, mean that the links with King Arthur **must** be explored further.

In Saint Armel, the last of the saltbeds were abandoned thirty years ago, and turned over to oyster basins. The first Saturday in April sees the Miss Pearl festival at neighbouring Gildas-de-Rhuys. Gildas was Arthur's contemporary. Breton cider, mussels and oysters are recommended. There are no dedications to Arthmael in Wales, but there was a chapel in Cornwall and he was commemorated annually at Stratton. His cult spread extremely rapidly from Brittany to Normandy, Touraine and Anjou.

The website 'Catholic Online Saints' gives the following entry: *'St Armagillus d.c. 570. Feastday August 16. Welsh missionary, called Armel, Ermel and Ervan, and a cousin of St Samson. He studied under Abbot Carentmael joining the abbot in missionary journies to Brittany, France. The missionaries founded Saint-Armel-des-Boscheaux and Plou-Ermel or Plouharzel. Connor, a local chieftain, forced them to leave the mission until 555. Connor was slain in battle that year, allowing their return. Armagillus is honoured in a Cornish church, St Erme.'* Samson's mother was Anna ferch Tewdrig, the sister of Meurig, which makes him Arthur's cousin. Arthur ap Meurig disappeared from Wales around 540 after the Battle of Camlan, and Armel was known as a warrior-saint in Brittany. The dispossessed Breton family of Amwn Ddu had married into Arthur's family, and many fought for him. Arthur had given lands to Carannog who went to Brittany with monks. Probably Carannog was Carentmael. It seems that a strong case can be made for Arthur and Armel being the same person. It would not have been in the interests of the princes of Wales and Henry VII to publicise the fact, as they were of the House of Gwynedd, not of the Silurian House of Gwynlliwg and Glwyssing.

*Emyr Llydaw, also known as Budic II, was forced to flee from the throne of Cornouaille in Armorica (Brittany) by the oncoming Franks. He married St Teilo's sister, although some sources state that he married Arthur's sister. One son, St Ismael, followed Teilo as Bishop of Menevia. Another son, Euddogwy, became Bishop of Llandaf. His son Amwn Ddu married Anna, the sister of Arthmael ap Meurig, and fought for the historical Arthur. Anna has been described as *'the sister of the High King of Britain'*. Budic's son Hywel Mawr, or Riwal Mawr, is featured in Arthurian legend, and it may be that his mother was Gwyar, Arthmael ap Meurig's sister. Budic's son Alan Fyrgain, also fought for Arthur. Gwyndaf Hen, another son, married into Arthur's family, his wife being Gwenonwy, Arthmael ap Meurig's sister and he fought for Arthur's knights. It also seems that Arthur's grandfather Tewdrig had helped Budoc I to regain his Breton throne, and this may be the king remembered by Margam Abbey's 6th century Bodvoc Stone. The ties between the family of Arthmael ap Meurig ap Tewdrig, the Romanised-Silurian high-kings of Britain, and the royal family of Armorica certainly bring us closer to accepting the Arthmael-Arthur-Armel connection.

**Ploermel is near the area of Brocielande and the magical Foret de Paimpont. Brocieland was the expanse of territory given to St Armel by Ithael after Armel helped him regain his throne from Conmire. Why is Armel's land so intrinsically linked with Arthur? This area has been sympathetically developed to link Arthurian legends with the site. It is where Merlin was imprisoned in a pool by Morgan le Fay, where the knights of the Round Table met at Comper Castle, where knights tramped across the wastelands seeking the Grail. Comper Castle has been made into an Arthurian exhibition centre, the Abbey at Paimpont features effigies of the Welsh founding saints of Brittany, and a tree in the forest has been painted gold. Sights include a wonderful walk along the Val Sans Retour (Valley of No Return), the Fontaine de Barenton, the Fontaine de Jouvence (Spring of Eternal Youth), Comper Castle and its lake, the Etang Bleu (Blue Lake), the Etang du pas du Hout, Le Temple Helouin megalith, the Lac de Tremelin and the Tombeau de Merlin (Merlin's Tomb dolmen). Le Point-du-Secret on the southern fringe of the forest may hold the clue to the burial-place of Arthur/Armel.

FOOTNOTE:
The author has just discovered 'Les Prenoms Celtiques' by Albert Deshayes, and has translated the entry upon Saint Armel as: *'Saint Arthmael was born in 482 in Wales. He emigrated to Armorica and landed on the shore at Leon. His was the foundation of the hermitage of Plou-Arzel. He made himself close to the King of France, Childebert I, and he stayed for six years in his palace (in Paris) before coming to Brittany. One after another, he had obtained two Breton parishes which took his name: Plouarzel and Ploermel. His name is also used at Ergue-Armel in Quimper and at Saint-Armel. It was Armel, near Rennes, who accomplished a number of miracles, and he died in 552. At Ploermel, a fountain (holy well?) is dedicated, and the local church possesses a stained-glass window depicting the saint. He is invoked for the cure of gout and rheumatism, and wet nurses prayed to him to have milk. Different scenes in the life of the saint feature in the windows of Plouarzel Church.*

Etymology: Composed of the old Breton (Welsh) term arth (meaning 'bear', taken in the sense of being a warrior) and mael, 'prince', the name given to Arzel, Arhel but also Armel by the process of Frenchification.'

Thus this 'bear/warrior-prince' was welcome at the court of the King of France for 6 years, and was obviously of noble Welsh stock. Could this have been Arthur, after the Battle of Camlan in 539? Six years in honoured recuperation, at Childebert's court, before going to Brittany to repay his debt to the Breton family which supported him in Britain?

Another Breton source, *'Prenoms en Bretagne'* tells us the following (author's translation): *'Armel is in Brittany a Christian name of masculine origin. Its etymology is 'arz': (='ours') bear and 'mael': prince. St Armel came from Wales in the 6th century. He is often represented with a dragon kept on a lead, and which is wearing a stole. The legend of the dragon is frequent in Brittany, and is found concerning other saints. He is the founder of Ploermel: Plou-Armel.* (Plou, like cil and llan in Welsh means a holy foundation). *He has also given his name to Saint-Armel (Ille-et-Vilaine), Saint-Armel (Morbihan), Ergue-Armel (Finistere). The Breton form of his the name is Arzhel, from which Plouarzel is formed (Finistere), where he has been supplanted by Saint Eloi. The evangelisation of Brittany was not easy: persecuted, Armel was exiled for a time at the court of King Childebert 1st. Armel is honoured for several deeds; he made water come from the earth, which could cure men and animals. He is represented among other saints in the Bishop's Palace at Rennes in the Breton monument (calvary?) 'Breiz d'ha Bugale' of Saint Anne of Aurac.*

Feminine form; Armel, Arzhela, Arzela, Arzhelenn, Arzhelez, Armela. Armelle is the Frenchified form. We have also found the derived names Ermel and Hermet from Saint Armel'.

Finally, from two more Breton sources, *'Une Toponomie du Finistere'* and *'Les Noms des Saints Bretons'* (J. Loth, 1910), Plousarzel is the parish of Arthmael, and *'according to the traditional Life, he was born in Great Britain and came ashore in Armorica in the region of Ac'H, a part of lower-Leon, between the Point St-Matthieu and the Aberwrach river ('mouth of the witch' - Breton is identical to*

Welsh in this instance). He came into the former Roman garrison town of Vorganium, Ososmi, on the Finistere coast (not Carhaix, which was Vorgium), and which is now called Coz-Castell-Ac'H. Ploermel has his relics, but his tomb is in the borough of St-Armel, where he died abbot of the second monastery founded by him. His patronage is ancient at Ergue-Armel. Arthmael is made up of 'arto', or 'ours' = bear, and 'maglo', meaning chief.

ARTHUR - ARTHMAEL AP MEURIG AP TEWDRIG d. 539 after Camlan, 547* or later in 570
ARTHWYS, ATHRWYS, ARTHUS, ADRAS, ARMEL? ARZEL?
EUROPE'S GREATEST LEGEND

Too much has been written on Arthur, this most potent of Western legends, that has been based upon mediaeval French romances. In truth, he was a 6th century Romano-Celt warlord from Glamorgan and Gwent, and books by Barber and Pykitt, and by Blackett and Wilson have paved the way for a radical assessment of the man and his times. The author's 'The Book of Welsh Saints' associates over 100 6th century Welsh saints of the Age of Saints with Arthur, and a book linking him with the great St Arthmael (Armel) of Brittany will appear in 2002. John Morris, in his magisterial 'The Age of Arthur' footnotes that Arthmael was the most important of all the Welsh emigrants to Brittany in the 6th century, but *'little is known of him'*. The Bretons know Armel as a warrior-prince from Glamorgan, and his appearance there coincides with the disappearance of Arthur from Wales.

The time of Arthur is the most debated area of British history, *'The Age of Saints'* in Wales, yet *'The Dark Ages'* across the rest of Europe. Arthur was a Celtic warlord, around whom the mythology of Guinevere, Merlin, Lancelot, The Holy Grail and the Round Table revolve. He fought back the Saxon threat from the East, and the Pictish threat from the North and West. It appears, after studying around sixty books on the legends surrounding Arthur, that he was Prince Athrwys, or Arthmael - the Bear Prince (Athruis ap Meurig ap Tewdrig). His son Morgan became King of Glamorgan.

'Journey to Avalon - the Final Discovery of King Arthur' (by C. Barber and D. Pykitt) makes a persuasive claim that Arthur's court of Gelli-weg was Llanmelin Hillfort, the ancient capital of the Silures, that overlooks Caerwent Roman town. In the Welsh Triads, Gelliwig in Cernyw was one of Arthur's three principal courts. Cernyw was once part of the coastal area of South-East Wales. Cornwall was not known as Cernyw until the 10th century, hundreds of years post-dating the Triads.

At Coed Kernew, just west of Newport, the church was founded in the sixth century by Glywys Cernyw, a son of Gwynlliw Filwr (the Warrior).

Gelliwig means small grove, and Llanmelin's previous name was Llan y Gelli (church of the grove). Llanmelin is situated in Gwent-is-Coed, Gwent below the Wood (now called Wentwood), where Arthur's uncle and chief elder Caradoc Freichfras (Sir Craddock) ruled when Arthur was campaigning. Barber and Pykitt believe that Caer Melin, as Llanmelin was known to the Romans, and where Scapula was defeated by the Silures in 53 AD, was the site of the fabled Camelot.

Nennius, from South-East Wales, wrote around the end of the eighth century about Arthur and his famous twelve battles. Arthur is also referred to in *The Gododdin'*, written around the end of the sixth century, early Welsh poetry, some of the Lives of the Saints, and in the sixth-century Welsh Triads of the Islands of Britain.

Many of the characters in Arthurian legend previously appear in Welsh legend and literature. Merlin was identified with Myrddin in Welsh history, both St Illtud and Gwalchaved with Sir Galahad, both Gwalchmai and St. Govan with Sir Gawain, Cei with Sir Kay, and Peredur and Bedwyr in 'The Mabinogion' with Sir Percival and Sir Bedivere. Peredur, who glimpses the Holy Lance and Grail in 'Peredur, Son of Erawc', has an uncle Bran the Blessed, who is the model for 'The Fisher King'. Eigyr passed into legend as Igraine, the mother of Arthur, and both Gwenhwyfar and Gwendoloena the flower maiden as Guinevere. The Welsh prince Medraut ap Cawrdaf became Mordred, and the Druidic goddess Morgen has been associated with Morgen le Fay. Morgen was the patroness of priestesses, who lived on Avalon, Bardsey Island, with nine sisters. Peredur, or Pryderi, brought about the devastation of South Wales by sitting on a Perilous Mound, but as Percival, in 'Didot Perceval' causes enchantments to fall on Britain by sitting on the Seat Perilous at King Arthur's Court.

Sir Lancelot may be based on Maelgwn Gwynedd, or Llwch Llawinawg, Lord of the Lakes, and Sir Tristram with Drustanus, the son of Marcus Conomorus, a prince of Glamorgan. Sir Howel is identified with Howel (Riwal) Mawr of Ergyng, who fought Lancelot, became Dux Britannorum after Arthur's death, and was buried at Llanilltud Fawr. The fabulous Castell Dinas Bran, perched high on the rocks overlooking Llangollen, is identified with Grail Castle. Both Bran (from the Mabinogion) and the Fisher King had wounds which would not heal, and King Bran is associated with the castle. Bran also had a magical 'cauldron of plenty', which is identified with the Holy Grail. Another of the Thirteen Treasures of Wales seems to be identical with Excalibur. Lloegr was the Welsh name for England, and Logres is the name of England in Arthurian legend. Pendragon, the title first taken by Arthur's father Uther and then by Arthur, is a combination of the Old Welsh 'dragwn', dragon/leader, and the Brythonic-Welsh 'pen', or head.

At the top of Snowdon, there was a tumulus commemorating one of Arthur's victims. Arthur sailed across Snowdonia's Llyn Llydaw on his way to Avalon, after fighting Mordred at Bwlch y Saethau ('Pass of the Arrows'). Bedevere threw Excalibur into Llyn Llydau, which seems to be a continuation of the Celtic throwing away of a dead warlord's weapons into water, which was sacred to them. Avalon seems to be Afallach, the sacred and holy isle of Bardsey off the Llyn Peninsula. Barber and Pykitt believe that Arthur recovered from his wounds at the monastery of Bardsey, and went to Brittany, where he was known as St. Armel. Barber and Pykit also state that Arthur was born in 482 at Boverton (Trebeferad), a Roman camp site in the Vale of Glamorgan, fought his final British battle at 'Cadlan' on the Llyn Peninsula where Mordred (Medraut) had territories, recovered from his wounds at Bardsey Island, and died in 562 at St Armel des Boschaux.

A persuasive case for the final Battle of Camlan being at Maes-y-Camlan (Camlan Field), just south of Dinas Mawddwy, has been made in a little booklet by Laurence Main. This local tradition was recorded in Welsh by a local bard in 1893. In the area are two Camlans, Bron-Camlan, Camlan-uchaf and Camlan Isaf. Across the valley from Maes Camlan are Bryn Cleifion and Dol-y-Cleifion (Hill of the Wounded and Meadow of the Wounded). The nearby ridge overlooking the Dyfi river is Cefn-Byriaeth (Mourning Ridge) where graves were discovered. Five miles east is the site where Mordred's Saxon allies are said to have camped the previous night, and the stream there is still called Nant-y-Saeson (Saxon Stream). The date was 537 in the Welsh Annals, but the Celtic Church may have dated this from the crucifixion of Christ, making it 574. Arthur ap Meurig ap Tewdrig was married to Gwenhwyfar, and his son Gwydre was killed by the Twrch Trwyth (the Irish Boar, in the Tale of Culhwch and Olwen in 'the Mabinogion') at Cwm Cerwyn, near Nevern. Nearby are the Stones of the Sons of Arthur (Cerrig Meibion Arthur). Arthur had supposedly returned from Brittany to defeat Mordred. Again tradition states that he survived the battle, but was grievously wounded while resting after he had won (by Eda Elyn Mawr, according to Harleian mss 4181 entry 42). Arthur was soon succeeded as Pendragon by Maelgwn Gwynedd, sometimes identified with Lancelot.

At Ogmore Castle was found a sixth century memorial stone recording a land grant by Arthur. It is now in the National Museum, and the Latin inscription reads 'Be it known to all that Arthmail has given this field to God to Glywys and to Netart and to Bishop Fili'. And in the holy church of St Illtud at Llanilltud Fawr, just a few miles away, the famous Pillar of Abbot Samson reads:

> 'In the name of the MOST HIGH GOD
> was begun the cross of the Saviour which
> Samson the Abbot prepared for his soul
> And for the soul of king Iuthahel
> And for Artmal the dead'

We must remember that Armel and Samson helped Iuthael regain his throne in Brittany, and that Arthur owned the lands of Glamorgan where Ogmore and Llanilltud Fawr lie. Why no academic wishes to formally associate Arthur with the Samson Pillar and Wales is unbelievable. Of course, St Illtud is known as Illtud Farchog (Illtud the Warrior-Knight) and was supposed to have fought for Arthur and for Arthur's uncle, Pawl Penychen.

A recent book by Adrian Gilbert, Alan Wilson and Baram Blackett ('The Holy Kingdom', Bantam Press, 1998) agrees with much of the Barber and Pykitt research, but strangely makes no reference to their work. The author is researching the area from St. Donat's Castle (the seat of Caractacus) through Llanilltud Fawr (the centre of monastic learning), Boverton (the possible birthplace of Arthur) and Llancarfan Monastery through to Caerleon, Caerwent and Llanmelin Hill Fort. This strip of the Vale of Glamorgan, the Roman forts of Cardiff and Caerleon, and the inland Church of St. Peter super Montem, seems to hold the key to all the Arthurian legends. 'The Holy Kingdom' makes the case for 'Caer Melyn' just north of Cardiff, being Camelot. The sulphur springs nearby colour the water yellow, so Caer Melyn means Yellow Fortress. As 'mellitus' means honey-coloured in Latin, perhaps it was corrupted to Caer Mellitus and hence to Camelot. The author's preference is for Arthur to have been based at Dinas Powys fort, with a 'palace' at the great Roman villa at Caermead outside Llanilltud Fawr, but far more research will be undertaken on this topic. The Gilbert book seems to drift off into the hiding of the 'True Cross' in Wales, but also reveals the finding in Glamorgan of a stone inscribed 'Rex Artorius Fili Mauricivs', 'King Arthur son of Maurice' (Meurig). If this stone is not a forgery, then it is essential that public and university resources are directed towards enlightening these 'Dark Ages'.

Arthur's links with the West Country are extremely tenuous, and based upon

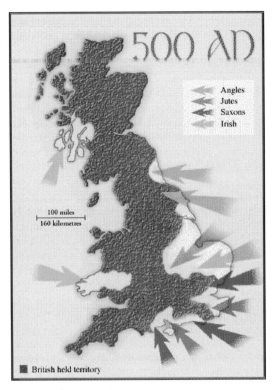

Arthur's Kingdom

romances from the Middle Ages. The placing of Arthur, Merlin and the knights of the Round Table firmly in Wales can be a tremendous boost to the tourist industry. All it needs is someone in power with the vision and courage to challenge and change things. Unfortunately this is not the type of person who clambers to the top in politics or tourist boards. English Heritage has recently been trumpeting the find, of a piece of slate from Tintagel in Cornwall, as proof of Arthur in the sixth century being an English reality. Cornwall was Welsh-British at this time. The rough inscription *'Pater Coliavificit Artnogov'* means *'Artnogov, father of a descendant of Coll, has had (this building) constructed'.* According English Heritage it is *'the first evidence of a link between the Arthurian legend and historical fact'* (Daily Telegraph August 7, 1990). Yet again publicity tries to overwhelm historical truth. Arthmael ap Meurig ap Tewdrig is known and recorded in history but does not 'fit' with the English tourist industry and its promotional power. It is so easy for the relevant authorities – the Welsh Office, Welsh Tourist Board and various local councils to promote Arthurian tours and holiday breaks in Wales. Why not promote Wales as 'The Kingdom of Arthur ?' It will pull in more tourists than dreamy scenes of empty beaches and deserted hills.

The Easter Annals describe Arthur's final battle in 539 after 12 victories, at Camlann, *'in which Arthur and Medraut (Mordred) perished.'* However, we still are unsure if Mordred was his enemy or fighting alongside him, or indeed if Arthur died here. One of the problems with Arthur is that of the suspicion of the early Roman Church with this fabulous hero, known across Europe. As a result the Catholic monk writing the Life of Cadog describes him as being lustful and perverse, and the Life of Padarn makes him out to be a mean despot. There are other unflattering references in many of the later religious sources. Certainly his contemporary, Gildas, had no cause to love Arthur because he executed Huail, the brother of Gildas.

In the Triads, Arthur is recorded as one of the *'three red chieftains of Britain'* and also as one of the *'three heroic supreme sovereigns of Britain.'* The 6th century Llywarch Hen, one of *'the three wise-counselling equestrians of Arthur's Court'* called Arthur a great warrior, as did Nennius, writing three hundred years later. A

10th century copy of Nennius, by Mark the Hermit, called him *'dux belli'* (war leader) and *'belliger Arthur'* (warlike Arthur). All these references predate the mediaeval French romances.

'The Genealogy of Iestyn ap Gwrgan' seems to confuse Arthur with Adras:
'Adras, the son of Meyryg, was a very heroic sovereign, who frequently put the Saxons to flight; killing and destroying them. He enacted many laws and ordinances for civil and ecclesiastical government; and was the first who instituted a class of Equestrians (mounted knights), *for the maintenance of correct comportment in war, and due discipline at arms; and also to guard well the country, watch carefully its enemies, and to establish an efficient system of communications with regard to hostilities and legislation.*

Morgan, the son of Adras, called Morgan the Courteous, and Morgan of Glamorgan, was a renowned king, and an Equestrian of Arthur's court, and of the Round Table. He was Arthur's cousin; particularly handsome; extremely courteous; and so cheerfully kind and merciful, that, when he went out to war, no one, old and strong enough to bear arms, would remain at home; hence it was that he acquired the designation of – Morgan the Courteous. It was he that gave the appellation – Morganwg – to his country; which name it has retained to this very hour.'

'He erected a Court at Margam, a place which he raised to a Bishoprick; which retained that distinction during the lives of five bishops, when it became united to Llandaff.' Morgan's grave was found between Margam and Kenfig.

It seems that Margam was originally called Morgan, and there is still a noble mansion there. An important but little-known fact relating to Morgan was related by Edward Mansel of Margam, a man of Norman descent, in his 'Account of the Conquest of Glamorgan' of 1591. Robert Fitzhamon was the Norman who conquered much of Glamorgan from its last prince Iestyn ap Gwrgant:

*'Before the time of Robert Fitzhamon there was one Chief Lord of Glamorgan whose were the high Royalties, and he assembled the other Lords every month to his Court where all matters of Justice were determined and finally settled, these Lords sat in Judgement on all matters of Law, with twelve Freeholders from every Lordship to give opinions after what came to their knowledge, and the Bishop of Llandaff sat in the high Court as a Councellor of Conscience according to the Laws of God, this Court was formed they say by Morgan (c.515-570?) who was Prince of the Country **after King Arthur** in the manner of Christ and his twelve apostles, and this form of Law was kept by Sir Robert Fitzhamon according to the old usage of the Country, after the High Court was held, which lasted three days, the Courts of the twelve Lordships were held in turn, and from them an appeal might be made to the High Court in the Country, the Lord and his yeomen in the same form and manner as in the High Court.*

After the winning of the Country by Sir Robert Fitzhamon, he took to him his twelve knights to supply the places in his Courts of the Lawful and right Lords of the twelve Lordships, which caused discontent insomuch that Welsh Lords took arms under Pain Turberville and Caradock ab Iestyn and Madoc his Brother, and they came to Cardiff Castle and surrounded it insomuch that it was on the point of being taken when King Henry the first going to the top of the Raven Tower to enquire concerning the tumult which was heard, he saw the place all encompassed by fierce armed men, whereupon he called a parley when Pain Turberville told him the reason saying that if rightful orders were not made, to restore the Laws of

Morgan the first, that he and Robert Fitzhamon should feel at the ears very soon of what stuff the Castle walls were of at the heart on which all in the Castle counselled together, and it was seen best to yield to the Country that request.' **This may be the origin of 12 man juries.**

Arthur's 'Saying of the Wise' is:

> *'Hast thou heard the saying of Arthur,*
> *The Emperor, the mighty sovereign ?*
> *"There is no devastation like a deceiver".'*

He is also named as one of *'the three red ravagers of the Island of Britain'*, along with Rhun ap Beli and Morgant the Wealthy. There are several triads referring to Arthur. From 'Gereint fab Erbin' there is:

> *'At Llongborth I saw Arthur's*
> *Brave men, they hewed with steel,*
> *Emperor, leader in toil'*

In 'Mi a Wum' is recorded:

> *'I have been where Llachau was slain,*
> *The son of Arthur, terrible in songs,*
> *When ravens croaked over blood'*
>
> and also:

> *'What man is the porter ?'*
> *"Glewlwyd Great-Grip,*
> *What man asks it ?"*
> *'Arthur and Cai the Fair.'*
> *"What retinue travels with you ?"*
> *'The best men in the world.'*

Arthur is also mentioned in 'Preidu Annwn', 'Cad Goddau', and finally in this marvellously evocative verse from 'Y Gododdin', the story of the British defeat at Catraeth and the oldest extant British poem:

> *'He charged before three hundred of the finest,*
> *He cut down both centre and wing,*
> *He excelled in the forefront of the noblest host,*
> *He gave gifts of horses from the herd in winter.*
> *He fed black ravens on the rampart of a fortress*
> *Although he was no Arthur.*
> *Among the powerful ones in battle,*
> *In the front rank, Gwawrddur was a palisade.'*

*This 547 date is intriguing, for Maelgwn Gwynedd died of the Bubonic Plague (the Yellow Death) in this year. Arthur was recorded as having a festering wound in his groin. This is one of the classic symptoms of the plague, along with the weeping yellow pustules under the armpits.

NOTE ON ARTHUR'S KNIGHTS OF THE ROUND TABLE
(from The Book of Welsh Saints)

It is interesting to note how many Welsh saints were related to, or served, Arthur in some way. A medieval text 'Deuddeg Pedwar Marchog ar Hugan Llys Arthur' gives his 24 knights at court as: Gwalchmai (i.e. Gawain), Drudwas, Eliwlod, Gwrgi (i.e. Bors), Perceval, Galahad, Lancelot, Owain, Menw, Tristan, Eiddilig, Nasiens, Mordred, Hoel, Blaes, Cadog, Petroc, Morfran ap Tegid, Sanddef, Glewlyd, Cyon, Aron, Llywarch Hen and Bedwyr (Bedivere). Of these, Gwalchmai/Gawain, Bors, Perceval, Galahad, Lancelot, Tristan, Mordred and Bedwyr/Bedivere are included on the thirteenth century Winchester Castle Round Table forgery. Also of these we can count as Welsh saints Aron, Cadog, Petroc and Llywarch Hen. It is still unsure whether Arthur fought with or against Mordred at Camlan in 539. Instead, it may have been the forces of Maelgwn Gwynedd that ambushed him.

If we can cross-relate the knights mentioned above with the saints mentioned in this book with Arthurian connections, we have the following reference list in alphabetical order:

St Alan Frygan ab Emyr Lydaw, whose troops deserted Arthur on the eve of Camlan. He married into Arthur's family; St Allgo ap Caw appears as Calcas ap Caw in the Mabinogion, fighting for Arthur. From Glamorgan, he went to Anglesey, from which he was forced to flee by Maelgwn Gwynedd; St Amwn Ddu ab Emyr Llydaw married into Arthur's family and may be the origin of the Black Knight; St Angar, Angawd ap Caw is mentioned in the Mabinogion as Arthur's knight; St Aron (Aaron) ap Cynfarch, father of St Ciwg, was given lands by Arthur. A saint of this name left Wales in the early 6th century and settled at St Malo; St Baglan ab Ithel Hael is given as Sir Balan, and was related to Arthur. Baglan is culted in Brittany and therefore may have fought for Armel/Arthur there; Bishop Bedwyn, Sir Baudwin was said to be one of Arthur's first knights, made a constable of the realm and one of the governors of Britain, but ended his life as a *'physician and hermit'* St Bedwyn was also called a 'comeregulus' (count-ruler), and Arthur had a brother called 'Comereg'. He was bishop of Cernyw (east Glamorgan/Gwent); Bedwyr Bedrynant (of the perfect sinews) was Cai's companion and the model for Bedivere, mentioned in Culhwch and Olwen. The warrior with Cai (St Cynan) most documented with Arthur, he died fighting for him (Armel?) in France; Bors' father was said to also be named Bors, who married Evaine, and his brother was Sir Lionel and cousin Sir Lancelot. He was said to be the father of St Elian Wyn, but Elian's father was Gallgu Rieddog. Bors has been identified with St Gwrgi; St Brioc may possibly been Arthur's brother Frioc, or Brioc the grandson of Brychan; Sir Breunor ap Dunawd Fawr is the brother of Sir (St) Deiniol and Sir Dinadan, and is known as the Black Knight; St Brynach was given land by Meurig (Arthur's father), and argued with Maelgwn Gwynedd; St Cadfan is known as a 'warrior saint' in Brittany, Armel's cousin, and possibly helped Arthur and Samson overcome Conmire; St Cado ap Geraint fought with Arthur at Badon Hill, was a great friend of Caradog Freich Fras (his brother-in-law), is linked with Guinevere and fought in Brittany; St Cadog (497-577) is linked with Arthur's family and disputed lands with Rhun ap Maelgwn and Rhun ap Brychan. He sheltered an enemy of Arthur. In a 1999 Western Mail article, Lawrence Main reckons St Cadog to be Sir Galahad. He goes on to reason that *'since Cadoc's father was Gwynlliw and Sir Galahad was the son of Sir Lancelot, it seems obvious that Sir Lancelot was Gwynlliw, a neighbour of King Arthur and a notorious womaniser;* St Caffo ap Caw, brother of Gildas,was killed by Maelgwn Gwynedd's men in Glamorgan or Anglesey; St Cai ap Cynyr Farchog may have became Sir Kay, and Landygai is on the north Wales coast; St Caradog Freich Fras ab Ynyr Gwent and Madrun is mentioned in the Arthurian triads, and became 'Sir Caradoc Bris Bras'. He married Amwn Ddu's sister, and became a knight of Arthur. One of Arthur's *'three cavaliers of battle'*, he fought in Brittany (for Armel ?). His brother 'Turquine' wanted to kill Lancelot; St Carannog ap Corun was given lands by Arthur, and went with Armel to Brittany; St Cawrdaf ap Caradog Freichfras ab Ynyr Gwent is given in the Mabinogion as Arthur's counsellor. His 'cor' was near Penllin, at Miskin; St Caw fled from his kingdom in the North of England, and has 21 children listed in the tale of Culhwch and Olwen. Many became knights of the round table in mediaeval reworkings of the life of Arthur ap Meurig ap Tewdrig, who gave some of them lands in 'Siluria', i.e. South-East Wales; Cedwy *'of Arthur's court'* is St Cedwyn ap Gwgon Gwron ap Peredur, the half-brother of St Ceidio and Caradog Freichfras; St Cenydd was a baby at a feast held by Arthur to celebrate Christmas; St Cywyllog ferch Caw was the wife of Mordred, and given lands by Maelgwn Gwynedd; St Cybi argued with Maelgwn Gwynedd, although his monastery lands were given by this king; St Cynan Gefnhir (or Cian) ap Cynwyd may be Cyon, a *'knight-counsellor to Arthur'*, who in the Winchester lists is one of the 24 knights; St Curig was a contemporary of Arthur, known as Curig the Knight, and is remembered in Brittany; Cynan, also known as St Kea is possibly Cai (Sir Kay) ap Lleuddyn Luydog from Lothian, who died in 550, a cousin of St Beuno. He was in Brittany at the same time as Armel; St Cynddilig ap Nwython was summoned to Arthur's coronation, with his brother Rhun; St Cynddilig ap Gildas attended Arthur's coronation according to Geoffrey of Monmouth; St Cyndeyrn is mentioned as Arthur's chief bishop in the North; St Cyngar's father, Geraint, died fighting for Arthur; St Cynidr appears to be the St Keneder who was with Cadog in his confrontation with Arthur; St Cynin ap Tudwal Befr was a warrior in early triads and the brother of Sir Ifor who was linked with Arthur as a knight; Cynlas Goch ab Owain was assassinated by Maelgwn Gwynedd when he tried to break his overlordship; St Cynwyl ap Dunawd fawr was the brother of Deiniol, and escaped from Camlan with Sandde Bryd Angel and Morfran ap Tegid; Cystennin (Constantine) ap Cado ap Geraint took over the High Kingship from Arthur after Camlan; Sir Danadan was possibly St Dunawd Fawr, St Dingad or St Dunwyd; Sir Daniel was possibly St Deiniol Fawr,with a brother Sir Breunor, known as the Black Knight. Deiniol may have been with Maelgwn Gwynedd at Llaniltud Fawr. He also witnessed a land grant by Maelgwn to Cyndeyrn; Derfel Gadarn ap Hywel Mawr ab Emyr Llydaw survived Camlan. He was said to be the brother of Armel, and also of Christiolus, Sulien, Rhystud, Dwywan and Dwyfael; Dewi, St David, was thought by Giraldus Cambrensis and Geoffrey of Monmouth to be Arthur's uncle. In his time, Arthur's knight Caradog Freichfras pushed the Irish out of Menevia; Sir Drudwas could be St Trydwas; St Dwyfael ap Hywel Mawr was one of Arthur's knights; St Dyfrig possily crowned Arthur; St Dywel ab Erbyn fought for Arthur, mentioned in Culhwch and Olwen and the Black Book of Carmarthen; St Edern ap Nudd is mentioned in the Dream of Rhonabwy and the tale of Geraint ab Erbin; St Einion's father Owain Ddantgwyn was treacherously killed by Maelgwn Gwynedd; St Elffin was rescued from Maelgwn Gwynedd's Deganwy Castle by

Taliesin; St Elidyr fought Maelgwn Gwynedd or Rhun ap Maelgwn; Eliwlod was one of the 24 knights, a grandson of Uther and nephew of Arthur, and perhaps the original of Sir Lancelot. Could this be St Eliquid or St Eiliwedd/Almedha ? St Endellion was said to be Arthur's god-daughter; King Erbyn of Domnonia's sons Geraint, Dywel and Erinid fought for Arthur. Erbyn asked Arthur for Geraint to return to the West Country to take over the kingship; St Ernin (Hernin) was linked to Conmire, who Armel fought in Brittany; St Euddogwy was given land by Arthur; St Eugrad ap Caw fought for Arthur in Culhwch and Olwen, as 'Ergyryat'; St Ffili is mentioned on a stone at Ogmore in connection with Arthmael/Arthur; St Geraint ab Erbyn was killed at Llongborth fighting for Arthur; St Gildas ap Caw's brother Hywel killed Gwydre ap St Gwenafwy, so he was executed by Arthur; St Gildas arbitrated in a dispute concerning king Melwas, Gwenhwyfar and Arthur; Gwalchmai has been associated with Gawain/Gofan, and as Arthur's nephew, killed by Lancelot or Mordred; St Gwen has been identified with Gwenhwyfar (Guinevere); St Gwenafwy's son was stabbed by Huail, which caused Arthur to execute Huail; Gwenhwyfar (Guinevere, Gwenhaf) founded Amesbury Church after her affair with Lancelot (or Maelgwn Gwynedd or Medrod), and St Mylor's relics were taken there; St Gwernabui was given land by Arthur; Gwgan Gwron ap Peredur features in Arthurian triads and married St Madrun; Gwrgi (Bors), the brother or son of Peredur saw the aftermath of the battle of Arderydd c.580; St Gwrst witnessed a land grant by Maelgwn; St Gwrthl was a chief elder who recognised Arthur as overlord, and was killed in Cardigan, possibly at Penbryn (Llongborth); St Gwyddno was present when Arthur's son Llacheu was killed; St Gwyndaf Hen married into Arthur's family; St Gwynlliw 'the Warrior' has been identified with Lancelot, and is Cadog's father; Hywel ap Caw was killed by Arthur; St Hywyn ap Gwyndaf was Arthur's nephew; Sir Iddo was identified with the warrior-saint son of Cawrdaf but he was possibly St Iddon ab Ynyr Gwent; Sir Ifor was the brother of St Cynin, and the son of Tudwal Befr and Nefydd; St Idloes, with St Sadwrn was one of Arthur's knights; St Illtud Farchog (the knight) attended Arthur's court with the warrior St Cadog; St Kea was linked with Arthur, Gildas, Gwenhwyfar and Mordred, but may be the same saint as Cai; St Lorcan Wyddel is mentioned in Arthurian triads; Sir Lucan (Lorcan?) was said to be the brother of St Bedwyr; St Llywarch Hen may be a later addition to the list, but his son was Sandde who escaped the slaughter at Camlan; St Mabon, the brother of St Teilo, was a follower and servant at Arthur's father's court; St Maglorius went to Brittany with Samson at the same time as Armel, and was the nephew of Amwn Ddu and nephew of Arthur; Maelgwn Gwynedd appears to have become High King (Pendragon) after Camlan, and is mentioned as Arthur's chief elder in St David's; St Maelog ap Caw is one of the knights in Culhwch and Olwen; St Maglorius was a nephew of Arthur who went at the same time as Arthur/Armel to Brittany; St Malo, a kinsman of Arthur, had major problems with Conmire in Brittany at the same time as Armel was there; St Marchell was Arthur's aunt; St Mechnyd ap Sandde was a knight; Medrod married Cywyllog ferch Caw, who was given lands by Maelgwn; St Meugan seems to have intervened in a dispute between Maelgwn and Cadog. He was related to Arthur; St Meurig, Arthur's father has been placed as Uther Pendragon; St Mewan was in Brocielande, a friend of Judicael at the same time as Armel; Morgan Mwynfawr ('gentle and great') was a knight, and Arthur's son, blessed by St Cawrdaf; St Ninnoc was Arthur's grandmother; Sir Nwython was probably St Nwythen ap Gildas, mentioned in Culhwch and Olwen; Owain ab

Urien Rheged was one of Arthur's knights; St Padarn argued with Arthur and Maelgwn; Peredur became Sir Percival, and was Pryderi ap Dolar mentioned in The Gododdin and the Arthurian triads. His son was St Dwyfael, Sir Dwyfael who fought for Arthur was probably Hywel Mawr's son; St Petroc (Pedrog) was St Cadog's nephew, one of the *'three just knights of court'*, one of the seven knights who survived Camlan, and known as *'Paladruellt'* (*'splintered lance'*); St Piran was

King Arthur

mentioned in Arthurian legend as being appointed Archbishop of York; Rhun ap Gildas was said to have been summoned to Arthur's coronation; St Sadwrn was a knight and nephew of Emyr Llydaw; St Samson was Arthur's cousin or uncle and Armel's cousin, and helped Armel overcome Conmire; Sandde Bryd Angel has been identified by some as St Padarn – he escaped from Camlan; St Talhaearn is linked in a 'saying of the wise' with Arthur and said to be the chaplain of Emrys Wledig; St Tathan is Arthur's brother-in-law; St Tathana's legend states that the court of Arthur's father Meurig was at Boverton; St Tegfedd ferch Tegid Foel, of Penllyn, was with Derfel Gadarn after Camlan, and said to have been killed by Illtud so Arthur's

tomb was not revealed; St Teilo was given the land where Tegfedd was killed for settling Arthur's dispute with Cadog; St Tewdrig was Pendragon, as was his son St Meurig, Arthur's father; St Trillo witnessed a land grant to Maelgwn, along with Deiniol, Gwrst and Rhun ap Maelgwn; Turquine wanted to kill Lancelot - he was the brother of St Caradog; St Tydecho ap Amwn Ddu, the nephew of Arthur, was persecuted by Maelgwn; St Teithfallt, Arthur's great-grandfather, is claimed to be Emrys Wledig (see Tyfodwg); St Umbrafael, the brother of St Amwn Ddu, married Arthur's sister Afrella; St Winnoc was the son of King Judicael, helped by Armel/Arthur to regain his throne; and St Ynyr Gwent is linked with Arthur, and went to Brittany.

Thus we have around 110 saints of the early-mid 6th century whose stories intertwine around the family of Arthur ap Meurig ap Tewdrig and the legends of King Arthur and St Armel.

Taliesin's poem 'The Graves of Warriors' gives us the following enigmatic lines:
'The grave of the horse, the grave of the Fierce-One,
The grave of Grim-Visaged red-sword,
The grave of Arthur, a mystery of the world.'

If Arthur was Armel, and went to Brittany to help his Breton kinsmen, this problem re-occurs. Armel's tomb at Ploermel is empty. Another translation of 'Englynion y Beddau' (Verses of the Graves) is:
'There is a grave for March, a grave for Gwythur,
A grave for Gwgawn Red-Sword;
The world's wonder a grave for Arthur.'

It is a difficult translation, which either means that he had a wonderful burial-place, or that no-one will ever know where he is. The 'Pointe du Secret' on the fringe of Paimpont Forest may hold a clue to this mystery. Walter Map, writing in 1135, said that Arthur was buried in the Black Chapel, Blackfriars Monastery just outside Cardiff Castle, near the banks of the Taf. A 7th century grave is there, but the author has seen no references to this possibility for Arthur's burial place.

NOTE ON ARTHUR'S SON

Lacheu fab Arthur appears in the Black Book of Carmarthen as in battle against Cai Wyn. Also Gwyddno Garanhir claims he was present when Llacheu was killed. He is often mentioned elsewhere as a fearless warrior, and was supposed to have died 'below Llech Ysgar'. An aforementioned early poem commemorates this:

> 'I have been where Llacheu was killed,
> Son of Arthur, marvellous in songs,
> When the ravens croaked over blood .....
> I have been where the warriors of Britain were slain,
> From the East to the North;
> I am alive, they are in their grave.'

Stones called the 'Sons of Arthur' may indicate that others of Arthur's offspring died, just leaving the young Morgan, causing the leadership of Britain to pass to Constans (Cystennin), then to Maelgwn. These two standing stones, Cerrig Meibion Arthur, stand near Cwm Cerwyn in the Preseli Hills, where Arthur fought the Twrch Trwyth and his son Gwydre and another son died. Near here is the unusually elliptical stone circle, Bedd Arthur. One tradition is that Morgan was Arthur's youngest son, born of the third of the ladies named Gwenhwyfar that Arthur married. His rise to favour irked Modred, who was Arthur's nephew, foster-son and hopeful successor. The same story tells us that Modred was the incestuous offspring of Arthur and his sister Gwyar (Morgan le Fay).

NOTE ON ARTHUR'S FATHER, Meurig ap Tewdrig ap Teithfallt, King of Morgannwg

King Tewdrig was martyred at Tintern in 470, but Meurig had taken over his kingdom prior to this date, and is thought to have been Uther Pendragon, the Dux Bellorum or leader in battle of the British against the Saxon and Pict invaders. Pendragon was an honorific title, and Uther's children included Arthur and Anna. Meurig was the father of King Arthur, and was excommunicated for breaking an oath and killing a rival, but canonised after his death for founding many churches. He married Onbrawst ferch Gwrgant Mawr, to reunite Glwyssing and Gwent with Ergyng. (Glamorgan, Gwent and Hereford/Worcester was the heartland of the Silures).

His children included Arthwys (Athrwys/Arthmael/Arthur), whose son was Morgan Mwynfawr, whose son was Eunydd. Eunydd's descendants ruled Glamorgan until the Norman Conquest. Meurig's daughter Anna married Amwn Ddu ab Emyr Llydaw, the dispossessed Breton prince. Amwn became a saint, and friend of Illtud and Dyfrig. Amwn's children were the important saints Tydecho, Tathan and Samson, who returned to Brittany. Another of Meurig's daughters was Afrella, who married Umbrafael ab Emyr Llydaw. Meurig's third daughter was Gwenonwy who married Gwyndaf Hen ab Emyr Llydaw, King of Brittany. Their children were Meugan (Meigant) and Hywyn. Hywyn was a confessor at the monastery on Ynys Enlli, where Arthur possibly went to recover after Camlan. The marriage of three daughters of Meurig to the three sons of Emyr Llydaw (Budic II of Brittany) gives credence to the claim that Arthur-Arthmael-Armel fought with his kinsmen in Brittany. It appears that after the Bretons supported Arthur, he helped Hywel Mawr and Budic II regain their lands, and then overcame Conmore for Iuthael to gain the Breton throne.

Meurig gave lands to the church around where his father Tewdrig was buried at Mathern, as recorded by Godwin, Bishop of Llandaf in 1615. Under Meurig's protection Llandaf and Llancarfan were founded, and he gave lands to both. It appears that he controlled most of Hereford, all of Monmouth and most of Glamorgan, i.e. the ancient kingdom of Siluria, and he seems to have ruled from Caerleon. After Meurig treacherously slew Cynvetu, Euddogwy summoned the bishops of Llancarfan, Llandough and Llanilltud to excommunicate him, but he was pardoned for giving lands to Llandaf, where he is buried. He may have founded the monastery at Llanfair Misgyn, Miskin. King 'Mouric ap Teudiric' is recorded as granting Roath in Cardiff (Reathr) to Gourcinnim for a sword with a gilded hilt valued at 25 cows. A smithy of this time has been recorded at nearby Dinas Powys in the Dark Age fort. Meurig's kingdom of Glwysing may have included Brecon as a vassal kingdom. There is a 13th century church at Alltmawr in Brecon dedicated to Mauritius, which may be his foundation.

Pwll Meurig, a mile or so from Chepstow, was his holy well, and famous for miracles. It ebbed and flowed with the tide like many Welsh coastal wells. The legend is that people used to stand on a magical log in the well to wash their faces. The well was flooded by the River Severn and the log floated out to sea, but always returned on the fourth day. Meurig's father Tewdrig also had a famous holy well. Barber and Pykitt believe that Meurig is buried on Mynydd y Gaer in Glamorgan, possibly on a site near Arthur's grave.

FOOTNOTE:
Dependent often upon the author's nationality, the sites of Arthur's battles as recorded by Nennius are in the West Country, the East of England, the Lake District, Yorkshire and Scotland. We could equally make a hypothesis that all of his battles were consistent with his being based in South Wales, fighting against the westward aggression of the Saxons, the sea-borne invasions of the Irish, and against other Britons from North Wales and Cumbria. Even the 'lost' Vandals who sailed from North Africa, are said to have invaded Wales at this time. If nothing else, the following list may just stimulate more Welsh interest in the place-names of fields, rivers and valleys. Around 830 Nennius wrote the 'Historia Brittonum'. He mentions the following battles by the 'dux bellorum', the 'magnanimous' Arthur.

'The first battle was in the mouth of the river which is called Glein' - 'Glein' stems from the Brythonic-Celtic, or Welsh, for 'clean', (today's 'glan') and there were many rivers thus named across Britain. 'Glyn' is a river valley. The village Gleiniant is on the river Nant-y-Gleiniant (Gleiniant stream) just north of Llanidloes in mid-Wales. The mouth of the Gleiniant meets the river Trannon just outside Trefeglwys, where there are the remains of a Roman road from Caersws to Pennal near Machynlleth. Arthur's cavalry would have made use of Roman roads.

'The second, third, fourth and fifth (battles) on another river which is called Dubglas and is in the region Linnius' - Aberdulais outside Neath is at the mouth of the Dulais River, and Pontarddulais near Swansea spans another river Dulais. Just north of the two are Llyn y Fan Fach and Llyn y Fan Fawr, and the region 'Linnius' may refer to 'the district of lakes'. This is at the western frontier of the traditional kingdom of Glamorgan and Gwent, and there had been Irish settlement in the west of Wales. Another candidate could be Ilchester in Somerset, then British and similarly under threat from the Saxons. The area round here was the Roman 'Lindinis' which may have been corrupted to Linnuis. The men of Domnonia, the West Country, fought for Arthur. The River Dulas (Black Brook) is described in the *'Brut'* as runing between Caer Efrog (Wroxeter) near the Welsh border in Shrophire, and Caer Fuddai, near Machynlleth. There is an Afon Dulas (Dulas River) near Machynlleth.

'The sixth battle on the river which is called Bassas' - Some historians place this as near Baschurch, between Oswestry and Shrewsbury in Shropshire, on the Welsh borders. Bassaleg outside Newport is another contender. Many battles were fought in this area between Saxons and Britons. Barber and Pykitt make a case for the Roman fort of Letocetum, now called Wall-by-Lichfield, outside Lichfield in Staffordhire. Basingwerk on the North-East Wales coast, is also a candidate.

'The seventh battle was at Cat Coed Celidon'. - 'Cad' is Welsh for battle, 'coed' for wood or forest, and Celidon has been named as Coed Celyddon, the Caledonian Forest. While this area of Scotland, like Cumbria, was still British at this time, there are candidates nearer Wales for the site. Blake and Lloyd (in *'The Keys to Avalon'*) believe the area to lie between Corwen, Cerrigydrudion and Denbigh in North Wales on the evidence of King Mark and Cernyw's association. Cernyw however was also the area just east of Cardiff, so it may have been there, between the Roman forts of Caerleon and Cardiff.

'The eighth battle was near the fort Guinnion, where Arthur bore the image of the Holy Virgin, mother of God, upon his shoulders, and through the power of our Lord Jesus Christ, and the Holy Mary, put the Saxons to flight, and pursued them with great slaughter' - Caer Guinn or Caer Gwent is the modern Caerwent, the remarkable walled Roman town near Caerleon and the Silurian camp of Llanmelin. This is near the later eastern limits of the kingdom of the Silures. Barber and Pykitt believe that Cats Ash near Caerleon is the site of this battle. If 'Guinnion' has been Latinised from the Welsh Gwynion, there is a site in Denbigh known as Caeaugwynion Mawr. There is a castle mound nearby, possibly Guinnion Fort. In the Berwyn Mountains there is also a hillfort named Carreg Gwynion.

'The ninth battle was fought in the City of the Legion' - Caerleon - Caer Legionis, or possibly the other great Roman fortress on the Welsh borders at Chester, near where a great later battle occurred in 613.

'He fought the tenth battle on the shore of the river called Tribruit' - This is properly spelt Tryfrwyd in 'The Black Book of Carmarthen'. Cai Hir, Arthur's foster-brother, fought against Garwlwyd, presumably under Arthur. This may be on the Severn near the border at Gloucester.

'The eleventh battle was on the hill called Agned' - Sources place this battle at the Roman fort of Bravonium, modern Leintwardine on the Welsh borders between Knighton and Ludlow. Barber and Pykitt place it at Catbrain hill-fort, just north of Bristol. Blake and Lloyd believe the site to be the hillfort outside Chester known as Maidens' Castle, from evidence in the *'Brut y Brenhinedd'* ('Chronicle of the Kings').

Another site given for the eleventh battle was *'Mons Beguion'*, (only in the Vatican ms. of the *'Historia Brittonum'*), and this is possibly a corruption of the Brewyn, where Urien Rheged fought. The Berwyn Hills or Bravonium/Leintwardine are the candidates for this battle.

'The twelfth was a most severe contest, when Arthur penetrated to the hill of Badon. In this engagement, nine hundred and forty fell by his hand alone, no one but the Lord affording him assistance. In all these engagements the Britons were successful' - This could be outside Bath, where another crucial battle between Germans and British occurred around 603, or at Mynydd Baedan outside Bridgend in Glamorgan. It was here that the advance of

the Saxons was finally halted. Lloyd and Baker suggest a hill-fort outside Buttington, North of Welshpool.

The final battle of Camlan appears to have been in Merioneth, where there are two river Camlans, possibly a battle between the Britons of North and South Wales for overlordship of the country. Certainly Maelgwn Gwynedd of North Wales was described as the 'Pendragon' after Arthur's disappearance after Camlan.

The only other battle associated with Arthur in Britain was at Llongborth, where Geraint fell, which many have placed as Portsmouth, for some reason, but there is a Llongborth in Ceredigion. 'Elegy for Geraint', said to be by Llywarch Hen, describes this battle:

> Before Gereint, the enemy's scourge,
> I saw white horses, tensed, red.
> After the war cry, bitter the grave...
>
> Before Geraint, the enemy of tyranny,
> I saw horses white with foam,
> After the war cry, a terrible torrent.
>
> In Llongborth, I saw the clash of swords,
> Men in terror, bloody heads,
> Before Geraint the great, his father's son.
>
> In Llongborth I saw spurs
> And men who did not flinch from the dread of spears,
> Who drank their wine from glasses that glinted...
>
> In Llongborth I saw the weapons
> Of warriors, and blood fast-falling,
> After the war-cry, a fearful return.
>
> In Llongborth I saw Arthur's
> Heroes who cut with steel.
> The Emperor, ruler of our labour.
>
> In Llongborth Geraint was slain.
> Heroes of the land of Dyfneint,
> Before they were slain, they slew.
>
> Under the thigh of Geraint swift chargers,
> Long their legs, wheat their fodder,
> Red, swooping like milk-white eagles...
>
> When Gereint was born, Heaven's gate stood open;
> Christ granted all our prayer;
> Lovely to behold, the glory of Britain.

Gereint's feast date is May 16. In the Book of Llandaf, Geraint founded the church at Magor near Newport. There is also Gerrans in Cornwall dedicated to Geraint, but this may be another saint. A martyr who died in battle, St Geraint is remembered in the old text 'The Sayings of the Wise':

> 'Hast thou heard the saying of Geraint,
> Son of Erbin, the just and experienced?
> "Short-lived is the hater of saints."

The Anglo-Saxon Chronicle places Gereint's death in 501, when 'Port and his two sons, Bieda and Maegla, came to Britain at the place called Llongborth, and slew a young Welshman, a very noble man.' Some think, following Bede's mis-dating of the coming of the Saxons by 20 years, that this battle was actually fought in 480. Others believe that it was fought in 510. Welsh tradition places Llongborth at Penbryn beach, near Aberporth in Cardigan rather than Portsmouth. (Llongborth means 'harbour' in Welsh). A farm inland is called Perth Geraint (at Bedd Geraint, Geraint's Grave) where he was said to be buried after the battle. Nearby is a standing stone inscribed *'Corbalengi iacit Ordovs'* denoting Corbalengus of the Ordovices tribe. In this parish John Jones wrote that there is a Llech yr Ochain (the Stone of Grief), near a well named Ffynnon Waedog (the Bloody Well). However, Barber and Pykitt place the battle on the Severn Estuary, near Magor (and Port-is-Coed, or Porthskewett to where Geraint moved his court). Merthyr Gerein (Geraint's Martyrdom, or Shrine) was an ancient chapel on a hillock known as Chapel Tump near Magor, the church Geraint founded.

Geraint may have held lands in Wales as well as the West Country, as there was a castle ruin named Dyngeraint (Dinas Geraint). Just seven miles from Penbryn is Cilgerran (Geraint's Retreat), with its magnificent castle overlooking a bend in the River Teifi. Provisions could be brought by boat to this site from Aberteifi (Cardigan). Cilgerran castle was known as Dyngeraint up to 1130 when Gilbert de Clare, first Earl of Pembroke, completed his Norman castle there.

Some claim that Geraint was the grandfather of Gildas, and also of Geraint who is mentioned in the Life of Teilo. A cousin or kinsman of Arthur, in legend Geraint defeated Edern ap Nudd in revenge for his slight on Gwenhwyfar (Guinevere), and married Enid, the daughter of Yniwl Iarll. In Arthurian legend, it was Geraint who encountered the 'Sparrow-Hawk Knight'. Chretien de Troyes wrote the mediaeval poem 'Erec and Enide' about Geraint's marriage. Geraint's son Cado carried on fighting the Saxons for Arthur after his father's death. Wherever we move in the circles around the hundreds of 6th century Welsh saints, we find derivations of Arthurian legend. Wherever we look upon maps of Wales and its borders, we find the evidence for Arthur and his battles.

SAINT BEUNO 7th century (d. 660 according to Cressy, and d. 642 according to Baring-Gould and Fisher)
PATRON SAINT OF COMPUTER TECHNICIANS

Feast Day April 21 (also 20)

The son of noble parents, Bugi (Hywgi) ap Gwynllyw Filwr and Perfferen ferch Llewddyn Luydog of Edinburgh (Dinas Eiddyn). Beuno was educated at Caerwent by Tangusius. He was related to Cadog and Mungo (Kentigern). In many ways, he is the North Wales equivalent of St David.

More dedications have been made to St Beuno in North Wales than to any other saint. It seems that he moved from a base in Powys to proselytise north-west Wales. The story is that he heard a man shouting to his dog in English, and determined to move until he was out of range of the Saxon tongue. Associated with founding a monastery at Clynnog in Caernarfonshire in 616, until the end of the eighteenth century pilgrims came to his burial place, where an oratory was built over his grave. It was excavated in 1914. His relics had been translated to Eglwys y Bedd, a new church, and a place of great miracles. The land had been given by his convert King Cadfan to him. Other sources say Cadwallon or Cynon gave him the land. Beuno's Vita was written by the anchorite of Llanddewi Brefi in the early fourteenth century based upon older works. As an old man, Beuno instructed Gwenfrewi with St Senan, and the instruction was continued by St Deifer.

Leland stated that Beuno was buried in the chapel adjoining the church and that one could still see a stone with an incised cross, indented by the saint's thumb. There is a holy well nearby. There used to be seats around it, and it was especially recommended for children with epilepsy and rickets, as well as impotency. A cure would come if one slept on a tombstone above the well overnight. Babies were placed on a bed of rushes on the font. Pennant described seeing there *a feather bed, on which a poor paralytic from Merionethshire had lain the whole night* after first washing in the well water. Epileptics favoured bathing in the water, then covering Beuno's tomb with rushes and sleeping on it. People with eye diseases scraped debris from the chapel walls, and mixed it with his well water to drink. In the later 17th century it was still held that a sick person laid on Beuno's tomb on a Friday would either recover or die within three weeks.

At his church at Clynnog on the Llyn, bulls bearing a certain mark were sacrificed *the half to God and to Beuno*, noted by John Ansters in 1589 – *as that people are of the opinion, that Beuno his cattell will prosper marvellous well*. The custom finished in the 19th century. The cattle cult came down from the Celtic worship of 'Audhumla', the primal cow. In the Celtic Northern Tradition, the primal cow is responsible for the creation of the world. 'Sacred beasts' with 'Beuno's mark' were given to the church wardens on Trinity Sunday, and the sale proceeds were placed in *Cyff Beuno*, *Beuno's Chest*, which still can be seen at Clynnog. This ancient oak chest, carved from a single piece of oak, gave rise to the local saying when someone tried to do something difficult: *Cystal I chwi geisio tori Cyff Beuno* – *You might as well try to break into Beuno's Chest.* One of the reasons for the custom of driving local bullocks to the church to dedicate them to him, was the pecuniary motive of achieving higher prices at market. The late mediaeval church of Clynnog Fawr stands on the site of St Beuno's oratory. Beuno died there after seeing a vision of angels descending from and ascending back to heaven. The church and shrine stand on ancient megaliths, one of which can be seen in the nave floor, and others of which are in the foundations. The site may have been a standing circle.

An early Christian inscribed stone at Llanfeuno-under-Clodock (Llanveynoe) in Archenfield (Ergyng) is close to the Roman road between Gobonium (Abergafenni) and Kenchester. The Hiberno-Saxon cross reads *Haefdur fecit crucem istam.* This church is now dedicated to Peter. Beuno is also remembered at Berriew and Betws Cedewain in Montgomeryshire near another Roman road to Caersws, and is said to have been a descendant of the princes of Powys of this area, centred on Mathrafal. North of here, Gwyddelwern near the Roman road to Caer Gai is also dedicated to Beuno, with his holy well. There is a late mediaeval 'waggon roof' in Gwyddelwern church.There is another St Beuno's Well at Betws Gwerfil Goch nearby. Further north, Whitford church was originally dedicated to Beuno, there was an old chapel of his in Llanasa, and Beuno's holy wells at Holywell and in Tremeirchion parish between Prestatyn and Denbigh. Many of these sites are near Roman remains. At Tremeirchion, the church is now that of Corpus Christi, has an 800-year-old yew, and once possessed a healing cross. Ffynnon Beuno's overflow here passes through the mouth of a carved stone head. There is mediaeval stained glass, and a remarkable 14th century canopied tomb to Dafydd ap Hywel ap Madog, Dafydd Ddu Arthro o Hiraddug (Black David, teacher of Hiraddug). This vicar of Tremeirchon was a bard, writer and sooth-saying propher, like Sion Cent of Kentchurch. Beuno's healing well lies in a nearby hollow, with water gushing from the mouth of the roughly carved stone head of unknown age. Another interesting well was Ffynnon Nantcall in Clynnog parish – it was said to cure melancholia.

In north-west Wales, Beuno is remembered at Aberffraw (the court of the princes of Gwynedd) and Trefraeth in Anglesey, and at Clynnog Fawr, Pistyll, Botwnnog and Carnguwch on the Lleyn peninsula. Aberffraw has an eleven feet dolmen called Dinas Dindryfal. There still exists Ffynnon Beuno in Malt House Lane, Aberffraw. There is also Ffynnon Bryn Fendigaid near Aberffraw, where a fish was kept for divination purposes, near some chalybeate springs where a woman named Gwladus was martyred at Croes Ladys. In Gwynedd, Llanycil is dedicated to him, with another holy well, near Caer Gai roman fort, as is Penmorfa with a holy well, just off the Roman road between Segontium and Tomen-y-Mur. Ffynnon Ddeuno no longer flows, but his ruined chapel can be seen at Gatwen Farm, Broughton, Brecon. In Gwyddelwern, Merioneth, was Ffynnon Gwern Beuno. At Berriew (Aberrhiw), Powys, there is Beuno's standing stone, Maen Beuno, which was said to be Beuno's first pulpit.

One day, walking the banks of the river, he heard a Saxon calling to his hounds on the other bank. He rushed back to his monks and addressed them *'My sons, put on your clothes and shoes, and let us leave this place for the nation of this man I heard setting on his hounds has a strange language which is abominable and I heard his voice. They have invaded this land and will keep it in ownership.'* From Montgomeryshire this early Welsh Nationalist travelled north and was given land at Clynnog.

E.G Bowen, in *'The Settlements of the Celtic Saints in Wales'*, draws attention to the fact that his disciples mentioned in his Vita founded churches near his. Guilsfield near Betws Cedewain, and Berriew are dedicated to Aelhaearn; Llandenan and Llanwyddelan to Lorcan Wyddel; and Llwchaearn is remembered at Llanllwchaearn and Llamyrewig. Near Gwyddelwern was an old chapel dedicated to Aelhaearn, and Cwyfan's Llangwyfan is nearby. In Flintshire, the Lleyn Peninsula and Anglesey his dedications are near those of St Winifred, Gwenfrewi. In the Lleyn and Arfon, saints Aelhaearn, Cwyfan, Edern, Deiniol Fab and Twrog have dedications close to Beuno's churches, and in Anglesey churches of Cwyfan, Deiniol Fab, Dona, Ceidio, Edern and Twrog are close to his dedications. Aelhaiarn founded Llanaelhaiarn in Caernarfon and Merioneth, and Cegidfa (now called Guilsfield, near Welshpool) in Montgomery. He was a servant of St Beuno. The ascetic Beuno used to walk into a cold river to pray, and Aelhaearn followed him once, standing behind him. Beuno did not know who was behind him, and called on a pack of savage animals which tore Aelhaearn apart. Beuno put the body together again, all except an eyebrow, which he replaced with the iron tip of his staff. Aelhaearn means *'the iron eye-brow.'*

Beuno's dedications include: Berriew (Aber-Rhiw) and Betws in Montgomery; Llanycil and Gwyddelwern in Merioneth; Clynnog Fawr, Carngiwch Chapel, Pistyll Chapel, Penmorfa chapel, Dolbenmaen chapel in Caernarfon; Aberffraw chapel and Trefdraeth chapel in Anglesey; Llanfeuno chapel to Clydog (Clodock) Hereford; Llanfaenor near Skenfrith in Monmouthshire should be called Llanfeuno. King Ynyr of Gwent gave Beuno three estates in Ewyas including Llanfeuno. Morgan Hen, King of Glamorgan, restored Llanfaenor in 980. A new church was built on the site in 1853.

The 'Sayings of the Wise' record:

> *'Have you heard the saying of Beuno*
> *To all who resort to him ?*
> *From death, flight will not avail".'*

Clynnog has an interesting cromlech with 110 cup-shaped hollows in its capstone, called Bachwen Clynnog Dolmen, and a nearby standing stone is known as Maen Dylan. Also Penarth Dolmen stands in a field named Caer Goetan. At Berriew, Maen Beuno is a leaning standing stone on the Severn's banks. Llanycil in Merioneth is dedicated to Beuno and had three standing stones, but none seem to have survived.

The loveliest of the legends surrounding Beuno is that he dropped his book of sermons walking across the Menai Strait sands from Anglesey. (The strait could have been passable at this time – it appears that water levels have risen forty to sixty feet in the last 1500 years). When he reached Clynnog Fawr, a curlew was in his cell, sitting by the book. Beuno prayed for God's everlasting protection of the curlew, and this is why its eggs are so difficult to find, as the colours match those of the ground upon which they have been laid.

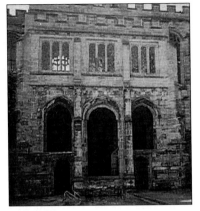

St. Beuno's Stone is at Holywell
(photograph courtesy of WTB)

Beuno's history of bringing back to life four or five decapitated victims has made him the 'Patron of Computer Technicians', who are frequently asked to do the impossible at once. Their web page bears the motto 'Illum Posse Dicere.' His most famous resurrection was that of St Winifred, Gwenfrewi, at the holy well with the longest unbroken record of pilgrimage in Europe. Gwenfrewi was the daughter of Prince Tefydd and Gwenlo. Legend is that she suffered from the unwanted attentions of Prince Caradog ab Alan, from Hawarden (Penarlag in Flintshire). On Mid-Summer's Day, she fled from him but he caught up with her at the church door before she could gain sanctuary. Because she had spurned him, he cut off her head, whereupon the earth opened up and swallowed him. Her uncle, St Beuno, restored her head to her shoulders and she lived the rest of her days as a nun at Gwytherin in Denbighshire. Where her head fell to the earth at Holywell (Treffynnon, Welltown), a spring of water gushed forth. Some sources say that she became abbess of a nunnery at Holywell, and others that she then followed Beuno to Clynnog, then she moved on to Bodfari, Henllan and finally became a nun under St Eleri in Gwytherin near Llanrwst. She died fifteen years after her head was restored to her body.

A legend says that Beuno asked Gwenfrewi to send him a rain-proof woollen cloak each year on the feast day of John the Baptist, the anniversary of the day upon which she was brought back to life. She placed it on a stone in the river, and each year the stone would sail down the river and across the sea to her uncle, and reach him in a perfectly dry condition. St Beuno's chapel was erected just above where St Margaret's Chapel now stands in Holywell, but the site is now dedicated to St James.

ANEURIN BEVAN November 15 1897 - July 6, 1960
FOUNDER AND ARCHITECT OF THE NATIONAL HEALTH SERVICE

'Nye' Bevan was born in Tredegar, one of the ten children of a miner, David Bevan. A poor performer at school, he was made to 'repeat' a year before he left to work in a colliery, aged 13. Like many other poor youngsters in the Valleys, he received most of his learning from the local Workingmen's Institute Library. He joined the South Wales Miners' Federation, and aged just 19 became chairman of his Miners' Lodge. His employers, the Tredegar Iron and Coal Company, saw him as an agitator and sacked him, but with the support of the Miners' Federation, the company was forced to re-employ him, on the grounds that he had been fired because of 'victimisation'. In 1919 he won a scholarship to study at the Central Labour College in London, and spent two years studying economics, politics and history. He read the *Communist Manifesto*, took up the ideas of Marx and Engels, and was also given lessons to cure his stammer.

Bevan returned to Tredegar in 1921, but the company refused to re-employ him, so for three years he was without work. In this time he acted as an unpaid adviser to people with financial and health problems. However, in 1924 Bevan managed to find work at the nearby Bedwellty Colliery, but this lasted only a few months as the colliery closed. In 1925 his beloved father died of pneumoconiosis - the dreaded disease of miners in Wales. Luckily, in 1926, Nye obtained another job, as a union official, his wages of £5 a week being paid by the members of the Miners' Lodge. With the General Strike of May 3rd, 1926, Bevan soon became one of the leaders of the South Wales miners.

The *National Health Service*, the jewel that was pioneered in Britain and copied in civilised countries all over the world, was largely based upon the example of a Welsh valley community scheme. Tuberculosis and Pneumoconiosis were rife in nineteenth century Wales, but in Tredegar was established the Workmen's Medical Aid Society (with its own doctors), in the 1890's. Workers paid three old pence in the pound, equivalent to just over one per cent of their income, for dentistry services, spectacles and midwives. Its doctors included AJ Cronin, who wrote about the scheme and its effects in 'The Citadel'. In 1923, Aneurin ('Nye') Bevan was elected to the Hospital Committee, allied to the Medical Aid Society, and as Minister of Health just over three decades later, he *launched the National Health Service*. It is thought that Tredegar is the model that inspired the creation of the NHS.

In 1928, Bevan was elected to Monmouthshire County Council, and in 1929 easily beat the opposition in Ebbw Vale to become its Labour candidate in the next General Election. He became a Labour MP in 1931, and in World War II was frequently a *'one-man opposition'* to Winston Churchill. His maiden speech in Parliament was an attack on Winston Churchill, his main enemy in the General Strike, the man who sent troops into South Wales. One of the most attractive aspects of Nye's personality was that he never tried to disguise his roots - not for him the claret-smooth old boy networks of miner's son Roy 'Woy' Jenkins. Nye Bevan was unequivocal in his attachment to the working classes: *'No amount of cajolery, and no attempts at ethical and social seduction, can eradicate from my heart a deep burning hatred for the Tory Party.......So far as I am concerned they are lower than vermin.'*

Aneurin Bevan

Bevan was one of the most outspoken opponents of Ramsay MacDonald's National Government, violently arguing against 'Means Testing' for the poor, and in 1934 married a fellow left-wing Labour MP, Jennie Lee. They became active for The Relief of the Victims of German Fascism, before the War, and helped set up the left-wing socialist weekly newspaper, *Tribune*. In 1938 he visited the Republican Government in Spain, witnessing the fight against Franco's Fascism. At the start of the War, he campaigned strongly for his implacable foe, Winston Churchill, to replace Neville Chamberlain and his Government. He also used his influence as Editor of Tribune and leader of the left-wing MP's in the House of Commons to shape Government policies. He advocated nationalisation of the coal industry, was against heavy censorship and the locking-up of foreign nationals, and spoke for a Second Front to help Russia against Germany.

After the War, Bevan was made Minister of Health, and 1946 saw his revolutionary National Insurance Act, instituting the Health Service from 1948, and beginning compulsory wage contributions to fund sickness, maternity and old age benefits and pensions.

Bevan resigned as Minister of Labour from the post-war Attlee Government in 1951 over charges being introduced for teeth and spectacles. However, the real reason was the foreign and defence policy of the Labour government. The scale of the arms budget, forced upon Britain by the U.S. government during the Korean War, was unsustainable. Even his enemy Winston Churchill later acknowledged that Bevan was right. In the last fifty years, political machismo has forced Britain to throw away ten per cent of its wealth every year into the bottomless pit of 'defence' spending. Thus less investment, on a cumulatively exponential scale, is available for education, health, science, pensions etc., etc. It is no surprise that the economic success stories since the second world war, Germany, Japan and Switzerland, have restricted defence budgets. Nye later became Shadow Foreign Secretary to Hugh Gaitskell, and was Deputy Leader of the Labour Party when he died of cancer.

It is odd that major politicians brought up in Wales, such as Michael Heseltine, Michael Howard, Roy Jenkins, and Geoffrey Howe have adopted upper-crust English accents. Bevan refused to do so. Neil Kinnock, as Leader of the Labour Party, saw no need to change his voice. Kinnock was severely attacked by the national media as being *'the Welsh Windbag'*, much as Lloyd George had been criticised in the early part of the century as *'the Welsh liar'*. Kinnock's oratory in his speech in Bridgend, just before Labour lost the 1983 General Election, is comparable to Bevan's and must be recounted for posterity – few Labour politicians can empathise with the man in the street like this, including the present Prime Minister, Anthony Blair –

'If Margaret Thatcher wins on Thursday she will become more a leader than a Prime Minister.

That power produced arrogance, and when it is toughened by Tebbitry and fawned upon by spineless sycophants, the boot-licking tabloid Knights of Fleet Street and placemen in the Quangos, the arrogance corrupts completely.

If Margaret Thatcher is re-elected as Prime Minister on Thursday, I warn you.
I warn you that you will be quiet when the curfew of fear and the gibbet of unemployment makes you obedient.
I warn you that you will have pain – when healing and relief depend upon payment.
I warn you that you will have ignorance - and then talents are untended and wits are wasted, when learning is a privilege and not a right.
I warn you that you will have poverty – when pensions slip and benefits are whittled away by a government that won't pay in an economy that can't pay.
I warn you that you will be cold – when fuel charges are used as a tax system that the rich don't notice and the poor can't afford.
I warn you that you must not expect work – when many cannot spend, more will not be able to earn. When they don't earn, they don't spend. When they don't spend, work dies.
I warn you not to go out into the streets alone after dark or into the streets in large crowds of protest in the light.
I warn you that you will have defence of a sort – with a risk and at a price that passes all understanding.
I warn you that you will be home-bound – when fares and transport bills kill leisure and lock you up.
I warn you that you will borrow less – when credit, loans, mortgages and easy payments are refused to people on your melting income.
If Margaret Thatcher wins on Thursday –
I warn you not to be ordinary
I warn you not to be young
I warn you not to fall ill
I warn you not to get old'

(Speech at Bridgend, June 7 1983, as reported in The Daily Telegraph, June 8, 1983). This is not the 'soundbite of three' approach to politics – it is a poetic approach to man's sensibilities – Margaret Thatcher won the British elections, but never won the Welsh electorate.

Aneurin Bevan, 1897-1960, is commemorated in a statue at the West end of Cardiff's Queen Street. There are several websites devoted to Bevan's sayings, all of which refer to him as an 'English' politician. Just some are repeated here - they demonstrate the shining wit and unswerving idealism of one of the very, very few politicians who never betrayed the electorate:
It is an axiom, enforced by the experience of all the ages, that they who rule industrially will rule politically;
I read the newspaper avidly. It is my one form of political fiction.
Freedom is the by-product of economic surplus.
Stand not too near the rich man lest he destroy thee - and not too far away lest he forget thee;
You call that statesmanship. I call it an emotional spasm;
We know what happens to people who stand in the middle of the road. They get run down;
This island is made mainly of coal and is surrounded by fish. Only an organising genius could produce a shortage of coal and fish at the same time;
The Prime Minister has an absolute genius for putting flamboyant labels on empty

baggage (on Harold MacMillan);
I am not going to spend any time whatsoever in attacking the Foreign Secretary....
If we complain about the tune, there is no need to attack the monkey when the organ grinder is present (in the House of Commons, to Prime Minister Anthony Eden and Foreign Secretary Selwyn Lloyd).
And the following are just some of his comments across the benches, directed at Churchill:
He is a man suffering from petrified adolescence;
The worst thing I can say about democracy is that it has tolerated the right honourable gentleman for four and a half years;
The Prime Minister has very many virtues, and when the time comes I hope to pay my tribute to them, but I am bound to say that political honesty and sagacity have never been among them;
I welcome this opportunity of pricking the bloated bladder of lies with the poinard of truth;
He never spares himself in conversation. He gives himself so generously that hardly anyone else is permitted to give anything in his presence;
The Tories always hold the view that the state is an apparatus for the protection of the swag of the property owners... Christ drove the money changers out of the temple, but you inscribe the title deed on the altar cloth.
All Tories are vermin...... The whole art of Conservative politics in the 20th century is being deployed to enable wealth to persuade poverty to use its political freedom to keep wealth in power.

LLYWELYN BREN d. 1318
LLYWELYN THE UGLY, LLYWELYN AP RHYS AP GRUFFUDD AB IFOR BACH, LORD OF SENGHENYDD AND MISKIN

The ancient lordship of Senghenydd was the most eastern of Glamorgan's 'cantrefs', lying between the rivers Taf and Rhymney. Then from the important Roman fort and port of Cardiff it headed north including Caerphilly. In 1093 the Normans conquered Iestyn ap Gwrgant, the last king of Glamorgan (Morganwg), and in the commote of Cibbwr, which included Cardiff, built a castle on the site of the Roman camp. The two other commotes of Senghenydd remained controlled by their Welsh lord, Senghenydd-is-Caiach (Caerffili to the river Caiach), and Senghenydd -uwch-Caiach (the region north of the river). In 1158, after an attempt by the Normans to take yet more lands, Ifor ap Meurig (Ifor Bach) scaled the walls of Cardiff Castle at night. Although it was defended by 120 men-at-arms, the Lord of Senghenydd carried off William, Earl of Gloucester, his wife Hawise and son Robert. Any Welsh rulers captured by Normans were normally tortured and blinded, but Ifor held the grabbing Norman prisoner until he had signed to give back stolen lands, and make compensation with additional lands. He then released the hostages. Senghenydd stayed in the hands of its native rulers, except for the Norman presence in Cardiff and across the Vale of Glamorgan, under Gruffudd ap Ifor (d.1211) and his son Rhys ap Gruffudd (d.1256).

Gruffudd ap Rhys was Lord in 1262, a document describing him as holding the two commotes of Senghenydd. However, because of the threat posed by Llywelyn ap Gruffudd, the last prince of Wales,Gruffudd ap Rhys was ejected by Gilbert de Clare, Lord of Glamorgan, in 1266. In 1268 the Norman began building the great fortress of Caerffili, probably on the site of a Roman fort. This was despite the signing of the Treaty of Montgomery of 1267, when England's French rulers recognised Llywelyn as Prince of Wales. From

Caerffili Castle besieged by Llywellyn Bren
(photograph courtesy of WTB)

Gwynedd, Llywelyn II therefore invaded and took over Upper Senghenydd, preparing for an attack upon the new castle rising at Caerffili. There was now an attempt at a treaty between Gilbert de Clare and Llywelyn at 'Monks' Bridge' (Crickadarn in Brecon), with hostilities ceasing for a time, with no incursion by either side over the River Caiach. However, de Clare completed his castle, which led Llywelyn to attack and destroy it on October 11th, 1270. Another, much stronger, castle was erected and Llywelyn returned with his army in October 1271 and laid siege. A treaty was arranged whereby the King's men took over Caerffili, while both armies moved away. However, de Clare by a ruse regained it from its custodians, the men of the Bishops of Lichfield and Worcester. Henry III died in 1272 without resolving the breaking of the treaty, and other Marcher Lords combined with de Clare to push Llywelyn back towards Brecon from Glamorgan. War with the new King Edward in 1276-77 forced Llywelyn back to Gwynedd, and his death by treachery in 1282 meant that the massive castle of Caerffili was now safe in French hands. In 1294-95 Senghenydd was devastated in a Welsh uprising, as was the town of Caerffili and its mills burnt, but the castle held out until the King's army came to Wales.

Not until 20 years later did Caerffili come under siege again. Llywelyn ap Gruffydd ap Rhys, the son of the Welsh Lord of Senghenydd ejected in 1266, had a stronghold at Gelligaer, yet another Roman fort. He had considerable property in Senghenydd, holding high office under Gilbert de Clare, being *'a powerful personage in those parts......* (having) *great mastery in that country.'* Problems started when de Clare was killed at Bannockburn in 1314. As the last of his line, the Crown took over his lands, from Neath to the Wye, the richest and most fertile part of Wales at the time.

As a vassal lord, Llywelyn had been virtually 'custos' of Glamorgan, acting as an adviser to the young Norman lord. With de Clare's death, the king appointed Ingelram Berengar, Bartholomew de Badlesmere and Payn de Turberville in rapid succession as his 'keepers' in Glamorgan. There was a spontaneous uprising, lasting from July to September 1314 across Glamorgan, forcing extra garrisons in many castles, and causing damage to Caerffili Castle. Llywelyn Bren had complained to the king about the tyranny of the new land-ownership. The men of Senghenydd were no longer entitled to collect firewood, many other ancient customs had been over-ridden, and lands had been taken from him in Senghenydd and Whitchurch (where there was a Welsh castle) near Cardiff. Edward II agreed with Llywelyn's claims, ordering that the lands be given back to one of his sons.

Payn de Turberville, Lord of Coity, was appointed 'custos' of Glamorgan in 1315, succeeding Badlesmere. He hated Welshmen, being in constant conflict with

Llywelyn's kinsmen, the lords of Afan, whose territories he coveted. Llywelyn was removed from his offices, and sought justice from the weak homosexual Edward II, who sided with his fellow-Norman. Appearing at Court, he was ordered to face parliament at Lincoln on a charge of inciting the Welsh to rebellion. Fearing arrest on a charge of treachery, Llywelyn rushed home from London, and because of Turberville's oppressive regime, found no difficulty in starting a great revolt that flashed through the Vale of Glamorgan. It is claimed that 10,000 men joined Llywelyn, and at one time it looked as if it would develop into a national revolt. Many people in Senghenydd died, and 31 burgages in Caerffili were burnt. He had returned to his base of Castell Coch, which the Normans had taken, and they refused to hand it over. Gathering around a thousand supporters, he scaled the castle walls and started a revolt that lasted nine weeks. In the Vale of Glamorgan, he destroyed the castles at Sully, Barry, Old Beaupre, Kenfig, Flemingston, West Orchard and East Orchard. He besieged the mighty Caerffili Castle, (the largest in Europe outside that of Windsor) but was eventually surrounded by two English armies.

In February 1316, King Edward assembled an army of mercenaries from Glamorgan, West Wales, Gloucester and the Forest of Dean at Cardiff Castle. Humphrey de Bohun approached Caerffili with another royal army, from Brecon. Other marcher lords joined in, as did Badlesmere. On March 12 a force of 150 men-at-arms and 2000 footmen, under the command of William de Montague, Henry Earl of Lancaster, and John Giffard marched north from Cardiff to relieve the siege of Caerffili Castle. Lady de Clare was trapped there, and there was strong opposition to the army at Thornhill. The troops seems to have flanked this opposition by way of Rudry, dislodging the Welsh from the hill-ridge as they made their way to the massive castle. In the face of converging armies, and after suffering heavy losses, Llywelyn retreated to Ystradfellte in the Vale of Neath. There, with two of his sons, he surrendered to de Bohun, on March 20th, 1316. To save his followers, he surrendered knowing his fate, saying *'It is better for one man to die than for a whole population to be killed by the sword.'* He was taken first to de Bohun's Brecon Castle, then to the Tower of London, where he and his sons were joined by his wife Lleuci, another son, and other Welsh prisoners. His lands and goods were seized and the inventory of stock confiscated still exists*. Lleucu was granted an allowance of 3 pennies a day for upkeep in her captivity, and her three sons 2 pence each. De Bohun and other Marcher Lords interceded with King Edward on Llywelyn's behalf and his life was spared.

Evans in 1908 noted that Llywelyn Bren killed all the tax collectors in each village, ridding villagers of their unfair burdens, and *'killed so many of the English and Normans, that no Englishman even thought of remaining in Glamorgan.'* The rebellion was put down by forces under the Earl of Hereford, Lord Mortimer of Wigmore and Rhys ap Gruffydd. Llywelyn Bren surrendered on condition that no harm came to his men, and they were allowed to return to their homes. After imprisonment in Brecon, Llywelyn and his two sons were taken to the Tower of London in 1316, but not treated unkindly, and set free in 1317. He received a full pardon on June 17th, 1317 and returned to Wales to lawfully recover his lands. Glamorgan had been devastated, and the heavy fines imposed upon the rebels were impossible to pay, leading to land forfeitures. Llywelyn's wife and sons seem to have been joined the barons De Bohun, Mortimer et al who invaded Despenser's territories in 1321.

The Despensers had now taken over Glamorgan, and had seized his estates in his absence. Lord Despenser, the favourite of Edward II captured the Welshman on his return home and illegally murdered him, despite the King's Pardon. This was one of the charges by the barons that led to Despenser's execution. Llywelyn's widow led another rebellion, that led to several Norman castles being burned. Sir William Fleming was hanged for carrying out Despenser's orders, and laid to rest alongside Llywelyn at Greyfriars in Cardiff. Another version is that Fleming acted as deputy to Sir Bartholomew Badlesmere as Custos of Glamorgan in which capacity he executed Bren, but more likely he was hung for taking part in the Barons' Revolt against the Despensers.

Hugh Despenser had appointed Payn Turberville of Coity Castle to be Custodian of Glamorgan. Sir William Berkerolles of East Orchard was Despenser's sub-lord, given full powers over the estates of Llywelyn Bren. This was done to evict Bren from his rightful possessions across Glamorgan. The Normans had found it far easier to subdue these flatter and richer southern parts of Wales, where reinforcements from the sea were available during their slow and uneven conquest. (The Normans only took four years to conquer England, but three-hundred and fifty to completely subdue all of Wales).

However, Berkerolles owed Llywelyn Bren his life from 1316, as Llywelyn had previously protected him in the Welsh attack at Caerffili, where thirteen Norman soldiers on Berkerolle's bodyguard were killed.

Ystradfellte Falls, where Llywellyn surrendered.
(photograph courtesy of WTB)

Llywelyn Bren was dragged through the streets of Cardiff, then slowly and barbarously executed at Cardiff Castle by the order of Despenser to Berkerolles, whose life Bren had previously saved. He was hung drawn and quartered, according to Despenser on the orders of King Edward II, but Despenser had received no such authority King Edward II. He wanted Bren out of the way, and had made Berkerolles execute him to distance himself from the disgusting event. Thus Despenser was executed himself on August 25th, 1320 near the Black Tower of Cardiff Castle, and was buried in the adjoining Greyfriars Monastery ruins, alongside Llywelyn Bren. The full charge against Despenser reads *'That he did wrongfully adjudge Llywelyn Bren, causing him to be beheaded, drawn and quartered to the discredit of the King and contrary to the laws and dignity of the Crown'*. Bren's grieving widow attacked the castles of Cardiff, Caerphilly and St. Quintin's. Cardiff City Council unforgivably allowed an office block to be built on the ruins of Greyfriars, which has now been converted into the Hilton Hotel.

Iolo Morganwg gives us a note on Llywelyn Bren and his destruction of the castles of St Athan and Flemingstone, taken from the manuscript of John Philip of

Treoes, near Bridgend:

'*Llywelyn Bren, the Aged, called Llywelyn the Ugly, demolished many castles of chieftains, namely, the castles of St Georges, the castle of Sully, the castle of Tregogun (Cogan), the castle of Foulke Fitzwarin, the castle of Barry, the castle of St Athan, the castle of Beaupre, the castle of Kenfig, the castle of Ruthyn, the castle of Gelli Garn, and the castle of Flemingston; - and he killed such numbers of English and Normans, that no Englishman could be found who would so much as entertain, for a moment, the idea of remaining in Glamorgan. At this period, there was in each town and village a sort of land steward, called preventive mayor; but Llywelyn the Ugly had them all hanged; and the chieftains were obliged to discontinue such appointments, because no person whatever could be found to undertake such office, either for money or goods.*'

Rice Merrick in 1568 makes the following entry concerning the Llywelyn Bren rebellion:

'*De Johanne Flemyng:*

Sir John Fflemynge, Knight, to whose lott fortuned the Lordships of Wenvo, St George's, Constantine Waules, Fflemyngstone, and Llanmays; Who gave unto his younger Sonne the Mannour of Constantine Waules and Fflemyngstone, of his name soe called, which Parcells continue at this day in his Name and lineage. The Lordshipps of Wenvo, St George's and Llanmays, discended to his eldest Sonne (and for difference was named Fflemynge of Wenvo, the other Fflemyng Melyn), whose issue Male enjoyed the same until the tyme of Edward the 2nd that Sir William Fflemyng, being Sheriffe, and cheife Ruler of Glamorgan and Morganwg, in the tyme of Sir Hugh Spencer, the Sonne, then Lord thereof. When the fortune of Spencers altered, his misfortune approached; for hee was executed at Cardiff, for that, as it was supposed, hee had wrongfully adjudged Llewellen Brenn, of Senighenith, to death, and, as it is said, caused a Jebet to be raysed by the Black Towne, within a little Wall that enclosed about the Prison, then called Stavell & oged, and there caused him to be hanged; for which cause (as some affirmeth) hee was attaynted by the Statute of Rutland.

This Sir William Fflemynge was buried in the White ffryars without the North gate of the Towne of Cardiff, whose Tombe, in a faire Stone, at the Suppression thereof, together with Llen Brenn his Tombe, made of wood, was defaced. (This is where the Pearl Building, now the Cardiff Hilton Hotel stands. Obviously the monastery was ransacked during the Reformation, and in the 1960's Cardiff Council unfortunately sold the land for development on the ruins.) *Robert Ffabyan, in his CHRONICLE, alleadgeth another Cause of his death; affirming, that hee was executed at Cardiff, in Wales in the 14 yeare of Edward 2, among a great number of Barons that were in diverse places put to death. After whose death, his Inheritance discended to his only Daughter; who marryed Malifand, of Pembrochshire, being one of the King's Mynyons. The issue male of Malifand continued and enjoyed Fflemyng's inheritance, untill that Edmund Malifand, who marryed with Margarett, Daughter to Sir Mathew Cradog, Knight, in the time of H. 7. Dyed without issue.*'

Despenser had been captured near Llantrisant in 1326 and executed. (When Caerffili castle surrendered in 1326, £14,000 was found hidden in barrels which belonged to Despenser, plus tons of silver-plate. In 1327 the estates of Senghenydd were restored by Edward (under Mortimer pressure) to Llywelyn's sons, Gruffydd, John, Meurig, Roger, William and Llywelyn. Edward II was shortly after brutally put to death with a red-hot poker in Berkeley Castle, and Despenser was captured and executed as a traitor at Hereford.

*Stock included 374 cows, 114 steers and heifers, 113 sheep, 84 pigs, 71 goats, 69 oxen, 41 calves, 29 mares, 9 'affers', 7 colts and 3 bulls. Possessions included 10 gold rings, a gold clasp, military garments, brass pots, Welsh chairs, armour, brass chandeliers, a saddle and 8 silver spoons.

FOOTNOTES:
(i) The vast majority of Norman lords and kings were illiterate. Among Llywelyn Bren's confiscated possessions were three books in Welsh, one copy of *'Roman de la Rose'*, four other books, a missal (mass book), a diurnal (service book for the day's holy offices) and two 'manuals' (office books of the medieval church).

(ii) In 1104 Gerald treacherously slew Hywel ap Goronwy to take Ystrad Tywi and Gower (Gwyr). Hugh Mortimer blinded Rhys ap Hywel in 1148, to take over his territories around Bridgnorth in what is now Shropshire. Blinding was a common Norman practice – King Henry II personally took out the eyes of his child hostages, the two sons each of the great Owain Gwynedd and The Lord Rhys. The terrible punishment of hanging, drawing and quartering while still alive was another Danish-French innovation in English law, invented for the punishment of Prince Dafydd, Llywelyn II's brother).

RICHARD BURTON November 19 1925 - August 5 1984
RICHARD WALTER JENKINS Jr. - 1960'S FILM SUPERSTAR

Born Richard Jenkins, he came from the same neighbourhood as Anthony Hopkins and after Oxford University trained at RADA. A superb stage actor, he also received seven Academy Award nominations and twice married Elizabeth Taylor prior to his death from a stroke and brain haemorrhage in 1984. His villa where he was buried, on Lake Geneva, was called 'Pays de Galles' (French for 'Wales'), and *'Sospan Fach'* was played at the funeral of this hard-drinking Celtic genius. Burton was survived by a young widow, Sally Hay (Burton) whom he married a year before his death. His first wife was Sybil Williams, to whom he was married from 1948-1963. He married Elizabeth Taylor twice, from 1964-1974 and 1975-1976. He was married to Susan Hunt, the former wife of the racing driver James Hunt from 1976-1982.

The second youngest of a Welsh miner's 13 children, he grew up Welsh-speaking in Pontrhydyfendigaid near Port Talbot, Glamorgan. He was adopted by his former schoolteacher Philip Burton, who discovered and nurtured Burton's acting talents, and helped him win a scholarship to Oxford. By 1949 he was seen as one of Britain's most exciting theatrical talents, and film director Phillip Dunne remembers him in London in *'The Lady's Not for Burning'*. *'He "took" the stage and kept an firm grip on it on every one of his brief appearances'*, eclipsing the star, John Gielgud.

His performances in the West End in the early 1950's, notably as Hamlet, made his name, but he is better known for his total of around 60 films. Apart from his brooding good looks and pale blue eyes, Burton had a marvellously rich speaking voice. 20th Century Fox signed Burton, hoping to make him into the 'new Olivier'.

He began an affair with Liz Taylor, the wife of the crooner Eddie Fisher, while filming Cleopatra in 1962. Taylor was critically ill, postponing the filming, and the

Richard Burton

star playing Antony, Stephen Boyd, walked away for the film. When Liz Taylor's heart stopped after an emergency tracheotomy, she had a near-death experience, when she *'knew there was a new love awaiting my return'*. Burton was brought in for Boyd, and the greatest love affair Hollywood has ever known was ignited. Burton's own cabal of Welsh drinking partners, the actors Stanley Baker and Donald Houston, the opera singer Geraint Evans, the harpist Osian Ellis and the singer-comedian Harry Secombe, all tried to make Burton stay with his Welsh wife, Sybil. All five met Burton and Taylor in a bar near Borehamwood film studios to make him see sense, but ended up singing Welsh songs instead. A cable from Laurence Olivier to Burton at the height of the Cleopatra scandal read *'make up your mind, dear heart. Do you want to be a great actor or a household word?'* Burton tersely cabled back *'Both'*.

With Elizabeth Taylor he starred in *Cleopatra* (1963), *The VIP's* (1963), *The Sandpiper* (1965), *Who's Afraid of Virginia Woolf* (1966), *Doctor Faustus* (1967 - Burton also directed), *The Comedians* (1967), *The Taming of the Shrew* (1967), *Boom* (1968), *Hammersmith is Out* (1972) and *Under Milk Wood* (1973).

Burton's 'best' films are possibly 'Becket', 'Equus' and 'Who's Afraid of Virginia Woolf', with his role as a fallen priest opposite Ava Garner in 'Night of the Iguana' possibly his greatest screen performance. Burton once said *'I want an Oscar - I've won all kinds of little Oscars but not the big one.'* Sadly, despite a record seven nominations (with Peter O'Toole), he never was awarded the accolade. He had been nominated for Best Supporting Actor for *'My Cousin Rachel'* in 1952. Then came a run of six nominations for Best Actor - *'The Robe'* (1953), *'Becket'* (1964), *'The Spy Who Came in from the Cold'* (1965), *'Who's Afraid of Virginia Woolf'* (1966), *'Anne of the Thousand Days'* 1969, and *'Equus'* 1977. For *'Anne of the Thousand Days'* he received the colossal sum of a million dollars and a percentage of the gross take, up from just half a million dollars for *'The VIP's'* in 1963. We can see here just how much of a Holywood 'superstar' he was in the swinging '60's. For the 1966 Oscar Awards ceremony, Taylor and Burton had co-starred in *'Who's Afraid of Virginia Woolf'*. Liz Taylor was awarded her second Best Actress Oscar, and Burton was beaten by Paul Scofield in *'A Man for All Seasons'*. Richard Burton refused the attend the awards, having been let down in the two previous years. Other notable 1960's films which included Burton were *'Where Eagles Dare'*, *'The Comedians'*, and *'What's New Pussycat'*. His awards included Best Actor for *'Virginia Woolf'* in the British Academy Awards, and Best Actor for *'Becket'* and *'Look Back in Anger'* given by the New York Film Critics Circle.

He made many mediocre films, being 'driven' a little like today's Michael Caine. Both came from humble backgrounds and felt that it was somehow not normal not to be working full-time. Burton admitted *'I've done the most awful rubbish in order to have somewhere to go in the morning...... I've played the lot: a* homosexual, a sadistic gangster, kings, princes, a saint, the lot. All that's left is a Carry On film. That's my ambition.' He admitted to a drink problem all his life, and said 'My father considered that anyone who went to chapel and didn't drink alcohol was not to be tolerated. I grew up in that belief.........When I played drunks I had to remain sober because I didn't know how to play them when I was drunk.'

However, it was on the stage that Burton really commanded, being seen as the true heir to Laurence Olivier. Sir John Gielgud said 'He was marvellous at rehearsals. There was true theatrical instinct. You only had to indicate. Scarcely even that.' In his last film, '1984', released in his final year, 1984 we can glimpse what a truly great actor he was. At Burton's funeral service, Brook Williams read that most moving of Dylan Thomas's poems, written to his dying father, 'Do not go gentle into that good night'. Paul Scofield read 'Death is Nothing at All', by an unknown author:

> Death is nothing at all;
> I have only slipped away
> Into the next room.
> Whatever we were to each other,
> That we still are.
> Call me by my old familiar name,
> Wear no forced air of solemnity
> Or sorrow;
> Life means all that it ever meant.
> Why should I be out of mind
> Only because I am out of sight?
> I am waiting for you
> For an interval,
> Somewhere very near,
> Just around the corner.
> All is well.

FOOTNOTE:
Burton shared a pathological hatred of Winston Churchill with Aneurin Bevan. Both were the sons of miners who had known Churchill send troops into keep order among the starving miners in South Wales. Burton played Churchill in a film 'The Gathering Storm' in 1974, and also played his voice in that brilliant TV documentary series 'Winston Churchill - The Valiant Years' in the 1960's. Of the latter role he was reported in the New York Times in 1974 as saying 'In the course of preparing myself... I realised afresh that I hate Churchill and all of his kind. They have stalked down the corridors of endless power all through history... What man of sanity could say on hearing of the atrocities committed by the Japanese against British and ANZAC prisoners-of-war "We shall wipe them out, every one of them, men, women and children. There shall not be a Japanese left on the face of the earth"? Such simple-minded cravings for revenge leave me with a horrified but reluctant awe for such single-minded and merciless ferocity.' The official BBC response to the New York Times banned him from future radio of television productions with the corporation. Its spokesman wrote 'As far as I am concerned, he will never work for us again... Burton acted in an unprofessional way.'

SAINT CADOG c.497– 577
CATWG, CADOC, CATHMAEL, CADFAEL, FOUNDER OF LLANCARFAN

Feast Day September 25 and February 24
Patron of the deaf in Brittany

An important Welsh saint and missionary, who like Dyfrig, Teilo, Beuno, Gwenfrewi and Padarn could have been Wales' patron saint. Venerated in South Wales, he probably visited Cornwall (but less likely Scotland), and was influential in Ireland because he instructed Finnian at Llancarfan. He seems to have been a contemporary of Gildas, David and Samson. According to Cressy he was taught by Tathan at Caerwent. He was associated with Arthur, and was said to have attended his court with the warrior-saint Illtud.

His parents, King Gwynlliw (Gunleus) and Gwladys, lived at Stow Hill in Newport, where St Woolos Cathedral (a corruption of Gwynlliw) now stands on the remains of a Celtic fort. Cadog was first named Cadfael (Battle Prince). He took his father's crown when Gwynlliw was converted. There are two versions of his death. One is that he was killed fighting the Saxons at Weedon* in Northants, where there is now a huge church. A more plausible story is that the Welsh hid his relics during the Norman invasion of Glamorgan, and used this story as a smokescreen when the great monastery of Llancarfan was placed under St Peter's of Gloucester. Gwynlliw is said to have left his kingdom to Meurig, the son of King Tewdrig. Meurig had married into Gwynlliw's family, and was the father of Arthur.

There are at least fifteen dedications to him in South Wales, and one in Cornwall. Most are found around his foundation of Nant Carban (Llancarfan) in what was Glywyssing, (east Glamorgan), and around Llangattock-nigh-Usk in Gwent. Near Llangattock-nigh-Usk were Llangattock Lenig, Llangattock Lingoed and Llangattock Feibion Afel (Llangattock Vibon Avel – referring to the sons of Abel or Afel). Pendeulwyn (Pendoylan) in Glamorgan, Llangattock (just outsde Cardiff's Pontprennau estate), Llancarfan with its two chapels at Llanfeithin and Liege Castle, Pentyrch, Llanmaes, and Cadoxton-juxta-Barri are sites of his. There are also churches at the Roman sites of Gelli-gaer (with a chapel at Brithdir) and Caerleon. Other dedications include Llangadog Crucywel, Llanysbyddyd outside Brecon, Llangadog near Llandovery and Cadoxton-juxta-Neath. The latter church had chapels at Aberpergwm and Creinant. Furthest west, there is a St Cadog's chapel in Llawhaden (Llanrhiadain). Cadog's churches are also to be found north of Cydweli and in Cheriton and Portheinon on the Gower Peninsula. Penrhos under Llandeilo Crosseny in Monmouth, and Trefethin under Llanofer in Monmouth also were his. Penrhos came for a time to be under St Michael, but somehow soon returned to Cadog, and the place was known as Llancaddoc Penrhos in a list of Abergavenny churches in 1348. St David is now the patron saint of Raglan church, but again this is considered a Cadog foundation. Raglan has a superb battlemented tower, and the tombs of the Marquises of Worcester and Dukes of Beaufort. Many of the Somerset family monuments there were destroyed by Cromwell's forces after the siege of Raglan Castle in 1640.

There are few remains of Llangadog near Amwlch in Anglesey, but a church in Cambuslang near Glasgow is still dedicated to Cadog – probably another Cadog. He had a large chapel near Harlyn Bay near Padstow, now in ruins, with one of Cornwall's most famous holy wells. There was also a holy well in St Just near the river Fal, once called Fenton Cadoc (Ffynon Cadoc) and now called Venton-Gassick.

He is celebrated in Brittany, from the Lannion Peninsula to Vannes, with a famous monastery on the Ile de Cado, off the Quiberon peninsula. A beautiful islet with a 12th century chapel on the Etel estuary in Brittany was named Saint-Cado

One of St. Cadog's foundations. at Cadoxton, Barri
(photograph courtesy of WTB)

after a 6th century *'prince de Glamorgant'*, who returned to Wales and was martyred. He was the patron saint of the deaf, and those afflicted used to lie on a stone 'bed' inside his chapel. The church at Pleucadeuc east of Vannes is Cadoc's. The prefix Pleu (or Plou, or Plo) dates from before the eighth century and indicates an early centre of Celtic Christianity, much as Llan often does in Wales. This Cadoc may be the son of Brychan however.

Llancarfan Church is dedicated to St Cadoc who founded the 6th century Nant Carban monastery here. Here he instructed Finnian of Clonnard, and prayed with him on the island of Flat Holm. Lifris wrote that the rocks around the island, known as the *'wolves',* were real wolves who were turned to stone when they swam across the water to try and take Cadoc's sheep. Llancarfan church was given to the Abbey of St Peter, Gloucester, by Robert Fitzhamon around 1107. Cromwell's soldiers broke the churchyard cross. It is very odd that no ancient stones are to be found here, unlike at nearby Llanilltud Fawr and Llandough. Cadoc was baptised Catmail, and it is thought that the ruined church of Lancatal (Llancadle) near Aberthaw may be his foundation.

Llanmaes Church is an old Celtic foundation, now dedicated to Cadoc, as is Cadoxton juxta Neath and Cadoxton juxta Barry (formerly Tregatwg). At Cadoxton-juxta-Neath, Cadog found on the banks of the river Nedd a wild boar, bees in a hollow tree, and the nest of a hawk at the top of the tree. He sent these as gifts to King Arthfael (Arthur) who granted him land to build a church. However, Llanmaes was previously dedicated to Fagan, and was called Llanffagan Fach. The parish register of Cadog's church at Llanmaes records several centenarians, including Elizabeth Yorath, who died in 1668 aged 177. Another record reads *'Ivan Yorath buried Saturdaye ye XVII day of June anno dni 1621 et anno regni vicessimo primo anno aetatis circa 180. He was a sowdiar in the fight at Boswoorthe and lived at Llantwit major and he lived mostly by fishing.'* So this soldier was a veteran 44 year-old in Henry VII's Welsh forces in 1485, and lived another 136 years!

Cadoc's Life, by Lifris, is the most complete of all the Lives written in Wales. Lifris's father was Bishop Herwald (1056-1104) and it is probable that Lifris was the last abbot of the great Llancarfan foundation before the Normans stripped it. Gildas is said to have copied the 'Life' when he stayed with Cadoc, and Caradoc of Llancarfan, who wrote Gildas' Life, states that it was still in the great church of Cadoc in 1150, covered with silver and gold. This original was probably destroyed to hide land ownership details by the Normans. Cadoc is linked to Arthur by giving sanctuary to a man who killed some of Arthur's men. Nine cattle of the ancient breed of Glamorgan cattle (red, with a white stripe along the backbone – they can still be seen at Margam Abbey Park) were given in settlement. Cadog also argued with Maelgwn Gwynedd and Rhun ap Maelgwn, and Rhain Dremrydd ap Brychan. These were times of the men of north Wales pillaging in the south, after Arthur's fateful battle at Camlan.

In the 6th or 7th century, Ilias ap Morlais, with the approval of King Ithael, gave a mansion in the middle of Abermynwy (Monmouth) and land to Dyfrig, Teilo and Euddogwy, and in the hand of Bishop Berthgwyn, the fourth Bishop of Llandaf. However, in 1075 Withnoc founded a priory there and mentions the church of Cattwg in Monmouth, and this may be the same church originally dedicated to the three saints. It seems to have been in the priory churchyard, but the present building is dedicated to the Virgin Mary. Heth, in his description of Monmouthshire, says that the school now stands on the site, and that it was known as Geoffry's Chapel – a beautiful bay window there is still called Geoffry's Window. It was a catholic chapel until the middle of the 18th century, and is believed to have been where Geoffrey of Monmouth studied.

Between Llangaddock and Bethlehem is a six feet standing stone supported by two others. At nearby Sythfaen is a ten feet Neolithic standing stone, and Coitan Arthur lies at Pont-yr-Aber also near Llangaddock. It is said to have been thrown here by Arthur from Pen Arthur Isa Farm on Cerrig Pen Arthur. Cadoc's memorial may have been at Landyfaelog Fach, where there was once a stone inscribed CATVC. Cadog's 'Saying of the Wise' was *let the heart be where the appearance is.*

At Llangatwg in Brecon is Ffynnon Gatwg, near the church. Francis Jones also notes his Glamorgan wells at Gelligaer (near the Roman camp), Pendoylan church, Aberkenfig, 'Kibwr' Castle and Court Colman. Near Llancarfan is Dyfrig's Well and the healing well Ffynnon y Fflamwydden (Flamebearer's Well) for erysipelas (fever with an infectious skin disease). Several streams meet in Llancarfan, under the brooding Iron Age encampment, and it is an area noted for wells. Francis Jones gives several sources to study, and mentions pin and rag wells to cure King's Evil, and a rag well still used in the early 20th century where a paste was made from soil and well water to cure erysipelas. John Aubrey of nearby Llantrithyd mentions seeing crutches by wells in Llancarfan. The Breach Well was still being used for erysipelas before the Second World War, where rags and pins were used as well as bathing.

* This attribution to Weedon, with its remarkable church, comes from the fact that it seems to have been called Beneventum. However, the Breton writer Albert le Grand places Beventum as Venta, or Caerwent, where Cadog was originally taught by Tathan. Barber and Pykitt have also noted Professor Bury's identification with Caerwent in his edited 'Muirchu's Life of St Patrick.' Perhaps, therefore, Patrick came from Caerwent as it was possibly the earliest major centre of Christian learning in Britain.

KING CADWALADR ap CADWALLON c. 630 - d. 664 or 688
CADWALADR FENDIGAID, SAINT CADWALADR THE BLESSED, HIGH KING OF BRITAIN

Feast Date November 12, October 9

Cadwaldr was the last king to hold the title of Gwledig, the *'High King'* of Britain who had authority over the other Celtic kingdoms. His father was King Cadwallon Llew (the Lion), the son of Iago ap Beli. In 633, allying with the Anglian King Penda of Mercia, King Cadwallon's army had defeated and killed Edwin King of Northumbria at Heathfield. Edwin had grown up with Cadwallon, under the protection of Iago, but in 626 drove the 'gwledig' into exile, and was baptised in 627 by Rhun ab Urien. In 633, Cadwallon resumed his title of 'Dux Brittaniarum' from the 'Bretwalda,' Edwin. Cadwallon ravaged from his base in North Wales as far as York, Edwin's former capital, where he killed Osric and defeated an army of Angles.

Cadwallon, *'the last hero of the British race'* was later killed in the last of his sixteen battles and forty skirmishes at *'Heaven's Field'* (Catscaul) in 635 by Oswald* (see 'An A-Z of Wales and the Welsh'). By this battle, with great losses on both sides, the British were finally pushed out of Northumbria. The Angles had attacked at night, when the British were unprepared. The Venerable Bede, who despised the Christian British, and always took the side of the pagan Anglo-Saxons in his accounts, said that Cadwallon tried to *'cut off all the race of the English within the borders of Britain.... Nor did he pay any respect to the Christian religion which had newly taken root amongst them; it being to this day the custom of the Britons not to pay any regard to the faith and religion of the English.'*

Although Cadwallon's son's nick-name was *'Cadomedd'**, 'battle-shunner'*, Cadwaladr led the British against invaders from Wessex from 634, after his father was killed fighting Oswald of Bernicia. It appears that he carried on the battles against the pagan Northumbrians. It may be that his men were present alongside Penda's heathens at King Oswald's final defeat at the Battle of Maes Ogwy (Oswald's Field) in 642. Despite his reluctance to face a larger army, Cadwaladr was forced to lead his people to a bad defeat, against Cenwalh, King of the West Saxons, at Peonne in Somerset in 658.

The tradition is that he was ill for most of his reign, and that Civil War raged, then a famine, then a great plague in 664, which possibly killed him. However, he may have escaped to the court of King Alain Hir in Brittany, from where he sent his son Ifwr back to regain the British throne. At this time the tradition is that Cadwaladr went on a pilgrimage to Rome, where he died in 688. His body was brought back to Llangadwaldr on Anglesey.

There are churches dedicated to Cadwallader in places named Llangadwaladr as far apart as Bishopston (also known as Bishton or Tref Esgob, and formerly called Llangadwaladr) under Llanwern in Monmouthshire, Llangadwaladr under Llanrhaiadr in Mochnant in Denbighshire, and Llangadwaladr in Anglesey. Magor

Cadwaladr the Blessed

(Magwyr) in Monmouth has been rededicated to the Virgin Mary. Michaelston-y-Fedw in Glamorgan was rededicated to Michael. There was also a Capel Llangadwaladr under Llanddeiniol Fab in Anglesey.

The Anglesey church, Eglwys Ael, contains a stone with a Latin epitaph to his grandfather, King Cadfan. The 7th century inscription reads

'CATAMANUS REX SAPIENTISIMUS OPINATISIMUS OMNIUM REGUM'
(Cadfan the King, wisest and most renowned of all kings)

He died in 625. Cadwaladr died of the plague in 664, and was called by the bards 'Bendigaid', and one of the three blessed sovereigns of Britain. On his tomb there are three intertwined fish, and a single fish on either side of a carved cross.

His 'Saying of the Wise' is:
Have you heard the saying of Cadwaladr,
King of all Wales;
"The best crooked thing is the crooked handle of a plough."

'The Red Dragon' of Cadwaladr was the standard borne by Henry VII on his way to Bosworth Field, and earlier used by Owain Glyndŵr as a mark of the kingship of the Britons. Gildas referred to it, the 'Insularis Draco', being carried earlier by another Gwedig, or High King, Maelgwn Gwynedd. It is the oldest national flag in the world. (See 'An A-Z of Wales and the Welsh' for full details).

The Welsh national flag is not featured on the Union Flag (Union Jack) of the United Kingdom, which superimposes the blue and white saltire of St. Andrew, and the red and white crosses of St. Patrick and St. George. The British flag thus features representation from Northern Ireland, England, and Scotland, but none from Wales. The Welsh Flag consists of two horizontal stripes, white over green, with a large red dragon passant. Green and white are the traditional Welsh colours, worn by the Welsh bowmen at the Battle of Crecy. The Red Dragon, one of the most ancient badges in the world, was brought to Britain by the Romans, who had copied it from the Parthians, and it was later used by both British and Saxon kings. Traditionally it was King Arthur's flag, and it was definitely the standard of Cadwaladr, from whom the Tudors were descended. Owain Glyndŵr adopted the 'red dragon of Cadwaladr' as his standard and the national flag of Wales.

The word "draig" or dragon was used in Welsh poetry to symbolise a warrior or leader. Pendragon, as in Uther Pendragon, meant a head, or chief leader. A legend dates from the eighth century about a fight between a Red Dragon ('Y Ddraig Goch') representing Wales and a White Dragon representing England foretelling the triumph of the red dragon. The red dragon of the Celts was their flag and symbol against the Saxons for 600 years after the Romans left Britain.

The White Dragon of the Saxons was last seen in battle against the Normans at Hastings in 1066. 'Y Ddraig Goch', 'the red dragon', was widely accepted as the oldest flag in the world at the international conference of flag makers in South Africa in 1987, according to the President of the Flag Institute. Flagmaker Robin Ashburner makes the point that it is the only flag to have remained unchanged in the last 1,000 years – 'the Welsh will be the only people to enter the next millennium with the same flag as they entered the current one'. (Denmark also claims the oldest flag, dating from 1219, but the 'father of flag science', or vexillology, Dr Whitney Smith of Massachusetts, supports the Welsh flag. The dragon came from China via the Romans, and when the Western Roman Empire was set up, the dragon symbol was used by the local chiefs in Britain. It was the Welsh symbol long before Offa built the dyke between the Saxon and Welsh kingdoms.)

The Welshman Henry Tudwr invaded England, through Wales, to end the Wars of the Roses. With the 'Red Dragon of Cadwaladr' as his standard, his smaller army defeated and killed the last Plantagenet King Richard III, at Bosworth Field. Henry used as his livery colours green and white, and on these colours his retainers painted the red dragon. When Henry became Henry VII of England in 1485, he decreed that from henceforth the Red Dragon should be the official flag of Wales. Henry even set up the official herald's position of Rouge Dragon Pursuivant to protect the flag. For a time the Dragon coexisted on the English Crown's royal crest with the Lion, but was replaced by the Unicorn of the Scottish Stuarts on the accession of James I in 1603. *Thus neither the Welsh flag nor the Welsh emblems of daffodil and leek appear in a united British context.*

There was no red rose of Lancashire during the Wars of the Roses, and the White Rose of Yorkshire was one of Edward IV's badges. It seems to have been Henry Tudor's idea to amalgamate the two into the Tudor Rose when he ended the wars and married Elizabeth of York. Henry VII balanced his Greyhound emblem of Richmond and Lancaster on the Tudwr royal arms, with the Red Dragon of Wales and Cadwaladr. To him the dragon showed his 'Trojan' descent and gave his kingship and the Tudor dynasty a legitimacy distinct from the houses of Lancaster and York.

* Oswald, or Oswallt, lived from 604-64, converted to Christianity late in life, and is commemorated on August 5. The Anglian King of Northumbria was martyred at Oswestry (Croes-Oswallt) and is remembered there, just over the present border in Shropshire but under the see of St Asaf. The church is only smaller than Ludlow of all the old 'Border' parish churches. In 634 King Oswald had defeated the Celtic King Cadwallon at Heavenfield near Hadrian's Wall. At the age of 38 he was killed at Masefield in present-day Shropshire by the Mercian army of Penda, avenging his ally Cadwallon. Oswald's body was dismembered, but his brother Oswy later retrieved the head and hands which he took back to Lindisfarne and Bamburgh castle respectively. An eagle took one of his arms and where it dropped King Oswald's Well bubbled forth, a place of pigrimage renowned for healing. St Aidan, when he had originally blessed Oswald, said *'may this hand never wither with age.'* One arm was *'uncorrupted'* for almost a millennium until it was destroyed in the Reformation. A wooden hand in Oswald's church at Lower Peover near Knutsford in Cheshire is a medieval 'glove' used to indicate that a free-trading fair was under way. Ffynnon Oswallt was a famous healing well in Whitford, Flintshire. It was situated in a field known as Aelod Oswald (Oswald's Limb), the name commemorating the king's dismemberment.

** Note that Ellis Peter's name for her Welsh monk in the series of books on Cadfael alluded to his crusading past. *'Cadafael'* means 'battle-seizer'.

CARACTACUS 1st century
CARATACUS, CARADOC, CARADAWG, 'AN ETERNAL MEMORIAL TO THE MERCY OF ROME'

Wales was never completely subdued by the Romans. Two of their four British legions were stationed on the borders, at Deva (Chester) and Isca Silurum (Caerleon). Isca was built, with Venta Silurum (Caerwent) to keep the Silures down, while Caerfyrddin (Carmarthen) was the heartland of the Demetae tribe. In 78AD, Tacitus remarked that it was necessary to exterminate almost *'the entire race'* of the Ordovices of mid-Wales and Gwynedd. When the British Catuvellauni tribe of the south-east of England, based around Colchester, were defeated by Aulus Plautius in 43AD, their leader fled to the Silures of south-east Wales. This was Caradog (the Caractacus of Roman history), our first Celtic hero identified with Wales. Caradog led a series of attacks by the Silures against the new Roman provinces in 47 and 48AD. Tacitus recorded that Scapula received the submission of the Deceangli of north-east Wales on the River Dee in 49AD, enabling him to pressurise the Silures. In the same year a fort was established at Gloucester, with others at Usk and Clyro.

Caradog continued resistance, with a joint alliance of Silures and Ordovices, but was defeated in 51AD, his wife and children captured, and he fled to Queen Cartimandua of the Brigantes in north-east England for support. She chained him and handed him over to the Romans. Caradog's father had been Cunobelinus of the Catuvellauni (Shakespeare's Cymbeline), the strongest of the Brythonic kingdoms of England, but the first to be attacked by Rome. The site of Caradog's last stand against Rome is still not known, but it appears to have been in the north-east of Wales, near the upper River Severn.

The Silures kept fighting after Caradog's capture, and defeated the Twentieth Legion in 52AD. In 57AD, Nero ordered that Anglesey, the chief centre of British discontent, be taken, and Tacitus descibes the burning of the sacred Druidic groves. The Iceni then rose under Buddug (Boadicea), preventing the Romans from finishing off the conquest of Wales. From 69-78AD there was another great push against the Silures and the Ordovices, by Julius Frontinus, then Julius Agricola. Three of the four Roman legions were now opposed against the Welsh borders. The XX legion was at Uriconium (Wroxeter), the XX Augusta Legion at Isca, and the XX Adiutrix Legion at Deva. The Silures were beaten by 75AD, and the Ordovices almost slaughtered out of existence by 84AD.There had been at least thirteen separate campaigns against Wales and its borders between 48 and 79AD, which explains the multiplicity of Roman villas, forts, fortlets, marching camps, roads and civil ruins dotted over much of Wales.

Caradog, captured and shown by Claudius in the famous triumph in Rome, was not recorded as a saint, but has an important place in the legends of early Christianity in Wales. His father Bran was supposed to have been kept hostage at Rome for 7 years, and returned with the saints Ilid, Cyndaf, Arwystli Hen and Mawan who preached the gospel in the 1st century from around 58. His daughter Eurgain, or Eigan, was recorded as the first female saint in Britain, who founded its first monastery at Llanilltud Fawr. Another daughter, Gwladys Claudia may have been extremely influential in the early Christian church in Rome. Caradog was said to have returned with Eurgain to his base at Dunraven Castle or St Donat's, and there is an ancient farm, Cae Caradog, near Dunraven. Caradog's great-grandson Lleurwg ap Cyllin was said to be the saint who erected the first church in Britain, at Llandaf, and sent to Rome for Elfan, Dyfan, Medwy and Fagan to evangelise Britain. Whatever the truth, Christianity was well-established in Wales in the second century, and remained as the religion through the Dark Ages of England and the rest of Europe. It seems more likely, however, that the father of Caractacus was the Cymbeline recorded by Shakespeare (Cunobelinus, King of the Catuvellauni). Suetonius called Cunobelin son of Tasciovanus, 'Rex Britanniorum', and he was friendly with Rome. Unfortunately his death led to a power-struggle between his sons Caractacus, Togodumnus and Adminius, because of the *'cyfran'* principle of inheritance (gavelkind). Adminius appealed to Rome, as did the ousted Verica, King of the Atrebates. This led to the Roman invasion of 43 AD.

Caractus' fight against the Romans was well-documented by Tacitus. Many sources place him as the son of Cunobelinus, the fabled Cymbeline, and some equate him with Arvigarus, and even Arthur. His tribe, the Catuvellauni were pushing hard against their neighbours, the Atrebates, whose king Verica asked the Emperor Claudius for military assistance. In 43 AD Caractacus and his brother Togodumnus were defeated by Claudius' army on the river Medway in Kent. Publius Ostorius Scapula became governor in 47AD, and attempted to force the Celtic tribes into a 'proper' state of submission to Rome. Caractacus again fought against Rome with the Trinovantes in the south-east of England, but was forced back to join the Silures in south-east Wales. The Iceni of the east coast rebelled and were defeated, then Scapula marched against the Deceangli of north Wales, fighting them until he had to head north to deal with the Brigantes in Yorkshire. The great fort of Gloucester (Caerloyw) was built to push back the belligerent Silures. Next Scapula returned to try to take Caractacus, who using guerrilla tactics retreated with the Silures to join up with the Ordovices of Powys. Eventually, Caractacus believed that he had found an excellent defensive position, descibed by Tacitus as following:

Then Caractacus staked his fate on a battle. He selected a site where numerous factors – notably approaches and escape routes – helped him and impeded us. On one side there were steep hills. Wherever the gradient was gentler, stones were piled into a kind of rampart. And at his front there was a river without east crossings. The defences were strongly manned.........The British chieftains went around their men, encouraging and heartening them to be unafraid and optimistic, and offering other stimulants to battle. Caractacus, as he hastened to one point and another, stressed that this was the day, this the battle, which would either win back their freedom or enslave them forever.... Then every man swore by his tribal oath that no enemy weapons would make them yield – and no wounds either.....

This eagerness dismayed the Roman commander disconcerted as he already was by the river-barrier, the fortifications supplementing it, the overhanging cliffs, and the ferocious crowds of defenders at every point .... After a reconnaissance to detect vulnerable and invulnerable points, Ostorius Scapula led his enthusiastic forces forward. They crossed the river without difficulty, and reached the rampart. But then, in an exchange of missiles, they came off worse in wounds and casualties. However, under a roof of locked shields, the Romans demolished the crude and clumsy stone embankment, and in the subsequent fight at close quarters the natives were driven to the hill-tops. Our troops pursued them closely.'

Caradog's family was led in triumph before the Emperor Claudius in Rome, usually the precursor to a public execution of captured opponents. However,

Tacitus records the famous sparing of his life by the emperor, noting Caractacus' defence:

'*Had my lineage and rank been accompanied by only moderate success, I should have come to this city as a friend rather than prisoner, and you would not have disdained to ally yourself peacefully with one so nobly born, the ruler of so many nations. As it is, humiliation is my lot, glory yours. I had horses, men, arms, wealth. Are you surprised I am sorry to lose them ? If you want to rule the world, does it follow that everyone else welcomes enslavement ? If I had surrendered without a blow being brought before you, neither my downfall nor your triumph would have become famous. If you execute me, they will be forgotten. Spare me, and I shall be an everlasting token of your mercy.*'

Many experts place the hill-fort of Old Oswestry as the place of battle, but it may have been the Breiddin near Welshpool or Cefn Carnedd near Llanidloes. The '*exceptionally stubborn*' Silures kept on resisting Rome, forcing a legion to be based at the new fort of Isca (Caerleon). The Deceangli and Ordovices rose again and were almost exterminated. Huge forts had to be built at Uriconium (Wroxeter) and Deva (Chester) to attempt to subdue the Welsh tribes, and the Romans cut through to Anglesey, the heart of European druidism in 60 AD. A garrison was established on this holy island but Boadicea (Buddug) led a revolt in England, so the Romans could not consolidate their gains in Wales. In 71, Petilius crushed the Brigantes, and between 74 and 78 the might of Rome turned once more against the Silures of Glamorgan and Gwent.

Caractacus in Rome

They had fought Rome from 49 and were regarded by Tacitus as courageous, stubborn, powerful and warlike. Ostorius Scapula had said that they must be annihilated or transplanted. When he died, '*worn out with care*', the Silures destroyed a Roman legion. However, the construction of Caerleon in 75 meant that the Silures came to an accommodation with the governor, leaving their hillfort capital of Llanmelin and settling in the new Roman town of Caerwent. The Silures became the most Romanised of the Welsh tribes, paving the way for Meurig and Arthur to become Pendragons in the years after the Romans left Britain. With south-east Wales secure, Agricola moved north to avenge a Roman defeat by the Ordovices and '*cut to pieces the whole fighting force of the region*'. Again, Anglesey was ravaged. The next 300 years were by no means peaceful in Wales, but the great stone forts at Chester, Caerleon, Carmarthen (Moridunum) and Caernarfon (Segontium) controlled a semi-quiescent people until the legions left around 400 AD. Unlike more 'settled' colonies of Rome, very few Roman villas have been found in Wales, and those that have are mainly attributed to Romano-Celts. Professor Euros Bowen noted that several Roman villas were found near the sites of Cadog's Llancarfan, Illtud's Llanilltud and Dyfrig's foundations. Tathan was also active at Caerwent, which leads to Bowen's conclusion, that the group of Celtic saints largely confined to south-east Wales represent a church that was locally established in late Roman times. This was the only part of Wales where Roman urban and country house culture was rooted, and Romano-British estates carried on the Christian tradition rather than relied on missionaries from Gaul.

There seems to be a mystery about the great monastery and religious centre of Llanilltud Fawr, Lantwit Major. It appears that St Illtud, after his vision on the banks of the nearby Dawen (Thaw), founded his monastery on the site of the earliest Christian monastery in Britain, which may even been still in existence at this time. Further research is needed, but if this is the case, Wales can claim something very special in world history – the oldest educational establishment in the world up until 1100 and the Norman invasion.

Uniquely, Caradog had been pardoned by the Emperor Claudius, and after seven years' captivity is said to have been allowed to return to his base at St. Donat's, near Llanilltud Fawr. Caradog's residence in Rome was known as 'The British House' and was the first house used for Christian worship in Rome. It is thought that his daughter Eurgain married a Roman, as did Gwladys (Claudia). It is thought that Eurgain brought Christianity to Wales, founding a monastic settlement called Cor Eurgain in Llanilltud Fawr. Another version is that she stayed in Rome, and the Cor was set up in her honour, first at Llanilid around 60 AD then transferring to Caer Mead* (Cor Eurgain) Roman villa at Llanilltud. One story was that Caractacus came back to St Donats with Eurgain and was buried at Llanilltud. St Paul was said to be a friend of Eurgain and Gwladys, and in legend came as St Ilid in 61 and 68. Gwladys is mentioned in Epistle 2 Timothy 4-21 as Claudia. (Paul was said to have visited Galicia, which may be Wales rather than the Spanish province). Other versions relate Ilid as Joseph of Arimathea.

A Welsh tradition is that Christianity first came to Britain with St Paul who came here with Eurgan (Eurgain). She had married Lucius in Rome and with him founded the first university at Llanilltud about 68 AD, known as Cor Eurgain, where Illtud's later monastery stood. The church was endowed by King Cyllin whose son had been converted by Eurgain. It was burned by Irish pirates in 322 and rebuilt by St Theodosius, Tewdws or Tewdrig. Then it was known as Cor Tewdws, or the college of Theodosius in Caer Wrgan. It was associated with Emperor Theodosius. (Other sources tell us that Tewdws is an alternative of Tewdrig, the martyred grandfather of Arthur). There is a record that the Irish attacked and destroyed Caer Wrgan in the fifth century. Caer Wrgan is the old name for Caer Mead, the huge Romano-Celtic villa just a mile north of Llanilltud Fawr. Cor is a very early version of Llan, meaning a monastic college. Cor Tewdws is marked on an 18th century map of Llanilltud as being a field north of the monastery site of Illtud.

'Achau y Saint' notes that the College of Caerworgorn was founded by Cystennyn Fendigaid (Constantine the Blessed) and soon destroyed by the Irish, at which time its principal was Padrig. This was Padrig Maenwyn, son of Mawon of the Gower peninsula, who was taken into captivity. This tradition is possibly fictitious. However, Caer Worgan was just a few hundred yards north of Cor

Tewdws. Perhaps after the sacking of the villa, a new building was erected, just north of the existing church. Theodosius II, the Great, was a contemporary of Cystennin and supposed to have founded it, but it was more likely to have been named in his honour by a Romano-British principal.

* It may be that, as well as the monastery (re-founded later by St Illtud) the Irish destroyed the fabulous fifteen-room Roman villa at Caer Mead, a mile from Llanilltud. After Macsen Wledig left with the legions in 383, this was taken over by the local prince or king, and there is evidence of 41 Christian burials on the site in the Age of the Saints. It is thought that the kings of Glamorgan and Gwent, from Tewdrig through his son Meurig to his son Arthmael or Arthrwys, may have used it as their palace. Arthmael, the Arthur of legend, has always been associated with being born at nearby Boverton, which claims to the Caput Bovium of the Romans (Cowbridge being Bovium). The Caer Mead site covers two acres, and one room (the court ?) was a massive 60 by 50 feet. There are mosaics there, and coins pottery and glass were discovered. Excavated in 1888, it has since been covered over and ignored, when it could hold the key to the legend of Arthur. A gold torc was found early in the 19th century, but sold for £100 and melted down. CADW should excavate this priceless site, at present merely humps in the ground, but is severely financially constrained.

WILLIAM CECIL, K.G. September 13 1520 - August 5 1598
LORD BURGHLEY, LORD HIGH TREASURER, THE ARCHITECT OF ELIZABETHAN ENGLAND, 'THE MAN THAT DOES EVERYTHING'

Cecil came from a Welsh family whose name was Anglicised from Seisyllt in the service of the Tudors, after Henry VII toppled Richard III in 1485. William's father Richard of Burghley in Northampton married a local heiress, and thus gained the manor of Bourne. Richard was a Groom of the Wardrobe at Court, and William served as a page there, before he entered St John's College, Cambridge in 1535. He married in 1541 when he went to Gray's Inn to practise law, but his wife died in 1543, leaving him a son, Thomas. William Cecil was rewarded by Henry VIII in 1542 for defending royal policy, and given a place in the Court of Common Pleas. In 1543 he entered Parliament, aged just 23.

After a second marriage in 1545, he joined an influential Protestant circle at court. When Edward VI succeeded to the throne, Cecil joined the household of the Protector, the Duke of Somerset, becoming his secretary in 1548. However, Somerset fell from power, Cecil was caught up in his disgrace, and despatched to the Tower of London for two months in 1549. Nevertheless, the abilities of Cecil were so highly regarded that he gained royal favour and became one of two secretaries to the young king, who gave him a knighthood in 1551. Cecil had acted as a go-between between the two main rivals for power over the young Edward, Edward Seymour, Duke of Somerset, and John Dudley, Earl of Warwick. When Somerset fell from power the second time, in 1551, it was Warwick who proposed Cecil's knighthood, and Cecil committed himself to Warwick, who now became Duke of Northumberland. However, when Northumberland proposed altering the succession, Cecil sided with the judges on the Tudor side, although fearing arrest and contemplating flight. Only on the royal command of Edward did Cecil capitulate to Northumberland's demands. He deserted Northumberland on Edward's death to side with the Tudors.

He met Mary Tudor as representative of Edward's council, and she called him *'a very honest man'*. Cecil was now offered a post in Queen Mary's court, but unlike most of his colleagues, preferred to withdraw from the Catholic milieu until Elizabeth's (possible) Protestant accession. His backing for Elizabeth, when it looked as if she was more likely to be executed than succeed to the throne, was something that kept the two very close throughout the next forty years. He immediately became her principal secretary and chief adviser on her accession in 1558. His first act was to persuade the reluctant Elizabeth to intervene in Scotland and sign the treaty of Edinburgh, to remove French troops from there.

William Cecil

Cecil was a superb statesman, but first helped Elizabeth to get the state on a sound economic footing, including adopting a new coinage in 1561. Elizabeth operated a rotating court, spending her time at the stately homes of various subjects. With her vast army of retainers, this saved enormous sums of money, and ensured that no one individual became too rich. Her subjects vied with each other to offer the most splendid sojourn at their estates, which helped add to the pomp and panoply of the Elizabethan period, while costing her nothing. To heal the terrible religious divisions (her half-sister predecessor Mary had executed 500 Protestants), Cecil and Elizabeth worked together on a compromise settlement to establish the Anglican Church in 1559. Cecil also ended the expensive war with France, organised an efficient secret service to snuff out Catholic attempts on Elizabeth's life, and dramatically strengthened the army and navy.

He was Chancellor of the University of Cambridge from 1559, and survived an attempt to sack him as Elizabeth's Secretary by the jealous Lords Leicester and Norfolk in 1568. He had introduced Norfolk into the council to balance Leicester's power. John Dudley's son, Robert Earl of Leicester, became emotionally close to Elizabeth, weakening Cecil's position. Despite threats of resignation, Elizabeth came round to keep siding with Cecil and rewarded him with the lucrative mastership of the Court of Wards in 1572. She had created him first Baron Burghley in 1571. In 1572 he also became Lord Treasurer and a Knight of the Garter. His loyalty, industry and judgement were indispensable to the Queen - he was her mainstay throughout most of her reign. While opposing Dudley, Cecil was sympathetic to Protestant desires for Elizabeth to marry and produce an heir, resisting Mary Stuart's claims to succeed. He recommended the Habsburg suitor, the Archduke Charles. In the early 1570's, Cecil was in diplomatic overdrive, aiding the Dutch while soothing Spanish feelings, and trying to achieve a French alliance. He knew that war would overstrain England's finances, and thereby endanger the Tudor monarchy. Cecil said *'a reign gaineth more by one year's peace than ten years' war'*.

In 1568, Mary Stuart, Queen of Scots, fled to England. The Ridolfi Plot to put Mary on the English throne, with a Spanish invasion, led to Norfolk's execution. The close attention paid to Mary Queen of Scots by Cecil later led to the discovery of the Babington Plot, and her trial for treason and execution in 1587. Equally, Cecil's insight into Spanish intentions led to preparations for naval resistance which helped beat the Armada in 1588. Cecil's elder son, Thomas, commanded a ship in the English fleet. Cecil had previously put out peace feelers to the Duke of Parma, the Spanish commander in the Netherlands, in 1585, again earning Leicester's enmity. Nonetheless, Cecil tried for peace with Spain again in 1587. The former Spanish ambassador to Elizabeth's court summed up his feelings about Britain's chief economist and diplomat '...*the man that does everything*'.

Elizabeth's principal councillor now presided over the coaching of his son Robert, born in 1563, towards the post of Elizabeth's secretary, which he took in 1596. Thus the '*reign of the Cecils*' continued. William Cecil retired with ill health, but still remained active, urging peace with Spain for fear of a costly war against a Franco-Spanish alliance. He died in 1598 before negotiations were concluded, and is buried at St Martin's Church, Burghley. The consummate master of Renaissance statecraft, famed over Europe, his talents as a diplomat, statesman and administrator were unparalleled. Of himself he said '*I have gained more by my temperance and forebearing than ever I did with my wit*'. A contemporary observation of Cecil showed that he kept his thoughts and feelings under control: '*he had no close friends, no inward companion as great men commonly have...nor did any other know his secrets.; some noting it for a fault, but most thinking it a praise and an instance of his wisdom. By trusting none with his secrets, none could reveal them*'.

Burghey House is probably the most magnificent Elizabethan building in Britain, built between 1565 and 1587, and still lived in by his descendants. At one point he had been offered an earldom by Elizabeth, but refused on the grounds of its great expense. Overworked and in ill-health, Cecil was an expert in finances, religion and socio-economic policy. He also co-ordinated the Privy Council, which met almost every day, and was the queen's Chief Councillor and Secretary; he managed Parliament and presided over the Exchequer as well as being a J.P. in five counties; Britain's de facto Foreign Secretary and chief diplomat, he made Britain respected as a European power; and he was ruthless with any opposition to his beloved queen. Without Cecil, it is difficult to envisage an Elizabethan Age.

FOOTNOTES:
(i) Cecil's grandfather was David 'Sysill', who married Alice Dicksons. Their son was Richard 'Cyssell', who married Jane Heckington. So we appear to have transmuted through 4 generations from 'ap' Seisyllt>Sysill>Cyssell>Cecil.
(ii) It appears that the Cecils were responsible for keeping the young Elizabeth away from *Bloody Mary's* court, in Hatfield House, for her own safety away from the intrigues of court. She seemed to know him well, for upon his appointment as her sole Secretary, she told him '*This judgement I have of you, that you will not be corrupted by any manner of gift and that you will be faithful to the State and that, without respect of my private will, you will give me that counsel which you think best.*' He remained her chief councillor to his death, when Elizabeth was at his bedside. '*No prince in Europe hath such a counsellor as I have in mine*', she once had said. She knew that he always gave his best advice, and would not be swayed by pressure. In turn, he knew how to put up with her extremes of temper by tactically retreating - he advised a younger man '*Good my Lord, overcome her with yielding.*'

JOHN CHARLES December 27 1931 -
THE GENTLE GIANT, IL GIGANTE BUONO

Charles rivals George Best and Billy Meredith as the greatest footballer produced in the British Isles, and could play in attack or defence, standing almost 6 foot 3 inches and weighing nearly 14 stone. His preferred position was centre-forward, but he was equally proficient as a centre-half, and may be unique in sometimes playing centre-forward for a club and centre-half for his country, and vice-versa. He left Swansea for Leeds in 1949 aged just 18, being chosen personally by the Leeds manager Major Frank Buckley. Charles was capped for Wales in 1950, aged just 18. He would have made more than 38 appearances, but Juventus were always reluctant to release their leading scorer. From Manselton in Swansea, Charles was renowned for his shooting and heading abilities, starting his career with Swansea.

This superb Welsh footballer was the *first British transfer over £50,000* when he left Leeds in 1957 for a distinguished career with Juventus from 1957, where he was nick-named *'il Gigante Buono'*, *'the gentle giant'*, and is still remembered with affection. £67,000 was a record transfer fee for a British player at the time. He scored 93 goals there in just 155 games, contributing to the winning of three championships and two Italian Cups. Charles scored 29 goals in his first season, being crowned *capocannoniere (top scorer)* in the league. This was in a defensive-oriented game, where goals were hard to score. A statue of him stands outside the ground, and he also played for AS Roma, scoring 4 goals in 10 games in 1962. His appearance on the streets of Turin used to be greeted with spontaneous applause, and he said *'If you go to play in another country and you don't reach out to the people, you are going to make your life a misery. I took to the Italians right away, and they took to me. I got on well with my team-mates and I liked to mix with the supporters in the little cafes. It was a wonderful slice of my life and I still have strong relationships from that time.* In 1958 Charles was voted Italy's Footballer of the Year, and was also one of the few non-Italian players chosen to play in the Italian National League XI. In this year, he was valued by Juventus at £150,000, over twice what they paid a year earlier, making John Charles the most valuable player in the world. A Newspaper headline in Italy of April 14th, 1959 read alongside a picture of John: *'A Magnificent 6'3" Chink of Welsh Marble bestriding the pitch in the No. 9 Zebra shirt of Juventus'*. 40 years later, Italian supporters of Juventus still voted John Charles as one of the ten greatest foreigners ever to wear the famous black and white stripes. A canvas portrait of him still hangs in the players' lounge in the club. In Italy, all players were treated equally, but there were win bonuses. Charles said *'Everybody got the same wage but when you played against Torino, Milan and Inter the president would come in and say "Right, you're on £500 bonus if you win." I had four kids. I couldn't bring up four kids on £18 a week. So we put that little bit extra into it to win matches.'* Agnelli offered Charles the massive sum of £18,000 to stay with Juventus instead of returning to Leeds, but Charles said *'At the time I was thinking of my kids' education - I didn't realise they were better off in an English school in Italy and being able to speak Italian. We got used to Italy. I never had to wear an overcoat there.'*

The problem is that every Welsh soccer-playing schoolboy wants to be a goal-scorer, to be in the limelight, ever since John Charles scored 42 goals for Leeds in the 1953-54 season. In 297 league games he scored 151 goals for Leeds. Charles scored Wales' first ever World Cup goal, in the 1958 1-1 draw with Hungary. He was not fit for the Wales team that narrowly lost in the World Cup quarter-finals in 1958, 1-0 to Brazil. He had been severely and constantly kicked in the preceding game, because of his influence on the Welsh team. It is fair to say that if he had been able to play, and get on the end of the constant stream of crosses served up by Cliff Jones, Wales could have won and been known world-wide. Such is the power of football. Brazil went on to win this World Cup in Sweden, starring the young Pele. John Charles' brother Mel was a noted international who played against Brazil, voted the best half-back in the tournament, and a long-time Arsenal player.

John Charles returned to Wales to play for Cardiff in 1963, aged 32, and scoring on his debut on August 24 against Norwich City. He scored 19 goals in 66 games, leaving in 1966. It is impossible to recall any other player in history who could play

centre-forward and centre-half with equal distinction at international and top club level, he rivals Billy Meredith as the greatest footballer ever produced by Wales, and is possibly the greatest sportsman of the nation. At the same time as banging in 42 goals as centre-forward for Leeds United, in the same season he was Wales' centre-half. There will never be another player like him. At 18, he had been the youngest player to pull on a Welsh shirt. In 1997, 25 international football writers assembled to draw up a list of the greatest footballers ever. No-one else in the top 25 had regularly played in two positions. He was never booked or sent off in his long career. John Charles was voted 9th in Football's Hall of Fame. If he had been

John Charles

Brazilian, he would have been voted first. In 1999, the respected Football Weekly placed Charles in its top 50 players of the century. Also in 1999 Swansea University gave John Charles an honorary MA. Charles said *'I had to leave school young, so it's unbelievable that I'm here today. You see things like this on television then it happens to you. It's unbelievable. I feel honoured because it's come from my home town. It's all so unexpected, and I am surprised. Football is football, but to have an honour from outside football, I think, is terrific.'* John Charles is not in the best of health, and there is a campaign for him to receive a knighthood for his services to the game. He lives on a state pension in Leeds, having given away all his mementoes and awards to charities over the years. However, he still tries to return to Italy every year to stay with old friends. He commented in 1999 *'They still recognise me over there. Last year I was sitting in a car and a boy, who was about 14, said, "Giovanni, come sta?" (John, how are you?)'.* In 1995 the author was trying to explain to several female pensioners at an outside café table in Reggio Emilia, near Bologna, that he was from Wales, in reasonable Italian. Thwarted, he tried the usual litany of Tom Jones, Shirley Bassey and 'rugby', with no joy. At last one of the old ladies realised, and said 'Ah, John Charles' and the others happily repeated the name, realising that the author came from the same area a Il Gigante Buono. This was 35 years after John Charles had left a rival club over a hundred miles away.

FOOTNOTE:
It is worth mentioning the matches in the 1958 World Cup. Wales had finished second to Czechoslovakia in their qualifying group, and beat Israel 2-0 home and away to reach the final rounds. Their manager was Jimmy Murphy, Matt Busby's assistant coach at Manchester United, and the team left London not expecting very much. That superb Tottenham Hotspur winger Cliff Jones said *'We were badly organised for a competition like the World Cup where preparation is half the battle. Jimmy hadn't been able to study any of our opponents, we'd had very little practice together and when we flew out we weren't even sure John Charles would (be allowed by Juventus) to play for us.'*

In the three seasons before John Charles had joined Juventus, the club had finished 7th, 9th and 9th in Serie A. In Charles' first season, they won the Championship, so the owner Umberto Agnelli did not want to lose him to Wales, and forbade him playing in the qualifying rounds. At the very last minute, Agnelli and the Italian FA relented and let Charles join the Welsh team in Sweden. The Swedish organisers wanted the great man to play, to help ticket sales, and Jimmy Murphy snapped *'How can I stage proper rehearsals without knowing whether he will turn up?'*. Three days after the Welsh team arrived in Sweden, John Charles turned up in their hotel for breakfast, having caught an overnight flight. He walked into a rapturous and incredulous reception. His brother Mel remembered *'I'll never forget it. John walked in. he looked like a Greek god because he was so tall and bronzed. The selectors saw him; threw down their knives and forks, stood up and started singing "For he's a jolly good fellow, for he's a jolly good fellow". It was like a kids' party.'*

The first match was against the 1954 finalists, Hungary, who were expected to win comfortably. They took the lead after five minutes, and spent the rest of the match chopping down the danger man, Charles, from behind. However, the much-abused centre-forward scored a brilliant header 20 minutes from time, and then Wales were mysteriously refused an obvious penalty when the great Ivor Allchurch was felled in the penalty area. Although Wales should have won, Murphy was ecstatic about the result. Wales 1 Hungary 1

The second match, in Stockholm, pitted Wales against Mexico, and most of the Swedish crowd supported the exotic Mexicans. Charles remembered *'We came out on to the pitch and saw all these people wearing sombreros. All you could hear was Messico! Messico! It didn't really affect the players though. Once you get started you don't notice the crowd.'* In a poor game, Allchurch volleyed a goal from a Webster cross, and Mexico equalised in the last minute. Wales 1 Mexico 1.

The next game was against the World Cup hosts, Sweden, and although Wales should have won the previous two matches, they knew they needed only to draw to go through to the next stage. Packing their defence, Wales survived in another poor game. Wales 0 Sweden 0.

Faced with a barrage of criticism after the Swedish match, Jimmy Murphy stated *'Those people who say we can't attack can expect a shock.'* However, again against Hungary Wales were 1-0 down at half-time, but dominated the second half. After two penalty appeals by the Welsh, Ivor Allchurch scored one of the best goals of the tournament. John Charles chipped the ball forward and Allchurch curled the ball into the top corner of the net. Again Charles was being savagely attacked, with no protection from the referee, and Wales needed to win to go through. With just 14 minutes left, Terry Medwin of Tottenham Hotspur scored to progress. Wales 2 Hungary 1.

The quarter-final was against the eventual winners, Brazil, and Charles, the Welsh talisman and Europe's best footballer, was too injured to play. The Brazilian team featured the household names of Pele, Didi, Garrincha and Zagalo. Wales attacked from the kick-off, with Webster missing two simple chances. Medwin and Jones, the wingers from the remarkable Spurs double-winning side of 1961, supplied a constant stream of crosses into the penalty box, but their was no John Charles to convert the opportunities into goals. Extra time looked a distinct possibility, but just 17 minutes from the end the 17-year-old Pele scored his first World Cup goal, which he later called the most important of his whole career. His shot was not clean or hard, but deflected off right-back Stuart Williams past the goalkeeper Jack Kelsey of Arsenal. To go out of the World Cup to a poor goal was terrible. Mel Charles commented *'I felt terrible. If it was a great goal I wouldn't have complained, but it wasn't - it was like a golf putt.'* Thus Wales lost its greatest chance in the modern age of international recognition. Wales 0 Brazil 1 There is an excellent book by Mario Risoli, *'When Pele Broke Our Hearts'*, published by Ashley Drake, which tells the story of Wales and this World Cup.

TOMMY COOPER   March 9 1922 - April 15 1984
THE COMEDIAN'S COMEDIAN

Possibly the greatest British comedian of all time, he was held in massive regard by contemporaries such as Eric Sykes, *'who bowed to no-one when it came to comedy'*. Born in Caerphilly, he moved with his parents to the West Country at an early age. He had not been expected to survive as a premature baby, but his grandmother helped keep him alive of a mixture of brandy and condensed milk. Aged 8, his auntie Lucy bought Tommy a magic set, and he spent the next eight years perfecting tricks. His first job was on board a boat as an apprentice shipwright, and he gave his first public performance there. It was disastrous. The coloured handkerchiefs, which were supposed to pour from a cylinder, were steadfastly stuck, no matter how he tugged them. A card fell out of his sleeve, and Cooper fled the stage in tears. However, he calmed down and analysed what went wrong, recalling years later *'I got stage fright. That's why it all went wrong. But then I thought to myself, well it might all have gone wrong but I got a laugh. Perhaps I should concentrate on that.'*

Aged 18, Tommy Cooper was called up in 1940 for the Second World War. The sickly baby was now 6 feet 4 inches, with size 13 boots when he joined the Horse Guards. He remembered *'On the first day there I put my foot in the stirrup but the saddle slipped and I ended up underneath the horse's belly. Everyone was sitting on their horse except me.'* In the Middle East, Cooper was wounded in the arm, and joined the concert party entertaining the troops. While entertaining the troops in NAFFI in Cairo, he had forgotten the pith helmet that he usually used for his act. To improvise, Cooper whipped off the fez of a passing waiter, and used that instead. This raised such a laugh, that the red fez became his trademark ever after.

He left the Army in 1947, to concentrate upon becoming a professional, incompetent buffoon (and thus could have had an alternative career in politics). As a full-time Music-Hall comic, he made his television debut on December 24th 1947 on the Leslie Henson Christmas Eve Show. Television did not really take off in Britain until the late 1950's, and Cooper honed his skills in live Variety Theatre, living hand-to-mouth at stages. After this initial break-through, it was almost a year before Cooper had a booking, in November 1948 at the Collins Music Hall, Islington. He toured the variety circuit, low on the bill, supplementing his income by working as a barrow-boy in the Portobello Road market until 1950. His next break was at the famous Windmill Theatre, where so many of Britain's post-war comedians learned their trade, competing with the main attraction, half-naked stationary ladies. In one week in 1950 he performed 52 shows there. Between 1951 and 1952 he was at the London Hippodrome, and also starred in the BBC TV series 'It's Magic'.

However, by the mid-50's his act had developed to the extent that he was appearing in one-off television specials such as Sunday Night at the London Palladium and Saturday Showtime. In 1957, his first TV series, Life with Cooper appeared. This was 'live' on a Monday night for a trial of 12 weeks. Of course, Tommy Cooper's act was ideal for live television - it did not matter if things went right or wrong, as his persona and professional training in the music halls enabled him to easily 'paper over the cracks'. The series was such a success that half-way through he was offered another series by ATV, Cooper's Capers, which ran in 1958. He was thereafter a constant feature of British television with guest appearances and his own shows such as Cooper's Half-Hour and Life with Cooper. During all this time, he kept touring the country appearing in clubs and perfecting his act as *'the comedian's comedian'*.

1957 had seen a successful debut season at the Hotel Flamingo in Las Vegas, and he turned down a season at America's famed 'Radio City Music Hall' because he was 'booked solid' for two years in England. Cooper returned to America in 1967 to record two Ed Sullivan shows. At the time this was the most influential show on American television, and Sullivan introduced him as *'the funniest man to ever appear on this stage.'* For years, Cooper was the most impersonated man in the UK, he was so famous.

Cooper could make an audience howl with laughter just by appearing on the stage, with his big, clumsy persona and perspiring face which could switch from joyful to lugubrious in an instant. His act revolved around magic tricks going wrong (- he was, incidentally, a superb magician and member of the Magic Circle),

Tommy Cooper

and simple, slightly corny, jokes. Paul Daniels, the leading British magician, reminisced: *'He did a great after-dinner speech at the Water Rats (the charity sponsored by entertainers). This great big man just stood up. That's all he did. He just stood up and the place was in absolute hysterics and a man standing up. Now, I don't care how much you study comedy, you can't define that, the ability to fill a room with laughter because you are emanating humour. After several minutes of laughter he turned to his wife and said, "I haven't said anything yet." And the whole place went up again.'*. He was given a Variety Club lunch by his peers in 1977 in honour of his 30 years in show-biz. As mentioned, this huge man always wore his red fez when performing. Cooper stood up in front of the 400 honoured guests from the entertainment industry, and on cue, each one reached into their pockets and pulled out a hidden fez which they placed on top of their heads. Cooper stared at them, puzzled, for a few minutes, waiting for the laughter to die down, reached into his pocket, pulled out a fisherman's yellow 'sou'wester' hat and donned it. *'Everyone fell about again.'*

It is impossible to summarise the act - it was a one-off by a much-loved man in his favourite element, and his enjoyment shone through any kind of material. *'Unforgettable'* is the best word to describe him, and there are several websites devoted to his jokes. Fellow-Welshman Anthony Hopkins' favourite party act is to adopt the Cooper persona and run through a string of his one-liner gags. Some of the author's favourite Cooper jokes are:

'I'm on a whisky diet - I've lost three days already.'
'I was cleaning out the attic the other day with the wife. Filthy, dirty and covered with cobwebs...but she's good with the kids.'
'I slept like a log last night - I woke up in the fireplace.'
'So a fella goes to the Doctor and he says "I keep thinking I'm a dog". The Doctor says "Well lie on the couch". The fella says "I'm not allowed!"
'I was in Margate last year for the Summer Season. A friend of mine said, "You want to go to Margate, it's good for rheumatism." So I did... and I got it.'

There are at least 12 videos easily available of Cooper, plus the film 'The Plank' in which he starred with Eric Sykes, possibly the best British comedy film ever. One problem with Cooper, is that in line with his shambolic personality, he was terribly unpunctual, driving directors to despair in rehearsals. Sykes, a known stickler for professionalism and time-keeping, and incidentally probably the most under-rated British comic ever, said that they had decided to meet at a pub near the film studios at 12 noon. *'So noon comes and goes and there's no sign of Tommy.'* Eric Sykes told the producer that he was very annoyed, and that he was going to have harsh words with Cooper if he turned up at all for the production meeting. The pub had filled up to maximum capacity by 12.45, when the front door swung open, and standing there was Tommy Cooper, wearing just a bowler hat and pair of pyjamas. He walked up to their table in the crowded pub, ordered a drink, and simply said *'I'm sorry I'm late. I couldn't get up.'* Sykes and the producer dissolved with laughter.

However, Cooper's other problem was more serious - alcohol - his long-suffering wife said once *'There's only one trick that Tommy always does successfully. It's making a drink disappear.'* His fatal coronary, on stage during a live television broadcast at Her Majesty's Theatre, had the audience believing it was part of the act. He fell back gracefully, disappearing through the curtains and died ten minutes later on his way to hospital. Jimmy Tarbuck, the show's host, commented *'As usual, he was supposed to make a mess of the last trick. He was wearing a long cloak from which he was supposed to start bringing out large objects. Then a ladder would come through his legs, followed by a milk churn and a long pole. When Tommy fell backwards, I thought he'd put another gag in. I thought he was going to do some levitation trick from under his cloak. We all expected him to get up and we waited for the roar of laughter. It was terrible when he didn't.'*

It is impossible to do justice to Cooper in words, but there is a true story which sums the man up, when he met the Queen after a Royal Command Performance. The dialogue went as follows:

Cooper *'Do you think I was funny?'*
Queen   *'Yes, Tommy.'*
Cooper *'You really though I was funny?'*
Queen   *'Yes, of course I thought you were funny.'*
Cooper *'Did your mother think I was funny?'*
Queen   *'Yes, Tommy, we both thought you were funny.'*
Cooper *'Do you mind if I ask you a personal question?'*
Queen   *'No, but I might not be able to give you a full answer.'*
Cooper *'Do you like football?'*
Queen   *'Well, not really.'*
Cooper *In that case......do you mind if I have your Cup Final tickets?'*

OLIVER CROMWELL April 25 1599 - September 3 1648
OLIVER WILLIAMS, LORD PROTECTOR 1649 - 1648

Cromwell's Day September 3 (Houses of Parliament Memorial Service)

In the English Civil War, Oliver Cromwell's New Model Army was the element that swung the war towards the Parliamentary forces and led to the Inter-Regnum. Cromwell was the son of Sir Henry Cromwell. Henry Cromwell's father was Richard Williams, a Welshman who took the name of his uncle and patron, Thomas Cromwell.

Morgan Williams of Llanishen, now a northern suburb of Cardiff, moved to London to become a brewer and innkeeper. He married a daughter of Walter Cromwell of Putney. Their son Richard adopted his mother's name, as Thomas Cromwell was of great importance in Henry VIII's court. Richard Williams was made a baronet and Privy Councillor in 1527, and his sons and grandsons signed their names as *'Cromwell alias Williams'*. In his early years so did his great grandson, Oliver Cromwell, who overthrew King Charles 1 and set up the parliamentary republic in Britain. There is a tradition that Oliver Cromwell was born on the Margam Abbey estate, rather than at Huntingdon, and that there is no record of his birth in England. (If any reader can elucidate, please contact the author).

Cromwell spent a year in Cambridge University before his father died in 1617, whereupon Oliver went to the Inns of Court in London to study law. He married in 1620 and returned to St Ives in Huntingdon to lease a farm. He was an MP for Huntingdon in the 1628-29 Parliament, probably as a result of aristocratic patronage from his wife's family, and was most probably *'the poorest man in Parliament'*. He seems to have had some kind of mental breakdown in 1630, after which he became a Puritan, convinced that God wanted him to do something important with his life. In 1636, he inherited a large estate in Ely from his wife's uncle, and the post of local tax collector of tithes for two Ely parishes. Aged 37, he was now a man of property and some standing locally.

In 1640 he entered the 'Short Parliament' of April 1640, and served through the 'Long Parliament' (August 1640-April 1660) as MP for Cambridge. In the Short Parliament Cromwell made a name for himself as a firebrand, being one of the first to call for the established church to be pulled up *'root and branches'*, declaring that parliament, not King Charles I, should appoint generals, and proposing annual parliaments, not dependent upon the king's whim. The parliament was dissolved in uproar, but Charles was financially destitute from his dealings with Scotland and had to re-summon Parliament.

The Long Parliament refused to help him until the Triennial Act was passed in 1641. It ensured a summoning of Parliament every three years, and another bill that year abolished the income-raising devices of the courts of Star Chamber and High Commission. In 1642, a volunteer force led by Cromwell (illegally) prevented the moving of silver plate from Cambridge University to swell the king's war-chest at York. Also in 1642, Parliament further took power from the Catholic Charles, abolishing the episcopacy, putting the army and navy under parliamentary control, and declaring that the bill would become law without Charles' signature. The Protestant House of Commons, made up of wealthy tradesmen and property-owners, resented any type of taxation funding royalty and wars. King Charles went to Parliament to arrest John Pym and four others, but they had fled. Charles travelled north to raise his standard against the forces of Parliament at Nottingham on August 22, 1642. The First Civil War had begun. Fighting under the Earl of Manchester in the Eastern Association, Cromwell's first 60-strong cavalry detachment were noted at the battle of Edge Hill in 1642. He had been commissioned as a Captain of Horse in 1642, and had become a Colonel of Horse then Lieutenant-General of Horse in 1643. In 1645, the three parliamentary armies were combined, and all officer-MP's expected to stand down and concentrate upon their work at Westminster. However, there was disagreement about who should command the cavalry, and Cromwell was commissioned on a series of 40-day contracts. Under Fairfax's New Model Army, Cromwell became Lieutenant-General of the Cavalry, his highly trained troops being called 'Ironsides' by Charles' cavalry commander, Prince Rupert. The Ironsides had fought superbly at Marston Moor in 1644, and at Naseby in 1645, both where Cromwell led the charges. In the fighting, Cromwell spent all but five of the forty-five months of the war actively in the field. However, in 1644 he appeared in Parliament to condemn his military chief the Earl of Manchester for supporting a negotiated settlement with the King. Cromwell wanted outright victory and an imposed settlement.

By 1646, Parliament controlled England, with the king in captivity. In 1647 Cromwell was given a long-term commission to replace his temporary contracts. With other army leaders, he tried to negotiate seriously with Charles I, but the king duped them, and another Civil War sparked later that year. The Second Civil War was mainly centred on South Wales, and Cromwell led forces through the area to besiege Pembroke Castle. After the suppression, Cromwell wanted Charles I to abdicate in favour of one of his sons, but the king refused. It appears that Cromwell made enemies in holding out against the king's execution. He was then sent to Ireland to suppress rebellion and then to Scotland. Fairfax refused to make an attack on Scotland, so Cromwell, summoned from Ireland, was appointed as his successor as Lord-General of the Army in 1650. The storming of Drogheda and Wexford have been recently proven (by an Irishman) not to be the massacres that later Stuart propaganda told us about. He finally overcame the Scottish army of

Oliver Cromwell

Charles II at Worcester in 1651, his last battle, triggering off the famous search for Charles before he escaped to the Continent. Cromwell had led his Ironsides into 20 battles and countless skirmishes, and never been beaten.

The splintering of English society was mirrored in a squabbling Parliament made up of Dissenters, Levellers, Puritans et al, when Cromwell took action in November 1648. With troops, he ejected 110 MP's, another 160 refused to attend again because of his action, and he was left with a 'rump' of MP's barely quorate for making decisions. Cromwell reluctantly became head of a new executive council to rule Britain, defined by a new Constitution. His 'Rump Parliament' dismantled the royal machinery of government, abolishing the monarchy, Privy Council, Courts of Exchequer, Admiralty and House of Lords. An executive Council of State and the Rump Parliament now ruled England. Cromwell said *'misrule is better than no rule, and an ill government, a bad government, is better than none.'*

However, the Rump came to see itself as a self-perpetuating oligarchy, and in 1653 Cromwell returned with his army to clear the House of Commons of all MP's. In the House of Commons, he shouted *'Ye are grown intolerably odious to the whole nation; ye, who were deputed here by the people to get grievances redressed, are yourselves become the greatest grievance... Your country therefore calls me to cleanse this Augean stable, by putting a final period to your iniquitous proceedings in this House; and which by God's help, and strength he has given me, I am now come to do; I command ye therefore, upon the peril of your lives, to depart immediately out of this place; go, get out! Make haste! Ye venal slaves be gone!'* The army called for a new Parliament of Puritan Saints, which was just as bad as the Rump, and that was dissolved by Cromwell in 1653. Just like Charles in 1629, Cromwell chose to rule alone, but his permanent army of 35,000 men and two trade wars with the Dutch gave him the same financial problems as Charles. Another Parliament was reconstituted, this time with an Upper Chamber full of Cromwell's supporters, with veto power, but the Commons stayed hostile to Cromwell. Oliver Cromwell became Lord Protector of the Realm instead of Lord General of the Army. The title of King had been suggested. However, his attempts to placate the various needs of Britain's first standing army, the nobility, Puritans and Parliament had alienated all his sources of support. Upon his death, his son Richard succeeded him in 1658, but the Commonwealth was in trouble and Charles II returned from exile in 1660. Cromwell's foreign policy made Britain a major player in Europe, and he beat the Spanish at the Battle of the Dunes in 1658 and occupied Dunkirk. He made peace between Sweden and Denmark, allied with France against Spain, and captured Jamaica from Spain.

FOOTNOTE:
Cromwell was deeply religious and believed that he had been blessed by God to change the iniquities of his country. The Parliamentary cavalry at first was no match for Rupert's Cavaliers, men used to horses. He gathered a thousand hand-picked Puritans, farmers used to horses and the land, and drilled them mercilessly in cavalry manoeuvres, although he had no experience of warfare. His regiment was named 'Ironsides' in the Roundhead army, and was never beaten once, despite being outnumbered often. His army would recite the Westminster Confession and march into battle singing the psalms of David - God was on their side, stiffening their backbone. Cromwell's main tactic was a fast, shock cavalry charge into the centre of the advancing army, cutting straight through the lines, and then circling to either right or left, wheeling the mass of opposition soldiers into a mob without formation, creating confusion for his foot-soldiers to destroy them. His discipline meant that his cavalry participated right through the battle, unlike Rupert's which usually charged and then scattered. Cromwell's regular troops preached, prayed, paid fines for drunkenness or profanity, and charged the enemy singing hymns.

DAFYDD AP GWILYM   c.1320-c.1380
WALES' GREATEST POET, THE NIGHTINGALE OF DYFED

He is the most celebrated Welsh poet, who is said to be buried under the old yew tree, in the churchyard adjoining the ruins of Strata Florida Abbey. (Another tradition places his body at Talley Abbey). Indeed, he is *'one of the greatest of all European mediaeval writers'*. Many of the Welsh princes are also believed to be buried with him at Strata Florida Abbey, the Anglicised version of *'Ystrad Fflur'*, *'The Way of the Flowers'*. He innovated in his use of language and metrical techniques. The seven-syllabled rhyming couplet form known as *'cywydd'** became his true metier. His reputed birthplace at Brogynin near Llanbadarn Fawr is marked by a celebratory plaque. He not only developed the cywydd but also introduced new themes and attitudes into Welsh poetry. He was a contemporary of Boccaccio and of the generation preceding Chaucer**.

Dafydd spent a great deal of time at his uncle Llywelyn's house, Cryngae in Castell Newydd Emlyn (Newcastle Emlyn). He described his uncle as a warrior, poet, linguist, scholar and teacher, who lived in a white-washed house with lamps burning brightly, with seats covered with gold silk, and in which fine French wine was drunk from cups of gold. Llywelyn ap Gwilym was a Constable, deputy to Earl Talbot, in charge at Newcastle Emlyn in 1543. In two *'awdlau'* Dafydd acknowledges his debt to his cultured uncle, describing him as a poet, a linguist and one who possessed *'all knowledge'*. Dafydd's father, Gwilym Gam ap Gwilym ab Einion, came from a family of power in the 14th century which had sided with the King of England for many decades. Dafydd's great-great-grandfather, another Gwilym had been Constable of Cemaes in 1241, assisting the French in their attack on Maredudd ab Owain of Ceredigion, and receiving lands as a reward.

Dafydd possibly was 'in exile' for some of his life, but was recognised as a great poet even in his own day. He could write in the traditional manner of the older poets, the *'Gogynfeirdd'*, although it was difficult, but moved towards a different type of diction and choice of themes. His impact was not unlike that of Wordsworth's simple manner upon the stultifying classical-based poetry of his day.

He lived in the bleak years after the loss of Llywelyn the Last, when Welsh independence had been seemingly extinguished, but his work includes funny tales of amorous adventures, as well as original nature poetry, and religious and metaphysical poems of varying form and structure. So little is known of his life, except that he was a linguist and a member of an aristocratic family, but his *'awdlau'* (odes) and *'cywyddau'* (rhymed couplets) show that he had been trained in bardic art and connected historically with 'the poets of the princes'. His 'new poetry' had initially been developed in Provence and France, spread by bands of young men known as 'clerici vagrante' or 'cleri' - in Wales they were wandering scholars known as *'Y Gler'*.

Strata Florida Abbey, where Dafydd is buried.
(photograph courtesy of WTB)

Dafydd followed their themes of nature and love, many of his poems being devoted to the golden-haired Morfudd and the raven-haired Dyddgu. *'In the work of Dafydd ap Gwilym, almost for the first time in European literature, we find nature poetry which is the result of direct observation and of personal experience and meditation. In his nature poetry Dafydd makes use of a technique which is chararacteristic of one type of the older traditional poetry, namely "dyfalu". "Dyfalu" is a technical term; in general it means to describe, but the "description" is carried out in many forms, by direct "word-painting", by comparison, by contrast, and in a host of other ways. Dafydd's poetry shows him to be a master of this technique; his variations on a single piece of description are almost bewildering, and throughout it all runs a vein of healthy, happy laughter.'*

Ted Hughes and Seamus Heaney named their verse compendium for young people 'The Rattle Bag' after Dafydd ap Gwilym's poem. Many of the features of his poetry cannot be translated into English, but 'Morfudd fel yr Haul' (Morfudd like the Sun) in cywydd form begins with the lines:

Gorllwyn ydd wyf ddyn geirllaes,	*I woo a softly spoken girl,*
Gorlliw eiry man marian maes;	*Pale as fine snow on the field edge;*
Gwyl Duw y mae golau dyn,	*God sees that she is radiant*
Goleuach nog ael ewyn.	*And brighter than the crest of foam,*
Goleudon lafarfron liw,	*White as the glistening garrulous wave's edge,*
Goleuder haul, gwyl ydyw.	*With the sun's splendour; gracious is she.*

English translations cannot to justice to Dafydd ap Gwilym's mastery of the technicalities of cynghanedd and cywyddau, and how he brought light-heartedness into poetical formalities, but the following two partial poems are from 'The Seagull' and from his famous 'Merched Llanbadarn' (The Girls of Llanbadarn):

I love her with the full force of passion;
Ah men, not Merlin, with his fine flattering lip, nor Taliesin,
Did love a prettier girl,
Sought-after like Venus, copper-haired,
Surpassing beauty of perfect form...
Oh, seagull, if you ever see
The cheek of the fairest maid in Christendom,
Unless I have the most tender greeting,
That girl will be the death of me....

I bend before this passion; a plague on parish girls!
Since, o force of my longing, I have never had one of them!
Not one sweet and hoped-for maiden,
Not one young girl, nor hag, nor wife,
What recoil, what malicious thoughts,
What omission makes them not want me?
What harm is it to a thick-browed girl to have me in the dark, dense wood?
It would not be shameful for her
To see me in a den of leaves.....

* The cywydd is a Welsh verse form, a short ode in rhyming couplets, with one rhyme being accented and the other un-accented. Each line has 7 syllables and has

to contain some form of *'cynghanedd'*. Cynghanedd itself is a complex system of alliteration and internal rhyme. The cywydd has similarities with the verse form used by French 'trouveres' (troubadors) and 'jongleurs' (wandering scholar-singers), and a great deal in common with the earlier *'bardd teulu'*. This was the poetry of the second grade of bard in the Welsh bardic system, the bard of the king or prince's 'war-band' or 'family'. Cywydd was the leading Welsh verse form, from the 14th until the 17th century.

**Remember that Chaucer's decision to use English, rather than Latin of French *'represented perhaps the most significant moment in our (English) national culture'* (-Peter Ackroyd). English, as an 'understandable' and written language, only dates from Chaucer's work of 1400. By that time Welsh was already over a thousand years old, and Dafydd ap Gwilym's work can be read today in its original form far more easily than Chaucer's.

SAINT DAVID, DEWI SANT 520 - March 1 589 (Dates of birth are variously given between 460 and 520, death between 544 and 589) *THE WATERDRINKER, PATRON SAINT OF WALES*

Feast Day March 1, July 10 in Brittany
Canonised 1119 or 1124 by Pope Calixtus
Emblem - a dove; Flag – a gold saltire on a black background
David is the only Welsh saint canonised and culted in the Western Church.

Dewi ap Sant (Sanctus) ap Ceredig ap Cunedda was the great grandson of Cunedda who came from the North Country to conquer North Wales, and the grandson of the founder of Ceredigion. Geoffrey of Monmouth believed that he was King Arthur's uncle, as did Giraldus Cambrensis. He was possibly born in Henfynyw in Cardigan, where the church is dedicated to him, Ffynnon Ddewi lies nearby. It seems that his original monastery, on land inherited from his father, was at Henllan in Dyfed, and Dewi moved to Menevia, St Davids, later. The Irish 'Catalogue of the Saints' of 730 records that Irish monks *'received the mass from Bishop David, Gildas and Teilo'*, and they influenced monastic development in Ireland. His uncle was St Carannog and his aunt St Ina. His cousins were said to be saints Cenau, Dogfael, Pedr, Gwynlle and Afan.

Legend says that his father Sant was told by an angel to save some land for David, thirty years before he was born. Also at this time St Patrick was going to settle in Glyn Rhosyn (Vallis Rosina, Vale of Roses) near the sea in Pembrokeshire, when an angel told him to leave it, as the place was reserved for a boy to be born in thirty years' time. Patrick was so upset at his God preferring an unborn child to him, that God had to take Patrick to a cliff rock still known as Eisteddfa Badrig (Sedes Patricii, Patrick's Seat), to show him that God wanted him to look after all of Ireland instead.

Many sources state that Dewi was born on the site of St Non's Chapel, baptised at Porth Clais, and educated at Hen Fynyw or Henllwyn (Vetus Rebus), with St Teilo, studying under Peulin (Paulinus). St Illtud's Life however says that David,

Gildas, Samson and Paulinus studied under Illtud. Dewi is said to have founded twelve monasteries, from Croyland to Pembrokeshire, and including Glastonbury and Bath.

It was claimed that Dewi made a pilgrimage to Jerusalem, where he was made a bishop, and took a principal part at the councils of Brefi (in Cardigan) and Caerleon. At Brefi he was recognised as primate of all Wales to replace Dubricius (Dyfrig), and he moved the see from Caerleon to Menevia (Mynyw, or St Davids in Pembrokeshire). Much of this information stems from a document of around 1090 which attempted to make St David's independent of Canterbury, but may not be reliable. All sources agree, however, that his principal seat was at St David's, where he died. There is a legend that he died in the arms of his pupil and great friend, Maedoc of Ferns. The great Irish saints claimed to be taught by David included Maedoc, Finnian of Clonard, Senan of Scattery Island, Findbar of Cork and Brendan of Clonfert.

The most famous tradition about David is that the ground rose at his feet at the Synod of Brefi in 545. David had never preached before, but was persuaded by Deiniol and Dyfrig to do so, where the church now stands at Llanddewibrefi. He was heard as clear as the bell as far away as Llandudoch (St Dogmael's). He was known traditionally as *'The Waterman'* as he and his monks were ascetic teetotallers and vegetarians. His last words were said to have been *'Lords, brothers and sisters, be happy and keep the faith, and do those little things you have seen me do and heard me say.'*

The story that David went with Teilo and Padarn on pilgrimage to Jerusalem, is mentioned in the Lives of all the other saints. It was recounted that the Patriarch John III of Jerusalem advanced him to the Archbishopric of Mynyw, Menevia, and gave Dewi the gifts of a staff, bell, golden tunic and portable altar. In David's Welsh Life, however, he is consecrated Archbishop in Rome when Peulin tells the Synod of his holiness. The

St. David's Cathedral
(photograph courtesy of WTB)

'Brut Dingestow' says that at this time there were just three archbishoprics in Britain and David succeeded Dyfrig (Dubricius) at Caerleon, not Mynyw (Menevia, or St David's). The other two cathedrals were London and York. One of Merlin's prophecies was that *'Menevia shall be dressed in the shadow of the City of the Legions'*. Geoffrey of Monmouth agrees with this, but one Triad tells us that the three Archbishoprics of 'Ynys Pridein' (the Island of Britain) were St David's, Canterbury and York.

Dewi is culted in Hereford, Gloucester, South Wales, Devon, Cornwall and Brittany, where he seems to have travelled after the great plague of 547. He was invoked to cure sick children in Brittany. David was recognised as patron saint of Wales only when the bones of Gwenfrewi were removed to England. Bishop Asser's Life of Alfred, written around 893, mentions the famous monastery and parish of

Holy David. About 1120 Pope Callistus II approved David's cult. A letter sent by the Chapter of St David's to Rome around 1125-1130 claims that St David's had been a metropolitan see since the beginnings of Christianity in Britain. Two pilgrimages to David at Mynyw equalled one to Rome, and three equalled one to Jerusalem. St David's Cathedral was rebuilt in 1275, largely from offerings taken at his shrine, which William the Conqueror, Henry II and Edward I and Queen Eleanor had visited.

David is associated with over fifty known churches in South Wales, most in the south-west. Glastonbury was claimed to be founded by David. In St David's Cathedral is a cross-slab with Latin crosses. At Llanddewi Brefi, probably Dewi's original monastery, are four stones. Two are cross-marked, and one inscribed to Dallus Dumelus. Another inscribed stone reads:

HIC IACET IDNERT FILIUS IACOB
I QUI OCCISUS FUIT PROPTER
PRAEDAM SANCTI DAVID

'Here lies Idnert son of Jacob who was killed because of the despoiling of St David'.

A 1693 recording fills in the words David and Jacob. This stone dates from around the 7th century, possibly carved after St David's was ransacked. One of the stones has been 'Christianised' and is called St David's Staff, which Dewi and Dyfrig leaned upon at he famous Synod of Brefi. At St David's Cathedral are also a number of Celtic cross-slabs. One stone had been used as a gate-post and has an inscription to 'Gurmarc'. They came from a holy well at Pen Arthur Farm a few miles away.

The church of St Mary and St David in Kilpeck in Herefordshire was formerly dedicated solely to St David. Its amazing carvings and rare 'sheel-na-gig' draw visitors from all over Britain. The present church dates from around 1140, but some Saxon stonework survives. In Cardigan Blaenpennal, Capel Dewi (Llandysul), Henfynyw, Llanarth, Llanddewi Aber-arth as well as Llanddewi Brefi are David's churches. At Llanddewi Aberarth, just north of Aberaeron, there are two Celtic stone fragments embedded in the wall of the west porch. Probably 10th century, they were found in the 1860 rebuilding of the church, and are parts of what has been called the *'finest cross in Wales.'* The inscription is faded on one, and the other stone has key patterns and intricate Celtic knotwork. In the church is an 11th century *'hogback'* stone, the only one in Wales and of a type only found in 'Viking' Yorkshire. 'Bangu' was David's portable bell was kept in Glascwm Church, one of the first twelve churches he founded.

The following dedications can be noted:
Pembroke – St David's cathedral, Whitchurch, Brawdy, Llanychllwydog, Llanychaer, Maenor Deifi, Bridell, Llanddewi Velfrey, Hubberston, Prendergast;
Carmarthen – Abergwili, Bettws, Henllan Amgoed, Abergorlech, Llanarthney, Llangadock, St David's Carmarthen, Llanycrwys, Meidrim;
Glamorgan – Llanddewi in Gower with a holy spring, Llangyfelach, Ystalyfera, Bettws, Laleston;
Monmouth – Llanddewi Fach, Llanddewi Skirrid, Bettws, Raglan, Llangeview, Llanthony (formerly Llanddewi Nant Honddu), Llangeview, Trostre;
Hereford – Much Dewchurch, Little Dewchurch, Kilpeck, Dewsall;

Cardigan – Bangor Teifi, Henllan, Bangor, Blaenporth, Henfynyw, Llanddewi Aberarth, Llanarth, Llanddewi Brefi, Blaenpenal, Capel Dewi;
Brecon – Garthbrengi, Llanfaes, Llanwrtyd, Llanddewi Abergwessin, Llywel, Trallwng, Maesmynys, Llanynys, Llanddewi y'r Cwm, Llanddulas;
Radnor – Creguna, Gladesbury, Glasgwm, Llanddewi Ystrad Enny, Llanddewi Fach, Heyope (Llanddewi Heiob), Whitton (Llanddewi yn Hwytyn).

Many churches were rededicated to David after he became patron saint of Wales, but there are no North Wales dedications to him in the traditional 'Six Counties', and precious few in Catwg's territory of Glamorgan, Glywyssing. In Monmouthshire there is Capel David near Abergafenni, Raglan, Llanddewi Rhydderch, Llanddewi Fach and Llanddewi Ysgryd. Llangadog Church in Carmarthenshire seems to have been previously dedicated to David. Llanarthne is now rededicated to David, and St Llywel's church at Llywel now also has dedications to David and Teilo. Near the great Carreg Cennen Castle, at Trapp on The Black Mountain, are earthworks and stone rubble of an ancient chapel dedicated to David.

It seems that David travelled to Ireland, and also that he and Teilo evangelised parts of Cornwall and Brittany. Near Llanfeuno in Hereford, Kilpeck, Dewsall, Little Dewchurch and Much Dewchurch are all dedicated to David. In Devon (Dumnonia was still British until around 900), there were dedications at Tilbruge (Thelbridge), Ashprington and Painsford, St David's chapel to Heavitree in Exeter and also in Cornwall at Dewstowe (Davidstow). His mother Non had a dedication at Altarnon, and at Plenynt (Pelynt, Plint) in Cornwall and Bradstone in Devon.

The political power of the bishops of St David's probably swayed the choice of Dewi as the patron saint of Wales – as stated there is not one dedication to him in North Wales. Research by the Reverend Rice Rees in the 1830's showed that *'in the original Diocese of Llandaff he has but two chapels, and only three in what is supposed to have been the original Diocese of Llanbadarn; all the rest, including every one of his endowments, are in the district of which, as Archbishop of Menevia, he was himself the Diocesan. The Cathedral of St David's is in the territory of his maternal grandfather, the neighbourhood of Henfynyw appears to have been the property of his father, and Llandewi Brefi is situated on the spot where he refuted the Pelagian heresy.'* The patron saint of Wales might well have been Gwenfrewi, if not for the removal of her relics to Shrewsbury. Better claims as patron saint can possibly come from Dyfrig (especially), Beuno, Teilo, Illtud and Cadog. His fight against the Pelagian Heresy probably assisted in his canonisation by the Roman church in the 12th century. Some of their foundations were later rededicated to David, such as Llangadog in Carmarthen. To the author, Pelagius (q.v.) was a far more attractive religious thinker than any popes of his knowledge – Christianity based on equality and natural goodness, rather than referent and political power, would have caused fewer deaths over the centuries.

There is a tradition that Arthur allowed Dewi to move the seat of his archbishopric from Caerleon to Menevia. Geoffrey of Monmouth states that he was honourably buried on the instructions of Maelgwn Gwynedd in Menevia, soon after Arthur's death, whom he thought died in 542. Archbishop Usher thought that David died in 544 aged 82. Maelgwn Gwynedd, according to the Annales Menevensses died in 547 during the great plague. In David's time's Caradog Freichfras (the son of a grand-daughter of Brychan) recovered Brecon from the

Picts, and featured as Sir Carados Bris Bras in later Arthurian romances. Urien Rheged cleared out Pictish and Irish settlers from the lands between the rivers Towy and Neath, and his descendants ruled these territories. He was known as Sir Urience in Arthurian mythology. It seems that David took the opportunity in establishing churches in these reclaimed territories.

February 28 is St David's Eve, and one of the favourite nights for the Cwn Annwn (Hounds of Annwn, the Underworld) to take to the skies. They race and howl across the firmament, and are the souls of the damned, hunting for more souls to feed to the furnaces of Hell. Anyone who hears them will soon meet death. Sometimes they are seen as huge dogs with human heads. This is a pre-Christian belief that lasted in rural Wales until the nineteenth century. There was a mass sighting of this spectral pack of dogs (probably geese) in Taunton, Somerset in 1940.

In the Gwaun valley in Pembrokeshire, Old St David's Day (March 12) was the occasion where the wax candle on the table was replaced by a wooden one, signifying that supper could be ate without candle-light. Like the custom at Tregaron, it was a symbol of the end of the winter nights. At this time, farm workers were also entitled to three meals a day, until Michaelmas when it reverted beck to two meals.

Some old sources say that it was David who convinced the Welsh to wear a leek* in their caps to identify each other in battle. David's spirit visited King Cadwallon's army at Hatfield Moors in 633, telling the army to put leeks in their hats, so they could recognise each other in the battle, and Edwin of Northumbria was beaten. Certainly the Welsh had the first uniform, (green and white) in European warfare (see the author's 'The A-Z of Wales and the Welsh'). Michael Drayton, in his 1612 'Polyolbion' however puts the Welsh leek into perspective in that David was a vegetarian water-drinker:

> As he did only drink what crystal Hodney yields,
> And fed upon the leeks he gathered in the fields.
> In memory of whom, in each revolving year,
> The Welshmen, on his day, that sacred herb do wear.'

In Shakespeare's 'Henry V', Pistol threatens the Welshman Fluellen:
'Tell him I'll knock his leek about his pate upon St Davy's Day', but later Fluellen forces him to eat the leek. In the same play, Fluellen refers to the Welsh service to the Black Prince at the battle of Poitiers:

'If your Majesties is remembered of it, the Welshmen did good service in a garden where leeks did grow, wearing leeks in their Monmouth caps; which your Majesty knows to this hour is an honourable badge of the service; and I do believe your Majesty takes no scorn to wear the leek upon St Tavy's day.'

Shakespeare described the habit of Welshmen wearing leeks and daffodils on St David's Day as 'an ancient tradition begun upon an honourable request.' An interesting correlation between the leek and St David's Day is found in Hone's 'Every-Day Book, Table Book and Year Book' (four Volumes, 1839) in which March 1st is the flowering day of the leek. The traditional Welsh daffodil will flower on March 7th. Dewi's 'Saying of the Wise' is as follows:

> 'A glywaist ti chwedl Dewi
> Gwr llwyd llydan ei deithi
> Goreu defawd daioni.'

'Hast thou heard the saying of St David,
The venerable man of extended honour ?
"The best usage is goodness".'

There are evocative remains of palaces of the bishops of St David's at Lampey, St David's and Abergwili. William Barlow, the monoglot English bishop from 1536-1548, tried to have the see moved to Carmarthen. He therefore stripped the roof of his palace at St David's to pay for his daughters' marriages, and built the 'new' palace at Abergwili. Intriguingly, Owain Glyndŵr in his Pennal document to Charles VI of France in 1406, wanted St David's to be accepted as a metropolitan church. Its authority would have covered the other Welsh dioceses, plus those of Exeter, Bath, Hereford, Worcester and Lichfield. Also, appropriation of Welsh churches by English monasteries would be annulled, only Welsh-speakers were to be appointed to ecclesiastical office in Wales, and two universities were to be established in North and South Wales. (The difficulties of transport and communication between the north and south in Wales are still in existence because of the nature of Welsh geography).

Maen Dewi, an eight-foot menhir was on the edge of Dowrog Common in 1912, stnading by a cottage known as Drws Gobiaeth (The Door of Hope). There was also a rocking stone, now destroyed, near St David's still intact in 1919. Other notable monuments in the area of the abbey include a stone circle inside the prehistoric camp on St David's Head, Trecenny Standing Stone, and two dolmens of the slopes of Carn Llidi. A seven feet Christianised standing stone can be found in Dewi's church at Bridell, made up of porphyrite greenstone from the Preselis, with Ogham and cup markings. It is inscribed *'Nettasgru Maqui Mucoi Breci'* *(Nettasagus son of the descendants of Breci)* and was probably carved in the 5th or 6th century.

David's dedication at Abergwili in Dyfed is surrounded by standing stones such as Pentre Ynis, Pant y Glien and Merlin's Stone. The last two are both in fields called Parc y Maen Llwyd (Grey Stone Park). Carreg Fyrddin (Merlin's Stone) carried his prophecy that a raven would drink human blood off it. In the 19th century a man digging for treasure was killed when the stone fell on him. At Dewi's Hubberston, there is also a standing stone.

David had many holy wells in Wales, and the author is indebted to Francis Jones' seminal work for the following listing:

Anglesey: Llangammarch; and near Llanddewi Abergwesin Church;
Cardigan: Capel Dewi, Llandysul (used for brewing beer for the fair); Llandygwydd; near Llanarth on the ford of Afon Ffynnon Ddewi; Henfynyw; and near Gogoyam, Llanddewi Brefi, where the well was in a cottage itself called Ffynnon Ddewi; Llandysilio-go-go;
Carmarthen: Llwyn Dewi healing well near Whitland; and Pistyll Dewi near Llanarthney;
Glamorgan: Llangyfelach; Southerndown; and Newton Nottage (where there was also his chapel and Dewiscwm has been renamed The Rhyll);
Pembroke: near St David's; near St Lawrence; Mabws Fach Farm in Mathry; Llanrheithan; St Dogwell's parish (formerly called Llantydewi); Brawdy, Whitchurch; Fishguard; Llanychllwydiog; Maenclochog; Manordeifi; Llanddewi Velfrey; Pistyll Dewi at the Cathedral; Porthclais where David was baptised; Newport; Haverfordwest; Cosherston; Harglodd Isa Farm;
Radnor: Ffynon Ddewi in Llanbadarn Fynydd.

There are many traditions associated with these wells, again they are noted in Jones' work. The author wished to take photographs of many of these sites and their associated ruins, but finance and publishing deadlines did not allow it. Perhaps such work would stimulate the authorities to refurbish some of these shrines – they represent over 1400 years of history which few other countries can show.

St David's Cathedral and its Bishop's Palace are in a hollow below the City of St David's, and it was thought that the bones of David and Justinian were still there. However, they were possibly destroyed when the shrines were smashed in the Reformation, and the relics were analysed as being only 1000 years old, which means that they may be those of St Caradog of Llancarfan. The tombs of Edmund Tudor (Henry VII's father), Bishop Gower and Rhys Grug can be seen, as well as those attributed to the Lord Rhys and Giraldus Cambrensis. There is a Millennium appeal to restore the cloisters, West Front stonework, organ and 14th century gatehouse, for which over £4 million is needed (telephone 01437-720204).

*There is a note on the virtues of the leek in the 13th century herbal manuals of the physicians of Meddfai, 'Meddygon Myddfai':

'The juice is good against the vomiting of blood. It is good for women who desire children to eat leeks. Take leeks and wine to cure the bite of adders and venomous beasts. The juice of leeks and women's milk is good against pneumonia. The juice with goat's gall and honey in equal parts, put warm into the ear, is good for deafness. It will relieve wind of the stomach, and engender strange dreams.' This fascinating cornucopia of mediaeval Welsh recipes gives another cure for excessive vomiting of placing one's testicles in vinegar. For irritability it recommends frequent partaking of celery juice to relieve the mood and induce joy.

DONALD WATTS DAVIES CBE FRS June 7 1924 - May 28 1999
THE COMPUTER PIONEER WHO MADE POSSIBLE THE INTERNET

Born in Treorchy, the son of a clerk at the coalmine, Davies is remembered as *'the scientist who enabled computers to talk to each other, and thus made possible the Internet'*. He started his career in a small team at the National Physics Laboratory, under the scientific genius Alan Turing, the man who first conceptualised computer programming.

At Imperial College, London, Davies gained a first in physics in 1943, and a first in mathematics in 1947, working with the famous Klaus Fuchs on atomic research at Birmingham University between his two degrees. Turing's group developed one of the first stored-programme digital computers in the world in 1950. Commended for a Commonwealth Fund fellowship in 1954, Davies' senior officer described him as *'outstanding not only in intellectual power but also in the range of his scientific, technical and general knowledge. He is equally unusual in his ability to apply this knowledge to mechanical and electrical design and even to the actual construction of complex equipment. He is, for example, one of the very small number of persons who could draw up a complete logical design of an electronic computer, realise this design in actual circuitry, assemble it himself (with a high probability that it would work as designed) and then programme it and use it for the solution of computational problems.'*

Working at the National Physical Laboratory, Davies coined the term *'packet switching'* in 1966 for the data transmission which is fundamental to the workings of the Internet. He also led a team that built one of the first functioning networks using packet data. He was reported in The Guardian in 1997 as saying that it was inefficient for a computer to send an entire file to another computer in an uninterrupted stream of data, *"chiefly because computer traffic is 'bursty' with long periods of silence. So, in November 1965, I conceived the use of a purpose-designed network employing packet-switching in which the stream of bits is broken up into short messages, or 'packets', that find their way individually to the destination, where they are reassembled into the original stream."*

The work of his team was presented at a 1967 conference in Tennessee where Lawrence Roberts (also of Welsh extraction) of the Advanced Research Projects Agency (part of the US Department of Defence) presented a design for creating a computer network. This led to the Internet prototype, the ARPANET. Unfortunately, like most British breakthroughs, funding was not available for a wide area network experiment by Davies, but his scientific papers were used world-wide, especially in America by Roberts and others to develop the technology. (The British are excellent at invention, but finance for innovation to market has always been the greatest problem - in a high interest rate economy, which favours financial institutions making easy profits, there is no desire to 'risk' investments outside the financial sector. A London government is virtually controlled by the City of London and the Bank of England, which in turn has switched Britain to a service-sector, loan-expensive economy). He developed a UK version of the ARPANET, mainly laboratory-based. His packet-switched network, Mark 1, served the NPL from 1970, replaced with his Mark II in 1973, which remained in operation until 1986, but it never was assisted in any way to develop the scale of the ARPANET. ARPA's designers used his self-routing method for messages, as the transport mechanism of the ARPANET, and the ARPANET evolved into the Internet.

Donald Watts Davies

Paul Baran at RAND had also been working on computer networks, and one of his parameters was the same as Davies' packet size of 1024 bits, which became the industry norm. Although Tim Berners-Lee has been called 'the father of the internet', it was the serendipitous marrying-up of the independent work of Davies, Roberts and Baran which made the Internet a practical proposition.

Davies later moved into data-security systems, working for teleprocessing systems, financial institutions and government agencies. He received the British Computer Society Award in 1974, was made a Distinguished Fellow of the BCS in 1975, and published several books upon communication networks, computer protocols and network security. He was made a Fellow of the Royal Society in 1987. He pioneered work in the 1980's on Smart Cards, as he believed they would be useful components in the secure operation of financial services over open networks.

Smart Cards were derided in the USA at the time as a French aberration, and as being only usable in off-line situations. The chip card with metal contacts was newly invented, and seen as unreliable and expensive compared to established contact-less portable data carriers like the magnetic stripe card and the bar code label. Disagreeing, Davies and his team at NPL managed to get substantial funding from the banks, EFTPOS, American Express, The Post Office, Texas Instruments and other companies. By the mid-80's the TTCC (Tokens and Transactions Control Consortium) had moved quickly into delivering solutions, focusing on high-speed encryption and authentication of sender and recipient. Regulation of secure access to, and private communication across, an open network by authorised users was enabled by what we now call an Intranet. An early application of the PC encryption card was found in the EFTPOS (Electronic Funds Transfer at Point of Sale) terminals in supermarkets. Of course, supermarkets can now use this payment method build up databases of customer needs and patterns of shopping, and also to directly input these retail purchases, to trigger their own stock fulfilment systems.

IDRIS DAVIES 1905 - 1953
THE MINER-POET, THE WORKING-CLASS POET

In 1926, the miners refused to work an extra hour a day, coupled with large pay cuts of 16-25%. On 30 April, 1926, those miners refusing the terms were locked out and the pits stopped producing. On 3rd May, the General Strike, called by the TUC, began. The mood in South Wales was almost revolutionary at this time, and when the TUC called off the strike just nine days later, the Welsh were left to fight on, alone and betrayed. Almost a quarter of a million men stayed away from the pit-heads. Police were called in from outside Wales to keep order, until the starving miners were forced back to work at the end of 1926. The effects on that South Walian generation solidified a feeling of 'us against the world' for decades. Idris Davies summed up the mood of the times, in a verse from 'Gwalia Deserta':

'Do you remember 1926 ? That summer of soups and speeches,
The sunlight on the idle wheels and the deserted crossings,
And the laughter and cursing in the moonlit streets ?
Do you remember 1926 ? The slogans and the penny concerts,
The jazz-bands and the moorland picnics,
And the slanderous tongues of famous cities ?
Do you remember 1926 ? The great dream and the swift disaster,
The fanatic and the traitor, and more than all,
The bravery of the simple, faithful folk ?
"Ay, ay, we remember 1926," said Dai and Shinkin,
As they stood on the kerb in Charing Cross Road,
"And we shall remember 1926 until our blood is dry."......'

The problem here is that death wipes out memories. Young people at university have absolutely no idea of German and Japanese atrocities of two generations ago.

The horrors of the First World War, the terrible poverty of the 1920's and the like simply do not exist for many people. It is *'cogito, ergo sum'* in action - 'I think therefore I exist' but the corollary is that 'It only matters if I know about it'. Knowledge is the only weapon ordinary people have in their armoury against pollution, unnecessary wars, corrupt politicians, multinational over-pricing and the like. Davies could see this, and cared for his fellows.

Rhymney-bred Idris Davies was a miner as a fourteen year-old, who became a London teacher and extra-mural lecturer. In a 1937 notebook he mentions an accident as a miner: *'I looked down and saw a piece of white bone shining like snow, and the flesh of the little finger all limp. The men supported me, and one ran for an ambulance box down the heading, and there I was fainting away like a little baby girl.'* From a Welsh-speaking home, he learned English in the local elementary school. At the colliery, a fellow-miner introduced Davies to the works of Shelley, and Davies realised that he could use the poetic medium to politicise people, proselytising socialism and human dignity. In 1926, aged 21, he lost a finger in a pit accident, and almost immediately the Great Strike started. With no work, Davies matriculated via a correspondence course to gain acceptance at Loughborough College and then at Nottingham University, qualifying as a teacher. In 1932 he was teaching in the East End of London. After many attempts, he managed to be transferred back to his beloved Rhymney Valley to teach in 1947, but was found to be suffering from stomach cancer in 1951.

He was the poet of the valleys, and died aged only forty-eight, in 1953. His 'Gwalia Deserta' was published in 1938 with his poems recommended by T. S. Eliot........ *'They are the best poetic document I know about a particular epoch in a particular place, and I think that they really have a claim to permanence.'* The long and unified dramatic poem described the desert that industrial South Wales had become in the 1920's and 1930's. His other great work was 'The Angry Summer' of 1943.

'Gwalia Deserta' shows a socially and politically committed poet, full of the imagery of mining-valley life in the terrible days of the 1930's. Much of his work describes the impact of the Industrial Revolution, and its terrible decline, upon his beloved countryside and people. A Celtic Christian Socialist, he epitomised Welsh bardic tradition with a respect for fellow mankind, rather than for wealth based upon prosperity..... *'Any subject which has not man at its core is anathema to me. The meanest tramp on the road is ten times more interesting than the loveliest garden in the world. And instead of getting nearer to nature in the countryside I find myself craving for more intense society'.*

Idris Davies is the most approachable of all Welsh poets writing in English, and verse XV of his 'Gwalia Deserta' was set to music by Pete Seeger and also recorded by The Byrds amongst many others -

O what can you give me ?
Say the sad bells of Rhymney.

Is there hope for the future ?
Cry the brown bells of Merthyr.

Who made the mineowner ?
Say the black bells of Rhondda.

And who robbed the miner ?
Cry the grim bells of Blaina.

They will plunder willy-nilly,
Say the bells of Caerphilly.

They have fangs, they have teeth !
Shout the loud bells of Neath.

To the south, things are sullen,
Say the pink bells of Brecon.

Even God is uneasy,
Say the moist bells of Swansea.

Put the vandals in court !
Cry the bells of Newport.

All would be well if - if - if -
Say the green bells of Cardiff

Why so worried, sisters, why ?
Sing the silver bells of Wye.

Not until 1994 were Davies' complete poems collected in hardback, and are now available in paperback. 'The New Welsh Review' recorded the 1994 publication as follows: *'the poet, who in his lifetime, was usually treated with condescension and frequently accused of being merely a propagandist for socialism and of writing journalism, is central to the study of Anglo-Welsh poetry - more crucial, in fact, than Dylan Thomas or even R.S. Thomas... this splendid volume... must be saluted: it is surely a major landmark in Anglo-Welsh studies.'* And 'Poetry Review' said *'he has a claim to be recognised as one of the outstanding working-class poets of the century... an important work of publishing and scholarship'.* Ignoring the slightly derisory connotations of 'working-class', we can see that Davies is slowly receiving the acclaim that he deserved in life.

He summed up many of his countrymen's attitudes to the more strict sects in his poem 'Capel Calvin'..................

'There's holy holy people
They are in capel bach -
They don't like surpliced choirs,
They don't like Sospan Fach.

They don't like Sunday concerts,
Or women playing ball,
They don't like Williams Parry much
Or Shakespeare at all.

They don't like beer or bishops,
Or pictures without texts,
They don't like any other
Of the nonconformist sects.

And when they go to Heaven
They won't like that too well,
For the music will be sweeter
Than the music played in Hell.'

'The Collected Poems of Idris Davies', edited by Islwyn Jenkins, is published by Gomer, and the author recently purchased a copy for £4.95. It is a truly wonderful and moving book, ending with his 'Psalm', which begins with the lines:

'Make us, O lord, a people fit for poetry,
And grant us clear voices to praise all noble achievement.'

HYWEL DAVIS 1680? - 1719
'THE CAVALIER PRINCE OF PIRATES'

'Ah!' cried another voice, that of the youngest hand on board, and evidently full of admiration, 'he was the flower of the flock, was Flint!'
'Davis was a man, too, by all accounts,' said Silver. 'I never sailed along of him; first with England, then with Flint, that's my story; and now here on my own account, in a manner of speaking.'
'Treasure Island', Robert Louis Stevenson, 1883.

Milford Haven's Hywel Davis was mate on a slave ship Cadogan in 1718 which was captured by Captain Edward England, en route from Nassau in the Bahamas to the island of Madagascar. Defoe wrote that England tried to get Davis to join his crew, but *'Davis resolutely answered that he would sooner be shot than sign the pirates' articles. Upon which England, pleased with his bravery, sent him and the rest of the men on board the snow Cadogan (a small brig), appointing him captain in the room of Skinner (who had been shot) and commanding him to pursue his voyage. He also gave him a written paper sealed up, with orders to open it when he should come to a certain latitude..... This was an act of Grandeur like what princes practise to their admirals.... The paper contained a generous deed of gift of the ship and cargo to Davis and the crew, ordering him to go to Brazil, dispose of the lading to the best advantage and make a fair and equal dividend with the rest.'*

Skinner had been pelted with bottles by the pirates for being a brutal captain, before being put out of his misery by a musket-shot. However, most of the crew refused to follow this course of action, so Davis took the slaver on to Barbados, where he was charged with being a pirate and imprisoned for three months. Released for lack of proof, Davis found that his name had been blackened by the events, and could not get passage on any ship as a mate. He decided to head for the pirate stronghold of New Providence, but Woodes Rogers had offered an 'Act of Grace' to the pirates, and there was still no future for him.

Rogers took pity on him, and Davis sailed on the Buck, a sloop full of New Providence's former pirates, with cargo for trading with Spanish and French possessions in the Indies. However, the simmering and resentful Davis started a mutiny at Martinique, and was elected captain *'over a large bowl of punch.'* He then made a speech, according to Defoe *'the sum of which was a declaration of war against the whole world.'* At a bay called Coxon's Hole in the east coast of Cuba, the pirates careened the Buck, and stripped her ready for pirate action. With his crew of just thirty-five men, Davis then took a French ship. He is later said to have *'played the (pirate) game because he was given the name'.* He was noted for his mercy, affability and good nature, unlike most other pirates.

The pirates sailed from the Caribbean to the Guinea Coast, plundering and acquiring a new and better ship, King James. After attacking the island of Sao Tiago, Davis set sail for Gambia, sailing into the harbour with English ensigns flying, and most of his crew hidden below decks. He went ashore to see the Governor at the Royal African Company fort, pretending to be a friendly merchantman fleeing from the French. He noted the defences, and being entertained by the Governor at dinner that night drew his pistols and gave a signal for his men to over-run the fort. Having looted Gambia, there was then an equally successful attack on Sierra Leone, with Davis now commanding three pirate ships.

One of Davis' cleverest exploits was the capture of two French ships in 1719. He forced the prisoners from the first ship to masquerade as pirates and hoisted a dirty tarpaulin as a black pirate flag. Bluffed into believing that the captured French ship was another pirate boat, the second ship, with 24 guns, struck its colours. Davis looted the two ships, then released them and their crews, and sailed to the Portuguese Cape Verde Islands. He flew the English flag to enter the port, and pretended to be an English privateer with a letter of marque to fight the Spanish. He was welcomed, indeed *'caressed by the Governor and inhabitants.'* For five blissful weeks the pirates enjoyed themselves – *'no diversion was wanting which the Portuguese could show or money could purchase.'* Five pirates stayed and settled there, including a Monmouthshire man who married a local girl.

Davis now took the Buck to Gambia, taking the guise of Liverpool traders. Captain Davis, the ship's master and the surgeon 'dressed like gentlemen' instead of the normal pirate dress. They took dinner with the Governor of Gambia Castle, saying that they were *'bound for the river of Senegal to trade for gum and elephant's teeth (ivory).'* Davis had taken a 'hamper of European liquor' to dinner, as a present for the Governor, and took him prisoner. The pirates escaped with ivory and bars of gold. It appears that Davis destroyed the trading post, because George Lowther sailed as second mate in March 1721 of the Royal Africa Company ship 'Gambia Castle, under Captain Charles Russell. It was *'carrying stores and a company of soldiers to the river Gambia, on the African coast, to garrison a fort some time before captured and destroyed by Captain Howel (sic) Davis, the pirate'* (Lowther mutinied at Gambia in June, and took 33 prizes in 17 months according to Dow & Edmonds. He soon consorted with Captain Edward Low – the two were vicious and vindictive partners in piracy. Low took 140 vessels in 20 months.)

In 1718 Snelgrave reported that *'Captain Howell Davis came in the river (Gambia) with a Black Flag showing, which said flag is intended to frighten honest merchantmen into surrender on penalty of being murdered if they do not'* Captain Snelgrave wrote in his 'A New Account of Some Parts of Guinea, and the Slave Trade' that when Hywel Davis captured his ship, they drank the looted claret and brandy from bowls, before throwing bucketfuls of the precious alcohol at each other, and ended up by swabbing the decks with the drink. (As Bart Roberts commented later, a pirate's life was to be a short and happy one.)

In 1719, the fort of St James on the Gambia was bombarded by Davis – one of the men sheltering was to become Governor Plunkett who was captured by Black Bart after his Sierra Leone fort at Brent (or Bence) Island was bombarded. Davis now met the pirate captains Thomas Cocklyn (also from New Providence) and La Bouche and formed up for a joint cruise 'on the account.' Hywel Davis was elected commodore by the pirates, but wisely refused the honour as *'strong liquor stirring up a spirit of discord, they quarrelled ....Since we met in love, said he, let us part in love, for I find that three of a trade can never agree.'*

The Buck now took another seven Dutch and English prizes in the next few months, taking gold dust, ivory and slaves. He relegated the Buck to a consort ship, and sailed a captured vessel that he renamed the King James, with 26 guns. Davis was a Jacobite, which explains the name. In the King James he fought a long battle against a well-armed Dutch ship, formerly in the navy of George, off Cape Three Points. The battle lasted from mid-day to mid-morning, with both ships suffering severely. On capturing it, he made repairs and put 32 cannon and 27 swivel guns aboard and renamed it the Royal Rover. He disposed of the Buck, and now had two very powerful ships to rove the seas.

Around June 5th 1719, the Royal Rover and King James nosed into the slaving harbour of Annambo on the Gold Coast, flying the black flags, drums beating and trumpets blaring. The three English slave ships moored there immediately struck their colours. Davis took their cargoes of slaves, gold and ivory – like most pirates he always tried to avoid a fight and consequent damage to his ship, crew and the precious booty of the prize ships. Also there was always the chance of obtaining fresh crew members and 'sea-artists', or a better ship. Equally, merchant traders, although often well-armed, knew that if they surrendered immediately, quarter was nearly always given. They had no real desire to fight for the ship's owner or a hated captain. As a former merchant seaman and captain, Davis knew this, and had therefore deliberately drawn up his Ship's Articles to give quarter when it was asked for, that is when a ship struck her colours (lowered her flag).

The Royal Africa Company's fort opened fire on the ships but its cannon were designed for short-range work against attacking natives. Pirate attacks were rare off this coast. The shot fell harmlessly out of range. Davis looted the three slave vessels, and he gave one of them to the captain of the Dutch ship, releasing him and his crew. One of the English ships captured was the Princess, a slaver whose second mate was a man of Pembrokeshire, like Davis. Something about the tall, dark John Roberts captured Davis' imagination, but he was proud of never having 'forced' a man to become a pirate. He took Roberts off the Princess, to allow him time to make a decision whether to join the crew or not. Roberts was also from Pembrokeshire, for which reason Davis may have wished to learn something about home. ('Black Bart Roberts' soon became the most successful and feared pirate of them all).

Sailing east, the next day the pirates plundered another Dutch ship bound for Holland. After just one broadside from the Royal Rover, it surrendered. Davis as usual 'gave quarter' as he had stipulated in his Ship's Articles. It was a great prize, with the *'Governor of Accra on board, with all his effects.'* Apart from merchandise, there was over £15,000 in coin aboard. Davis now rid himself of the other two captured slavers, selling them off, and let those that wanted leave his ships. Roberts and thirty-four other merchant seamen decided to stay with Davis. Black Bart Roberts must have been bemused how easy the pirate life was, and he had heard of the bloodless trickery of Hywel Davis in his past exploits.

More ships were taken on the Guinea Coast, off the Bight of Biafra and the Bight of Benin, but off Cameroon the King James had to be abandoned because it was leaking badly. It had been badly damaged in the battle with the first Dutch ship a few weeks earlier. It was abandoned, and the crew transferred with the guns to the Rover, now renamed The Royal Rover. The Royal Rover sailed to the Isle of

Princes (Principe, off Gabon), where Davis claimed to be captain of an English man-of-war sent to bring piracy to a halt in the area. The Portuguese Governor officially welcomed him, and the pirates found a sandy cove to careen the ship. With just one ship left, it had to be fast and seaworthy. The pirate ship had been saluted by the fort's twelve cannons overlooking the harbour, and Davis had been greeted personally by the Governor of Prince's Island. Davis and his men felt safe. In the evenings, they spent their booty on women and drink in the little settlement on the main harbour. Because of their free-spending ways, the Governor must have soon known that they were pirates rather than the poverty-struck and impressed men of His Majesty's Navy.

No-one knows whether Davis intended to repeat his trick at Gambia, tricking the English Governor, or just rest and carouse a while, as he had done at the Cape Verde Islands under its Portuguese Governor. It may have been that the pirate just wanted to careen his ship and spend his loot. Careening was a laborious, and necessary process, carried out every three months or so. On a sandy beach, the topmasts were taken down (and perhaps replaced) and all the guns removed. By blocks and tackles, the ship was attached to trees (or another ship) and pulled over onto her side. The hull was then cleared of debris, repairs made, and coated with tallow and pitch. The process was repeated on the other side. This hard work was often accompanied by evenings of whoring, gambling and drinking. It appears that this was the case – he would not have allowed his men to get out of hand if his motive had been to capture the Governor of Prince's Island by subterfuge.

Tragedy now happened for Davis. Esquemeling recounts that a Portuguese negro swam ashore and told the Governor that he was to be invited on Davis' Royal Rover and held to ransom. It seems more likely however that the Governor was afraid of being reported to Portugal for consorting with, and profiting from pirates, on his poor little island. The Governor probably suspected Hywel Davis was a pirate, but there were huge profits to be made from trade with such a ship. They had few outlets for their stolen merchandise, accepted low prices, and usually spent the proceeds very quickly. The Royal Rover was to leave harbour after a few weeks, on a Monday morning. Davis had promised to pay the Governor a farewell visit on the Sunday morning, and went his chief surgeon and a handful of other crew. There was no-one at the Government House, and on his return the party was ambushed. Three were immediately killed, including the surgeon. Davis was shot four times but still fought back. After the fifth bullet wound he fell to the ground but still shot and killed two Portuguese soldiers. The Portuguese swarmed over his dying body and cut his throat to ensure he was dead.

Just one pirate managed to flee to the waiting boat, which was rowed quickly to the Royal Rover. Without a captain, there had to be an election of someone agreed by the whole crew. However, Davis' ship was very different from other pirate vessels. The hardest and most experienced pirates, such as Thomas Anstis (who later captained his own pirate ship), and Valentine Ashplant (the former captain of a brig), had formed themselves into what they called The House of Lords. They had assumed powers not available to the rest of the crew, or Commoners. They could go ashore at will, walk the quarter-deck and parley with the captains of prize ships. They referred to each other as 'my fellow noble' and greeted others as 'my noble lord'. It was this House of Lords which first debated who among them should be the new captain. They democratically chose John Roberts.

A new ship's surgeon and other officers were next appointed to replace those lost at Prince's Island. After this it was down to the serious business of avenging the death of Hywel Davis. One of the Lords, Walter Kennedy, had been voted as one of Roberts' lieutenants, and he led a band of thirty men up the hill to attack the fort. The settlement on Prince's Island was only a couple of streets with wooden shacks, and the fort guarded both this and the harbour. The Royal Rover fired broadsides at the fort, while the pirates attacked, but the Portuguese fled before they reached the walls. The fort was fired, and its 12 cannon thrown into the sea. Kennedy's band returned, as agreed, to the ship.

The pirate council on board then decided that it wanted to destroy the town as well. Roberts, being the captain only in times of aggression (or being chased) agreed, but only on condition that the town could be taken at minimum risk. To get to the settlement on land would mean passing through dense forest, perfect for an ambush. The Royal Rover could not sail into the shallow harbour without stripping itself of goods and armaments, leaving the pirates defenceless if things went wrong. He therefore took a nearby French ship, stripped it of everything removable and mounted twelve guns on it. He put other guns on rafts which the French ship towed towards the town. Once in the harbour and just off the town, it was bombarded at length until it had been virtually levelled. For good measure, two Portuguese ships in the harbour were also ransacked and set alight. Roberts restored the French ship to her captain and sailed southwards, away from 'The Isle of Princes' and its burning settlement. Hywel Davis had been avenged.

JEFFERSON DAVIS June 3 1808 - December 5 1889
PRESIDENT OF THE CONFEDERATE STATES OF AMERICA

Jefferson Davis Day June 3 (Alabama, Florida, Georgia and Mississippi)

John Davies emigrated from Wales to Philadelphia in 1701. His son Evan married a Welsh widow named Jane Williams, and the couple had a son, Samuel. The family moved to Augusta, Georgia, when Samuel was a boy, and her two Welsh sons by her earlier marriage enlisted in the Revolutionary army. Young Samuel Davies followed as a mounted gunman, later forming his own infantry company, fighting the British in Georgia and the Carolinas. At the end of the war, he was granted land in Georgia, then moved to Kentucky to breed racing horses on 600 acres of land, later known as Christian County and now as Todd County. Here, in 1808, the last of his ten children was born, and named Jefferson, after the great Welshman just finishing his second term as President of the United States.

The cradle, in which his mother Jane rocked the Jefferson Davis, is in The Confederate Museum in New Orleans. (At some stage the spelling of Davies changed to Davis).When the child was three years old, the family moved to Louisiana, and in 1812 to Mississippi. While Welshman Thomas Jefferson had created the new country of the United States, Jefferson Davis grew up to almost break it in two. A graduate of West Point, Jefferson Davis served in the Indian Wars, and was wounded becoming a hero in the Battle of Buena Vista against the Mexicans. He held his position here, saving Zachary Taylor from an ignominious

Jefferson Davis

defeat. Davis then eloped with Taylor's daughter Sarah, who died shortly after their marriage in 1835. He later married a Welsh lady, the daughter of a Mississippi aristocrat and plantation owner. In 1838 he was elected to the House of Representatives, during which time he again served under Taylor in the Mexican-American War, and sat in the US Senate from 1847 to 1851. Davis was Secretary of War under President Franklin Pierce from 1853 until 1857, when he returned to the Senate, becoming leader of the Southern Democrats. The German-born abolitionist Carl Schurz said that Davis met every expectation of what *'a grand personage the War Minister of this great Republic must be'*. As unofficial 'spokesman for the South, Jefferson, however viewed the Southern states as *'a country within a country'*.

In 1860 South Carolina issued a declaration of secession from the USA. By January 1861, Georgia, Florida, Alabama, Mississippi, Florida, Louisiana, Texas and Arkansas had also seceded from the union. Virginia and North Carolina soon followed. Jefferson Davis was elected in February 1861 as President of the Confederate States of America. The ensuing bitter Civil War lasted from 1861 to 1865, with the vast military capability of the Union North eventually overcoming the Confederate Southern states. After 1861, Davis wished to serve in the Confederate Army, but became President of the Confederate States of America fighting against the Northern Union states under President Lincoln.

The great and brutal battles of Manassas (where Davis took the field), Appomatox, Shiloh, Gettysburg, and the two battles at Bull Run echo through history, and the South has still not forgotten Sherman's devastation. 359,528 Union and 258000 Confederate troops had died in the young republic. The turning point in the war, more than any other, was the mass-production of the Springfield rifle in Connecticut. It had greater accuracy and three times the range of the old smooth-bore rifle. On the fateful third day of Gettysburg, 12,000 Confederate soldiers had mounted one last, great, Napoleonic assault on the Union lines. All but 300 were mown down before they reached the Northerners.

John Morgan's 'Alligator Horsemen' were the most hated and feared of all the Confederate soldiers. Courageous guerrillas, led by a Welshman, no atrocities can be held against their name in this dirty war. By 1865, the Second Kentucky was a scattered regiment of foot soldiers, as the Union rampaged through the Southern States. Even now, they were so highly rated that they were the chosen elite troops, to assist the Welsh Confederate President Jefferson Davis, in his flight from Richmond, before his capture. After his capture near Irwinville, Georgia, Jefferson Davis was put in shackles and imprisoned. His Welsh wife, Varina Howell, fought for his early release after two years in poor conditions. Davis refused to request the official pardon which would restore his citizenship. A private businessman and author after his release, Davis died in New Orleans aged 82.

The 'New York World', not a Southern sympathiser, called Jefferson Davies *'the best equipped man, intellectually, of his age, perhaps, in the country'*. Joseph McElroy, in his biography of Davis, says that *'Lincoln sought to save the Union; Davis did not wish to destroy the Union; he sought to preserve states' rights, under his interpretation of the Constitution.'* Like Jefferson before him, the right to liberty justified revolution for Davis - for him the Civil War was not about slavery but about freedom for the states and their individuals. He *'was convinced that Lincoln's aim was to convert a Federal republic of sovereign states into a consolidated nation with the right to dominate the states, the old idea which had precipitated the American Revolution.'* In the South, the Civil War is still referred to as 'The War of the States'.

The *'demon of centralisation, absolutism and despotism'* which is *'well-known by the friends of constitutional liberty'* had modern parallels in Chancellor Kohl's ideas for a united Europe with national sovereignty being subverted to central committees. A central over-riding bureaucracy could not work for Russia, so the European Union seems to be struggling against the natural flow of history. Welsh people from Glyndŵr to Thomas Jefferson to Jefferson Davis have always been rightly suspicious of both centralisation of power and rule by procedure and committees. Interestingly Lincoln had said that if he could win the Civil War without freeing the slaves, he would. Lincoln's main reason for pursuing this course of action **'was not to free the slaves, but to cause discomfiture to the South in the Civil War'** (Brian Walden, BBC TV, 13th January, 1998). The distinction of Jefferson Davis being pro-slavery and Lincoln being anti-slavery has been a useful myth to help centralise power in Washington.

JOHN DEE July 13 1527 - December 1608
BLACK JACK, 'THE MAGUS OF HIS AGE'

At Cefn Pawl near Beguildy was born Ieuan Ddu, John Dee, Black Jack, who became Elizabeth I's tutor, a man respected at court who was also a noted mathematician, antiquary, astronomer, philosopher, geographer, propagandist, astrologer and spy. How many people these days can put that on their business card?

John Dee was better known back in Powys as a magician and practitioner of the Black Arts than as a court adviser to Queen Elizabeth. Born in 1527, in Mortlake, Surrey, his father Rowland Dee was from Pilleth in Radnorshire, and worked as a 'gentleman server' to Henry VIII. John Dee said that he was a native of Beguildy, near Knighton in Radnorshire, and his diary shows his friendships with the Herberts, Morris Kyffin and John David Rhys (the grammarian-physician 'John Davies') among other notable Welshmen of the day. He taught the soldier-writer Morris Kyffin in London, c.1579-1580. Dee claimed descent from Rhodri Mawr, and to be a cousin of Blanche Parry. (Parry was also related to William Cecil [q.v.], who drew up her will and was her executor. She was *Chief gentlewoman of the Queen's most honourable Privy Chamber and Keeper of her Majesty's jewels.)* John Dee went to St John's College Cambridge in 1543, and was nominated as a foundation fellow of Trinity College Cambridge in 1546, before in 1546 moving to Louvain (Leuven)* in modern-day Belgium because science and mathematics were better established there. He believed that English humanism was not scientific enough, and made contact with some of the finest minds in mathematics and geography, such as Mercator, Ortelius and Gemma Phrysius. *'An astounding polymath..... the lectures of this twenty-three-year-old at Paris were a sensation; he* *was to be courted by princes all over Europe. He returned to England with navigational devices like the balestila or cross-staff, was taken up by the Queen, the retinue of the Earl of Leicester and the Sidneys, and was at the heart of the Elizabethan Renaissance'.*

He was a student in Louvain until 1550. Dee then lectured mathematics at Paris *'to enormous acclaim'* when he was twenty three, and in 1551 returned to the court of Edward VI. By the skin of his teeth he escaped the Marian persecution of Protestants, and returned to London to be taken into the heart of Elizabeth's court. With Blanche Parry and William Cecil having the queen's ear, this may have helped Black Jack to operate smoothly in Elizabethan court circles. He became a consultant of Elizabeth in State affairs, including giving advice on the Julian Calendar. He declined lectureships at the College of Reims and Oxford in 1554. *'With his remarkable library at Mortlake, (Dee) became the thinker behind most of the ventures of the English in their search for the North-East and North-West Passages to Cathay, pouring out treatises, maps, instructions, in his characteristic blend of technology, science, imperialism, speculation, fantasy and the occult'* ('Welsh Wizard and British Empire' by Gwyn Alf Williams). He was imprisoned by Queen Mary for trying to 'enchant' her, and a London mob sacked his fabulous library in 1583 as the den of a black magician. He is said to have been the model for both Shakespeare's white Prospero and Marlowe's black Faust.

Dee invented the term *'The British Empire'* for Queen Elizabeth in 1576 to prove her right to North America which has been 'discovered' by the Welsh prince Madog ap Owain Gwynedd. (i.e the Brythonic Celts, or the British, were the founders of her empire). His *'Titles'*, now lost, formed his concept of a British Empire for Elizabeth. It was based upon the polar maps of his friend, Gerard Mercator, and the work of William Lambard and the Venetian Zeno brothers. Dee claimed Scandinavia, the Arctic and America for Elizabeth. He used the Madoc story to justify the American claims. Dee also advised Drake upon his circumnavigation, and schemed a North-West Passage with Gilbert. After being caught up in spiritualism and alchemy, Dee disappeared to Bohemia, Prague and Poland from 1584-1589, returning to be given the wardenship of Christ's College, Manchester, remaining there until 1604. In 1587-88 Dee was spreading prophecies from Prague about *'the imminent fall of a mighty kingdom and fearsome storms'*. These reached the Vatican via Dee's patron, the Emperor Rudolph, and were reprinted across Holland, undermining the morale of its Spanish occupying army. Dee's exultant letter to Queen Elizabeth on the Armada's defeat in 1588 justifies his

John Dee

predictions. James I refused Dee's petition to clear him of the slander that he was *'a conjuror or caller or invocator of spirits'*. While Dee sometimes brought suspicion on himself by his dazzling intelligence across many fields of knowledge, the whispering campaign against him started with a wonderful stage device in the Cambridge production of an Aristophanes play. People saw his brilliance as proof of collusion with the occult. The Dictionary of Welsh Biography states: ... *it would seem certain that if he had adhered to pure science and steered clear of the esoteric or occult, he would rank amongst the foremost British pioneers of science'*.

Most of his 79 treaties remain in manuscript, but his works on hieroglyphics were published across Europe, and his *'Diary'* in England after his death. Dee also published the work of Euclid, and prepared an edition of Robert Recorde's mathematical studies, Recorde being a fellow-Welshman and inventor of the 'equals' (=) sign. *'The Grounde of Artes'* ran to 26 editions by 1662. As well as augmenting Recorde's writings, Dee wrote the seminal *'Mathematical Preface'* to Billingsley's translation of Euclid in 1570. His preface has been called a *'landmark in mathematical thought.'* Dee's *'Memorials pertayning to the Perfect Arte of Navigation'* was published in 1577.

*Even now, Louvain is a noted university city, and having visited there over a dozen times on business, I can vouch for the fact that it has the best selection of beers in the world - it is also the home of Stella Artois, which is admired as a drink as much by the locals, as Mateus Rose is by the Portuguese.

FOOTNOTE:
The British rejected the Gregorian Calendar in 1583, after Secretary of State Walsingham, on behalf of the Privy Council, passed a copy of the papal bull to *'the court magus'*, John Dee. *'Dee was the obvious choice as advisor. One of the leading scientific figures in England, and possessed of one of the largest private libraries in the country, he had a command of the latest astronomical learning (Copernicus included), as well as of current antiquarian and historical writing, both necessary for an understanding of the calendar issue. He had been imprisoned under Mary, had given astrological advice as to the date of the queen's coronation, had acted as an agent for Walsingham, and with him was among the advocates of a 'blue water' foreign policy combining Protestant alliances with voyages of exploration and colonisation'* (-Dr Robert Poole). Dee dropped everything to work on the problem, and delivered a 62-page illuminated treatise to the Lord Treasurer Burghley (q.v. William Cecil). Cecil visited Dee to try to persuade him to advise conformity with the rest of Europe by revising the English calendar. Dee agreed to a panel of three learned university men to discuss the treatise further, one of whom (Thomas Digges) was a former pupil of Dee's and a friend of Cecil. Despite further pressure from Cecil Dee rejected the papal calendar as it dated from the first council of the Christian church rather than from the time of Christ.

SAINT DEINIOL d.c. 550
DEINIOL WYN, THE BLESSED, DEINIOL AIL, DANIEL

Feast Date September 10, 11, 21, 22, December 10, possibly November 21

Deiniol was a hermit who lived on Daniel's Mount in Mynyw in Pembroke, who became Bishop of Bangor. He was said to have been uneducated and illiterate, and suddenly became endowed with complete religious knowledge when he said his first mass in the cathedral. However, his parents were the famous Dunawd Fawr and Dwywe ferch Gwallog ap Llenog, which made his illiteracy unlikely. He probably assisted his father in the foundation of Bangor-is-Coed. Deiniol and Dyfrig were said to be the two clerics who persuaded David to take part in the Synod of Brefi in 545, which makes him an extremely important figure in the early Christian church.

He founded Bangor Fawr (Bangor Deiniol) on the Menai Straits, where the cathedral is dedicated to him. He was the abbot but Maelgwn Gwynedd raised the place to an episcopal see, and Deiniol was the first bishop, possibly receiving the consecration from Dyfrig. He was buried on the Isle of 20,000 Saints, Bardsey (Enlli).

As founder and first Bishop of Bangor in Arfon, his diocese covered Gwynedd, and there is a dedication in Denbigh at Marchwiel outside Wrexham. Churches are also associated with Deiniol at Llanuwchllyn, and at Llanfor near Bala in Merionethshire. Wakes were held here on September 11, and a great fair at the former on September 22 until this century. Itton in Gwent was formerly called Llanddeiniol. St Deiniol's Ash is in Clwyd. Llanddeiniol in Cardiganshire is near Llanddewi Brefi, where Deiniol was associated with St David. There are few southern dedications like this. Hawarden in Flint is dedicated to Deiniol, and there were chapels at Worthenbury in Flint, and St Daniels under Monktown (Monkton) in Pembroke. Hawarden Fair was held on September 10th, and on the 21st when the dates changed in 1752.

Gwynfardd wrote about the privileges of St David at Brefi, that he had such joy:

> 'To have around him, about his plains,
> Men liberal and kindly disposed, and fair towns;
> He ensured protection to a quiet people,
> The tribe of Daniel, highly exalted, their equal
> Exists not, for lineage and morality and courtesy.'
> ('A bod o'l gylchyn, cylch ei faesydd,
> Haelon, a thirion, a theg drefydd;
> A gorfod gwared lliwed llonydd,
> Llwyth Daniel oruchel, eu hefelydd
> Nid oes, yn cadw oes, a moes, a mynudydd.')

At Bod-Deiniol farmhouse on Anglesey is Bedd Branwen, also sometimes called Bod-Deiniol. This is said to the burial-place of Branwen, whose tale in the Mabinogion involves the invasion of Ireland and the death of Bran. There is a Daniel's Well in Bangor, Caernarfon, Ffynnon Ddeiniol was in Penbryn parish, Cardigan, and Ffynnon Ddeiniol was in Bangor Monachorum parish, Denbigh. In

Flint there was a Ffynnon Daniel in Bangor-is-Coed parish, and another near Llanfor churchyard in Merioneth.

Deiniol fled the Yellow Plague in 547 and is remembered in Brittany at St Denoual and Plangenoual in the Cotes du Nord. Ploudaniel is south of Lesnevin, Kerdaniel is near St Fiacre south of Guincamp, and Pleu Daniel lies between Paimpol and Treguier.

SAINT DYFRIG c. 465 - c.546
BISHOP DUBRICIUS, 'DUBRIC THE HIGH SAINT, CHIEF OF THE CHURCH IN BRITAIN'

November 4 and 14 (translation May 29)

In the Life of Dyfrig (Vita Dubricii), his mother is Eurddil or Eurduila, daughter of King Peibio of Ergyng (Archenfield district in Herefordshire). His father was said

Llandaff Cathedral, where Dyfrig is the founder Saint
(photograph courtesy of WTB)

to be a king of Ergyng (Archenfield) called Pepiau, so his genealogy is confused. As Pabiali ap Brychan was also known as Papai, this may then be justified. He may have been born in Madley on the Wye near Hereford, which was Welsh-speaking until the eighteenth century. Other sources say that he was born at Mochros on the Wye in the same county, or on the banks of the Gwaun near Fishguard (Abergwaun) in Pembroke. He was of the line of Brychan, probably a grandson. King Peibio was known as 'King Dribbler', and when he discovered that Eurddil was pregnant threw her into the river in a sack. Three times the current threw her back on the shore. He then decided to burn her, but she was found next morning unharmed, cuddling the infant Dyfrig.

Dyfrig's own estate was called Ynys Eurddil, or Ynys Ebrdil (also Miserbdil) which was probably Mochros. Most sources say that his first foundation was at Archenfield (based on the Roman city of Ariconum). Another version is that he wandered along the Wye looking for the best place, and saw a wild white sow with piglets in a meander of the river. He called the site Moch-rhos, or Mochros (Moor of the Pigs), modern-day Moccas. Associated with St Illtud and St Samson, Dyfrig was extremely important in southeast Wales and Herefordshire, and it appears that David succeeded him as primate of Wales. He had religious centres at Hentland, Whitchurch, Madley, Moccas and Caldey Island. His chief church was centred at Hentland, just outside Ross-on-Wye, and the village itself rests on a Roman site. At a farm called Llanfrother there, were found traces of an ancient establishment. In Archenfield (modern Herefordshire) the church at Whitchurch, and chapels at Ballingham and Hentland are dedicated to him. It seems fairly certain that he and his disciples moved west after the battle of Dyrham, when Gloucester, Bath and probably Caerwent were destroyed. Their monasteries in Ergyng and Ewyas were wasted, and they sought refuge at Llandaf with Teilo, and at Llanilltud Fawr and Llancarfan.

In the 7th century Life of Samson he is a famed churchman (many of the details of the Welsh saints come from the Breton Lives, as Welsh records were destroyed during the four-hundred year fight against Anglo-French domination. Destruction of land titles and deeds, usually recorded on church manuscripts, allowed Norman and Angevin lords to take over Welsh territories legally). Known as 'papa' Dubricius, he was said to have ordained Samson as a deacon at Llanilltud Fawr. Some sources say that Dyfrig was taught himself by Germanus of Auxerre but Dyfirg was a century too late, so this may mean he was a follower of Garmon's teaching. Certainly, he seemed to have been a strong opponent of Pelagianism and persuaded his friend David to preach against it at the Llanddewi Brefi synod. Samson's Life claims that Dyfrig was an abbot at Enlli, and Geoffrey of Monmouth claimed that he crowned the 15-year old Arthur at Silchester. Geoffrey of Monmouth states that there were 200 philosophers in his college at Caerleon, studying science and astronomy.

Stone at Caewent, the Roman town associated with Dyfrig
(photograph courtesy of WTB)

Other later medieval records place him as bishop of Caerleon from 490 on succeeding Tremorinus, the founder of Llandaf and again as the saint who crowned Arthur. On Caldey Island was found a stone inscribed 'Magl Dubr', tonsured servant of Dubricius, where it seems Dyfrig was for some time the abbot there. There are also dedications to him at Gwenddwr, south of Builth in Breconshire and at Porlock in Somerset. Porlock was formerly '*ecclesia Saint Dubricius*' in a deed of 1476. There are at least six churches clustered in Archenfield dedicated to Dyfrig. Hereford's Saint Devereux is a corruption of Dubricius.

Dyfrig retired to Enlli, but a Norman bishop of Llandaf had his bones translated to Llandaf in 1120 for the greater honour of his cathedral, where he was one of the four titular saints. The relics reached the Lleyn penisula mainland on May 7 and arrived at Llandaf on May 23, where his reliquaries (his head and one arm encased in silver) drew pilgrims until the Reformation. They were removed in 1538 and lost. Tennyson called him *'Dubric the high saint, Chief of the church in Britain'.* Dyfrig's most famous well is near the ancient monastery site of Garnllwyd at Llancarfan, where Cadog was presiding at this time. Ffynnon Dyfrig can still be found in the woods known as Coed Ffynnon Dyfrig, and nearby at Llanfeithyn he had another healing well. These survivals certainly seem to authenticate his stay, possibly with Teilo, at Llancarfan. There is a case to be made that Dyfrig founded the colleges of Llancarfan, Caerworgan (Llanilltud Fawr) and Caerleon, and that he should have been made the patron saint of Wales for the effects that these monasteries had upon Celtic Christianity. His effigy lies in Llandaf Cathedral.

GARETH OWEN EDWARDS July 12 1947 -
THE GREATEST RUGBY PLAYER OF ALL TIME

'Kirkpatrick to Williams. This is great stuff. Phil Bennett covering, chased by Alistair Scown. Brilliant, oh that's brilliant. John Williams, Bryan Williams, Pullin, John Dawes, great dummy, David, Tom David, the halfway line. Brilliant by Quinnell, this is Gareth Edwards, a dramatic start, what a score! Oh that fellow Edwards'. Every Welshman remembers Cliff Morgan's increasing crescendo of a commentary on that day when the Welshmen in the Barbarians team magically carved through the invincible All Blacks' defence on January 27th, 1973. From Phil Bennett fielding a long kick and dangerously side-stepping and jinking three times under his posts, the ball went to the truly great JPR Williams, who was high-tackled around the neck by Bryan Williams. However, JPR who managed to pass the ball to the English hooker John Pullin who immediately transferred to Dawes. Gareth Edwrds at this time is near the ball, but not involved. Welsh captain John Dawes took the ball on, with a dummy cutting through defenders, then that wonderful flanker Tommy David received his pass, and burst over the half-way line. He is forced to flip the ball one-handed to his left. Derek Quinnell, the father of the current internationals Scott and Craig, caught the very low pass at speed and flipped it up to wing John Bevan near the touchline. However, the pass is intercepted by Edwards, who has joined the movement like a guided missile from nowhere, sprinting outside the New Zealand full-back and just making it over the try-line near the corner flag.

25 seconds of magic, which the referee later admitted he could have stopped because of two New Zealand high tackles. Because of the preponderance of Welshmen in the Barbarian team against the unbeaten All-Blacks, in the final match of their tour, it seemed like a home match at Cardiff Arms Park. The Baa-Baa's won 23-11 in a fabulous game of open aggressive rugby, the like of which we shall never see again unless rugby returns to the understandable laws of the 1970's. (The great game has been radically altered by law changes to make it a contest between battering rams, with hard-contact thuggery being the aim of the game rather than ball-movement and grace. The lock-picker's toolbox of amateur rugby, where we can analogise the screwdriver, pliers, spanner et al to the swerve, scissors, pace-change, dummy, side-step etc., has been replaced by the Irish hammer of heavily padded professional men simply crashing into each other).

Gareth Edwards of Gwaun-Cae-Gurwen made a record 53 consecutive appearances for Wales from 1967 to 1978, when he retired after scoring a remarkable 20 tries for his country. A poll of 200 players, coaches, managers and writers across the globe, to find the greatest rugby player of all time, was published by 'Rugby World' in October 1996. The highest Englishman, at 12th, is Fran Cotton. Top was Gareth Edwards, (followed by Serge Blanco) and three other members of *'the golden team'*, Gerald Davies, Barry John and J.P.R. Williams, are all in the top 10. Another poll, of internationals and coaches, carried out across the world before the 1999 World Cup, also placed Edwards as the 'greatest-ever', over 20 years after his leaving the game. Edwards won three Grand Slams, 5 successive Triple Crowns, captained Wales 13 times and scored 20 tries.

Gareth Edwards

He went on three British Lions tours, including the successes of New Zealand in 1971 and South Africa in 1974. He won 5 triple Crowns and 3 Grand Slams. His try mentioned previously, in the 1973 Barbarians defeat of New Zealand, was manufactured almost entirely by Welsh players, and is arguably the most memorable try in recorded history. Edwards was also a key member of the British Lions team that beat New Zealand in 1971 and South Africa in 1974, winning 10 Lions' Caps. Both tours featured some of the greatest flowing rugby ever seen, which makes it all the more odd that the rules were altered to make the game more like rugby league, and far more unattractive as a spectacle in the last decade.

Remembered for the 1971 and 1974 Lions Tours, Edwards was a youngster on the 1968 tour to South Africa. However, he believes it was the true turning-point in his personal career. He had a long pass, but he knew that it could be bettered, so tended to run with the ball sometimes when a pass was a better option. On his first appearance with the legendary John outside him at fly-half, Edwards has asked 'The King' how he wanted the ball given to him. John famously responded, *'Just throw it, I'll catch it'*, which did not really help Edwards much. At this time, Cardiff's Arms park was also used by the international team, and by Cardiff Athletic (The Rags), with games never being called off because of 'bad conditions' and as a result it was like a quagmire for most of the rugby season. Edwards recalled that he had no confidence in his passing, and that Ken Catchpole (Australia) and Chris Laidlaw (New Zealand) could put spin on the ball. South Africa gave him his first opportunity to learn to pass like these maestros - *I had three months in perfect conditions and could practise virtually every day. From that time, I never looked back and it changed my game almost overnight. Though it took me quite a long time to perfect the long spinner, my confidence came right back. I did not have to worry about my pass any longer. Everything was right for me after that tour.'*

Edwards' Cardiff and Wales partnership with Barry John heralded the 'Golden Age' of Welsh rugby in the 1970's. From 1969-1979 there were only three seasons when Wales did not finish top of the 5 Nations Championship, winning 3 Grand Slams, 6 Triple Crowns and never losing at the Arms Park. In 1971 at Stade Colombes, tries from John and Edwards gave Wales a 9-5 victory (3 points for a try) after losing 5-0. This gave Wales their first Grand Slam since 1952. Edwards' greatest individual try is thought to be against Scotland in 1972. Wales were leading 16-12, with Edwards already having scored, when Gareth broke from a scrum in his own 25-yard area, near the touch-line. He passed the Scottish wing-forward and scorched up the touch-line until faced by the Scottish full-back, chipping over him. Kicking the ball on through the mud, the cover closed on him, and he just made the try-line by the corner-flag. The great comedian Spike Milligan remembers standing up and roaring at his television set, willing Edwards on to score. It was Wales' biggest victory for 41 years.

The author recently met Edwards, now a director of Cardiff Rugby Club, and used to watch him and Barry John play for Cardiff. Both were amateurs in those days, and received nothing for playing for Wales or Cardiff. Edwards said *'you had to win for Wales - you couldn't go home otherwise'*, and that crowds did not realise that often players played when suffering injuries. There was no alternative to winning. The Welsh Rugby Union has consistently ignored the men whose skills, intelligence and backbone made Welshmen everywhere stand tall. Not just Edwards and John, but of their era the sublime Gerald Davies, the invincible J.P.R. Williams, the 'Pontypool Front Row', Mervyn Davies,

Rugby's Millennium Stadium at Cardiff
(photograph courtesy of WTB)

John Taylor - the list goes on. Even today's players know all their names and grew up in their shadow - why cannot these legends, for that is their value to Wales, meet the Welsh team before every match to help motivate them?

Edwards has had a successful career since his 1978 retirement from the game, in business, broadcasting and writing. His most beloved pastime apart from his family is fly-fishing on the Welsh rivers. A natural athlete, he won the All England Schools 400-yards hurdles when at Millfield. He could break out of tackles, seeing them as a personal affront, and went fearlessly for the try line like a terrier when other scrum-halves would pass or kick. The author is proud to have watched Gareth Edwards in his pomp for Cardiff and Wales. Other players have been able to match Edwards in parts of his game, but none in its totality - he simply had no weaknesses as a rugby footballer. To appreciate Gareth Edwards, one has to watch videos - writing cannot do him justice.

5-Nations Champion 1969, 1970, 1971, 1975, 1976, 1978
Triple Crown 1969, 1976, 1977, 1978
Grand Slam 1971, 1976, 1978
British Lions 1968 South Africa, 1971 New Zealand, 1974 South Africa
FOOTNOTES:
The great player and coach Carwyn James spoke to the Barbarians players on the morning of their match against the unbeaten All-Blacks, probably the most unpopular touring side ever to visit the British Isles. The following is taken from a Stephen Jones' article in The Sunday Times, June 13, 1999, entitled *'The Try for All Seasons'*: *'People expected us to win,*

but also in a certain style' said Edwards. *'I have never felt so weak at the kick-off, because of the pressure'.* *'I remain convinced'* JPR Williams said, *'that the whole thing really was Carwyn's try...He soothed us, told us to enjoy it. And I'll never forget his last words - to insist to Phil Bennett, who was full of trepidation, to go out and play just like he did for Llanelli'.* Bennett was told by James that he could *'sidestep this lot off the park'.* Jones goes on to describe the build up to Edwards' participation in the try *'......... David had made his boisterous surge, Quinnell had handled the ball delicately, on his fingertips and handed it on towards John Bevan on the left wing. More dazzling microseconds as Bevan shaped to catch the ball, still with the defence in reasonable shape; and suddenly, Edwards came to the scene from nowhere, at a pace so blistering that he added another gear to a movement that was already at high speed.*

But where had he been? Why so late at the party? *'Even though the game was only a few minutes old I was feeling weak with the pressure. I was running round like I had no legs and never really feeling part of it. When Phil fielded the ball I was 50 yards away in the other corner, running back towards our line'.* Indeed, the first contribution which Edwards made to the move lay in avoiding his own onrushing colleagues. At one stage, he was probably as much as 25 yards behind the ball. *'I was still asking myself why didn't someone kick the ball out, so I could get my second breath'.*

But instincts were quickly aroused. 'John Dawes got the ball, and like the poacher I was, I thought that if I chased there could be something on'. There was. Edwards spotted a running line down the left wing and the ball gradually moved back towards that flank of the field. Edwards is the greatest rugby player that I have seen in my life. He was also one of the fastest, a marvellous athlete and sprinter. Bennett and the others have conjured marvellously. But that final ingredient, which takes the try from possible to certain, is raw pace. Suddenly, it is as if all the rest had been treading in treacle after all. Edwards snatches the ball form the outstretched fingers of Bevan and covers the final 33 yards at searing speed. *'I was 20 yards back initially but when I caught up I was in full stride. I know John Bevan was screaming for it and maybe he was earmarked by some of the defence. But it doesn't matter who Derek was trying to pass to. I was in full print stride when I caught it. By the time I got round Joe Karam, the only thing I thought about was my hamstrings. Never before had I felt I had run so fast.'* A later try by JPR Williams passed through more pairs of hands, but this was the try that everyone always remembers.

(ii) Cardiff Rugby Football Club is the most famous rugby club in the world, still playing at the Cardiff Arms Park, and mention should be made here of its record against the 'Big 3' touring teams. Cardiff always plays the 'first team' of South Africa, New Zealand or Australia, as the match is regarded very much as an 'international' by these teams. Other British teams often play the touring team's 'seconds'. Against South Africa, the statistics are skewed because the author saw the 13-0 defeat in 1960, where the Cardiff fly-half Tommy McCarthy was stretchered off early on to a horrible, and unpunished late tackle, forcing Cardiff to play with 14 men (no substitutes, then) in the mud against the dirtiest team ever to tour Britain. However, that caveat aside, the record against South Africa is Won 1, Lost 6, average score 8-10 (taking out the 1960 match, the average score would be 8-8). Against New Zealand, Cardiff have Won 1, Lost 8, average score 8-15. However, against Australia, Cardiff have never lost - Won 6 Lost 0, average score 15-8. (The full Welsh team's record against Australia is Won 8, Lost 11). So in all matches, Cardiff have won 8, lost 14, with an average score of 8-10. This is why touring teams want to play their best sides at the Arms Park - no other team in Britain can touch Cardiff's record. It is a tragedy that professionalism and new Southern Hemisphere rules have disfigured the game, and that some current Cardiff players do not realise the heritage of the club.

(iii) It is well worth recording in full 'The Times' report of Edward's first Triple Crown. The reader may note that Wales scored 7 tries, worth 3 points each, three converted, a drop goal and two penalties, to three penalties by a good English team. Scorers were not included, except for the superb Cardiff centre and wing, Maurice Richards, who scored 4 tries in this match before joining rugby league. In today's scoring, the result would be (on a poor pitch)

Wales 50: England 9. Anyone who believes that rule changes, enforced on rugby by the Southern Hemisphere countries (to favour prolonged contact on the Rugby League pattern), have improved the game, should watch a video of this match. No child watching the 1999 World Cup in Wales would wish to take up rugby, or come away with a set of heroes to emulate - it was incredibly boring, and featured more incredibly stupid refereeing errors than the author has seen in a lifetime of watching rugby. Two of the tries scored by Australia against Wales makes one think that match-fixing has not been confined to football and cricket. Awesome incompetence by the referee and his linesmen is the most Christian way to view any recording of that match. The other point about the new rules is that there is not one child in Britain who came away from watching the World Cup with any hero to emulate. The game is simply no longer attractive, the only interesting game being the semi-final upset where France beat New Zealand. However, let us return to better days. Wales had not won the 5-Nations Championship since 1966, and went on to dominate the game for a decade:

'WALES WIN THE TRIPLE CROWN April 14 1969

At last Wales proved on Saturday that they were unquestionably the best rugby team in this year's international championship by winning it for the first time since 1966 and the Triple Crown into the bargain. Hitherto they had suggested it, but three goals (converted tries), a drop goal, two penalty goals and four tries to England's three penalty goals at Cardiff, stamped them with that priceless quality of being able to pull out their best when it was needed.

Now the Welsh dragon can at least embark upon its south Pacific tour with its tail up. This morale booster must have been doubly sweet to the Welsh coach, D.C.T.Rowlands, who was their captain when they last won the Triple Crown in 1965. The congratulations showered upon him were well earned. He will be the first to admit, however, that he has had currently exceptional quality to mould without which the best teaching in the world can fail.

This was Wales's biggest victory over England for 47 years, and in the championship they have scored 79 points, including 14 tries, or an average of three and a half a match. Nobody could deny that this was positive stuff, a capacity which made their kicking in some earlier matches rather puzzling. On Saturday they let rip with some authority, and four tries for Richards alone were more in an international match than most people can remember.

The pattern of victory was set by the Welsh forwards, well led by Brian Thomas, and with Delme Thomas, who came for Brian Price, in outstanding form. From the first scrummage their pack, in which the front five were entirely predominant over their opposite numbers, pushed England all over the place. They had command of the line-out, and as a whole were more effective in the loose.

No wonder therefore that Wales were well set up for their glorious spree in the second half, after appearing a little low in the first period against a wind off the Taff violent enough to send bandsmen's caps bowling down the field.

Edwards, captain and scrum-half, again showed how he has already perfected most of the tricks of his trade. John's intuitive directional sense, which threads him through apparently impenetrable defensive jungles, was a great nuisance to England.

Both wings were in form, and the quick-witted swift-moving Richards had help with some of his tries from the centre where Jarrett also kicked a dozen points and Dawes brought with him his usual air of orderly rationality.

Quite simply England did not have enough of the ball to have much of a chance. When they did have possession for some time in the first half, with the wind behind them, they wasted too many opportunities to run the ball. In this Wales taught them a most painful lesson after the interval.'

GERAINT EVANS CBE 1922 - 1992
'A GREAT ACTOR IN THE BRITISH TRADITION, AS WELL AS A GREAT SINGER IN THE ITALIAN ONE' - *New York Times*

Born in Cilfynydd, near Pontypridd, he made his Covent Garden debut as the Night Watchman in *Die Meistersinger* in 1948. After this small start, he went on to assume all the leading bass-baritone roles in the classical repertoire. His father was conductor of the local church choir, and Geraint sang as a boy-soprano there. His father recognised his talents and encouraged him with violin lessons. By the age of 17, Geraint's voice had mellowed to a baritone, and he was invited to appear as a soloist in a performance of Medelssohn's *Elijah*. The notable choral director Idloes Owen saw this performance and was so impressed that he invited Evans to join his Owen's Lyrian Singers, and to undertake serious vocal training. However, World War II interrupted his studies, and after Royal Air Force service, he was stationed in Germany in 1945.

Evans now trained with the famous German bass Theo Hermann, who had heard him singing on his own show on British Forces Network Radio. After further study at London's Guildhall School of Music and in Geneva with Fernando Carpi, Hermann arranged for Evans to meet the musical director of the Royal Opera, Covent Garden. He was immediately offered a contract. His debut in *Die Meistersinger* was followed some years later by a starring role as the cunning town clerk, Sixtus Beckmesser, in the opera.

Geraint Evans

Evans was Papageno in *The Magic Flute*, Leporello in *Don Giovanni*, Figaro in *Le Nozze di Figaro*, Mozart's finest operas, and also appeared in all Benjamin Britten's works. In 1960, while singing *Figaro* at La Scala, many Milanese thought that he was a Sicilian, because of his flawless Italian diction. He appeared in Donizetti's *Lucia di Lammermoor* with Joan Sutherland and took the title role in Donizetti's *Don Pasquale*. This latter role was for his 25th season at Covent Garden in 1973, where he delighted the audience with *'his superb characterisation and beautiful belcanto singing.'* Of his performance as Leporello at the Met, the critic Irving Kolodin wrote *'the most artfully sung servant in decades... acted with typical English* (sic) *conviction that to be a fine servant is no less a distinction than to be a worthy master.'*

His greatest role was the title role in Verdi's *Falstaff*, *'which he sang in every opera house in the world.'* Evans also stage directed the Welsh National Opera, and companies in Chicago and San Francisco. A warm and friendly man, he was greatly respected by all those who worked with him. A CBE was conferred in 1959.

In the 1960's the notes to the recording *The Royal Family of Opera* are as follows: *'Thee is a selected list which grows slowly over the years of opera artists who are not content to master only the vocal art, but who also devote equal energy to perfecting the theatrical side of opera's nature. These are the true opera artists, and Geraint Evans is certainly among their limited number. It has often been said that he could be famous as an actor if he ever decided to stop singing, and certainly anyone who has experienced his Falstaff, Wozzeck, Leporello or Figaro knows this to be true. He is the master of many vocal styles, although Falstaff and the Mozart roles have perhaps become his most sought-after specialities. At his first performance at the Met in the role of the fat knight, the enthusiasm of the audience was equalled only by that of the conductor of the evening, Leonard Bernstein. Evans is a perfectionist, every detail of make-up, costume, gesture and facial expression serves, when added to his vocal and musical mastery, to create a complete character.'*

'Sir Geraint Evans earned his place in operatic history by being consistent, working tirelessly to improve his performances and by his sheer longevity on the great stages of the world. He also was noted by his fellow performers as being a warm and friendly colleague.'

GWYNFOR EVANS 1912 -
'WALES' GREATEST LIVING PATRIOT'

President of Plaid Cymru - The Party of Wales - for 36 years from 1945 until 1981, and now its 'Honorary president', Gwynfor was the first member of his party to be elected to Parliament, in 1966. A devout Christian and a pacifist, he was almost treated as a pariah in the House of Commons because of his insistence that Wales was a nation which needed to preserve its language, and which needed its own parliament. Fortunately, Gwynfor Evans knew the history of Wales, what had been done to it, and its remarkable culture, heritage and contribution to Christianity and civilisation. This compares dramatically with a later Welsh political leader, Neil Kinnock, who sadly believed that Wales did not have *'much of a history'*. The problem, as always, is that people only believe what they are told - the inquiring mind will find that history is always written by the attackers. From the anti-Druid propaganda of the Romans to today's times, the media follows the masters, and what went before is wiped out.

Gwynfor Evans graduated at Oxford and Aberystwyth, and took over as president of Plaid Cymru in 1945. To some extent the growth of Plaid was helped by the Conservative government of the 1950's. Responding to its election pledges, it attempted to create a sinecure phantom Ministry of Welsh Affairs in that decade, headed by the first of a long line of English Tories, Sir David Maxwell Hamilton-Fyfe. His strange attitude towards Wales and the Welsh earned him the epithet across Wales was *'Dai Bananas'*. He was followed by others of the ilk of Sir Henry Brooke, Sir Keith Joseph, the miming John Redwood and the adolescent William Hague. Wales was given a Secretary of State position in the Cabinet in 1964. Evans moved away from Saunders' Lewis vision of Plaid Cymru, towards more political activity, environmentalism, European federalism and social democracy on the Scandinavian model.

Born in Barri, Glamorgan, a town of few Welsh-speakers, his father owned the department store, Dan Evans, which still runs in the run-down main street (Holton Road) of the town*. Gwynfor was a conscientious objector in World War II, which turned many local people against him, and he moved to Carmarthenshire. Imprisoned several times for trying to keep the language alive, his daughter Meinir was twice imprisoned herself in London's Holloway gaol, and her husband Ffred Ffrancis himself spent five years in prison. Ffrancis was leader of Cymdeithas yr Iaith Gymraeg (the Welsh Language Society), the formation of which by a younger generation in the 1960's Gwynfor calls *one of the proudest chapters in the history of Wales*. The movement, by court protests at wanting trials in Welsh, by daubing English road-signs in Wales, and by a programme of civil disobedience, eventually was rewarded with Welsh being awarded official language status. The Welsh Language Act of 1967 will not secure the language, but will help slow its destruction. Some readers should probably be made aware that Welsh was 1400 years old when Chaucer was trying to write the first barely recognisable English. If we say the Shakespeare's language is the start of modern English, it is around a fifth of the age of Welsh.

Apart from his other efforts to raise the profile of the Welsh language, Gwynfor knew that it was necessary to be a language of the media - there simply had to be a Welsh television channel. The author was recently in Galway, speaking to a Gaelic radio station, and realised that Ireland needed a Gaelic 'soap-opera' on TV to help its dying language. 'Pobol y Cwm' has that distinction on Sianel Pedwar Cymraeg (Welsh Channel 4), and people should remember that Gwynfor Evans almost died from a hunger-strike to get a Welsh language TV channel. The bellicose Prime Minister, Mrs Thatcher, had promised one, but reneged. After her U-turn,

Gwynfor Evans

when Gwynfor was close to death, someone scrawled in letters three feet high, on the wall of the Thames Embankment facing Westminster, *'GWYNFOR 1 - THATCHER 0'*. Another of Gwynfor's achievements is the popularity of Welsh-medium schools, where teaching is carried out in the Welsh language. As he said in 1996, *'the way to annihilate a nation is to obliterate its culture. The way to delete its culture is to destroy its language'*. He also believes that *'the nation-state is now so powerful it can kill a culture merely by ignoring it.'* This author, however, believes that nation-states are increasingly powerless, and that stateless multinational companies control economies, labour forces and politicians.

His greatest sorrow was the drowning of Trywerin, *'except for the campaign for a Parliament for Wales, Trywerin was the most important of our battles'*. The beautiful valley of Cwm Trywerin was made into a reservoir for Liverpool, despite overwhelming opposition from the Welsh people. (Presently the Welsh pay more for water than the English who use water from Welsh reservoirs). As Trywerin is now surplus to Liverpool's requirements, perhaps it could be drained and the land returned as National Park to Wales. Passive demonstrations, encouraged by Gwynfor, were no good, and there was some sabotage against transformers used in the dam's construction, and against the following Clywedog dam for Birmingham's needs. All Welsh MP's voted against the Trywerin tragedy and the wiping out of the 100%-Welsh-speaking community of Capel Celyn, except for Sir Henry Brooke, the Tory Minister of Welsh Affairs.

It is fair to say that the precarious survival of the language, and the existence of a National assembly since 1999, despite its lack of power**, have been in no small part due to Evan's influence and stance. Because of him, Plaid Cymru is a real opposition to the Labour Party in Wales, despite the recent 'softening' of its nationalist stance. The rise of Plaid is of massive importance to Wales because it gives real opposition at last to the Labour Party in Wales - hopefully some of Britain's resources can be diverted into the nation as a result - its schools and colleges are massively under-funded compared to those in England, and the wealth per person (GDP per capita) is around three-quarters that of England's. Wales has always been neglected by the Tories when in power at Westminster, because it is not a source of parliamentary power for them. Labour has ignored it for exactly the opposite reason - it can count upon Wales for seats in Parliament, and does not need to offer 'sweeteners'.

'For the Sake of Wales: the Memoirs of Gwynfor Evans' has been translated by Meic Stephens, and is a marvellous book (published by the Welsh Academic Press). Its reviewer in the American-Welsh newspaper Ninnau said *'there are not enough superlatives in my vocabulary to express what I believe to be the value of "For the Sake of Wales", especially to the North American Welsh, or others of the Greater Welsh Nation throughout the world, who want to come home to their Welshness'.* And Manon Rhys, in her preface to the original publication in Welsh in 1982 wrote *'This is the story of one of the great souls of Twentieth-century Wales.'* Dafydd Elis Thomas writes in the introduction *'It is not political ideas, or religious conviction, or moral authority or personal integrity (although all these are virtues in the person of Gwynfor Evans) which shine most clearly through this book. It is, rather, a love of people everywhere, expressed in an open and positive caring for the national community of Wales and its constituent parts.'*

*The author grew up in Barri - as of writing, the beautiful Town Hall on the main square has been semi-derelict and mainly unoccupied for over 18 years, since the council moved into grand new offices. The roof of the once-superb library, which forms part of the building, recently collapsed. Barri has huge infrastructural problems, which politicians seem unable to face. One of the main problems of Cardiff's growth is that it has sucked resources from its neighbouring hinterland - to the east Newport, to the north Caerffili and the valleys, and to the west Barri have all been ill-served by their elected representatives for decades. *'Mapping Social Exclusion,'* a report by the national (British) Assembly, underestimates the problems of the Welsh economy, for which there seem to be few practicable solutions. Among its findings are that half of all households have incomes below £10,000; 40% of Welsh people have no savings; 22% of people have no qualifications; 18% of households with dependent children have no earned income!; 10% of the population is being treated for depression or anxiety; nearly 9% of homes are unfit to live in; 26% of people of working age are dependent on state handouts; the GDP per capita is around 20% below Europe's.....and so on. The legacy of colonisation and being run by London is not a happy one for Wales.

Recent steel redundancies may just get Welsh people thinking about their politico-economic future, and bring about a massive anti-Government protest vote in forthcoming elections, but it is beyond the wit of politicians to cure economic problems. Very little British industry is now domestically owned. Transnational companies avoid taxation wherever they operate, and pay no corporate taxes. If a government wishes to tax them, they move on to another country, and even blackmail governments to stay operating in any country. The author has presented several conference papers concerning multinational tax avoidance (Japanese companies operating in Wales are a specific case in point). As a result, a higher taxation burden falls upon the working man, via indirect methods - this is why the UK has the highest personal taxation burden, the highest car, oil and food prices, in Europe, despite among the lowest wages. Governments can no longer tax industry, which results in a double-edged sword - the highest personal taxation in history, and a lessening provision of a welfare state. By welfare I do not mean social 'scrounging', but the provision of quality education, pensions, medical care, old age health provision, and decent rail, road, communications, water and sewage infrastructures. Thatcher's selling-off of nationalised assets (which belonged to the nation, and the revenues of which kept taxes down) merely disguised the reality of Britain's sick, foreign-owned economy. The future is not just bleak for Wales, but also for England. And of course, where do top British politicians go when they retire from politics, despite having no business experience? Onto the boards of various multinational companies.

**The Scottish Assembly has far more power than the National Assembly (which should be called the 'British Assembly'), because the Prime Minister and Cabinet which agreed to the legislation were overwhelmingly Scottish at the time. Of the 22-man cabinet, the only Welshman was the placid Alun Michael as the ineffectual Minister for Wales. The Prime Minister (Blair), Chancellor of the Exchequer (Brown), Foreign Secretary (Cook), Minister of Defence (Robertson), Lord Chancellor (Irvine) and Defence Minister (Robertson) were all Scottish, filling 6 of the 7 most powerful Cabinet places (-the Home Secretary, Straw, was English). If we add Dewar (Scotland) and Smith (Culture), the Scots had 8 of the 22 Cabinet places.

JOHN EVANS   christened April 14 1770 - May 1799
THE MAN WHO OPENED UP AMERICA

Jefferson's friend and protegé, a fellow-Welshman called Meriwether Lewis, opened up the American West, with fellow explorer William Clark. Lewis commanded and completed the first overland expedition to the Pacific Coast and back (1803-1806). They had used the maps of John Thomas Evans of Waunfawr in Gwynedd, who had explored the Missouri Valley in 1792 for the first time, looking for Prince Madoc's Welsh Indians. They almost definitely would not have discovered the route to the Pacific Ocean, a decade later, without the work of Evans. Jefferson personally sent Evans' maps to Meriwether Lewis, and used them when making 'The Louisiana Purchase'.

The plan for the young weaver, John Evans, to find 'Welsh Indians' or 'Madogwys' descended from Madoc ap Owain Gwynedd, had been inspired by

Iolo Morganwg, who was going to go with him to America. There had been an outbreak of 'Madoc Fever' across Wales at the time, but Iolo was too ill to go. Evans arrived in America in 1792, after paying £20 to travel 'steerage', with letters of introduction to several Welshmen of influence in Philadelphia, but they warned him that the Indian tribes were dangerous, and told him to forget his quest. At this time, apart from the Indians, England, America, France and Spain were all manoeuvring to gain chunks of the sub-continent. Undeterred, Evans moved down to St Louis, in Spanish territory, saying that he wished to explore inland for Welsh Indians. Thinking he was an English spy, the Spanish threw him into prison for some time in 1795. They came to realise that he had no love of the English, and offered him work as an agent for Spain. He was released on the representations of John Rice Jones, a prominent New Orleans businessman who had previously employed him as a surveyor. The Spanish saw Evans as being able to take over Welsh-Indian (Mandan) territory for them, especially as he spoke their language.

The French had ceded Louisiana to Spain in 1764, and before that date there had only been one expedition, under Bourgmont in 1714, partially along the Mississippi and Missouri Valleys. After this time, no European successfully ascended the Missouri River beyond the Platte River until Jacque d'Eglise brought back stories of incursions by English traders from Canada into upper Louisiana. Alarmed by the threat to its sovereignty, Spain decided to promote exploration prior to settlement in the upper Missouri River. In 1793, Spain chartered the *'Company of Discoverers and Explorers of the Missouri'*, familiarly known as the 'Missouri Company' to exploit the fur trade in the region. A prize was offered to the first Spanish subject to reach the Pacific Ocean via the Missouri River. The Spanish sponsored four separate parties to reach the Mandan villages, before the one led by John Evans in 1796 finally succeeded. (Incidentally, two years later the Welsh cartographer David Thompson mapped the upper Missouri and upper Mississippi for the first time - he will be noted in another book in this series).

Evans had entered the service of Spain and Jacques Clamorgan* and reached the Mandans, enduring a terrible winter with them. He held the Mandans for Spain against the Canadians, thus helping to fix the current American-Canadian border. The Mandans put Evans up for 6 months, and protected him against French traders. The Mandans may be the remnant tribe of Prince Madoc's 1170 voyage (see Meriwether Lewis, Jefferson, John Dee and Madoc ab Owain Gwynedd). Why would they protect a starving 'white man'? In ill-health, Evans had to leave the Mandans because of financial troubles in the Spanish Missouri Company which supported his expedition.

He travelled further than any white man before him along the Missouri River and mapped the whole of his journey. He travelled 1,800 miles in 68 days, arriving back in St Louis in July, 1797. He wrote a terse note within a much longer letter to Samuel Jones of Pennsylvania that there were no Welsh Indians between latitudes 30 and 40. The brevity of this note is strange, as the discovery of the 'Madogwys' was the very raison d'etre of his being in the USA. Dr Islyn Thomas made a speech in New Jersey in 1967, quoting the great-grandfather of one Arthur T. Halliday as saying that he was convinced that Evans was lying - *'he never returned to Philadelphia because he lied to his friends about the Indians'*. A postscript to this 1803 memorandum, just 4 years after Evans' death, said that Evans *'when heavily in strong liquor bragged to his friends in St Louis that the Welsh Indians would keep their secret to their graves because he had been handsomely paid to keep quiet on the subject. He added that in a few more years there would be no more trace of any Welsh ancestry or language as time and disease would eventually remove all traces.'* It appears that as an employee of Spain Evans may have held their line, against America being settled by the British before Columbus' claim to the New World.

Evans lost his possessions in Mississippi floods, and died, possibly of drink or fever, in New Orleans, aged only 29. There is a rumour that the basement of a French museum in St Louis holds documentation and correspondence concerning Evans' 1800 mile round-journey.

*Charles Morgan seems to be related to the family of Morgans who were influential in the West Indies at this time.

BILL FROST 1850 - 1935
THE FIRST MAN TO FLY

Upon 26th July, 1998, 'The Sunday Times' carried a long feature *'Welsh airman beat Wrights to the skies'*. Andrew Alderson writes that Welsh carpenter, Bill Frost, flew in Summer 1896.........

'Until now, history has credited the Wright brothers with conquering the skies. But new evidence suggests that their famous flight was not the first. Seven years before them, Frost is said to have set off in a "flying machine" from a field in Pembrokeshire and stayed in the air for 10 seconds. Newly discovered documents reveal that Frost, from Saundersfoot, Pembrokeshire, applied to register a patent for his invention – a cross between an airship and a glider – in 1894. It was approved the following year and detailed how the invention was propelled upwards by two reversible fans. Once in the air, the wings spread and are tilted forward "causing the machine to move, as a bird, onward and downward." A fan is used to help the aircraft "soar upward", while the steering is done by a rudder at both ends.

Crucially, locals in the Welsh seaside resort insist that the aircraft was built and flown within a year of the patent being approved. Yesterday experts on both sides of the Atlantic believed that the name of William Frost, not the Wright Brothers, deserves pride of place in aviation record books as the first pioneer of manned, sustained and powered flight. Historians, descendants and a former neighbour of Frost are convinced that only his modesty – in failing to acclaim his role or having a photograph of the flight – meant his achievements went unacclaimed. Roscoe Howells, the historian and writer, used to be a neighbour of Frost in Saundersfoot and heard an account of the flight from the inventor himself. "He became airborne, so he said, and I would never believe that Bill Frost was a liar or romancer," said Howells. "His flying machine took off, but the undercarriage caught in the top of a tree and it came down into a field. If he hadn't caught it in the tree, he would have been right over the valley over Saundersfoot and it would have been death or glory." Nina Ormonde, Frost's great-great-granddaughter, said: "Our family has always known that he was the first to fly, he flew for 500 to 600 yards. But Bill gave up on it and there is no point in our revelling in the glory because it was his achievement." Frost's flying machine was 31 feet long and made of bamboo, canvas and mire mesh, with hydrogen-filled pouches to attain "neutral buoyancy".

The later flight by Orville Wright in 1903 lasted just 12 seconds. Alderson describes Bill Frost as a carpenter and builder on the nearby Hean Castle estate, who was a deacon of the chapel and founded the local male voice choir. *'His determination to fly his aircraft after the initial flight was defeated by bad luck and lack of money. Although he repaired his machine after hitting the tree, it was later ripped from its moorings and damaged by gales, apparently in the autumn of 1896. He later travelled to London and tried to get funding from the government's war department. According to Frost's descendants, he received several approaches from foreign governments for the rights to his patent, but refused on the grounds of patriotism. The revelations about Frost's design and flight have been uncovered by Jill Waters, a producer, and Patrick French, a presenter, for radio 4's Flying Starts, to be broadcast on Saturday.*

"The Wright Brothers had the benefit of independent witnesses, log books full of technical data and, most important, photographic evidence," said French. *"Yet there are compelling reasons for thinking that the first person to fly was Bill Frost."* In an interview given in 1932, three years before his death, Frost described himself as *"the pioneer of air travel".* Then aged 85 and blind, he spoke of his lack of funding after the war department dismissed his efforts, arguing *"the nation does not intend to adopt aerial navigation as a means of warfare".*

Jeff Bellingham, a Gloucester-born mechanical engineer now living in Minnesota, first discovered Frost's invention after reading Howells' local history book and deciding, on a whim, to see if the inventor had a patent. Today, a century on, there is a new race. Bellingham intends to build a replica, first a quarter-size and later a full-size one, of Frost's aircraft. "I believe it will fly and that afterwards people will acknowledge history books are wrong," Bellingham said'. Bellingham is looking for sponsors in the Lake Elmo area of Minnesota to build a £25,000 quarter-size model of the 1896 craft. Having tracked down the patent, Bellingham also intends to build a £180,000 full-sized replica and fly it from the same field in Saundersfoot. Bleriot crash-landed in Dover in 1909, a full thirteen years after Frost's flight. Some people claim that Gustave A. Whitehead flew in 1901 in Connecticut, before the Wright's first controlled powered flight in 1903. However, there are no claims for such a flight prior to Frost's in 1896.

According to T.G. Sticking's *'The Story of Saundersfoot'*, Frost's machine was *'a triplane, but made only one flight - on a night when a gale was raging - when it took to the air, unpredictably, and landed two miles away, in pieces!'* Designed to take to the air by means of a horizontal fan, with the assistance of a cylinder filled with hydrogen, once in the air the machine would glide for a while on its wings. When more height was required, the wings would be tilted upwards and the fan used again. The 'Pembrokeshire Herald and General Advertiser' on October 11th 1895 stated that Frost had a provisional patent for his flying machine invention, and had been engaged on the project since 1880, a period of fifteen years. He gave a press interview in 1932, when blind and poor, just three years before his death, claiming to have flown. He said that as a carpenter aged 28, in 1876, he had been momentarily lifted off the ground in a high wind, when carrying a long plank. From then on he had become obsessed with trying to fly, and in the early 1890's had been seen by onlookers running around a filed with a sheet of zinc strapped to his head. His wife and daughter had recently died, and people put it down to temporary madness induced by grief. A devout chapel man, people believed his story that he had built the plane in his garden workshop at St Bride's Hill, and that he had flown in it. His original patent description of August 30th, 1895, reads: *'The flying machine is constructed with an upper and lower chamber of wire work, covered with light waterproof material. Each chamber formed sharp at both ends with parallel sides. The upper large chamber to contain sufficient gas to lift the machine. In the centre of the upper chamber a cylinder is fixed in which a horizontal fan is driven by means of a shaft and bevelled gearing worked from the lower chamber. When the machine has been risen to a sufficient height, then the fan is stopped and the upper chamber, which has wings attached, is tilted forward causing the machine to move as a bird, onward and downward. When low enough it is again tilted in an opposite direction which causes it to soar onward and upward, when it is again assisted if necessary by the fan. The steering is done by a rudder at both ends.'*

JOHN FROST May 25 1784 - July 27 1877
PIONEER OF BRITISH DEMOCRACY

Chartist Memorial Day April 10

A new working-class militancy was a strong breeding ground for the doomed Chartist Movement, a campaign for basic human rights in the 19th century. The 1838 People's Charter called for universal male franchise, payment of MP's, equal electoral districts, secret elections and the abolition of property qualifications to vote. Most activity supporting Chartism, trying to stop wealthy landowners buying votes from the enfranchised few, took place in the industrialised parts of South Wales. Newport's Chartist Uprising ended when troops killed twenty-four Chartists. The seven thousand marchers, mainly miners, came down Stow Hill to be met by a hail of bullets by soldiers hiding in The Westgate Hotel. Queen Victoria knighted the mayor, who gave the order to shoot the marchers, whose **eight ringleaders were sentenced to be hung, drawn and quartered.** This is only in 1839! The political show-trial was called by Michael Foot *'the biggest class-war clash of the century'.* Public protest led to the sentence being commuted to transportation for life without a last meeting with their families. The historian, Macaulay, called the ringleaders **'great criminals.........who would, if their attempt had not been stopped at the outset, have caused such a destruction of life and property as had not been known in England for ages.'** These words come from a man who believed universal suffrage to be incompatible with civilisation as he knew it. He thought democracy would hurt the English property-owning classes.

   Just like the Merthyr Rising, there was negligible publicity in England. As Coupland says: *'Nothing happened in England to match the march of some five thousand Welshmen down from the coal valleys through the darkness and drenching rain of a winter night to Newport..... nobody remarked that the trouble was suppressed by English soldiers who were paid to do it and shot down twenty Welshmen and wounded several others in the doing.'*

   The leader of the Newport Rising was born in Newport, a Welsh-speaker whose father died and who was raised by his grandparents. After a very short time at school, John Frost was apprenticed as a boot-maker to his grandfather, but left

John Frost's Chartists at Newport

home at 16 to become a tailor in the nearby town of Cardiff. Aged 22, he had made enough money to return home and start his own business as a draper and tailor, and just three years later, in 1809, became a burgess for Newport. Over the next eleven years he married and had eight children, and he voraciously read to catch up on his lost education. As a leading businessman and official, he read and was strongly influenced by the writings of the libertarians Tom Paine and William Cobbett. However, in 1821 he accused a Newport solicitor of being responsible for his exclusion from his uncle's will, and was sued and fined £1000 for libel in 1822. He continued to accuse the solicitor of malpractice and in 1823 imprisoned for six months. Told he would receive a long prison sentence if he repeated his allegations, Frost turned his anger against the solicitor's close friend, Sir Charles Morgan, owner of the great Tredegar House in Newport. An 1830 pamphlet accused Morgan of treating his tenants badly, and advocated that votes for all (universal suffrage) and secret ballots were the only means of curbing the power of the aristocracy. Inspired by Cobbett, Frost established a left-wing periodical, *'The Welchman'* in 1831.

For the next five years, Frost devoted himself to leading the movement for universal suffrage in Newport. In 1835 he was voted one of Newport's 18 councillors and also made a magistrate, in 1836 being elected mayor. However, his aggressive behaviour led to his replacement as mayor in the following year. Frost also served Newport as a Guardian of the poor and as an Improvement Commissioner. He now focussed upon campaigning for the People's Charter, becoming a national leader. In 1839 he made several inflammatory speeches at the Cartists' First National Convention, so Lord John Russell, Home Secretary, had Frost removed as a magistrate, because he was advocating violence to achieve democracy. Frost wrote in The People's Charter: *'The time is fast approaching when there must be no neutrals; the question will be who is for good and cheap Government, and who is against it'*

In 1838 Henry Vincent had been imprisoned at Monmouth Assizes for 12 months, for making 'inflammatory' speeches supporting Chartism. Frost toured South Wales calling for a massive protest meeting to show the strength of feeling against this sentence. His plan was to march upon Newport to demand Vincent's release. Queen Victoria and her ministers were frightened that such a march could be repeated across Britain, threatening the stability of the German monarchy and its government, so major preparations were made to defuse the march. Frost had told the crowds *'Does any man expect that members put into the House of Commons by bribery, and perjury, violence and drunkenness will ever make laws favourable to the people.'* (Under the 'rotten borough' system whereby very few people could vote, their voting could be 'bought' by substantial largesse including free alcohol - the richest man usually won the election - as Frost said: *A bad system cannot produce good men. We do not look for figs from thistles'*).

When the 7000 marchers arrived in Newport they discovered that several Chartists had been arrested and taken to the Westgate Hotel in the town centre. On the night of November 3, 1839, they gathered outside the hotel, chanting *'free the prisoners'*. After a few moments, soldiers place inside the hotel were ordered to fire into the crowd, when over 20 were killed and scores wounded. The marchers fled back up to the Valleys, and a man-hunt started for all those involved.

One million, four hundred thousand people signed a petition asking for the pardon of the ringleaders, but most died as convicts in Australia. Lord Melbourne, after Cabinet discussions, decided to commute the sentences of hanging, drawing and quartering to transportation for life. The trial judge also asked for commutation - there was only one sentence for 'treason', which he had had to pronounce. John Frost went to Tasmania, where after hard labour he worked as a clerk and as a schoolteacher. In 1846 Thomas Duncombe pleaded for Frost to be freed, in the House of Commons. In 1854, Duncombe persuaded Lord Aberdeen, the Prime Minster to release Frost. Aberdeen stipulated that Frost was not allowed back into Britain, and Frost's daughter Catherine joined the Chartist in the USA, which he toured making speeches against the British system of government.

John Frost, former Mayor of Newport and JP, was fully pardoned in 1856 when he was seventy-one and returned to be honoured in Newport, being carted through the town in a flower-bedecked carriage. It was drawn by his former Chartist comrades. His wife Mary died just a year later, after their 17-year parting. The main square in Newport is now named after him, and you can still see bullet holes in the Westgate Hotel. He soon retired to Bristol, where he wrote articles for newspapers on subjects such as the horrors of deportation, universal suffrage and prison reform. Frost died aged 93, and is buried at Horfield Parish Church, Bristol. The Corn Laws were repealed in 1846, making bread cheaper, and 1867's Great Reform Bill doubled the electorate, adding another one million voters. At last some working people could vote - Chartism had helped change British history.

Frost himself said *By the struggle of these men, we now enjoy five of the six demands of the people's Charter covenants in our constitution. I do hope one day the last of these will be included, whereby we can at least get rid of a third of the House of Commons every year, by vote.*

FOOTNOTES:
(i) The Anglicisation of Newport and its environs since this time has been rapid. John Frost had addressed the Chartists in Welsh, and Gwent, even on its Herefordshire borders, was a Welsh-speaking county. A few years earlier, Iolo Morganwg had stated that Gwent had the highest proportion of monoglot Welsh speakers of all the counties in Wales. (It is now probably the most Anglicised county).

(ii) In 1847, the Government's official 'Report on the State of Education in Wales' at least apportioned some blame for the rise of Chartism '*I regard the degraded condition (of the people of Monmouthshire) as entirely the fault of their employers, who give them far less tendance and care that they bestow on their cattle, and who with few exceptions, use and regard them as so much brute force instrumental to wealth, but as no wise involving claims upon humanity*'............ '*Brynmawr contains 5000 people, nearly all of whom are the lowest class........Not the slightest step has been taken to improve the mental or moral conditions of this violent and vicious community*'. At this time, the ironmasters and colliery owners like Crawshaw Bailey were living in heavily defended castles and mansions, guarded from the hatred of their employees.

GILDAS c.498 - c.570 or 583
ABBOT GILDAS BADONICUS, GILDAS THE WISE, GILDAS-DE-RHUYS OF MORBIHAN, GWELTAS, THE FIRST BRITISH HISTORIAN, 'THE SECOND APOSTLE OF IRELAND'

Feast Date January 29 (also January 28) - The 'rain-saint' of Brittany

Gildas, son of Caw, wrote '*De Excidio et Conquesta Britanniae*' ('*Concerning the Ruin and Conquest of Britain*') in 540, which was extensively used by Bede. His epithet 'Badonicus' came from the fact that he was born in the year of the great victory over the Saxons at Mount Badon. **Gildas was the first British historian,** and it seems more than likely that he wrote 'De Excidio' at Llanilltud Fawr or nearby Caer Worgan. In 'De Excidio' is quoted the letter from the Britons to Aetius in Gaul asking for assistance against the pagans. He drew lessons from the Roman occupation of Britain, and denounced five contemporary 'tyrants', the kings named as Constantinus of Domnonia, Aurelius Caninus, Vortipor of Dyfed, Cuneglasus of North Wales and the lowest of them all, Maelgwn Gwynedd (Magloconus).

Gildas wrote accusingly that the decadence of British rulers and clerics had led to Anglo-Saxon successes in Ynys Pridein, the Island of Britain. After the remaining Roman troops left in 410 to protect the Empire in Europe, the Romanised Celts of the island were increasingly subject to attacks by the Picts of Scotland, Scots of Ireland (Goidels) and Saxons of Germany. During these disintegrating and troubled times, the British were increasingly pushed back westwards into the areas now known as Strathclyde, Cumbria, Wales and the West of England. The brunt of the attacks on Celtic Wales in this period were from the sea-borne Goidels, and from the Germanic tribes pushing ever westwards.

Gildas was taught by St Illtud at Llanilltud Fawr, and visited Ireland, influencing the development of its church. The Irish High King, Ainmire was so concerned about the decline of Christianity in Ireland that he had requested Gildas to organise its revival in 570. Gildas took monks from St David's (Menevia) and Llancarfan to carry out the task, including (his brother?) St Aidan, who joined the King of Leinster's retinue. Gildas was known as **'the second apostle of Ireland.'** St Columbanus wrote to Pope Gregory the Great about '*Gildas auctor*' who was asked to give advice on church doctrine to '*Vennianus auctor*' (probably Finnian of Clonard). Finnian founded the monastic order in Ireland before his death in 548.

Cadog possibly refused to arbitrate between Gildas and David for the see of Menevia. Cadog went with Gildas to Ronech and Echni (Steep Holm* and Flat Holm). Possibly the wild leek and entire-leaved paeony still found there are remnants of the early monastic settlements. On Steep Holm, where Gildas is said to have stayed, there is a well and chapel, and he lived on birds' eggs and fish. In 530-534 he stayed at Glastonbury, where he was said to have arbitrated in a dispute between Arthur, and King Melwas of Somerset who had taken Gwenwyfar – he halted Arthur's siege.

He returned when he heard that his eldest brother Huail (Hywel) had been killed by King Arthur**. He was reconciled with Arthur, who asked for his pardon, then went to Armorica for ten years where it is claimed that he wrote his 'Epistle' admonishing the British kings for their vices***. There are also claims that it was written in Glastonbury around 540-544. It certainly seems to date from around the time of Camlan and Arthur's possible death. When Gildas returned from Brittany, Cadog asked him to direct the studies in Llancarfan for a year. Like Cadoc, he then went to a small island (perhaps Flat or Steep Holm, or even Barri Island), intending to spend the rest of his days in prayer, but was disturbed by pirates. His lack of reference to Arthur is legendarily excused by the story that he threw the pages concerning the King into the sea after Huail's death. However, it could be that the main purpose of the book was to chastise the retreating Welsh chiefs rather than praising the good who fought for their country. There is also doubt that Arthur was present at Badon Hill – 498 may be too early, and it seems that Ambrosius led the British forces, possibly assisted by another chieftain called Arthmael. Arthur was around 16 at this time, probably old enough to fight (when life expectancy was far shorter) but too young to assume any real battle command.

According to Breton tradition Gildas ended his days in Brittany, founding the monastery near Rhuys near Morbihan, and dying on the Island of Houat. Gildas-de-Rhuys neighbours Saint Armel, which again shows his links with Arthur. Exiled from Paris, Pierre Abelard was abbot at Gildas-de-Rhuys in 1126, writing to Heloise *'I live in a wild country where every day brings new perils'*. Showing remarkable acuity, he quickly fled as he realised that his brother monks were trying to poison him.

On the Gulf of Morbihan Gildas was known as a 'Breton' monk called Gweltas, and there is a 'Bonnes Fontaine' under the Grand Mont where the Romanesque abbey-church is situated. This well is where Gildas first stepped on the mainland. The Rhuys Peninsula, 17 miles south of Vannes, has an exceptionally mild climate, and was renowned for its wine and its 6th century monastery. The Ile St Gildas, off Treguier on the Cotes-d'Armor, has St Gildas' Chapel, two dolmens and a shrine to St Roch. In 919, because of Viking raids the monks at Rhuys fled to Locmine with the body of Gildas. The Isle of Houat, off Quiberon

Gildas-de-Rhuys
(photograph courtesy of WTB)

in Brittany, also has a church dedicated to St Gildas. With fellow Welsh saints Herve and Eloi, prayers were given to Gildas in Brittany for sick horses. His feast day is still celebrated in Vannes, and in Carhaix his festival has assumed the character of St Cerwydd's and is a fateful rain-day. Some other dedications include St Gildas south of Chateaulin, St Gildas-des-Bois north of St Nazaire, St Gueltas between Lamballe and Plancoat, and St Gildas north of Carhaix-Plouguer.

Llanildas near Llanilltud Fawr became Y Wig Fawr (The Great Wood) and is now known as Wick. It seems a pity that our first historian is not remembered in his own country, and perhaps Wick could re-assume its original name. His brothers were said in his Life to be St Allgo (Allectus), St Eugrad (Egreas), St Maelog, Guillin and he had a sister Peithien (Peteona). Old Welsh sources claim he had five sons, Cenydd, Maidoc (Aidan), Dolgan, Nwython and Gwynno. The sons of St Cenydd were St Ffili and St Ufelwy.

A fragment of one of his letters remains: 'Abstinence from bodily food is useless without charity. Those who do not fast unduly or abstain overmuch from God's creation, while being careful in the sight of God to preserve within them a clean heart (On which, as they know, their life ultimately depends), are better than those who do not eat flesh or take pleasure in the food of this world, or travel in carriages or on horseback, and so regard themselves as superior to the rest of men: to these **death has entered through the windows of their pride.**' He also left a 'lorica', a kind of charm prayer for every part of the human body, asking for protection of the teeth, tongue, mouth, throat, uvula, windpipe, root of tongue, etc., etc. Gildas' 'Saying of the Wise' is: *fortune will never favour the hateful'*.

It is well worth quoting parts of 'De Excidio' to show the feeling with which Gildas wrote of his times. Interestingly he calls Vortigern 'unlucky' in the first extract (from Chapters 23 and 24), when he invited the Saxons into Kent to act as mercenaries, against the constant attacks from Ireland and Scotland. In the second extract, from Chapter 25, we can see his great admiration for Emrys Wledig, Ambrosius Aurelianus, who pushed back the ravaging Saxons for a time.

'They first landed on the eastern side of the island, by the invitation of the unlucky king, and there fixed their sharp talons, apparently to fight in favour of the island, but alas ! more truly against it. Their mother-land, finding her first brood thus successful, sends forth a larger company of her wolfish offspring, which sailing over, join themselves to their bastard-born comrades. From that time the germ of iniquity and the root of contention planted their poison amongst us, as we deserved, and shot forth into leaves and branches'............... *'For the fire of vengeance, justly kindled by former crimes, spread from sea to sea, fed by the hands of our foes in the east, and did not cease, until, destroying the neighbouring towns and lands, it reached the other side of the island, and dipped its red and savage tongue in the western ocean*............... *So that all the columns were levelled with the ground by the frequent strokes of the battering-ram, all the husbandmen routed, together with their bishops, priests and people, while the sword gleamed, and the flames crackled around them on every side. Lamentable to behold, in the midst of the streets lay the tops of lofty towers, tumbled to the ground, stones of high walls, holy altars, fragments of human bodies, covered with livid clots of coagulated blood, looking as if they had been squeezed together in a press; and with no chance of being buried, save in the ruins of the houses, or in the ravening bellies of wild beasts and birds; with reverence be it spoken for their blessed souls, if, indeed, there were so many found who were carried, at that time,*

into the high heaven by the holy angels. So entirely had the vintage, once so fine, degenerated and become bitter, that, in the words of the prophet, there was hardly a grape or ear of corn to be seen where the husbandman had turned his back.'

'Some, therefore, of the miserable remnant, being taken in the mountains, were murdered in great numbers; others, constrained by famine, came and yielded themselves to be slaves for ever to their foes, running the risk of being instantly slain, which truly was the greatest favour which could be offered them; some others passed beyond the seas with loud lamentations instead of the voice of exhortation. "Thou hast given us as sheep to be slaughtered, and among the Gentiles hast thou dispersed us." Others, committing the safeguard of their lives, which were in continual jeopardy, to the mountains, precipices, thickly wooded forests, and to the rocks of the seas (albeit with trembling hearts), remained still in the country. But in the meanwhile, an opportunity happening, when these most cruel robbers were returned home, the poor remnants of our nation (to whom flocked from divers places round about our miserable countrymen as fast as bees to their hives, for fear of an ensuing storm), being strengthened by God, calling upon him with all their hearts, as the poet says, - "With their unnumbered vows they burden Heaven," that they might not be brought to utter destruction, took arms under the conduct of Ambrosius Aurelianus, a modest man, who of all the Roman nation was then alone in the confusion of this troubled period left alive. His parents, who for their merit were adorned with the purple, had been slain in these same broils, and now his progeny in these our days, although shamefully degenerated from the worthiness of our ancestors, provoke to battle their cruel conquerors, and by the goodness of our Lord obtain the victory.' It is hardly surprising from this contemporary writing, that the Celtic Church refused to evangelise the Saxons in later years, incurring the wrath of Bede.

* On Steep Holm, on the beach near the monastery ruins, was found a Celtic 'god-head', whose 'shouting aspect' signifies a symbol of life. It could have been placed in a wall as a talisman or fixed into the mouth of an island spring which emerges from the cliff face. It may have been venerated by some of the Celtic soldiers who made up the Roman garrison there. Steep Holm was known as Ronech in Gildas' time, and Flat Holm as Echni. Barri (Ynys Peirio) was also a hermit island. Gildas and Cadoc probably used the Roman ruins on Steep Holm as a base for their hermitage. They were said to live on fish and the eggs of sea-birds. The edible plant known as Alexanders still grows on the island, as do wild leeks and nettles, which would have complemented their diet. A few times a year one can travel to Steep Holm by the world's last ocean-going paddle-steamer, and walk around for a few hours. Flat Holm can be reached most days of the year from Barri harbour.

The Saxons renamed the islands Bradanreolice and Steopanreolice ('Broad', and 'Steep Place of Burial'). Isolated offshore islands around Wales were regarded as sacred burial sites by the early Welsh. John Leland (c.1506-1552) quoted from an old document, now lost, that Saint Cadoc the Wise stayed on Flat Holm ('Echin', sic) and Gildas on Steep Holm ('Ronnet', sic) respectively. Leland also states that on Steep Holm Gildas began writing 'De Excidio'. There was a Roman signal station upon Steep Holm, in sight of the Roman harbour of Cardiff, and also within site of the Roman supply base of Classis Britannica, the Roman fleet, at Cold Knap in Barri. This latter Roman naval defence base, protecting the Channel from Irish attacks, is of great historical importance, and some remains can still be seen.

Steep Holm has the remains of a mediaeval priory, and Mary Collier's 1972 book on the 'Ghosts of Dorset, Devon and Somerset' repeats a 19th century recollection: *"But although the religious house at Glastonbury was once his home, his ghost haunts Steep Holme. Maybe he loved the little island. He is not seen, but on moonlight nights he is heard nearby the ruin of the Priory, just the slow footsteps of somebody walking along, which are called 'St Gilda's Tread'."* The 'tread' has also been heard throughout the 20th century, a noise like the 'slow crunching of gravel', although there are no gravel paths, and the reports predate the introduction of Muntjac deer in 1977.

** In Ruthin today, Maen Huail in St Peter's Square is supposed to be the stone upon which Huail was executed by Arthur. It seems that Arthur may have given lands to atone for this deed, as Gallgo, Maelog, Eugrad and Peithien all had foundations in Radnorshire. Rowland's 'Mona Antiqua' makes Caw the father-in-law of Modred, which again would place Gildas with his kinsmen antipathetic to Arthur.

***The tone of Gildas' attack upon the remaining kings of the British people can be seen in the following extract:

Britain has kings, but they are tyrants; she has judges, but unrighteous ones; generally engaged in plunder and rapine, but always preying on the innocent; whenever they exert themselves to avenge or protect, it is sure to be in favour of robbers and criminals; they have an abundance of wives, yet are they addicted to fornication and adultery; they are ever ready to take oaths, and as often perjure themselves; they make a vow and almost immediately act falsely; they make war, but their wars are against their countrymen, and are unjust ones; they rigorously prosecute thieves throughout their country, but those who sit with them at table are robbers, and they not only cherish but reward them; they give alms plentifully, but in contrast to this is a whole mountain of crimes which they have committed; they sit on the seat of justice, but rarely seek for the rule of right judgement; they despise the innocent and the humble, but seize every occasion of exalting to the utmost the bloody-minded, the proud, murderers, the concubines and adulterers, enemies of God, who ought to be utterly destroyed and their names forgotten. They have many prisoner sin their gaols, loaded with chains, but this is done in treachery rather than in just punishment for crimes ....'

GIRALDUS CAMBRENSIS c.1146 - 1223
GERALD OF WALES, GERALD THE WELSHMAN, GERALD DE BARRI

Giraldus was an extremely important figure in Welsh church (and social) history. His father was William of Manorbier, and his mother was Angharad, the daughter of Gerald de Windsor and the famous Nest ferch Rhys ap Tudur. Rhys ap Tudur was Lord of Deheubarth. Gerald's family was also related to The Lord Rhys, Rhys ap Gruffudd. The youngest son of this Norman-Welsh marriage, Gerald was educated by his uncle David Fitzgerald at St David's, at St Peter's Gloucester, then at the University of Paris. As archdeacon of Brecon, he was the favourite to succeed his uncle at St David's in 1176, but Henry II refused to recognise his nomination by the Welsh canons and enforced the election of the Englishman, Peter of Lee.

Bitterly disappointed, Giraldus returned to France and became a lecturer in the University of Paris. He mediated in a dispute between Rhys ap Gruffydd and the king, and accompanied Prince John to Ireland in 1185, when he wrote 'Expugnatio Hibernica' and 'Topographica Hibernica.' 1188 sees him with Archbishop Baldwin touring Wales to recruit for the Crusade, the journey of which is recounted in 'Itinerarium Cambriae'. In 1194 he completed 'Descriptio Cambriae', left the Crown service and went to Lincoln to further his studies.

Giraldus was offered the bishoprics of Llandaf and Bangor, and those of Ferns and Leighlin in Ireland, but he only wanted St David's. On the death of Peter de Lee in 1198, yet again the King and the Archbishop of Canterbury opposed the appointment of Giraldus, although the chapter wanted him to succeed. The dispute widened to one where Giraldus wanted the recognition of St David's as a metropolitan see separate from Canterbury, and three times in five years Giraldus took the arduous journey to Rome to see the Pope and plead this case. His Welshness, energy, learning and intelligence were seen as a dangerous combination by the Plantagenets, a French-speaking illiterate dynasty not noted for subtlety. Gerald maintained that it was the fear of the effect that it would have on the national politics in Wales that prevented his appointment. (The Pope was not too anxious to have a Welsh Church independent of Canterbury - at this time its importance to the survival of Christianity was better-known than today - and dissent weakens power). Giraldus never succeeded in his ambition, but was buried in his beloved St David's.

Geoffrey of Monmouth's works helped put Wales on the literary map of Europe. Gerald helped cement this foundation of Welshmen writing important works in Latin. His writings reflect experiences gained on his travels as well as his knowledge of the authorities on learning. The Welshman's writings were prolific, but it is generally agreed that his most distinguished works are those dealing with Wales and Ireland, with his two books on his beloved Wales the most important: "Itinerarium Cambriae" and "Descriptio Cambriae". Professor Davies tells us that Giraldus, whom he calls *'an admirable story-teller'*, is the only source for some of the most famous of the Welsh folk tales including the

Manorbier Castle, where Gerald was born.
(photograph courtesy of WTB)

declaration of the old man of Pencader to Henry II: *This nation, O King, may now, as in former times, be harassed, and in a great measure weakened and destroyed by your and other powers, and it will also prevail by its laudable exertions, but it can never be totally subdued through the wrath of man, unless the wrath of God shall concur. Nor do I think that any other nation than this of Wales, nor any other language, whatever may hereafter come to pass, shall on the day of severe examination before the Supreme Judge, answer for this corner of the earth.*

It was Giraldus who also wrote (of the Welsh) that *'If they would be inseparable, they would be insuperable'*, and that, unlike the English hirelings, who fight for power or to procure wealth, the Welsh patriots fight for their country. He had pleasant things to say about the poetic talents of his people, too: *In their rhymed songs and set speeches they are so subtle and ingenious that they produce, in their native tongue, ornaments of wonderful and exquisite invention both in the words and the sentences... They make use of alliteration in preference to all other ornaments of rhetoric, and that particular kind which joins by consonance the first letters or syllables of words.*

Gerald could not have predicted the later perfection of cynghanedd, the complex system of sound correspondence that has characterised the strict-metre poetry of the Welsh for so many centuries and that is still practised today, especially in competitions for the eisteddfod chair. Cynghanedd did not become a formal system with strict rules until the fourteenth century, but its uniquely Welsh forms had been honed for centuries before that. Giraldus also penned the following words that give so much pride to Welsh singers of today, especially those who participate in the immensely popular Cymanfoedd Ganu (hymn-singing festivals) held throughout Wales and North America: *'In their musical concerts they do not sing in unison like the inhabitants of other countries, but in many different parts. . .You will hear as many different parts and voices as there are performers who all at length unite with organic melody.'*

Gerald appears to have been a friend of Walter Map and Geoffrey of Monmouth, two other 12th century chroniclers and is one of the more attractive figures in British history.

Before the Nonconformist fever, the harp was often used with a 'pibgorn' (pipe) and 'crwth' (Celtic violin). There was also a primitive Welsh bagpipe, the 'pibacawd'. From over eight centuries ago, Giraldus Cambrensis gives us the following description in his 'The Journey Through Wales' (Penguin Classic p236)..........

'Guests who arrive early in the day are entertained until nightfall by girls who play to them on the harp. In every house there are young women just waiting to play for you, and there is certainly no lack of harps. Here are two things worth remembering: the Irish are the most jealous people on earth, but the Welsh do not seem to know what jealousy is; and in every Welsh court or family the menfolk consider playing on the harp to be the greatest of all accomplishments.'

The 'Life' of the recluse Caradog Fynach, who died in 1125, was written by Giraldus Cambrensis but has been lost. This hermit-saint from Brecon was harpist and keeper of the hounds to Prince Rhys ap Tewdwr in the eleventh century, but lost the dogs. He then fled from Dyfed and Rhys ap Tewdwr to Llandaf Cathedral and was ordained. The histories attribute miracles to him, healing tumours by touching, turning fish into coins for the poor, and halting a chasing Viking longship. His tomb-effigy can now be seen in St David's Cathedral. For many years after his death, his body did not decay and laid in state in the cathedral. William of Malmesbury recounts trying to steal a finger of Caradog as a relic, but the hermit jerked his hand away. Bones were recently analysed in the hope that they were those of St David and St Justinian (Iestyn), but were dated at around 1000 years old, so may be those of Caradog.

St Caradog's Chapel at Newgale near St David's is now a mere hollow in the sands above the beach, but was still standing at the start of the nineteenth century. It was possibly built to commemorate Caradog's funeral procession across the sands to St David's Cathedral, when Gerald of Wales recounts that a storm failed

to wet the coffin. A letter survives of
Pope Innocent III in response to a
request by Gerald to have Caradog
canonised. Caradog is one of the
few Welshmen to have been
officially sanctified by Rome, along
with Dewi, Sadyrnin, Cyfelach and
Gwryd, before the martyrs of the
Middle Ages. Giraldus Cambrensis
took the 'Life' to read it to Pope
Innocent III in Rome, to get
Caradog canonized. The Pope
appointed the abbots of Whitland,
St Dogmael's and Strata Florida as a
commission to inquire into the case,
upon May 8, 1200.

Giraldus Cambrensis

There are several superb publications of Gerald's life and works, including
CADW's 'A Mirror of Medieval Wales', and Penguin Classic 'Gerald of Wales - The
Journey Through Wales/The Description of Wales'. It is not known when his 'The
Life of St Ethelbert' was published, but his other works appeared on the following
dates:

1188 The Topography of Ireland; and The Conquest of Ireland
1191 The Journey Through Wales
1194 A Description of Wales; and The Life of St David
1195 The Life of Galfridi (Geoffrey) Archbishop of York
1197 The Jewel of the Church
1198 The Life of St Remigius (Remi)
1208 De Rebus a Se Gestis (Autobiography)
1213 The Life of St Hugonis (Hugh)
1216 A Book of Invectives; and A Mirror of Two Men
1218 The Rights and Status of St David; and The Instruction of a Prince
1220 The Life of St Ethelbert

OWAIN GLYNDŴR 1355 or May 28th, 1354 - September 20th 1415
OWAIN AP GRUFFYDD - LORD OF GLYNDRFRDWY,
WALES' GREATEST HERO

For some Welshmen, Millennium Day was be September 16, 2000, Glyndŵr's Day,
six hundred years since a company of nobles gathered in his manor at Glyndyfrdwy
to proclaim Owain Glyndŵr Prince of Wales. No other Welsh leader is referred to
simply by his surname. Owain Glyndŵr is the Welsh leader 'sans pareil', the name
a rallying cry for all things Welsh. The group of people who regularly set alight to
English holiday homes in remote areas of Wales from the 1960's to the 1980's
called themselves *'Meibion Glyndŵr'*, *'The Sons of* Glyndŵr'*. Glyndŵr not only
lit up Wales with a united rebellion against overwhelming odds, but also his
mysterious disappearance from history left an unbeaten feeling in Welsh hearts. He
was the last *'Mab Darogan'*, *'Son of Prophecy'* for the Welsh bards, before Henry

Tewdwr (Tudur, or Tudor) took the English crown in 1485 from the last of the
Angevins, Richard Plantagenet.

There are numerous Welsh legends about Glyndŵr's birth. They include the fact
that his father's horses were standing in blood up to their fetlocks in their stables,
and that the baby would cry at the sight of a weapon, and only stop when he could
touch it. The legends are referred to in Shakespeare's *'Henry IV, Part I'*:

> '..........*At my birth*
> *The front of heaven was full of fiery shapes;*
> *The goats ran from the mountains, and the herds*
> *Were strangely clamorous to the frighted fields.*
> *These signs have marked me extraordinary,*
> *And all the courses of my life do show,*
> *I am not in the roll of common men.'*

Glyndŵr could trace his heritage back to Rhodri Mawr, who was head of the royal
houses of Gwynedd, Powys and Deheubarth. He was born around 1353, and some
say he was educated at Oxford. It is known that he studied for seven years at the
Inns of Court in Westminster. Later he became squire to the Earl of Arundel and
Henry Bolingbroke, later Henry IV. Fluent in Latin, English, French and Welsh, he
served King Richard II in his 1385 Scottish campaign. He also may have fought on
the Continent for the English King, but records are incomplete. Aged around forty-
five, after a life of service to the crown, it appears that he returned to Wales to retire
to his great family estates at Glyndyfrdwy (an area of the Dee Valley, between
Llangollen and Corwen), and at Cynllaith on the other side of the Berwyn Hills.
(Glyndyfrdwy means valley of the river Dee, and was shortened to Glyndŵr, valley
of water). At Sycharth, in Cynllaith, was Glyndŵr's chief house, protected by
moats, with nine guest rooms, resident minstrels and bards, fishponds, deerpark ,
dovecot, vineyard, orchards, mill, wheat fields and peacocks. His income from his
estates, around £200 a year, had enabled this faithful servant of the English Crown
to settle down in 1398 with his wife Margaret, and nine or so children.

But just four years later, in 1402, the English had burnt down both the manor
houses at Sycharth and Glyndyfrdwy, of this fifty year-old nobleman. It is difficult
to describe the desolation Glyndŵr must have felt about the destruction of
Sycharth, in particular - all that is left is the moat, in one of the most beautiful parts
of Wales - his family bard Iolo Goch (who died about 1398) has left us a full
description, which ends:

> '*Seldom has there been seen there*
> *Either a latch or a lock,*
> *Or someone playing porter,*
> *No lack of bountiful gifts,*
> *No need, no hunger, no shame,*
> *No-one is parched at Sycharth.*
> *The best Welshman, bold leader,*
> *Owns this land, Pywer Lew's line,*
> *Slim strong man, the land's finest,*
> *And owns this court, place to praise.'*
> (translated by Joseph Clancy)

1399 had been the turning point in Glyndŵr's existence. King Richard II had sailed to Ireland when he heard that the exiled Henry Bolingbroke, son of John of Gaunt, had landed in England. Richard returned via Milford Haven and made for Conwy, choosing Wales as his base for a battle. However, he was met by Henry Percy, Earl of Northumbria, who assured him that Bolingbroke meant no insurrection, but just wanted to inherit his father's lands and title. Richard rode to Conwy Castle to listen to Bolingbroke's request, but was ambushed, forced to 'abdicate' in favour of Bolingbroke, who became Henry IV. King Richard was spirited away to Pontefract Castle and disappeared from history. Richard's royal baggage train, still at Conwy, was seized by Henry's troops, but then 'liberated' by local Welshmen, who recognised treason when they saw it. Henry IV therefore was not over-enamoured of the Welsh, and it also appears that Glyndŵr might have been a squire to Richard II, as well as to Bolingbroke. Owain Glyndŵr had also in the past fought for King Richard, and Henry Bolingbroke was obviously dubious as to his loyalty to an usurper.

King Richard's abduction and murder ruined Glyndŵr's idyllic existence after just one year of retirement. His income from his estates was around two hundred pounds a year, but in 1399 Reginald Grey, Lord of Ruthin, stole some of his Glyndyfwrdwy lands. Glyndŵr was legally trained, and decided to fight Grey with a lawsuit in the English Parliament. A proud and loyal man, of royal blood, extremely tall for his times, he wore his hair down to his shoulders against the prevailing fashion of cropped hair in London. His case was dismissed with the comment 'What care we for barefoot Welsh dogs !'

Even Shakespeare referred to Glyndŵr as a brave and cultivated man -

> ' a worthy gentleman,
> Exceeding well read, and profited
> In strange concealments, valiant as a lion,
> And wondrous affable, and as bountiful
> As mines of India',

and he gives Glyndŵr these lines:

> 'For I was trained in the English court,
> Where, being but young, I framed to the harp
> Many an English ditty lovely well
> And gave the tongue an helpful ornament.'

We can see that Owain Glyndŵr was not the type of man to be thrown out, and treated like a dog, by an ignorant French-speaking English Parliament. The new king, Henry IV now raised taxes in Wales, and his aggressive (and illiterate) Marcher Lords like Grey urged him to settle the growing unrest there. Henry was preoccupied with Scotland, however, and instructed his barons to offer free pardons to law-breakers, hoping to defuse the situation. Lord Grey offered a pardon and a position as master forester to Gruffydd ap Dafydd, who had stolen some of his horses. The Welshman gave himself up, as requested, at Oswestry, but was lucky to escape alive.

He sent a letter to Grey about the betrayal.........

I was told that you are in purpose to let your men burn and slay in any land which succours me and in which I am taken. Without doubt as many men as you slay for my sake will I burn and slay for yours. And doubt not that I will have bread and ale of the best that is in your Lordship'.

Lord Grey sent a copy to the Prince of Wales, the future Henry V, together with a copy of his reply to Gruffydd, threatening him

' I hope we shall do thee a privy thing, a rope, a ladder, and a ryng (noose), high on gallows for to hang. And thus shall be your ending.'

Grey could not be trusted, as we shall see - he desperately wanted more land in Wales. When Henry IV summoned each noble to bring a quota of men to fight in Scotland, Grey did not pass on the message to Owain Glyndŵr. His absence from the army, just after the Parliamentary slighting, would hurt Glyndŵr's standing further in Henry's eyes. Henry's army was badly beaten. The king now allowed Grey leave to proceed against his *'treacherous subject'*, Glyndŵr.

Lord Grey decided that a frontal assault was unlikely to succeed, and therefore arranged a meeting to discuss Glyndŵr's grievances. Glyndŵr agreed, but knowing Grey's record, asked for only a small band of men to accompany the Marcher Lord. Grey agreed, and arrived to open discussions at Sycharth. Luckily, Iolo Goch, the famous house-bard of Glyndŵr, was told of a much larger band of Lord Grey's horsemen, hidden in the woods outside the house, waiting for the signal to attack. Iolo Goch entertained the host, and singing in Welsh alerted Glyndŵr to the threat. Owain made an excuse and fled his beloved Sycharth to his other estate, further west at Glyndyfrdwy, just before Grey's troops arrived.

Here on 16th September 1400, Glyndŵr took the 'Red Dragon' of Cadwaladr and Wales as his standard. This is now celebrated as Glyndŵr Day across Wales, with events and the wearing of red and gold ribbons - his heraldic colours. Aged almost fifty, he was proclaimed Prince of Wales, by Welshmen flocking to Glyndyfrdwy. Students from Oxford and Cambridge, labourers, noblemen and friars came to support him, resenting English wrongs. On 18 September, Glyndŵr's small, poorly armed force rode into Lord Grey's base of Ruthin, looted the fair and fired the town. No-one was killed, but fourteen rebels were captured and hanged. Glyndŵr's band soon learned about fast-moving warfare. By 24 September, they had fired and looted Denbigh, Flint, Hawarden, and Rhuddlan, and were moving on to Welshpool. However, the Sheriff of Shrewsbury had raised men from the Border and Midlands, and beat Glyndŵr's little force decisively on the banks of the Vyrnwy River. On 25 September, Henry IV arrived in Shrewsbury with his army, and dismembered Goronwy ap Tudur, a local nobleman, sending his limbs along the Welsh borders to Chester, Hereford, Ludlow and Bristol, *as an example* to those thinking of supporting Glyndŵr.

Glyndŵr was now in hiding when his aggrieved cousins, Goronwy ap Tudwr's kinsmen on Anglesey, Gwilym and Rhys Tudwr, started a second rebellion. Near Beaumaris, at Rhos Fawr, the Tudur army was defeated but managed to melt away before it was destroyed. Henry IV then destroyed Llanfaes Abbey, as its Franciscan monks had supported the Welsh rebels. Henry marched to the coast at Mawddwy and returned to Shrewsbury. The small Welsh army watched him all the way, not strong enough to face the Plantagenet force. Henry offered a pardon to Glyndŵr's brother, Tudur, which he accepted. However, Owain Glyndŵr was excluded from terms, and all his lands given to the Earl of Somerset, John Beaufort. It looked as if Glyndŵr's days were numbered at the end of the year 1400.

The Marcher Lords were allowed to take any Welsh land that they could by force of arms or subterfuge. On top of this, in 1401, the English Parliament passed laws that no Welsh person could hold official office, nor marry any English person. The Welsh could not live in England, and had to pay for the damage caused by the 1400 rebellions. This racial purity enforcement enraged the Welsh of all classes.

Glyndŵr was back now at Glyndwfrdwy, isolated with few supporters, as Gwynedd had accepted the royal pardon. Other noble Welsh families sent envoys to King Henry, complaining about the brutality and taxes of the Marcher Lords. However, the situation looked bleak until the Tudur brothers once more decided to change the rules of the game. They emerged from hiding in their Anglesey stronghold. While the garrison of Conwy Castle was at church outside the walls, on Good Friday 1401, two of their men posed as labourers, gained access to the castle and killed the two gatekeepers. Gwilym and Rhys Tudur, with a band of just forty men, fired the town and took control of Conwy Castle. Henry Percy, nicknamed Hotspur, controlled North Wales, and needed to get them out of the castle. After weeks of negotiations, the Welsh were starving. Both sides agreed to a sad compromise. The Tudurs were guaranteed free passage back to Anglesey upon the giving up of some of their force. It is said that Gwilym selected them in their sleep - they were later drawn, hanged, disembowelled and quartered while alive by Hotspur, their remains being scattered about Wales as a warning against further rebellion. However, this piece of history may be later anti-Tudor propaganda.

Many Welshmen again started returning from England to Wales, and were backed by supporters of King Richard (by now probably dead) with donations to the Welsh cause. A man called William Clark had his tongue pulled out for daring to speak against Henry IV, then his hand cut off for writing against him, then he was beheaded. By May 1401, another small band of men had joined Glyndŵr, but he was routed by Hotspur near Cader Idris. He was forced to move South to the slopes of Pumlumon and raised his standard again where Nant-y-Moch reservoir now corrupts the land. With around four hundred men only, he rode down to loot and burn Llandrindod Wells, New Radnor, Cwmhir Abbey and Montgomery. Welshpool resisted and Glyndŵr returned with the remains of his little band (- just one hundred and twenty men, according to Gruffydd Hiraethog), to the safety of the Pumlumon (Plynlimon) foothills and caves.

Unknown to him, an army of fifteen hundred Flemings from the settlements in South-West Wales - the 'Englishry' south of the Preseli Hills - was marching to exterminate this threat to their livelihoods. They surrounded him and charged downhill at Glyndŵr's trapped army at Hyddgen on the Pumlumon foothills. Glyndŵr's army knew that they either died there and then, or would be slowly disembowelled if captured. The incentive was enough, and they halted and reversed the Flemings' charge. News spread all over Wales that the Welsh had won a real battle at last.

Hotspur, disillusioned by a lack of support from Henry in Wales, now took his North Wales peace-keeping army back to Northumberland. This was Glyndŵr's opportunity to traverse all Wales, hitting Marcher Lord possessions and those of their sympathisers. These years are described by Sir John Wynn in his 'History of the Gwydir Family' -

'beginning in Anno 1400, continued fifteen years which brought such a desolation, that green grass grew on the market place in Llanrwst.........and the deer fled in the churchyard'.

'In 1400 Owain Glyndŵr came to Glamorgan and won the castle of Cardiff and many more. He also demolished the castles of Penlline, Landough, Flemingston, Dunraven of the Butlers, Tal-y-Fan, Llanbleddian, Llanquian, Malefant and that of Penmark. And many of the people joined him of one accord, and they laid waste the fences and gave the lands in common to all. They took away from the powerful and rich, and distributed the plunder among the weak and poor. Many of the higher orders and chieftains were obliged to flee to England'.

The king saw that Wales was turning to Glyndŵr, and that his Marcher Lords could not control any parts of the country. In October 1401, Henry marched to Bangor in North-East Wales, then West to Caernarfon in Gwynedd, then South, looting the abbey at Ystrad Fflur (Strata Florida) near Aberystwyth. Henry carried on to Llandovery, butchering any Welshman he caught, while Glyndŵr's men picked off his outriders and made constant assaults on his baggage train. At Llandovery, Henry *publicly tortured to death* Llywelyn ap Gruffydd Fychan for refusing to betray Glyndŵr's whereabouts. A memorial is to be erected to this loyal Welshman - it is time that Wales celebrated its heroes - how many people know that this event occurred?

While his supporting bands harried the King's army, Glyndŵr unsuccessfully attacked Caernarfon and Harlech castles. Facing a professional army with mere volunteers, and holding no castles of consequence, Glyndŵr made overtures to the Scots, Irish and French for desperately-needed assistance against their mutual '*mortal enemies, the Saxons.*' He even asked Hotspur to try to arrange a peace with Henry IV. The King was inclined to agree, but Lord Grey hated Glyndŵr, and Lord Somerset wanted more Welsh estates, so they agreed to use peace talks as a device to capture Glyndŵr. Fortunately, Hotspur, an honourable Northerner, refused the Norman request to be part of this treacherous charade.

1402 started off well for Owain Glyndŵr. On January 31, he appeared before Ruthin Castle, challenging Grey to fight. Grey was captured, trussed up and carried away to be imprisoned in Dolbadarn Castle. Perhaps Glyndŵr should have killed the man who was the cause of all his troubles, but he immediately ransomed him for £10,000. Some money was raised immediately, and his son was given in surety for the rest. Raising this ransom effectively ruined Grey, who signed an agreement never again to attack the man he had made an outlaw. (If positions had been reversed, the Norman Lord Grey would have tortured Glyndŵr before hanging, drawing and quartering him. The Welsh did not believe in such bestiality. We can also see that when Glyndŵr captured Lord Mortimer in battle, Mortimer eventually married Glyndŵr's daughter in captivity, and died fighting for him against the English.)

Soon after, Glyndŵr survived an assassination attempt by his cousin, Hywel Sele of Nannau, probably on the orders of King Henry. An arrow was deflected by the armour under his jerkin, and Hywel Sele was killed and placed in a hollow oak tree. Throughout the rest of the year, Glyndŵr ravaged North Wales (leaving alone Hotspur's estates in Denbigh), and then moved against Powys, controlled by the great Marcher Earls, the Mortimers.

On St Alban's Day, June 22nd, 1402 at the Battle of Pilleth (near Knighton), Edmund Mortimer's English knights and Herefordshire levies charged uphill at Glyndŵr's army. Mortimer's Welsh archers poured volley after volley of deadly arrows into the English charge, apparently in an unrehearsed expression of support for Glyndŵr. (Much of western Herefordshire and Worcestershire was Welsh-speaking at this time). Up to two thousand of Mortimer's troops were killed on the slopes. Rhys Gethin, Rhys the Fierce, had drawn up his men hidden behind the top of the hill, so Mortimer had underestimated the Welsh force of four thousand, as well as having been unable to control his Welsh archers. Mortimer was captured in the battle, but Henry IV accused him of treason and would not ransom him. Hotspur, Mortimer's brother-in-law, was incensed that a villain like Lord Grey could be ransomed, whereas Henry had set his mind against the innocent Mortimer.

In Shakespeare's 'Henry IV Part I', a horrified courtier recounts

> .... *'the noble Mortimer,*
> *Leading the men of Hereford to fight*
> *Against the irregular and wild Glendower,*
> *Was by the rude hands of that Welshman taken;*
> *A thousand of his people butchered,*
> *Upon whose dead corpse there was such misuse,*
> *Such beastly, shameless transformation*
> *By those Welsh women done, as may not be,*
> *Without much shame, retold or spoken of.'*

Forget this propaganda against Welsh women - after this event Henry IV passed legislation banning English men marrying Welsh women. Who would have wanted to marry such harridans if the atrocity stories were true ? A contemporary entry in 1402 in the *'Annales Henrici Quarti'* tells us of the extent of Glyndŵr's reputation at this time: *'(Glyndŵr) almost destroyed the King and his armies, by magic as it was thought, for from the time they entered Wales to the time they left, never did a gentle air breathe on them, but days turned into nights, rain mixed with snow and hail afflicted them with a cold beyond endurance.'*

Glyndŵr at last had freedom to do whatever he wanted - he attacked and burnt Abergavenny and Cardiff, and the ruins of his sacking of the Bishop's Palace at Llandaf in Cardiff can still be seen. He besieged Caernarfon, Cricieth and Harlech castles. This forced Henry IV to totally ignore his Scottish problems and assemble three armies, totalling a massive one hundred thousand men, on the Welsh borders. The bards had been singing of Glyndŵr's supernatural powers, and during Henry's advance into Wales, appalling weather conditions forced all three armies to return to England by the end of September. It was thought at the time that Glyndŵr could command the elements, and well as possessing a magic Raven's stone that made him invisible - even the English troops ascribed magical properties to this guerrilla partisan. Again, this is referred to in Henry IV Part 1:

> *'Three times hath Henry Bolingbroke made head*
> *Against my power. Thrice from the banks of the Wye*
> *And sandy-bottomed Severn have I sent*
> *Him bootless home, and weather-beaten back.'*

In 1402, the imprisoned Edmund Mortimer married Owain Glyndŵr's daughter, Jane. Mortimer's nephew, the young Earl of March, had a far better claim to the English throne than Henry IV, and no doubt Glyndŵr was hoping that Henry Bolingbroke would be killed and Wales made safe with an English king as an ally. His big problem was that Hotspur captured the Scots leader, the Earl of Douglas, at the battle of Homildon, securing England's northern border. With his Scottish problems solved, this allowed Henry IV to plan to finally subdue Wales. Glyndŵr, on his part, wanted complete control of Wales before Henry struck.

In 1403, Owain Glyndŵr kept up his blockade of the Northern Welsh castles, while attacking Brecon and Dinefwr and trying to displace the Flemings from Pembrokeshire. Glyndŵr's able lieutenants were the three Rhys's; Rhys Gethin (the Fierce), Rhys Ddu (the Black), and Rhys ap Llewellyn. The latter had real reason to hate the invading English - it was *his* father, Llewelyn ap Gruffydd Fychan, who had been slowly killed in front of Henry IV at Llandovery in the dark days of 1401, for refusing to lead him to Glyndŵr. Later in 1403, a Welsh army was beaten at Laugharne by Lord Thomas Carew. Glyndŵr also sadly learned of the deliberate demolition of his manors and estates at Sycharth and Glyndyfrdwy by the Prince of Wales, Henry of Monmouth, who later won undying fame at Agincourt.

Hotspur, meanwhile, wanted to ransom the Earl of Douglas, but Henry demanded him as a prisoner to secure the ransom. Coupling this insult with the argument over Edmund Mortimer's ransom, Hotspur allied with Edmund Mortimer, Douglas and Glyndŵr to form an army near Chester. At the bloody Battle of Shrewsbury, Hotspur was killed, despite the havoc wrought by his Chester archers. This tragedy happened before he could link up with Glyndŵr. Henry then went to Northumberland to suppress a small uprising by Hotspur's father, Earl Percy of Northumberland. Glyndŵr ravaged Herefordshire in Henry's absence.

The enraged King Henry now passed legislation that *any Welshman found in any border town would be executed.* He marched through South Wales to Carmarthen, but like the previous invasion, Glyndŵr did not come to the party. Henry returned to England and within a week Glyndŵr had taken Cardiff, Caerphilly, Newport, Usk and Caerleon. Some French troops were assisting Glyndŵr by now, and his army had grown to at least 10,000 men-at-arms.

By 1404, Owain Glyndŵr's main focus was the taking of the seemingly impregnable 'Iron Ring' of castles in North Wales. He won over the starving Harlech garrison by pardons or bribes when it had only sixteen men left. The great castles of Cricieth and Aberystwyth then fell, and at Machynlleth, in The Parliament House, Owain Glyndŵr held his first Parliament. Envoys came from France and Spain, and an ambassador was sent to France. Dafydd ap Llewelyn ap Hywel, Davy Gam ('squint-eyed') tried to assassinate him here for Henry IV, and was surprisingly imprisoned rather than cut to pieces. (This again demonstrates the humane Welsh attitude of the times towards prisoners. Davy Gam later was knighted by Henry V as he lay dying at Agincourt). Another Welsh Parliament was held in Dolgellau in 1404.

Glyndŵr now took a small army to again pillage Herefordshire, but the Earl of Warwick captured his standard at Campstone Hill near Grosmont Castle. Glyndŵr just escaped capture. Fortunately, the English did not pursue the defeated troops, which regrouped and beat Warwick at Craig-y-Dorth, three miles from Monmouth, and chased them back into the fortified town. Glyndŵr was in the South-East awaiting a French invasion fleet of 60 vessels under the Count of March, who for some reason never landed. Glyndŵr returned to his court at Harlech. In Anglesey, Owain's forces were now beaten at the battle of Rhosmeirch, and also lost Beaumaris castle.

In 1405, Rhys Gethin burned Grosmont Castle in Monmouthshire, but was then decisively beaten by Prince Henry, using Welsh archers. Glyndŵr sent his almost identical brother, Tudur, and his son Gruffydd to restore the situation by attacking Usk Castle where Prince Henry had established himself. In the battle of Pwll Melin, two miles away, Tudur and Abbot John ap Hywel of Llantarnam were killed. Gruffydd ab Owain Glyndŵr was imprisoned in the Tower of London in disgusting conditions until he soon died. Three hundred prisoners were beheaded in front of the citizens of Usk, as an example pour les autres.

After the Welsh defeats at Grosmont and Usk, Henry now offered a pardon to those who renounced the rebellion, and thereby regained full control of South-East Wales. He then gathered an army of forty thousand at Hereford to advance into mid and North Wales. Another English force took Beaumaris and control of Anglesey in the far North. At this time, Archbishop Scrope of York led a rebellion in the North of England. Henry diverted his forces to Shipton Moor where he beat back the Northern rebels. This gave Glyndŵr some breathing space, and he gathered ten thousand men in Pembrokeshire to wait for an invasion fleet of one hundred and forty French ships. Around five thousand Frenchmen arrived at Milford, joined with Glyndŵr and sacked the English/Fleming town of Haverfordwest, but could not take the castle. They next looted Carmarthen and then took over Glamorgan, leaving Glyndŵr back in control of most of Wales.

In August 1405, he moved on to attack England, *its first invasion since 1066*. Henry raced to Worcester to face the threat of Glyndŵr, who was camped on Woodbury Hill. There were some skirmishes, but Glyndŵr had no lines of supply, so he retreated back to Wales, following a scorched earth policy. Henry's starving army was forced to call off the pursuit, freezing as the bitter winter took hold. Again, the terrible weather was blamed upon Glyndŵr's supernatural powers. **This had been Henry's *fifth* invasion of Wales, and still** Glyndŵr **seemed untouchable.**

1406 began with a treaty between the dead Hotspur's remaining Percy family of Northumberland, Earl Mortimer and Glyndŵr. This 'Tripartite Indenture' divided England and Wales between the three Houses, with Glyndŵr possessing Wales and gaining a 'buffer zone' on its borders. At his second Machynlleth Parliament, Glyndŵr wrote to Charles VI of France, asking for recognition, support and a 'Holy Crusade' against Henry for pillaging abbeys and killing clergymen. In turn, Glyndŵr promised the recognition by St Davids of the French-based Pope Benedict XIII. (Welsh Parliaments were also held in Pennal, Harlech and Dolgellau). Glyndŵr also asked Papal permission to place two universities, one each in North and South Wales, to build a future for his country. This letter was signed '*Owain by the Grace of God, Prince of Wales*', and is in the French National Archives.

However, Henry IV was wasting away through syphilis or leprosy, which enabled his son Henry, the 'English' Prince of Wales to take control of the Welsh campaigns. He beat a Welsh army, killing yet another of Glyndŵr's sons in March, and retook South Wales, fining the landowners heavily to support his thrust into North Wales. North Wales, being fought over for five years, had neither financial nor manpower reserves to support Glyndŵr, but he still held around two thirds of the land Wales, and castles at Aberystwyth and Harlech. At his time, he almost disappears from history except for bardic references of him roaming the country.

In 1407, Prince Henry besieged Aberystwyth Castle with seven cannon. One, 'The King's Gun' weighed four and a half tons. Rhys Ddu held out and Henry returned to England. Glyndŵr reinforced the castle, while England unfortunately signed a peace treaty with France. In this year, Owain's great ally, Louis of Orleans, was murdered in mysterious circumstances in Paris. It may have been the work of English spies.

1408 saw another blow for Glyndŵr. His ally, the old Earl of Northumberland, Hotspur's father, was killed at the Battle of Braham Moor by Prince Henry's forces. The Prince then re-entered Wales, bombarded Aberystwyth into submission, and by 1409 had also taken Harlech, Glyndŵr's last bastion, capturing his wife and family. Edmund Mortimer, the former enemy who became his son-in-law in captivity, died (probably of starvation) in Harlech, fighting for Glyndŵr. Owain had just managed to escape from Harlech as the besiegers moved in. It must have been a difficult decision to leave his family there, while he tried to round up support rather than be cornered. A sad footnote has been the discovery noted in John Lloyd's 1931 book 'Owen Glendower' – he *'left behind him in the castle one little personal relic which has recently been unearthed in the course of excavations, viz. a gilt bronze boss from a set of horse harness, bearing the four lions rampant which he had assumed as prince of Wales'*. The four lions rampant, counter-charged in gold and red, were the ancient arms of the princes

Harlech Castle where Glyndŵr's family was captured (photograph courtesy of WTB)

of Gwynedd. Glyndŵr was more a descendant of the Houses of Deheubarth and Powys than Gwynedd, but he had needed that provenance, that in effect died out with the vicious assassination of Owain Llawgoch, to be accepted throughout Wales.

The last gasp of Glyndŵr's revolt occurred near Welshpool Castle when a raiding party under Phillip Scudamore, Rhys Tudur and Rhys Ddu was beaten and the leaders captured. After the usual revolting, slow, barbarous executions, Scudamore's head was placed on a spike at Shrewsbury, Rhys ap Tudur's at London, and Rhys Ddu's at Chester. This disgusting ritual torture was never practised by the Welsh when they captured prisoners, but Normans and Plantagenets believed that payment to the church would get them to heaven, whatever their sins.

In 1413, the Plantagenet Prince of Wales succeeded as Henry V, and in 1415 offered a pardon to Glyndŵr and any of his men. In 1416, he tried again, through Glyndŵr's remaining son Maredudd, who himself accepted a pardon in 1421. It thus appears that Glyndŵr was still alive a few years after his last recorded sighting. Gruffydd Young, in the Council of Constance in France, was still working for Owain Glyndŵr in 1415, stating that Wales was a nation that should have a vote in ending the papal schism. Glyndŵr would have been around sixty-five years old at this time, having spent his last fifteen years in constant warfare against the English crown.

Some say Owain died in a cave in Pumlumon (Plynlimon), where it all started, mourning the death of all but one of his six sons. Other believed he ended his days with his daughter Alice and her husband John Scudamore in Golden Valley in Herefordshire. The present owner of the Great Hall of Kentchurch, Jan Scudamore, has been besieged with people asking permission to search her estate for the remains of Glyndŵr. Many identify him with Siôn Cent of Kentchurch, a poet, magician and mystic whose grave can still be seen, half in and half out of Grosmont church. Other stories have him dying at Monnington Court, near Kentchurch, at Monnington-on-Wye in 1415, in the deep oakwoods of Glamorgan and on a mountain ridge in Snowdonia. The bards raided Arthurian legend to put him sleeping with his men in a cave to be awakened again in Wales' hour of greatest need. One bard stated that Glyndŵr *'went into hiding on St Matthew's Day in Harvest (1415) and thereafter his hiding place was unknown. Very many say that he died: the seers maintain that he did not'*. The author's researches confirm that he died at one of his daughter's houses, at Scudamore's mansion or at nearby Monnington, where he had been disguised as a shepherd, upon September 16th, 1415, aged 61, almost exactly fifteen years from the start of his war on September 20th, 1400. Recently in 2000, however, the Scudamore family of Monnington Court revealed that Glyndŵr had been buried on their land, and that the family had divulged to always keep his secret.

Glyndŵr's greatest problem had been that he was up against the greatest soldier of his age, Harry of Monmouth, who within a few years was to win at Agincourt with Welsh archers, and be recognised as the future King of France. Henry cut his teeth against a massively under-resourced Glyndŵr, who had no incomes to pay his troops and relied on volunteers against a vastly superior professional force. However, Owain could still point to a career where he set up his own law-courts and chancery, tried to form the first Welsh universities, summoned parliaments, sent envoys to foreign courts and nominated bishops. However, this last battle between the 'Welsh' Prince of Wales and the 'French-Plantagenet' Prince of Wales could have only one ending.

Repressive laws were enacted after the rebellion to stop any future threat from Wales to the English crown. No-one with Welsh parents could buy land near the Marcher towns, own weapons, become citizens of any towns or hold any offices. *In lawsuits involving a Welshman and an Englishman, the Englishman decided the verdict and the sentence. Gatherings of Welsh people were forbidden, and an Englishman marrying a Welsh woman became legally Welsh, forfeiting all his rights of citizenship. No Welshman could be a juror.* These and many more impositions, on top of the already harsh regime of the Statute of Rhuddlan of 1282, ensured Harri Tewdwr great popular support in his move to gain the crown of England in 1485.

Massive taxes were raised to pay for the invasions of the two Henry's, but Welshmen were not allowed to help each other to harvest their fields, causing major food shortages. If merchants of any towns were robbed in Wales, and the property was not returned within a week, they could retaliate upon *any* Welshman that they could seize. Much of the above is taken from the excellent book by Richard Sale, 'Owain Glyndŵr's Way' (published by Hutchinson), which gives a background to Wales, details of Glyndŵr's life, and a description of the long-distance footpath that commemorates the man. The best summary of Glyndŵr is by the noted English historian, G.M.Trevelyan... *'this wonderful man, an attractive and unique figure in a period of debased and selfish politics'*. The French historian, Henri Martin, calls Glyndŵr a man of courage and genius. Most English encyclopaedias do not mention him - one of the truly great, principled and forward-thinking men in British history. Welsh schools have not taught the history Glyndŵr in any depth whatsoever, for over a hundred years, but his name still inspires Welshmen all over the world.

J.E. Lloyd puts Glyndŵr into his proper perspective in the Welsh national psyche:

*'Throughout Wales, his name is the symbol for the vigorous resistance of the Welsh spirit to tyranny and alien rule and **the assertion of a national character which finds its fitting expression in the Welsh language**......... For the Welshmen of all subsequent ages, Glyndŵr has been a national hero, the first, indeed, in the country's history to command the willing support alike of north and south, east and west, Gwynedd and Powys, Deheubarth and Morgannwg. He may with propriety be called the father of modern Welsh nationalism.'*

I have managed to return to Wales after a career in England and overseas. I bought part of an old barn, part of which was built from the ruins of West Orchard Castle (known locally as 'the humpy field'). The doorway, now a window, has the arch from the old entrance to the castle. According to local legend, Glyndŵr destroyed West Orchard, so my 'East Barn' has now been renamed 'Porth Glyndŵr', and I touch the old stone for good luck every day. He is also said to have stayed at East Orchard Castle. 'Cofiwch Glyndŵr' means ' Remember Glyndŵr' and is a slogan for the Welsh Nationalist movement - he still lives. Glyndŵr is the undefeated symbol of Wales, with his red dragon of Cadwaladr - he is the equivalent of Jeanne d'Arc and William Wallace and el Cid for Welsh people everywhere.

After Owain Lawgoch's (Yvain de Galles) assassination in 1378 on the orders of the English crown, the royal House of Gwynedd was extinct. Glyndŵr was then *'un pen ar Gymru'*, the only head of Wales, as he was the direct descendant and link between the dynasties of Powys and Deheubarth. Glyndŵr symbolically adopted Owain Lawgoch's heraldic device of the four red lions rampant of Gwynedd. As his ambassador had told the French king, Glyndŵr was the 'rightful' heir of Lawgoch, or the princes of Gwynedd and Wales. Owain Glyndŵr united Wales both politically and symbolically. Elen ferch Thomas had a brother, Owain ap Thomas, who died childless in 1360, so the first son of her marriage to Gruffydd Fychan, Owain Glyndŵr, had no rivals as the leader of the Welsh resistance.It was thought that Owain Lawgoch, the sole heir to the Royal House of Gwynedd, had been assassinated before he could marry. (However, the author has found traces of a leader of a French war-band, Edouart d'Yvain who overlapped with Llawgoch's assassination, and the Owain Llawgoch Society believe that he may have married a French-woman, so the Royal House of Gwynedd may still be extant!)

Although Glyndŵr had briefly won political, cultural and ecclesiastical independence, before final defeat and the harshness of the laws of a revenging English king, the wars had been a personal disaster for him. His closest brother Tudur had died at the Battle of Pwll Melyn in 1405. His son Gruffydd was captured there, and spent the remainder of his years imprisoned in the Tower of London and Nottingham Castle. Some sources say that he died of the plague in the Tower of London in 1410 - he just vanished from history, like so many other captured descendants of Welsh princes. Glyndŵr's wife, two daughters and three grand-daughters were taken into imprisonment after the fall of Harlech Castle. His son-in-law, Edmund Mortimer, with a good claim to the English crown, died at

Harlech. Mortimer's wife, Owain's daughter Catherine, died in prison with two of her daughters, and all were buried in St Swithin's Church in London around 1413. (Only the churchyard remains, soon to be covered with another office-block for paper-pushers). Her son Lionel, Owain's grandson and a claimant for both Welsh and English crowns, died, where or when is unrecorded. Owain Glyndŵr's closest lieutenants and comrades-in-arms, Rhys Ddu, Rhys ap Llywelyn, Rhys Gethin and Phillip Scudamore had been tortured to death.

It appears that only one relative survived the carnage, his son Maredudd, who had hidden with him when the rebellion was crushed. When Maredudd ab Owain eventually accepted the King's pardon upon 8th April, 1421, it had been twenty years and six months since Owain Glyndŵr had proclaimed himself Prince of Wales. These two decades of fighting against overwhelming odds, of reclaiming Cymru from the Normans, are neglected in all British history books. This British hero has been excised from the history of Britain even more effectively than William Wallace was.

Glyndŵr had no funeral elegy from the bards – he was probably a broken man – but in Welsh mythology his disappearance from history, rather than his capture and execution, gave the poets and gives the nation a hope for the future – Glyndŵr is THE Welsh hero par excellence. This is a story of culture, humanity, nobility, treachery, courage, bitter defeat, glorious resurgence and a mysterious finale. Can anyone think of a better story for a Hollywood epic ? It was not until 1948 that a Parliamentary Act, declaring Glyndŵr to be a proscribed traitor, was repealed. Perhaps a blockbuster film could start with this scene.

Cymdeithas Owain Glyndŵr has attempted a geophysical survey at the mound at the deserted village of Monnington Straddel, near Monningon Court Farm, an ancestral seat of the Scudamores in Herefordshire's Golden Valley. Afirmation of the site was given by Sir John Scudamore of Kentchurch, a direct descendant of Sir John Scudamore and Alice ferch Owain Glyndŵr. A painting by Jan van Eyck at Kentchurch may be of the mystic poet-priest Sion Cent or his contemporary Owain Glyndŵr.

The Sunday Times ran a poll of 100 world leaders, artists and scientists, published on November 28th, 1999, asking for the names of the most significant figures in the last 1000 years. In 7th place was Owain Glyndŵr. (The list started with Gutenberg, Shakespeare, Caxton, da Vinci, Elizabeth I and Faraday in the first six places. Newton, Lincoln and Galileo followed Glyndŵr in the Top 10). Thus even today he is regarded above Churchill, Mandela, Darwin, Bill Gates and Einstein. Among the voters were President Clinton and Boris Yeltsin.

*The author is not very convinced that many of these attacks on holiday homes were carried out by Meibion Glyndŵr - at this time MI5 was at its most paranoid, and like the Brecon 'bomb-factory' incident, the political inspiration for these events seems to have come the area around Westminster.

FOOTNOTES:
1. From Thomas Pennant's 'Tour in Wales' of 1778 (abridged by David Kirk) we are told that Glyndŵr's father was Gruffudd Fychan and his mother Elena '(of royal blood and from whom he afterwards claimed the throne of Wales). She was eldest daughter of Thomas ap Llywelyn ap Owain, by his wife Elinor Goch, or Elinor the red, daughter and heiress of Catherine, one of the daughters of Llywelyn last Prince of Wales. **She probably was concealed by some friend on the death of her father,** otherwise the jealousy of (King) Edward about the succession would have made her share the fate of her sister (Gwenllian) who perforce took the veil in the convent of Shrewsbury.'

2.Glyndŵr's death date has remained a mystery, but T.D. Breverton has recently come across three separate sources with the same date, in his researches for 'The Book of Welsh Saints' (published September 15th, 2000 by Wales Books, ISBN1-903529-01-8. This information has been passed to the Owain Glyndŵr Society, Cymdeithas Owain Glyndŵr, at 37 Glanyrafon Road, Pontardulais, Swansea SA4 1LT.

T.J. Llywelyn Prichard wrote 'The Heroines of Welsh History' in 1854, in which he quotes the Rev. Thomas Thomas, vicar of Aberporth writing 'The Memoirs of Owain Glyndŵr'.

Our hero terminated his hopes and fears on 20th of September, 1415, on the eve of St Matthew, in the 61st year of his age, at the house of one of his daughters; but whether of his daughter Scudamore or of his daughter Monnington is uncertain. Prichard also mentions Glyndŵr's Life in the Cambrian Plutarch by John Humphreys Parry, but I have been unable as yet to source either book.

Marie Trevelyan of Llanilltud Fawr wrote 'The Land of Arthur' in 1895, dedicated to Llywelyn ap Gruffudd, and states that Glyndŵr was born on May 28th, 1354 (so we also have a birthdate!), and *on September 20th, 1415, this celebrated 15th century leader of the Welsh people, and last hero of Welsh independence, died in Herefordshire. According to the MSS of the Harleian Collection, Glyndŵr's body, which was entire and of "goodly stature" was discovered at Monnington in that shire, during the restoration of the church in 1680. But his resting place remains unmarked and unrecognised.* The May birthdate gives festival opportunities, and the Sept 20th date gives feast-week opportunities to fit in with Glyndŵr Day of Sept 16.

Also, a 'penny booklet' recently acquired by the author is *Hanes Owain Glyndŵr, Tywysog Cymru,* by Thomas Pennant o'r Downing, printed by H. Humphries at Caernarfon around 1900, gives the same death date of September 20th, 1415. It points out that the king sent Sir Gilbert Talbot from Porchester to arrange a pardon for Glyndŵr and his supporters in 1415, but Owain's death delayed its implementation until it was agreed with Meredydd ab Owain Glyndŵr in 1416.

D.W. GRIFFITH Janury 22 1875 - July 23 1948
'THE PIONEER OF CINEMA', 'THE FATHER OF FILM'

The father of the epic movie, David Lewelyn Wark Griffith - DW - used to boast of his Welsh ancestry from Gruffydd ap Llewelyn, King of Wales. His father had been a Cofederate veteran, who regaled the young Griffith with tales of bravery and the devastation of the Southern States in the Civil War. Born in Kentucky, a favourite domicile of expatriate Welshmen, he made hundreds of short films before his masterpieces 'The Birth of a Nation' (1915) and 'Intolerance' (1916). Other major films made between 1918 and 1922 were 'Hearts of the World', 'Broken Blossoms' and 'Orphans of the Storm'. 'Hearts of the World' broke new ground by showing war scenes actually filmed at the front in World War I. Griffith revolutionised cinema techniques, innovating the fade-in, fade-out ('dissolve'), close-up and flashback. He elevated moving pictures from an invention to an artistic medium, his epics and masterpieces being seen and copied all over the world.

Not happy at just being an actor in a film, Griffith was a director who made over 450 'short' films between 1908 and 1913. Many big stars had their break at this time, and gained their experience with him, Mary Pickford alone appearing in over 100 of his movies. Other stars 'made' by Griffith included Mack Sennett,

Mabel Normand, Lionel Barrymore and Dorothy Gish (Lilian's sister). His assistant directors included Erich von Stroheim, W.S. van Dyke, Tod Browning and Raoul Walsh, all who became top directors themselves. Influenced by European films, Griffith's first full length movie was 'Judith of Bethulia' in 1914, but his next film 'The Birth of a Nation' in 1915 aroused massive controversy. The intimate story of a family torn apart by the Civil War, it featured epic war scenes, and was the most ambitious film ever made. Strongly pro-South, he was forced to alter his views for future works.

Griffith wanted to make a historical blockbuster, and 1916's pacifist 'Intolerance' wove together Babylon, Christ's passion, the St Bartholomew's Day Massacre and a story set in contemporary California. The linking theme was man's intolerance to man. He moved away from the linear narrative of 'The Birth of a Nation', pioneering a new type of film-making, with the stories being told in a parallel mode, and moving back and forwards in time. It infuriated many Americans, who expected the type of film that Mack Sennett was making with his Keystone Cops - easy-to-follow plot lines with clear-cut heroes and villains. The film was critically acclaimed in Europe and Russia, but made losses in America. As a result, the amazingly opulent and sexy Babylonian sequence was re-cut and released as 'The Fall of Babylon' to try to make profits. His vision of peace was not wanted by a nation preparing for fighting the First World War.

D. W. Griffith

After this epic, Griffith focussed on smaller films, with Lilian Gish in the wonderful 'Broken Blossoms' in 1919 and in 'Way Down East' in 1920. In the former she is threatened by a drunken father, and in the second she insists that her dead baby is baptised. These touching films showed that he could handle, with masterful technical efficiency, intimate story-lines, but the 'Roaring Twenties' saw a different style of film-maker take over. Both films were made for United Artists, but after 1921's 'Orphans of the Storm' with Dorothy Gish, both Gish sisters never worked with Griffith again.

In 1915, Griffith had linked up with the other producers Mack Sennett and Thomas Ince, to form Triangle Studios, and the venture lasted until 1919. Its biggest stars, William S. Hart and Douglas Fairbanks, walked out in 1917, after which losses started accumulating. In 1919, Griffith was asked to become part of a daring plan to liberate the screen artist from studio control, and the producer-director joined the fledgling United Artists, co-founding it with the mega-stars Douglas Fairbanks, Charlie Chaplin and Mary Pickford.

In the 1920's Griffith made several features for United Artists, focussing upon his protegé Carole Dempster as the leading lady. 'America' in 1924 showed the pride and pitfalls of ambitous patriots in America's history. 'Isn't Life Wonderful', also in 1924, gave Dempster her greatest role desperately trying to survive in the ruins of post-War Germany. W.C. Fields starred in 'Sally of the Sawdust', a comedy-drama in 1925. He had left his three former partners at United Artists to produce this film. Griffith's last film, in 1931, was only his second 'talkie', 'The Struggle', an ambitious film examining the disease of alcoholism. A film before its time, it sealed his fate, and his last years were wasted as he could not finance more movies. As an example of a hugely talented man, a inspiring pioneer lauded in his lifetime and then wilfully ignored, we can compare him to Orson Welles.

GRUFFYDD AP CYNAN 1055 - 1137
KING OF GWYNEDD, 'PRYDAIN BRIAWD' (THE POSSESSOR OF BRITAIN)

From Gruffydd ap Llywelyn ap Seisyllt's death in 1063, there was almost permanent fighting between the Welsh princes. The laws of Gavelkind meant that kingdoms and princedoms were constantly being broken up between all male heirs, legitimate and illegitimate. Gruffydd ap Cynan, grandson of Iago of Gwynedd, landed in Anglesey to reclaim his lands from Trahaiarn, in 1075. (His father had died fighting with Gruffydd ap Llywelyn against Harold of Wessex in 1063, when Gruffydd ap Cynan was just eight years old). He defeated Trahaiarn at the Battle of Waederw and recovered Merioneth as well as Gwynedd, but there was a revolt against him because of the conduct of his Irish mercenaries. Gruffydd tried again in 1076, but was forced off Anglesey. In 1081, he returned once more, allying himself with Rhys ap Tudwr to try and heal the land after the depredations of the Earl of Chester and vicious Robert of Rhuddlan.

The carnage in Wales only relented with the victory of Rhys ap Tewdwr (of the royal house of Deheubarth), and Gruffydd ap Cynan (of the royal house of Gwynedd) at the battle of Mynydd Carn in 1081, when Trahaiarn was killed. William the Conqueror, on a pilgrimage to St David's in 1081, recognised Rhys ap Tewdwr's right to Deheubarth.

However, in his attempts to gain the throne of Gwynedd, Gruffydd ap Cynan was captured by Hugh the Fat, Earl of Chester and held as a prisoner in chains at Chester for twelve years. Hugh the Fat had bribed Meirion Goch to bring Gruffydd to a meeting in 1082, where peace might be arranged between the Welsh and Normans. In 1094, the Earl of Chester had ordered that Gruffydd be displayed in chains at Chester market place so the people could see the fall of the great Prince of Gwynedd. In the bustle of the market, he was rescued by Cynwrig Hir. A blacksmith knocked his chains off and the small rescue party managed to escape to Aberdaron, and sail back across to Ireland. Gruffydd soon returned to Wales, with his fellow prince, Cadwgan ab Bleddyn, He ravaged parts of Shropshire and Cheshire, and defeated the Normans in the woods of Yspwys. William II (William Rufus) invaded Wales in 1095 to restore order, but the Welsh retreated to the hills, and William returned to England. In 1096, Gruffydd defeated Norman armies at Gelli Trafnant and Aber Llech. William led another fruitless invasion in 1097 against Gruffydd and Cadwgan.

In 1098 the earls of Chester and Shrewsbury campaigned in a concerted attack against them, and invaded Anglesey, but Gruffydd and Cadwgan fled to Ireland.

Norman cruelty led to a fresh revolt, and just then the Scandinavians descended upon Anglesey. The earls were beaten on the banks of the Menai River by the force led by Magnus Barefoot, King of Norway, who personally killed Red Hugh, the Earl of Shrewsbury. Gruffydd now moved back in 1099 to restore and consolidate his Gwynedd power base as the Normans retreated, reigning over Anglesey and the kingdom known as Gwynedd uwch Conwy.

In 1114, King Henry I invaded with three forces; in South Wales under Strongbow, Earl of Pembroke; in North Wales under Alexander of Scotland, and a force under himself against Powys. In a difficult holding campaign Gruffudd fought no battles, and lost no land, but decided to parley with Henry. As a result, Gruffydd submitted to him, and promised to give up his son-in-law Gruffydd ap Rhys, the other patriotic leader, in order to keep the peace. However, it appears that Gruffudd ap Cynan warned Gruffudd ap Rhys of his agreement. The Chronicles tell us that Gruffudd ap Cynan quietly sent a messenger to Pembroke Castle to warn Nest that her brother's life was in danger, so Gruffudd ap Rhys first fled to Aberdaron. A boat then took him to the safety of the great forest of Ystrad Tawy in Deheubarth. (Gruffudd ap Rhys was the son of Rhys ap Tudwr, the co-victor of Mynydd Carn. He later avenged the murder of his wife Gwenllian ferch Gruffudd ap Cynan, defeating the Normans outside Cardigan).

Llynnau Mymbyr, Snowdonia, the heart of Gruffudd's Kingdom
(photograph courtesy of WTB)

Gruffudd ap Cynan ruled Gwynedd quietly until 1121, when he moved with King Henry quickly to take over Powys, which was riddled with internal disputes. He later took over Deheubarth. His sons Owain and Cadwalladr cemented his grip on most of Wales. Gruffudd ruled over a peaceful Wales until his death, blind and ailing, in 1137. The work of some poets of his time is preserved in 'The Black Book of Carmarthen', and the court poetry of his bard Meilyr* survives. His biography was written just twenty years after his death, declaring Gwynedd to be the *'primus inter pares' ('first among equals')* of Welsh kingdoms. Gruffudd was buried in Bangor Cathedral to the left of the high altar, and his son, the heroic poet-prince Owain Gwynedd succeeded peacefully. During Gruffudd's lifetime, his sons took Meirionydd, Rhos, Rhufoniog and Dyffryn Clwyd for Gwynedd.

Gruffudd's wife Angharad ferch Owain ab Edwin, survived him by 25 years, receiving half his goods, as was Welsh custom. His daughter Gwenllian was executed by the Normans after the battle of Maes Gwenllian. Her son, Rhys ap Gruffudd (see Yr Arglwydd Rhys) fought with Owain Gwynedd against the Normans, and took over leadership of Welsh resistance upon his death. Thus Gruffudd's descendants carried on the fight for Wales for sixty years after his death, to the death of Rhys ap Gruffudd in 1197. Just thirteen years after this, Welsh leadership had passed to Llywelyn the Great, of the House of Gwynedd. In 1485, Gruffudd ap Cynan's descendant, Henry Tudor, became the first Welsh King of England.

Buried in Bangor Cathedral, Gruffudd ap Cynan's elegy was sung by Meilyr, his pencerdd (chief bard). In 1094, Gruffudd's *'harpist (and) chief of song'* was noted in his twelfth century biography** as being killed in the battle of Gellan, retreating from Aberlleiniog. It seems clear that Gruffudd was a cultured man, and the traditional lore of the Welsh bards was that he drew up regulations to govern their craft. This is mentioned in a statute concerning the 1523 Caerwys Eisteddfod, almost four centuries after his death.

*Meilyr Brydydd (fl. c. 1100 - c. 1137) was Gruffudd's chief court-poet at Aberffraw, the traditional seat of the kings of Gwynedd, on Anglesey. He seems to be the earliest of the 'gogynfeirdd' (early poets) and his son Gwalchmai, and Gwalchmai's own sons Meilyr and Einion, represent the first-known line of hereditary poets. In Anglesey, the place-names Trewalchmai and Trefeilyr, Tre'r Beirdd (Place of Bards) and Pentre'r-Beirdd (Head Place of the Bards) recall these poets of almost a millennium ago.

**He is the only medieval Welsh prince whose biography has survived. All the others were burned by invading land-thieves or lost. His 'Historia' tells us that two of his brothers were kings of Ulster, and also tells us *'Oh dearly beloved brother Welshmen, very memorable is King Gruffudd, who is commended by the praise of his earthly pedigree and the prophesy of Merddin (Merlin)....... Intimate friends of Gruffudd say that he was a good man of middle height, fair-haired, hot-headed, with a round face of good complexion, large shapely eyes, fine eyebrows, a comely beard, a round neck, white skin, powerful limbs, long fingers, straight shanks, and fine feet. He was skilled and eloquent in several tongues. He was noble and merciful towards his people, cruel towards his enemies, and very gallant in battle...... Then he increased all manner of good in Gwynedd, and the inhabitants began to build churches in every direction therein, and to plant the old woods and to make orchards and gardens, and surround them with walls and ditches and to construct walled buildings and to support themselves from the fruit of the earth after the fashion of the Romans. Gruffudd on his part, made great churches for himself in his chief places, and constructed courts and gave banquets constantly and honourably. Wherefore, he also made Gwynedd glitter ten with lime-washed churches like the firmament with stars.'*

The Chronicle of Ystrad Fflur, written by the monks of Strata Florida Abbey, tell us of the turmoil following 1066, the years in which Gruffudd came to power and the 'French', i.e. Normans started to seriously attack Wales.

1066 In this year Harold, the son of Earl Godwin, raised himself through oppression to the very height of kingship over the Saxons. And while he was enjoying the glory William the Bastard and a mighty host came after him; and after a mighty battle and a slaughter of the Saxons despoiled him of his kingdom and his life.

1069 In this year was the battle of Mechain fought between the sons of Cynfyn, Bleddyn and Rhiwallon, and the sons of Gruffudd, Maredudd and Ithel. And there the sons of Gruffudd fell and Rhiwallon ap Cynfyn. And Bleddyn ap Cynfyn rules. And Maredudd ab Owain ab Edwin ruled in the south.

1072 in this year Maredudd ab Owain was slain by the French and Caradog ap Gruffudd ap Rhydderch on the banks of the Rhymni.

1073 The French ravaged Ceredigion and Dyfed. And Menevia and Bangor were ravaged by the Gentiles (Vikings).

1074 The French ravaged Ceredigion

1075 Bleddyn ap Cynfyn was slain through the evil-spirited treachery of the princes of Ystrad Tywi; and it was Rhys ab Owain who slew him. And after him Trahaearn ap Caradog ruled over Gwynedd; and Rhys ab Owain and Rhydderch ap Caradog held the South, and Gruffudd ap Cynan took Anglesey. Thereafter was the battle of Camddwr between the sons of Cadwgan, Goronwy and Llywelyn, and Caradog ap Gruffudd, and Rhys ab Owain and Rhydderch ap Caradog. Also in this year was the battle of Bron-yr-Erw between Gruffudd ap Cynan and Trahaearn.

1076 Rhyddrch ap Caradog was slain by Meirchion ap Rhys ap Rhydderch, his cousin, through treachery

1077 In this year was the battle of Gweunytwl between the sons of Cadwgan and Rhys ab Owain

1078 In this year was the battle of Pwllgwdig in which Trahaearn obtained the victory and Rhys ab Owain fled like a wounded, frightened stag before the hounds. And at the close of the year Caradog ap Gruffudd slew Rhys and Hywel, his brother.

1079 In this year Rhys ap Tewdwr began to rule

1080 In this year Menevia (the St David's area) was pillaged

1081 In this year was the battle of Mynydd Carn, in which Trahaearn ap Caradog was slain by Rhys ap Tewdwr and Gruffudd ap Cynan. And thereafter Gruffudd ruled in Gwynedd. And William, king of England and Wales and much of France, came to Menevia on pilgrimage.

1087 In this year William the Bastard, prince of the Normans and King of the Saxons and the Britons and the Scots, died after exceeding great glory in this changeable world.

1088 In this year Rhys ap Tewdwr was expelled from his kingdom by the sons of Bleddyn. And he fled to Ireland. And after he gathered a fleet there, he gave battle at Llech-y-crau and there killed two sons of Bleddyn.

1089 In this year the shrine of David was taken by stealth and despoiled

1093 In this year Rhys ap Tewdwr, king of the South, was slain by Frenchmen who were inhabiting Brycheiniog - and with him fell the kingdom of the Britons. And within two months the French over-ran Dyfed and Ceredigion - and made castles and fortified them.

1094 In this year the Britons being unable to bear the tyranny and injustice of the French, threw off the rule of the French, and they destroyed their castles in Gwynedd and inflicted slaughter upon them. And the French brought a host to Gwynedd and Cadwgan ap Bleddyn drove them to flight with great slaughter at Coes Yspwys. And at the close of the year the castles of Ceredigion and Dyfed were all taken except two

1095 William, king of England, moved a host against the Britons but he returned home empty-handed and having gained naught

1096 The French moved a host into Gwent and the Britons slew them all at Celli Tarfawg. And thereupon the French raided Brycheiniog and they were slain by the *sons of Idnerth ap Cadwgan at Aber-Llech. And the warband of Cadwgan ap Bleddyn despoiled the castle at Pembroke.*

1097 William moved a great host without number against the Britons. And the Britons, placing their trust in the Lord of Heaven, avoided the assault of the French. And the French returned home dejected and empty-handed.

1098 In this year the French moved a third time against the men of Gwynedd. For fear of treahery, Gruffudd ap Cynan fled to Ireland.

1099 Cadwgan ap Bleddyn and Gruffudd ap Cynan returned from Ireland. And, after making peace with the French, they received a portion of the land and the kingdom.

1100 In this year died William, king of England, who would do nothing just nor anything that appertained to the commandments of God. He died without heir because he had always used concubines. And thereupon Henry, his brother, took the kingdom.

(In 1102-1103 Henry seized Maredudd ap Bleddyn and Iorwerth ap Bleddyn by treachery and took their princedom, but Maredudd escaped in 1107 and reclaimed it. In 1106 Hywel ap Goronwy was *'slain by treachery of the French'* In 1108 was noted the Flemish colony settled in Pembroke).

1114 Henry moved a host against the men of Gwynedd and above all to Powys. And Gruffudd ap Cynan made peace, paying a large tribute. And Owain ap Cadwgan did likewise and thereafter he joined the king in Normandy

1115 Henry made one from Normandy - his name was Bernard - bishop of Menevia in contempt of the clerics of the Britons

(In 1116 Gruffudd ap Rhys took Narberth and ravaged the Gower, and in 1121 Henry moved into Powys, forcing Owain ap Cadwgan to pay tribute).

1137 In this year died Gruffudd ap Rhys, the light and excellence and strength of all south Wales. And Gruffudd ap Cynan, prince of Gwynedd and head and king and pacifier of all Wales, ended his temporal life in Christ after receiving extreme unction and communion and confession and repentance for his sins, and becoming a monk and making a good end in his perfect old age. And for a third time the sons of Gruffudd ap Cynan came to Ceredigion and burned castles.'

GRUFFYDD AP LLYWELYN AP SEISYLL 1007- August 5 1063
'HEAD, SHIELD AND DEFENDER OF THE BRITONS' - THE ONLY WELSHMAN EVER TO RULE OVER THE WHOLE OF WALES

Royal succession was important in Welsh history. Cunedda (c.440 AD) established the main tree of descent, dividing Wales between his eight sons, whereby Meirion received Merioneth, Ceredig had Ceredigion (Cardiganshire) etc. In line from Cunedda were Maelgwn Gwynedd (died 547), Cadwaladr ap Cadfan (defeated by Offa of Mercia in 634), Rhodri Mawr (who united Wales against the Norse invaders, and died in 878), Hywel Dda (who established the Laws, and died in 950), and Gruffydd ap Llywelyn, (killed by Harold before Hastings).

Maredudd ap Owain ap Hywel Dda had briefly recreated the Kingdom of Wales from 986 to 989, after the schisms that followed his grandfather's death around

950. Later, Llywelyn ap Seisyll ruled Gwynedd from 1018 to 1023, and had beaten the Prince of Deheubarth to establish himself as King of Wales. Llywelyn's mother, Angharad, was a great-grand-daughter of Hywel Dda. Llywelyn was killed in 1023, through the jealous treachery of Madog, Bishop of Bangor. Anarchy again restarted upon his death, with all the Welsh princes reasserting their independence. His son, Grufydd ap Llywellyn, was also Maredudd's grandson (on his mother, Angharad's side), but had to flee to France, where he stayed for sixteen years.

'Brut y Tywysogion' ('The Chronicles of the Princes') records that between 950 and 1100 28 Welsh princes met violent deaths and four were blinded. In a hundred years, nearly fifty Welsh rulers were tortured, incarcerated, murdered or slain in battle. Wales was racked by internal warfare and invasions by the Mercians until Gruffydd returned from France, and beat Earl Leofric (Lady Godiva's husband) at Rhyd y Groes (near Welshpool) on the Severn in 1038. In 1039, he killed Iago ab Idwal to regain Gwynedd and gain Powys. He ravaged Cardigan and carried off the wife of Hywel ab Edwin, Prince of Deheubarth. Gruffydd had gathered forces and won a battle at Pencader and sacked Llanbadarn Fawr in 1041 to control Cardigan for a time. However, Prince Hywel in 1042 defeated a host of *'black gentiles'* (Danes based in Dubin) invading Cardigan at Pwlldyfarch. Gruffydd won another battle at Newport in 1044 to gain South-East Wales, Gwent. Also in 1044,

he killed Hywel ab Edwin at the battle of Carmarthen, when Hywel had allied with Dancs from Ireland to gain his revenge. In 1047, around 140 of Gruffudd's warband were killed by treachery in Ystrad Tywi, so he ravaged through Pembroke and Ystrad Tywi. With control of South Wales, Gruffydd now turned aggressively on the Saxon invaders. In 1052 he crushed the Saxons and their Norman mercenaries near Leominster in Hereford. He caused the death of Gruffydd ap Rhydderch to gain the remains of Deheubarth in 1055. Gruffydd was now master of almost all of Wales.

Rhuddlan Castle, the site of Gruffydd ap Llywelyn's Court
(photograph courtesy of WTB)

1055 was an eventful year. Harold of Wessex, son of Earl Godwin, ensured that the Earldom of Mercia went to his brother. The deposed Earl, Leofric's son Aelfgar, allied with Gruffydd and Gruffydd married his daughter, Ealdgyth. The allies burned Hereford, and Gruffydd took possession of Whitford, Hope, Presteigne, Radnor, Bangor-Is-Coed and Chirk, beating a small Saxon army. These lands, across Offa's Dyke, had been in Saxon possession for three-hundred years until the border stabilised. Bishop Leofgar of Hereford assembled a mixed force of Norman settlers and Saxon-English. He crossed the Dyke, but was killed by Gruffydd and his army destroyed on Jun 16th, 1056 in the valley of the Machawy. Gruffydd had now settled his court at Rhuddlan, an area heavily settled by Mercians, and from North-East Wales now reconquered large parts of the Earldom of Chester over Offa's Dyke, including much of Flintshire and Denbighshire.

In 1056-1057 Gruffydd drove Cadwgan ap Meurig out of Morgannwg, to control the last princedom. Gruffydd ap Llywelyn became **the only Welshman ever to rule over the whole of Wales.** From 1057 until his death in 1063, the whole of Wales recognized his kingship. In the same year, Aelfgar needed Gruffydd's help to regain Mercia again, and in alliance with the Viking Magnus Barefoot's fleet, they triumphed. However, Harold of Wessex, one of the greatest generals of the time, had been occupied defeating MacBeth in Scotland and uniting Wessex, Mercia, East Anglia and Northumberland for eight years before he unfortunately turned the Saxon war machine of the House of Godwinson against Gruffydd.

Gruffydd's brutality against rival Welsh families was well-known - he defended it as *'blunting the horns of the progeny of Wales so they do not wound their mother'* (see Walter Map's 'De Nugis Curialum' of 1180). As such, when Harold and his brother Tostig of Northumbria attacked by land and sea, much support faded away and the other royal houses saw the opportunity to reclaim their princedoms of Deheubarth, Morgannwg, Powys and Gwynedd. It was winter, and Gruffydd's *'teulu'*, or bodyguard, had returned to their lands for the winter, not expecting any attack. Harold feinted to attack from Gloucester, and raided the South Wales coast with a fleet based in Bristol. Harold made a long forced march with lightly armed troops to the North (similar to his superb march from the Battle of Stamford Bridge in Yorkshire to Hastings three years later). Most of Gruffydd's forces were separated from him, in the South. He had been caught out by the fast-moving Saxons.

Harold struck so rapidly at Rhuddlan, Gruffydd's seat of government, that the unprepared Gruffydd only just escaped by sea. He was pressed back towards Snowdon, and a reward of three hundred cattle offered for his head. He was killed by one of his own men, Cynan ap Iago, according to the Ulster Chronicle (the son of Iago, who had been killed by Gruffydd). The king's death on August 5th 1063 had been made possible by the treachery of Madog, the very same Bishop of Bangor who betrayed Gruffydd's father, Llywelyn, forty years earlier.

Gruffydd's head was carried to Harold, who married his widow and made Gruffydd's brothers his regional commanders in Wales. Harold refused to pay the traitor Madog, and his ship was sunk carrying him to exile in Ireland. Harold did not annexe any Welsh land, and in part because of this victory, he was elected King of England over the claims of Edward the Confessor's nephew and rightful heir. Soon the Saxon enemy was to be replaced by a far more powerful force - the Normans. The Brut y Tywysogion, the Welsh Chronicle of the Princes, lamented Gruffydd as the *'head, shield and defender of the Briton, perished through the treachery of his own men.....the man erstwhile thought invincible, the winner of countless spoils and immeasurable victories, endlessly rich in gold and silver and precious stones and purple apparel.'* The Anglo-Saxon Chronicle recalls Gruffydd ap Llywelyn as *'King over all the Welsh race.'* During his reign he extended Welsh territories back into Hereford, over Offa's Dyke, and united the Welsh nation. It is to him that Wales owes its debt of lasting resistance to the Danish-French Normans who destroyed the Anglo-Saxons.

Harold went on to Hastings in 1066, and the Saxons of England were completely under the Norman yoke by 1070. (Note that the Welsh-speaking British region of Cumbria was only annexed to French-controlled England in 1170. The Welsh-speaking county of Cornwall had been annexed by the Saxons for England in 930). However, Wales kept its independence against the Normans for two centuries, until the death of Dafydd, and the 1282 Statute of Rhuddlan. From then, the Welsh were relatively subdued until the Glyndŵr rebellion gave independence again for a decade from 1400. Then, in 1485, the Tudwrs took over the English crown from the Plantagenets.

FOOTNOTE:
From the Chronicle of Ystrad Fflur, the relevant dates of Gruffudd's time are as follows:

'1035 *Maredudd ab Edwin was slain by the sons of Cynan. Afterwards a cross was raised for him at Carew (-which can be seen today outside Pembroke's Carew Castle). And the Saxons slew Caradog ap Rhydderch.*

1039 *Iago of Gwynedd was slain. And in his place Gruffudd ap Llywelyn rules who throughout his reign hounded the Pagans and the Saxons in many battles. And first he defeated Leofric of Mercia at Rhyd-y-Groes.*

1041 *In this year was the battle of Pencadair where Gruffudd defeated Hywel ab Edwin, and he seized Hywel's wife and took her for his own*

1042 *In this year was the battle of Pwlldyfach where Hywel defeated the Gentiles. And in that year Gruffudd was captured by the men of Dublin (Vikings)*

1043 *Hywel ab Owain, king of Glamorgan, died in his old age*

1044 *Hywel ab Edwin gathered a fleet of the Gentiles of Ireland to ravage the kingdom. And Gruffudd encountered him and there was a mighty battle at the mouth of the Tywi. And there Gruffudd prevailed and Hywel was slain.*

1045 *In this year there was great treachery and deceit between the sons of Rhydderch, Gruffudd and Rhys, and Gruffudd ap Llywelyn*

1047 *About seven score of Gruffudd ap Llywelyn's Teulu (warband) were slain through the treachery of the leading men of Ystrad Tywi. And thereafter Gruffudd ravaged Dyfed and Ystrad Tywi.*

1049 *All Deheubarth was ravaged*

1052 *In this year Gruffudd ap Llywelyn fought the Saxons and their French allies (Norman mercenaries) at Llanllieni.*

1056 *Gruffudd ap Llywelyn took Gruffudd ap Rhydderch's kingdom and his life. And after that Gruffudd moved a host against the Saxons, with Ranulf as their leader. And after bitter, fierce fighting the Saxons turned to flight. And Gruffudd pursued them to within the walls of Hereford and there he massacred them and destroyed the walls and burned the town. And with vast spoil he returned home eminently worthy.*

1058 *Magnus, son of Harold, ravaged the kingdom of England with the help and chieftainship of Gruffudd ap Llywelyn, king of the Britons*

1059 *In this year died Owain ap Gruffudd*

1063 *In this year Gruffudd ap Llywelyn was slain, after innumerable victories, through the treachery of his own men. He had been head and shield and protector to the Britons*

HOWELL HARRIS   January 23 1714 - July 21 1773
'THE FATHER OF METHODISM IN WALES', 'THE GREATEST WELSHMAN OF HIS AGE'

Whether we regard the great Methodist Revival in Wales as something that destroyed much of the fabric and tradition of Welsh society, or as a unique massive spiritual upheaval in Wales that helped save the language, it is certain that it altered irrevocably the nature of Wales and its people. There was a complete renewal of the Welsh people in all aspects of the national life and character. At the core was Howell Harris, of whom the great Sir Owen M. Edwards (to be featured in *'Another 100 Great Welshmen'*) wrote *'Whatever else can be said of Harris's oratory and genius and of his strange projects, the awakening of Wales from a sleep that was paralysing its national vigour can be attributed to him more than anybody else.'*

Howell Harris

In 1738, Harris began his mission in North Wales, as one of a trio of leaders across the nation, the others being Daniel Rowland of Llangeitho and Howell Davies, the 'Apostle of Pembrokeshire'. His father had come from Llangadoc in Carmarthen, to Talgarth in Brecon, around 1700, and was known as Howell Powell alias Harris. He married Susanah Powell of Trefeca-fach in 1702, and Howell was their third son. (His eldest brother Joseph went to the West Indies, wrote navigational treatises and became Assay-Master at the Royal Mint in the Tower of London, and his other brother Thomas also made his fortune in London, returning to become Sheriff of Brecknock and a land-owner).

Howell went to Llwyn-llwyd Academy (like William Williams, q.v.), and from 1732 until 1735 was schoolmaster at Llangors and Llangasty. In 1735, he was completely overwhelmed by the preaching of Pryce Davies, vicar of Talgarth, and began to evangelise. Joseph Harris returned from London to take Howell to St Mary Hall, Oxford, to matriculate. However, Harris left Oxford in days and applied for holy orders in 1736, which was refused several times because he was preaching 'irregularly'. Harris consulted Griffith Jones (q.v.), who had suffered the same problems, and in 1737 began working with Daniel Rowland, soon converting William Williams and Howell Davies (noted above, who was recommended by Harris to work with Griffith Jones).

1742 saw the formation of various societies into an Association, which formed an alliance with the English Methodist movement. This Association influenced all phases of Welsh religious life, and created as its permanent body the Calvinistic Methodist, or Presbyterian Church of Wales. Harris sided with Whitefield when he broke with John and Charles Wesley on the issue of Calvinism versus Armenianism. In the famous Welsh-English Calvinistic Association meeting at Watford, Caerffili, in 1743, Whitefield presided over Harris, Williams of Pantycelyn, Rowland and John Powell. From now on were the formative years of Welsh Calvinistic Methodism, where societies were organised, zones arranged for preachers, and associations set up to control the movement. Harris was *'its organising genius, without any doubt'*, and the system's foundations remain today.

He tried to heal the breach between Whitefield and the Wesleys, and preached at Moorfields in Whitefield's absences. Harris, unusually, always tried to attend conferences called by the Wesleys. His great contribution to British Methodism was his vision of an evangelical movement encompassing not only the conflicting Methodist groups, but also the Moravians.

In 1744, Howell Harris married Anne Williams of Ysgrin, Radnorshire, which her parents fought to prevent, and they went to live in his mother's cottage at Trefecha. In the 1740's he had drifted towards Moravian doctrine, and in 1750 the Welsh Methodists spilt into two movements, the other supporting Daniel Rowland's views. Harris now appeared to become unmanageable. After so many years trying to heal wounds, he would stand no interference, and quickly lost supporters. Almost alone, he retired to Trefecha in 1752, where his health and balance were restored. After his massive work from 1735-1750 in altering the religious complexion of Wales, he turned inwards, and set up a religious community based upon the Pietistic Institution at Halle, Germany. He pulled down his home, to build an edifice where he and his followers could live, work and worship together. Members of 'The Family' placed all their possessions with the community, and in a few years over a hundred people were following trades and crafts at Trefecha. Members of the Family took over local farms, and Harris helped found the Breconshire Agricultural Society, the first in Wales.

By 1763, in the new spirit of revival fanned by Rowland's ministry and William Williams' hymns, a more subdued Harris was welcomed back into the evangelist fold, and embarked on a series of preaching tours. Massive crowds of his former converts went to see the great man. In 1768, the Countess of Huntingdon opened a college for preachers at Trefecha. Harris was now an ill man, and after a few years of suffering died in 1773, to be buried in Talgarth Church. The Dictionary of Welsh Biography concludes:

'His greatest contribution to the welfare of the people was his preaching. This was the means of waking the humbler classes of Wales from their torpid slumber and of revealing to them their spiritual endowments. He was, indeed, one of the makers of modern Wales. In spite of his cross-grained and dictatorial temper, his unceasing enthusiasm and his unbounded desire to save souls carried everything before him in the early days of the religious renaissance. The influence which he has had on the life of his people proves that he was the greatest spiritual force in his generation and many believe that he was the greatest Welshman of his age.' The historian Dr R.T. Jenkins also wrote 'It is difficult to believe that Howell Harris was not the greatest Welshman of his century.' Finally, the Rev. G.T. Roberts in his biography of Harris stated: 'This powerful evangelist, able organiser, and great Methodist was God's gift to Wales, and very few men have so deeply and so permanently influenced the religious life of the Principality as Howell Harris.'

HENRY VII OF ENGLAND AND WALES
January 28 1457 - April 21 1509
HARRI TEWDWR, HENRY TUDOR, EARL OF RICHMOND, THE FIRST OF THE TUDOR DYNASTY

The Welsh supported the Lancastrian cause in the Wars of the Roses, and many died in the slaughter at Mortimer's Cross in 1461. One of the Welsh captains, Owain ap Maredudd ap Tudur (Owen Tudor), was captured and beheaded by the Yorkists, and his head placed on the steps of Hereford Cathedral. Here '*a mad woman combed his hair and washed away the blood from his face, and got candles and set them round his head, all burning, more than a hundred.*' This may have been an act of clairvoyance, because Owen Tudor's grandson, Henry, founded the Tudor dynasty that united England and Wales. Henry's father, Edmund, died in Yorkist imprisonment in Carmarthen just three months before Harri Tudur was born in 1457.

Born in Pembroke Castle, of royal Welsh descent, one of Henry's ancestors was Llewelyn the Great's Justiciar, Ednyfed Fychan, whose heraldic arms were three severed Saxon heads. Brought up by a Welsh nurse, Henry Earl of Richmond was lucky to be alive, even before he raised the Red Dragon of Cadwaladr upon Bosworth Field. He had been born posthumously to Edmund Tudor, his mother being Margaret Beaufort, the sole inheritor of the Lancastrian claim to the crown of England.

Pembroke Castle, where Henry Tudor was born (photograph courtesy of WTB)

Harri Tudur was only fourteen in 1471, the year that the Lancastrian King Henry VI was murdered and his son Prince Edward killed. Suddeny Harri was the prime Lancastrian claimant to the English crown in the continuing Wars of the Roses. His uncle Jasper Tudur (the Earl of Pembroke) only just managed to help him flee to Brittany, then still a country independent of France, and with a similar language to Welsh. Mayor Thomas White of Tenby hid young Henry in cellars which can still be seen. The new English King Edward IV asked for Harri to be handed over, but died soon after and was succeeded by Richard III of York, who killed Edward IV's two sons, the '*princes in the Tower*'.

In 1483, Harri Tudur pledged his band of followers that he would marry Edward IV's daughter Elizabeth of York and thus unite the warring Lancastrian and Yorkist factions. His own lineage went back through his grandfather Owain's marriage to Catherine, widow of Henry V, to the Royal Houses of Gwynedd and Gruffydd ap Cynan, and that of Dinefwr and Rhys ap Tudur.

In September 1484, Harri barely escaped with his life as he was warned that a group of Breton nobles were going to take him to Richard III. He crossed the border into France, and with the Earls of Oxford and Pembroke, the Bishop of Ely and the Marquis of Dorset, prepared to invade Britain. He borrowed money from France, and with two thousand mainly Welsh, Breton and French troops, landed near his birthplace in Pembrokeshire. Henry Tudur moved through Wales gathering support. Rhys ap Thomas gathered the men of Deheubarth and met Henry at Shrewsbury. So did the men of Gwynedd under Richard ap Hywel of Mostyn. While pleading his cause at Mostyn, King Richard's men from nearby Flint Castle arrived and Tudur had to escape by a back window. A stained glass commemoration panel in Mostyn Hall can be seen, and Henry presented the family with a silver bowl and ewer after the Battle of Bosworth.

Many Welshmen believed that Harri was the promised 'mab darogan', 'son of prophecy', to free Wales from the English. Glyndŵr's rebellion had paved the way for this nationalist upsurge. The Lancastrian forces crossed the Severn near Shrewsbury, finally meeting Richard's numerically superior army at Bosworth Field in Leicestershire. This was one of the strangest battles in history. A rag-tag army of French and Breton convicts and misfits, supported by Welsh contingents, moved into the heart of England. From the west, Henry's force, watched by Richard's mounted scouts, had moved from Lichfield to Leicester, and was making its slow progress towards Bosworth Field. It had swollen from 2,500 to 4,500 soldiers on its journey across Wales. The Earl of Shrewsbury brought 500 men to the scene. From the east of England, Lord Norfolk's loyalist army of 4,000 men was approaching in the opposite direction. Percy of Northumberland was bringing Richard's 3,000 troops from the north. Richard with 6,000 followers was hurrying from the south, and another two armies of the Stanley brothers also arrived at the same time. Of the six main armies, three were uncommitted at the start of the battle. Apart from the Stanleys, related to Henry but committed by hostages to Richard, Henry's 4,500 men faced a potential 13,500 Yorkists. Henry had a fresh horse, ready to flee the battle-field and fight again, probably upon Jasper's instructions.

The Yorkist contingents under the Stanley brothers had pledged to assist Richard III, mainly as Lord Stanley's son was held hostage by Richard, but held back from the battle. The battle was started by the Earl of Oxford attacking the Duke of Norfolk's army. Lord Thomas Stanley led his 4,000 men towards Northumberland's position on a nearby hill. Oxford's forces were soon beaten back. Around half an hour into the battle, Richard could see Henry and Jasper Tudor, with the standard of the Red Dragon, on the slopes behind Oxford's tired forces. Richard took a great gamble. At the head of a hundred men, he charged across to this position, passing William Stanley's army. The Red Dragon was cut down, and the standard-bearer, Sir William Brandon was killed. In this melee, part of the army of 2,500 men under Sir William Stanley charged to help Henry. Lord Thomas Stanley held his 4,000 men back. Equally, the army supporting Richard under the Earl of Northumberland refused to engage the Lancastrian army, watching the battle develop. Richard and his small force was quickly overwhelmed and Richard killed. The forces of the Lancastrian Earl of Richmond, Henry Tudur, eventually overcame the rest of the Yorkist army of Richard III. Rhys ap Thomas was said to have been knighted on the battlefield for killing Richard of York with his great battle-axe, and supposedly put Richard's crown on Henry's head. Richard III was the last king to die in battle, which was decided by the Stanleys siding with Henry. (The superbly carved medieval bed of Sir Rhys ap Thomas can be seen in St Fagan's Castle, at The Museum of Welsh Life, Cardiff).

Richard's death effectively ended the battle, and Henry's marriage and diplomacy effectively ended the Wars of the Roses. His wife Elizabeth of York was herself a descendant of Llywelyn ap Iorwerth (q.v.) A Yorkist invasion force mainly composed of Irish and Germans was bloodily defeated in 1487 at Stoke. The impostors to the throne, Perkin Warbeck and Lambert Simnel were dealt with. By the standards of the age Henry was extremely merciful to the defeated Yorkists, with few of the executions that had followed previous battles. Despite several threats to the crown, Henry Tudur laid the basis for a stable constitutional monarchy. By the cunning Treaty of Etaples, he took money from the French in return for not fighting them. He built trade and alliances, and under his Royal Commission John Cabot reached Nova Scotia in 1497.

Aged only fifty-two, Henry Tudur died at Richmond in 1509, leaving a peaceful country, full treasury and an uneventful succession. The *'founder of the new England of the sixteenth century'*, Francis Bacon called him *'a wonder for wise men'*. The great historian G.M. Trevelyan pointed out to the influence of Bosworth Field and the Tudors: *'Here, indeed, was one of fortune's freaks: on a bare Leicestershire upland a few thousand men in close conflict foot to foot....... sufficed to set upon the throne of England the greatest of all her royal lines, that should guide her through a century of change down new and larger streams of destiny.'*

King Henry VII

Henry's success had been largely due to Welsh support, and the emissary for Venice reported to the Doge that ......

The Welsh may now be said to have recovered their independence, for the most wise and fortunate Henry VII is a Welshman'.

And Francis Bacon commented that *'To the Welsh people, his victory was theirs; they had thereby regained their freedom.'*

Henry VII had brought up his eldest son and heir, Arthur, as a Welsh speaker. Arthur was married with great ceremony to Catherine of Aragon in 1501, cementing the Spanish alliance. Arthur's untimely death gave the nation Henry VIII and changed the course of British history – without it Britain would probably still be a Catholic country. And Henry VIII's daughter Queen Elizabeth I oversaw the greatest flowering of culture, in the British Isles, under this Tudor dynasty. For the first time Britain became a real player on the world stage in the arts. Bosworth Field marked the end of medieval England and the beginning of more modern government, with a conscious attempt to integrate Wales into England.

WILLIAM HERBERT 1423 - July 27 1469
WILLIAM AP WILLIAM AP THOMAS, EARL OF PEMBROKE, THE FIRST STATESMAN OF A NEW ERA

He was the son of William ap Thomas ap Gwilym ap Jankyn, a minor member of the Welsh gentry, who had married Elizabeth Bloet, widow of Sir James Berkeley around 1406. She was the only daughter and heiress of Sir John Bloet, whose family had held Raglan since 1174. Her son James owned Raglan Castle, which William ap Thomas held as a tenant. Elizabeth died in 1420, and in 1425 James agreed that William ap Thomas, who had sided with the English against Owain Glyndŵr, could hold the castle for the rest of his life. By this time, William ap Thomas had married Gwladys ferch Syr Dafydd Gam (called by the bard Lewis Glyn Cothi, '*y seren of Efenni*', '*the star of Abergafenni*'). 'Davy' Gam had not only tried to kill Glyndŵr, but had fought at Agincourt, being knighted by the King as he lay dying). The first husband of Gwladys, Sir Roger Vaughan, had also died in 1415 at Agincourt.

By 1421, William was steward of the lordship of Abergafenni. By his marriages, William ap Thomas had acquired lands and wealth from the two heiresses, and was knighted by King Henry VI when the king was just five years old. It was unusual for a Welshman to be knighted, and this border family was seen very much as a 'buffer' against future Welsh insurgencies. William ap Thomas was now known as '*Y Marchog Glas o Went*', '*The Blue Knight of Gwent*', and in 1432 bought Raglan Castle outright for 1000 marks from his stepson James. He rebuilt the castle on a grand scale to match what he had seen while fighting in France in the same contingent as Davy Gam and Sir Roger Vaughan. Through his family connections to the Duke of York became the chief steward of his estates in Wales in 1442-1443. As Sheriff of the counties of Cardigan, Carmarthen and Glamorgan, William was now a powerful man. He died in London in 1445, being buried in the Benedictine priory church of Abergafenni, and Gwladys died in 1454. The legend is that she was so loved that 3000 knights, nobles and peasants followed her body from Coldbrook House to the Herbert Chapel at St Mary's Priory Church. The mighty Raglan Castle passed to William ap William. William ap William's father and grandfather had fought in France for Henry V, and William himself fought in France, under the great Welsh warrior Matthew Goch.

William ap William anglicised his name, and was known as William Herbert after a remote Norman ancestor. The Herberts became an important dynasty in Britain. He married Anne Devereux, and had four children. Originally a Lancastrian, then a prominent Yorkist, he fought in France for Henry VI's doomed claim to the English crown, and was raised to the peerage in 1462 as Lord Herbert of Raglan by Edward IV for his help in raising him to the kingship. (William

Raglan Castle, home of William Herbert
(photograph courtesy of WTB)

had marched to London with the Earl of March, who was then proclaimed King Edward IV). For a Welshman born of Welsh blood, this was unique in these troubled times of the Wars of the Roses. His power in holding Wales for the Yorkists enabled Edward to put down rebellion in the rest of his kingdom. However, Jasper Tudor*, Earl of Pembroke, was Henry VI's half-brother from Owen Tudor's relationship with Catherine de Valois. Jasper had custody of his nephew Henry Tudor, Earl of Richmond. In 1468, William Herbert took Harlech castle, and with it Henry Tudor, the Lancastrian claimant to the English throne, and sent him to be confined at Raglan. Jasper fled to Brittany, and William was rewarded with the great title of Earl of Pembroke.

The bard Guto's Glyn urged Herbert to now unite Wales and free it from English rule.

Na ad arglwydd swydd i Sais	My Lord, don't give the English office
Na'l bardwn i un bwrdais;	Not pardon to a burgess;
Barna'n iawn, brenin ein iaith	King of our language**, be aware
Bwrw yn tan ein braint unwaith...	Their rights were once thrown in the fire...
Dwg Forgannwg a Gwynedd	Join Glamorgan and Gwynedd,
Gwna'n un o Gonwy i Nedd.	Unify from Conwy to Neath

Herbert's rise to power paralleled that of the Woodville family, the relations of Edward IV's wife Elizabeth. In 1466, Herbert's son and heir married Elizabeth's sister, and their daughter Maude was put forward as a possible bride for Henry Tudor, to bring him into the Yorkist fold. With the Lancastrian insurrection of 1469, Edward IV commissioned the Herberts to suppress the Lancastrian rebels. William Herbert marched east to intercept the Lancastrian advance on London. The rising had been secretly instigated by the Earl of Warwick, a Yorkist, but jealous of Herbert's position of power. The rebel army was superior to Herbert's but the Welsh refused to be pushed back. On July 23rd, a cavalry force led by the Earl of Devon, and by Richard Herbert, William's brother met a superior northern contingent, and after fierce fighting, fell back. They joined Herbert's main force at Banbury. King Edward did not reinforce Herbert, and Lord Rivers refused to help***. After heavy casualties on both sides on July 25th, the disaffected Richard, Earl of Warwick suddenly appeared on the scene with the king's army and sided with the Lancastrian rebels. The Yorkist Earl of Devon immediately fled with his army, leaving William Herbert, Earl of Pembroke, and his brother Sir Richard Herbert of Coldbrook, alone at the Battle of Banbury, on July 26, 1469.

The chronicler Hall wrote: *'Pembroke behaved himself like a hardy knight and expert captain; but his brother Sir Richard Herbert so valiantly acquitted himself that with his poleaxe in his hand he twice by fine force passed through the battle of his adversaries and returned without mortal wound. When the Welsh were on the point of victory John Clapham, esquire, servant of the earl of Warwick, mounted on the eastern hill with only 500 men and gathered all the rascals of Northampton and other villages about, bearing before them the standard of the Earl of Warwick with the white bear, crying A Warwick! A Warwick!'* Now terribly outnumbered, the 18,000-strong Welsh army of the Herberts was defeated, around 170 Welsh men of note killed and the Herbert brothers unlawfully executed by the vindictive Warwick. They were summarily beheaded at Northampton upon July 27th.

William had pleaded with Warwick, the 'Kingmaker' to save Richard. Hall wrote: *Entreaty was made for Sir Richard Herbert both for his goodly person which excelled all men there, and also for his chivalry on the field of battle. The earl when he should lay down his head on the block said to John Conyers and Clapham "Let me die for I am old, but save my brother which is young, lusty and hardy, mete and apt to serve the greatest prince in Christendom." This battle ever since has been, and yet is a continual grudge between the northernmen and the Welsh'.* Sir Richard's body was immediately brought to the Herbert Chapel, and he was interned in the place meant for his brother William. The tomb-effigies can be seen today at Abergafenni. Herbert's half-brother, Tomas ap Rhosier, was also slain. His home was the mansion of Hergest, in Welsh-speaking Herefordshire. Another patron of bards, he was the keeper of the great 'Llyfr Coch Hergest, 'The Red Book of Hergest'.

The cream of Welsh aristocracy was killed at Banbury (also known as the Battle of Edgcote). Guto'r Glyn wrote *'Let us hasten to the North to avenge our country. My nation is destroyed, now that the earl is slain'.* And Lewis Glyn Cothi said *'This greatest of battles was lost by treachery; at Banbury dire vengeance fell upon Wales'.* H.T. Evans called Herbert *'The first statesman of a new era, and the most redoubtable antagonist of the last and most formidable of the old'* (i.e. Warwick).

*The great warrior Jasper Tudor will appear in 'Another 100 Great Welshmen' in 2002.

**William Herbert was said to be more fluent in Welsh than English, and a noted patron of bards and harpists. On his death, the bards sang *'Raglan was our tongue's vineyard'.*

***Earl Rivers' support could have swung the battle - he was captured at Chepstow and executed with his son at Kenilworth on August 12th. The Earl of Devon was taken in Somerset and also beheaded at Kenilworth. King Edward was seized near Kenilworth by Warwick. Edward IV later managed to depose Henry VI and Warwick was slain at the battle of Barnet, on Easter Day, 1471. With Edward's forces was the young son of William, the new Earl of Pembroke. Guto'r Glyn called for national rejoicing and said that the death of Warwick was just retribution for Herbert's execution.

SIR ANTHONY HOPKINS December 31 1937 -
PHILIP ANTHONY HOPKINS, HOLLYWOOD SUPERSTAR

Filming Shakespeare's violent 'Titus Andronicus' in 1999, Anthony Hopkins was quoted as saying *'To Hell with this stupid business, this ridiculous showbiz, this futile, wasteful life. I look back and see a desert, a wasteland, all those years in a false environment.'* His Welsh co-star Matthew Rhys spoke of the pressure of filming, saying that Hopkins' part was *'horrendous'*, trying to find reasons for the actor's decision to take a *'long, long rest'* and leave acting completely. However, a quality cast and $15,000,000 has made him reconsider his decision, to star as

Hannibal Lecter. 'Hannibal' is the long-awaited follow-up to the film which catapulted Hopkins into the big league in 1991, 'The Silence of the Lambs'. In it, he played a psychopathic cannibal. His other 2001 films include 'Hearts in Atlantis' and 'The Devil and Daniel Webster'.

The voice of Port Talbot-born Hopkins has an uncanny resemblance to that of Richard Burton, born just a few miles away. His films since 'Silence' in 1991 include 'Dracula' (1992), 'Howards End' 1992, 'Freejack' (1992), 'Chaplin' (1992), 'Spotswood' (1992), 'Shadowlands' (1993), 'The Trial' (1993), 'The Innocent' (1993) 'The Remains of the Day' (1993), 'Legends of the Fall' (1994), 'The Road to Wellville' (1994), the title role in 'Nixon' (1996), 'Surviving Picasso' (1996), 'August' (1996), 'Amistad' (1997), 'The Edge' (1997), 'Meet Joe Black' (1998), 'The Mask of Zorro' (1998), 'Instinct' (1999), 'Mission Impossible 2' (1999) and 'Titus Andronicus' in 1999. With such a punishing schedule of starring in 22 films (and TV work) in 9 years, it is little wonder that Hopkins considered taking time out.

The only son of a baker, he did not enjoy school at Cowbridge, and still considers himself as a 'loner' and 'outsider'. After two years' military service, he went to RADA, where by his own admission he had a drink problem which persisted for many years. Aged 37, in 1978 he sought help and gave up alcohol after it destroyed his first marriage. His breakthrough movie role had been as the scheming future Richard the Lionheart in 'The Lion in Winter' in 1968, and other films included 'Hamlet', 'The Looking Glass War', 'When Eight Bells Toll', 'Young Winston', 'A Doll's House', 'All Creatures Great and Small', ''A Change of Seasons', 'Juggernaut', 'A Bridge Too Far', 'Magic', 'International Velvet', 'The Elephant Man', 'The Bounty', '84 Charing Cross Road', 'The Good Father', 'A Chorus of Disapproval', and 'Desperate Hours'. He was knighted in 1993, having received the CBE in 1991. Upon April 13, 2000, he officially became a resident of the USA, which caused some controversy in Wales.

Beginning as a theatre actor, he played Julius Caesar at the Old Vic, and was awarded a British Theatre Association and Observer Award for his role in the National Theatre's 'Pravda' in 1985. He won Emmies for his TV work in 'The Lindbergh Kidnapping Case' (1976) and 'The Bunker' in 1981. 'The Tenth Man' drew a Golden Globe nomination, a National Board of Review Award and a New York Film Critics Association Award. 'The Lion in Winter', his second film, drew a British Academy Award nomination, as did 'Magic' in 1978, which also had a Golden Globe nomination. 'The Silence of the Lambs' won Hopkins his Oscar, a British Academy Award, various critics awards and a Golden Globe nomination. He was also nominated for an Oscar for 'Shadowlands' and 'Nixon'. His role in 'Nixon' also won him a

Anthony Hopkins

Golden Globe nomination and a Screen Actors Guild award nomination. For 'The Remains of the Day' he received a British Academy award. For 'Amistad' where he played the American-Welsh president John Quincy Adams (q.v.), he was nominated for an Oscar, and said that he felt a real affinity with the man and the role. '*You can't go anywhere with the character until you know the lines. I go over my lines 200, 250 times. Learn it so cold so that you can do it, almost parrot-fashion. And in the process of doing that, you learn the rhythms of the speeches, and from reading the text of the actual speech he gave to the Supreme Court, you can hear how he must have said it and you can begin to feel like John Quincy Adams.*'

For further information on Hopkins, Burton, Stanley Baker and a host of Welsh entertainers, see 'The Dragon Entertains - 100 Welsh Stars', by Alan Roderick, ISBN 1-903529-026, Glyndŵr Publishing, 2000).

DAVID EDWARD HUGHES May 16 1831 - January 22 1900
THE FIRST MAN TO TRANSMIT AND RECEIVE RADIO WAVES, TELEPHONE PIONEER, POLYMATH MUSICIAN, INVENTOR, SCIENTIST AND PHILOSOPHER

A prime example of an unknown Welsh contribution to science is that of David Hughes, who *invented the teleprinter* (from 1855, this telegraph-typewriter was widely used*). In 1878 he invented the microphone and also the induction balance. In 1879, he held an experiment in Great Portland Street. At one end of the street he had a spark transmitter to generate electro-magnetic waves, and at the other a 'coherer', a piece of equipment to receive the waves. He had proposed the theory to Clark Maxwell, and the President and Secretary of the Royal Society witness the success of the experiment. **A Welshman had proposed and demonstrated the first radio transmitter and receiver in the world, and thereby proved the existence of electro-magnetic radiation.** The English committee was not impressed, however, and attributed the effects to Faraday induction rather than electro-magnetic radiation. A polymath, from 1850-53, Hughes had been a Professor of Music at Bardstown College, Kentucky, and he left a fortune to four London hospitals. Most of his £470,000 will went to the hospitals, but some smaller amounts were bequeathed to a number of technical societies. (Readers might note that Bardstown was where the Evan Williams family set up American bourbon whisky production, and the area has strong Welsh linkages.)

Born at the cottage now known as Green y Ddwyryd, in Corwen, his work is mentioned in biographies of the great inventors Morse, Preece (another Welshman), Heavenside and Lodge. As the 'Daily Post' recorded following an exhibit of David Hughes in Denbigh County Library in 1999, '*Italian-born Gugliemo Marconi is world famous as the inventor of the wireless radio and German scientist Heinrich Hertz attained fame by giving his name to radio frequency waves. Yet, eight years before Hertz, Welshman D.E. Hughes became the first person in the world to transmit and receive radio waves. That same year he developed a radio system to transmit signals from Lavernock near Cardiff to Bream in Somerset. His work failed to satisfy colleagues' demands for proof and his achievements went unrecognised for years.*'

His father, also named David Hughes, was an accomplished musician, and all his children were considered child prodigies. He started giving concerts with Joseph Tudor (David Edward's brother), when Tudor was only five, playing in all the UK's major cities as well as before royalty. Each child, David Edward, John Arthur and

Margaret (an accomplished harpist) joined the travelling concert party with their parents, and when the family emigrated to America, gave concerts in all of New England's principal venues. However, Joseph tragically drowned, and after a few months the family started touring America, Canada and the West Indies before settling in Virginia to live. David Edward Hughes' virtuosity at the piano had attracted the attention of Herr Hast, an eminent German pianist, who procured him a professorship of music at St Joseph's College, Bardstown, Kentucky. Apart from his musical gifts, his accomplishments in physical science and mathematics made him the natural choice for the chair of natural philosophy at the same college. Thus at the age of 19 he held two professorships.

He also taught philosophy before he invented the printing telegraph when he was just 23. His keyboard enabled the corresponding letter to be printed at a distant receiver, working a little like the 'golfball' typewriter, before any typewriter was invented. Hughes mechanism became the genesis of the modern teleprinter, telex system and even the computer keyboard is its direct descendant. This was patented in 1855, when he was 24, and this caused several small telegraph companies to merge and form West Union Telegraph Co., to exploit telegraphy across the USA using the 'Hughes System'.

David Edward Hughes returned to Europe, where his telegraph system became the adopted standard. He became one of the most highly decorated scientists of the period, honoured by most European nations. He was awarded a Grand Gold

David Hughes

Medal at the 1867 Paris Exhibition, the Royal Society Gold Medal in 1885, and the Albert Gold Medal of the Society of Arts in 1897. No other person received all three of these distinctive honours. For inventing the microphone and printing telegraph, plus other inventions, Napoleon III created Professor Hughes a Chevalier of the Legion of Honour. His other titles included: The Order of Saint Meurice and Saint Lazare (Italy); The Order of the Iron Crown (Austria), which carried with it the title of Baron; The Order of Saint Anne (Russia); The Noble Order of Saint Michael (Bavaria); Commander of the Imperial Order of the Grand Cross of the Medjidie (Turkey); Commander of the Royal and Distinguished Order of Carlos III (Spain); The Grand Officer's Star and Collar of the Royal Order of Takovo (Servia); and Officer of the Royal Order of Leopold (Belgium). Hughes had travelled Europe, implementing his system, in the year after his return from America.

Hughes' invention of the 'loose-contact' carbon microphone in 1877 made practical telephony a possibility for the first time - he refused to take out patents but gave the invention to the world. Wheatstone in 1827 had been the first to use the term 'microphone', and Hughes revived it in 1878 for his invention. He discovered that a loose contact in a circuit containing a battery and telephone receiver would give rise to sounds in the receiver, which corresponded to the vibrations impinged upon the diaphragm of the mouthpiece or transmitter. This invention was vital to telephony and later to broadcasting and sound recording. He revealed his secrets to the Royal Society at London on May 8, 1878, and to the general public in June of the same year. In 1879, Hughes discovered that when a stick of wood covered with powdered copper was placed in an electrical circuit, the copper would adhere when a spark was made. This started off the invaluable technology of powder-coating. His research into the experimental theory of magnetism was a major contribution to electrical science, and his papers on this and other subjects brought him many honours and medals, as well as Fellowship of the Royal Society. In 1886 he was President of the Institution of Electrical Engineers. All of this time, he was composing and playing works for concertina, violin, piano and harp, and some of his inventions had musical applications. His telegraph was internationally used until the 1930's, and his microphone is the fore-runner of all the carbon microphones now in use.

In 1900, 'The Electrician' noted '*It is with profound sorrow that we have to announce the death, on Monday evening last, of Professor D.E. Hughes. His death, at the age of 69 years, deprives the world of one of its most accomplished electricians, the electrical profession of one of its most honoured and respected members and a worldwide circle of admirers of a genial and well-beloved friend. It truly can be recorded that David Hughes lived without making a single enemy, and died mourned by all whose good fortune it has been to come within the cheery circle of his friendship.*'

*The editor of the New York Associated Press summoned Hughes via telegram from Europe to New York. The American Telegraph Company used Morse technology, charging exorbitant rates for the transmission of news. His editors took up Hughes' instrument in opposition to Morse, and introduced it on the lines of several companies. The Western Telegraph Company then took over those companies, and editors were once again faced with high prices.

FOOTNOTE:
In britannica.com, Hughes is referred to as an 'Anglo-American', which is patently wrong.

LLEWELLYN MORRIS HUMPHREYS 1899 - November 23 1965
MURRAY THE CAMEL, MURRAY THE HUMP, PUBLIC ENEMY NO. 1

Eminent in the sense that he made the Mafia what it is today, Murray Lewellyn Humphpreys was probably the only Welsh mobster in America's gangland. (Incidentally the cosy gang of quango members who control Welsh life is known as the 'Taffia'). He was initially known as Murray the Hump, and by extension as Murray the Camel. Lean, tall, dapper and handsome, with a brooding manner, he was the first of a new breed of racketeer, part criminal and part businessman. He was Al Capone's favourite side-man, and Capone once said '*Anybody can use a gun......... the Hump uses his head. He can shoot if he has to, but he likes to negotiate with cash when he can. I like that in a man.*' The trademark of the Capone gang was the Thompson submachine gun, affectionately known as the '*Chicago Chopper*' or the '*Chicago Tie-Breaker*'.

Brian Humphreys and Ann Wigley married in a Methodist chapel in China Street, Llanidloes. Both were from Carno, just nine miles from Newtown, and they struggled to make a living there, on a hilltop farm called Y Castell. After a few years they emigrated, and Llewellyn Morris Humphreys was born in their small house in North Clark Street, Chicago. He was named after his uncle Llywellyn Humphreys, a JP, chapel deacon and county councillor back home in Wales. Aged 7, Llewellyn had left school and was selling newspapers on a street corner, during a time of great violence between newspaper proprietors in the city. He had a benefactor, however, Judge Jack Murray, and in his youth Humphreys adopted Murray as his Christian name, as no-one could say Llywellyn properly. Murray Humphreys, as he was drawn in from the streets into Al Capone's ubiquitous Mob, became Murray the Hump, then Murray the Camel, either because of the association of Hump with Camel, or from his penchant for wearing elegant camel-hair coats and always carrying a walking stick. His first position was as a 'torpedo' (hired gunman or assassin), and it is believed that he shotgunned to death Roger Touhy, a bootlegger and Capone's enemy, just 23 days after Touhy's release from prison.

The Camel was the architect of the infamous St Valentine's Day Massacre of 1929. Tony Accardo was Capone's chief bodyguard, nicknamed 'Joe Batters' by Capone after he had beated to death a rival mobster with a baseball bat. Accardo and 'Tough Tony' Capezio were given the contract to kill Weiss after the Weiss-Moran gang had made an attempt to kill Capone. They machine-gunned him on the steps of the Holy Name cathedral, where both had worshipped as children. Bugsy Moran was now the main target. The Camel discovered that Bugsy Moran bought his liquor stocks from the Genna Brothers, and got Angelo Genna to call Moran to take a delivery on February 14, at 10.30 in the morning. To ensure the whole Moran Gang would be there, Genna told them it was an extra large delivery, requiring many men to shift it for distribution. The Hump then borrowed a police paddywagon from the captain of the police auto-pound, and two uniforms from a corrupt officer. 'Machine Gun' Jack McGurn and Louis 'Little New York' Campagna wore the police outfits, and 'Joe Batters' Accardo and 'Tough Tony' Capezio wore overcoats. Believing that it was a police raid, Bugsy's men dropped their weapons and faced the wall, knowing that Moran's connections would make sure any charges were dropped. The 5-man assassination squad dressed as policemen wiped out 7 members of Bugsy Moran's opposition gang at a garage warehouse, in the street where 'The Hump' was born. Bugsy missed it because he had luckily overslept, while Capone had a safe alibi at his Florida holiday-home.

In 1931 Capone was in Cook County Jail for income tax evasion, receiving visits from senators and city dignitaries. A newspaper report mentioned Murray 'The Camel' Humphreys calling on 'Snorky' Capone in his new 'office' to bring him up-to-date on the latest 'take'. Prohibition was repealed in 1933, and the Syndicate's best source of illegitimate income died up overnight. Some mobsters went legitimate and stayed in the distilling business, but others returned to their core businesses of vice and gambling. 1933 saw Humphreys take a 11-year 'rap' for tax evasion, but he only served 3 years. In 1936, Humphreys, the youngest member of the Capone Syndicate, left Leavensworth Jail, returning to his rightful place as a gang leader in the rackets. In 1943 his colleague Frank 'The Enforcer' Nitti was charged with tax evasion and committed suicide. In 1944 'Big Bill' Thompson, the most colourful and corrupt mayor Chicago had ever seen, died. Thompson left more than $2million in shoe-boxes, but his highest salary had only been $22,500 p.a.

Aged 48, Alphonse Capone died of syphilis in 1947, and the Hump attended the funeral as the 'heir apparent', along with Jack 'Greasy Thumb' Guzic. (Eliot Ness of the 'untouchables', his main enemy gone, drifted into alcoholism by 1948, and died heavily in debt in 1957, aged just 54.) Bugsy Moran had lost power. Many other racketeers managed to dodge the law under Capone's protegé Murray the Camel, who had succeeded Al Capone as Public Enemy No. 1. Under Humphreys, the rackets continued to thrive in Chicago. With the demise of boot-legging, Humphreys led the mob into the semi-respectability of liquor distribution and running saloons. However, he held on to the control of gambling and prostitution via political pay-offs. While more respectable and discreet, Humphreys moved the mob into the control of unions and financial institutions, moving also into thoroughly legitimate spheres and entertainment. Capone's 'syndicate' was now called 'the outfit', the name by which the Chicago rackets are known today. He was in control of 70% of racketeering in Chicago, making about $80 million a year.

The FBI credits Muray the Camel with the technique of money-laundering, investing crooked money in legitimate business, and it was certainly Humphreys behind the introduction of gambling into Las Vegas, Nevada. ('The Godfather' film is an excellent depiction of this period). In 1959 the mob accountant husband of the 37-year-old Betty Jean Vine found out that she was having an affair with the 60-year-old Humphreys. Allegedly Humphreys murdered him with an ice-pick, then divorced his part-Cherokee wife Mary and married the younger woman. He visited Wales just once, in 1963, under an assumed name. Two years later he died, just after the FBI issued a warrant for his arrest.

His daughter Luella lives on a fortified ranch outside Oklahoma City, and remembers him as a loving and devoted father. For one of her teenage birthday parties at the swish Humphreys residence in Chicago, the guest singer was Frank Sinatra.

FOOTNOTES:

1.Nicknames are a Mafia phenomenon. Apart from 'the Hump', or 'the Camel', there was Vincenzo de Mora, known as 'Machine-gun' Jack McGurn. Other well-known mobsters were Paul 'the Waiter' Ricca, 'Tough Tony' Capezio, 'Bugsy' Moran, Louis 'Little New York' Campagna, Frank 'The Enforcer' Nitti, Jake 'Greasy Thumb' Guzik, Tony 'Joe Batters' Accardo, 'Big Jim' Colosimo, Sam 'Mooney' Giancana (also known as 'Momo', he shared a mistress with President Kennedy), Frank 'Strongy' Ferraro, Sam 'Teets' Battaglia, Felix 'Milwaukee Phil' Alderision, Joey 'O'Brien' Aiuppa, Joey 'The Clown' Lombardo, Carl 'Tuffy' Deluna, Tony 'The Ant' Spilotro, Sam 'Wings' Carlisi, John 'No Nose' DiFronzo, 'Trigger' Mike Coppola, Frankie 'The X' Esposito, Sammy 'The Bull' Gravano, John 'The Dapper Don' Gotti, 'Big Paul' Castellano, 'Jackie 'Nose' D'Amico, 'Tony Roach' Rampino, 'Jelly Bean' DiBono, 'Gas Pipe' Casso, Vincente 'Chin' Gigante, Benny 'Eggs' Mangano, 'Fat Tony' Salerno, 'Fat Tony' Pronto, 'Fat Angelo' or 'Fatso' Ruggiero, 'Crazy Joe' Gallo, Joey 'The Check-Casher' Ingrassia, Jimmy 'The Weasel' Fratianno, Angelo 'The Ape' Annunciata, 'Tony Ducks' Corallo, Vincent 'Jimmy Blue Eyes' Alo, 'Shot Pants' Cacioppo, Frankie 'The German' Schweihs as well as Al 'Scarface' Capone.

2.A new book claims that the Kennedys 'bought' the 1960 Election with Mafia help ('The Dark Side of Camelot' by Seymour Hersh). Jeanne Humphreys, the Camel's widow, claimed that of the five Mafia leaders who agreed to a deal with Joe Kennedy, to financially support his sons win crucial votes against Nixon, the Hump was the only one who dissented. He regarded Kennedy as a *'four-flusher'* from Prohibition days, who could not be trusted. His fears were justified as Giancana was wiretapped by the FBI in the 1960's, who recorded him saying that he had been double-crossed by the Kennedys.

HYWEL DDA 890 - 950
HYWEL AP CADELL AP RHODRI AP MERFYN FACH - HYWEL DDA - HYWEL THE GOOD OF DEHEUBARTH

In 918, Hywel ap Cadell ap Rhodri Mawr ruled Dyfed, and in 920 took over Seisyllwg when his brother Clydog died, so his lands covered the kingdom of Deheubarth, South-West Wales from the Dyfi to the Tawe. His wife was Elen ap Llywarch, by which marriage he claimed Dyfed, and his child Owain. Hywel made a pilgrimage to Rome in 928, and gained control of Brecon by 930. Then from his power base in Deheubarth, this grandson of Rhodri Mawr added Powys and Gwynedd to his kingdom, to largely reunify Wales in 942. In 942 Idwal Foel had been killed by the Saxons, so Hywel was now supreme among the Welsh princes. In 'Brut y Tywysogion', Hywel was described as *'the chief and most praiseworthy of all the Britons.'*

The only Welsh king to earn the epithet *'Dda', 'the good'*, he peacefully unified much of Wales by inheritance, marriage, alliances, and diplomatic relations with Alfred the Great of Wessex. Upon the death of Idwal Foel of Gwynedd, Hywel drove out Idwal's sons and took over Gwynedd and Powys. He led no invasions into England, and coexisted peacefully with Aethelstan upon his succession after Alfred's death. It had helped that Alfred's chief advisor, Asser, was a former monk at St. David's. Hywel understood the power of his larger neighbour, despite strong calls from the bards to ally against them. He had seen the death of Idwal and witnessed the final extinction of the Brythonic kingdom of Cornwall, and wished to keep Wales intact. Hywel Dda's quiet diplomacy and conciliation helped give Wales another three centuries of independence against its larger neighbour. Hywel was the first Welsh ruler to issue his own coins.

The assembly called by Hywel in 930 at Y Hendy Gwyn (Whitland) was *one of the first of its kind in Britain.* In 942 the assembly finally established a legal code for all of Wales, 'Cyfraith Hywel', codifying the common laws of all the different kingdoms. This legislation was only destroyed in 1536 with the Act of Union with England, where laws based upon the right of the individual of any sex were replaced by laws based upon male machismo, property ownership and class structure solidification. At Whitland today, one can visit the Hywel Dda Gardens and Interpretative Centre. Cyfraith Hywel was the name by which the native law was known to the Welsh in medieval times, and the extent of its use is

Hywel Dda

reflected by the survival of around forty lawbooks dating from before 1536. The first generation of these books, some in Latin and some in Welsh, dates from the middle decades of the 13th century. (The Peniarth manuscript of this period is in the National Library of Wales and has wonderful illustrations of the king and some 24 court officials).

Welsh Law gave precedence to the woman's claim in any rape case; marriage was an agreement, not a holy sacrament, and divorce was allowed by common consent, with an equal share of land and possessions; illegitimate children had the same rights as legitimate children; there was equal division of the land between all children upon the death of parents. (This last law contributed to the strife among Princedoms and Kingdoms - everyone had a claim somewhere, and most tried to rebuild what their parents had - the Normans were clever at playing off one heir against another and gaining in the long run). Under Hywel's Laws, farming was a communal affair (reminiscent of Robert Owen eight hundred years later), and *the man did not have unrestricted control over his wife as a possession, unlike all the other 'civilised' European countries.*

In the Celtic Church, as well as outside, there was a tradition in Wales that women had a real social status - a woman's rights to property under Cyfraith Hywel were not granted in English law until 1883. A woman also had a right to compensation if her husband hit her without any cause. In English law, the woman was the property of the husband, a chattel, whereas a divorced Welshwoman received half the property. It is typical of the Laws that the queen had special privileges - there is no mention of a queen in early English, Irish or Germanic laws.

Doctors were liable for the death of patients unless the family had agreed to the course of treatment. Contracts were stronger than legislation in civil disputes. In criminal procedings, *recompense by the offending family network, and reconciliation, took precedence over revenge.* The laws tried to achieve social harmony, with none of the English elements of public whipping, trial by fire or boiling water, torturing, gibbetting, burning of witches or disembowelling being known in independent Wales. The rate of execution in *'primitive'* 12th century Wales was proportionately less than a quarter than that endured under modern English law in the 19th century. Under the entry upon John Frost we can see that the sentence given to the leading Welsh Chartists in 1839 was that they should be *'hung, drawn and quartered'* – this was for asking for democracy.

For theft there was no punishment whatsoever if the purpose was to stay alive - up to the late 18th century, children were hung in England for stealing a lamb. Children were of equal status - the law of Gavelkind meant shared inheritance amongst all children - a civilised and socially unique method of preventing massing of power and lands. Even more advanced was the law that illegitimate children received all the rights, including inheritance, of family offspring – 'Cyfraith Hywel' states that the youngest son has equal rights to the oldest, and also that *'the sin of the father and his wrongdoing should not be set against the son's right to his patrimony'*, so illegitimate children had equal rights. A boy came of age at 14, free of parental control, and a father could be chastised for hitting him after this age. A girl came of age at 12, and like the boy could decide whether she wished to stay in the father's household. She could not be forced into marriage, nor arbitrarily divorced. Rhiannon, in the Mabinogon story of Pwyll, Prince of Powys, refuses to marry, saying *'every woman is to go the way she willeth, freely.'*

Professor Dafydd Jenkins has noted that aspects of Hywel's laws, that were superseded by English law in 1536, are being reintroduced as enlightened reforms in the 1990's, such as reparation to the victims of crime. **Compensation of the victim was more important than punishment of the offender.** For damage unwittingly done, redress had to be made. Even for murder, the Welsh state was active in seeking compensation for the victim's family, to remove the need for vengeance and feud. Obviously, the far-extended Welsh family-clans exerted pressure on their members to toe the line, as if any of them offended, all had to pay something. All the checks and balances were in place under this system to make society enforce its own social code.

Unlike many societies, there were no differences in morality requirements for the sexes - a Welsh woman could heavily fine her husband on an *increasing* scale for adultery, and also divorce him for it. A woman could even divorce her husband for *'stinking breath'*. She had property rights not given under English law until the Married Woman's Property Act of 1870. In France and the rest of Britain, wife-beating was a recognised right of the husband - in Wales there had to be a definite, very serious offence, and then the punishment was limited to just three strokes of a rod. **The Welsh have possibly been the most civilised race in the world in their attitudes towards women from the Dark Ages of the fifth century to the present day.** The author made the old joke at a recent international conference that the real reason was that we feared them so much, and that we even put them on our national flag. The truth is however, that there are not many Paul Gascoignes and O.J. Simpsons in Wales - the social hubris attached to being known as a wife-beater would be too much to bear in our society. We do not make them international superstars or celebrities. The Welsh might have some faults, but hitting women is generally not one of them.

The Laws were fair to all men and women - violence to the person was averted at all costs, and responsibility shared by the offenders' relatives, which made for social order. Not until the Act of Union in 1536 and after did we see the disgusting system that is known as British justice imposed on Wales. The 'torture until you confess' treatment was recently still used to get a confession in IRA bomb cases - with never a comeback on corrupt policemen, politicians, lawyers and judges who use the system to their best advantage. The twin elements that define a nation are its language and legislation - the London government wiped out a humane system of laws based on social responsibility and replaced it with one based upon class, property, prestige, repression and violence. They almost wiped out the language by similar methods.

Hywel's death in 949 or 950* saw the resumption of Viking attacks, and the laws of gavelkind meant that princes fought against princes with no national unity until the accession of Gruffydd ap Llewellyn in 1039. There were ninety years of murder and mayhem and internal power struggles against a background of Saxon, Mercian and Norse invasions. But the Laws lived for six-hundred years, and their ethos of human equality is slowly replacing the property-based spirit of English laws. The finest book upon what was the finest legal framework in history is by Dafydd Jenkins, 'Hywel Dda, The Law', published by Gomer Press in the Welsh Classics series.

*The relevant dates prior to, and after Hywel's death, from the Chronicle of Ystrad Fflur, show the upheaval in Wales caused by his death:
910 In this year Cadell ap Rhodri died and Asser
914 In this year the Black Gentiles took Cyfeiliog, bishop of Ergyng
916 In this year Anarawd ap Rhodri, king of the Britons, died
918 In this year Ireland and Anglesey were ravaged by the men of Dublin (Vikings).
920 In this year Clydog ap Cadell was slain by Meurig, his brother
922 In this year was the battle of Dinas Newydd
922 In this year Hywell ap Cadell submitted to Athelstan
929 In this year Hywel ap Cadell made pilgrimage to Rome
935 In this year Gruffudd ab Owain was slain by the men of Ceredigion
942 In this year Cadell ab Arthfael was poisoned. And Idwal ap Rhodri and Elisedd, his brother, were slain by the Saxons

945 In this year Hywel ap Cadell ordered the laws to be codified
949 In this year Hywel Dda ap Cadell the head and glory of all the Britons died.
And then there was the battle of Carno between the sons of Hywel and the sons of
Idwal
952 In this year Dyfed was laid waste twice by the sons of Idwal, Iago and Ieuaf.
And the Gentiles slew Dwnwallon
954 In this year there was a great slaughter between the sons of Hywel and the sons
of Idwal at the place called Gwrgystu: the battle of Conwy Hirfawr. And after that,
Ceredigion was ravaged by the sons of Idwal.

FOOTNOTE: ON THE LAWS OF HYWEL DDA
There is a tradition that the tribal laws and customs were codified by Dyfnwal Moelmud long before Hywel, but the earliest manuscripts date from the 12th and 13th centuries, extracts made by practising lawyers, the earliest from the time of Llewelyn the Great. There were slight differences between North, West and South Wales, known as the Venetian, Dementian and Gwentian Codes, and they stayed in force in entirety until Edward I's Statute of Rhuddlan in 1283, and many provisions remained until the period of the Tudors in the 16th century.

Many Welsh laws and traditions are noted in the ancient 'Triads', expressions where objects are grouped in threes. *We know of nothing similar in any other country,* and some of these sayings may date back to the time of the Druids, who committed the old laws to memory. Triads are found in the oldest Welsh manuscripts such as the Mabinogion, bardic poems, the 12th century Black Book of Carmarthen, ancient versions of the Welsh Laws, and the 14th century Red Book of Hergest. Examples are:

Three things a man experiences through litigation: expense, care and trouble.
Three things which cannot be hidden: love, hatred and pride.
Three things not easily restrained are the flow of a torrent, the flight of an arrow, and the tongue of a fool.
Three things a good liar must have: a good memory, a bold face, and a fool to listen.
Three things that will take a good man unawares: sleep, sin and old age.
The strength of a bard is his muse, that of a judge is his patience, that of a lawmaker his patriotism.

The amazing fact that the laws were written in Welsh as well as Latin helped ensure that the language thrived. To keep a culture, history, laws, literature, religion, language and community must intertwine and be respected. These Welsh laws, first written down over a thousand years ago, according to Saunders Lewis fashioned : *'lively forms of the mind of every poet and writer in Wales until the sixteenth century, and also directly influenced the shape and style of Welsh prose. This implies that the language had already reached a philosophical* **maturity unequalled in its period.** *It meant that it had a flexibility and positiveness which are the signs of* **centuries of culture.** *This means that there is a long period of development behind the prose of the Cyfreithiau (Laws).'*

From the Laws, we find that Welsh kings had a servant called a 'Foot-Holder'. This anti-stress kit consisted of a man holding the king's feet in his lap, from the moment the king sat down to eat in the evening, until he went to bed. At this time, the king had no power, as he was no longer king while his feet were off his kingdom. He could therefore relax, and not have to make any decisions, while his power passed to the 'Foot-Holder'. The 'Foot-Holder' could now grant pardons to criminals, arbitrate in disputes and the like, while the king drank quietly to oblivion and threw chicken drumsticks at the harpist.

SAINT ILLTUD c.475 - 525/537
ABBOT ILLTUD, ILLTYD FARCHOG, ELTUT, ILDUT, HILDUTUS, ILLTUD THE WARRIOR

Feast Date November 6 and 7, February 7 (Cressy)

He attended Arthur's court and was known as a knight and warrior with Cadog, before he became a saint. One source states that he trained at the monastery of Cassian near Marseilles and was ordained by Germanus of Auxerre. The son of Bicanus ab Emyr Llydaw, and thus of Breton origin, he built a church and later a monastery under the protection of Meirchion (Meurig) prince of Glamorgan (and Arthur's father). Illtud's wife was Trinihid, and was associated with Llanrhidian in Gower and Llantrithyd near Illtud's great monastery. Llanrhidian Church has 'The Leper Stone', a Celtic slab found embedded in the doorway in the 19th century. Illtud's name Eltut, according to a Norman source, was *'Ille ab omne crimine tutus'* – *'the one safe from all evil'.*

In the Vita of Cadog, it is stated that Illtud became a monk when fifty soldiers under his command were swallowed up into the earth. As these were probably cavalry, this may have occurred in the swamps and marshes around Llancarfan at the time. No less than seven named streams flow into Llancarfan and the ford is often flooded there. Llanilltud Fawr is on the site of a monastery founded (or refounded) in the late 5th or early 6th century by Illtud, and is mentioned in the 7th century Life of Samson – Samson was taken by his parents Bicanus and Rieingulid to Illtud's famous monastery, and 'magister Eltut' was described as:

'of all the Britons the most accomplished in his knowledge of all the scriptures, both the Old Testament and the New testament and in every branch of philosophy, poetry and rhetoric, grammar and arithmetic: and he was most sagacious and gifted with the power of foretelling future events.'

His father was a military nobleman and his mother the daughter of Anblaud, Amlawdd Wledig, king of Britain. His aunt was said to be Igerna, Arthur's mother. After serving as one of Arthur's knights, Illtud then served Paul of Penychen, king of Glamorgan and son of Glywys. Thankful for his deliverance he went to St Cadog, and left his wife. Illtud, when he turned to religion, was admonished by an angel to send his wife away into the night and refused to ever communicate with her again. Leaving Paul's residence at Penllyne or Pentre Meurig, he slept on the banks of the Naduan (- the Dawen, or Thaw), then became a monk on the banks of the next river west, the Hodnant. Named by some as the original Sir Galahad, one of the 'Sayings of the Wise' triads refers to him :

'Hast thou heard the saying of Illtud,
The studious, golden-chained knight:
Whoso doeth evil, evil betide him.'

An important saint, operating mainly in the south-east of wales, his brother was possibly Sadwrn. His 'Life', written in 1140, is not as important as the references in 'The Life of Samson' written around 650. He founded the monastery at Caldey island, Ynys Pyr, which was formerly called Llan Illtud. His 'bangu' (holy bell) was recovered from King Edgar's army, and his name was called on to protect the people of North Wales from Marcher Lords in the late 11th century

In 1080 Llanilltud's tithes and advowson were seized by Robert Fitzhamon and conferred onto the new Norman abbey of Tewkesbury, and this was confirmed by 1106 and 1180 charters. The church is unique in Wales, and was once extremely large. John Wesley noted after teaching there on 25th July 1777, *'About eleven I read prayers and preached in Llantwit Major Church to a very numerous congregation. I have not seen so large or handsome a church since I left England. It was*

Llanilltud Fawr Church
(photograph courtesy of WTB)

sixty yards long but one end of it is now in ruins. I suppose it has been abundantly the most beautiful as well as the most spacious church in Wales.' Several wall-paintings survive in the church, as well as the famous memorial stones, and the church is well worth visiting.

The church at Llanhamlach in Breconshire is dedicated to St Iltud and St Peter. There is also Capel Illtud (also called Llaniltud) on the Roman road between Brecon and Neath in Defynnog parish. Near Cadoxton-juxta-Neath is Llantwit-juxta-Neath (Llanilltud Nedd), and Ilston in Gower was formerly called Llanilltud Gwyr, shortened to Eltut's Town by Flemish-Norman settlers and hence Ilston. He is also the patron of Oxwich on the Gower, and his holy well is at Llanrhidian on the peninsula. He is the patron of Penbre in Carmarthen. There is a Llanelltud near Dolgellau, and he had a cult in Brittany. Llanelltud in Merionethshire may have started with a cell of one of Illtud's disciples. Llantrisant Church in Glamorgan is dedicated to Illtud, Gwynno and Tyfodwg.

According to Ecton, Llanhari, Llantrithyd, Llantwit Fardre, Lantwit under Neath were his in Glamorgan, plus Llanhiledd in Monmouth (with nearby Mynydd Llanhilleth) and Lantwood or Llantwyd in Pembroke. Capel Illtyd under Dyfynog in Brecon and Llanelltyd under Llanfachraith in Merioneth was also his. Ffynnon Illtud remains near the runed cairn called Ty Illtyd at Llanhamlach. Another Ffynon Illtud can be seen at Llanwonno in Glamorgan, and St Illtyd's Well at Llanrhidian, Gower, was said to have spouted milk in 1185.

Many churches and chapels in Brittany commemorate Illtud, such as Lanildut, Loc-Ildut and St Ideuc. *'Meme les volailles ont leur saint: saint Ildut'* (Bretagne, Le Culte des Saints, internet source CyberOuest ©Vannes). Illtud was the patron saint prayed to for success with poultry. Coadout church south of Guincamp, in Treguier diocese has a statue of Ildut. A local tradition is that he used to meet and pray with Briog at a ruined dolmen near there. A song to Ildut is still sung at his pardon there. Landebaeron is dedicated to St Maudez, but also has a stature of Illtud and a silver reliquary with his skull. Doble notes several other dedications such as Ploerdut's chapel of St 'Iltut'. Aber-Ildut is north-west of Renan.

Some sources state that he taught David, as well as Samson, Maelgwn, Gildas and Pol Aurelian and he is buried at Bedd Gwyl Illtyd in Brecon. Bedd Gwyl Illtyd means the grave of St Illtyd's Eve. The 'bedd' lies near Llanilltyd Church and Mynydd Illtyd. It was the custom to keep watch there on the night before his feast day. At Llanilltud Fawr, there is a torchlight carnival procession featuring dragons every Bonfire night, the eve of Illtud's day, which by happy coincidence keeps the custom of his celebration alive. The Celtic carved stones in Llanilltud Church are not properly displayed, but are among the most important in the British Isles.

Illtud was noted in history as having invented a special plough. The fields all around his monastery are full of limestone rock and therefore difficult to till. Before his time it was customary in Wales to cultivate fields by using a mattock and an over-treading plough (*'aradr arsang'*), implements used by the Irish on similar soils for centuries after. Wrmonoc's Breton Vita of Pol Aurelian describes in fabulous terms how Illtud regained lands from the seas to assist his cultivation, and some of the Hodnant valley and at nearby Aberddawen/Llanfabon was reclaimed at a very early date by earthen banks acting as sea walls.

Illtud's cave on the banks of the Ewenni river can still be seen, where he slept at night. There was also supposed to have been a retreat at Llanhamlach, three miles east of Brecon, recorded by Giraldus Cambrensis, where Illtud's *'mare that used to carry his provisions was covered by a stag, and produced an animal of wonderful speed, resembling a horse before and a stag behind.'* It is believed by some that he was born near Brecon. Arthurian legends place Illtud as one of the guardians of the Grail, and as Arthur's cousin. Nennius in his 8th century 'Marvels of Britain' recorded that when Illtud was praying in his cave near the sea he saw the body of *'the once and future king'* Arthur, whom Illtud had to bury in a secret place. This story is related to his chapel at Oxwich on the Gower peninsula. Illtud *'was praying in a cave near the sea and a boat came in bearing two men and the body of a holy man, an altar floating above his face. When Illtud went to meet them, they took out of the ship the body of the holy man, the altar still stood suspended and never moved from its position. Then the men in the boat said to Illtud "This man of God charged us to bring him to thee and to bury him with thee, and that thou should not reveal his name to anyone lest men swear by him"*. Arthur did not want anyone to swear vows at his tomb – an eery precursor of the 'lost' king of Wales, Owain Glyndŵr, eight centuries later.

It is a little-known fact that Llanilltud was ear-marked for the site of the first University of Wales. However, a hotel-building project in Aberystwyth ran into difficulties, and a huge new building was suddenly made available at the right price. The site of Llanilltud monastery and church is near the first century Cor Eurgain (Caer Worgorn), succeeded by the Cor of Tewdws (Theodosius), where foundations can still be seen on the field marked Cor Tewdws in 19th century maps. The Life of Pol de Leon says that Illtud had also a monastery on Ynys Pyr, which appears to be Barri (Ynys Peirio), rather than Caldey Island. A monastery site was marked upon maps of Barri until the railway station was built there, when the island was rejoined to the mainland in the docks construction.

Maen Illtud at Llanhamlach is also known as Ty Illtyd, a dolmen thought to be Illtud's hermitage. There are over 60 inscribed crosses inside the burial chamber, possibly made by a recluse. A standing stone at Llanhamlach stands opposite Peterstone Court. There are several holy wells dedicated to Illtud. Two in Glamorgan could not be located by Francis Jones, but another four are noted, including those at Michaelstone, Llansamlet and Llanwynno.

IOLO MORGANWG   March 19th, 1747-December 18th, 1826
EDWARD WILLIAMS, SAVIOUR OF WELSH CULTURE

(Note the following is taken from the author's 'The Secret Vale of Glamorgan' ISBN 1-903529-00X, which also contains a long appendix upon Edward Williams.)

Upon June 21st, 1792, an itinerant stonemason named Edward Williams proclaimed a Gorsedd of the Bards of the Island of Britain, at Primrose Hill in London. Using his bardic name of Iolo Morganwg, he went on to lay out another circle of stones at the Ivy Bush Hotel in Carmarthen in 1819, re-starting the ancient tradition of the eisteddfod. A National Eisteddfod was held in Liverpool in 1929, and in 1900 a Gorsedd of Bards was formed in Brittany, and in 1928 a similar Gorsedd was started in Cornwall.

Iolo Morganwg's Eisteddfod recreation

Born at Pennon, Llancarfan, he was the son of Edward Williams of Gileston and Ann Mathew of Llanmaes, who had married in St Tathan in 1744. Soon after Edward's birth, they moved to St Tathan, but from 1756 the family lived in a tiny thatched cottage in Flemingston, and Iolo trained as a stonemason, eventually moving to Cowbridge, where a plaque in the High Street commemorates him. Iolo states that he learned to read by watching his father cut inscriptions on gravestones, as he did not attend any school. His mother also probably taught him, and he says that he was taught in the bardic crafts by Edward Williams of Llancarfan. It was thought that his mother married 'beneath her station' as she had been brought up by her distant relatives, the Seys, in Boverton Place. Other Glamorgan bards such as Rhys Morgan, Lewis Hopkin and Sion Bradford influenced his childhood. The Rev. Edward Pritchard had lived in the same tiny Flemingstone cottage, which had one room downstairs, and two minute box bedrooms open to the rafters. It was held on lease from Lady Charlotte Edwin, and the height of the bedrooms was only 4 feet at the sides, rising to around 6 foot in the middle. By 1850, the cottage was demolished. It had been situated in the yard of Gregory Farm, where the barn is now.

The Rev. David Williams writes: *'Edward junior was trained as a stonemason but realised that his true craft lay elsewhere, in the history and culture of Wales. He was a life-long sufferer with asthma and this, too, may well have inclined him away from manual work to more literary pursuits. Although it is sometimes stated that he was self-taught, his studies were guided by John Walters, Rector of Llandough and Vicar of St Hilary - a noted scholar and lexicographer. He was also helped in his studies by another clergyman, Thomas Richards of Coychurch, and it was through his studies with the latter that he became fascinated with the bardic tradition and saw himself as its true heir. He adopted the bardic name of Iolo Morganwg, the name by which he is best known....... His Unitarian beliefs did not prevent his having his children baptised at Flemingston Church, nor was he refused burial in the churchyard. The date of his funeral is recorded as taking place on December 20th 1826.* He was buried just outside the West end of the Church and the extension of the building in 1858 meant that his burial spot now lies within the Church building. To mark the place there is a memorial wall tablet to him and his son, Taliesin. This was erected by 'Caroline, Countess of Dunraven' among other admirers. Close to it is a memorial window depicting Christ among the doctors. This was given by Iolo's great grandson, Mr Illtyd Williams of Middlesborough whose family long maintained an interest in the Church'. As a young man, Iolo had the opportunity to read ancient Welsh manuscripts which had been collected by John Walters of Llandough and Thomas Richards of Coychurch, which gave him a great interest in the structure and vocabulary of the Welsh language.

Professor G.J. Williams wrote the following, which was delivered posthumously on the BBC Welsh Home Service in 1963:

'Iolo was, in his early years, a romantic poet, and throughout his life, a romantic dreamer. Everybody agrees that he was the greatest authority of his day on the subject of Welsh literature and on many aspects of Welsh history. He was also an authority on such subjects as horticulture, agriculture, geology and botany and, in his old age, he was prepared to lecture on metallurgy in the school which his son had opened in the new industrial town of Merthyr Tudful. His manuscripts show that he was a musician who had composed scores of hymn tunes, and that he took great delight in collecting folk-songs. He was a theologian who helped establish the Unitarian denomination in South Wales, and a politician who revelled in the excitement of the early years after the French Revolution.'

Edward Williams was responsible for retrieving much material upon early Welsh history, but has been portrayed as a fraudster by nearly all sources. As a result, the author has been extremely careful in using his material. However, it seems time for a careful study of his life's work – vitriol was heaped upon him for daring to say that British history predated the Germanic invasions. Hanoverian apologists such as Bishop Stubbs hated any church predating the Roman Catholic conversion of the pagan Saxons. A very major reassessment of Iolo is needed, preferably not by professional historians, blinkered in their ways and minds by what they have been taught. Iolo Morgannwg is a shining beacon of Welsh history. He tried to 'kick-start' the engine of a dying culture, for which the many of the 'crachach' (snobs) of the time hated him. Vitriolic attacks often have a reason that stems not from academic integrity, but from dislike of change. For many academics to change their thinking, to go back to original sources, to approach a problem differently, requires a change in our educational system. Why has no academic looked at the pre-medieval histories of saints and placed them into context with King Arthur? Why has no academic re-visited Iolo's copious writings and analysed them properly?

The Rev. David Williams writes: *'The cottage in which he lived was demolished not long after his death and in the space it occupied there now stands the barn of Gregory Farm. The manuscripts which once filled the house were carefully preserved and are now kept at the National Library of Wales at Aberystwyth. They are so numerous that any scholar would find it a daunting task to read through tem and they bear eloquent testimony to the man's industry.'*

Again from David Williams *'His love of his home village is evident by the way that he boasts "The lands in the parish of Flimston are some of the best of the best part of our County. The soil is strong and deep, considerably more so than in some of the adjacent parishes. William Hooper, a very good farmer and my valuable friend in that parish, was nearly, if not the first that introduced what we call good liming." "The lily of the valley grows in the woods here in the parish of Flimston..... and the white hyacinth." However, he did not get on well with all his neighbours: "I think that native farmers are, in plural, the greatest slovens and the most ignorant of men, even in their own profession, of any living." "The Glamorgan farmers are, except comparatively a few, far less intelligent and, as is usually the case, far more self-conceited, than those of Breconshire." This is, perhaps written in one of those spells of bad temper for which he was well-known and which led him to quarrel violently with even the best of his friends. A tendency which led Theophilus Jones of Brecon to refer to him as "mad Ned". The object of his spleen was sometimes Thomas William, founder of Bethesda'r Fro and a noted Welsh hymn writer. He lived in Flemingston Court in Iolo's lifetime, but the later had little time for him and pilloried him in the verse: "Song of the Hypocritical Preacher".*

As well as Jennett Francis, Iolo noted *'John Harry's age ascertained from register. A lying old devil as ever was. Swore by his God that he was 118 years of age and could remember King David." "Catherine Rees alias Jenkins of the same parish, died about 1768 at about 100 or more - an illiterate rustic. She could give no interesting account of anything that had happened in her day, only that men and women of all ages in her young days had the general habit of smoking. She remembered Morris Dances by women, all in breeches, continuing with companies of men dancers. She lamented the discontinuance of Sunday dancing." He also noted the depopulation of the Vale in this time "After looking at St Athan and Flimston, let the mournful (for he must be so) observer proceed to the next village of Boverton....... And observe what were once populous places. The numerous farm houses and cottages in ruins will give an idea similar to no other but that of the recent depredatory approach of an invading army having passed through the country, beating down all before him."*

Little known is the fact that Iolo and John Evans of Waun-fawr planned in detail to visit the tribe of Welsh Indians, the Mandans, supposed to be descendants of Prince Madoc's expedition. Iolo dropped out in 1792, leaving Evans to explore the Missouri alone. Evans is regarded as the greatest explorer in America, along with Meriwether Lewis, the Welsh leader of the Lewis and Clark expedition which crossed the continent. Another point about Iolo's life is that he said that Wil Hopcyn (1700-1741) was the author of the haunting 'Bugeilio'r Gwenith Gwyn' (the song known in English as 'Watching the Wheat'), but it seems that Iolo himself wrote the poem. Iolo's son Taliesin later told the tragic tale of Wil Hopcyn and Ann Thomas of Llangynwyd, the 'Maid of Cefn Ydfa', and connected the song to this story.

Much has been written on Iolo, but little in this century - it seems that only in the later 1990's has a pride in being Welsh reappeared in the national psyche. It is to be hoped that dissertation students spend time quarrying among Iolo's voluminous writings rather than wasting their time reinventing the wheel in ever more abstruse and obtuse terms. Details of his life from the Dictionary of Welsh Biography are as follows. After training as a stonemason, he journeyed in North Wales, 1771-72, then went with his brothers to London in 1773. He met Owen Myfyr and other members of the Society of Gwyneddigion, and studied the manuscripts of the Morrises of Anglesey. The poet Robert Southey wrote:

'Iolo, Iolo, he who knows
The virtue of all herbs of mount or dale,
Or greenwood shade, or quiet brooklet's bed;
Whatever lore of science or song
Sages or bards have handed down.'

Awbery notes that in London Iolo met Prime Minister Pitt, and the great Dr Johnson, who tried to humiliate him. He worked as a mason in London and Kent, went to Bristol in 1777, married in 1783 and met financial difficulties. His father-in-law gave him some land at Tredelerch (Rumney in Cardiff) to farm, but Iolo was in Cardiff Gaol in 1786-1787. In August 1786 he had been taken to court in Cowbridge by two of his many creditors, Dr John Walton and Evan Griffith of Penllyn. Unable to pay up, Iolo was set free at the Great Sessions of August 1787.

After spending time in Trefflemin (Flemingston, Flimstwn), Iolo returned to London for most of the years between 1791 and 1795. In London he presented the Prince of Wales with a poem on his marriage in 1795, and supposedly attended the ceremony wearing a leather apron and carrying a trowel. In London he was in contact with Unitarian leaders and sympathisers of the French Revolution, and accused of preaching sedition. It is said that he was examined by Pitt, who declared him innocent and restored his research papers to him. On leaving London, Iolo wrote:

'No more of London's hateful noise,
Ye maddening crowds adieu;
Detested art, ungenial joys
I dwell no more with you.
Hail ! Dear Glamorgan, let me meet
Once more the favoured place
I fly with gladdened soul to greet
My native soil again.'

In 1795 Iolo was back in Trefflemin, and in 1796 was given a contract by the Board of Agriculture, to describe the condition of lands and farms in Glamorgan and Carmarthenshire. This was his great opportunity to rescue old manuscripts and parchments from outlying farms and manors. He assisted Gwallter Mechain (Rev. Walter Davies*) in a report on Welsh agriculture. Before this, Iolo had opened a shop in Cowbridge, where he sold books and groceries. Because of the fears engendered by the French Revolution, the House of Commons proscribed the selling of Tom Paine's 'The Rights of Man' (which should even now be compulsory reading for politicians and employers). He wrapped a Bible in paper, writing on the outside, 'The Rights of Man', and displayed it in his shop

Iolo Morganwg

window. A man bought it, hoping to report Iolo to the authorities, but Iolo told him *'My friend, that book contains the best and dearest rights of man.'* Tom Paine had subscribed to Iolo's publication of poems in 1794, along with two other friends, Hannah Moore the reformer, and Robert Raikes, the founder of Sunday Schools.

At his shop from 1795-1796 Iolo declined to sell any sugar that had been associated with slavery, campaigning for its abolition. His sugar, he proclaimed, was *'East India sweets, uncontaminated by human gore.'* By this time, the stone-dust he had inhaled through masonry work was giving him severe breathing difficulties. The shop is where R. S. Bird's shop was, and an inscription was placed on the wall in 1926.

It reads:
Er cof am
Edward Williams, (Iolo Morganwg),
1747-1826, Saer Maen, Bardd Rhyddid,
Hynafhiaethydd, ac un o Gymwynaswyr Mwyaf
Llen a Hanes Cymru

Y maen hwn a osodwyd yma gan adrannau
Dwyrain a chanolbarth Morgannwg o undeb
Genedlaethol y cymdeithasau Cymraeg, ben
Can mylnedd ei farw ar yr 17fed o Ragfyr 1826,
I nodi'r ty y bu Iolo Morganw yn gwerthu
Llyfrau ynddo.
Y Gwir Erbyn y Byd
A translation of the above is:

In memory of Edward Williams (Iolo Morganwg),
1747-1826, Stone Mason, Bard,
Historian, and one of the Greatest Benfactors
Of Welsh History and Literature.

This stone was placed here by the East and Central Glamorgan Division of the National Union of Welsh Society to commemorate the centenary of his death on 17th December 1826, and to mark the house where he sold books.
Truth Against the World

Around the time he had his shop, Iolo wrote a libellous poem on the Cowbridge sexton, which rivalled his slurring ditty on 'Cowbridge topers'

Here lies interred upon his back,
The carcase of old surly Jack
Fe dyngwys lawer tra fu fyw (He attracted many whilst alive)
Myn crog, myn Crythraul, a myn Duw, ([swearing] By the Cross, by the Devil and by God)
With many a curse and many a damn,
Da gwyddai'r Diawl ag yntau pam, (The Devil and he knew best)
But now he struts, a blustering blade,
Lle mae'r iaith honno'n iaith y wlad. (Where that language is the language of the land)

Appointed as an editor of the Myvyrian Archaiology, in 1799 he travelled through North Wales again, collecting materials. He was a leading figure in the formation of the Unitarian Association in South Wales in 1802, and was still in contact with friends in London until around 1805. Known now as a principal authority on Welsh history, he succeeded in making the Gorsedd of Bards an integral part of an eisteddfod in the grounds of Carmarthen's Ivy Bush Hotel in 1819. Maxwell Fraser stated that Iolo had devised the Gorsedd ceremonial at Primrose Hill in 1791. He published very little in his lifetime, and died at Trefflemin on December 18th, 1826, aged 81. Many of his hymns were published after his death. Much of the vituperation heaped upon his research was unfounded, and the work of Hanoverian apologists who could not believe that Britain had a history before the Saxons came from Germany. The Dictionary of Welsh Biography entry concludes as follows:

Iolo was a versatile man. He took an intelligent interest not only in the literature of Wales but also in such subjects as agriculture, gardening, architecture, geology, botany, politics, the history of religion, theology, etc. He was an excellent poet and he has a special place in the history of romantic verse in Wales. The most strange thing about him was his complex mind - but it would be out of place to treat that subject here. After the death of Iolo his son, Taliesin, bound his papers into volumes; those volumes are now in the National Library.' The author would make a plea here, in the interests of scholarship, that they be scanned and placed on CD for purchase and study.

THOMAS JEFFERSON 1743 - July 4 1826
THE AUTHOR OF THE DECLARATION OF INDEPENDENCE

Born in Albemarle County, Virginia, he inherited from his father 5000 acres of plantations, and from his mother a position in society. After studying at the College of William and Mary, he read law, and in 1772 married a widow, Martha Waynes Skelton. He took her to live in his partly finished mountain-top home, Monticello. *'He was also an architect, builder and carpenter. Into his stately Virginia home, Monticello, went gadgets that were designed to save time and energy for its occupants. He built a circular staircase to save space. He also installed a dumbwaiter to save the servants many needless trips up and down the stairs. There were folding tables, and chairs than folded back into the walls when not in use. Sliding panels were built into some of the walls so that dishes and other small objects could be passed from one room to another with ease. He designed a trick bed. From one side he emerged to his study, from the other, to his breakfast. During the day the bed was raised out of the way.'*

Jefferson's original draft of the Declaration of Independence was severely pruned by Congress, and North Carolina and Georgia were responsible for the removal of anti-slavery promises. Jefferson said that his father came from the Snowdon foothills, and a US State Department official unveiled a plaque at Llanfair Ceiriog in 1933, *'To the Memory of a Great Welshman, Thomas Jefferson'.*

Jefferson used all his powers when he drafted the Declaration of Independence*, imbued with the Welsh traditions of social equality.............his original draft declares *'We hold these truths to be sacred and undeniable; that all men are created* *equal and independent, that from that equal creation they derive rights inherent and inalienable, among which are the preservation of life, and liberty, and the pursuit of happiness.'* In the same year, 1786, he wrote a bill establishing religious freedom, and in the years that followed endeavoured to make his words reality. Jefferson was very proud of his Virginian statute, where he enshrined the separation of the church and state, as he believed in religious liberty - a politically-aligned religion would mean minority persecution. He believed that *'the care of human life and happiness........is the first and only legitimate object of good government.'* This belief in the welfare of citizens is alien to present Western governments, which seem to kow-tow to the multinational business interests which control them.

He had succeeded Benjamin Franklin as Minister to France in 1785, and his sympathy for the French Revolution brought him into conflict with Alexander Hamilton, when Jefferson was Secretary of State in 1793, so he resigned from Washington's Cabinet. Two political parties began to emerge, Jefferson's Democrat-Republicans and Hamilton's Federalists, and Jefferson opposed a strong Federal government and championed the rights of states. He was a reluctant candidate for the presidency in 1796, yet came within 3 votes of selection. He was appointed Vice-President, although at the time an opponent of President John Adams (q.v.) In 1800 he tied with Aaron Burr for the presidential candidacy, but with Hamilton's support was elected President.

Thomas Jefferson

As third President after George Washington, from 1801-1809, Jefferson negotiated and signed the Louisiana Purchase of vast French territories from Napoleon. For $15 million, **the USA** *doubled in size* - a cost of under 3 cents an acre. The sale included over 600 million acres, most of the 13 states in the middle of America, from the Gulf of Mexico to the Rocky Mountains and Canadian border. It was a diplomatic and political triumph, ending the threat of war with France, and opening up the land west of the Mississippi for settlement, allowing the colonies to eventually reach the Pacific. By acquiring the heart of the continent, he secured the independent future of the fledgling USA. Some objected to the purchase as it was not provided for in the Constitution, but Jefferson later admitted that he had stretched his Presidential power *'till it cracked'*, for *'what is practicable must often control what is pure theory.'*

In his first term, Jefferson cut back upon central army and navy expenditures and cut the government budget, allowing him not only to reduce the National Debt by one third, but also to eliminate the unpopular tax on whiskey. He also sent a naval squadron to suppress the Barbary Pirates who were harassing American ships in the Mediterranean. In his second term he fought to keep America neutral in the Napoleonic Wars, although both England and France interfered with American merchantmen. Jefferson had been the first President to be inaugurated in Washington, and he called his new residence, The White House, 'a great stone house, big enough for two emperors, one pope and the grand lama in the bargain.' He walked to his inauguration in a home-spun grey suit, as bad weather had delayed the arrival of an expensive velvet suit and a new $6,000 carriage.

The Library of Congress purchased Jeffferson's 6,500 volume book collection for almost $24,000 to replace those burned by the British, but he died in relative poverty. On July 4, 1826, there was a ceremony in the House of Representatives to celebrate 50 years of independence. Jefferson's friends were soliciting money for his relief, with little success, at the ceremony. Jefferson died that same day, along with his friend John Adams

J. F. Kennedy at a dinner honouring Nobel Prize winners said '*I think this is the most extraordinary collection of talent, of human knowledge, that has ever gathered together at The White House - with the possible exception of when Thomas Jefferson dined alone.*' This greatest and most unassuming American president composed his own epitaph........*Here was buried Thomas Jefferson, Author of the Declaration of American Independence, of the Statute of Virginia for Religious Freedom, and Father of the University of Virginia.*'

* Another Welshman, the one-legged lawyer Gouveneur Morris (1755-1835), wrote the final draft of the Constitution and as such is commemorated on a plaque on Philadelphia Town Hall, along with William Penn, Jefferson, and the Welshmen Robert Morris and John Marshall. Gouveneur Morris was later Minister to France and a senator:

'Perpetuating the Welsh heritage, and commemorating the vision and virtue of the following Welsh patriots in the founding of the City, Commonwealth and Nation: William Penn, 1644-1718, proclaimed freedom and religion and planned New Wales, later named Pennsylvania;
Thomas Jefferson, 1743-1826, third President of the United States, composed the Declaration of Independence;
Robert Morris, 1734-1806, foremost financier of the American Revolution and signer of the Declaration of Independence;
Gouverneur Morris, 1752-1816, wrote the final draft of the Constitution of the United States;
John Marshall, 1755-1835, Chief Justice of the United States and father of American constitutional law.'

AUGUSTUS JOHN   January 4 1878 - October 31 1961
SOCIETY PAINTER, 'SUPREME DRAUGHTSMAN' AND BOHEMIAN

Augustus John and his sister Gwen John (1876-1939), from Tenby, Pembrokeshire, have many paintings in Welsh art galleries. Augustus John shocked even the

Bohemian art world with his behaviour and promiscuity. A student at the Slade in the 1890's, he was invited to paint the Queen (now the Queen Mother) in 1937. He suggested that he stayed at a pub near Windsor Castle, where she would visit secretly for sittings, an offer she refused. He failed to complete the canvas, and it was first seen publicly in 1961. In the 1940's he was offered a knighthood. His wife had died, and he was told that he must marry his long-time mistress Dorelia. He had lived and procreated with her for 40 years, so he proposed - and she demurred, thus depriving him of his recognition. His portraits and paintings can be found in Stockholm, Washington, Sydney, Detroit and Dublin. For 30 years he had been *the* portrait painter of British society, hailed as *'the last of the Old Masters'*, but was a wild child until the end. Dylan Thomas' wife, Caitlin, was one of the many artist's models who found herself compromised in a relationship with him*. His sister Gwendoline's intensely expressive paintings can also be found in major galleries.

Augustus John

John was at the Slade School of Art from 1894-1899 with his sister Gwen. It appears that his personality changed in 1897, when he injured his head after diving into the sea on holiday. From being the quiet and studious son of a solicitor, John started dressing in a Bohemian manner, grew a beard and began drinking heavily. His paintings became more adventurous, and his friend Wyndham Lewis said that John had become a *'great man of action into whose hands the fairies had placed a paintbrush instead of a sword.'* The most talented artist of his generation, in 1898 he won the Slade Prize, and his first exhibition was in 1899. John married in 1901 but was widowed in 1907. His wife Ida had died giving birth to their fifth child. He had met Dorelia McNeill in 1904, and from 1907 she was his lifelong companion and the subject of many of his paintings and drawings. Augustus John had developed a nomadic lifestyle, living in a horse-drawn caravan and often camping out with gypsies, and his famous picture of Dorelia of 1908 *'The Smiling Woman'* depicts her as a gypsy. With his large family, he toured Wales, painting Welsh gypsies and visited Provence in 1910, returning to produce post-impressionist landscapes. Dorelia was constantly producing children, and *'when, in 1909, they all settled for a few nights in a field near Cambridge, J.M. Keynes reported "John is encamped with two wives and 10 naked children".'* He appears to have had many illegitimate children, known as 'demi-Johns'.

Aged 26 at the start of World War One, he was now the best-known artist in Britain, with an international reputation. His friend Lord Beaverbrook interceded to obtain John a post in the Canadian army as an officer, and he was given permission to paint whatever he liked on the Western Front. He was the only officer in the Allied Forces, save for King George V, to be allowed to keep his moustache and beard. Unfortunately, after two months he was involved in a brawl and sent home in disgrace. Beaverbrook's intervention saved John from a court-martial, and he was sent back to France. He was also at the Versailles Peace Conference where he painted the portraits of several delegates.

In the 1920's John was Britain's leading portrait painter, and his subjects included Thomas Hardy, George Bernard Shaw, Tallulah Bankhead, Dylan Thomas and T.E. Lawrence (of Arabia). His two-part biography is *'Chiaroscuro'* (1952) and *'Finishing Touches'* (published posthumously in 1964). Critical opinion seems to be that his creativity was diminished after the War, and he took an easy route by painting the rich and famous. However, it may be that the huge financial burden of supporting his large official and 'unofficial' families forced him to take the easy money. Interestingly, John always affirmed that he never grew his famous red beard at all and that it simply appeared of its own accord, after his bathing accident at Giltar Point, Tenby. He hated his solicitor father (his mother died when John was young), and it appears that it was an act of rebellion against him. He said to another artist, Nina Hamnett, *'We are the sort of people our fathers warned us against'*. His lecherous reputation was such that it was said that, whenever he walked down Chelsea's King's Road, he used to pat the heads of all the children, just in case it was one of his.

*John was supposed to have 'forced' himself on his female models, including a 16-year-old irish dancer, Caitlin MacNamara, when he was 52. Whatever the truth of the matter, she rapidly became his mistress. Augustus John and Caitlin were to visit Richard Hughes at Laugharne's Castle House, and Dylan Thomas engineered an invite to meet the great man in July 1936. The day deteriorated on a trip to Carmarthen, with John becoming increasingly irritated with the behaviour of Dylan and Caitlin. After a drunken fight, Dylan was left in a carpark in Carmarthen while John and Caitlin returned to Castle House for dinner. This was the first meeting of Dylan Thomas and his wife-to-be. It was thought that Dorelia would have been tired of his many affairs and their Bohemian lifestyle, but the Welsh novelist Richard Hughes once heard her

Tenby Harbour
(photograph courtesy of WTB)

say *'There's one thing about John that I've never got used to, not after all these years... I don't know what to do about it... Time after time...he's late for lunch'*.

BOBBY JONES   March 17th, 1902 - December 18th 1971
ROBERT TYRE JONES JR., 'THE GREATEST AMATEUR GOLFER EVER'

Perhaps the greatest golfer in history, Bobby (Robert Tyre) Jones had Welsh roots. A qualified lawyer from Atlanta, he won the US Open four times and the British Open three times. After winning the 'Grand Slam' of the US Open, the British Open and both Amateur Championships in his golden year of 1930, he retired from the game as there were no challenges left. He was just 28 years old, and he went on to build the Augusta National Golf Course and found the Masters Tournament.

As an amateur, he won the US Open in 1923, 1926, 1929 and 1930, the US Amateur Open in 1924, 1925, 1927, 1928 and 1930, and the British Open in 1926, 1927 and 1930. The first golfer to win the US Open and the British Open in the same year (1926), he was the only player ever to score what was then the Grand Slam of golf, taking the open and amateur titles of both the USA and Britain in 1930, in which year he retired, aged just 28.

From Atlanta, Georgia, Jones was a sickly child of rich parents. Not until 5 years old could he eat solid foods, and to help him develop, his family bought a summer home next to the fairways at Atlanta's East Lake Country Club. At 6, he was using sawn-off golf clubs, and at 7 mimicking the swing of Stewart Maiden, the country club pro golfer. Maiden said *'He was never lonesome with a golf club in his hands. He must have been born with the soul of a perfectionist.'* Aged just 11, he shot an 80 on the old course at East Lake and showed the card to his proud father, who wept as he hugged his son.

Jones was a short-tempered, club-throwing youth, but acquired an even disposition in his 20's, being unruffled on any golf course. He first entered a major tournament, the US Amateur aged 14, as a golfing prodigy, and won his first two matches before going out in the 3rd round. A 1940 article in The Saturday Evening Post reported that *'Bobby was a short, rotund kid, with the face of an angel and the temper of a timber wolf. At a missed shot, his sunny smile could turn suddenly into a black storm cloud....... Even at the age of 14 Bobby could not understand how anyone could ever miss any kind of golf shot.'* However, Bobby had not won anything by the time he was 20, which led many to doubt his ability to make the grade. Jones later said of this time that *'I was full of pie, ice cream and inexperience. To me, golf was just a game to beat someone. I didn't know the someone was me.'* His low-point came in the 3rd round of the 1921 British Open, when he committed the unpardonable sin of picking the ball up on the 11th green. He had already taken over 50 shots, and said some 50 years later *'It was the most inglorious failure of my sporting life.'*

The breakthrough came in the 1923 US Open at Inwood, New York. He was leading easily

Bobby Jones

with three holes left, but with a sequence of bogey-bogey-double bogey he dropped four shots and allowed Bobbie Cruickshank to tie with him. Jones said *'I didn't finish like a champion - I finished like a yellow dog.'* In the 18-hole play-off, both men were still tied going into the par-4 final hole. Both missed the fairway with their drives, and Cruckshank laid up on the fairway with his second shot. Jones could do likewise, playing safe, or aim from loose dirt at the edge of the rough, over water to the green. Jones used to describe a dangerous shot, that only a golfer with real guts could achieve, as *'sheer delicatessen.'* Using a 2-iron, he drilled the ball over the water to within 8 feet of the pin and two-putted for his first major. That shot, and this win, made him unstoppable in the years to come, and he won most of his championships easily.

An exception was the 1929 US Open, when he again finished poorly, probably relaxing too much. With 6 holes to go, Jones led by 6 strokes, but Al Espinosa went 2-under-par for the final 6 holes, while Jones bogeyed the 12th and triple-bogeyed at 15th. He missed the green on the 18th and needed a 12-foot putt for a tie. With his famous putter, *'Calamity Jane'*, he just made the putt to tie for a play-off. As if determined to show that he was far better than Espinosa, Jones won the 36-hole play-off the next day, by a massive 23 strokes.

In the 1920's he was alongside Bill Tilden, Babe Ruth and Jack Dempsey in the pantheon of American sporting giants. In his final year of 1930, no-one knew that he was retiring, but Jones was expected by the nation to achieve the *'impregnable quadrilateral'* Grand Slam. In the British Amateur at St Andrews, he won all his eight matches, although three by only one stroke. Two weeks later, he won his 3rd British Open at Royal Liverpool, Hoylake, by just two strokes. It was on his return that New York gave him his ticker-tape parade - the people assumed that the first-ever Grand Slam was in the bag, although with two tournaments to play.

At the US Open at Interlachen, Minneapolis, Jones led with two holes left, but a double-bogey on the 71st hole cut his lead to just one. However, on the 18th, he single-putted from 40 feet for a birdie to win his 4th US Open Championship. Jones then easily won the US Amateur in Philadelphia, surrounded by Marine bodyguards who protected him from his fans. Herbert Warren-Wind wrote *'in the clubhouse, after a talk with his father, he began to digest the reality that the grand Slam was factually behind him and with it the ever-accumulating strain he had carried for months. When he appeared for the presentation he looked years younger.'*

Two months later he retired, winner of 13 major championships, a record that stood for over 40 years. Warren-Wind wrote *'There were no worlds left for him to conquer.'* A graduate from Georgia Tech and Harvard University, Jones now practised law full-time, only playing once a year in his Masters tournament. Towards the end of his life, Bobby Jones suffered from syringomyelia, a fluid-filled cavity in the spinal chord which caused at first pain, followed by loss of feeling and muscle atrophy. Confined to a wheelchair by this nerve disorder, and condemned to a slow death, he weighed between five and six stone when he died in 1971. Warren-Wind commented *'As a young man, he was able to stand up to just about the best that life can offer, which is not easy, and later he stood up with equal grace to just about the worst.'*

From the Bobby Jones Golf Tournament website (see footnote), we read the following:

'Most of the world called him Bobby. His mother called him Robert, his father

called him Rob and he insisted that his friends call him Bob. To the British he was
Bonnie Bobby. He never turned professional, but on a part-time basis he took on
Walter Hagen and the rest of the then best golfers. **He was the greatest of all,**
In 1930, when he was 28 he won the US Open, US Amateur, the British Open
and the British Amateur Championships. He then retired from competitive golf to
raise his young family and continue his business career. In the eight years preceding
the **retirement he won 62% of the national championships he entered,** *in the*
largest golfing nations there are, Great Britain and the US. No amateur or
professional golfer has come close to compiling such a record nor is it likely that
anyone ever will.

In 1971, at the age of 69, he succumbed to Syringomelia, which he had fought
for 22 years. He would call the disease Hell. When an old friend suggested he had
made a good adjustment to the condition, he answered, "If adjustment means
acceptance, I'd say no. I still can't accept this thing. When it first happened to me
I was pretty bitter, and there were times when I didn't want to go on living, so I
had to face the problem of how I was going to live. I decided I'd just do the very
best I could."

At a time when Babe Ruth was king, Jack Dempsey was the Heavyweight
Boxing Champ, Red Grange was scoring touchdowns almost at will, and Walter
Hagen was stopping to smell the roses, Bobby Jones was just as deserving of his
fame. He did it all and didn't get paid for it.'

FOOTNOTE:
Welsh Americans since 1979 have been running the Bobby Jones Golf Tournament at Ann
Arbor (twinned with Brecon), open to all those citizens named Robert, Bob, Bobby or
Roberta Jones. Entrants are given nicknames such as 'Computer', 'Too-Tall' and 'Hubcap'
to distinguish them. Over 350 'Bobs' from 38 states and 4 countries have participated in the
20 tournaments to date, raising over $100,000 for syringomelia research, recovery and
rehabilitation.

DAVID JONES November 1 1895 - 1974
POET-PAINTER, ACCORDING TO T.S. ELIOT ON THE SAME LITERARY
LEVEL AS EZRA POUND, JAMES JOYCE AND ELIOT HIMSELF

David Michael Jones was born in Brockley, Kent, the son of James Jones, a printer's
manager. Jones' knowledge of print, and his remarkable gifts in calligraphy and
printing, probably stem from this connection. His grandfather had come from
Wales to work as a mast and block maker in Surrey. Aged just 7, his 'Dancing Bear'
sketch gained public attention, and his pictures began to be exhibited at the Royal
Drawing Society. At 16, David Jones enrolled at Camberwell Art College. Jones'
intention was to become a 'painter of Welsh history' or an animal illustrator, but
his teachers opened his eyes to French Impressionists and the Pre-Raphaelites.

However, the Great War interrupted Jones' studies, and he enlisted in January
1915, serving in the horrors of the Western Front with the Royal Welsh Fusiliers,
from 1915 to 1918. Jones was wounded at the Somme at the Battle of Mametz
Wood in 1916. The regiment was exhausted by forced marches, and some of the
men were barely conscious before the conflict, and Jones was carried wounded and

uncoscious from the front. His experiences, quite naturally, dramatically affected his later literary output. After demobilisation, Jones received a grant to study art once more, at the Westminster School of Art. However, his years under fire in the army jarred with the placid environment of the art school, and Jones sought an answer by converting to the Roman Catholic church in 1921. He met the engraver/sculptor Eric Gill, who wished to form *'a company of craftsmen living by their work and earning such reputation as they had by the quality of their goods'*, and moved out of London to join him, learning wood and copper engraving.

He illustrated *'Gulliver's Travels', 'The Rime of the Ancient Mariner'* and other books, and worked on his watercolours while travelling around Britain, sometimes staying with Gill near Llanthony Abbey, sometimes with his parents, and sometimes at Benedictine monasteries. His delicate water colour washes and elegant calligraphy took him away from the mainstream of British art, and a reassessment of this most multi-talented man is overdue. Kathleen Raine describes the *'Turneresque evanescence'* of his 'Manawyddan's Glass Door' in her wonderful appreciation of his writings, poetry and art, 'David Jones and the Actually Loved and Known'. His luminous, visionary watercolours, redolent of Arthurian mysticism and the legends of The Mabinogion, can be seen in the Tate Gallery and many other museums.

In 1937, David Jones wrote 'In Parenthesis' ('seinnyesit e gledyf ym penn mameu'). TS Eliot wrote that he was *'deeply moved'* by the typescript and that it was 'a work of genius' in his introduction to it. Part poem, part book, it mingles Jones' cathartic experiences in the First World War with Arthurian legend, Welsh mythology and the Roman occupation of Britain. *Eliot places Jones in the same literary representation as himself, Ezra Pound and James Joyce.* Jones, a writer, painter, calligrapher and illustrator, was obsessed with the way technocracy has taken us away from faith and sacrament. The intensity of inspiration from

Llanthony Priory, an inspiration for David Jones
(photograph courtesy of WTB)

his historical roots is probably only rivalled by Arthur Machen and W.B. Yeats.

The great poet Stephen Spender, in his New York Times book review of 'In Parenthesis', said *'This work of a poet-painter has its every word chiselled out of experience, and is probably the World War I monument most likely to survive.'* And the review in the Times Literary Supplement stated *'This is an epic of war...but it is like no other war-book because for the first time that experience has been reduced to a "shape in words"... the impression still remains that this book is one of the most remarkable literary achievements of our time.'* The work is a mixture of poetry and prose, a painting of words which TS Eliot called *'a work of genius'.....'When "In Parenthesis" is widely enough known - as it will be in time - it will no doubt undergo the same sort of detective analysis and exegesis as the later works of James Joyce and the Cantos of Ezra Pound'.*

'You can hear the silence of it:
you can hear the rat of no-man's-land
rut out intricacies,
weasel-out his patient workings
scrut, scrut, scrut,
harrow-out earthly, trowel his cunning paw'

Also according to the great poet W.H.Auden, David Jones' 'The Anathemata' was *'very probably the finest long poem written in English this century'.* This considered meditation on the history and mythology of Celtic-Christian Britain was intelligent, ambitious and influenced T. S. Eliot's own work. Jones' 'Epoch and Artist' is dedicated to Saunders Lewis, the Welsh Nationalist writer. All his writings show his alienation against the world of machines, existentialism, modernism and the analytical philosophy that eradicates metaphysics and the signposts of history. From Jones 'Epoch and Artist' we read *'A man can not only smell roses (some beasts may do that, for lavender is said to be appreciated in the Lion House) but he can and does and ought to pluck roses and he can predicate of roses such and such. He can make a signum of roses. He can make attar of roses. He can garland them and make anathemata of them. Which is, presumably the kind of thing he is meant to do. Anyway, there's no one else can do it. Angels can't nor can the beasts. No wonder then that Theology regards the body as a unique good. Without body: without sacrament. Angels only; no sacrament. Beasts only: no sacrament. Man: sacrament at every turn and all levels of the "profane" and "sacred", in the trivial and the profound, no escape from sacrament.'*

GRIFFITH JONES   1683 (May 1 1684 christened) - April 8 1761
THE MAN WHO MADE WALES THE MOST LITERATE EUROPEAN NATION

Born at Pant-yr-Efel, Penboyr, Carmarthenshire to John ap Gruffydd and Elinor John, after primary education in his village, he became a shepherd. Wishing to become a clergyman, he then went to Carmarthen Grammar School. From 1707 he applied several times for ordination but was rejected until 1708 when he was made deacon, and then a priest in 1708 at Penbryn, Ceredigion. He was curate at Penrieth, Pembroke in 1709 and Laugharne, Carmarthen in the same year. At Laugharne he became master of the S.P.C.K. school (founded by Sir John Phillips of Picton Castle), and in 1711 was appointed rector at Llandeilo-Abercywyn, Carmarthenshire. He was now known as a superb preacher, and people travelled for miles to hear him, leading to a formal complaint by the English Bishop William Ottley of St David's in 1714, about his *'going about preaching on weekdays in Churches, Churchyards, and sometimes on the mountains, to hundreds of auditors'.* Several times between 1714 and 1716 Griffith Jones was summoned before the bishop's court in Carmarthen to answer charges of ignoring church laws and customs, i.e. popularising Christianity. Even today, this is frowned upon by the Church, which seems to prefer men from the grey world of pointless committees to real men of faith and action.

Becoming a corresponding member of the SPCK in 1713, Jones was chosen to become a teacher and missionary in India, but declined the appointment, and in 1716 Sir John Philipps appointed Griffith to become rector of Llanddowror, Carmarthenshire. Jones worked hard to support the SPCK, and supported a new edition of the Welsh Bible for a decade. In 1718 he travelled around Wales, England and Scotland with Philipps on a preaching tour, before marrying Philipps' sister in 1720. In 1731 Griffith wrote to the SPCK proposing a *'Welch School'* at Llanddowror, as the number of SPCK schools in Wales had started to decline. Griffith Jones began the *'circulating schools'* movement sometime between 1731 and 1737, by which later date there were 37 schools with 2,400 scholars.

Schools were held for three months in the same place, usually in winter when farm-workers and children had more time available to study. Often the village church was used, if the rector would agree. Schools were also run in barns, storehouses and even a windmill. Night schools were also available for those who could not get any time off in the day, and pupils were taught to read the Welsh Bible and to learn the Church Catechism. SPCK religious texts were used to teach literacy, and any funds raised were spent on teaching, not on buildings. All the schoolmasters were trained by Griffith Jones personally at Llanddowror, and he insisted that they were members of the Church of England.

The movement was essential in giving the Welsh opportunities for literacy - by the time he died in 1761, it was estimated that 158,000 people between the ages of 6 and 70 had learned to read, out of an estimated Welsh population of 480,000 (in 1750). This percentage of literate Welsh people was *probably higher than any other European nation of the time, and probably the world,* despite the grinding poverty. The annual report, *'Welch Piety'*, recorded that over 3495 schools had been set up by Jones's death, a wonderful success story. In that actual year, the 210 existing schools taught 8023 pupils. The Miners' Institutes of the 19th century assisted this desire for literacy, with their wonderful library collections. One has been shifted, stone by stone, to the Museum of Welsh Life at St. Fagans. The major contribution that Jones made was to save the life of the Welsh language – he taught the nation to read, and imbued it with a sound knowledge of Bishop Morgan's wonderful Welsh translation of the Bible. His Holy Day in the Church in Wales is April 8th, the date of his death. Of course, some parts of Wales were not visited by the schools, and the teacher moved on after three months, and into this vacuum the Sunday schools came. This idea from England was seized upon in Wales, by the rapidly-growing nonconformist sects, and operated upon the day that everyone was available. They gave a huge impetus to the Welsh language before the provision of state education, and then became rather peripheral to education in Wales.

After his death, Bridget Bevan carried on his work with training masters for the schools until her death in 1779. Griffith Jones' schools were attacked by some church dignitaries, because of his connections with Whitfield and other Methodist leaders, with a series of indignant pamphlets. The schools helped the Methodist Revival in Wales, and nearly all its early leaders came into contact with Jones. Both Griffith and his wife Margaret are buried in Llanddowror Church. The circulating schools were an immense achievement, unparalleled elsewhere in the world, and created armies of readers conversant with the standard language of the Bible. This made possible the awakening of interest in education among the Welsh in the 19th century.

INIGO JONES July 15 1573 - June 21 1652
THE FOUNDER OF CLASSICAL ENGLISH ARCHITECTURE, THE FIRST AND GREATEST OF 'ENGLISH' RENAISSANCE ARCHITECTS

Wales is about castles and churches, not great mansions and palaces. However, the great Inigo Jones has many houses and bridges attributed to him in Wales. He founded classical English architecture, designing the Queen's House at Greenwich, rebuilding the Banqueting Hall at Whitehall, and laying out Covent Garden and Lincoln's Inn Fields. He also designed two Danish royal palaces and worked with Ben Jonson, introducing the proscenium arch and movable scenery to the English stage.

He was the founder of the English school of classical architecture, bringing features of Rome and Renaissance Italy to Gothic England. Jones was Surveyor of the Kings Works from 1615-1635. His father was a cloth worker, and Jones appears to have been apprenticed as a joiner in St Paul's churchyard before he appears in 1603 as a 'picturemaker' in the household accounts of the fifth Earl of Rutland. In 1605 he was employed by Queen Anne to provide costumes and settings for a Whitehall masque. It is fairly clear that by now he had been to Italy, probably visiting theatres in Florence, and had acquired skills as a draftsman and architect*. In 1608 he designed the New Exchange in the Strand for the Earl of Salisbury, and a spire for St Paul's Cathedral. His main activity until 1640, however, appears to have been designing stage settings, costumes and decorations for masques for the Court, in which he worked with Ben Jonson until an argument in 1631.

In 1611, Jones was appointed Surveyor to the heir-apparent, Prince Henry, who died in the following year. In 1613 he was with the fourteenth Earl of Arundel visiting Italy and the houses of Palladio, before returning in 1614. He was made Surveyor of the Kings Works in the following year, and as an architect of outstanding skills, changed the focus of the appointment from one of maintenance to one of improvement. He started work on the Queen's House in Greenwich in 1617, and it was not completed until 1635. (King James' wife died in 1619, and the project was put 'on hold' for 17 years until Charles I married). In 1619 he began building the replacement Banqueting House at the palace of Whitehall, after fire had destroyed the old one. It was finished in 1622, and Rubens added the ceiling paintings in 1635. The Banqueting House was a setting for formal banquets and court masques, based on the

Inigo Jones

design of a Roman basilica, and is still used as a venue for state occasions.

Inigo Jones' most famous ecclesiastical design was the Queen's Chapel at St James Palace (1623-25, now Marlborough House Chapel). From 1625, Jones worked on converting Somerset House into a residence for Charles I's new queen,

Henrietta Maria. He also made major changes to St Paul's Cathedral, but unfortunately it was destroyed in the Great Fire of London in 1666**. As the king's agent, Jones influenced the design of London houses and the development of London. He created London's first 'square' or piazza in Covent Garden in 1630, and designed the church of St Paul's on Palladian lines. Other sources state that the first square in London was his design for Lincoln's Inn. Coleshill and Amesbury were amongst the country mansions he designed. It now appears that Wilton House, attributed to Jones, was the work of his pupil and nephew, James Webb, and Jones acted as an advisor.

Civil War in 1642, and the seizure of the king's houses in 1643 meant that Jones was no longer employed. He was among the defenders at the siege of Basing House, from which he was rescued wrapped in a blanket. Jones regained his properties in 1646, and was buried in the Church of St Benet, Paul's Wharf. Inigo Jones was a master of classical design, who broke the mould of Jacobean architecture in Britain. Most of his architectural drawings and masque designs survive, in collections at Worcester College, RIBA and Chatsworth House.

*It appears that he lived in Venice at this time, and Christian IV of Denmark induced him to leave Italy and accept an appointment at the Danish Court. Buildings are named as having been designed by Jones in both Denmark and Italy, but proof is difficult at present.

**In 1997, more than 70 stones from Inigo Jones' 'lost' portico of the old St Paul's Cathedral were found beneath the present cathedral. Christopher Wren used the blocks in his foundations.

MICHAEL DANIEL JONES   March 2 1822 - December 2 1899
THE FOUNDER OF THE WELSH COLONY OF PATAGONIA, FATHER OF THE MODERN WELSH NATIONALIST MOVEMENT, 'THE GREATEST WELSHMAN OF THE 19TH CENTURY'

Jones was born in the Manse, Llanuwchllyn, Merioneth, the son of another Michael Jones, who was minister of 'Yr Hen Gapel' (the old chapel) there. There was a huge theological controversy which split the congregation, and the minister later became Principal of the Independent College at Bala. After being educated by his father, Jones spent a few months as a draper's apprentice in Wrexham. However, Michael D. Jones wished to follow his father into the ministry, and went to Carmarthen Presbyterian College (1839-43) and then Highbury College in London. In 1847, he went to America, in the midst of the great emigration caused by the poor harvests and agricultural depression of 1840-1850. He stayed with relatives in Cincinnati and was asked to stay for some time as a minister. While there, Jones set up a society to give financial assistance to poor people from Wales who wished to emigrate, and several branches of 'The Brython Association' started across the United States. This was to be the genesis of Jones' life mission, to establish a Welsh-speaking 'Welsh Colony' for emigrants who wished to escape from the oppression of Tory landlords across Wales. He wanted a Welsh state where: '... *a free farmer could tread on his own land and enjoy on his own hearth, the song and the harp and true Welsh fellowship...There will be chapel, school, and parliament and the old language will be the medium of worship, of trade, of science, of education and of government. A strong and self-reliant nation will grow in a Welsh homeland.'*

Returning to Wales, Michael D. Jones became pastor of Independent churches in Carmarthenshire. His father died in 1853, and Michael was asked to succeed him as minister of Bala, Tyn-y-Bont, Soar, Bethel and Llandderfel, and as Principal of Bala College. However, a constitutional dispute meant that for a time a rival college operated in Bala, before moving to Bangor in 1886. This was known as *'the Battle of the Two Constitutions'* (1879-85). Jones wanted the subscribers to be able to control the government of the college, whereas his antagonists wanted the controllers to be representatives appointed by the churches of each county of Wales. (Bala was the major Welsh-speaking college at this time). The problem was exacerbated by

Bala Lake
(photograph courtesy of WTB)

Jones' financial support for the Patagonian Colony. He was forced to sell off Bodiwan, which was his home and also the seat of the college to meet his debts, and the so-called *'Decapitation Committee'* held at Shrewsbury dismissed Jones from the Principalship. Jones resigned from Bala College in 1892 to allow it to also move to Bangor, the new Bala-Bangor College later became the University of Wales there.

In South America the existence of the Welsh-speaking colony, in Patagonia, stopped Chile claiming vast expanses of land from Argentina in 1865. One hundred and fifty three Welsh emigrants had boarded the sailing ship Mimosa and landed at Port Madryn there in the same year, trekking forty miles to found a settlement near the Chubut River. In 1885, some families crossed four hundred miles of desert to establish another settlement in Cwm Hyfryd at the foot of the Andes. Y *Wladfa* ('The Colony'), founded by the reformist preacher Michael D. Jones, was to be a radical colony where Non-conformism and the Welsh language were to dominate. Jones was deeply concerned about the Anglicisation of Wales - to preserve the heritage his people would have to move. He is regarded as the *founder of the modern Welsh nationalist movement.* The Argentine government was anxious to control this vast unpopulated territory, in which it was still in dispute with Chile, so had granted one-hundred square miles for the establishment of a Welsh state, protected by the military.

For ten years after 1865, this Welsh state was completely self-governing, with its own constitution written in Welsh. The immigrants owned their own land and farmed their own farms – there was to be no capitalist state with its hated landlord system. *Females were given the vote – the first democracy in the world to show egalitarianism, and this fifty years before British suffragettes started to try to change the British system. Boys and girls aged eighteen could vote, over a century*

*before they could in Britain. Voting was by secret ballot and all were eligible –
two more democratic innovations.* The language of Parliament and the law was
Welsh, and only Welsh school books were used.

Back home in Wales, the use of Welsh was forbidden in schools. 'Y Wladfa' was
'the first example of a practical democracy in South America', and the first example
of a practical, egalitarian, non-discriminatory democracy in the world. There were
massive problems in the settlement at first, until the native Teheulche Indians and
their chief taught the Welsh to catch guanaco and rhea, from the prairies. Also, the
Indians would exchange meat for bread, going from house to house saying *'poco
bara'* - Spanish for 'a little' and Welsh for 'bread'. This was a 'green colony'
whereby both sides gained. The Welsh taught them to break in horses, and they
showed the Welsh how to use bolas to catch animals. By controlling the waters in
the Camwy Valley, the settlers began to prosper. Unlike unsuccessful Spanish
settlers before them, they had very few problems with the native Indians, who still
empathise with the Welsh. When two Welsh settlers were killed in the Chubut River
uplands in 1883, Lewis Jones, the leader of the colony, refused to believe it. He told
the messenger *'But John, the Indians are our friends. They'd never kill a
Welshman.'* It transpired that an Argentine patrol had trespassed on Indian land,
and the Welsh were tragically mistaken for the Indians' Argentine enemies. The
bodies had their sexual organs stuffed into their mouths.

The colony grew to three thousand people by the time Welsh immigration halted
in 1912, *and had been **the first society in the world to give women the vote**.*
Interestingly, the Welsh code of law established by the settlers was the first legal
structure in Argentina, and its *'influence in modern-day Argentinian law can still
be seen'*. Three hundred and fifty people are currently learning Welsh in Patagonia,
helping the language to survive there, and plans are underway with teacher
exchanges to double this figure. However, only five thousand still speak the
language regularly, most of them in their later years. The success of the colony
attracted immigrants from Spain and Italy in the first decades of the twentieth
century, and the Welsh influence is declining steadily.

The Eisteddfod Fawr is still held in Chubut, financially supported by the
Argentinian government. It gives around a quarter of a million pounds a year to
support eisteddfodau in Gaiman, Trefelin and Trelew in recognition of the service
performed by the early settlers. Gaiman is the 'most' Welsh town in Patagonia,
with signs on the road approaching *'Visit Tŷ Llwyd, the Welsh Tea House'*, *'Stop
at Tŷ Gwyn'* and *'Come to Tŷ Te Caerdydd'*. In Tŷ Te Caerdydd, a costumed group
from the local school sometimes dances, and the traditional Welsh tea is served by
Welsh-speaking, Welsh-costumed staff. Bruce Chatwin's curious travelogue, *'In
Patagonia'*, gives a flavour of the place, with characters like Alun Powell, Caradog
Williams, Hubert Lloyd-Jones, Mrs Cledwyn Hughes and Gwynneth Morgan.

In the 1920's, President Fontana was the first President of Argentina to visit the
region. On horseback – there were no roads or trains – the official party could not
cross the river into Trelew. A tall, strong, red-haired youngster called Gough
offered to help, and lifted him up and carried him across the raging river, to the
town reception. A couple of years later the boy was in the ranks of conscripts in
the main square in Buenos Aires, waiting for the president to address all those
required to carry out their National Service in the military. The president stepped
out onto the square, surrounded by his generals and bodyguard, when a Welsh
voice rang out loud and clear *'Hey, I know you !'* Gough broke ranks and started

striding towards the president, waving his arms. A hundred guns trained on him before President Fontana broke into a smile and shouted to his guard that this big red-haired youth was indeed not dangerous, and known to him.

I am indebted to a friend, Rene Griffiths, for the above story. He has a ranch near Butch Cassidy's* old farm in Cholila, and is fairly certain that the gang carried out a maximum of two robberies in South America, simply because of the distances involved (at Rio Gallegos, and Villa Mercedes de San Luis in 1905). Butch and Sundance, under their aliases, were accepted into the community and Welshmen helped them get started in horse-breeding. Incidentally, Benetton has bought huge tracts of Patagonia to farm sheep, and Sylvester Stallone and other Hollywood stars have ranches there. Rene showed me a photograph of the lake on his land, where he wants people to come for fishing holidays. I idly asked how long it was - ten miles was the answer. There is a huge scale to these lands. I also asked if there were any problems with the cattle stock when he visited South Wales - he answered *only mountain lions*.

Jones was almost broken financially by the strain of supporting the settlement in Patagonia - he had envisaged it as the pattern for an independent Wales, and laboured, travelled, wrote, addressed meetings, collected money and lost his son there. He also fought against the oppression of Tory landlords - he hated servility, and beat the candidate of Sir Watkin Williams Wynn as representative on the county council for Llanuwchllyn in 1889. This was a tremendous victory for Welsh radicalism. He is buried at Yr Hen Gapel. His vision, hope and enthusiasm helped develop Welsh patriotic feeling into a vigorous, practical nationalism. The great poet Gwenallt, in 'The Historical Base of Welsh Nationalism', described Michael D. Jones as *'a saint, a great and large-hearted Congregationalist; the greatest Welshman of the 19th century; and the greatest nationalist after Owain Glyndŵr.'*

* Butch Cassidy and the Sundance Kid in Patagonia were alleged to have formed a gang comprised of Welshmen, and Cassidy's old farm is still ranched. Their best friend was a Welshman called Daniel Gibbons, who helped them purchase horses. A son of Michael D. Jones, a grocer called Llwyd ap Iwan, was said to have been killed by the gang in 1909, in Arroyo Pescado in Northern Patagonia. However, it appears to have been a couple of renegade drifters from the USA that carried out this act. It was this pair, named William Wilson and Robert Evans, that were also killed in the shoot-out with the Argentine military at Rio Pico, not the famous American outlaws. The Bolivia deaths were the fiction of a screen-writer. Butch, Sundance and Etta appear to have spent their time peaceably - they had no need of money at first - and were assisted by the Welsh to settle in.

Butch Cassidy bought 12,000 acres near Cholila in 1901, and the following year Sundance and his 'wife', Etta Place arrived. However, in 1907 one of their gauchos saw Butch's picture in a Buenos Aires paper, although he could not read, and told everyone around him that this was his 'boss'. A couple of days later, Sheriff Perry (of Pinkerton's Detective Agency), heard the story and made his way down to Patagonia from the capital. The gaucho had showed the outlaws the picture in the newspaper, and they escaped with Etta Place over the Andes into Chile, just two days before Pinkerton's detectives arrived on the scene. According to his sister, Butch died in the 1930's in Washington State, and Etta Place seems to have died in Denver some time after 1924.

TOM JONES June 7 1940 -
'JONES THE VOICE'

Thomas Jones Woodward ('Tom Jones'), from Trefforest near Pontypridd, signed the largest contract in British television in 1968, receiving an estimated nine million pounds for eighty-five shows spread over five years. 'It's Not Unusual' and 'What's New Pussycat' were probably his greatest hits.

The son of a miner, his unique and powerful voice ranges from baritone to tenor. He was forced to marry early, aged 16, and found himself a father at that early age. (His son Mark Woodward became Tom's manager on the death of Gornon Mills in 1986). After an assortment of dead-end jobs, including working in a paper-mill, labouring on building sites, cutting gloves and selling vacuum cleaners door-to-door, by 1963 he had his own group, Tommy Scott and the Senators. At this stage the songwriter Gordon Mills saw him and recalled *'The first few bars were all I needed to hear - they convinced me that here was a voice that could make him the greatest singer in the world.'* However, the overtly sexual nature of Jones' performances made a breakthrough difficult, and the band, now called Tom Jones and the Squires, struggled to make it in London, with Mills as manager. In 1964 there was a record contract with Decca, and Jones' second release, written by Mills, was *'It's Not Unusual'*. The record was considered *'too hot'* by the BBC, which banned it. Only when it reached the charts, reaching number one, by repeated plays on that great pirate radio station, Radio Caroline, did the BBC relent and play it.

Jones' career now took off. In 1965 he opened for the Rolling Stones, and toured with the Spencer Davis Group. He had a hit record in 1965 with the theme to the James Bond film *'Thunderball'*, and also with *'What's New Pussycat'*, but then his successes dried up for a year until he bought an album by another man of Welsh extraction, in a New York record store. Tucked away on Jerry Lee Lewis' album *'Country Songs for City Folks'* was the record which has since been identified with Jones and Wales, *'Green Green Grass of Home'*. A year later another hit arrived with *'I'll Never Fall in Love Again'*, and in 1967 Tom Jones was in Las Vegas. He recalled *'I went to see Frank Sinatra at Caesar's Palace. He had a reputation of not introducing anybody, so I sat there with my parents and my wife was with me and a bunch of friends. He said, "Ladies and Gentlemen, I would like to introduce you to the number one singer in the world who is in the audience tonight, and I'm his number one fan.*

Tom Jones

Tom Jones." Well that was it. I stood up and I mean it was fantastic, and then I went backstage to see him. My parents and everybody went into the bar area. I said I'll go back and say hello to Frank. I went back to see him and he said "Are we going to have a drink?" All of a sudden I'm walking with Frank Sinatra through Caesar's Palace'.

Then came a song which somehow or other has come into the singing at rugby matches in Wales, and sung by choirs and Welshmen everywhere. It was written for P.J. Proby, who turned it down and gave it to Jones' manager, Gordon Mills. 'Delilah' reached number 2 in the charts in 1968 and led to an appearance on the Ed Sullivan Show. Jones remembered with some hilarity that the lyrics had to be altered for America's prurient viewers at the time. The part about killing his faithless girlfriend was passed for singing, but *'At break of day when the man drove away I was waiting'* had to be altered to the nonsensical *'At break of day I was still cross the way I was waving.'* Otherwise viewers would know that a man and woman had spent the night together. Elvis used to warm up for his shows by singing *'Delilah'*, and developed a warm friendship with Tom. When *'The Green Green Grass of Home'* became a hit for Tom in 1966, Elvis would call around radio stations requesting the song to be played. In 1968, Tom Jones starred for four weeks in the Flamingo in Las Vegas, appeared at the Hollywood Bowl, and toured the world, including Australia. On his return he had a three-year contract for a TV series, *This is Tom Jones. Help Yourself* was another 1968 hit for him.

1969 saw six of Jones' previously released albums declared 'gold', and 1970 saw another gold album and a gold single, *'Without Love'*. In 1971, the album and single *'She's a Lady'* went 'gold', followed in 1972 by the gold album *'Live at Caesar's Palace'*. Over the next few years, many previous recordings would go 'platinum'. After a few years, *'The Boy From Nowhere'* reached number 2, and put Jones back in the popular frame again. He covered Prince's 'Kiss' with the Art of Noise in 1988. In 1992, he was the special guest at the Glastonbury Festival, and in the same year, really made it to the big time, appearing as himself on 'The Simpsons'. In 1994, the album *'The Lead and How to Swing It'* was a great success. The album 'Reload' in 1999 went to the top of the charts, and gave Tom several hit singles. He performs with Chrissie Hynde (The Pretenders), Iggy Pop, Cerys Matthews (Catatonia), Robbie Williams, Van Morrison, the Stereophonics, The Cardigans and Mousse T.

MERIWETHER LEWIS August 18 1774 - October 11 1809
'UNDOUBTEDLY THE GREATEST PATHFINDER AMERICA HAS EVER KNOWN'

Born to a Virginia planter family, Lewis briefly assumed the management of his late father's plantation before joining the state militia in 1794 to help put down Pennsylvania's Whiskey rebellion. Lewis stayed on as an officer in the regular army, serving on the frontier in Ohio and Tennessee, and becoming captain in 1800. He then became paymaster for the First Infantry Regiment. An old family friend and neighbour, Thomas Jefferson, now appointed his protegé in 1801 as his Private Secretary, with the idea that Lewis was the ideal man to led a transcontinental voyage of discovery. Later, Jefferson would write that Lewis was *'brave, prudent, habituated to the woods and familiar with Indian manners and character'.*

Thomas Jefferson had promoted three expeditions to attempt reach the Pacific, in 1783, 1787-8 and 1793. For this latter expedition, Lewis had volunteered. As

President in 1802, he was worried about Alexamder Mackenzie's reaching the Pacific from Canada for the North-West Company. Jefferson knew that the British could then easily move down the west coast of the sub-continent, and move inland from many points. Jefferson's Louisiana Purchase had been completed in 1803. After Congress approved of his plan to reach the Pacific in 1803, he appointed his secretary Meriwether Lewis to lead a 'Corps of Discovery'. The aim of the expedition was *'to make friends and allies of the far Western Indians while at the same time diverting valuable pelts from the rugged northern routes used by another nation (Britain)... and bringing the harvest down the Missouri to the Mississippi and thence eastward by a variety of routes.'* Lewis knew the Western frontier through military experience, and his family had been linked with the neighbouring Jeffersons in Albemarle County for at least three generations. Jefferson sent Lewis for geographical, cartographical and surveying lessons, after which Lewis appointed his Virginian friend William Clark as co-captain of the expedition. Lewis then spent several weeks in New Orleans talking to Indian traders with knowledge of the Missouri River.

The President had told Congress that he expected Lewis and Clark to discover a *'mountain of salt'*, 180 miles long and 45 miles wide (around the size of Wales!) They made contact with new Indian tribes, and found 'new species' such as prairie dogs, horned lizards, coyotes, bighorns, sage grouse, porcupines, jack rabbits, trumpeter swans, steelhead salmon trout, mule deer and pronghorn antelopes. One hundred and twenty two animals new to science were discovered, along with one hundred and seventy new types of plant.

At least two of the 12-strong Lewis and Clark party, Sergeant Ordway and Private Whitehouse, believed that they would find Prince Madoc's fair-skinned Indian descendants, still in possession of Welsh treasure. They met light-skinned Indians in The Flatlands of Montana and Dakota, speaking a strange *'gurgling kind of language spoken much through the throat'*, and Whitehouse was *'sure of it'* that they were the lost Welsh tribe. The party had begin its trail up the Missouri river in Spring 1804, following the Madogwys, or Mandan route, and by October reached the Mandan villages in what is now North Dakota. The Mandans gave them food, military protection, and information about the way ahead, and put up the party for the terrible Dakota winter in their earth lodges. They were then assisted by Sacagawea, the Shoshone wife of a French-Canadian trapper. Not until 6 months later, in April 1805, did the party move out up the Missouri again. By late September, the small party was taken in by the Nez Perces for shelter in September, before reaching the Pacific in November.

Lewis wrote to Jefferson via a trapper to Cohokia, *'In obedience to your orders we have penetrated the continent of North America to the Pacific Ocean, and sufficiently explored the interior of the country to affirm with confidence that we have discovered the most practicable route which does exist across the continent by means of the navigable branches of the Missouri and Columbia Rivers.'* He wrote that a party must travel by boat 2,575 miles up the Missouri to the Great Falls of Missouri, then portage (carry the boats and equipment) 18 miles across land, travel 200 more river miles, and then cross the Bitterroots (*'tremendous mountains which for 60 miles are covered with eternal snow'*). Finally, the boats could be used again for 640 miles down the Snake, Clearwater and Columbia rivers to the Pacific Ocean. Once Jefferson knew this, he pushed US negotiations and claims of sovereignty over the western lands bordering the Louisiana Purchase.

Meriwether Lewis

Over the two years, four months and ten days Lewis took to reach the Pacific Coast and return, the expedition encountered over forty Indian tribes, including the Oto, Missouri Osage, Yankton Sioux, Omaha, Teton Sioux, Arikaras, Mandans, Hidatsas, Flatheads, Nez Pierce, Shoshoni, Warapams, Chinooks, Clatsops, Walla Walla, Crow, and the tribe feared most by all the other Indians, the Blackfeet. At Lemhi Pass in Idaho, Lewis had become *the first white man to cross the Continental Divide,* and he named the Missouri River canyon in Montana, *'The Gates of the Mountains'.* Americans can now follow his trail, stopping at isolated campsites.

Lewis had followed the Missouri to its source, crossed the unknown Rockies, and followed the Columbia River to Pacific Ocean, returning overland to St Louis from 1804-1806. He had designed a collapsible canoe, 'The Experiment', to transport equipment around rapids. According to his biographer, S.E. Ambrose, in 'Undaunted Courage', Meriwether Lewis was **'the first great American celebrity after the Revolutionary War - a superstar in today's terms.'**

Thomas Jefferson rewarded Lewis with the governorship of the huge new territories acquired by the Louisiana Purchase, but it looks like he acquired syphilis, drank to obsession, drifted into debt and committed suicide in Tennessee in 1809, aged just 35. Controversy now rages as to whether he was murdered, as his family believed, and experts from George Washington University wish to dig up his bones. The main account of his death comes from an innkeeper, Mrs Grinder, who recounts hearing two shots, then finding Lewis with bullet wounds in his head and chest, using a razor, *'busily engaged in cutting himself from head to foot'.* Robbery by the innkeeper may be a motive, and pathologists wish to look at the angle of bullet entry into his bones to assess whether it was murder.

For those interested in conspiracy theory, Lewis had stopped at the log cabin known as Grinder's Stand, in the Tennessee Mountains, on his way to Washington, where he hoped to clear up debts to the War Department, incurred while serving as America's first governor of the vast Louisiana Territories, which cut a swathe across the middle of modern America (see Jefferson). The Territorial Secretary, Frederick Bates, was jealous of Lewis, and raised a problem over the expenses incurred in sending the Mandan Chief Sheheke home. The new Madison Administration refused to honour a $500 voucher, and the Secretary of War sarcastically wrote to Lewis that his 'friend' Jefferson was no longer in office. According to the website salon.com, after sorting out the financial problem, *'then he planned to deliver the priceless journals of his great expedition, which had come to a triumphant conclusion three years earlier, to his Philadelphia publishers.'* Except for two servants, who were trailing behind with the heavy trunks, and Major James Neely, who was away rounding up stray horses, Lewis was travelling alone, and booked into the inn by himself. Mrs Grinder's husband was away at the time. Thus the only account we have is Mrs Grinder's, who changed her story several times. Sometimes she said that she was alone, and other times that her family were witnesses. About 3 in the morning, she was woken up by the sound of a gun shot from the guest cabin. Then there was a heavy thud, with the words *'Oh Lord'* shouted. A few minutes later, Lewis called *'Oh Madam! Give me some water and heal my wounds!'.*

Mrs Grinder said in one version that she was alone and feared to enter his room, although he spent the night begging for water and assistance. At dawn, Mrs Grinder and her servants entered Lewis's cabin, and he was lying across the bed. Lewis showed them where the bullet had entered his body, but he also had a gunshot wound in his head. Lewis asked them to put him out of his misery, offering his money to them, but they sat down for a few hours and watched him die. One of Mrs Grinder's stories is that he died on the bed, and another that he crawled outside to die. The forensic scientist James Starrs believes that there is no way that Clark could have shot himself in the head and chest, and then razored himself from head to foot. And importantly, William Clark, his oldest friend, knew that as an experienced soldier, Lewis would have killed himself quickly and cleanly. A neighbour of the Grinders told Clark that the entry point for the bullet wounds were from Lewis's back, which he saw when he helped lift him into a coffin. Some suspicion falls on Major Neely as well as Mrs Grinder (or her allegedly absent husband, who had been seen nearby). Neely is indicted in the above website as taking Lewis's money and possessions - his wallet was never found, and Lewis's half-brother had to regain his horse and rifle from Neely.

SAUNDERS LEWIS 1893 - 1985
PATRIOT, INTELLECTUAL, ACTIVIST, FOUNDER OF PLAID CYMRU, 'THE GREATEST FIGURE IN WELSH LITERATURE IN THE 20TH CENTURY'

John Saunders Lewis was brought up in the strong Welsh community of the Wirral, on the west bank of Liverpool's Mersey River. He fought alongside Irishmen in the First World War, which activated his sense of nationalism, being rightly convinced that the survival of the language was the key to the survival of the nation. His studies at Liverpool University had been interrupted by the war, where he served as an officer with the South Wales Borderers in France, Italy and Greece. He returned to take a first in English, before undertaking a dissertation upon English influences upon classical Welsh poetry. In 1922, he was a lecturer in Swansea University's Department of Welsh.

During the National Eisteddfod in Pwlleli in 1925, representatives from 'Y Mudiad Cymreig' ('The Welsh Movement') and 'Byddin Ymreolwyr Cymru' ('The Army of the Welsh Home Rulers') met to join and form 'Plaid Cymru' ('The Welsh National Party'). Saunders Lewis was a founder and in 1926 its President.

In 1936, with two friends, he set fire to a hangar at the RAF bombing range of Penberth, at Penrhos on the Llyn Peninsula. Little damage was caused, and the three turned themselves into police the next day for their token act. The Welsh jury in Carmarthen **acquitted** the three - Saunders Lewis had said in court *'What I was teaching the young people of Wales in the halls of the university was not a dead literature, something chiefly of interest to antiquarians, but a living literature of the Welsh people. This literature is therefore able to make demands of me as a man as* *well as a teacher.'* **The English authorities could not accept the verdict of a Welsh jury, and had the three retried in London, giving them nine months in prison.**

The Welsh former Prime Minister, David Lloyd-George, railed against the injustice of it all - *'They yield when faced by Hitler and Mussolini, but they attack the smallest country in the kingdom which they misgovern. This is a cowardly way of showing their strength through violence......This is the first government that has tried to put **Wales on trial at the Old Bailey**.......I should like to be there, and I should like to be 40 years younger.'* Saunders Lewis was asked if he wanted to see a bloody revolution, and answered *'So long as it is **Welsh blood and not English blood**.'* He died in 1985, a poet-philosopher-nationalist-pacifist, still without much honour in his own land - the majority of Welsh youngsters have never heard of the man, who did more than anyone since Bishop William Morgan to keep the Welsh language alive. Lewis said *'to acquiesce in the death of a language which was the heritage of our forefathers for 1,500 years, is to despise man. Woe betide the society that despises man.'* Saunders Lewis would have hated the fields of holiday home caravans on the Llŷn Peninsula, and the colonisation in progress at present. From the dock at his trial in Caernarfon he declaimed *'It is plain historical fact that, from the 5th century on, Llŷn has been Welsh, of the Welsh, and that as long as Llŷn remained un-Anglicised, Welsh life and culture were secure. If once the forces of Anglicisation are securely established behind as well as in front of the mountains of Snowdonia, the day when the Welsh language will be crushed between the iron jaws of these pincers cannot long be delayed. For Wales the preservation of the Llŷn peninsula from this Anglicisation is a matter of life or death.'*

Saunders Lewis was the major figure of both Welsh-language politics and literature of the 20th century, who in Plaid Cymru set out to create a culturalist nationalist party. He could not see the possibility of creating a Welsh nation-state, unlike Gwynfor Evans (q.v.), but aimed to preserve Welsh language and tradition. He wanted a rural economy rather than large-scale capitalism and socialism, with small-scale private ownership, redistribution of wealth, and deindustrialisation. He saw Wales as part of a European federation of peoples, not a Europe of nation-states. He was forced to resign as Plaid Cymru president in 1939.

Saunders Lewis

After Lewis' release from prison and his sacking from his lectureship, he supported himself by farming, occasional teaching, and journalism. Saunders Lewis had been shamefully blacklisted by the University of Wales for his nationalism - not until 1952 was he accepted back into acadaemia, at Cardiff University's Department of Welsh. Constantly writing in Welsh, he retired to his home in Penarth in 1957, to devote himself full-time to writing. His astonishing output is listed in detail in *'The New Companion to the Literature of Wales'*, edited by Meic Stephens. Apart from his

contributions to political journalism and literary criticism, the 'Companion' notes:
'The writings of Saunders Lewis are informed by a love of Wales seen in the context of European Catholic Christendom. He had a profound knowledge of Latin, French and Italian literature as well as English and Welsh...His own most important contribution to Welsh literature was as a dramatist. Apart from a handful of comedies in which Welsh institutions are gently but tellingly satirised, his plays explore such weighty and often sombre themes as the imperatives of honour, the responsibilities of leadership, the nature of politics and the conflict between "eros" and "agape"... Apart from "Siwan" (1956), which he described as a poem, Saunders Lewis published no more than 53 poems in all but some of them are undoubtedly among the finest Welsh poems of the 20th century. They deal, in a variety of metres both traditional and innovatory, with the predicament of Wales, the glory of nature, and the call of God.'

A partial translation (by Gwyn Thomas) of Lewis's bleak 'Y Dilyw' of 1939 reads:

'The tramway climbs from Merthyr to Dowlais,
Slime of a snail on a heap of slag;
Here once was Wales, and now derelict
Cinemas and rain on the barren tips;
The pawnbrokers have closed their doors,
The pegging clerks are the gentry of this waste;
All flesh had corrupted his way upon the earth.'

In 1979, the Welsh people voted against a National Assembly. A 1996 poll gave 2:1 opposing the Assembly. In 1997 the referendum for a Welsh Assembly was passed by the tiniest minority, mainly because Welsh Nationalists threw everything into supporting the proposal - they see it as a half-way house to full devolution and independence for Wales. That other Tory-free zone, Scotland, also voted for limited independence, but have their own Parliament, with far greater powers than the Welsh Assembly. Without Saunders Lewis, even this small measure of independence from London would not have been achieved.

In 1962, Lewis made his infamous radio speech, *'Tynged yr Iaith'*, forecasting the death of the Welsh language by 2000. This stimulated the formation of Cymdeithas yr Iaith Gymraeg. As much as Gwynfor Evans, Lewis was responsible for the Welsh Language Bill by his incessant work in stemming the twin inflows of ignorance and apathy. Twice nominated for the Nobel Prize for Literature, during his lifetime and after his death in 1985, the literary talents of this poet, dramatist, literary historian and critic have been compared to those of T.S. Eliot and W.B. Yeats.

Idris Davis (q.v.) wrote of Lewis:
'Though some may cavil at his creed
And others mock his Celtic ire,
No Welshman loyal to his breed
Forgets this prophet dares the fire,
And roused his land by word and deed
Against Philistia and her mire.'

And the late, and similarly-minded R.S. Thomas wrote:
'And he dared them;
Dared them to grow old and bitter

As he. He kept his pen clean
By burying it in their fat
Flesh. He was ascetic and Wales
His diet. He lived off the harsh fare
Of her troubles, worn yet heady
At moments with the poet's wine.

A recluse, then; himself
His hermitage? Uninhabited
He moved among us; would have led
To rebellion. Small as he was
He towered, the trigger of his mind
Cocked, ready to let fly with his scorn.'

OWAIN LLAWGOCH 1330? - August 31 1378
YVAIN DE GALLES, THE LAST OF THE LINE OF GWYNEDD, 'THE LAST HEIR OF THE TRUE PRINCE OF WALES', FREEBOOTER, ADMIRAL, GENERAL, CHEVALIER OF FRANCE

Owain ap Thomas ap Rhodri was known in Wales as Owain Lawgoch (Llaw Goch = Red Hand), and on the continent as Yvain de Galles. (He was nick-named 'red hand' because of his presence on battlefields across Europe). Owain was the grandson of Llywelyn II's brother, *and the sole heir of the Princes of Gwynedd.* Born about 1330 on his father's estate at Tatsfield in Surrey, in 1350 he bound himself to the service to the King of France, and became his protegé. He constantly proclaimed himself the true heir of Aberffraw (the court on Anglesey of the Princes of Gwynedd), and only de Guesclin features more highly in French literature as an enemy of the English at this time. Described by Edward Owen as *'possibly the greatest military genius that Wales has produced',* he crossed to England in 1365 to claim his inheritance, but was forced to return to France, fearing for his life.

Many Welshmen followed him, including Ieuan Wyn, who took over Owain's company of soldiers after his death. Owain still features in the folk literature of Britanny, France, Switzerland, Lombardy and the Channel Islands. With his father executed by the King of England, 'Owen of Wales' had been brought up at the court of King Philip VI of France, and was one of the most noted warriors of the fourteenth century. Described as *'high-spirited, haughty, bold and bellicose'* (Barbara Tuchman, 'A Distant Mirror'), he had fought heroically against the English at Poitiers in 1356 (somehow surviving against all the odds). Owain campaigned in the Lombard Wars of the 1360's, for and against the Dukes of Bar in Lorraine, and with Bertrand du Guesclin in the campaigns of the 1370's. In 1366, he had led the Compagnons de Galles (Company of Welshmen) to fight Pedro the Cruel in Spain.

An Anglesey man, Gruffydd Sais was executed, and his lands confiscated by the crown in 1369 for contacting *'Owain Lawgoch, enemy and traitor',* and in the same year Charles V gave Owain a fleet to sail to Wales from Harfleur. It was sadly repulsed by storms. The French King Charles now gave Owain 300,000 francs, another fleet and 4000 men to win back his land. Owain proclaimed that he owned

Wales '*through the power of my succession, through my lineage, and through my rights as the descendant of my forefathers, the kings of that country*'.

Taking Guernsey from the English, Owain captured the legendary Captal de Buch, the Black Prince's comrade, hero of Poitiers and one of England's greatest soldiers. Owain had taken a Franco-Castilian landing party to The Channel Islands and overpowered him at night. Such was the Captal's reputation that King Charles V kept him in prison in the Temple in Paris without the privilege of ransom. Both King Edward of England and delegations of French nobles repeatedly asked Charles to ransom him if he promised not to take up arms against France, but the King refused and the noble Captal sank into depression. He refused food and drink and died in 1376.

Owain prepared to invade Wales after his seizure of Guernsey, but sadly a message came from the French king to help the Spanish attack the English-occupied La Rochelle in 1372. Owain responded and fought again against the English (who had killed both his great-uncles Llywelyn and Dafydd, as well as his father). Owain never had another chance to return to Wales. The signed treaty of Paris between Owain Llawgoch and King Charles V of France, of May 10th, 1372, still survives. It begins '*Owain of Wales, to all those to whom these letters shall come, greetings. The kings of England in past times having treacherously and covetously, tortuously and without cause and by deliberate treasons, slain or caused to be slain my ancestors, kings of Wales, and others of them have put out of their country, and that country have by force and power appropriated and have submitted its people to divers servitude, the which country should be mine by right of succession, by kindred, by heritage, and by right of descent from my ancestors the kings of that country, and in order to obtain help and succour that country which is my heritage, I have visited several Christian kings.......*'

In 1375, Owain took part in the successful siege of Saveur-le-Comte in Normandy, where for the first time cannon had been used really successfully to break the English defences. He then took a contract from the great Baron Enguerrand de Coucy, Count of Soissons and Bedford to lead four hundred men at a fee of four hundred francs per month, (with one hundred francs per month going to his assistant, Owain ap Rhys). Any town or fortress taken was to be yielded to De Coucy. Again, the treaty contract survives, dated October 14th, 1375.

The capture of Duke Leopold of Austria was to be worth 10,000 francs to Owain, who attracted 100 Teutonic knights from Prussia to his banner. With The Treaty of Bruges, English knights also came to offer their services under the leadership of Owain. Probably around 10,000 soldiers eventually formed an army for De Coucy and Owain. The knights wore pointed helmets and cowl-like hoods on heavy cloaks, and their hoods called '*gugler*' (from the Swiss-German for cowl or point) gave their names to the 'The Gugler War'.

The companies making up the army plundered Alsace, and took ransom of 3000 florins not to attack Strasbourg as Leopold retreated, ordering the destruction of all resources in his wake. He withdrew across the Rhine, relying on the Swiss to stave off the attack, although the Swiss hated the Hapsburgs almost as much as they hated the Guglers. The invaders were allowed entrance to Basle, but their forces became increasingly scattered as they sought loot in the wake of Leopold's depredations. Near Lucerne, a company of Guglers was surrounded by the Swiss and routed. On Christmas night a company of Bretons was ambushed by citizens of Berne, city of the emblem of the bear. On the next night, the Swiss attacked the

Abbey of Fraubrunnen, where Owain was quartered, setting fire to the Abbey and slaughtering the sleeping *'English'*. Owain swung his sword *'with savage rage'* but was forced to flee, leaving 800 Guglers dead at the Abbey.

Ballads tell of how the Bernese fought *'40,000 lances with their pointed hats'*, how *'Duke Yfo (Owain) of Wales came with his golden helm'* and how when Duke Yfo came to Fraubrunnen, *"The Bear roared 'You shall not escape me ! I will slay, stab and burn you !' In England and France the widows all cried 'Alas and woe!' Against Berne no-one shall march evermore !"*

The following details are fully recounted in 'Froissart's Chronicles'. In 1378, Owain was conducting the siege of the castle of Mortagne-sur-Gironde* near the Atlantic coast. There were chains across the river here, protecting the English-held Bordeaux from sea attacks by the French. As usual, early in the morning, he sat on a tree stump, having his hair combed by a new squire, while he surveyed the scene of siege. His new Scots manservant, James Lambe, had been taken into service as he had brought news of *'how all the country of Wales would gladly have him to be their lord'*. But with no-one around, Lambe stabbed Owain in the back with a short spear, and escaped to Mortagne - the English king had paid £20** for the assassination of the person with the greatest claim to the Principality of Wales, the last of the line of Rhodri Fawr. Norman and Angevin policy had always been to kill Welsh male heirs and put females of the lineage into remote English monasteries, as we can see in the case of Llywelyn the Last (Llywelyn Olaf). It seems that Owain was buried at the chapel of St Leger, his possible headquarters during the siege. Owain's men swore to continue the siege and avenge their lord, but were surrounded by an English relieving army under Neville. In respect to their valour, the survivors of Owain's company were given a safe-conduct to leave Mortagne, and rejoined the main French forces. The details of the siege of Mortagne and of Owain's assassination are vividly illustrated in Froissart's Chronicles.

Owain Lawgoch was only second in valour to Bertrand du Guesclin in Europe through these years, a mercenary operating away from home compared to a national hero. His is an amazing story, yet he is unknown to ninety-nine per cent of Welshmen, only mentioned as an aside in specialist text-books. His importance to King Edward III of England is shown in a payment of 100 francs and in the Issue Roll of the Exchequer dated December 4, 1378: *'To John Lamb, an esquire from Scotland, because he lately killed Owynn de Gales, a rebel and enemy of the King in France............... By writ of privy seal, &c., £20.'* However, with Owain Lawgoch's death, the prior claim to the heritage of Llywelyn the Great and Llewelyn the Last passed on eventually to another Owain, Glyndŵr, another *'Mab Darogan' ('Son of Prophecy')* of the Welsh bards. When Owain Glyndŵr, in 1404, requested French help against England, he reinforced his case by referring to Owain Lawgoch's great service to the French crown.

*Owain was supposed to have been buried at Mortagne, but there are persistent legends concerning his burial at Llandybie church. He is connected with a legend at Llyn Llech Owain, a lake near Llandybie, and is also said to lie with his men in a cave under the marvellous Carreg Cennen Castle near Llandybie. He will be awoken by a bell to save Wales. There is a possibility that Ieuan ap Wynn, his second-in-command at Mortagne, returned to Wales with Owain's heart for burial. Ieuan took over the war-troop and changed his heraldic coat-of-arms to Owain's, adding a *'bend gules'*. Members of Owain's company were still serving in France until 1396, and French and Breton troops arrived in Wales in 1402 to fight for Owain Glyndŵr. It may be that Ieuan or other veterans came with them, and Owain Glyndŵr had adopted Llawgoch's heraldic badge as Prince of Wales. In early September, 1378, Ieuan Wyn and Llawgoch's men met up with the main French forces at Saintes, and had taken Owain's body with them. On the way, at Cozes, they again buried his body, but kept his heart preserved in a small casket. The French-Breton force that supported Glyndŵr attacked Llandovery and Dynefwr Castles, burned Llandeilo and took Dryslwyn Castle, before besieging Carreg Cennen. It may be that the casket-bearer was wounded, or that Llandybie was a convenient holy site for burying Llawgoch's heart in his homeland.

" " As well as the £20 blood money, there were expenses to be paid. A letter from Sir John Neville, Governor of Aquitaine, to Richard Rotour, Constable of Bordeaux noted the payments made to Lambe's assassination squad, three of whom were killed by Owain's men while Lambe effected his escape. Part of the letter is translated as... *'they, in the country of the French, and, especially for the great and perilous adventure in which they risked life and limb to bring about the death of Owain of Wales, traitor and enemy to the King our said Lord. By which deed they diminished the evils and destruction wrought on the lands of the subjects of the King our Lord.... Owing to the great profit and service they have rendered in this recent foray to Mortagne....The said John Lamb and his companions have as outgoings the sum of 522 livres and 10 sous of current money, in payment for coats, helmets, hauberks, arm harness, gauntlets and many different harnesses and clothes purchased in the town of Bordeaux, to arm and array themselves.'* There is also the receipt and letter signed by John Lamb.

FOOTNOTES:

1. Wales Books (Glyndŵr Publishing) has commissioned a book upon Llawgoch - *'The History of a Legend'*. Anyone with information upon possible descendants of Llawgoch in France, or upon his life can contact the Secretary, Cymdeithas Yvain de Galles, 2 Lon Slwch, Aberhonddu, Powys LD3 7RL with information.

2. The author has found an *'Edouart d'Yvain'* mentioned as a minor warlord in France towards the end of Owain's life - could it be his son, and the line of Gwynedd still be extant in France? The Llawgoch society has also uncovered the intriguing information that Owain probably married a French woman, the 'Lady Elinore'. Marie Trevelyan, the early 19th century historian from Llanilltud Fawr, tells us that *'there were several Welsh military leaders at this time, and these included Edouart Yvain, probably a son of the redoubtable Yvain de Galles; Jehan Wyn, Yvain Greffin, and Gay Robin ap Ledin, Welsh deserters from the armies of Edward III appear as renowned captains of cosmopolitan banditti and freebooters, one of whom was the famous and much dreaded Chevlier Rufin'*. If anyone can trace Edourt Yvain, please contact the Yvain de Galles (Owain Llawgoch) Society at the above address. It appears that Jehan Wyn was Ieuan Wyn, Owain's second-in-command. Gay Robin ap Ledin is probably Robin ap Bleddin who was in a company billeted at St Jean d'Angely in May 1392. The 'dreaded Chevalier Rufin' must be one of the several persons called Gruffydd (often anglicised to Griffin) who appear in muster lists of the time, possibly Gruffyd ap Madog, who was with a company at St Jean d'Angely in April 1396.

3. On Sunday 31stAugust 2003, at Mortagne-sur-Mer, near Bordeaux, the above Society will be unveiling a memorial to Owain, Yvain de Galles, at Mortagne-sur-Gironde. The site is just within what was the main land gate of the old castle, so Owain will have symbolically achieved his objective. The monument will be a gift of the people of Wales to the people of

Mortgagne and France, and will be insured and maintained by the local council. The area surrounding will be planted with daffodils. Welsh people are invited to contribute and attend this important occasion, the 625th anniversary of the assassination of our last Prince of Wales. (There are many camp and mobile-home sites along this stretch of coast-line, and this author is combining his attendance with a family holiday in the area. Eurosites, Haven and Eurocamp all offer accommodation nearby). A donation of £1 will ensure that a daffodil bulb is planted, and the contributor's name will be recorded in perpetuity in a commemorative book to be given to the citizens of Mortagne. The society is looking to raise a fund of £20,000 for the monument, and would welcome assistance in fund-raising, and in gaining new members for this terrific cause.

DAVID LLOYD GEORGE   January 17 1863 - March 26 1945
ONE OF THE GREATEST STATESMEN OF THE 20TH CENTURY, 'THE MAN WHO WON THE WAR', 'THE GREATEST PRIME MINISTER SINCE PITT'

The son of William George of Pembrokeshire and Elizabeth Lloyd, his schoolmaster father died a year after David's birth in Manchester, and the family returned to Wales to live with Richard Lloyd, David's uncle at Llanstumdwy, Caernarfonshire. Richard Lloyd was a Welsh-speaking Nonconformist shoemaker, deeply resenting English dominance over Wales, and had a lasting influence on his nephew. David did well at school, passed the Law Society examinations, and in 1879 was articled to a firm of solicitors in Porthmadoc in 8179, before setting up his own law practice in Criccieth. In 1888 he married Margaret Owen, and was an active member of the Disciples of Christ Chapel in Criccieth. His reputation grew as a fiery orator in Welsh and English in church, and as a man who was willing to defend people against those in authority. Joining the local Liberal Party, David became an alderman on Caernarfonshire County Council. A great supporter of Land Reform, he took part in demonstrations against church tithes.

From 1890-96, Lloyd George had been leader of the Welsh Home Rule Campaign, but the failure of the Cymru Fudd movement was assured in 1896, when businessmen from Cardiff and Newport blocked the Liberal party's support for Welsh self-government. Lloyd George now turned his attentions from Welsh affairs to *'the country as a whole'*.

In 1890, Lloyd George had been selected as the candidate for the Conservative parliamentary seat of Caernarfon Borough. He fought on a platform of religious equality in Wales, land reform, graduated taxation, free trade and a local veto in granting licences on alcohol. He won by just 18 votes, and at 27 became the youngest member of the House of Commons. His great powers of oratory brought him to the attention of Liberal leaders in the House, but because of his radicalism, and his opposition to the Boer War, they felt he would lose his seat in the 1900 election. However, Lloyd George won comfortably - he was seen as the most important figure in Parliament defending Welsh rights. He also incurred the displeasure of the Liberal bigwigs in supporting the 1902 Education Act, in particular for assisting John Clifford's National Passive Resistance Committee. Over 170 Nonconformists had been sent to prison for refusing to pay their school taxes - Lloyd George advocated free schooling for all.

The Liberal Party had surged into power in Wales with its opposition to landlords and anti-establishment policies, and by the turn of the 20th century was virtually in total control. In the 1906 election, the Liberal Henry Campbell-Bannerman became the new Prime Minister, appointing the capable Lloyd George as President of the Board of Trade. David impressed him so much, that in 1908 he was promoted to become Chancellor of the Exchequer. Previously as Minister for the Board of Trade (1905-1908) he was responsible for the passing of three important acts involving merchant shipping, the production census and patents. *He introduced* Old Age Pensions *(1908) and National Health Insurance (1911)* when Chancellor of the Exchequer from 1908-1915. A fierce opponent of the Poor Law, the Chancellor wanted to *'lift the shadow of the workhouse from the homes of the poor.'* The rejection of his budget by The House of Lords, with its Conservative majority, in 1909-1910 led to *Parliamentary reform and a lessening of the nobility's power.* Lloyd George toured the country, making speeches in working-class areas, against the 'nobles with no nobility' who were using their privileged position to hurt the poor and stop old age pensions. He called it a *'war budget. It is for raising money to wage implacable warfare against poverty and squalidness.'* Because of the ensuing unpopularity of the House of Lords*, the Liberal government managed to cut its powers in the 1911 Parliament Act. The 1911 National Insurance Act gave the British working classes the first contributory system of insurance against illness and unemployment. All wage-earners between 16 and 70 had to join the health scheme, the worker paying 4d a week, the employer 3d and the state 2d. In return there was free medical attention and medicine, and workers were guaranteed 7 shillings a week for 15 weeks in any one year, if they were unemployed. The Conservative opposition and the House of Lords declaimed Lloyd George as a *'socialist'.* His measures formed the basis of the Welfare State that until recently gave a reasonable safety-net to the disadvantaged in Britain.

A radical Welsh nationalist and a pacifist, he had compared the Boers, in their fight against the Empire, to the Welsh. He only moved from pacifism with the invasion of Belgium by Germany in 1914. Even so, with three other senior members of the Government, he had written to the Prime Minister, Herbert Asquith, that he intended to resign rather than be party to a war declaration. The other three resigned, but Asquith managed to convince Lloyd George to stay on, as the country needed him. In August 1914, the South Wales Miners' Federation proposed an international miners' strike to *stop the outbreak of war,* and there continued to be an anti-war movement in the South Wales mining areas. A massive increase in food prices, coupled with record profits for coal-owners, caused a demand for a new wage agreement in 1915 which was refused, so the South Wales miners went on strike. They were opposed by the Government, coal-owners, Great Britain Miners' Federation and the national newspapers, and the government threatened to imprison any

David Lloyd George

strikers. However, the strike was solid. The then Minister of Munitions, David Lloyd George, intervened and settled the strike, acceding to most of the demands of the South Wales Miners' Federation.

As Minister of War from 1915-1916, Lloyd George was put in charge of the total war effort, and found it difficult to control the poor and wasteful tactics of his generals of the Western Front. Lloyd George argued strongly with the dinosaur Douglas Haig, commander in chief of the BEF, and with General Robertson, chief of the imperial general staff, about their using men as cannon-fodder. When at last Lloyd George's proposal was accepted, that the French and British forces fight under one joint commander, the war turned decisively the allies' way. However, he was more successful with the navy, when he with great difficulty persuaded them to use the convoy system to ensure adequate imports of food and military supplies. The Coalition Government was impressed by Lloyd George's capabilities and began to question Asquith's leadership in these days of crisis. In December 1916, Lloyd George agreed to collaborate with the Conservatives to remove Asquith, a decision which split the Liberal Party. Lloyd George was now Prime Minister, and his Coalition Party won the 1918 General Election, Asquith losing his seat. In 1916, Lloyd-George was welcomed into No. 10 Downing Steet by Maurice Hankey, later War Cabinet Secretary. '*I congratulated him*' said Lord Hankey later, and he replied slowly '*You are shaking hands with the most miserable man on earth.*' However, Lloyd George was now virtually a prisoner of the Conservative party after the war, and although he promised progressive reforms in education, housing, health and transport, he was unable to effect them. He was defeated in the 1922 election. For the rest of his career he was a campaigner, but with no power base - the Tories did not want change, and the Liberals distrusted him as the man who broke up their party. Just two months before his death, he received the title Earl Lloyd-George of Dwyfor.

By his forceful policy he was, as Adolf Hitler later said, '**the man who won the war**'. One of the 'Big Three' at the peace negotiations, he was shown to be a brilliant diplomat. Lloyd George mediated a settlement with Germany mid-way between Woodrow Wilson, and the more punitive actions desired by Clemenceau, as France had lost so much in the Great War. His defeat in 1922 was mainly due to his ceding of 'The Irish Free State' - *the modern day Eire was given its independence by him* against strong opposition by the Conservatives in his government. Lloyd George is also notable in world history for approving the Balfour Declaration, promising the Jews a national state in Palestine. **So Wales has had a world statesman who has changed the face of the twentieth century.**

*In an editorial for '*Udgorn*' in 1888, Lloyd George wrote of the House of Lords: *This institution is at odds with the spirit of the age... the true basis of any government is the voice of the people... the House of Lords has won for itself a reputation as the arch enemy of every reform... a man of the weakest understanding or with the most tarnished of characters may sit in this noble house... it is readily conceded even by Tories that the House of Lords should be reformed, however total abolition of this place is the only reform worth fighting for... to include the fall of this God of oppression among the victories of liberty would give reason to rejoicing for generations to come.'*

FOOTNOTE:
The only other 'great' British Prime Minister of the 20th century was a war-leader but no reformer, Winston Churchill. On Lloyd George's death in 1945, Churchill told the Commons: *He was the greatest Welshman which that unconquerable race has produced since the age of the Tudors. Much of his work abides, some of it will grow greatly in the future, and those who come after us will find the pillars of his life's toil upstanding, massive and indestructible.'* A statue is planned for Lloyd George, next to Churchill's, in Parliament Square.

LLYWELYN AP IORWERTH AB OWAIN GWYNEDD
1173 - April 11 1240
LLYWELYN FAWR – LLYWELYN THE GREAT

Dolbadarn Castle was built by Llywelyn's father, Iorwerth, around 1170, and it was there (or Nant Conwy) that this last true Prince of Wales was born in 1173. He never claimed the title, but was content to be overlord of Wales, being recognised as Prince of Gwynedd and Lord of Snowdon. His grandfather was the great Owain Gwynedd.

Professor T. Tout has called Llywelyn *'certainly the greatest of the native rulers of Wales.........If other Welsh kings were equally warlike, the son of Iorwerth was certainly the most politic of them.......While never forgetting his position as champion of the Welsh race, he used with consummate skill the differences and rivalries of the English........Under him the Welsh race, tongue and traditions began a new lease of life.'*

Llywelyn gained possession of part of Gwynedd in 1194, when Richard I, The Lionheart, was King of England. Aged just 22, Llywelyn beat his uncle Dafydd at the battle of Aberconwy. On the death of his cousin Gruffydd in 1200,

Dolbadarn Castle, the site of Llywelyn's birth
(photograph courtesy of WTB)

Llywelyn gained the rest of Gwynedd. Llywelyn wished to push out from his Gwynedd power base, to take over the kingdoms of Deheubarth (after the death of The Lord Rhys) and Powys. To help his plans, Llywelyn first allied with King John, who became King in 1199, and he married John's daughter, Joan in 1205. Equally, John wished to limit the ambitious Gwenwynwyn of Powys. Powys was traditionally the weakest of the three major princedoms of Gwynedd, Deheubarth and Powys, squeezed between the other Welsh houses and the English Marcher Barons. Llywelyn over-ran Powys while King John captured Gwenwynwyn at Shrewsbury. Llywelyn also pushed Gwenwynwyn's ally, Maelgwyn, out of Northern Ceredigion. Llywelyn then took the Marcher Earl of Chester's castles at Deganwy, Rhuddlan, Holywell and Mold. From this position of control of North

Wales, Llywelyn ap Iorwerth could then assist John on his invasion of Scotland in 1209.

However, by 1210, King John saw Llywelyn as an over-powerful enemy, and with Gwenwynwyn and Maelgwn invaded Wales. Llywelyn, deserted by other Welsh nobles, fell back towards his mountain base of Gwynedd, trying a scorched earth policy to starve John's army. However, Llywelyn eventually was forced to sign an ignominious peace treaty that just left him Gwynedd. The lesser Welsh rulers had preferred an absentee overlord rather than a native Welsh ruler, but the situation changed when they saw King John build castles near Aberystwyth, near Conwy and in Powys.

This threat of subjugation reunited the Welsh under Llywelyn in 1212, and John's castles were attacked and taken. Pope Innocent III gave his blessing to the Welsh revolt, and King Philip of France invited Llywelyn to ally with him against the English. True to form, *John hung all his Welsh hostages, including Maelgwyn's 7-year-old son.* By 1215, Llywelyn had captured many Norman castles and was in control of Pengwern (Shrewsbury). Llywelyn joined the English barons at Runnymede, *and his power was one of the major factors that persuaded John to sign the Magna Carta in that year.*

At Llywelyn's Parliament at Aberdyfi in 1216, he adjudicated on claims from rival Welsh princes for the division of Welsh territories under his overlordship, and his decisions were universally accepted. This was probably Wales' **'first Parliament'**. By 1218, Llywelyn had taken Cardigan, Cilgerran, Cydweli (Kidwelly), Llansteffan and Carmarthen castles, and was threatening the Marcher castles of Swansea, Haverfordwest and Brecon. John had died in 1216, and in 1218 Llywelyn's pre-eminence in Wales was recognised by the new English king Henry III, at The Treaty of Worcester.

However William, Marcher Earl of Pembroke, seized the castles of Carmarthen and Cardigan in 1223, as the English barons moved in concert to push Llywelyn back to Gwynedd. Hubert de Burgh, justiciar of England, pushed into Powys, but was beaten by Llywelyn at Ceri in 1228. Hubert consolidated his hold on Marcher Lordships, and by 1231, Llywelyn was forced to go on the offensive, pushing down to South Wales and burning Brecon and Neath. Pembroke and Abergavenny were also taken. Henry III invaded Wales and was lucky to escape with his life when Llywelyn launched a night attack on Grosmont Castle. By the Peace of Middle in 1234, Llywelyn was once more recognised by the English as pre-eminent in Wales, calling himself Prince of Aberffraw and Lord of Snowdonia. As we have seen, he had to be conscious of the feelings of his subject rulers in the rest of Wales. It was almost a quarter of a century earlier, that they had turned on him to support King John.

At this height of his powers, Annales Cambriae records *'The Welsh returned joyfully to their homes, but the French* (i.e. the Norman-English), *driven out of all their holds, wandered hither and thither like birds in melancholy wise'*. Llywelyn had been very much helped in his dealings with the English through his marriage to Joan, the daughter of King John, and spent his later years building up the prosperity of Wales. Llywelyn helped religious foundations, and supported a great flowering of Welsh literature. The earliest known text of 'The Mabinogion' was written down, and the imaginative brilliance of the bards can still be read today. They praised the strength and peace their lord had brought Wales against the 'French' king and his Norman barons. Dafydd Benfras said he was *'his country's strongest shield'*, Einion ap Gwgan hailed him as *'the joy of armies......the emperor and sovereign of sea and land'*, and Llywarch ap Llywelyn wrote *'Happy was the mother who bore thee, Who are wise and noble.'*

Aged sixty-eight, this great lord of Snowdon died as a monk at Aberconwy Abbey in 1240, worn out and crippled. Llywelyn ap Iorwerth ab Owain Gwynedd had inspired a revision of the 'Laws' of Hywel Dda, reorganized the administrative machinery of Wales, maintained cordial relations with the Pope and the English Church, and brought peace and prosperity to a united Wales. He had also ensured that Henry III recognised his son by Joan, Dafydd, as rightful heir. His remarkable diplomatic and military skills were celebrated by all the Welsh poets of the times.

However, Gruffydd, Dafydd II's elder brother, was still imprisoned in the White Tower in London. He died on St David's Day, 1244, trying to escape on a rope of knotted sheets. In 1245 Henry III reneged on his promises and again invaded Wales, but was defeated by Dafydd in the only significant battle at Deganwy, and retreated back to England. Upon the tragically early death of Dafydd ap Llywelyn Fawr in 1246, a new power struggle took place to control Wales, only to

Conwy Castle, the site of Llywelyn's burial
(photograph courtesy of WTB)

be resolved by Llywelyn the Last. Mystery surrounds Dafydd II's death. It may be that he was poisoned on Henry's orders.

Years later, Llywelyn's great stone sarcophagus was removed from Aberconwy Abbey, as King Edward I symbolically built his great castle of Conwy over the abbey. It went to the Gwydir Chapel in the Church of St Grwst in Llanrwst. The present Chapel is said to have been designed by Inigo Jones. However, Llywelyn's bones were not allowed to be taken away, and left under the new castle of Conwy. His bard, Dafydd Benfras, wrote this moving lament at his death -

'Where run the white rolling waves
Where meets the sea the mighty river,
In cruel tombs at Aberconwy
God has caused their dire concealment from us,
The red-speared warriors,
Their nation's illustrious son.'

'Annales Cambriae' refers to his death....... *'Thus died that great Achilles the Second, the lord Llywelyn whose deeds I am unworthy to recount. For with lance and shield did he tame his foes; he kept peace for the men of religion; to the needy he gave food and raiment. With a warlike chain he extended his boundaries; he showed justice to all.....and by meet bonds of fear or love bound all men to him.'*

The 1240 entry in the Chronicle of Ystrad Fflur reads: *In this year the Lord Llywelyn ab Iorwerth ab Owain Gwynedd, prince of Wales, a second Achilles, died after he had assumed the order of Aberconwy; and he was buried honourably there.'*

LLYWELYN AP GRUFFYDD AP LLYWELYN FAWR
c1225 - December 11 1282
EIN LLYW OLAF - LLYWELYN THE LAST

The Welsh custom of 'gavelkind' meant that Llywelyn the Great's kingdom had to be divided among all his four male heirs, although Llywelyn had tried desperately for all the kingdoms to be united under his son Dafydd. Within a month of Llywelyn's death, in 1240, King Henry III moved against Dafydd, invading and reneging on his agreement, forcing him to surrender many of his father's gains. Dafydd yielded his elder brother, Gruffydd as a prisoner. Incarcerated in the Tower of London, Gruffydd died trying to escape, four years later. King Henry's treachery meant that Norman Marcher lords took Welsh territories, Gruffydd ap Gwenwynwyn took his realm back, and the king claimed the territories of Tegeingl, Carmarthen, Cardigan and Cydweli.

Llywelyn's father, Gruffydd, has a particularly tragic history - he was the illegitimate son of Llywelyn the Great, and was imprisoned as a hostage by King John from 1211-1215 after John defeated Llywelyn in battle. Then Llywelyn the Great saw Gruffydd as a problem for Dafydd's succession and locked him up in Deganwy Castle from 1228-1234. From 1239 to 1241 both Gruffydd and his son Owain Goch were held by Dafydd in Cricieth Castle. Finally, after Dafydd's defeat by Henry III, poor Gruffydd was to spend his last three years in the Tower of London. So Gruffydd ap Llywelyn Fawr ap Iorwerth was imprisoned by King John for four years, by his father Llywelyn the Great for six years, by his step-brother Dafydd II for two years, and then by King Henry III for three years, when he died trying to escape. From 1211 to 1244 Gruffydd spent fifteen of thirty-three years imprisoned. This sad history affected his son Llywelyn ap Gruffydd, in his view of Norman-Welsh relations, for the rest of his life.

Gruffydd's tragic death sparked the Welsh to react to Henry's overlordship. Assisted by Gruffydd's vengeful son, Llywelyn, Dafydd allied with all but two of the other Welsh princes (Powys and Gwynllwg). They attacked the Norman lands and regained the important border castle of Mold. Dafydd appealed to Pope Innocent IV for help, offering Wales as a vassalship in return for protection against the Norman-English. He called himself Prince of Wales, the **first** to use that title.

Henry III assembled an army at Chester and beat the Welsh on the banks of the river Conwy, *slaughtering all the Welsh prisoners*. An English army was recalled from Ireland to lay waste to Anglesey. Dafydd kept fighting from his Gwynedd fastnesses, and forced Henry to withdraw. One of the great tragedies of Welsh history is Dafydd's premature death in 1246, possibly from poisoning. Henry claimed all of Dafydd's land, because he had been promised it if Dafydd died childless. A Norman army now pushed up through the South, conquering Ceredigion, Meirionydd and Deganwy.

The leaderless men of Gwynedd immediately accepted Llywelyn and his eldest brother Owain Goch as rulers of Gwynedd. (Owain had been imprisoned in the Tower of London with their father, Gruffydd). However, after three years of warfare, the brothers had reached a point where the starving population could no longer support an armed force, and sued for an armistice. In April 1247 they were confirmed as lords of Gwynedd uwch Conwy (that part of Gwynedd west of the Conwy river and north of the Dyfi) and the status of Gwynedd reduced to an English vassalship, conforming to the matters of status of an English lordship. In this year, Matthew Paris recorded that *'Wales had been pulled down to nothing'*.

In 1256, 'Brut y Tywysogion' records that *'The gentlefolk of Wales, despoiled of their liberty and their rights, came to Llywelyn ap Gruffydd and revealed to him with tears their grievous bondage to the English; and they made known to him that they preferred to be slain for their liberty than to suffer themselves to be unrighteously trampled on by foreigners.'*

By 1255, Llywelyn ap Gruffydd ap Llywelyn Fawr, this grandson of Llewelyn the Great had won total control of Gwynedd. He had defeated and imprisoned his two brothers at Bryn Derwen. Poor Owain Goch, was incarcerated in Dolbadarn Castle for twenty years to ensure stability, but Dafydd escaped to England. ('Red Owen' thus spent twenty-three years incarcerated, eight more than his father). Llywelyn now pushed out all over Wales, beating back Henry III's army, while the men of Deheubarth beat royal forces near Llandeilo in 1257. This Battle of Coed Llathen was near Llangathen west of Llandeilo, and around 3000 English knights and soldiers were slain, and higher number than were killed at Hastings. The battle-site sign of crossed swords that existed in the 1950's has disappeared.

The ruling houses of Powys, Glamorgan and Deheubarth acknowledged Llywelyn as their lord in 1258, as he had not only pushed the Normans out of Gwynedd, but also out of most of Wales. Until 1262 there was a fragile truce, but Llywelyn went back on the attack to gain more of Wales, first from Roger Mortimer, and then part of the lordships of Brecon and Abergavenny. In 1264, he allied with Simon de Montfort, who was now in control of England after beating the king at Lewes. By the Pipton Agreement, de Montfort recognised Llywelyn, on behalf of the crown, as Prince of Wales and overlord of the other great men of Wales.

The English chronicler Matthew Paris wrote that *'the North Welsh and the South Welsh were wholly knit together, as they had never been before'*, and praised the courage and vigour of Llywelyn, saying *'Is it not better, then, at once to die (in battle) and go to God than to live (in slavery)?'* Later, King Henry III was forced, by The Treaty of Montgomery in 1267, **to recognize Llywelyn as Prince of Wales,** who in return recognised the suzerainty of the English crown. Llywelyn now had more control and influence in Wales than any prince since the Norman Conquest of England. However, where his relations with the devious Henry had always been poor, he was soon to come up against a new king of England who simply resented Llywelyn's very existence.

When Edward I succeeded to the English crown, Llywelyn, fearing the normal Norman-French treachery, did not attend the coronation. His father had died in London. Llywelyn also refused to pay tribute to Edward I, and built a new castle and town, Dolforwyn, against Edward's wishes. Llywelyn had sent a letter to Edward in1272 , stating that *'according to every just principle we should enjoy our Welsh laws and custom like other nations of the king's empire, and in our own language.'* Llywelyn was declared a rebel in 1274, and Edward invaded. Edward and his barons used violence to provoke rebellions all over Wales which were brutally crushed, while he pursued and harried Llywelyn, even forcing him to move, starving, from his mountain stronghold of Gwynedd.

In 1277, Edward had fifteen thousand six hundred troops in Wales, and Llywelyn was humiliated with the Treaty of Aberconwy when he sued for peace. He was stripped of his overlordship granted at the Treaty of Montgomery. In 1278, King Edward felt secure enough to release Elinor de Montfort, the betrothed

Hawarden Castle, attacked by Llywelyn
(photograph courtesy of WTB)

daughter of the great Simon de Montfort, from prison. He then attended her wedding to Llywelyn in Worcester Cathedral. (Years previously, Elinor had been captured with her brother, on her way to marry Llywelyn – the Plantagenets feared a dynasty that would be more popular than theirs).

However, after a peaceful interlude, Llywelyn's wayward brother Dafydd attacked Hawarden (Penarlag) Castle and burnt Flint in 1282, sparking off another war. Ruthin, Hope and Dinas Bran were quickly taken. Llywelyn had the choice of assisting his brother, who had been disloyal to him before, or supporting him. He fatefully chose the latter option, agreed at a Welsh 'senedd' ('senate') at Denbigh. Days before, Elinor had died on the birth of their first child, Gwenllian. Llandovery and Aberystwyth were soon taken as the revolt spread.

King Edward now assembled ten thousand soldiers at Rhuddlan, including a thousand Welsh archers. Navies with archers moved to the Dee and from Bristol. Other armies advanced under the Marcher Lords. The war first went well for the Welsh. The Earl of Gloucester was defeated by Llywelyn near Llandeilo, a force in Anglesey was smashed, and Edward was forced back from Conwy to winter in Rhuddlan. However, more English reinforcements, including fifteen hundred cavalry and Gascon crossbowmen arrived.

In 1282, a Welsh detachment of eighteen men was entrapped at Cilmeri, near Llanfair-ym-Muallt (Builth Wells). At this place on 11th December, Llywelyn was killed. His nearby leaderless army was then annihilated by Welsh bowmen in English pay. Llywelyn's head was cut off and sent to Edward at Conwy Castle, and later paraded through London with a crown of ivy, before being stuck up on the Tower of London. His coronet was offered up to the shrine of Edward the Confessor at Westminster Abbey. The 'Croes Naid' of his ancestors, believed to be a fragment of the 'True Cross', and perhaps the Welsh equivalent of Scotland's Stone of Scone, was taken to Windsor Castle and vanished during the English Civil War.

There is no understanding of how Llywelyn came to be so far detached from his main forces in his Gwynedd stronghold. Edward had offered him exile and an English earldom in return for unconditional surrender. With his small band, Llywelyn had been waiting for someone at Irfon Bridge, but longbowmen suddenly appeared and cut them to bits. Llywelyn escaped, only to be speared by Stephen de Frankton, before he could reach his main forces. Archbishop Pecham of Canterbury had been negotiating between Llywelyn and Edward on the terms of an end to the war, and the documentation still exists.

According to Pecham's later letters, a document was found on Llywelyn inviting him to go to the Irfon Bridge, sent by the Marcher Lords. This document disappeared, and also a copy sent by the Archbishop to the Chancellor. It looks like **Llywelyn was killed by Norman treachery*** – the treachery on the bridge is a recurrent theme in Welsh literature, and for centuries the inhabitants of Builth were known as traitors in Wales. ('Bradwyr Buallt', 'Builth Traitors' became a common term of abuse). Also according to Archbishop Pecham, de Francton's spear did not kill him, and Llywelyn lived on for hours, asking repeatedly for a priest, while his army was being slaughtered a couple of miles away. He was refused one, while his captors waited for the Marcher Lord Edmund Mortimer to come to the scene. According to 'The Waverley Chronicle', he executed Llywelyn on the spot. Probably he also took possession of the letter in Llywelyn's pocket at this same time. It may have been that de Franckton was given a large farmstead at Frampton, just north of Llanilltud Fawr, in the now 'safe' Vale of Glamorgan, in return for keeping quiet.

The plaque on his roadside granite monument at Cilmeri simply proclaims *'Llywelyn ein Llyw Olaf'* – *'Llywelyn Our Last Leader'*. His mutilated body lies in the atmospheric remains of the Cistercian Abbey Cwmhir, (Abaty Cwm Hir) which had a 242 feet nave, the longest in Britain after York, Durham and Winchester Cathedrals.

On Llywelyn's death, his brother Dafydd III pronounced himself Prince of Wales, and survived for ten months, using guerrilla tactics against Edward's forces in Snowdonia. Dafydd ap Gruffydd escaped from Dolwyddelan Castle before its capture, probably moving down to Dolbadarn Castle. For a month he then operated from Llywelyn Fawr's former castle, Castell y Bere and the Cader Idris foothills. Just before four thousand troops under William de Valence reached there, he was forced back to Dolbadarn, as Castell y Bere was captured. The net was closing in on him. An army from Anglesey and a force of Basque mercenaries moved to encircle Snowdonia. Upon promise of pardon, some of his own men gave him up. *After two-hundred years of struggle, the French-speaking Normans, with their Saxon troops and foreign mercenaries, had overcome the nation of Wales. It had taken them just months to overcome England.*

With Dafydd's capture, the English tried to destroy the dynasty of the Llywelyns of Gwynedd. Llywelyn's only child, the year-old Gwenllian, was incarcerated for the rest of her life in Six Hills monastery in Lincolnshire. A recent plaque marks her possible resting-place. His nephew Owain was imprisoned for over twenty years in a cage in Bristol castle until his death. The other of Dafydd's sons, Llywelyn, also died in Bristol Castle. In 1317, Aberffraw, the traditional home of the Princes of Gwynedd, was obliterated by the English – the last of the Welsh royal palaces to be demolished.

The Prince of Wales, Dafydd III, was dragged by horses through the streets of Shrewsbury, and at the High Cross *he was hung, drawn and the entrails ripped from his living body.* His corpse was then quartered, and his joints distributed to York, Winchester, Bristol and Northampton for display. The representatives of York and Winchester disputed over which city should have the honour of receiving the right shoulder - it went to Winchester. Dafydd's head was led on a pole through the street of London, with a crown of ivy, to the sound of horns and trumpets. It was spiked on the White Tower in London, next to his brother Llywelyn's. Conwy Castle was symbolically built on the tomb of Llywelyn the Great. By 'The Statute Of Rhuddlan', in 1284, Edward finally and formally took control of Wales.

In 1282, Gruffydd ab yr Ynad Coch's magnificent elegy to Llywelyn tells us

'Great torrents of wind and rain shake the whole land,

The oak trees crash together in a wild fury,
The sun is dark in the sky,
And the stars are fallen from their courses,'
and ends with
'Do you not see the stars fallen ?
Do you not believe in God, simple men ?
Do you not see that the world has ended ?
A sigh to you, God, for the sea to come over the land !
What is left to us that we should stay ?

Because of the loss of independence of Gwynedd and Powys after a thousand years, Gruffydd wrote:

"Oh God ! That the sea might surge up to You, covering the land !
Why are we left to long-drawn weariness ?
There is no refuge from the terrible Prison."

In 1294 there was a serious rebellion by Madog ap Llewelyn, but Edward defeated him, and the few privileges left to the Welsh in The Statute of Rhuddlan were rescinded. The bards longed for a 'Mab Darogan' to free Wales again - they had to wait a century for the great Owain Glyndŵr in 1400. Edward's Statute of Rhuddlan of 1284 bitterly punished and repressed the Welsh in their own lands, so the later rebellion by Glyndŵr, and the successful overthrow of the English monarchy by the Welsh Tudors (Tewdwrs, Tudurs) in 1485, were massively supported by all of Wales.

* 'The Treachery at the Ford' is a recurring theme in Welsh poetry. Appended to this book is part of some recent work by Anthony Edwards on the last days of Llywelyn. Anthony has published 'Letters of a Peacemaker - The Intervention of Archbishop John Peckham in the Welsh War of 1282', 'Ghosts on the Fairway - The Army that Vanished', 'The Massacre at Aberedw', 'Appointment at Aberdedw' and 'Marwolaeth Llywelyn ap Gruffudd - Y Gwirionedd'. Alone, it seems, he has spent years uncovering the deliberately facts behind the genocide of these times across Wales, the total annihilation of an army of 3000 Welshmen with no recorded English casualties, and the betrayal and strange death of Llywelyn. The relevant sequence letters in Peckham's correspondence are 'missing' from official archives. Glyndŵr Publishing wishes to publish a **new book concerning Llywelyn's last days** with Anthony Edwards (Hafodty Uchaf, Tregarth, Gwynedd LL57 4NT), so if any reader has fresh information, kindly contact Glyndŵr Publishing.

FOOTNOTES:

1. It appears that Twr Llywelyn, the ancient manor-house at Pen-y-Bryn, just north of Bangor, on the shores of Abergwyngeryn, overlooking the Menai Straits, is the lost palace of Llywelyn and his forebears. The Royal Commission on Ancient Monuments has called it *'the most important site discovered in Wales in this (20th) century'*, and the distinguished medieval archaeologist Professor David Austen has called it *'an immensely important site in the national psyche of Wales'*. More information is available from Kathryn Pritchard-Gibson at The Aber Trust, c/o Pen-y-Bryn, Abergwyngeryn, Bangor, Gwynedd LL33 0LA, and on the www.castlewales.com website.

2. Without the bards' Celtic oral tradition, much of Welsh history and heritage would have been lost forever. There has been a strong oral tradition that 500 Welsh bards were slaughtered after the death of Llywelyn II, because they may have inflamed the Welsh back

to rebellion against their new conquerors, the French kings of England. As well as the 'rounding up' of bards and the imprisonment and execution of their employers, Henry IV in 1403's Ordinance de Gales, forbade their existence. Thus truth becomes hidden. One of the most famous and most popular Hungarian poems celebrates this story, written by the famous poet Janos Arany (1817-1882). He was Professor of Hungarian Literature at the Nagy-Koros College, a notary, actor, editor and one of the founders of modern Hungarian poetry. The Austrian Emperor Franz-Josef defeated Hungary in its War of Independence (1848-49), then made his first visit there. He asked Janos Arany to write a poem to praise him, and this was the poet's nationalistic response. (The reference to Milford Haven is to the 'Mab Darogan', the 'Son of Prophecy', Henry VII.)

A Walesi Bardok

Edward kiraly, angol kiraly
Leptet fako lovan
Hadd latom, ugymond, mennyit er
A velszi tartomany

The Bards of Wales

Edward the King, the English King,
Astride his tawny steed -
'Now I will see if Wales,' said he,
'Accepts my rule indeed.

Are streams and mountains fair to see?
Are meadow pastures good?
Do wheat-fields bear a crop more pure
Since washed with rebels' blood?'

"In truth this Wales, Lord, is a gem,
The fairest in your crown:
The streams and fields rich harvest yields
The best through dale and down."

Edward the King, the English King,
Astride his tawny steed:
A silence deep his subjects keep
And Wales is mute indeed.

The castle named Montgomery
Ends that day's travelling;
And the castle's lord, Montgomery,
Must entertain the king.

With game and fish and every dish
That lures the taste and sight
A hundred rushing servants bear
To please his appetite.

With all of worth the isle brings forth
Of splendid drink and food,
And all the wines of foreign vines
Beyond the distant flood.

'You lords, you lords, will none consent
His glass with mine to ring?
What? Each one fails, you dogs of Wales,
To toast the English king?

Though game and fish and every dish
That lures the taste and sight
Your hand supplies, your mood defies
My person with a slight!

You rascal lords, you dogs of Wales,
Will none for Edward cheer?
To serve my needs and chant my deeds,
Then let a bard appear!'

The lords amazed, at him they gaze,
Their cheeks grow deathly pale;
Not fear but rage, their looks engage,
They blanch but do not quail.

All voices cease in soundless peace,
All breathe in silent pain;
Through the door bold, a harper, old,
Enters with grave disdain.

"Lo, here I stand, at your command,
To sing your deeds, O King!"
And weapons clash and shields crash
Responsive to his string.
"Harsh weapons clash and shields crash,
And sunset sees us bleed,
Raven and wolf our dead engulf -
This, monarch, is your deed!

A thousand lie, beneath the sky,
They rot beneath the sun,
And we who live shall not forgive
This deed your hand has done!"

'Now let him perish! I must have'
(King Edward's voice is hard)
'Your softest songs, and not your wrongs!'
Up steps a youthful bard.

"The breeze is soft at eve, that oft
From Milford Haven moans;
It whispers maidens' stifled cries,
It breathes of widows' groans.

You maidens, bear no captive babes!
You mothers, rear them not!"
The fierce king nods. The boy is seized
And hurried from the spot.

Unbidden then, among the men,
There comes a dauntless third.
With speech of fire he tunes his lyre,
And bitter is his word.

"Our bravest died to slake your pride -
Proud Edward, hear my lays!
No Welsh bards live who'll ever give
Your name a song of praise.

Our harps with dead men's memories weep.
Welsh bards to you will sing
One changeless verse - our blackest curse
To blast your soul, O King!"

'No more! Enough!' - cries out the king.
Enraged, his orders break:
'Seek through these vales all bards of Wales
And burn them at the stake!'

Soldiers ride forth to South and North,
They ride to West and East.
Thus ends in grim Montgomery
That celebrated feast.

Edward the King, the English King
Spurs on his tawny steed;
Across the skies red flames arise
As if Wales burned indeed.

In martyrship, with song on lip,
Five hundred Welsh bards died;
Not one was moved to say he loved
The tyrant in his pride.
'God's Blood! What songs this night resound
Upon our London streets?
The Mayor shall feel my irate heel
If any that song repeats.'

Each voice is hushed; through silent lanes
To silent homes they creep.
"Now dies the hound that makes a sound;
The sick king cannot sleep."

'Ha! Bring me fife and drum and horn,
And let the trumpet blare!
In ceaseless hum their curses come -
I see their dead eyes glare.......'

But high above all drum and fife
And trumpets' shrill debate,
Five hundred martyred voices chant
Their hymn of deathless hate......

MADOC ab OWAIN GWYNEDD 1134 - ?
DISCOVERER OF AMERICA?

Possibly born in Dolwyddelan Castle, Prince Madoc was smuggled to Ireland as a boy by his mother Brenda, daughter of the Lord of Carno in mid-Wales. Later in favour at his father's court, he married Annesta, a maid of honour at the court. According to legend, in the next three years he travelled to Ireland, Cornwall and Brittany, and in 1163 represented his father as emissary to the Lord of Lundy Island. In 1169, Owain Gwynedd died, and there was the likelihood of civil war between his many sons for the succession. His chosen successor was Hywel, who faced a coalition from his brothers Rhodri and Dafydd. Hywel was defeated, then Rhodri and Dafydd quarrelled and Madoc tried to broker peace between them. Madoc sailed to France to seek help from Louis VII, so that England did not invade North Wales while there was the succession problem. During his journey, however, Louis and Henry II made peace, and Madoc returned empty-handed.

Madoc and his brother Einion had three ships built, the flagship of the little fleet being the 'Gwennon Gorn'. Wood was felled from the great forest of Nant Gwynant in Caernarfonshire, and Viking practice was followed in the construction. The old stories state that stag horn nails were used instead of iron as they would not rot, and Madoc could use a lode-stone to navigate. The hulls were covered, like coracles, with cow hides tanned on oak bark. The ships were built at Abergele and they sailed from Llandrillo-yn-Rhos, near Llandudno. In 1170, thirteen ships and three-hundred men left the island still called Ynys Fadog (Madog's Isle) in the mouth of the River Glaslyn. In Welsh mythology, Madoc's ship, the 'Gwennan Gorn' still haunts the coast off Abergele. He picked up his brother at Lundy Island on the way to America, and returned several years later with a small crew. The others had been left to start a

Dolwyddelan Castle
(photograph courtesy of WTB)

colony in this fabulous new land. Prince Madoc then went again to America with ten ships filled with men and women. The fact that there are traditions associated with Alabama and Georgia, as well as North Dakota, may mean that the two parties never met up.

Madoc settled some of the company in America, and returned for his brother Rhiryd, Lord of Clochran in Ireland, as promised. Another band of settlers then left via Lundy, Rhiryd sailing in the 'Pedr Sant' (Saint Peter). An old stone found on Lundy Island read *'It is an established fact known far and wide, that Madoc ventured far out into the Western Ocean never to return'*. According to Indian legends, he went back to Wales a third time to bring more settlers, but never came back. The legend was first recounted outside Wales by Willem the Minstrel in the 13th century, and there was a flurry of interest in the legend, promulgated by John Dee (q.v.) in the 16th century to prove Elizabeth's rights to the New World. Sir

George Peckham wrote 'A True Reporte' in 1583. *'Madoc left the land in contention between his brethren and prepared certain ships with men and munitions, and sought adventures by the seas, sailing west, leaving the coast of Ireland so far north, that he came to a land unknown where he saw many strange things...After he had returned home, and declared the pleasant and fruitful countries that he had seen without inhabitants, none who heard him would believe and he was shunned by his countrymen.'* It seems that he did return once before returning, and during this time he is associated with finding the Holy Grail at Llanbabo Church. Peckham states that he took the 'Grail' to the spot where St Cybi ascended to Heaven. An up-to-date reading list is given on the www.madoc1170.com website, but influential works on Madoc were written by Herbert in 1677, Owen in 1777, Williams in 1791 and Burder in 1797.

It may be that the two bands of settlers never met, because one story then takes the settlers heading up north-west and becoming the Mandan Indians, and another relates to a white settlers heading down to Mexico and Aztec territories. Hernando Cortez, who captured Mexico, mentioned Madoc, as did Montezuma, the King of Mexico. Montezuma, in his treaty with Cortez, stated that his light-skinned people came from a little island in the north. The buccaneering explorers Walter Raleigh and John Hawkins also mention Madoc in their writings. This uncle of Llywelyn the Great is commemorated with a plaque at Fort Morgan, Mobile Bay, Alabama: *'In memory of Prince Madoc, a Welsh explorer, who landed on the shores of Mobile Bay in 1170 and left behind, with the Indians, the Welsh language'*. Tom McRae ('The Inditer', on the Internet) looked with his uncle for two 'stone cauldrons' on Mobile Bay recently. His uncle had seen them as a child, when they were known as 'Viking Tarpots'. Very early ships carried stone pots for ballast and storing food. When they landed, the cauldrons were used to boil resin from pine trees, to make pitch and 'caulk' the hulls of their ships.

On Columbus' return from his 1492 discovery of America, he stated that the people honoured a white man called Matec, and he wrote on his chart of the Gulf of Mexico *'these are Welsh waters'*. He also referred to one stretch of sea near the Sargasso as Mar di Cambrio (the Sea of Wales). For years, the early Spanish settlers in Nova Hispana (Florida) searched for the *'gente blanco'* who had reached America before them. One 1519 Spanish map labels Mobile Bay as Tierra de los Gales (Land of the Welsh). The Italian historian Peter Martyr (1459-1525) wrote about white Indians with brown hair, and said that Indians in Guatemala and Virginia revered *'Matec'*. The Dutch writer Hornius argued in 1652 that America had been peopled by many races, with the Welsh as a major component. The stone forts around Mobile Bay cannot be explained by the Indians. Catlin noted the similarity of Mandan forts along the Ohio and Missouri Rivers to Welsh structures. The largest is on top of Fort Mountain in north-west Georgia, near the headwaters of the Coosa River whose waters flow into Mobile Bay.

A major boost to the Madoc legend was the return to Wales, after a missionary tour, of the Reverend Morgan Jones in 1669. He stated that he and some companions were captured by Indians who threatened to kill them. Jones turned to his fellow missionaries and told them, in Welsh, to prepare themselves for death. The Indians heard and understood him, welcomed the missionaries as cousins and set them free. Chief Oconosta, in his tribal history of the Cherokees, told the story of the white tribe advancing along the Missouri River, building forts for protection as they travelled. Even the last settlements of the Mandans were surrounded by earthwork stockades to protect themselves from the Sioux.

The explorer George Rogers Clark was told by Chief Tobacco's Son of the Shawnee Indians that white men had been killed at a battle, in the thirteenth century, on the Falls of the Ohio, near Louisville Kentucky. The defeated colony moved on upriver along the Ohio, Missouri and Mississippi rivers. John Sevier, the founder of Tennessee, noted in 1810 the old stone hill-forts from Mobile to Kentucky and Tennessee. Ancient Roman coins were found in these forts. He questioned Oconosta, who had been a Cherokee chief for sixty years, in 1782. Oconosta related the story of the white Indians escaping from hostility with local tribes, moving from the Carolinas down the Tennessee to the Ohio then up the Mississippi and Missouri. Oconasta related that *'they are no more White people; they are now all become Indians, and look like other red people of the country.'* *'He had heard his grandfather and father say they were a people called Welsh, and that they had crossed the Great Water and landed first near the mouth of the Alabama River near Mobile and had been driven up to the heads of the waters until they arrived at Highwassee River.'* The explorer-painter George Catlin thought that the Mandans were the lost Welsh tribe, as their women were fair-complexioned, with hazel, blue or grey eyes. Some of the men had beards, unlike other Indian tribes. They did not use canoes like neighbouring Indians, but round boats like coracles. Catlin also said that some of their words were identical to Welsh, and this before he found out about the Madoc story. Catlin hailed from the Welsh stronghold of Wilkes-Barr in Pennsylvania, so he was easily able to check Mandan against Welsh words.

The Mandans, unlike other Indians, knew how to ride horses with bridles and saddles. Their lodges had once been oblong, rather than the circular ones favoured by native Indians. It was a matrilinear society, based upon agriculture, like the old Welsh society. Some beehive lodges are reminiscent of the styles used by Celts, as seen in the few Glamorganshire pigsties remaining. The Mandans had box-beds with skin curtains – box-beds with curtains were popular in Wales until 1800. Their rounded 'bull boats', made of skins and wickerwork, were almost identical to the Welsh coracles that have been used for the last two millennia. Anthropologists place their arrival on the Missouri at between 900 and 1400, the right time frame for Madoc's small band. The Mandans' legends said that they came from 'lower down' the Missouri. A string of strange stone 'forts' run down from their Heart River and Knife River territories down to Mobile Bay, on the Gulf of Mexico. Indians did not build forts, but Madoc was born in a castle. Up river from the Falls, at the mouth of Fourteen Mile Creek, a stone fortress once stood. In 1874, State Geologist E. T. Cox described the walled fortification on the 'Devil's Backbone' and drew a map of a pear-shaped enclosure. His assistant stated that a great deal of skill was necessary to build the walls without mortar. (The unique stone fortress was dismantled to build the Big Four Railroad Bridge. In 1898, a helmet and shield were found in Louisville, but were stolen. In 1799, six skeletons were unearthed in Jeffersonville, but have been lost.) The neighbouring Hidatsa tribe called the Mandans 'Gulf-people' because of their origins in the Gulf. These occurrences helped cement the connections between Madoc's settlers moving from Mobile and the Mandan tribe.

One of the first explorers to find the tribe, the French explorer La Verendrye in 1739, wrote *'The fortifications are not characteristic of the Indians....Most of the women do not have the Indian features.... The tribe is mixed white and black. The women are fairly good-looking, especially the light coloured ones; many of them have blonde or fair hair.'* The Mandan chief described their journey from further south, up the river. He described the tribe as *'white men with forts, towns and permanent villages laid out in streets'*. Many descriptions referred to the preponderance of brown and red hair, and blue eyes amongst the Mandans, and they were known as the 'white Indians' even by other Indian tribes. The other strange occurrence was the preponderance of beards among the tribe. All other Indian tribes are smooth-skinned, but the Mandans, with their very different language, were known to other Indians as *'the bearded tribe'*. Catlin also notes the preponderance of white hair amongst the older Mandans, a very rare occurrence in native Indians.

The Mandans were almost wiped out by smallpox in 1781 when half the tribe died, and then in 1837 it decimated them to just a few dozen survivors. These were enslaved by the Arikaras, and now no Mandan-speakers survive. The remnants live on the Fort Berthold reservation in the heart of the USA, and their ceremonial grounds have been covered by the Garrison Reservoir (so there is definitely something in common with Wales). The Mandans worship 'the Lone Man', a white man who started the tribe, and his shrine is 'The Ark of the Lone Man', a holy canoe. Mandan cosmology also centres of a great flood – Madoc's lands in Wales bordered Cantre'r Gwaelod, the 'lowland hundreds' lost to the sea.

The late Gwyn Alf Williams, with his hatred of imperialism, was dismissive of Madoc in his 1979 book 'Madoc: the Making of a Myth', but one can only reiterate the final lines of his book, where he met a surviving Mandan, Ralph Little Owl:

*'They came at last, those moments we had half-hoped for, half-feared, when a chill ran through us which was not the wind. Ronald Little Owl rehearsed the Mandan prophecies which had all come true, including one that old wolves would make the Missouri run backwards (as they have done). The last one, however, he would not tell us – "it would not be polite". The language ? "When I die, the Mandan language will have gone." And the Lone Man ? He bent his Asiatic face into the television lights and said, **"The Lone Man was the founder of our people. He was a white man who brought our people in his big canoe across a great water and landed them on the Gulf of Mexico."'***

Just twenty years later, eight hundred years of history has been consigned to the realms of legend. A recent book by Dana Olson refers to the fact that a colony of Welshmen is mentioned in 'Walum Olum', the chronological history of the Delaware Indians ...... *'That the country north of the Falls of the Ohio and adjacent to the river was inhabited by a strange people many years before the first recorded visit of a white man, there can be no doubt. The relics of a former race are scattered throughout this territory, and the many skeletons found buried along the river banks of the river below Jeffersonville are indisputable evidence that a strange people once flourished here.'* According to Olson, there is *'additional and convincing proof that Prince Madoc founded the first recorded settlement in America and established in what is now Clark County, Indiana, the longest surviving colony (1170-1837) before widespread immigration brought other white men to this country.'*

Charles Morgan, a Welsh West Indian known as Jacques Clamorgan, operated from St. Louis, and led The Missouri Company for Spain, trying to open up the unexplored American interior, win control of the fur trade, and reach the Pacific before the British and Americans. A French trader, Jaques d'Eglise, from St. Louis in 1790 had come across a tribe of Indians in the Upper Missouri, the Mandans, and had described them as *'white, like Europeans'*. Jacques Clamorgan organised a Spanish expedition to find them, headed by John Evans (q.v.) who could speak their language. The Mandans were known as the tribe who introduced the cultivation of corn to other tribes, who were the most skilful dressers and workers of buffalo hide, and the main source of glass beads for Indians. The colour white, and the White Buffalo were especially revered by the Mandan, who had a female society known as the White Buffalo Cow Society, whose leader wore a white buffalo robe. The Mandan were the most important of all the Missouri River tribes, culturally and in trade, living in fortified villages of circular earth huts, or lodges. They called themselves *'Numangkake'* (men), usually with the epithet of the name of their village (like Williams Pantycelyn!). *'Archaeological research suggests that during the period 1100-1400 the earliest manifestations of Mandan culture began to emerge. Their villages, which were to be found on terraces strung along the Missouri River for a distance of some 500 miles in present-day North and South Dakota, generally consisted of small, isolated settlements of between 15 and 40 households....'* Some appeared to have moved on to Montana with the Minnetarre (from Colin Taylor's 'The Plains Indians'. Several specialist books place the start of the special Mandan culture around 1100-1150, which gives another link with Madoc).

At least two of the Lewis and Clark party, Sergeant Ordway and Private Whitehouse, believed that they would find Prince Madoc's fair-skinned Indian descendants, still in possession of Welsh treasure. They met light-skinned Indians in The Flatlands of Montana, speaking a strange *'gurgling kind of language spoken much through the throat'*, and Whitehouse was *'sure of it'* that they were the lost Welsh tribe. The artist George Catlin painted some of these 'Welsh-speaking' Mandans before the tribe was decimated by the new white man's illness of smallpox in 1838. Scholars claimed that many of their customs, and their use of coracles for catching fish, 'proved' their Welsh ancestry. Professor Gwyn Williams also recounts that *'Mandan girls were celebrated for their good looks and amiability and were said to be more adept than most. They chattered endlessly even when making love – a fact which one later observer cited as further proof of their Welsh descent !'*

Madoc's story is recounted in Hakluyt's 'Voyages' (1582) and Lloyd and Powell's 'Cambria' 1584. Powel states that Peckham's source of information was Gutyn Owen, a well-documented Welsh monk-historian at Basingwerk Abbey in the 1480's. Abbey annals and Owen's writings were destroyed in the Reformation. John Dee, the Welsh *'magus of his age'* claimed America for Queen Elizabeth I on the basis of this tale, which was developed by Southey in his long poem 'Madoc' in 1805. 'Madoc' is based on Montezuma's statement to Cortez, that a white leader 'from the east' brought an American tribe south into Mexico.

FOOTNOTES:
1. The 12th century maritime archives *'The Black Book of Admiralty'* includes in its 1171 entries the ship *'Guignon Gorn'*, belonging to Madoc. The Flemish poet Willem van Hulst (Willem the Fleming) first wrote of Madoc's story, *'The Voyage of Madoc'* around 1200-1210, but no original copy survives. This is mentioned by the Dutch copyist Jacob van

Mearlant in 1255. Around 1200, the bard Llywarch ap Llywelyn also referred to his departure. Around 1450 Ieuan Brechfa wrote that Madoc had sailed in search of *'a fair land across the oceans, unknown and unproved'*, and in 1470 a Ruabon priest, Maredudd ap Rhys wrote that Madoc discovered a mysterious new land.

2. The author's notes on Madoc and America in *'An A-Z of Wales and the Welsh'* was noticed by Howard Kimberley of Maesteg, who runs the www.madoc.1170.com website. Madoc1170, of which the author is now a member, is an organisation dedicated to finding out the truth about Madoc and America, and will be commissioning DNA testing upon descendants of Owain Gwynedd and Mandans. The ongoing research will be published in a book by Bryn Griffith, to be published by Wales Books (Glyndŵr Publishing). If anyone wishes to become involved with this exciting and intriguing project, in Britain or America, or has relevant information, kindly contact Bryn or Howard via the Madoc website or via this publisher.

3. Catlin wrote of the curious stone forts along the Missouri made by the Mandans, of their unique coracles, their specialist skills in glass and pottery, their huts and other links with Wales, and came from Wilkes-Barre, an area full of Welshmen. Catlin thinks that the Madogwys became the Mandan, as they made great use of the red dye obtained from the Woodroff plant, which is known in Welsh as Mandon. He notes the places that they lived between the Gulf of Mexico and along the Missouri and Ohio Rivers, and gives us some intriguing language similarities in his appendices upon *'The Extinction of the Mandans'* by smallpox and *'The Welsh Colony'*: He wrote *'I have dwelt longer on the history and customs of these people than I have on any other tribe...because I have found them a very peculiar people. From the striking peculiarities in their personal appearance, in their customs, traditions and language, I have been led conclusively to believe that they are a people of a decidedly different origin from that of any other tribe in these regions.'*

ENGLISH	MANDAN	WELSH
I	Me	Mi
You	NeChi,	Chwi
He	E	Ef
She	Ea	Hi
It	Ount	(They =) Hwynt
We	Noo	Ni
They	Eona	Hwna (masc), Hona (fem)
Those ones	-	Yrhai Hyna
No, or, there is not	Megosh	Nagoes
Head	Pan	Pen
The Great Spirit	Mah ho Peneta	Mawr Penaethir

4. The Mandans can lay claim to being the only Indian tribe never to have been at war with the United States. Wales has never declared war on any other nation, only ever defending itself, in its 2000-year history, and as its colonists in Patagonia settled peacefully among the native Indians. Hopefully DNA testing can prove the link between Wales and the few remaining Mandans.

5. One of the most intriguing aspects of the story, apart from a shield and armour being found in the Missouri basin by early settlers, as well as a longboat, is the custom of the Mandan medicine-man. Yearly he visited the medicine lodge at each fortified Mandan camp, to open the medicine-lodge which had been closed all year. He was chiefly naked, and known as the *'Nu-mokh-muck-a-nah'* *(The first or only Man)*. His body was covered in white clay to give the appearance of a white man, and his robe was four white wolf-skins. On his head he wore a head-dress made of ravens' skins and he carried a large and sacred pipe. While the medicine lodge was ritually cleaned, he would visit each lodge in the village,

stopping and crying until the owner of the lodge appeared and asked what was the matter. He replied that *'he was the only person saved from the universal calamity; that he landed in his big canoe on a high mountain in the west, where he now resides; that he had come to open the medicine lodge, which must needs receive a present of some edged-tool from the owner of the wigwam, that it may be sacrificed to the water," for he says, "if this is not done, there will be another flood, and no-one will be saved, as it was with such tools that the big canoe was made."* The knives and spears were then thrown into the river from a high place, in the presence of the whole village, *'from whence they can never be recovered, and where they were, undoubtedly, sacrificed to the Spirit of the Water.'* Often the weapons were deliberately bent or broken, a seeming passing-on of the identical Celtic-Druidic ritual, unknown in other tribes. Also, the legend of Atlantis and Wales occurs in the bay off Prince Madoc's home (see the author's 'An A-Z of Wales and the Welsh'). On the other hand, it could be that the tradition of the flood was somehow also passed on to these Indians, whose rituals also included the worship of a dove, the symbol of peace. The visit of the Lone Man was the precursor to the ritual torture of young Mandan men as their rite of passage to adulthood, as depicted in 'A Man called Horse'.

6.It is difficult to halt writing on such an interesting topic, one has to read George Catlin's accounts - he was convinced that the Madans were the Madogwys. Areas for investigation for the new book on Madoc will centre on the language similarities; the unique Mandan craft of making blue glass beads; the unique coracle boats; the stone fortifications like Celtic hill-forts and native Welsh castles; the structure of the earth-lodges, identical to Welsh huts of the 12th century; the existence of a family tree of 30 generations, dating to the time of Madoc; DNA testing; contemporary accounts of the White Indians; interviews with Mandans; the practice of sacrifice of weapons to water; and the story of the Lone White Man, possibly Madoc himself. However, one more note from Catlin reads: *Notwithstanding the long familiarity in which the Minatarees have lived with the Mandans, and the complete adoption of most of their customs, yet it is almost an unaccountable fact, that there is scarcely a man in the tribe who can speak half a dozen words of the Mandan language; although, on the other hand, the Mandans are most of them able to converse in the Minataree tongue; leaving us to conclude, either that the Minatarees are a very inert and stupid people, or that the Mandan language (which is most probably the case) being different from any other language in the country, is an exceedingly difficult one to learn.'*

BILLY MEREDITH   July 30 1874 - April 19 1958
'FOOTBALL'S FIRST SUPERSTAR', 'THE WELSH WIZARD', 'OLD SKINNY', 'THE WIZARD OF THE WING', 'THE KING', FOUNDER OF THE PFA

In Football, *the oldest international in the world* was William Henry (Billy) Meredith from Black Park, near Chirk, who played right wing for Manchester City, Manchester United, and Wales. At twelve years old he was working in Black Park Colliery. The conditions marked him for life, and he decided to become a professional footballer, signing for Ardwick (Manchester City) for a £5 fee in 1894. He had played as an amateur for Chirk, then almost a season in 1894 as a part-timer for Northwich Victoria at the Drill Field, now the oldest surviving football ground in the world. (Northwich was a founder member of the Second Division). Meredith made his debut while still working down the pit. He scored twice on his home debut and quickly became the favourite player of the supporters. One Friday after working he took the 2am train on Saturday morning to Newcastle, arriving at 11, played a match and was back home at 10.30pm to go to work the next day.

This was his City debut on October 27th, 1894. In 1894, November 3rd saw the first-ever Manchester Derby football league match, with 'the Heathens' (Newton Heath, which became Manchester United) playing Manchester City at Ardwick. Both teams had met before in cup and Alliance matches, but this was the first League meeting. It was Meredith's first home fixture, and although he scored both goals, Newton Heath won 5-2.

This moustachioed lynchpin of the City team took them to promotion in 1899 and in the next year became their captain. He scored 29 goals in 33 games in his first season in the First Division, from his position on the right wing. (The Premier League is a recent invention). After temporarily dropping down to the second division again, Meredith captained the team again to promotion in 1903. His trademark was that he chewed a toothpick while playing. Originally, he had chewed tobacco to help him concentrate, but the lady who cleaned his kit complained about the difficulty of removing his stained spit from his shirt, and he took up the toothpick.

As captain, he took Manchester City to the Cup Final in 1904, scored the winner, and took the FA Cup back to Manchester for the first time. He had recently been voted the most popular player in the country by readers of 'The Umpire' magazine. The team finished second in the First Division. He had started to become a *'star'* and all on a maximum wage of £4 a week. However, a bribery scandal erupted in 1905, as the FA claimed that Meredith had paid an Aston Villa player £10. Meredith always denied the charge, but he and the entire City team was banned for a year before the suspension was quashed. Billy then stunned the football world by signing for City's newly-promoted bitter rivals, Manchester United, in late 1906 (with four other City players who had also been accused of corruption). They became the backbone of an excellent United team. The players had been paid £6-7 a week instead of the statutory £4, and 17 City players and 5 directors were suspended. Billy was thus not only involved in the bribe incident, but also in illegal bonuses with the rest of the team, and was lucky to play again. Meredith was signed first of the City players, by the great United manager Charlie Magnall. He thrilled the United crowds for fifteen years, and was their best player, drawing record crowds wherever they played. He also holds the 'oldest Manchester United player' record.

He was bought by the newly promoted Manchester United in October 1906, and has a place of honour in their football museum. Although officially a 'free transfer', Billy received a £500 signing-on fee, a massive amount of money. His first game was against Aston Villa on January 1, 1907, as his ban ran through all of 1906. The inspired Billy teased the Villa defence, and his cross to Turnbull won the match. They were on their way as a great team. By the end of the season, United had climbed from a lowly position in December 1906 to 8th in the table. As Bobby Charlton stated, Billy Meredith was their *'earliest star'*. Football at this time was a *'hard man's game'*, but Meredith missed hardly any matches as United won the League for the first time in 1908. In 1909 the Charity Shield was won, and in 1911 there was another League Championship. He was Manchester United's key player when they won the FA Cup for the first time in 1909, and he became soccer's first media personality, with personal appearances and product endorsements - **he was football's first 'superstar' in any country in the world.** United beat Brighton away, Everton at home, Blackburn away, then were losing at Burnley when a blizzard halted the match. United won the replay and beat Newcastle, the cup-holders in the semi-final. Newcastle won the league that year. In the final against Bristol City, Meredith was said to be the difference between the two teams at Crystal Palace in front of 70,000 fans. The players went to the Alhambra after the game to see the great comedian George Robey. Returning on the train to Manchester on Sunday, they were greeted by a brass band and 300,000 people lined the streets. 30,000 people had waited in the Clayton stadium for 3 hours to see the team. (Old Trafford was being built).

In his position of authority in the game, he formed and chaired the first meeting of the Professional Footballers' Association at the Imperial Hotel, Manchester.

Billy Meredith

Many players were banned from playing, and drifted back out of the union, to play for their FA clubs. However, Meredith and the United wing-half Charlie Roberts persisted and formed *'The Outcasts FC'* with other United players. Manchester United were suspended by the Football Association, but the new players' union survived by the skin of its teeth, and Meredith was the last player to return to play after the strike for better conditions. For a long time, only the United players had held out, but Tom Coleman of Everton walked out on his team and sided with the Manchester players, and soon after he was followed by the great north-east clubs of Newcastle, Middlesborough and Sunderland, then the rest of the Everton team and Liverpool. The FA backed down. The PFA, Professional Footballers' Association, was initially known as *'Meredith's Union'*, affiliated to the National Federation of Trade Unions.

However, World War 1 broke up the fine United side, with football being suspended from 1915-1918. In these years, Billy guested over 100 times for Manchester City and Stalybridge Celtic, with United's permission. In 1920 he had become the oldest international player on record, winning against England, aged 45 years and 8 months. In that year, Wales won the international championship for the first time, a fitting end to Meredith's international career. It was the first time that Meredith had been in a winning team against England. After 332 matches for Manchester United, Billy argued with the club (as they would not employ a full-time manager), and left on a 'free transfer', aged 48, to join Manchester City once more, as player-coach. According to the 'redcafe' website, his departure was *'the beginning of the end'* for United, and in the following season they finished 13th in the league, being ejected from the FA Cup in the first round. Meredith returned to Manchester City in 1921 for the final three years of a glittering career. Appearing for City, he was the oldest player ever in an FA Cup match, aged 49 years and 8 months in 1924 against Newcastle. In all he played 1568 matches, including 46 for Wales, still playing for Wales aged 45. Extremely quick, lean, and tall for the times

(5 foot 9 inches), Meredith was affectionately known as 'The Welsh Wizard' or 'Old Skinny' to the fans.

He played against England aged almost forty-six, in 1920, and his international career spanned a record twenty-six years, and four decades. Meredith was in the team for Wales' first victory against England, and was selected seventy-one consecutive times for his country from the age of twenty-one, but only played forty-six times because Manchester City often stopped him playing. Meredith played for thirty years in the English First Division and hardly missed a game until he was well into his fifties. Obsessed with training and fitness, he scored nearly five-hundred goals from his position of outside-right, and was a sporting celebrity in his seventies. In 1958 he sent a good luck telegram to Jimmy Murphy's United team in the semi-final of the FA Cup, in the weeks after the Munich Air Disaster, which wiped out the 'Busby Babes'. However, he died in that same year aged eighty-three, and is buried in an unmarked grave in Manchester. The great Stanley Matthews was compared with him, but Meredith could also score goals - he said Matthews *'would never have made the grade in my day'*. Billy has been compared to *'the (Stanley) Matthews, (Tom) Finney and (George) Best of his day, all rolled into one'*.

Upon his retirement, Billy Meredith took over a pub, although he was a teetotaller, and remained close to both Manchester clubs, scouting and also coaching at Old Trafford from 1931. In April 1925, over 15,000 fans turned up for Billy's testimonial, to see a Manchester XI draw 2-2 with a Glasgow XI. Billy played, aged over 50. In 1926, a full-length film was made of his career, with Billy starring and playing himself as a trainer. A fragment of 45 feet of this film was found a few years ago, so we have some footage of the great man.

MERLIN 5th - 6th century
ARTHUR'S WIZARD

Arthur's advisor, prophet and magician is basically a construct of Geoffrey of Monmouth's *'History of the Kings of Britain'*. Geoffrey combined the Welsh traditions of the prophet-bard Myrddin with a story from Nennius (q.v.). Geoffrey wrote *'The Prophesies of Merlin'**. Merlin became a popular figure in 13th century French works, and Thomas Malory made him Arthur's advisor in the 'Morte d'Arthur', and the creator of the Round Table at Caerleon for Uther Pendragon. Tennyson made him the architect of Camelot in 'The Idylls of the King'. The earliest known reference is in the prophetic poem 'Armes Prydain', The Prophecy of Britain, probably dating from around 900.

Myrddin Emrys, after whom Caerfyrddin, Carmarthen, was named, is the Merlin of Arthurian legend. Merlin's Oak, a leafless stump held up by iron struts, stood in the centre of Caerfyrddin until 1958 when it was removed to assist more carbon and lead pollution by modern traffic. Merlin had prophesied that Carmarthen would fall with the death of the tree, so it had been carefully preserved until the Philistines took over and uprooted it, along with fifteen hundred years of legend. (*'Llanllwch has been, Carmarthen shall sink, Abergwili will stand'*, and *'Carmarthen, you shall have a cold morning; Earth will swallow you, water in your place'*.) Another of his prophecies was that a bull would go to the top of St. Peter's Church in Carmarthen, and a calf was found at the top centuries later.

Carmarthen, Merlin's birthplace
(photograph courtesy of WTB)

The most famous wizard in the world, he was in Welsh folk tales long before the Arthurian cycle where he appeared as Arthur's councillor, and foresaw the hero's downfall. He became known as Merlin because the Latinized form of Myrddin would have been Merdinus, linked to the Latin for dung, Merdus (-the French 'merde'). He was also a poet and a prophet, forecasting that one day the Welsh would once again take over the land of Britain and drive the Saxons out. This shows remarkable foresight – the east side of the British Isles is dropping into the sea at three to four times the rate of that of the west side. In future millennia, England will have disappeared and Wales and its Cornish, Cumbrian and Strathclyde cousins will once again rule this island.

As a youth, Merlin was linked with Vortigern, King of Britain, who could not build a tower on Dinas Emrys. Merlin informed him that there was a problem because two dragons guarded an underwater lake. Recent archaeological excavation showed an underground pool. These red and white dragons were symbolic of the British against Saxon fight for Britain. In legend, he next advised Ambrosius Aurelius, the conqueror of Vortigern, to bring back the Giant's Ring of sacred stones from Ireland and erect Stonehenge. After the death of Ambrosius, his successor Uther Pendragon became besotted with Eigyr (Igraine), wife of Gorlois, so Merlin shape-shifted Uther into Gorlois and she conceived Arthur. After the Battle of Arturet, Merlin went insane and lived in the woods. He returned to advise Arthur. Welsh traditions say that he lies in chains in a cave under Bryn Myrddin, Carmarthen, or in a cave near Dinefwr castle, or buried on Bardsey Island, where he took the 'Thirteen Treasures of Britain' He is also thought to have been imprisoned in a pool in Britanny.

There were probably two Myrddins, one Myrddin Wyllt, a Celtic wizard who lived in the Scottish woods at the time of Vortigern, and Myrddin Emrys from Carmarthen, who lived at the time of Arthur.

The Breton link with Merlin and Arthur is interesting. There is a scenic tour in the 'Purple Country' of Broceliande, fifty-six miles of roads criss-crossing ancient sites and megaliths. The Barenton Spring is where Merlin first met Vivian the Enchantress. Merlin's Tomb is an old passage grave where he was imprisoned by Vivian. Also in the forest, the lake known as the 'Fairies' Mirror' is supposed to be used by Vivian to hold Merlin. Morgana le Fay imprisoned Arthur's unfaithful knights in The Valley of No Return. Comper Castle's lake is said to have been the home of Vivian, who brought up Lancelot under its waters, and the castle has an Arthurian exhibition. Paimpont Abbey celebrates the 6th century Welsh missionaries and 'founder-saints' of Britanny.

Merlin left behind a set of prophecies for the next millennium after his death. Thomas Heywood's 1812 book 'The Life of Merlin' links Merlin's prophecies

through all the events in British history, for example the Gunpowder Plot:
'To conspire to kill the King,
To raise Rebellion,
To alter Religion,
To subvert the State,
To procure invasion by Strangers.'

*'The Prophesy of Merlin' is in the Bodley 6943 ms, Magdalen College ms and elsewhere, and was used by Chaucer. The Magdalene version is as follows:

'When feythe fayleth in prestys sawys (when faith fails in priestly sayings)
And lordys will be londys lawys (and lords turn against God's laws),
And lechery is prevy solas, (and lechery is held as a privy solace)
And robbery is goode purchase (and robbery is a good bargain)
Then shall the londe of Albion (then shall England)
Be turned into confusion. (be turned into confustion)

When Goneway shall on Curtays call, (when rudeness calls upon courtesy)
Then Wallys shall rayke and hastely rise; (then Wales shall quickly rise)
Then Albion Skottlonde shall to hem fall; (and England Scotland fall to him)
Then waken wonders in every wise. (causing wonder in everyone)
The rede Irelonde foc shall rise with all (the red Irish fox shall rise with all)
With glayvys grownde, and gare men to agryse (with glaring grounds and cause men to attack?)
To fell and fende oure fomen all; (to battle all our enemies)
Sevyn shall sytt in youre asyse.' (seven will be taken to court)

FOOTNOTE:
A French scribe wrote in *'Vita Edward Secundi'*, 'The Life of Edward II, around 1330:
*'The Welsh habit of revolt against the English is a long-standing madness... and this is the reason. The Welsh, **formerly called the Britons**, were once noble, crowned with the whole realm of England; but they were expelled by the Saxons and lost both name and country. However, by the sayings of the prophet Merlin they still hope to recover England. Hence it is they frequently rebel.'*

THE MINER

There are no apologies for this entry. Each miner was as great a hero as any man in history, and came to symbolise Wales. 'Black Gold' originally referred to Welsh Black Cattle, when they were herded to England in the Middle Ages onwards. The discovery of vast amounts of the 'Black Diamond' or the other 'Black Gold' effectively changed the nature of much of Wales forever. The beautiful wooded valleys of Rhondda Fach and Rhodda Fawr were suddenly filled with tightly-packed terraced communities made up of workers from all over Britain and Ireland.

Since Mrs. Thatcher's decision to rely on subsidised foreign coal rather than the most efficient coal producing industry in the world, employment in the coalfields has collapsed. There were only 28 pits still open at the end of the strike which Thatcher used the police to help break. There are now only three pits of those twenty-eight left, and Tower Colliery only because the miners bought it to keep their jobs. Neil Hamilton, the deselected and disgraced former Tory Trade Minister, in response to the accusation that Wales would never vote Tory, said 'We got our own back by changing the constituencies and closing down the pits'. Tower Colliery is the only deep pit left in Wales, with just 240 employees, and a very limited life-span. There are two drift mines in Betws and Cwmgwili employing around another 220 men. There are some large-scale open-cast operations run by Celtic Energy, producing around 2.5 million tonnes per annum. It is a far cry from the 1930's when Wales produced a third of the world's consumption, and there were over 65 pits in The Rhondda alone. In 1913, over 250,000 men worked underground, now there are just 1500 colliers including overground staff. 40% of Welsh coal goes to one power station at Aberthaw, and at any contract renewal time we may see a switch to subsidised imports from Poland, Vietnam, Colombia or South Africa. Cardiff and Barry shipped a world record 13 million tonnes in 1913 - now nothing goes out. Colombia uses child labour in its mines and has a massive fatality rate.

The present total output of Welsh pits is around 3 million tonnes, compared to 57 million tonnes in the old days. Like all other mineral wealth, coal has been creamed off. The City of London has taken the money and run. When the pits were private, owners like the Marquis of Bute became multi-millionaires. When they were nationalised, the country made profits and did not have to import fuel, helping its Balance of Payments. Now there is nothing. All foreign coal that comes in is either heavily subsidised by governments or produced under inhuman conditions, as in Colombia. Ethics ? Morals ? or Free Trade ? (See Footnote).

The coal industry has been in decline since the change of propulsion from coal to oil in the shipping industry. As Home Secretary, Winston Churchill sent English troops to keep order in Tonypandy, an act that ensured his eternal unpopularity in the Welsh Valleys, despite his heroic role in the Second World War. In August 1914, the South Wales Miners'

Pit-head wheel, Pontlottyn
(photograph courtesy of WTB)

Federation proposed an international miners' strike to *stop the outbreak of war*, and there continued to be an anti-war movement in the South Wales mining areas. A massive increase in food prices, coupled with record profits for coal-owners, caused a demand for a new wage agreement in 1915 which was refused, so the South Wales miners went on strike. They were opposed by the Government, coal-owners, Great Britain Miners' Federation and the national newspapers, and the government threatened to imprison any strikers. However, the strike was solid. The then Minister of Munitions, Welshman David Lloyd George, intervened and settled the strike, acceding to most of the demands of the South Wales Miners' Federation.

Disputes continued, however, and in 1916 the Government took over control of the South Wales Coalfield. A year later, all other coalfields were effectively nationalised by the state, and in 1919 a Royal Commission recommended the continuation of nationalisation, as *being in the best interests of the state and miners*. After appearing to accept the Report, the Government handed back control of the industry in 1921 to the coal-owners. (Backhanders, bribes and corruption were as prevalent in the British political system as in any South American dictatorship. The only difference is that the British national press, xenophobic beyond belief, had always railed against 'Johnny Foreigner' while imprinting upon the population that 'British is Best'. Not surprisingly, all media barons end up as millionaires, honoured by the British government of the day with lordships and baronetcies. The Welsh have never believed the London-controlled media - they have always voted for the party of the people, Liberals then Labour, rather than the party of the English ruling classes). The coal-owners demanded lower wages, and on April 1, 1921, began a lock-out of the million miners in Britain who refused to accept the new terms. After three months, the South Wales Miners' Federation accepted defeat, after not being supported by the Transport Workers and Railwaymen, who reneged on their promise of solidity with the miners.

In 1926, the miners refused to work an extra hour a day, coupled with large pay cuts of 16-25%. On 30 April, 1926, those miners refusing the terms were locked out and the pits stopped producing. On 3rd May, the General Strike, called by the TUC, began. The mood in South Wales was almost revolutionary at this time, and when the TUC called off the strike just nine days later, the Welsh were left to fight on, alone and betrayed. Almost a quarter of a million men stayed away from the pit-heads. Police were called in from outside Wales to keep order, until the starving miners were forced back to work at the end of 1926. The effects on that South Walian generation solidified a feeling of 'us against the world' for decades. Once again, we return to Idris Davies to sum up the mood of the times, in a verse from 'Gwalia Deserta':

'Do you remember 1926 ? That summer of soups and speeches,
The sunlight on the idle wheels and the deserted crossings,
And the laughter and cursing in the moonlit streets ?
Do you remember 1926 ? The slogans and the penny concerts,
The jazz-bands and the moorland picnics,
And the slanderous tongues of famous cities ?
Do you remember 1926 ? The great dream and the swift disaster,
The fanatic and the traitor, and more than all,
The bravery of the simple, faithful folk ?
"Ay, ay, we remember 1926," said Dai and Shinkin,
As they stood on the kerb in Charing Cross Road,
"And we shall remember 1926 until our blood is dry."......'

Between 1921 and 1936, investment fell in the industry, and 241 mines were closed in South Wales, with the number of working miners falling from 270,000 to 130,000. One company owned 80% of anthracite coal production in South Wales, so kept the screw tight on employment and wages. In Dowlais, 73% of men were without work. 500,000 people left South Wales between the wars, looking for work. Edward VIII had made a famous visit to the coal-mining valleys in 1936, telling the 200,000 unemployed miners struggling through the Great Depression, *'Something must be done. You may be sure that all I can do for you I will.' Within 3 weeks he had abdicated,* never returning to Wales - the forked tongue of the Hanovers has been replicated in recent events regarding the marital fidelity of the entire clan.

H.V. Morton, in 'In Search of Wales', 1932, reports a South Wales miner in the 1930's as saying: *'Some of the worst cases of hardship I've known have been in homes where the father was trying to keep six children on £2 5s. a week and was too proud to accept help off anyone.......When you're on a shift you fall out for twenty minutes and eat bread and butter, or bread and cheese which your wife puts in your food tin......One day we were sitting like this talking when Bill didn't answer......He'd fainted. So I lifted him and carried him to the pit bottom to send him home, but before I did this I gathered up his food tin. There wasn't a crumb in it ! He'd been sitting there in the dark pretending to eat, pretending to me - his pal - Now that's pride.'*

In the 1960's seventy-four coal mines closed, and by 1985, only thirty-one were left. In 1996, only one deep pit, owned by the workers, is holding on at Tower. From 1948, with two hundred and fifty pits employing 113,000 miners, Wales has just one deep mine, with 240 colliers.

COLLIERY	CLOSED	JOBS LOST
North Celynen	March 1985	576
Abersychan	August 1985	424
Bedwas	August 1985	615
Markham	September 1985	606
South Celynen	September 1985	477
Aberpergwm	October 1985	317
Penrhiwceiber	October 1985	661
Abertillery New	October 1985	466
Maesteg St Johns	November 1985	888
Blaengarw	December 1985	727
Six Bells	March 1986	490
Nantgarw	November 1986	622
Ebbw Vale Cwm	November 1986	1259
Tonyrefail Coedely	November 1986	1259
Abernant	February 1988	845
Ynysybwl	February 1988	1130
Cynheidre	January 1989	1043
Oakdale	March 1989	873
Ebbw Vale Marine	March 1989	648
Merthyr Vale	August 1989	675
Trelewis	August 1989	296
Blaenant	May 1990	718
Penallta	November 1990	650
Maerdy	November 1990	777
Treharris	March 1991	766
Taff Merthyr	August 1992	688
TOTAL		18496

Big Pit, at Blaenafon, was sunk in 1860, but some galleries were worked for fifty years previously. It is now open as a mining museum, and the guided underground tour requires miners' helmets, and a three hundred feet (90m) drop in a pit cage to the coal seam. The Cefn Coed Colliery Museum in the Dulais Valley also simulates life underground, based at the Blaenant Colliery which was one of the last Welsh mines to close in 1990. The Rhondda Heritage Park is based around the former pits at Lewis Merthyr and Ty Mawr collieries in Trehafod.

Afan Argoed at Cymmer is the Welsh Miners' Museum, giving visitors an insight into the hardships of the old colliers and their communities. Little children pulled coal wagons 10-12 hours a day, 6 days a week, for two old pennies (less than one new penny) and were forced to repay one penny for the cost of their candles. Many ex-miners still suffer in

Big Pit, Blaenafon
(photograph courtesy of WTB)

agony from "The Dust" in their lungs, pneumoconiosis or silicosis, a few of which receive a pittance of a pension for it. All Welsh colliery records were removed to England by the NCB, to make it extremely difficult for NACODS (a small mining union) to prove rights to compensation for the survivors. The Labour Government is following the Tory pattern of holding on to Vibration White Finger and chronic bronchitis pay-outs. As disabled miners say, *'They're just waiting for us to die.'*

In the disastrous 1984 national miners' strike, the Welsh pits were the last to return to work. Maerdy, known as Little Moscow, was the last pit in the Rhondda, which closed in 1990. An Ogmore Vale collier defended the strike - *'Why on earth do they think we're fighting to defend stinking jobs in the pitch black ? There are no lavatories or lunch-breaks, no lights or scenery.........We're fighting because our community and our culture depends on it.'*

Of course, coal has been a mixed blessing for Wales – it attracted people from all over Britain to the unspoilt Welsh valleys, who assimilated into the Welsh culture. It gave jobs, albeit dangerous ones – miners' children were encouraged to 'improve' themselves and get into teaching rather than go down the pit. There is still a disproportionate number of Welsh people in British education at all levels. There were some terrible disasters, like the Senghenydd explosion. However, nothing in Welsh history hurt the nation as much as the Aberfan disaster of 1966. A coal slag tip, which the National Coal Board had been repeatedly warned was unstable, collapsed down a mountainside onto the village. The village primary school was drowned in black slurry, with one hundred and sixteen children and twenty-eight adults killed (- read the poem 'Chalice' which ends this book). A Disaster Appeal raised money for the remaining parents and the village, to build a new, smaller, school and make a memorial cemetery. £150,000 was taken out of the villagers' Disaster Fund by the Government to pay for the removal of the coal waste in 1967. In 1997, after thirty years' campaigning by Plaid Cymru, the Government repaid the money. However, they did not repay the £1.5 million it is worth now, but just the original £150,000.

The legacy of coal was that it changed South and North-East Wales and in two ways – the first is the obvious scarring of the landscape. Compare these two descriptions of the Rhondda Valley:

'The valley stretched for a distance of eight or ten miles between two nearly parallel lines of hills, broken by a succession of cliffs of singular beauty.....The emerald greenness of the meadows in the valley was most refreshing........ The air is aromatic with the wild flowers and mountain plants. A Sabbath stillness reigns.....it is the gem of Glamorganshire.' – C. Cliffe 1847.

'The river Rhondda is a dark, turgid and contaminated gutter, into which is poured the refuse of the host of collieries which skirt the thirteen miles of its course. The hills have been stripped of all their woodland beauty and there they stand, rugged and bare, with immense rubbish heaps covering their surface......The whole length of the valley has become transformed......the din of steel engines, the whirr of machinery, the grating sound of coal screens, and the hammering of the smithies proceed increasingly night and day, year in and year out. An unheard of wealth of industry and a great population have simultaneously sprung up together during the past sixty years......The industrial townships of this valley appear to be inseparably connected in one continuous series of streets of workmen's cottages to Pontypridd.' – Arthur Morris 1908.

So the valleys are scarred, but this population explosion in many ways reinvigorated Wales. Just from 1901 to 1910 the South Wales coalfield attracted 129,000 people, most from England. Wales was attracting immigrants at an annual rate of 4.5 per 1,000, almost as high as the new golden world of the U.S.A. This massive influx of immigration from England, Scotland and Ireland included my father's grandfather, who walked from Kent with his family to find work here at Barri Docks. His son married one of the Cadoxton Hyatts that originally worked at St Donat's Castle. My father met my mother, whose grandmother was a monoglot Welsh lady from near Trefeglwys in Montgomery. My mother's side of the family is pure Welsh. My father's family now only think of being Welsh – no-one has any English longing. People adapt to Wales. We find the Rabaiottis, McLucases, O'Briens and the Smiths advocating their Welshness to the trees. They came and they stayed. Their children have to leave Wales to find work, but even these grandchildren of 'settlers' have discovered *'hiraeth'* and return *'home'* to settle when they can.

FOOTNOTES:
1. The poem 'Chalice', about pit-disasters and the coal legacy is appended.

2. The doctrine of free trade dates from a 200-year-old theory, based upon two countries specialising in two goods for exchange. It does not take into account the fact that often goods are owned by virtually stateless multinationals across the world, who plough nothing back in the form of taxes into the countries in which they operate. British policy is to attract these multinationals with incentives such as free factories to create employment, however low-grade and unskilled. Support for domestic industry against these subsidised foreign competitors has been non-existent. The author compared Thatcher's treatment of native industry as *'the economics of Sparta'*. Sick babies were left on a mountain to see if they would live, just as UK companies have been left to wither, die and be taken over. Around

50% of Britain's manufacturing base, including all the 'choice' sectors, is now foreign-owned. Even the City of London is now virtually foreign-controlled. The latest news about Corus, a.k.a. British Steel, is cutting down on its Welsh operations, is no surprise. Although nominally a British-Dutch firm, most shares are owned by American companies, and short-term profits take precedence over long-term employment. The WDA's proud record in attracting call-centres to Wales ignores the fact that they are temporary unskilled jobs, paying just 58% of the national wage rate.

PRESIDENT JAMES MONROE April 28 1758 - July 4, 1831
'ERA-OF-GOOD-FEELING PRESIDENT', 'THE LAST COCKED HAT'

Born in Westmoreland County, Virginia, the son of Spence Monroe and Elizabeth Jones, he was President from March 4 1817 - March 3 1825. Monroe graduated from William and Mary College in 1776, and trained to be a lawyer. He served as a captain in the Continental Army in the American Revolution.

A Democrat-Republican, he served as a member of the Continental Congress from 1783-86, and as a Senator from 1790 - 94. In 1794 Monroe was appointed Minister to France, where he stayed until 1796, and was elected Governor of Virginia in which position he served from 1799-1802. He became Minster to France and England from 1803-1807, before being appointed Secretary of State by President Madison from 1811-1817. He was also Secretary of War from 1814-1815.

In 1816, Monroe easily beat Rufus King in the Presidential Election, winning 183 votes against 34, with 4 not cast. His salary was $25,000 to run the Presidential Office. He was the first US President to have been a US Senator, and his 1817 Inauguration was the first to be held outdoors. The White House was still being rebuilt after its burning by the British, when Monroe moved in, and upon January 1st, 1818 Monroe hosted a reception to mark its reopening. He had had to sell his own furniture to the government as the house was almost empty. In the uncontested 1820 election, Monroe gained 231 votes, with 3 not cast and just 1 vote for John Quincy Adams, who served as Monroe's Secretary of State from 1817-1825. Adams was not standing, but a vote was cast for him by the New Hampshire delegate, so that Washington would remain the only USA President elected

James Monroe

unanimously. The US Marine Band played *'Hail to the Chief'* at his 1821 Inauguration, the first time that song was played for a President. The band has played it at every inauguration since that time.

In 1818, the number of stripes on the US flag was fixed at 13 to honour the original colonies, and the Anglo-American Convention set the 49th Parallel as the border with Canada. In 1819, Florida was ceded to the USA by Spain, in exchange for the USA cancelling $5,000,000 worth of debts. In 1820, the Missouri Compromise forbade slavery above the latitude of 36 degrees and 30 minutes. In 1823, the Monroe Doctrine was delivered to Congress, warning European nations not to interfere with the free nations of the Western Hemisphere.

Long public service made Monroe a poor man (like Jefferson), and in 1830, Monroe was forced to move in with his daughter, where he died a year later. He is buried in Richmond, Virginia. Jefferson said of him: *'Monroe is so honest that if you turned his soul inside out there would not be a spot on it.'*

FOOTNOTE:
Of the first 6 presidents, 5 (James Madison, John Adams, John Quincy Adams, Jefferson and Monroe) were of Welsh descent. Of these, Jefferson, John Adams and Monroe all died on July 4, Independence Day. Madison missed it by a few days, dying on June 28th. Another man with Welsh antecedence must be noted as an American president, David Rice Atchison, who in reality was the 12th President, a Missouri senator. President James Polk had left the White House and Zachary Taylor was due to become President on March 4, 1849. However, March 4 was a Sunday, and Atchison became president 'pro tempore' of the Senate, serving under the provisions of the Senate for just one day until Taylor was sworn in. This Welsh-American was quite possibly the best ruler of any country in recorded history, not raising any taxes, telling any lies or starting any wars.

CAPTAIN HENRY MORGAN 1635? - August 25, 1688
THE GREATEST BUCCANEER

'Privateering' was the practice of the state commissioning privately-owned ships to attack enemy merchant ships. It came into its own with the sea-dog captains of the Elizabethan Age, men such as Drake, Hawkins, Frobisher and Raleigh. Legally sanctioned, it was fundamentally different from piracy, which preyed on all shipping, in that it focused upon enemy ships only. The Crown often sold privateering licences in return for a cut of the spoils. Many of the privateers who fought the Spaniards in the 17th century became known as buccaneers, from the French 'boucaniers', meaning sun-dryers of meat. *The most famous and successful of all the buccaneers was a Welshman, Henry Morgan.*

Henry Morgan was thought to have been a cousin of the Morgans that owned Tredegar Park outside Newport, the son of a gentleman farmer, probably from Llanrhymney. However, it seems that he was of lower station, as the Bristol Apprentice Books (Servants to Foreign Plantations) note *'February 9, 1655, Henry Morgan of Abergavenny, labourer, bound to Timothy Tounsend of Bristol, cutler, for three years to serve in Barbados on the like Conditions'*. This was the standard contract for emigration to the West Indies, and the 'conditions' referred to the fact that Morgan would be paid £10 after his three years of indentured service, when he would be free to work for anyone in 1658. He set sail from Bristol at the age of around twenty, bound for the West Indies to make his fortune. After another four years working in the sugar plantations of Jamaica, in 1662 he joined a ship heading to Jamaica to plunder Spanish ships and various enemy-occupied coastal towns. In 1655 Jamaica had been seized from Spain to serve as a base for free-booting American and British privateers to operate against Spanish America.

Morgan was so successful that within two years his share of the booty enabled him to buy his own ship. Aged just twenty nine, he now used Jamaica as his base, and from here he harassed the Spanish on the American mainland, and built up an enormous treasure trove. When the Spanish started attacking British ships off Cuba, the Governor of Jamaica asked Morgan to return and scatter the Spanish fleet. Morgan was then made Admiral of the Jamaican fleet of ten ships and five hundred men, because of his courage and success. By 1665, Morgan had made enough money to marry Elizabeth, the daughter of Edward Morgan of Llanrhymney, Deputy-Governor of Jamaica since 1664. It was this Morgan who was related to the great Morgan family of Tredegar House, Newport. From 1666, Morgan allied himself with Edward Mansfield, the famous buccaneer, and on Mansfield's death was elected 'admiral' of his buccaneer fleet. Governor Modyford of Jamaica gave Henry Morgan 'commissions' to attack the Spanish.

Well documented is Morgan's sacking of Puerto Principe (now Camaguey in Cuba) in 1668. In the same year, he looted and ransacked the largest city in Cuba,

Henry Morgan

Porto Bello, and Maracaibo in Venezuela. Morgan followed this up by crossing the Atlantic and he plundered some of Spain's richest coastal cities, but was eventually chased into open waters by the main Spanish fleet. Morgan and his privateers decided to turn and fight, and nearly annihilated the Spanish. On his return to his Jamaican base, Morgan had lost just eighteen men, and plundered a quarter of a million pieces of gold and silver coins, jewellery, silks, spices, munitions, weapons and slaves. Captain Morgan was just thirty three years old, with a reputation that had attracted seafarers from all over the West Indies to join his flag.

After his sacking of Porto Bello in Panama, Morgan attacked a French ship. It appeared that the French had given 'notes of exchange' to an English ship previously, in return for provisions. These notes had not been 'honoured' when presented for payment in Jamaica. Morgan positioned his flagship, The Oxford, in a bay in south Haiti, waiting for a sighting of the French ship. When it appeared, he invited the captain and officers to dine with them. Over the meal, he rebuked them for their treatment of the English ship, and imprisoned them. Morgan and his crew commenced carousing, firing guns into the air in their drunken dancing. Unfortunately, a spark of gunfire lit the powder magazine, and there was an explosion. Three hundred crew and the French prisoners were blown to bits.

Morgan and his officers were at the stern of the ship, and survived, being furthest away from the explosion. He returned to the site later, in The Jamaica Merchant, to try and salvage the ship, during which The Jamaica Merchant also sank. It now appears that The Oxford has been found, and salvage attempts have started. Also in 1669, the Spanish Capitan Pardal swore vengeance upon Morgan. After making a small raid on a Jamaican village, left the following note pinned to a tree near the smouldering village hall. '*I, Capitan Manuel Pardal, to the Chief of Privateers in Jamaica. I come to seek General Henry Morgan, with two ships and twenty-one guns. When he sees this Challenge, I beg that he will come out and seek me, that he may see the Valour of the Spaniards'*. Within weeks, Pardal was caught near the east coast of Cuba, and shot through the neck in battle.

On his return to Jamaica, Morgan was put in charge of thirty five ships and two thousand men. Aged thirty five, he decided to break the power of Spain in the West Indies by attacking Panama, their largest and richest town in the Americas. Meantime, Britain and Spain had negotiated peace in London and orders were despatched to him to call off any attacks on Spanish colonies. Morgan ignored the orders, reached the mainland in 1670, and marched across the Isthmus of Panama towards the city. In the course of this devastating raid, Morgan and his men succumbed to the heat and disease as they hacked their way through the jungle, destroying every fort and church in their path. By the time he reached Panama, in January 1671, Morgan had only a half of his original two thousand men left, but he attacked the defending force of twenty thousand Spaniards with such venom that they fled the city. One hundred and fifty mules were needed to take the booty back to the ships - Morgan went on ahead of the other buccaneer captains. He cleared off to the safety of Jamaica, with all of the greatest treasure proceeds in history, and was well on his way before the other privateers reached their ships.

The Spanish put a price on Morgan's head, and as the raid had occurred in peace-time, he was arrested and extradited to London in 1672. Governor Modyford had already been sent home to answer charges. Luckily for Morgan, the peace did not last and he was released after paying out a huge part of his treasure to the Crown. King Charles II knighted him and sent him back to Jamaica as Lieutenant Governor of the island, where Morgan died, a successful planter, at the age of fifty two in 1688. He was buried in Port Royal on August 26th, 1688.

FOOTNOTE:
The English translation publishers of Esquemeling's contemporary book, 'The Buccaneers of America' were sued by Morgan for calling him a 'pirate', and questioning his upbringing, in 1685. *This was the first ever recorded case of damages being paid and apologies being made for libel*. Subsequent editions feature the publisher's apologies. See 'The Book of Welsh Pirates' by T.D Breverton, published late 2001.

JOHN PIERPOINT MORGAN   1837- 1913
'THE MAN WHO SINGLE-HANDEDLY SAVED THE USA FROM BANKRUPTCY ON TWO OCCASIONS', 'THE MOST POWERFUL MAN IN AMERICA', 'THE CORSAIR'

After the Civil War, John Pierpoint Morgan built his father's firm into most influential private banking house in the USA. His company grew to be the most important force in American finance in the quarter-century before the First World War.

Morgan was born into a wealthy family in Hartford, Connecticut, and in 1854 his father Junius Spencer Morgan became a partner in George Peabody's banking house in London. Junius took over the firm when Peabody retired, naming it J.S. Morgan & Co. After completing his education at a Swiss finishing school and Gottingen University in 1856, his son worked in London for Junius. However, by 1857 John Pierpoint Morgan had left to work on Wall Street, initially selling

European securities underwritten by his father's firm. By 1862 John Pierpoint had opened his own firm. In 1863, however, Morgan was investigated by a Congressional Committee on Government Contracts. He had purchased and resold defective rifles to General Fremont's troops in St Louis. Firing the guns amputated the thumbs of the Union soldiers when fighting the Confederates, and the army refused to pay. Undeterred, Morgan filed a claim for $110, 000 (- he had paid less than $18,000 for the rifles). The committee report was scathing upon Morgan: *He cannot be looked upon as a good citizen, entitled to favourable consideration of his claim, who seeks to augment the vast burdens daily increasing, that are to weigh on the further industry of the country, by demands upon the Treasury for which nothing entitled to the name of an equivalent has been rendered... Worse that traitors in arms are the men who pretending loyalty to the flag, feast and fatten on the misfortunes of the nation, while patriot blood is crimsoning the plains of the South and bodies of their countrymen are mouldering in the dust.'* Morgan was considered a 'robber-baron' who made his fortune during the war, along with Gould, Armour, Rockefeller and Carnegie. Somehow Morgan emerged unscathed, and helped refinance the US Government after the Civil War, but several friends and colleagues were imprisoned for fraud.

As a financial advisor to national governments, the Morgan company established its presence in 1870, when it extended a daring £10 million loan to the besieged government of France in the Franco-Prussian War. (The firm was financial representative for Britain and France in both World Wars, and in 1988 issued $2.6 billion in bonds to finance long-term debt for Brazil, a model now widely used in the restructuring of debt for developing companies. It also arranged a similar deal for Russia). In 1871 Morgan merged with Drexel of Philadelphia. The new firm, Drexel, Morgan & Co., opened its offices on the corner of Wall Street and Bond Street, which is still now the headquarters of the Morgan Bank. In 1873, there was a Wall Street crisis, when the strongest survived, among them being Morgan. In the 1880's, Morgan sponsored the Edison Light Company.

The rapid expansion of American railways after the Civil War had led to price wars and fragmentation. Frequent mergers and bankruptcies had made the sector one with extremely complex financial structures, and Morgan realised the need to rationalise the industry, reorganising major companies such as the Baltimore and Ohio, the Chesapeake and Ohio and the Erie line. He brokered one agreement between two competing railroads by inviting both presidents upon his yacht for a cruise, and refusing to let them off, until they came to terms. His bank had financed the development of the railroad system to open up America, and by 1900 Morgan controlled one of the six major railway lines. A forbidding physical presence, his authority in the banking world was becoming the stuff of legend, even before he

John Pierpoint Morgan

took over J.S. Morgan & Co. on his father's death, and renamed it J.P. Morgan & Co. in 1890. John Pierpoint became senior partner with offices in London, Paris, New York and Philadelphia. After the 1893 financial panic, Morgan formed a syndicate to float a dollar bond issue for President Grover Cleveland to finance an increased gold reserve. He rescued the Gold Standard in 1895 and this stabilised the traumatic American economy.

In 1901, Morgan was instrumental in the creation of US Steel, the largest corporate enterprise in the world at that time, capitalised at $1.4 billion. He had bought out Andrew Carnegie's steel empire for $480 million, and combined it with several smaller companies, making the world's first billion-dollar company. Later he told an abashed Carnegie that he would have paid him $100 million more if he had asked for it. Also in 1901 Morgan was accused of starting a financial panic so that he could acquire cheap assets. In 1902 he created the International Harvester company, and also was instrumental in forming the famous General Electric (GE), and AT&T, as his pressures to merge formed the foundation for modern corporations. 1902 also saw the control of the White Star Line move from Britain, when it was purchased by the International Mercantile Marine Company (IMM) for $10 million. This vast shipping combine had been created by none other than John Pierpoint Morgan. IMM built the ill-fated Titanic in 1912. Morgan now controlled large chunks of the economy, including the Equitable Life Assurance Society. Morgan was attacked for creating monopolies ('trusts' he called them), but the Harvard business historian Alfred Chandler believed that Morgan replaced the invisible hand of competition with the visible hand of corporate management, paving the way for American economic dominance in the 20th century. Morgan and his partners sat on the boards of 112 huge companies, spanning finance, railways, transport and utilities.

In 1907, when a banking panic threatened to spin out of control, Morgan took command and rallied the other bankers to restore confidence. He locked a group of financiers into his library until they agreed to bail out the Trust Company of America, and thus saved a financial meltdown. Morgan also imported $100 million of gold from Europe to stop the run on the banks. Morgan wielded as much power as the President, and had turned Wall Street into his personal playground - it is thought that he was the source of the rumour which led to the crisis. This panic led to the creation of the Federal Reserve System in 1913, the year the Morgan died in Rome. Interestingly, the banking houses of Morgan and Rockefeller came to maintain and control the great intelligence services of the 20th century. Many agents of their banking houses worked for the US intelligence agencies. During World War I, one of the most important areas of agent authentication was the fabrication of passports, ID cards and other documents. J.P. Morgan's son, Commander Henry Spencer Morgan, ran the censorship and documents agency and compiled intelligence from mail, cables and telephone intercepts.

Towards the end of his life, Morgan began an affair with the beautiful Victoria Sackville-West, who wrote when she started seeing Morgan in 1911: '*I have never met anyone as attractive. One forgets his nose entirely after a few minutes, as his eyes are either twinkling or full of kindness and expression. He will be 75 next April! He is full of life and energy. A wonderful man.*' She was referring to Morgan's enormous, purple-veined proboscis, a result of untreated acne rosacaea. A surgeon had offered to operate, to which Morgan had responded '*If I come to New York with my nose cured, every street boy will laugh at me and split his sides laughing.'* However, his success with women was legendary. It was rumoured at the time that his real reason in financing a hospital for pregnant women was to cater to his mistresses.

He put together one of the greatest art collections in history, which he bequeathed amongst others to the Metropolitan Museum of Fine Art in New York, and his private library became the public Pierpoint Morgan library. In his last years, Morgan was asked by a congressional committee if money was not the basis of commercial credit. He replied *'No sir, the first thing is character... a man I do not trust could not get money from me for all the bonds in Christendom.'* This performance in 1912 was a tour de force, but it exhausted him, and in February 1913 he collapsed in Egypt of nervous exhaustion, babbling about conspiracies. A month later, he died in Rome.

Morgan's control of American public and private financing is without parallel. The 1998 'Forbes' survey put Bill Gates' worth, from his Microsoft shares, at $51 billion. However, Morgan controlled a percentage of American Gross Domestic Product many times that of Gates. *'Peter Drucker calculated recently that Morgan was rich enough to finance all of America's capital investments, whether private or public sector (except housing), for a period of four months – but that to do so today would take the fortunes of the top 60 American billionaires combined.'* (Daily Telegraph, 28th June 1998). He had been the driving force behind the railroad, shipping, telephone, electrical and steel industries in the USA, as well as the forming of the basis of modern multinational companies, making America the world leader in production.

FOOTNOTES:

1. Morgan stated that *'Compounding is the eighth wonder of the world'*, and Einstein reinforced his view, saying *The most powerful concept or principle in the world that I am aware of, is that of compounding.'* This refers to the impact of time upon the money that one accumulates through saving at a rate above inflation. As the Hudson Institute confirms, *'It takes 90% of the time to get half-way to your goal, the rest comes with a rush.'*

2. In 1934, H.G. Wells was interviewing Stalin for the International Herald Tribune, and referred to Morgan as a parasite who cared only for profit. Stalin demurred, saying *'We Soviet people learn a great deal from the capitalists. And Morgan, whom you characterise so unfavourably, was undoubtedly a good, capable organiser.'*

BISHOP WILLIAM MORGAN c.1545 - September 10 1604
TRANSLATOR OF THE BIBLE INTO WELSH

Celebrated in the Church in Wales on the anniversary of his death, Morgan was responsible for the survival of the Welsh language. William's father was John ap Morgan ap Llywelyn, and his mother Lowri ferch William ap John ap Madog. His place of birth at Tŷ Mawr, Wybrnant, Penmachno, Nant Conwy is open to the public. Educated at St Johns, Cambridge, he graduated in 1568, was ordained at Ely in the same year, took his MA in 1571, and his D.D. in 1583.

An Act of Parliament in 1563 was passed to allow the translation of the Bible and the Book of Prayer into Welsh *'because the English tongue is not understood of the most and greatest number of all her majesty's most living and obedient subjects inhabiting Wales'.*

It seems that from 1572-77 William Morgan held the ancient parish of Llanbadarn Fawr near Aberystwyth, then becoming vicar of Welshpool (1575-79), holding the sinecure of Denbigh (1575-96), becoming vicar of Llanrhaeadr-ym-Mochnant and also Llanarmon (1578-95). From 1579 Morgan was rector of Llanfyllin, and parson of Pennant Melangell (1588-95). There was some hostility to Morgan at Llanrhaeadr, from the family of his nephew Evan Meredith, over a wedding of a wealthy heiress to Robert Wynn of Gwydir. The Star Chamber recorded that Morgan was a conscientious man, harassed by the malice of his enemies. Despite his problems, the vicar completed his vast work of the translation of the Bible while at Llanrhaeadr, probably taking over 20 years to complete it. He revised Salesbury's translation of the New Testament, and was encouraged in his work by Archbishop Whitgift, who gave most financial support to his publishing of the Bible. John Davies and Edmwnd Prys also assisted Morgan (see footnotes).

Dr Gabriel Goodman of Ruthin had been chaplain to William Cecil (Lord Burghley, q.v.), and one of Cecil's executors. As Dean of Westminster, this famous churchman assisted greatly in the production of Morgan's Bible, allowing Morgan to stay with him in London between 1587 and 1588. Dedicated to Queen Elizabeth Tudor, Morgan's work marked the beginning of modern Welsh literature and helped spur the Nonconformist movement. Also in 1588, his translation of the Psalms was published. In 1595, Morgan was made Bishop of Llandaf, and moved to be Bishop of St Asaf in 1601.

His life was not without struggles, and he died a poor man, being buried at St Asaph. After his death *'an inventorie of all and singular the goodes and chattells'* of the churchman was made *'for the payment of the Debtes dewe by the said late Bishopp'*. From the *'Chamber where the Bishopp lay'* were taken *'two fether beddes' and 'one boulster'* worth ten shillings (50p), and a *'looking glasse'* worth 20 pence (8p). Also among his possessions were 40 tons of coal, and ten chickens worth three shillings. There is a memorial in the grounds of St Asaf Cathedral to the Bible's translators.

The 1588 Bible is the most important book in the history of Welsh language and literature, and its existence probably saved the language itself. At the time, there was *'alarming decay'* in the Welsh language, fragmenting into different dialects, idioms and styles with the lack of any central referent source. Morgan went back to sources like the Mabinogion and medieval romances, to escape the current corruption of the tongue, and what emerged was a language which avoided Salesbury's pedantry. Morgan used the vigour and purity of earlier works, but added flexibility to give a wider range of expression. He gave the language a new lease of life*, providing writers with a pattern. As the Welsh people learned to read the Bible through the schools of Griffith Jones (q.v.), and as every family tried to purchase one, the language of the Bible began to influence spoken Welsh. The language was reinforced around a central core, with the influence of preachers, and gave the Welsh people a real sense of national identity. *'Every Welshman who speaks Welsh is under a deep obligation to William Morgan'*.

Worth noting here is the fact that *'Welsh was the only non-state language of Protestant Europe to become the medium of a published Bible within a century of the Reformation. Perhaps it is mainly to this fact that much of the strength of present-day Welsh is owed, compared to Irish (which did not get its own Bible until*

1690 and where Catholic congregations did not have access to it, and Scots Gaelic (which had to wait until 1801)'. This information is sourced from that superb website, britannia.com, of which Peter Williams and other Welshmen domiciled in America can be justly proud.

*Meic Stephens wrote that *'The Bible of 1588 was as influential in keeping alive the idea of an independent Wales as the defeat of the Armada was in maintaining England's independence'*, and that since Morgan's language was that of the poets, *'contemporary and classical, natural and dignified'*, his Bible *'ensured the purity, accuracy and strength of the poetic vocabulary should live on.'* At this time the bards were facing extinction in Wales.

FOOTNOTES:

1. JOHN DAVIES 1567-1644 - Holy Day May 15
Dr John Davies of Mallwyd is one of the greatest Welsh scholars, given a Holy Day by the Church in Wales. Born in Llanferres, the son of David ap John ap Rhys and Elizabeth ferch Lewis ap David Lloyd, he graduated from Jesus College in 1593. He was close to Bishop William Morgan of Llandaf, whom he helped translate the Bible. He gained his divinity degree and doctorate from Lincoln College Oxford in 1608 and 1616 respectively. From 1604 he was rector of Mallwyd, and also gained the rector's post at Llan-ym-Mawddwy in 1614. He surrendered the sinecure of Darowen for the sinecure of Llanfor in 1621. From 1617 he was the prebendary of Llanefydd in the cathedral church of St Asaf. Davies is best known for his great Welsh-Latin Dictionary of 1632, which he compiled during his time as Rector at Mallwyd. His Welsh grammar, 'Antiquae Lingua Britannicae', was another magisterial work dating from 1620, and it is supposed that he was an active contributor to Richard Parry's Welsh Bible of 1620. He stayed at Mallwyd for 40 years, and his contribution towards the survival of the Welsh language cannot be underestimated.

2. EDMWND PRYS 1544-1623   Holy Day May 15
Given the Holy Day of May 15th (the same as John Davies), this archdeacon of Merioneth was possibly born at Llanfor in the same county. After St Asaf's Cathedral School, he went to St John's College, Cambridge, and in 1572 was given the living of Ffestiniog and Maentwrog. In 1576 he was appointed rector of Ludlow, and that same year made archdeacon. From 1576 until his death he lived at Tyddyn-ddu, Maentwrog. Llandenddwyn was given him in 1580, and he was made canon of St Asaf in 1602. Prys assisted William Morgan in his translation of the Bible, and published a book of psalms in 1621, *'the first Welsh book in which music was printed.'* He also wrote 'contemplative' poetry. His first wife was Elin ferch John ap Lewis of Pengwern, and his second wife was her cousin, Gwen ferch Morgan ap Lewis of Pengwern. 'The Dictionary of Welsh Biography' notes the distinguished children of the marriages.

JOHN NASH 1752 - May 13 1835
THE ARCHITECT OF THE REGENCY, THE MAN WHO CHANGED THE FACE OF LONDON

John Nash of Cardigan was apprenticed to Sir Robert Taylor, and lived in Carmarthen from 1784-1796, designing several local houses, as well as the Cardigan County gaol and the west front and chapter house of St David's Cathedral. He had previously gone bankrupt in London, so returned to Wales in 1783. After his second move to London in the 1790's, he designed the wonderful and superbly oriental Prince Regent's Pavilion at Brighton. He laid out *Regent's Park, Trafalgar Square, St James Park, Carlton House Terrace and Regent Street.* One of the greatest town planners, his 1779 patent for improvements to the piers and arches of bridges led the way for the introduction of steel girders in building. On his return to London, Nash had collaborated in a partnership with the landscape gardener Sir Humphrey Repton, but became employed by the Prince of Wales from 1798.

The beautiful house he designed in Llanerchaeron, near Aberaeron, is now a National Trust property. It is the finest example of a classical villa in Wales, being restored at a cost of over £2,000,000. The original house was remodelled by Nash, with a free-standing billiards room, home farm, superb granary, cow-byre etc., and forms the centre-piece of a rare example of a Welsh gentry estate of the period. Originally belonging to the Parry family, descendants of Llywelyn Fawr, it passed to the Lewis family in 1634, and Colonel Lewis commissioned Nash in the 1790's. John Powell Ponsonby Lewes left the estate in his bequest to the nation in 1989. Its 670 acres include two historic parks, three SSSI's, the unaltered farm complex and labourers' cottages. The estate's property manager says '*Llanerchaeron is nationally important, as estates have all but disappeared through dereliction, fragmentation, modernisation and development.*' Also in Wales, Nash roofed the Church of St Peters, and designed the great and beautiful houses of Nanteos (where the 'Holy Grail' was kept), Dolaucothi and Hafod.

John Nash

The Royal palace at Brighton was originally a large 18th century farmhouse, which Henry Holland transformed for the Prince Regent (later George IV) into a Palladian villa from 1787. However, the prince commissioned his favourite architect, John Nash in 1814 to create a more exotic vision, and by 1822 there was completed an extraordinary building, completely against the refined neo-Classical mode of Regency times. Said to have cost over £500,000, it is a mixture of Indian exterior and Chinese interior, with bulbous domes, minaret chimneys, silk wall-hangings, and an astonishing tribute to the versatility of John Nash. Apart from his church work, he built Gothic country houses and Palladian terraces. Nash acquired considerable wealth, and from 1798 built East Cowes Castle on the Isle of Wight, which influenced the early Gothic Revival school of architecture.

Nash's London was a mish-mash of architectures - the rich preferred to have their great houses in the countryside, and town houses in London. The city was a collection of unconnected suburbs. Prince George became regent as George III passed further and further into the dark realms of insanity, and decided that Britain needed a real capital city, as had been achieved in Paris. With Napoleon's defeat, Britain was now the greatest power and major trading nation in the world. In 1811, the prince selected John Nash to expand his leased income properties in London. In this year, Marylebone Park had reverted to Crown ownership, and the prince saw the chance to build upon it and make a rental property fortune. He loved Nash's work on the Prince's Royal Pavilion in Brighton, and asked him to design Regent's Park, a new housing development on Crown lands. Nash was in competition against two government architects, who proposed an inward-looking development, but Nash proposed keeping the (former Marylebone) Regent's Park, and connecting it to the rest of the city with a sweeping new street, Regent Street. He also linked the street to existing landmarks, opening up vistas rather than closing them off. The park was given a lake, the Regent's canal, a large wood and botanical area, and on the periphery shopping arcades and picturesque groupings of residences. The Prince Regent agreed, saying he was *'so pleased with this magnificent plan which will eclipse Napoleon's.'* In his 1811 plan, Nash said the street should constitute *'a boundary and complete separation between the streets and squares occupied by the nobility and gentry, and the narrow and meaner houses occupied by mechanics and the trading part of the community.'* Thus it would appeal to rich people who could afford to pay high rents to the Prince.

His bold and unpopular plan led to mass destruction of slums and houses, and he was mercilessly lampooned in the press until the completion of the project. Nash sliced through the city with Regent Street and new connecting streets, lining them with new buildings and pavilions. He planned, designed, and even acted as general contractor, bartering constantly with masons, carpenters and builders. Where Regent Street joined the Park, Nash designed the long and beautiful curve of houses known as Park Crescent. Designed to look like a palace, the crescent was a row of houses in a palace façade. The people of London came to love the 'Nash Terraces' in the area, and his system of inter-linking parks and landmarks. The Quadrant led into Piccadilly Circus. Nash gave London a shape totally unconnected to the old system of separate village squares, a *garden city* of villas, terraces, crescents, a canal and lakes. From Carlton House (Prinnie's home) and St James's Park to Regent's Park and its lake, on one side of Regent Street lies the original city of London, and on the other Westminster. The street was widened, and forced to twist and turn by Nash as he could not afford to buy up any of the more expensive West End properties to achieve his goal. Nash's elegant, neo-classical style, with its porticoes, pediments, statues and colonnades, became known as 'Regency' architecture.

In 1820, George IV decided to reconstruct Buckingham Palace, as his Carlton House was *'antiquated, run-down and decrepit'*, and gave John Nash a budget of £450,000 to achieve its transformation. Nash retained the main block, but doubled its size and faced the main block with mellow Bath stone, adding a new suite of rooms facing west to the gardens. In 1827 he demolished the North and South Wings, and rebuilt on a larger scale with a triumphal arch. In 1829, he was sacked (after George IV's death) because the cost of rebuilding had reached £500,000, and the building was completed in the 1830's by Edward Blore. Today's palace, however, is the work of Nash. During the building work, Nash redesigned Marble Arch in 1828, inspired by Rome's Arch of Constantinus. It was supposed to be the gateway to the Mall, but was too narrow for the State Coach to pass through, and moved to the top of Hyde Park.

Nash also cleared the slums and mazes of alleys to form Trafalgar Square as a lasting monument to Admiral Nelson in 1841, and designed Nelson's Column. In his work on Regent Street, he built the remarkable All Soul's Church in Langham Place, with its needle-shaped spire and colonnades. Apart from his work on St James's Park (1827-29) and Regent's Park and its terraces (1811-25), Nash's key works are: The United Services Club, Pall Mall 1827; Regent Street 1813-25; the Brighton Pavilion 1815-21; Royal Opera Arcade 1816-1818; Haymarket Theatre

1822-25; All Souls' Church, Langham Place 1822-1825; the Marble Arch (1828); Buckingham Palace 1821-30; Carlton House Terrace 1827-33; the Royal Mews 1825 and Trafalgar Square 1826-35. In 1825 he designed the Picton Monument in Carmarthen to Sir Thomas Picton (q.v.)

A generous patron of artists, Nash died at East Cowes in 1835, aged 81. He had changed the face of London forever and inspired new generations of architects. He was an almost exact contemporary of that other great architect, Sir John Soane (1753-1837), and the architects Pugin and Salvin trained under John Nash.

RICHARD 'BEAU' NASH   October 18 1674 - February 3 1761
'THE KING OF BATH', 'THE MASTER OF CEREMONIES', 'THE DANDY OF BATH'

Richard 'Beau' Nash was born in Swansea, son of Richard Nash of Pembrokeshire (possibly from the village of Llangwm), who had settled in Swansea as a partner in a glass-works. His mother was one of the Pembrokeshire Poyer family. Educated at Queen Elizabeth's Grammar School, Carmarthen, Beau Nash went to Jesus College, Oxford, but dropped out. He joined the army but found that it was too expensive and time-consuming, then went to the Middle Temple in 1693 to study law. He hardly attended, but somehow lived a sybaritic and hedonistic life, probably through his skills in gambling. In 1695 Nash organised a pageant for King William III at the Middle Temple, who was so impressed that he offered Nash a knighthood. Not having the means to support a title, Nash declined. From henceforward he lived by making huge wagers and gaming, and receiving gifts from women admirers.

The small town of Bath had been exploited by the Romans for its hot mineral springs, which pump out 250,000 gallons of water a day, but it was Nash who gave it its special social appeal. Queen Anne's visits in 1692, 1702 and 1703 to take the waters had improved Bath's social standing. Attracted to Bath in 1705, Nash organised a band, and took a lease of rooms 'for assembly'. A failed scholar, lawyer and soldier, he excelled in organising social ceremonies. He was a socialite with a penchant for order, cleanliness and propriety. He was first aide-de-camp to the master of ceremonies, a Captain Webster, who was soon killed in a duel*. Nash then transformed Bath into the fashionable centre of England. In 1706 he raised the fortune of £18,000 by subscription to improve the roads in the City around his 'Assembly Rooms'. The roads were paved, so gowns did not drag in the mud, beggars and thieves were driven out of Bath, and sedan chair drivers were fined for insolence. Nash drew up rules against the wearing of swords, duelling, informal dress, promiscuous smoking and the cheating of 'chairmen' (sedan-chair carriers) and lodging-house keepers. Nash, champion of the 'gentlemen of fashion' took to snuff and decried the use of pipes. He prohibited all smoking in public rooms and assemblies, and manufacturers started scenting snuff, as on the Continent, to meet a massive upsurge in demand. (Snuff mills across Britain, notably still in Kendal, were built by 1720 to meet the demand caused by Nash's fashion). He enforced his rules autocratically against noble and commoner alike.

Nash's 'rules' of 'polite society' were allied to a common dress code and the discouragement of 'hard drinking'. He was so successful in attracting both the aristocratic elite and the growing gentry class to his fashionable and safe town, that Bath's population grew from 3,000 in 1700 to 35,000 in 1800, swelled also by visitors in the 'Bath Season' of October to early June. (It became the 8th largest city in England). The rules and dress code encouraged sociability between the gentry and nobles, and made the less fashionably-minded feel at home. His *'Rules - by general consent determined'* are as follows:

I.   *That a visit of ceremony at coming to Bath, and another at going away, is all that is expected or desired by ladies of quality and fashion - except impertinents.*

II.   *That ladies coming to the ball appoint a time for their footmen's coming to wait on them home, to prevent disturbances to themselves and others.*

III.   *That gentlemen of fashion never appearing in a morning before the ladies in gowns and caps, show breeding and respect.*

IV.   *That no person take it ill that any one goes to another's play or breakfast, and not to theirs - except captious by nature.*

V.   *That no gentleman give his tickets for the balls to any but gentlewomen - N.B. Unless he has none of his acquaintance.*

VI.   *That gentlemen crowding before ladies at the ball, show ill-manners; and that none do so for the future - except such as respect nobody but themselves.*

VII.   *That no gentleman take it ill that another dances before them - except such as have no pretence to dance at all.*

VIII.   *That the elder ladies and children be contented with a second bench at the ball, as being past or not come to perfection.*

IX.   *That the younger ladies take notice how many eyes observe them - N.B. This does not extend to the Have-at-Alls.*

X.   *That all whisperers of lies and scandals be taken as their authors.*

XI.   *That all repeaters of such lies and scandal be shunned by all company - except such as have been guilty of the same crime. N.B. Several men of no character, old women and young ones of questioned reputation, are great authors of lies in the place, being of the sect of Levellers.*

"Beau" Nash, 1742

A superb conversationalist and wearing distinctive clothes, he was the arbiter of fashion and taste. From the start, he dressed the part, and moved with an exaggerated elegance, which soon earned him the nickname 'Beau'. Instead of the popular white wigs of the time, he wore a black wig, with a jewelled cream beaver hat set at a rakish angle. His coat was highly decorated with lace and braid, and left open to show his splendid waistcoat and ruffled shirt. Nash made Bath the playground of the English aristocracy, the most fashionable resort in the land. He was a bon vivant, and star of the show, with his huge white hat, parading around the paved streets in a carriage drawn by six grey horses, his progress announced by the blast of French horns. Although dismissed as a 'fop' and a 'dandy', he soon imposed his rules of polite society across the city. Nash encouraged the wealthy to invest in new buildings.** Nash initiated the buildings of the Pump Rooms, overlooking the King's Bath, where the company of rich people could assemble to gossip, as well as the Assembly Rooms, with a huge ballroom for the sparkling balls and adjoining card (gaming) room. Poor lodgings were replaced by luxurious ones. He even built a hospital, promoting the use of Bath's mineral waters.

In the Pump Rooms and the Assembly Rooms, the Master of Ceremony's word was law. He ridiculed the wearing of riding boots at fashionable gatherings. One of Nash's rules forbade the wearing of boots in the rooms at evening, and a country squire tried to defy him. Nash asked him *'Why have you not also brought your horse into the ballroom, since the four-footed beast is as well-shod as its master?'* Princess Amelia, the daughter of George II, was refused one more dance when he had decreed that the music should stop. In Constance Hill's biography of Jane Austen we read: *'When Miss Austen and her uncle had passed in also, they would find themselves in a long, lofty room lighted by tall windows, and having at each end a large semi-circular arched recess, one containing the musicians' gallery, the other a statue of Beau Nash standing in a niche above a tall clock. Beau Nash! who for fifty years "was literally the King of Bath", and of whom Goldsmith wrote: "I have known him on a ball night strip even the Duchess of Queensberry of her costly lace apron, and throw it to one of the back benches; observing that none but abigails appeared in white aprones; and when the Princess Amelia applied to him at 11 o'clock for one more dance he refused, his laws being as he said like those of Lycurgus - unalterable."* Dress Balls were held once a week and began at 6pm, when the eleven musicians on the first-floor gallery struck up. Between 6 and 8 there were minuets, a stately dance performed by couples alone: *'It is often remarked by Foreigners that the English nation of both sexes look as grave when they are dancing, as it they were attending the Solemnity of a Funeral.'* The more energetic country dances followed between 8 and 9 and required a freer dress, and the Rules of the Assembly Rooms noted: *'No Lady dances country-dances in a hoop of any kind and those who choose to pull the hoops off, will be assisted by proper servants in an apartment for that purpose.'* At 9 the dancers moved to the Tea Room for refreshment, and the entertainment continued with further country dances until 11, when the evening was ended by the Master of Ceremonies. Nash *'entering the ballroom. Orders the music to cease, and the ladies thereupon resting themselves till they grow cool, their partners complete the ceremonies of the evening by handing them to the (sedan) chairs in which they are conveyed to their respective lodgings.'*

An 'Assembly' was defined in 1751 as *'a stated and general meeting of the polite persons of both sexes, for the sake of conversation, gallantry, news and play.'* Guests amused themselves at cards, drank tea or walked around talking and flirting. The Assembly Rooms had been constructed by Nash for this purpose, with different rooms being used for tea-drinking, eating, gossiping, dancing and gaming. The Tea Room was used mainly for refreshments and concerts. Meals were served throughout the day, from public breakfasts, to supper during Dress Balls. Food on the side-tables included *'sweetmeats, jellies, wine, biscuits, cold ham and turkey.'* Tea was the favoured drink, usually drunk weak and without milk, but sometimes with arrack (fermented cocoa) and lemon. A foreign visitor noted that Bath's tea-parties were *'extremely gay'.*

Richard 'Beau' Nash

Sometimes, things got out of hand: *'The tea-drinking passed as usual, and the company having risen from the tables, were sauntering in groups, in expectation of the signal to attack, when the bell beginning to ring, they flew with eagerness to the dessert, and the whole place was instantly in commotion. There was nothing but jostling, scrambling, pulling, snatching, struggling, scolding and screaming.'*

In 1738 Nash welcomed the Prince of Wales to Bath, and set up an obelisk, inscribed by Alexander Pope, to mark his visit. Bath had become 'the place to be, and be seen', and Nash's presence and the social scene also drew in many of the architects who accomplished great buildings in the city. It was during his time that the city acquired its ranks of Palladian mansions and town houses, all built in the local honey-coloured Bath stone, in which all new buildings have to be clad, even today. The physical design of the wonderful city of Bath under the two John Woods is entirely due to Nash. The Woods created Queen Square, the North and South parades and the Royal Crescent. In 1820, Nash's Assembly Rooms were burnt to the ground. Also known as 'the Lower Rooms', they were situated on *'the Walks leading from the Grove to the Parades', with 'a Ball Room ninety feet long, as well as two tea rooms, a card room' and 'an apartment devoted to the games of chess and backgammon'. 'They were superbly furnished with chandeliers, girandoles, etc.'*

Two meetings with the preacher John Wesley have been recorded, both to the detriment of Nash. On one occasion, Beau jested to his friends that he would attend a prayer meeting and confound the Methodist 'ranter'. He entered the meeting, swaggering pompously, and a large audience had gathered to 'see the fun'. Nash asked Wesley by what authority he dared to preach, declaring that he was breaking the laws, and added *'Besides your preaching scares people out of their wits.'* Wesley responded *'Sir, did you ever hear me preach?'* and Nash replied that he had not. Wesley asked *'How the can you just of what you have never heard?'* *"By common report'.* answered Nash, to which Wesley responded *'Sir, is not your name Nash? I dare not judge you by common report. I think it is not enough to judge by.'* Nash then said *'I desire to know what these people come here for.'* A member of the congregation answered *'Sir, let an old woman answer him. You, Mr Nash, take care of your body. We take care of our souls, and for the food of our souls we have come here'.* Flustered, Nash left, and Wesley proceeded with his sermon. Desiring revenge, Beau Nash was walking down a narrow street in Bath, and saw Wesley walking through the crowds towards him. He rushed forwards, confronting the preacher, crying *'Make way, sir! I never give way to fools!'.* John Wesley calmly answered, *'Why sir, I always do'* and graciously stepped aside to make way for the red-faced rake.

However, tighter laws against gaming, in 1740 and 1745, reduced Nash's circumstances, and his income and influence waned. When gaming had been allowed, his position as Master of Ceremonies had made it difficult for him to absolutely ruin himself - he would have had to have shown control in the socially charged atmosphere of the gaming tables. The gambling tables were the main attraction for the idle rich, and attracted sharpsters (professional gamblers) as well, who exploited the more amateur players. Gambling was carried on at a fever-pitch, as illustrated in Connely's biography of Nash: *'Not even his loss of £1400 impaired his prestige as guardian of the games. His net reputation was that he was a winner, because of his "superior skill and dispassionate attention". Players who lost £20 to £200 begged Nash to tie them up, like Ulysses, lest they succumb to the siren sound of the dice, and the Master often caught hold of a player's dice-box in mid-air."* Bath became the centre for high-stakes gambling, and it was not uncommon for titled men and women to lose their entire estates at the gaming tables. The historian Lecky wrote that at Bath, gambling *'reigned supreme; and the physicians even recommended it to their patients as a form of distraction...among fashionable ladies the passion was quite as strong as among men.'* The city drew large incomes - the losses of the wealthy - from the tables, which were an integral part of funding municipal works and establishing the social character of the city.

Living in poverty towards the end of his life, Beau wrote a letter condemning gambling as folly, and a vice to be avoided at all costs. When he was 82, the corporation voted him an allowance of £10 per month. Upon his death, aged 87, there was a lavish ceremony paid for by the Corporation, and he was buried with much pomp in Bath Abbey. The entire city mourned his passing. An article upon Beau Brummell, one of Nash's successors as arbiters of fashion, notes of Nash: *'- a man of singular success in his frivolous style, made for a master of ceremonies, the model of all sovereigns of drinking-places, absurd and ingenious, silly and shrewd, avaricious and extravagant. He created Bath; he taught decency to "bucks", civility to card-players, care to prodigals, and caution to Irishmen! Bath has never seen his like again'* (-from Blackwood's Edinburgh Magazine, June 1844). Oliver Goldsmith wrote in his biography: *'The whole kingdom became more refined by lessons originally derived from him,'* and that he was *'the first who diffused a desire for society and an easiness of address among a whole people.'*

What is now known as Beau Nash House in Saw Close, was built in 1720 for Juliana Popjoy, his life-long mistress. Originally intended for her sole use, Nash took residence there after losing his own house in a gambling game. It is now Popjoy's Restaurant. Nash's original house is now the Garrick's Head pub, around the corner. Beau was accused, when he moved in with Juliana, of being a 'whoremonger'. He replied that you could no more call a man a whoremonger for having one whore in his house, than you could call him a cheesemonger because he had one cheese. Born in Wiltshire in 1714, Juliana Popjoy was thirty years younger than Nash. A contemporary caricature depicts her as *'Lady Betty Besom'* leaping over *'the sacred boundary of Discretion'* on her dapple-grey horse. She helped Beau receive Princess Mary and Princess Caroline at his magnificent house St John's Court (The Garrick's Head) in 1740. She nursed Nash in the last years of his life, and a notice appeared in the Gentleman's Magazine in 1777 announcing her death. She had lived for some years *'in a large hollow tree'* near Warminster, *'on a lock of straw, resolving never more to lie in a bed: and she was as good as her word unless when she made her short peregrinations to bath, Bristol and the gentlemen's houses adjacent; and she then lay in some barn or outhouse.'*

*Nash was responsible for the outlawing of the wearing of swords within the city walls, mindful of the fate of his precursor. This prompted Richard Sheridan to write in 'The Rivals': *'A sword seen in the streets of Bath would raise as great an alarm as a mad dog.'*

**Much of the investment capital came from the Bristol slave trade. The town, possibly the first in the world built solely for pleasure, relied on the arms and cloth sent to Africa, the slaves sent from Africa to the colonies, and the tobacco, rum, sugar and raw cotton that came from the colonies. This triangular trade in described in the next book by this author upon Welsh pirates and buccaneers. As a result, Nash himself noted *'Bath is become a mere sink of profligacy and extortion. Every article of house-keeping is raised to an enormous price...I have known a negro-driver, from Jamaica, pay overnight, to the master of one of the rooms, 65 guineas for tea and coffee to the company, and leave Bath the next morning, in such obscurity, that not one of the guests had the slightest idea of his person, or even made the least enquiry about his name.'*

FOOTNOTES:

1.Royal Tunbridge Wells claims that Beau Nash was also Master of Ceremonies there, and its present Master of ceremonies at the chalybeate springs dresses up as Beau Nash, but wears a white wig (see www.attractionsnews.com)

2.The rules and regulations which Nash imposed upon Bath's unruly sedan chair operators are the basis for the regulations which govern modern taxis.

3.Not everyone was enamoured of the glories of bath society under Nash. Smollett, in 'The Expedition of Humphrey Clinker' gives a Scottish perspective: *'Imagine to yourself a high exalted presence of mingled odours, arising from putrid gums, imposthumated lungs, sour flatulencies, rank armpits, sweating feet, running sores and issues, plasters, ointments, and embrocations, hungary-water, spirit of lavender, asafoetida drops, musk, hartshorn, and sal volatile; besides a thousand frowzy streams, which I could not analyse. Such… is the fragrant aether we breathe in the polite assemblies of Bath.'*

NENNIUS 8th- 9th century
'THE HISTORIAN OF THE BRITONS'

Nennius apparently had access to 5th and 6th century sources which no longer survive, for his early Latin compilation known as *'Historia Brittonum'*, giving an account of British history from Julius Caesar to the 7th century. In his preface he describes himself as a disciple of Elfoddw of Bangor, the *'chief bishop of the land of Gwynedd'* in 809. Elfoddw died in 809, having acceded in 768 to the Roman reckoning of the date of Easter. Internal evidence of Nennius' work points to his being from south-east Wales, and he acknowledges his debt to Gildas (q.v.) for the events prior to 540. After the preface, the sections are as follows: *'The Six Ages of the World'*; *'The History'*, *'The Anglo-Saxon Genealogies'*, Computations and the 28 Cities of Britain', and *'The Marvels of Britain'*. The date of the compilation is given by Nennius as the 858th year of the Lord's incarnation, dating from Christ's birth. However, the Chronicle of Ystrad Fflur puts the date at 823, dating from Christ's death. The author *'put together all he could find'* of the remnants of writings at this time. Of course, the Celtic bardic tradition was oral, and so we are extremely fortunate that this Bangor monk pulls together various Welsh records.

There is no real chronology, and Nennius is concerned to show the British, i.e. Welsh, in the most favourable light, portraying them as of noble descent, capable of heroic deeds, and treacherously driven out of their rightful territories by the Saxons. This had considerable relevance at the time, as Rhodri Mawr later fought to consolidate the remaining Welsh lands. The book gives some of the earliest mentions of Arthur, and has a famous passage on the earliest Welsh poets. We cannot overstate Nennius' contribution to our knowledge of British history, from a time when the nation was in terrible peril. He wrote at a time when Wales had been 'dulled' by the slaughter of monks at Bangor-is-Coed by pagans, a feat celebrated by the so-called 'Holy' Bede. Nennius is mentioned in the 9th century Irish *'Psalter of Cashel'*. His sources included Gildas, Eusebius, Jerome, Isidore and Prosper.

Nennius, in his 8th century 'History of the Britons', shows how important Wales and the West were in these times. No less than 16 of his list of 28 cities are from this area of civilisation, leaving 12 spread across the rest of England and Scotland.

The words 'Caer' or 'Y Gaer' normally means a camp or fortress in Welsh, and usually denotes a Roman camp ('castra') much as the suffic 'caster', 'cester' or 'chester' does in the English langauge. The Welsh word 'Dinas' meaning 'fort' is often attached to hill camps that precede the Roman invasions. The British/Welsh bases are as follows:

1. Caer-Caratauc, which is Cary Craddock in the parish of Sellack, Hereford (not Catterick in Yorkshire). This hillfort in Ergynge was said to be a palace of Caradog Freichfras, son of King Ynyr of Gwent.

2. Caer-Costoeint - Caer Soeint - Caernarfon (se Caer Segeint) or Silchester

3. Caer-Ddraiton is Din-Draithou in the Life of St Cadog, and is Dunster in Somerset. Cado entertained Arthur here, and another name was Din-Torre, the fort on the river Torre.

4. Caer-Guent is Caer Gwent or Caerwent, the Venta Silurum of the Romans. The walled Roman city became the capital of Gwent, replacing the Silures' hill-fort of Llanmelin nearby. Coin hoards from around 425 and burials denote continuing occupation throughout the 'Dark Ages'. Caerwent was 'given' by Caradog Freichfras to Tathan when he moved his main court to the more easily defended camp at Portskewett nearby. The Roman walls are remarkable at Caerwent, but it is by-passed by most visitors to Caerleon and Wales. The site covers 20 hectares and the walls once stood 20 feet high. They are around 12 feet wide at the base. The main road to South Wales ran through the East and West gates.

5. Caer-Guiragon is Worcester.

6. Caer-Guouthigorn is Little Doward hillfort at Ganarew, Hereford, supposedly the site of Vortigern's last stand, although he may have escaped to Brittany.

7. Caer-Guricon is Viroconium, Wroxeter, the capital of Powys under Vortigern but later sacked by the Anglo-Saxons, forcing the princes of Powys back to Mathrafal. The Roman remains here are excellent.

8. Caer-Legeion-guar-Uisc is Isca, Caerleon on the River Usk outside Newport, with some of the best Roman features in Europe.

9. Caer-Legion is Deva, Chester, where Arthur possibly fought. With Caerleon, this was the second great fortress on the Welsh borders as the Romans pushed out from Gloucester and Wroxeter. In 603 Augustine held his second conference with the British bishops here, and around 610 or 613 the British lost the great battle when Bangor-is-Coed was destroyed.

10. Caer-Meguaidd is Meifod at Mathrafal, the court of Powys (not Manchester).

11. Caer-Pensa-uel-Coyt is South Cadbury hillfort (not Pevensey)

12. Cae-Peris appears to be Caer Beris just outside Builth Wells, but may be Porchester

13. Caer-Segeint is the great fort at Segontium, Caernarfon the old capital of the princes of Gwynedd before they moved to Aberffraw, and forever linked with Macsen Wledig and Elen. The river Arfon flows to the sea at Caernarfon, which means 'fort on the Arfon/

14. Caer-(D)Urnac appears to be Wroxter, or possibly Dorchester

15. Caer-Luit-Coyt is Wall, outside Lichfield, retaken from the Saxons by Prince Morfael of Pengwern around 650.

16. Caer Merdin is Caerfyrddin, Carmarthen

The other towns listed by Nennius were probably Dumbarton, Canterbury, Colchester, Doncaster, York, Grantchester, Leicester, Carlisle, London, Manchester, St Albans, Ilchester and Silchester. Other towns at this time included Caer-Baddan or Aquae Sulia, Bath. King Ffernfael had his court here, and it was lost to the Saxons at the fateful battle at nearby Dyrham in 573. Ffernfael died, as did King Cyndyddan who had his capital at Caer-Ceri (Cirencester). Cirencester was the capital of the province of Britannia Prima, and Wales was Brittania Secunda to the Romans. The third British king to die at Dyrham was Cynfael of Caer-Gloui (Gloucester). Caer-Teim was Tamium, Cardiff, where king Ynwyl was mentioned in Gereint and Enid as living in the ruined palace (the Roman fort) while the new kings of Glywyssing settled themselves at Dinas Powys hillfort just west of the city.

The Prologue to the British Chronicles of Nennius is not only a marvellous piece of writing, but mentions that he has just taken published works, even from the 'enemy' Scots and Irish and not altered them - it is up to the reader to sort the wheat from the chaff:

'1.NENNIUS, the lowly minister and servant of the servants of God, by the grace of God, disciple of St Elbotus, to all the followers of truth sendeth health.

Be it known to your charity, that being dull in intellect and rude of speech, I have presumed to deliver these things in the Latin tongue, not trusting to my own learning, which is little or none at all, but partly from writings and monuments of the ancient inhabitants of Britain, and the chronicles of the sacred fathers, Isidore, Hieronymus, Prosper, Eusebius, and from the histories of the Scots and Saxons, although our enemies, not following my own inclinations, but, to the best of my abilities, obeying the commands of my seniors; I have lispingly put together this history from various sources, and have endeavoured, from shame, to deliver down to posterity the few remaining ears of corn about past transactions, that they might not be trodden under foot, seeing that an ample crop has been snatched away already by the hostile reapers of foreign nations. For many things have been in my way, and I, to this day, have hardly been able to understand, as was necessary, the sayings of other men; much less was I able in my own strength, but like a barbarian, have I murdered and defiled the language of others. But I bore about within me an inward wound, and I was indignant, that the name of my own people, formerly famous and distinguished, should sink into oblivion, and like smoke be dissipated.

But since, however, I had rather myself be the historian of the Britons than nobody, although so many are to be found who might much more satisfactorily discharge the labour thus impose on me; I humbly entreat my readers, whose ears I may offend by the inelegance of my words, that they will fulfil the wish of my seniors, and grant me the easy task of listening with candour to my history. For zealous efforts very often fail. May, therefore, candour be shown where the inelegance of my words in insufficient, and may the truth of this history, which my rustic tongue has ventured, as a kind of plough, to trace out in furrows, in the ears of my hearers. For it is better to drink a wholesome draught from a humble vessel, than poison mixed with honey from a golden goblet.

2.And do not be loath, diligent reader, to winnow my chaff, and lay up the wheat in the storehouse of your memory: for truth does not come from the manner in which it is spoken, but that the thing be true: and she does not despise the jewel which she has rescued from the mud, but she adds it to her former treasures.

3.For I yield to those who are greater and more eloquent than myself, who, kindled with generous ardour, have endeavoured by Roman eloquence to smooth the jarring elements of their tongue, if they have left unshaken any pillar of history which I wished to remain. The history therefore has been compiled from a wish to benefit my inferiors, not from an envy of those who are superior to me, in the 858th year of our Lord's incarnation, and in the 24th year of Merfyn, King of the Britons*, and I hope that the prayers of my betters will be offered up for me in recompense of my labour. I shall obediently accomplish the rest to the utmost of my power.'

*Merfyn Frych was the father of Rhodri Mawr (q.v.), who became High King in 844, which confirms the date of 'The History of the Britons' as 823, not 858.

IVOR NOVELLO   January 15 1893 - March 6 1951
DAVID IVOR DAVIES, FILM STAR AND MUSICAL PLAYWRIGHT, 'THE LAST GREAT ROMANTIC', 'THE WELSH GENIUS', 'THE VALENTINO OF ENGLAND', 'THE BRITISH ADONIS'

Born at Llwyn-yr-Eos ('Grove of Nightingales'), 95 Cowbridge Road East in Cardiff, his Welsh-speaking parents were David Davies and Clara Novello Davies. There is a blue plaque on the house, and a small lilac bush in the garden. The family moved later to nearby 11 Cathedral Road, a far grander property. His mother was named Novello after her godmother, a famous Italian singer, and Clara was the founder and creator of the Welsh Ladies Choir. Ivor was just six months old when he was taken to the 1893 Chicago World Fair with the choir, which won the Ladies Choral Competition and every solo prize for which they entered. On her return Madam Clara was invited to sing before Queen Victoria, and henceforth the choir was known as The Royal Welsh Ladies Choir. Ivor learned music from his mother, before entering the Magdalen College of Music in Oxford.

In 1914, he composed the most popular song of the Great World War, 'Keep the Home Fires Burning', and entertained the troops in war-torn France. In 1916, he became a pilot in the Royal Naval Air Service, surviving two crash landings. David Ivor Davies of Cardiff, Ivor Novello, not only wrote popular songs, but was an actor-manager, taking the romantic lead in his musicals such as 'Glamorous Night' (1935), 'The Dancing Years' (1939), 'Arc de Triomphe' and 'Gay's The Word' (1951). He also wrote the operettas 'Careless Rapture' (1936) and 'King's Rhapsody' (1949). His other musicals included 'Crest of the Wave' (1937), and 'Perchance to Dream' (1945).

He was the leading British silent movie star and a matinee idol through the 1920's, working with the great directors D.W. Griffith (q.v.), Alfred Hitchcock and Louis Mercanton, but the theatre remained his first love. The Frenchman Mercanton came to London looking for a leading man for his new film 'Call of the Blood' and saw a photograph of Novello, exclaiming *That's the actor I want!'* Upon discovering that Novello was not an actor, but a composer, he still pursued him to make the film and Novello became a great star. He became the heir to the romantic throne in the cinema left vacant by the death of Rudolph Valentino. His films were 1919 'The Call of the Blood' (Mercanton); 1920 'Miarka: The Daughter of the Bear' (Mercanton); 1922 'Carnival' (Knoles); 1922 'The Bohemian Girl' with Gladys Cooper (Knoles); 1923 'The Man without Desire' (Brunel); 1923 'The White Rose' (D.W. Grffith); 1923 'Bonnie Prince Charlie' (Calvert); 1925 'The Rat' (Cutts); 1926 'The Triumph of the Rat' (Cutts); 1926 'The Lodger' (Alfred Hitchcock); 1927 'Downhill' (Hitchcock); 1928 'The Vortex' (Brunel); 1928 'The Constant Nymph' (Brunel); 1928 'The Gallant Hussar' (von Bolvary); 1928 'The South Sea Bubble' (Hayes Hunter); 1928 'The Return of the Rat' (Cutts); 1930 'Symphony in Two Flats (Gundry); 1931 'Once a Lady' (McClintie, in the USA); 1932 'The Phantom Fiend [The Lodger]' (Elvey); 1933 'I Lived With You' (Elvey), 1933 'Sleeping Car' (Litvak) and 1934 'Autumn Crocus' (Basil Dean). Films of his musicals include 'Glamorous Night' in 1937; 'The Dancing Years' starring the Welsh actor Dennis Price in 1950, 'King's Rhapsody' starring Errol Flynn and Anna Neagle in 1955, and 'The Dancing Years', made for TV in 1977. 'Glamorous Night' had a West End revival in 1997.

Novello also had an 'electrifying stage presence', writing 24 plays and appearing in 14, including 'Henry V'. But his favourite genre was the musical - he appeared in six of the eight he wrote and composed over 250 songs. A little-known fact is that he co-scripted 'Tarzan the Ape Man' in 1932, and was responsible for the line *'Me Tarzan, You Jane'*, which was included after he said it in a mix-up in rehearsal, when the female lead accidentally quoted the lead's lines to him.

Ivor Novello

Novello's songs have survived as classics of musical theatre. Ivor Novello was the toast of the West End in the beginning of the 20th century, and his first 'hit', *'Keep the Home Fires Burning'* became almost an anthem of the troops suffering in Europe. He was one of the world's greatest songwriters, with *'Dreamboat'* and *'We'll Gather Lilacs'* being huge hits. He was probably never knighted because of a legal problem in 1944. An infatuated female fan tried to gain favour by obtaining for him a car licence under false pretences. A particularly vindictive judge gave the unwitting Novello a one-month prison sentence as an example. However, Novello emerged from gaol as popular as ever - he had almost single-handedly kept the theatres open during the dark days of the war years.

Novello was a naturally gifted star of stage and screen, also writing songs, operettas, plays and films. A gifted playwright, his dazzling musical shows helped keep West End London theatres alive in the traumatic years of the 1930's and

1940's. He was described as having *'the most beautiful profile in the world'*, and the excellent biography by James Harding is now available in paperback from the Welsh Academic Press. A modest, caring, self-effacing man, despite the epithets such as *'the Valentino of England'* bestowed on him by the American press, David Ivor Davies was devoted to his *'Mam'* until her death. Noel Coward, Novello's friend for 35 years, said in the introduction to *'Ivor Novello, Man of the Theatre'*, *'His death will be a personal loss to many millions of people.....For those who loved him there is no consolation except the memory of his charm, his humour and his loving generosity.'* In the same book, Peter Noble wrote: *'Even those other playwrights, actors and composers who were inclined to be jealous of his continued successes, could not but agree that he was a most charming and kindly man.'*

Novello died suddenly of coronary thrombosis in his flat above the Strand Theatre. Just four hours previously he had played the lead in his favourite and greatest musical, 'King's Rhapsody' at London's Palace Theatre. 7,000 people attended his funeral, overwhelmingly female. His first biographer, Peter Noble, called him *'the great Welshman who brought more happiness to more people through his many gifts than possibly any other man of our century'*.

OWAIN GWYNEDD 1109-1170
OWAIN AP GRUFFYDD AP CYNAN, 'THE BULWARK OF ALL WALES'

'The History of Gruffydd ap Cynan' was written in the thirteenth century, a hundred and fifty years after his death. Born around 1055, his family was exiled at the Irish court, and he married the daughter of the King of Dublin. He invaded Wales in 1075, beating Trahaern of Gwynedd. Trahaern won a second battle, and Gruffydd turned to piracy for six years. In 1081, with a fellow-prince, Rhys ap Tewdwr, he set out from St Davids and killed Trahaern at the battle of Mynydd Carn. Rhys took control of Deheubarth, but Gruffydd returned to piracy and ended up being imprisoned in chains by the Normans.

After his rescue, and Rhys' death in the Battle of Brycheiniog against the Normans in 1093, Gruffydd at last took control of Gwynedd and Deheubarth. King William II, William Rufus, invaded but was repulsed. The Marcher Lords attacked with revolting cruelty, but returned to their border fortresses. In 1099, King Henry I attacked Wales. Gruffydd, by diplomacy, evaded battle, and kept quiet until his peaceful death in 1137 at the age of eighty-two. He was ruler of most of Wales, and Bangor Cathedral holds a tomb believed to be his - the earliest tomb of a Welsh prince.

During the two hundred years of battles with the Normans and Plantagenets, three political entities in Wales remained fairly stable and relatively independent, the princedoms of Powys, Deheubarth and Gwynedd. Gruffydd's son, Owain Gwynedd extended his possessions over Offa's Dyke into England, and down into the other two princedoms. This ensured the predominance of the Princes of Gwynedd, Rhodri Mawr's descendants, in the continuing Welsh fight for independence. Owain ap Gruffydd thus became known as Owain Gwynedd. Owain's grandson was Llewelyn ap Iorwerth, Llywelyn the Great, whose own grandson was Llywelyn ap Gruffydd, Llywelyn Olaf (Llywelyn the Last).

Owain's reign saw the *strongest Norman attacks on Wales* - his whole reign was focused upon protecting Wales from the Marcher Lords. He was also known as Owain Fawr, 'Owain the Great', and repulsed an invasion by Henry II so easily *that no other Plantagenet king attempted to subjugate Wales until his death.* Gwalchmai, his pencerdd ('chief household bard') wrote in 'The Triumphs of Owain'........

'Owain's praise demands my song
Owain swift and Owain strong;
Fairest flower of Rhodri's stem,
Gwynedd's shield, and Britain's gem.....
Lord of every regal art
Liberal hand and open heart....
Dauntless on his native sands
The dragon-son of Mona stands'

Mona is the English translation of Mon (Anglesey), the holy island of Wales, where the princes of Gwynedd had their chief court at Aberffraw.

From his accession to the crown of Gwynedd in 1137, Owain Gwynedd was faced with major problems from his brother Cadawaladr, and Owain's sons Hywel and Cynan defeated him and forced him to flee to Ireland. In 1145, Owain lost his favourite son Rhun and fell into a long period of grieving. However, Hywel Hir and Cynan took the mighty Norman fortress of Mold (Wyddgrug) and razed it to the ground, restoring his spirits, and showing him that there was a war to be won. The castle was thought to be impregnable. In 1149 Madoc ap Maredudd, Prince of Powys, joined the Norman Earl of Chester to gain lands off Owain. Their army was slaughtered in a battle in the woods of Consyllt, but Madoc escaped to cause further trouble.

In 1156 Owain's brother Cadwaladr, and Madoc ap Maredudd now stirred the English king to invade Wales, to exterminate this over-powerful neighbour. Henry II's first campaign against Owain ended in a truce in 1157. Owain, with his sons Dafydd and Cynan, had waited for Henry's army in the woods at Coed Eulo (Cennadlog) near Basingwerk, on the Dee estuary. They almost took Henry prisoner, and the Earl of Essex threw down the Royal Standard and escaped through the woods. Knights from Henry's fleet ravaged Anglesey, trying to destroy the grain crops to starve Owain's people into submission. However, the invaders were driven back to their ships, and one of the King's sons was killed, while Henry waited for reinforcements at Rhuddlan. With the 1157 truce, Owain gave King Henry hostages, promising not to attack England, and allowed the King to keep the land around Rhuddlan.

In 1160, with the death of Madoc ap Maredudd, Owain attacked Powys and extended his influence in the east. In 1166, the Council of Woodstock tried to make the Welsh princes vassals, and there was an uprising led by Owain, and his nephew Rhys ap Gruffydd (The Lord Rhys) in South Wales. A monk of St. David's wrote *'All the Welsh of Gwynedd, Deheubarth and Powys with one accord cast off the Norman yoke.'*

Henry II had tried again to subjugate Wales in 1164, but failed, and Owain's son Dafydd captured the important King's castles of Basingwerk and Rhuddlan in 1166 and 1167. Henry's forces were vast, composed of Normans, Flemings, Gascons and Scots as well as English. Henry recaptured the castles, and set up to invade from a base in Shrewsbury. With his brother Cadwaladr back on his side, and The Lord Rhys, Owain called his forces to Corwen. Henry moved through the damp Berwyn Mountains, cutting a road through the heavy forests in Glyn Ceiriog to keep away Welsh archers and raiding parties. Even today the road is called 'Ffordd y Saeson', ('The English Road'). Welsh guerrilla attacks and bad weather defeated the Normans, and they retreated back to the shelter of Shrewsbury (Pengwern).

One violent attack by the Welsh guerrilla forces took place at a place now called 'Adwy'r Beddau' (The Pass of the Graves). Apart from Owain and his brother Cadawaladr and the men of Gwynedd, Henry was facing Rhys ap Gruffudd (The Lord Rhys, q.v.) and the men of Deheubarth, and Owain Cyfeiliog's supporters from Powys and the Gwent army of the sons of Madog ab Idnerth. The battle at Crogen in Dyffryn Ceiriog is recorded in no English history books. Owain then despoiled all the castles that the French-Anglo-Normans had built in Wales, including the mighty Rhuddlan Castle.

The Berwyn Mountains, where Owain defeated the French
(photograph courtesy of WTB)

King Henry, in his rage, killed all his prisoners. He also had four important hostages – Rhys and Cadwaladr, two sons of Owain Gwynedd, and Cynwrig and Maredudd, two sons of The Lord Rhys of Deheubarth. *He blinded them – 'and this the King did with his own hand'* according to The Chronicles. Few Welsh people know of this terrible event* – it is in hardly any British history books. One wonders what would have been written, if the Welsh had ever done this to English princes. As Cicero stated, *'To know nothing of what happened before you is to remain forever a child'*.

In 1165 Brut y Tywysogion tells us of Henry II crossing the Ceiriog Valley near Tregeiriog, en route for Ffordd Saeson across the moors in filthy weather. Welsh guerrilla tactics forced him back from his mission, which was *'to destroy all Britons.'* '.... *The king was greatly angered; and he moved his host into Duffryn Ceiriog, and he had the wood cut down and felled to the ground. And there were a few picked Welshmen, who knew not how to suffer defeat, manfully encountered him in the absence of their leaders. And many of the doughtiest fell on both sides. And then the king, and the advanced forces along with him, encamped on the Berwyn mountains. And after he had stayed there a few days, he was greatly oppressed by a mighty tempest of wind and exceeding great torrents of rain. And when provisions failed him, he withdrew his tents and host to the open land of the flats of England.'* On his return, he destroyed all in his path, and ordered all his Welsh hostages to be blinded and castrated.

In 1168, diplomatic relations were established between Owain Gwynedd and King Louis VII of France, to King Henry's impotent fury. Owain's ambassador to

France offered Louis help against the English. When he died in 1170, after thirty-three years as Prince of Gwynedd, Owain was hailed as *'the king and sovereign and prince and defender and pacifier of all the Welsh after many dangers by sea and land, after innumerable spoils and victories in war ......after collecting together into Gwynedd, his own country, those who had been before scattered into various countries by the Normans, after building in his time many churches and consecrating them to God'.*

His chronicler states also that his kingdom *'shone with lime-washed churches like the firmament with stars'.* Owain had encouraged monasticism, especially in Gwynedd, but he died excommunicated because he refused to divorce his wife, his cousin. Archbishop Baldwin of Canterbury, when he visited Bangor Cathedral in 1188, thus spitefully ordered Owain's bones to be moved from the Cathedral to the churchyard.

Madog, a son of Owain Gwynedd, was credited as being the Welshman who discovered America. Madog's sister, Gwenllian, was killed after battling the Normans at Cydweli , and may have been the author of the 'Mabinogion'. The Lord Rhys was Owain's nephew - see the entry on Rhys ap Gruffydd (Arglwydd Rhys). Rhys was the son of Gwenllian, and she was executed by the Normans when he was just four years old. Rhys ap Gruffydd, Prince of Deheubarth, now took the mantle of chief defender of Wales against the invading Normans.

The year 1169 in The Chronicle of Ystrad Fflur notes: *'At the end of this year Owain ap Gruffudd ap Cynan, prince of Gwynedd, the man who was of great goodness and very great nobility and wisdom, the bulwark of all Wales, after innumerable victories, and unconquered from his youth, and without ever having refused anyone that for which he asked, died after taking penance and communion and confession and making a good end.'*

* Giraldus Cambrensis tells us of Owain's restrained behaviour towards the burning of churches and the blinding of 22 hostages, including his sons. He had been urged to burn English churches in retaliation, but replied: *'I do not agree with this opinion: rather we should be grateful and joyful because of this. For we are very unequal against the English unless we are upheld by divine aid; but they, through what they have done, have made an enemy of God himself, who can avenge the injury to himself and to us at the same time.'*

ROBERT OWEN   May 14 1771 - November 17 1858
'THE FOUNDER OF SOCIALISM', 'THE FOUNDER OF INFANT SCHOOLS', 'THE MOST POPULAR MAN IN EUROPE', 'THE MODERN WORLD'S FIRST SOCIALIST'

In 1771, Trenewydd (Newtown) in Montgomeryshire produced a man who changed society across the world with his thoughts and actions. Karl Marx and Freidrich Engels both paid generous tribute to him in the development of their theories (see footnote). Engels wrote in *'The Condition of the Working Class in England',* 1844, that *'English socialism arose with Owen.'* The youngest son of the village postmaster, aged 10 he was apprenticed to a draper in Stamford, Lincolnshire. He spent all his spare time reading at his employer's library, before being appointed superintendent of Drinkwater's large cotton mill in Manchester, aged only 19. He soon transformed the factory into one of Britain's leading producers, making the first use in Britain of American sea island cotton, and making improvements in spun cotton quality. Aged 28, in 1799 he moved to David Dale's cotton mills in Lanarkshire as manager, marrying Dale's daughter in 1800 and buying a partnership in the firm.

When Robert Owen took over these cotton mills in New Lanark in Scotland, he improved housing and sanitation, provided medical supervision, set up a co-operative shop, selling at little more than cost price, and established *the first infant school in Great Britain*. Owen also founded an Institute for the Formation of Character and a *model welfare state* for New Lanark. He reasoned that character was moulded by circumstances, and that improved circumstances would lead to goodness. 500 of his employees were young children from the poorhouses and charities of Edinburgh and Glasgow, and Owen set up a model factory and a model village, where hours were considerably shorter than elsewhere in Britain (a 12-hour day, including one and a half hours for meal-breaks). The 'Gentleman's Magazine' recorded: *'the children live with their parents in neat comfortable habitation, receiving wages for their labour...The regulations here to preserve health of body and mind, present a striking contrast to those of most large manufactories in this kingdom.'*

The mills made a commercial profit, but some of his partners were displeased with the extra expenses incurred by Owen's philanthropic socialism, and in 1813 Owen organised a new firm. Its members were content with a 5% return on capital, and stockholders included the Quaker William Allen and the legal reformer Jeremy Bentham. The factories not only enhanced the workers' environment, but received international interest as they actually also increased productivity and profits. 1813 also saw the publication of Owen's *'A New View of Society'*, pleading for education for all as the key to social reform and improving working conditions. From 1816, his school at New Lanark took children from 3 to 10 years old, or to 13 if parents could afford for the child not to work. The 'play and learn' approach was the basis of his Utilitarian theory of education - nursery schools were Owen's original concept. Owen saw national education as freeing man from narrow views and the dogmatism of the church.

His example was largely responsible for bringing about The Factory Acts of 1819, but disappointed at the slow rate of reform in Sir Robert Peel's England, he emigrated to America in 1821 to set up another model community. From 1817 Owen had proposed that *'villages of co-operation'*, self-supporting communities run on socialist lines, should be founded, to *ultimately* **replace private ownership**. He took these ideas on co-operative living to America and set up the community of New Harmony, Indiana, between 1824 and 1828, before he handed the project over to his sons and returned to Britain. (Owenite community village experiments in England continued, in Hampshire, near Glasgow and in County Cork).

The experiment cost him £40,000, an absolute fortune in those days. The USA community failed without his inspiring idealism, but he carried on encouraging the fledgling trade union movement and co-operative societies. From 1929, Owen took over the development of co-operatives (the first had been formed in London in 1926). 1832 saw a failed attempt to set up a National Equitable Labour Exchange. In 1833 *he formed the Grand National Consolidated Trades Union.* He wanted to use the unions to change the economic system, to destroy capitalism and break the overwhelming power of the state. In 1835 he founded the Association of All Classes of All Nations, for which he is known as the founder of the socialist movement.

From 1834, Owen led the opposition against the deportation of The Tolpuddle Martyrs, a group of Dorset farm labourers, who had stopped working in a cry for higher living wages. Because of his criticisms of the organised religion of the day, where positions were granted as favours, he lost any support from those in power, whose families benefited from the system. He wrote about the barbaric nature of unrestrained capitalism in 'Revolution in Mind and Practice'- the glories of Thatcherite free trade, where Nike, Adidas and Reebok sportswear are made in totalitarian regimes using semi-slave labour, spring to mind today. He wanted political reform, a utopian socialist system, with a transformation of the social order. *People were all equal, there should be no class system, and individuals should not compete but co-operate, thereby eliminating poverty.*

He was a *fore-runner of the co-operative movement,* a great inspirer of the trades union movement, and probably the *modern world's first socialist.* Those that followed his teachings, who called themselves Owenites, *gradually changed their name to Socialists, the first recorded use of the term.* Owen is a Welshman of

Robert Owen

international stature, who is hardly acclaimed in his own land, but his socialism is a thread that runs through Welsh history from the Laws of Hywel Dda in the tenth century, to the election of the first Labour MP in Britain in 1910, to the whole-hearted support for the Miners' Strike in 1984, to the present state of left-wing support in Wales.

As the pioneer of co-operation between workers and consumers, his understanding of the 'value chain' and wealth creation has not been equalled until Michael Porter in recent years. The over-riding problem in Western society is that political leaders are insulated from the communities they represent - they are always several orders of magnitude richer than the common man, and do not understand the basic nature of wealth creation. Wealth comes from something being dug out of the ground, altered and transported, with value being added along the route. Every service is parasitic upon this process. It seems that Mrs Thatcher never realised that marrying a millionaire was not an option for most of society.

In April 1840, an editorial in 'The Cambrian' referred to Robert Owen *'The discontent of the lower and working classes has assumed a new form which threatens to become far more mischievous than mere political agitation, however fiercely carried on. We allude to the institution and spread of Socialism. Under pretence of improving the condition of the poor, Socialism is endeavouring, permanently, to poison their happiness, by depraving their morals, and depriving them of all those consolations flowing from the principles of religion. It is of little use to show that Mr. Owen is a lunatic.'*

Incidentally, a theme in this book is that the Welsh are terrible self-publicists. In 'The Witch Doctors' a 1997 'global business book award winner', we have reference to Robert Owen, ' *a Scottish mill-owner who thought there was money to be made by treating workers as if they were human beings (he would not employ any child under ten years old) and thus has been deemed to be "the pioneer of personnel management"* (quote from Urwick and Breech, quoted in Clutterbuck and Crainer) .... *Peter Drucker's enthusiasm for the well-being of workers led Rosabeth Moss Kantner to compare him to Robert Owen, the nineteenth century Scotsman who ordered his factory managers to show the same due care to their vital human machines as they did to the new iron and steel which they so lovingly burnished.'* So there we have it, the leading edge authors of 'The Witch Doctors', with other eminent management writers, all claim Owen to be **Scottish**. No wonder no-one knows about Wales on the world stage. Many websites even state that Owen was English.

His son, Robert Dale Owen, was prominent in the abolitionist movement in the USA, writing 'The Policy of Emancipation' and 'The Wrong Slavery'. He became Ambassador to Naples, but (like his father) returned to Newtown and died in 1858. 'Hiraeth' is a strong emotion. A memorial museum* is now in the house where his father was born. Owen's other sons were also notable in the history of the USA, David Dale Owen making the first geological survey of the American mid-west, and Richard Dale Owen serving with distinction in the Civil War and becoming a professor at Nashville University.

* Another museum in Newtown is in the High Street, with mementoes about W.H. Smith, the leading British newsagent chain (it also owns Do-It-All, Dillons, Waterstones, Virgin Records and Our Price Records), that started in 1792. Newtown also saw the *birth of the mail-order idea*, started by Sir Pryce Pryce-Jones in 1861 to sell Welsh linens. One of his more famous customers was Queen Victoria, the Anglo-German queen only remarkable in that her girth exceeded her height in her latter years. His business base, the Royal Welsh Warehouse is still being used. Keeping on the subject of Newtown, in the 18th century, Sir John Pryce of Newtown passed into history as a man who loved his wife so much that he slept in bed with her embalmed body after she passed on. His second wife had to sleep on the other side of the bed from the corpse. When this second wife died, Sir John settled down at night between two embalmed women.

FOOTNOTE:
Freidrich Engels wrote in *'Socialism: Utopian and Scientific': 'At this juncture, there came forward a manufacturer 29-years-old - a man of almost sublime, childlike simplicity of character, and at the same time one of the few born leaders of men. Robert Owen had adopted the teaching of the materialistic philosophers: that man's character is the product, on the one hand, of heredity; on the other, of the environment of the individual during his lifetime, and especially during his period of development. In the Industrial Revolution most of his class saw only chaos and confusion, and the opportunity of fishing in these troubled waters and making large fortunes quickly. He saw in it the opportunity of putting into practice his favourite theory, and so of bringing order out of chaos. He has already tried it with success, as superintendent of more than 500 men in a Manchester factory. From 1800 to 1829, he directed the great cotton mill at New Lanark, in Scotland, as managing partner, along the same lines, but with a greater freedom of action and with a success that made him a European reputation.*

A population, originally consisting of the most diverse and, for the most part, very demoralised elements, a population that gradually grew to 2,500, he turned into a model colony, in which drunkenness, police, magistrates, lawsuits, poor laws, charity, were unknown. And all this simply by placing the people in conditions worthy of human beings, and especially by carefully bringing up the rising generation. **He was the founder of infant schools,** and introduced them first at New Lanark. At the age of two, the children came to school, where they enjoyed themselves so much that they could scarcely be got home again. Whilst his competitors worked their people 13 or 14 hours a day, in New Lanark the working day was only 10 and a half hours. When a crisis in cotton stopped work for four months, his workers received their full wages all the time. And with all this the business more than doubled in value, and to the last yielded large profits to its proprietors.

In spite of all this, Owen was not content. The existence which he secured for his workers was, in his eyes, still far from being worthy of human beings. "The people were slaves at my mercy". The relatively favourable conditions in which he had placed them were still far from allowing a rational development of the character and of the intellect in all directions, much less of the free exercise of all their faculties. "And yet, the working part of this population of 2,500 persons was daily producing as much real wealth for society as, less than half a century before, it would have required the working part of a population of 600,000 to create. I asked myself, what became of the difference between the wealth consumed by 2,500 persons and that which would have been consumed by 600,000?'

The answer was clear. It had been used to pay the proprietors of the establishment 5% on the capital they had laid out, in addition to over £300,000 clear profit. And that which held for New Lanark held still to a greater extent for all the factories in England. "If this new wealth had not been created by machinery, imperfectly as it has been applied, the wars of Europe, in opposition to Napoleon, and to support the aristocratic principles of society, could not have been maintained. And yet this new power was the creation of the working classes". To them, therefore, the fruits of this new power belonged. The newly-created gigantic productive forces, hitherto used only to enrich individuals and to enslave the masses, offered to Owen **the foundations for a reconstruction of society:** they were destined, as the common property of all, to be worked for the common good of all.

Owen's communism was based upon this purely business foundation, the outcome, so to say, of commercial calculation. Throughout, it maintained this practical character. Thus, in 1823, Owen proposed the relief of distress in Ireland by Communist colonies, and drew up complete estimates of costs of founding them, yearly expenditure, and probably revenue. And in his definite plan for the future, the technical working out of details is managed with such practical knowledge - ground plan, frond and side and bird's-eye views all included - that the Owen method of social reform once accepted, there is from the practical point of view little to be said against the actual arrangement of details.

His advance in the direction of Communism was the turning-point in Owen's life. As long as he was simply a philanthropist, he was rewarded with nothing but wealth, applause, honour, and glory. **He was the most popular man in Europe.** Not only men of his own class, but statesmen and princes listened to him approvingly. But when he came out with his Communist theories that was quite another thing. Three great obstacles seemed to him especially to block the path to social reform:

private property,

religion,

the present form of marriage.

He knew what confronted him if he attacked these - outlawry, excommunication from official society, the loss of his whole social position. But nothing of this prevented him from attacking them without fear of consequences, and what he had foreseen happened. Banished from official society, with a conspiracy of silence against him in the press, ruined by his unsuccessful Communist experiments in America, in which he sacrificed all his fortune, he turned directly to the working-class and continued working in their midst for 30 years.

Every social movement, every real advance in England on behalf of the workers links itself on to the name of Robert Owen. He forced through in 1819, the first law limiting the hours of labour of women and children in factories. He was president of the first Congress at which all the Trade unions of England united in a single great trade association. He introduced as transition measures to the complete communistic organisation of society, on the one hand, co-operative societies for retail and production. These have since that time, at least, given practical proof that the merchant and the manufacturer are socially quite unnecessary. On the other hand, he introduced labour bazaars for the exchange of the products of labour through the medium of labour-notes, whose unit was a single hour of work; institutions necessarily doomed to failure, but completely anticipating Proudhon's bank of exchange of a much later period, and differing entirely from this in that it did not claim to be the panacea for all social ills, but only a first step towards a much more radical revolution of society.'

PADRIG c.390-461
ST PATRICK, 'THE MOST FAMOUS WELSHMAN IN THE WORLD'*, THE APOSTLE OF IRELAND

Feast Date March 17

Born in Bannaviem Tabarniae**, Bannventa, possibly modern Banwen near Neath, (near the village of *'Enon'*) he was the grandson of a priest named Potitus, and the son of a deacon and decurio (town councillor) called Calpurnius. Padrig was captured as a 16-year-old by Irish pirates organised by Hiall of the Nine Hostages, High King of Ireland. He was treated as a slave by a Pict in Antrim for six years. He either escaped or was freed, returned to Wales, received some training as a priest, and returned to Ireland around 430-433. From his Armagh base, he wrote the first literature identified with the early British church, following the simple Welsh monastic life and attempting to abolish paganism and sun-worship.

Another version is that Saint Patrick was born in Carmarthen or Pembrokeshire in 389, and was carried off by Irish raiders in 406, becoming Bishop of Armagh in 432, being consecrated by St Garmon at Auxerre. Recent evidence seems to point to his birth in Banwen. In St. Patrick's *'Confessio'* he states he was born at Banaven Taberiar, a small-holding near a Roman fort, which could be Tafarn-y-Banwen, a farm near an old Roman stronghold. This is also on the strategically important Sarn Helen, once a major Roman road through Wales. Local tradition says that Patrick came from Banwen, and there are placenames such as *'Hafod Gwyddelig'* (*'Irish Summerhouse'*) and a *'Nant Gwyddelig'* (*'Irish Stream'*). George Brinley Evans also points to the nearby Hirfynydd Stone, the extremely rare early Christian carving of a man in prayer, surrounded by Irish symbolic patterns. (Note that *'Gwyddelig'*, the Welsh for *'Irish'*, is similar to *'Goidelic'*. The Welsh were the Brythonic Celts, and the Irish were the Goidelic Celts). Cressy states that Patrick was born in Glyn Rosina, the valley of St Davids, in 361, and died at Glastonbury in 472, aged 111.

Rhigyfarch tells us that St David's father Sant was told by an angel to save some land for David, 30 years before his birth, where St Patrick was going to settle at Glyn Rhosyn (Valis Rosina, the Vale of Roses). Near the sea in Pembroke, near the main Pembroke-Ireland crossing, yet out of site of pirates, this is where St David's

Cathedral stands today. The angel also told Patrick to leave, angering him that God should prefer an unborn child. However, God took Patrick to the cliff-top, to the rock seat still known as Eisteddfa Padrig, to show him that God wished him to look after the whole of Ireland instead.

Iolo Morgannwg also names a Padrig as the son of Maewan, Principal of the monastery at Bangor Illtud, who was carried away by Irish pirates. Broadway, near Cowbridge, has also been linked with Patrick in legend, where he was supposed to have been born at Pedr Onen (Peter's Ash). Writing in the early 19th century, Marie Trevelyan believed that Patrick was known as Maenwyn (Holy Rock), and educated at Caerworgan (Llanilltud Fawr, near the great Romano-British villa of Caermead). It was here that the honorary Latin name of Patricius was given to him. She wrote of an ancient folk lament, which was only remembered by two people who lived miles apart, and which was sung at 'Mal Santau' (sic). Here she means 'Mabsantau', saints' feast day festivals. The song used to be familiar in Penmark, St Tathan and Llanilltud Fawr (Llantwit Major), and commemorated a boy called Maenwyn who was born at Nant-y-Tirion, Treberfaydd ('shining place', the old Caput Bovium of the Romans, present-day Boverton). The boy was caught in a nearby bog when the Goidelic Irish burned the monastery of Caerworgan. Many people believe that Arthur was also born at Boverton. In Evans' 'History of Glamorgan' we read '....*other writers doubt the existence of Eurgain, but all agree that a college was founded by the Roman General Theodosius (called by the Welsh, Tewdws) some time between the years 368 and 395 AD. The principal and chief teacher of this college (Llanilltud) now called Cor Tewdws, was one Balerius, a learned Roman Christina. He was succeeded by Patrick, a native of Glamorgan, and a former student of the college. The college prospered exceedingly until it was attacked, despoiled, and destroyed by some Irish pirates, who, when they retired, carried Patrick with them a prisoner. Patrick continued his good work in Ireland, preaching the Gospel boldly, and he is still loved by the Irish as their patron saint.*'

Under the sandy shoreline of Whitesands Bay lies the sixth century St Patrick's Chapel, which itself lies upon an older burial ground. A rectangular mound now stands in the field called Parc-y-Capel near the shore. Excavated in 1924, it is a single cell chapel with human remains below the west wall. Mrs Dawson mentions the nearby Tŷ Gwyn in 'Archaeologia Cambrensis' in 1888: *Tŷ Gwyn is situated above Porth Mawr, and about two miles from St David s. It stands on the south slopes of Carn Lidi, the purple rocks above it springing out of the heath, with here and there a gorse bush, like a puff of flame breaking out of the crannies of the rock. Below it, near the sea, are the foundations of St Patrick s Chapel, in the site of his embarkation. The foundations of the church of Tŷ Gwyn, the cradle of Christianity among the Southern Irish, are trodden underfoot by sheep and oxen, that wander over the wide cemetery where lie thick, in narrow coffins of unshaped stones, the bodies of the first inmates of that earliest Mission College in Britain. When we visited the spot in 1898, the farmer had torn up the grave slabs of the tombs in the cattle-yard, and the drainage of his cow stalls and pig stys soaked into the places where the bodies of the ancient fathers of the British and Irish churches had crumbled to dust.*' (Candida Casa, at Whithorn in Wigtownshire, followed the pattern set by Ty Gwyn. When books are written about the Irish saving Christianity in the Western world and not mention the fact that without Wales, Ireland would have remained pagan like England and Scotland, it is time to rethink how Wales can publicise its contribution to civilisation.) There is a nearby rock called Carn

Patrick. There was also a Paterchurch, or Patrickchurch, in Monkton, Pembrokeshire. One of the gates to St David's Cathedral is still known as Porth Padrig. Cefn Padrig is a ridge of coastline between Burry Port and Llanelli.

Llanbadrig in Anglesey has been claimed for another Padrig, but it is recorded that the Cistercian monks of Aberconwy Abbey (destroyed by the English) dedicated the ancient church to St Patrick of Ireland in 1250. (Llywelyn ap Gruffudd, the last Prince of Wales, had given the land to his church). There was an old 'serpent stone' there, a carving of coiled snakes, below the base of a niche which contained a statue of the saint. Patrick was said to have driven the snakes out of Ireland, but the stone vanished in the 19th century. In the late 19th century the building was restored, and an early 'ichthus stone' of blue granite was found in the churchyard. This is not found in Anglesey and denotes a place of worship from the Age of Saints. It is today placed in the west wall with its carving exposed. A rough path from the churchyard to a cave has always been known as Traed Padrig Sant, 'The Footprints of St Patrick'. This cave stands in a rocky cleft underneath the church, which itself is on a headland, and at the back of the cave is a spring with fresh water. Local tradition is that Padrig was travelling between Wales and Ireland and was shipwrecked here. In gratitude for his deliverance he built the church, as it had the required local water source.

Pawl Hen traditionally founded the great monastery at Whitland in Carmarthen, variously known as Alba, Rosnat or Tŷ Gwyn (being whitewashed), but some say that it was founded by Padrig before he went to Ireland. Perhaps Pawl Hen founded the famous school there in Patrick's monastery, which would explain the large numbers of Irish monks said to have studied there.

Some of the other Welsh saints associated with Patrick are noted in the author's 'The Book of Welsh Saints'. St Brioc was said to be a disciple of Garmon, along with Illtud and Patrick, and was a founder-saint of Brittany. St Carannog's Vita recounts in its 3rd lesson that the saint disguised himself as a beggar and followed Patrick to Ireland to evangelise, rather than take up his father's kingship and fight the invading pagan Irish. Sen Patrick, from the Gower Peninsula, was closely associated with Patrick and died in 493. St Seny, or Senanus, was Patrick's brother, founded Llansannan in Denbigh, Bedwellty and Llantrisant, and named his son Patrick. St Mel (d.488) was a Welsh follower of Patrick, and became Bishop of Ardagh after evangelising the area. Mechu and Muinis also left Wales with Mel to assist Patrick in his mission. All these three saints have been given Irish genealogies in the last two hundred years. Mel was possibly the son of Patrick's sister, Darerca. Patrick's British sisters, Lupida and Darerca were captured with him. Darerca's son Rioch also assisted Patrick and was consecrated as a bishop. Her other sons included Secundinus (Sechnallus), Menni and Auxilius, all who went to Ireland. Most of these British saints are now regarded as Irish, and Darerca's life has been distorted to make her a virgin, closely associated with Patrick and Bridget. Ieuan Gwas Padrig was a saint and disciple of Patrick who founded the church at Cerrig y Druidion, and has several holy wells. Abbot Ffinian studied at Llancarfan under Cadoc, where he had a chapel, became Ireland's leading religious leader after Patrick's death, laying out the organisation of the Irish church on the pattern of Llancarfan. Ffinian himself instructed the saints Columbus, Ciaran and Brendan.

Wherever Padrig was born, he himself claimed to have evangelised the Irish, and he visited Rome in 442 and later. According to the Annals of Ulster, he organised the church and founded the Cathedral Church of Armagh in 444, which became the administrative centre of Christianity. Between 412 and 415 he studied at Lerins, in France, and may have studied under St Garmon at Auxerre before he returned to Ireland in 431. St Patrice on the Loire is named after him, and local people believe him to be the nephew of Martin of Tours. Unlike St David, Patrick has never been officially canonised by the Catholic Church. In the Vatican Library, Biblietecha Sanctorum Vol. 10 notes that his cult started locally.

*For this quote I am indebted to Barry Tobin, a fluent Gaelic and Welsh-speaker, who has done much to pull Irish and Welsh culture together, as has Myles Pepper, the leader of the West Wales Arts Connection, based at Fishguard (Abergwaun).

**Some sources place Padrig as a Romano-Briton from Strathclyde. His 'Confessio' begins· *'I am Patrick, a sinner, most unlearned, the least of all the faithful, and utterly despised by many. My father was Calpornius, a deacon, son of Potitus, a priest, of the village Bannaven Taburniae; he had a country seat nearby, and there I was taken captive.'* His 'Epistola' is a message to a prince named Coroticus, in Ceredigion or Pembroke, who was trying to force Irish immigrants out of his Welsh lands.

FOOTNOTES:

1. The Breton writer Albert le Grand places Beneventum as Venta, modern Caerwent, where St Tathan taught St Cadog (q.v.), and from where Dyfrig (Dubricius, q.v.) oversaw the Welsh church. Professor Bury, in his 'Muirchu's Life of St Patrick' also believes the walled Roman town of Caerwent to be Bannaventum, the earliest major centre of Christian learning in Britain. The Breton Cressy noted a saint from the nearby Roman fort and camp of Caerleon, St Baccharius, who died in 460 - *'By Nation a Brittain* (i.e. Welsh) *and Disciple of St Patrick; he adicted himself to the study of litterature at Caer-leon.'* Another place associated with Bannaventum is Llansannor or the River Thaw near Llancarfan.

2. British history was rewritten in the 19th century to date from the Germanic invasions of the Saxons and Jutes. Before that were the 'Dark Ages' before Germanic civilisation came to the Isle of Britain. It is interesting that in British (not English) history, this period has always been known as 'The Age of the Saints'. (For those who wish to know why the history of Britain was rewritten, and how, please consult 'The A-Z of Wales and the Welsh' by this author. In 1903, Baring-Gould and Fisher eloquently expressed what these forgotten people gave to the heritage of Britain:

'For centuries, partly due to the sneer of Bede, and partly to the proud contempt with which the Latin Church regarded all missionary work that did not proceed from its own initiative, the English Church has looked to Augustine of Canterbury as the one main source from whom Christianity in our island sprang, and Rome as the mother who sent him to bring our ancestors to Christ. That he did a good and great work is not to be denied; he was the Apostle of Kent, where the Britons had all been massacred or from whence they had been driven. But Kent is only a corner of the island. And it was forgotten how much was wrought by the Celtic Church, even for the Teutonic invaders, **far more than was achieved by Augustine.**

It was the Church in Wales which sent a stream of missionaries to Ireland to complete its conversion, begun by Patrick......... It was from Ireland that Columcille went to Iona to become evangelist to the Picts. From Llanelwy went forth Kentigern with 665 monks and clerics to restore Christianity in Cumbria, which extended from the Clyde to the Dee. It was from Iona that the missioners proceeded who converted all Northumbria, Mercia, and the East Saxons and Angles. Honour to whom honour is due, and the debt of obligation to the **Celtic saints in the British Isles has been ignored or set aside hitherto.**

But they did more. To them was due the conversion of Armorica. Evidence shows that nothing, or next to nothing, was done for the original inhabitants of that peninsula by the stately prelates of the Gallo-Roman Church. They ministered to the city populations of Nantes and Rennes and Vannes, and did almost nothing for the scattered natives of the province. They were left to live in their heathenism and die without the light, till the influx of British colonists changed the whole aspect, and brought the people of the land into the fold of Christ.'

The Irish connection, with the Welshman Patrick and contributions from the way of Christianity in Wales, has never been truly assessed. The Irish, with their flair for publicity, can publish books like Thomas Cahill's *'HOW THE IRISH SAVED CIVILIZATION: the Untold Story of Ireland's Heroic Role from the Fall of Rome to the Rise of Medieval Europe'* (Sceptre 1995 paperback) – a Welsh book could have been written with the same title and probably more validity. (The book's title capitals are reproduced exactly). It totally ignores the fact that the Irish church was basically a Welsh construct upon a formerly heathen population. The church in Wales lasted from the earliest days of Christianity in the Western world through to the present day. **In all other European countries the Christian church was extinguished at some time,** including Ireland except for a few hermits clinging to rocks in the Atlantic. The survival of Christianity in Wales is as amazing as the survival of its language over this period, with such close proximity to England. In Ireland and Scotland, the language has all but died, despite their relatively greater distance from the power of the government of the south-east of England.

PELAGIUS (MORGAN) c385-c460's

Morgan (*'from the sea'*) was traditionally born in Bangor-is-Coed, the site of the famous monastery and was a lay monk there. In Montgomeryshire, however, he was said to be a native of Llanrhaeadr, who first preached his *'heretical'* ideas in the churchyard at Castle Caereinion. Some say that he was not British, but St Augustine, Prosper, Gennadius, Orosius and Mercador wrote that he was. A respected religious teacher in Rome in the 380's, he was forced to escape from the oncoming Goths, who eventually sacked Rome in 410. He was now living in Carthage, but the church leaders combined to get his ideas dismissed as heretical. Leaving another Briton, Caelestius (Celestine), he went to Palestine, and was supported by Bishop John of Jerusalem.

Pelagius was not a saint, but his vision of Christianity was far closer to the principles of humanitarian morals and ethics than the evolving Roman church of his times. In the early fifth century this Celtic monk denied the concept of *'original sin'*, the teaching that Adam's sin corrupted all of his descendants. This was a practical denial of the need for the established church to grant grace and salvation to mankind. He believed that men could by themselves, and their own Christian works be taken to heaven. He was condemned by Pope Innocent I and Zosimus, but his teachings affected European history down to Luther, Calvin and the Cathars. Paying for salvation was not the way to heaven. Following a leader was not the way to Heaven. Following the example of Christ was the only way for Pelagius. Salvation mainly lies with the person, who by acts of will and self-control could make himself or herself better, more acceptable to God and mankind in general. The doctrine was initially accepted by Jerome. Also, in the 4th century John of Cassian accepted it in his thirteenth conference. The Roman church later expunged this manuscript from John's writings. The supremacy of the human will over the grace of God, as decided by the power of the church, could simply not be accepted. As Augustine stated in his *'Sermons'*, *'Roma locutus est; causa finita est'* – *'Rome has spoken; the case is finished.'*

Pelagius had followed Origen's doctrine of 'free will', and in 401 settled in Rome lecturing upon mankind's natural dignity and the absurdity of 'original sin' as preached by Augustine. Thus priests who could absolve sins were unnecessary. A true believer could reach Heaven by his acts alone. *'Everything good and everything evil, for which we are either praised or blamed, is not born with us, but done by us'*, he wrote. When Alaric and his Visigoths invaded, Pelagius escaped to North Africa, where he met Augustine. Augustine later condemned Celestine (Celestius), the British follower of Pelagius, for heretical teachings. Pelagius now went to Palestine, where his teachings found favour, but Augustine persuaded the Church of Rome to condemn him in 417, which the Council of Carthage confirmed in 418. Many Italian bishops supported Pelagius, and they were banished alongside him. In 429 the bishops Germanus (Garmon) and Lupus (Bleiddian) were sent to Britain because of its adherence to Pelagianism, *'that noxious and abominable teaching that men had no need of God's grace.'* Pelagianism was formally pronounced heretical in 431. It was obvious that Pelagianism threatened the very core of the money-making authority of Rome. The British had already threatened Rome's civil power with the cavalry of Macsen Wledig (Maximus) and Cystennin (Constantine) across Gaul, and Morgan had to be stopped in his tracks.

Basically, Pelagianism took money away from the Roman Church, and thence economic and political power. Men were basically good, and the church was not needed for them to go to heaven. Mankind is God's masterpiece of creation, because it has the capacity to reason between what is a good and what is an evil act. If mankind freely chooses good, it deserves salvation. If mankind chooses evil, it breaks the contract that binds it to God. For these ideas, Pelagius was accused by Prosper of Aquitaine of denying the concept of Original Sin, and of claiming that man can avoid sin by the power of *'free-will without the aid of Divine Grace'*. It was therefore heresy to the church that infants who die unbaptised are not necessarily banned from heaven. The Roman church as a *'command and control'* system replicated that of any army, and Pope Celestine (d.432) saw the Pelagian Heresy as the greatest menace to the unity of the church in the West, with Britain as its stronghold. Prosper said that Pope Celestine called the Pelagians *'Enemies of Grace'* (- of course, a state of grace could only be achieved by submitting to, and paying, the Roman Church). Prospero also declared that Agricola, son of the Pelagian Bishop Severianus, was corrupting the churches of Britain around 429. Pope Celestine thus sent Germanus, Bishop of Auxerre, to the Isle of Britain, to try to extirpate the teaching, and a Briton, Palladius, to Ireland.

The ascetic Pelagius wrote two tracts and several letters that have survived. In one he states that *'It is not much to set an example to pagans; what is much better is to set such an example that even the saints can learn from you.'* His truth that all people, rich and poor, are created equal by God, never gained favour with the mainstream church, which preferred the North African theology of St Augustine. Augustine (354-430) said *'Salus extra ecclesiam non est'* – *'There is no salvation outside the church'* a doctrine still followed by many 'Christian' sects, which thus condemns those born in countries outside the ecclesiastical authority of the Christian church. As a result there is no Saint Morgan, but there should be. His ideas, based on Druidic and Stoic thought, were so widespread in Britain that in 429 Germanus of Auxerre had been asked to suppress them, as mentioned above.

Germanus returned in the 440's to try again, in the reign of Vortigern, a Pelagian Christian. This seems to have been the time of the famous *'Alleluiah'* victory at Maes Armon, near Mold in Flint. Vortigern kept Britain independent until 44?, but has been pilloried throughout history, partially because of the Germanic bias of academics since the Hanovers took the English throne, but mainly because the early chroniclers of the history of Britain were anti-Pelagians. Anti-Pelagianism gave us the terrible deeds of the Inquisition, Simon de Montfort's dreadful *'crusade'* against the Cathar *'perfecti'* in France, and led indirectly to the strict Calvinism that almost destroyed a thousand years of Welsh society and culture.

It is instructive to note that Pelagianism would have destroyed the Roman Catholic church by starving it of funding and power. The Roman system of confessions and the selling of indulgences and pardons produced a steady income stream and lands from those in power. Thus Norman barons could steal Welsh land, blind and torture children and women, but be forgiven by God and go to Heaven in exchange for money and endowments of land. Much of church land was taken by bloody means in Wales, via Normans and Angevins, from its original owners. The author is not a theologist, but it seems that Pelagius is nearer to Christ's teachings than the established church, and his acceptance would have led to a far more peaceful 1500 years of history.

The following extracts are taken from 'The Catholic Encyclopaedia' of 1913, and are added without comment. *'As all his ideas were chiefly rooted in the old, pagan philosophy, especially in the popular system of the Stoics, rather than in Christianity, he regarded the moral strength of man's will, when steeled by asceticism, as sufficient in itself to desire and to attain the loftiest ideal of virtue. The value of Christ's redemption was, in his opinion, limited mainly to instruction and example, which the Saviour threw into the balance as a counterweight against Satan's wicked example, so that the nature retains the ability to conquer sin and to gain eternal life even without the aid of grace. By justification we are indeed cleansed of our personal sins through faith alone but this pardon implies no interior renovation of sanctification of the soul. How far the sola-fides doctrine "had no stouter champion before Luther than Pelagius" and whether, in particular, the Protestant conception of fiducial faith dawned upon him many centuries before Luther probably needs more careful investigation. ...... To explain psychologically Pelagius's whole line of thought, it does not suffice to go back to the ideal of the wise man, which he fashioned after the ethical principles of the Stoics and upon which his vision was centred. We must also take into account that his intimacy with the Greeks developed in him, though unknown to himself, a one-sidedness, which at first sight appears pardonable. The gravest error into which he and the rest of the Pelagians fell, was that they did not submit to the doctrinal decisions of the Church."*

The article goes on to comment on the 'last traces of Pelagianism' which held on in Celtic Britain: *'After the Council of Ephesus (431), Pelagianism no more disturbed the Greek Church, so that the Greek historians of the 5th century do not even mention the controversy or the names of the heresiarchs. But the heresy continued to smoulder in the West and died out very slowly. The main centres were Gaul and Britain. About Gaul we are told that a synod, held probably at Troyes in 429, was compelled to take steps against the Pelagians. It also sent Bishops Germanus of Auxerre and Lupus of Troyes to Britain to fight the rampant heresy, which received powerful support from two pupils of Pelagius, Agricola and*

Fastidius. Almost a century later, Wales was the centre of Pelagian intrigues. For the saintly Archbishop David of Menevia participated in 519 in the Synod of Brefy, which directed its attacks against the Pelagians residing there, and after he was made Primate of Cambria, he himself convened a synod against them. In Ireland also Pelagius's "Commentary of St Paul" was in use long afterwards, as is proved by many Irish quotations from it.' (The Synod of Brefi was in 545, not 519, which makes Wales the last stronghold of Pelagianism).

SIR THOMAS PICTON 1758 - June 18 1815
THE HERO OF WATERLOO

A son of Thomas Picton of Poyston, Pembrokeshire, he was commissioned (aged 13) as an ensign in 1771 in the 12th Regiment, which was under his uncle's command. He was promoted to lieutenant five years later. Picton became a half-pay captain for 12 years, remembered only for his actions when the 75th Regiment was being disbanded in Bristol at the end of the American War. Some of the men began to protest, and Picton, a burly man of over six feet tall, drew his sword and plunged into the mob to arrest the ringleader. After these years of enforced idleness, in 1794 Picton sailed without orders to the West Indies, to press his services upon fellow-Welshman, Lieutenant-General Sir John Vaughan. He was 38 years old. With several actions against the Spanish, he was rapidly promoted. However, his first 'official' active service did not come about until the capture of St Lucia in 1796, where he distinguished himself by his bravery. He was promoted from captain to lieutenant-colonel. Picton was made governor of Trinidad when it was taken in 1797, and his nine-year tenure aroused much controversy.

Picton's major problem was that he lacked the resources to keep the island British - he had few men, and a paucity of funds. He literally had to rely on threats and corruption to keep control. He even entered an alliance with the island's French planters against the threat of invasion by French and Spanish fleets. In 1806, because of the complaints of new colonists entering the island, he was brought back to London to face a variety of charges. All charges were dismissed, except for the torture of a slave, which was dismissed on appeal* The inhabitants of Trinidad were so grateful for the benefits of his administration of the island, that they voted him £5000 when he left it, as a token of their esteem and gratitude. A few years later, fire ravaged the capital of Trinidad, and Picton returned the whole £5,000 to help repair the damage.

In 1809, Thomas Picton fought on the expedition to Walcheren, and was appointed Governor of Flushing when it was taken. However, a bout of fever forced him to return to England, where he was soon given a division to command by Wellington against Napoleon. Picton's reputation stems from his command of the *'Fighting'* 3rd Division in the Peninsular War. His bravery at the terrible battles of Badajoz, Vittoria and Ciudad Rodrigo made him popular with his men, and the public back in England. He had personally led his men up the breach at the walls of Badajoz. At Busacos, he caught up with the retreating Portuguese battalion on hearing of their defection. Still wearing his coloured nightcap, he had turned them around, shouting *'Forward'* and *'Hurrah'* to save the day. In the Battle of Vittoria, Picton's division sustained, for over four hours, an unequal attack from the main body of the French army. For this, he had received Wellington's warmest congratulations.

Picton's officers presented him with a silver dinner service, made by the greatest of the Georgian silversmiths, Paul Storr, in 1814. It cost the enormous sum of £1400 and has just been auctioned in New York for £200,000. One of the tureens has the inscription from his officers and staff *'in testimony of their respect for his distinguished military talents uniformly displayed during the campaigns of 1810, 1811, 1812, 1813 and 1814 as a memorial of their attachment arising no less from his publick than from his private worth.'* There follows a list of his battle honours - Busacco, Fuentes d'Onor, Ciudad Roderico, Badajos, Vittoria, Pyrenees, Orthes and Toulouse. He received the thanks of the House of Commons on seven occasions, and Carmarthen crowds turned out to meet him when he retired, aged 56, to Ferryside in 1814. His home was Iscoed, at Ferryside in the parish of St Ishmael's.

Possibly because of the Trinidad scandal, his name was the only one omitted from the list of generals raised to the peerage at the end of the campaign. Possibly another cause was Wellington's dislike of Picton's mixing with his officers and men. Wellington called him *'a rough foul-mouthed devil as ever lived,'* but Picton was Wellington's favourite companion during that gruelling campaign across Spain and Portugal. Extremely disillusioned, Picton had returned to Carmarthenshire, to contest an election and enter politics, but Napoleon escaped from Elba. Wellington hastily recalled Picton, as one of his most trusted generals, to command the 5th Division. Picton had been knighted in the same year.

Thomas Picton

Wellington's Dispatches note *'I had directed all of my army to march upon Les Quatre Bras; and the 5th Division, under Lieut. General Sir Thomas Picton, arrived at about half past two in the day, followed by the corps of troops under the Duke of Brunswick, and afterwards by the contingent of Nassau... At this time the enemy commenced an attack upon Prince Blucher with his whole force, excepting the 1st and 2nd corps, and a corps of cavalry under General Kellermann, with which he attacked our post at Les Quatre Bras...We maintained our position also, and completely defeated and repulsed all the enemy's attempts to get possession of it. The enemy repeatedly attacked us with a large body of infantry and cavalry, supported by numerous and powerful artillery. He made several charges with the cavalry upon our infantry, but all were repulsed in the steadiest manner... Picton.... highly distinguished (himself)....* (because of Blucher's withdrawal), *I retired from the farm of Quatre Bras upon Genappe, and thence upon Waterloo, the next morning, the 17th, at 10 o'clock.....*(a description of the Battle of Waterloo)....*I propose to move this morning upon Nivelles, and not to discontinue my operations....such advantages could not be gained, without great loss, and I am sorry to ad that ours has been immense. In Lieut. General Sir Thomas Picton His Majesty has sustained the loss of an officer who has frequently distinguished himself in his service, and he fell gloriously leading his division to a charge with bayonets, by which one of the most serious attacks made by the enemy upon our position was repulsed.'* Picton was loved by his men, as he was one of that very rare breed of generals who 'led from the front' - they knew that he would not ask them to do anything that he would not do.

An account of the battle reads: *'When Buonaparte was convinced that he had failed in his design upon Hougoumont, the fire of cannon and musketry became more terrible. Columns of French infantry and cavalry, preceded by a formidable artillery, advanced from all points, ascended the eminence on which the British were stationed, , and precipitated themselves upon their squares. In vain the French artillery mowed down entire ranks of their opponents. The chasms were instantly filled, and not a foot of ground was lost. "What brave troops!" exclaimed Buonaparte to his staff. "It is a pity to destroy them; but I shall defeat them at last." The British reserved their fire until the enemy had approached within a few paces, and then, with one well-directed volley, levelled whole squadrons of the French. Other troops, however, succeeded, and the enemy pressed on to closer and more destructive combat. The principal masses of the French were now directed on the left of the British, where the divisions of Generals Picton and Kempt were posted. Napoleon's object in this attack was to turn the left of the allies, and, by separating them from the Prussians, cut off the retreat of Lord Wellington in that direction. The Scottish regiments displayed all the heroism by which they had been distinguished in that battle of the 16th (Quatre Bras), and sustained the principal brunt of the attack.*

A strong column of the enemy advanced under a galling fire from the British artillery, without discharging a shot. They gained the height, and pressed on, resolved to carry the position. Sir Thomas Picton immediately formed his division into a solid square, and advanced to the charge. Appalled by the boldness of his manoeuvre, the French hesitated, fired one volley, and retreated. On this occasion, Sir Thomas Picton received a musket-ball in his temple, and expired without a struggle. After his lamented fall, it was discovered that he had received a wound in his hip, on the 16th (2 days prior to Waterloo, at Quatre Bras), which he had concealed from all except his valet, and which had assumed a serious aspect for want of surgical assistance.' Picton must have been in terrible pain from gangrene at Waterloo, but still wished to lead the Scottish 5th Division.

In bitter hand-to-hand fighting, Picton's *'thin red line'* had held at Quatre Bras, which saved the day for Wellington, but he had been was severely injured. A musket ball had broken two of his ribs, and he had a hip wound. Heavily bandaged under his uniform, Sir Thomas had concealed his wound to lead the charge of his men at Waterloo. Forty-five years a soldier, there are monuments to his memory in St Paul's Cathedral, where he is buried, and at Carmarthen. His place in the crypt of St Paul's Cathedral is next to Wellington's tomb, and Picton is the only Welshman buried in that Cathedral. His first monument at Carmarthen was designed by John Nash (q.v.) in 1825.

*This was a most strange affair, where it seems that a confession was sought from a slave girl, Louisa Calderon, the 10-11 year-old mistress of a Pedro Ruiz. She was supposed to have stolen money from Ruiz, in collusion with Carlo Gonzalez. Gonzalez was apprehended, and Picton imprisoned the girl, who was allegedly tortured to confess by a magistrate named Bagora.

RICHARD PRICE February 23 1723 - April 19 1791
'THE FRIEND OF THE UNIVERSE, THE GREAT APOSTLE OF LIBERTY', 'THE MOST ORIGINAL THINKER EVER BORN IN WALES'

Richard Price of Tŷ'n Ton, near Llangeinor in Glamorgan's Garw Valley was one of the most influential and original Welshmen in history. His father was Rhys Price, and he was educated privately before studying at the Rev. Vavasor Griffith's Academy at Talgarth, Breconshire. His strict father virtually disinherited Richard, because he did not have as orthodox religious views. (In Cadrawd's superb history of Llangeinor, he notes the extreme parental authority of the Prices of Tynton - Richard's cousin Ann Thomas was the ill-fated 'Maid of Cefn Ydfa', her mother being Rhys Price's sister). Richard was only 16, and in Talgarth, when he heard the news of his father's death, and he and his mother were forced to move from Tynton by his step-brother, and live in semi-penury in Bridgend. Richard several times walked between Bridgend and Brecon to see his family. His mother soon died, and Richard was left with £400 from his father's estate upon this event. He nobly donated all of the money to his sisters, although he had no means of support and was aged only 18. He could no longer stay in the Academy, so appealed to his uncle the Rev. Samuel Price, to join him in London. Richard appealed to his step-brother for assistance to reach London, but that individual merely loaned Richard a horse to reach Cardiff.

Price walked to London, sometimes hitching a lift on farm wagons. His uncle Samuel received him unfavourably, sending Richard out to very cheap and unhealthy lodgings in Pudding Lane. The Rev. Price placed Richard in Mr Coward's Academy in Moorfields, to be trained as a dissenting minister. However, long study and poor lodgings almost broke Richard's health, and he had to return to Glamorgan for the summer to recuperate. Upon returning to London, Price moved into better lodgings and studied Mathematics, Philosophy and Theology. He became attached to his tutor, John Eames, a friend of Isaac Newton, a noted mathematician and an FRS. Leaving Moorfields Academy, Price became a domestic chaplain in Stoke Newington, continuing his studies for 13 years, until his employer died. Fortunately, his employer left Richard Price a house in Leadenhall Street and another smaller property. During this time Price had gained fame as a noted preacher. From the age of 22, he had taken the lectureship at the Presbyterian Meeting House in Old Jewry. With his circumstances improved, Price was able to marry in 1757. He was devoted to his wife, who unfortunately within a few years had become a confirmed invalid. It was in 1756 that Price published his great work on moral philosophy, 'A Review of the Principal Questions and Difficulties in Morals.'

This work notably widened his circle of acquaintances, to include the Master of Pembroke College, the Bishop of St Asaph, and the great philosopher-historian David Hume. He was now aged 33, and had the audacity to challenge the work of Locke and Hume, arguing that 'morality is a branch of necessary truth', but Hume enjoyed the openness, modesty and friendship of Price, visiting him many times at his home in Stoke Newington. Professor Fowler, in his 'Principles of Morals' stated that Price had anticipated the conclusions of the German Imanuel Kant by 20 years. (It can be posited that the universally famous Kant, who spent his life in university pondering ethical science, knew of Price's work and plagiarised it.) Benjamin Franklin wrote to Price in 1767, congratulating him, and sending a glowing review of his work from Paris of the *'Bibliotheque des Sciences et des Beaux Artes'*. The brilliant scientist Joseph Priestley also joined Price's discussion groups, and became a great and lifelong friend. Price managed to get Priestley a post with the Earl of Shelburne, enabling him to experiment towards his position as *'the father of the science of chemistry'*. Lord Shelburne had been intrigued by Price's *'Dissertations'* and had become a firm friend of his - one of his letters to Price begins: *'When I write to you, my heart and pen go together.'* Priestley reinforced these feelings: *For the most amiable simplicity of character, a truly Christian spirit, disinterested patriotism, and true candour no man in my opinion ever exceeded Dr Price. I shall ever reflect upon our friendship as a circumstance highly honourable, as it was a source of peculiar satisfaction to me.'* Price was also a friend of the poet Samuel Rogers, and of his parents - the poet's biographer states: *But a man destined to European renown and worthy of it, was living near, and gave occasional help, this was Mr (afterwards Dr) Price, one of the most acute and enlightened minds the 18th century produced, the charm of whose character exerted a considerable influence on Rogers' parents, and a close friendship sprung up between them.'*

Thomas Bayes, a friend of Price's died, leaving a problem on the *'Theory of Probabilities'* unsolved, and Price took two years, working intermittently, to solve it. He published his paper in 1763 in *'Transactions of the Royal Society.'* A supplementary paper appeared in 1764's *Philosophical Transactions'*, leading to the great honour of election Fellowship of the Royal Society in 1765. His portrait still hangs there. Now known as a radical dissenter, unitarian minister and moral philosopher, Price had established his reputation as a preacher in Newington Green, London and Hackney, and followed up *'Principal Questions in Morals'* with *'The Importance of Christianity'* (1766). 1767 saw another four volumes of his work published, *'Dissertation on Miracles', Providence', 'Prayer'* and *'Junction of Virtuous Men in a Future State'*.

In 1769, he was made a D.D. by Glasgow University, and also published his celebrated *'Northampton Mortality Tables'*. Price had given a paper to the FRS in 1769 upon the *'Expectation of Lives'*, diffidently correcting errors made by the mathematician de Moivre. The difficulty of the work was said to have turned Price's hair white. In 1767 Price had been approached by a number of lawyers who had formed a plan for the provision of their widows. Price found it so defective, that he researched to correct the defective bases of many societies like that of the lawyers. His celebrated treatise on *'Reversionary Payments'* was dedicated to Lord Shelburne, and his *'Northampton Life Tables'* (the result of over 20,000 calculations on life statistics) formed the basis of new industry of 'Life Assurance' and pensions He was associated with the first such society to be established, the 'Equitable Assurance Society', its success being due to his advice, and his Bridgend-born nephew William Morgan, became its first actuary. More editions followed, with the 1772 publication containing an appeal to reduce the *'grand national evil'* of the National Debt. William Pitt was influenced by Price's writings on the National Debt. Among his many influential books is *An Appeal to the Public on the Subject of the National Debt* (1772). Price had been admitted to The Royal Society in 1765 for his work on probability (see footnote).

Richard Price was in touch with the political leaders in the New England colonies, the Welsh future-president John Adams, Arthur Lee and Benjamin Franklin among others, and urged an easing of measures by the British government. It is said that in 1874, Price advised the citizens of Boston to *'throw the taxed tea into the sea rather than submit to taxation without representation'* (q.v. Samuel Adams). War broke out in 1775, and in 1776 Price published *'Observations on the Nature of Civil Liberty - the Principles of Government, and the Justice and Policy of the War with America'*, pleading for justice and putting forward a plan to pacify the colonies. This pamphlet was a sensation, having to be reprinted several times, and selling an unheard-of 60,000 copies in 12 editions by the end of 1776. He argued that each community had the right to self-government, responsible only for carrying out their electors' wishes, and that denial of this responsibility constituted treason. How different to today, where MP's are only responsible to their lords and masters who dictate three-line-whip party policy.

Richard Price

The pamphlet was also translated into French and Dutch and went into several editions on the Continent. Price was attacked in print by John Wesley, the Archbishop of York, and the Bishop of London separately. Willam Morgan's *'Memoirs'* aptly commented *'The preachers of the Gospel of peace denounced their anathemas against the friend of peace and harmony, whose only aim was to prevent the ravages of war, attempting at least to point out the folly and injustice of it.'* King George III's brother, the Duke of Cumberland, supported Price, and told him at the Bar at the House of Lords that he had been *'reading the pamphlet until he was blind'*. Lord Ashburton interposed *'It is rather remarkable that Your Royal Highness should have been blinded by the book which has opened the eyes of all mankind.'*

Merchants in the City of London were hard-hit by the war, and the Court of Common Council gave the freedom of the City of London in 1776 for this work, in a gold box to the value of £50, in recognition of his work in trying to bring peace. Crowds flocked to Hackney to see Price preach, Priestley saying that he attained a greater celebrity than any other Dissenting Minister in the past, yet Price remained humble in his dealings with everyone. In 1777 there was another pamphlet on the American War, dedicated to the Lord Mayor and notables of London. Appended were more writings on the National Debt, and work on the debts and resources of France. It demolished the arguments of the critics of his former pamphlet, as did another pamphlet aimed against Burke and the Archbishop of York in the following year.

Price supported the American Revolution with several books. He was honoured in both France and America. This **'Friend of the Universe, the Great Apostle of Liberty'** was asked by the newly established American Congress, through his friend Benjamin Franklin, to accept American citizenship and to set up a financial system in the new republic. His strong moral and lobbying support of the new American democracy, and abilities in philosophy, insurance and national financing were such that the young republic sent him the following resolution *'In Congress 6 Octr 1778 Resolved, That the Honourable Benjamin Franklin, Arthur Lee, and John Adams Esqrs or any one of them, be directed forthwith to apply to Dr Price, and inform him, that it is the Desire of Congress to consider him as a Cityzen of the united States, and to receive his Assistance in regulating their finances. That if he shall* *think it expedient to remove with his family to America and afford such Assistance, a generous Provision shall be made for requiting his Services.'* This wonderful offer, to be in effect the first 'Chancellor of the Exchequer' of the USA, was declined, probably because of the serious illness of Price's wife. Yale University gave Dr Price an honorary LL.D in 1781.

1780 saw a collaboration with Horne Tooke to publish *'Facts'*, a damning indictment of Lord North's government, which helped bring about his downfall. Another publication on America was commented upon by President Washington in 1785 as *'being the best legacy he could leave them.'* Lord Shelburne succeeded Lord North as Prime Minister in 1782, and was advised by Dr Price upon the finances of the country. Price refused the post of Private Secretary, however. Shelburne was soon succeeded by William Pitt the Younger, who also took the post of Chancellor, and leaned heavily upon Dr Price's advice. Lecky, the historian, referred to Price's original 1772 publication on the National Debt as *'destined to exercise a profound and most singular influence on English financial policy.'* Pitt's major motive now in economics was the reduction of in Dr Price's term *'that monstrous accumulation of artificial debt.'* Pitt worked with Price to develop his 'Sinking Fund Scheme' of 1786 to reduce the National Debt. In 1786 Price helped found a new Academy at Hackney, where he would teach Morals, Mathematics, Astronomy and Natural Philosophy to educate Ministers and the sons of Dissenting Ministers. Unfortunately, his ailing wife died in September, greatly distressing Richard, and Lord Lansdowne wrote a sympathetic letter of condolence from Bowood House in Wiltshire. It is worthwhile noting its contents to show once again the character of Richard Price, the poor boy from Glamorgan, and his influence upon all levels of society:

'Though the post only allows me a moment, I cannot delay a day to assure you that you have not a relation who feels more sensibly the loss which you have sustained. Let me beseech you to command me in any shape, I will come instantly to London if I can contribute to your comfort, or will be happy to see you here, where no one shall come but as are agreeable to you. You will find Lady Lansdowne and me nearly alone. We dine at 5 o'clock as plain as you do in your own house, Lady Lansdowne plays for an hour on the harpsichord, and we go to bed at eleven. We'll consider and treat you as a father. Every person about the house reveres and respects you, and you'll make us very happy, which is the next best thing to being happy yourself.'

Price had continued corresponding with leading American statesmen, earning the opprobrium of the British security forces, and also wrote to the distinguished Frenchmen Turgenev, Necker (a popular minister to Louis XVI) and Condorcet. They all saw him not just as an expert on national finance, but had read his theories on liberty and civil government in their French translation. France was struggling with its economy. As well as with his former pamphlets, Richard Price now also provoked Burke's anger with his support for the French Revolution (*'A Discourse of the Love of Our Country'*) in 1789, where he sermonised *'Tremble, all ye oppressors of the world.............you cannot now keep the world in darkness'*. Price celebrated their *'ardour for liberty'*, and provoked Edmund Burke to write his *'Reflections on the Revolution in France.'* In poor health, Price had been asked to give the speech for the Anniversary of the English Revolution (see Cromwell), on November 4th, 1789, presided over by Earl Stanhope. Price's 'Love of Our Country' speech eulogised the establishment of a free constitution for

France (something that Britain still needs), stating *'Behold, the light you have struck out, after setting America free, reflected in France, and there kindled into a blaze that lays despotism in ashes, and warms and illuminates Europe!'* In the evening dinner, Doctor Price gave a congratulatory address to the National Assembly in Paris, hailing *'the glorious example given in France to encourage other nations to assert the unalienable rights of mankind, and thereby to introduce a general reformation in the governments of Europe and make the world free and happy.'* Price's speeches, enunciating the principles of the Revolution, were transmitted to the Duc de la Rochefoucauld and the French Assembly, who received it with loud applause.

Rochefoucauld personally wrote thanking the doctor, addressing him as *'the Apostle of Liberty'*. The discourse and speech were published in pamphlet form, and again caused a sensation. During the French Revolution, Price had corresponded closely with Thomas Jefferson (q.v.), the American Minister to France, and became a correspondent and supporter of Tom Paine. A year later, on July 14th, 1790, Price made another speech to commemorate the first anniversary of the French Revolution, promoting peace for ever between nations, as the French had promised. De la Rochefoucauld read the speech out to the National Assembly, who all stood to listen, their heads uncovered as a mark of respect to Richard Price. De la Rochefoucauld then read it again in his honour.

After Price's death upon April 19th, 1791, the Earl of Stanhope led the huge funeral procession, and Dr Priestley read the funeral service. The National Assembly and the Jacobins in France went into mourning. To summarise this most remarkable man, with his friend Joseph Priestley, Price had helped found the Unitarian Society. He influenced Mary Wollstonecraft, who wrote the important *'Vindication of the Rights of Women'*. His *'Review of the Principal Questions in Morals'* put an element of realism into the philosophy of the day, and was possibly the greatest of his theological and ethical treatises. He also drew up the first budget of the new American nation, and his expertise on demography and actuarial matters influenced the financial policies of William Pitt and Shelburne. Unwavering in his support for the American colonies, despite English opposition, however Price refused an offer of American citizenship. Price was also a great supporter of the French Revolution. This statistician, preacher and philosopher had a political influence upon radicals in both the Old and New Worlds. John Davies calls Price *'the most original thinker ever born in Wales'*. A friend of Presidents and Prime Ministers, he was is little-known in Wales.

*Samuel Rogers wrote of this vastly underestimated polymath, *'He was the most humane of men; to see distress was in him to feel an impulse to relieve it. All admired and loved him for the sweetness of his disposition and the unaffected sincerity of his manners.'* Price needs not just a new biography, but also an international society dedicated to his memory.

FOOTNOTES:
1. Without Richard Price, it is possible that Bayesian statistical analysis may have been overlooked in history. His friend, the Rev. Thomas Bayes was elected a Fellow of the Royal Society in 1742, but published very little. On his death aged 59 in 1761, Richard Price found among Bayes' papers an *Essay towards solving a problem in the Doctrine of Chances*. Price had it published by the Royal Society in 1763, and Bayesian estimation became a statistical technique for calculating how true a proposition is likely to be. Unlike classical statistics, for

the first time prior judgement is factored into the equation. Bayesian methods have grown in popularity for business forecasting, archaeological digs, courts cases, in analysing the results of drugs trials and improving the service of banks, amongst other uses.

2. Price's home, Tynton (Tŷ'n Ton), is in a bad state of disrepair. Formerly a mansion, it became a farmhouse, and stands on the southern slopes of Mynydd Llangeinor.

DR. WILLIAM PRICE March 4 1800 - January 23 1893
CHARTIST FREE-THINKER AND REPUBLICAN DOCTOR

Llantrisant in Mid-Glamorgan has a superb hill fort, and provided the Black Prince's finest archers for The Hundred Years' War. However, its main claim to fame is its 19th century doctor/druid, Dr. William Price, who proselytised not just vegetarianism, nudity, and free love, but also the unhealthiness of socks, the potential dangers on the environment from rapid industrialisation, revolution, republicanism and radical politics. *He refused to treat patients who would not give up smoking,* and prescribed a vegetarian diet instead of pills. Born at Rudry, on March 4, 1800, his minister father wanted him to be a churchman, but William wished to practise medicine. He studied under Dr Evan Edwards at Caerphilly for six years, during which time his father died. His guardian uncle Thomas secured him an appointment as a schoolmaster, but William refused the offer and enrolled at the Royal College of Surgeons in London. How he supported himself is unclear, but he astonished everyone by passing the examination of both College and Hall in just 12 months, the first student in history to do so. He spent another year studying anatomy, surgery, physiology and medicine, and Dr Price returned to Wales in 1821.

Practising at Nantgarw outside Cardiff (near the world-famous porcelain works, where there is a museum today), he acquired fluency in several languages including Hindi. A tall man, he dressed in a white tunic over a scarlet waistcoat and green trousers. Price let his hair grow into long plaits, and was of the opinion that doctors should be paid a regular wage for keeping people healthy - when they became ill, the doctor should then bear the expense of treating them. He often put patients on a natural, vegetarian diet, which he followed himself, and gave a public lecture in which he said *'Medical science has of all the sciences been the most unscientific. Its professors, with a few exceptions such as myself, have always sought to cure disease by the magic of pills and potions and poisons that attack the ailment with the idea of suppressing the symptoms rather than attacking the cause.'* Apart from the quacks and authorities of the medical profession (with their 'cursed regimes' of purging and bleeding), he also made enemies of the church, both established and Nonconformist, telling them that *'Man is greater than your God, for Man created God in his own image.'* He also wrote to a friend: *'Priests are paid to teach that the world of thieves and oppressors, of landlords and coal-owners, is a just world. Their theology is always that of the doctrine that the powers that be are ordained by God.'* During his practice, he also became associated with 'druidical rites' and deposited many researches into the Public Records Offices. He was the first doctor to be elected by a group of factory workers as their own general practitioner, being paid a weekly deduction out of wages paid at the

Pontypridd Chainworks. *This was the precursor of the miners' medical societies, which were, in turn, the origin of the National Health Service.*

A skilled surgeon, he attended Chartist rallies in a cart drawn by goats. In a speech on Pontypridd Common, he stated 'We *have tolerated the tyranny of those who oppress us - landlords, coal-owners, and the clergy - too long. We must strike with all our might and power. Let cowards go their way, for they have no part to play in this great struggle. Men of the valleys, remember that the principle behind Chartism is the principle which acknowledges the right of every man who toils to the fruits of his labours. The points embedded in this charter are our immediate demands. But ultimately we shall demand more. Oppression, injustice and the grinding poverty which burdens our lives must be abolished for all time. We are the descendants of valiant Welshmen and we must be worthy of the traditions which they have passed on to us.'* Price had moved from Nantgarw to Llantrisant by this time, and was elected leader of the Pontypridd and District section of the Charter. John Frost (q.v.) and Price's great friend William Jones were arrested after the Newport Rising, and a warrant issued for the arrest of Dr Price. He was thus forced to escape to France (in a frock) to live in 1839. The story is that Price was assisted up the gangplank at Cardiff Docks by a police inspector who was looking for him.

In Paris he was helped by his friend John Masklyn to set up in practice, and he consorted with the great writer-philosopher Heinrich Heine. Price spent seven years in Paris, becoming something of a society doctor, with his fresh approach to medicine, and returned to Eglwysilan near Pontypridd in 1846. He still ranted against the medical profession - *'Some call it recognised science, but I call it recognised ignorance!'* A campaigner against tobacco, he threw a man's clay pipe out a railway carriage, and told the offender that he would follow it, if he complained. He held druidic ceremonies at the rocking stone near Pontypridd, which were considered satanic by the local Methodists, and began building a Druidic Temple near it. A case of trespass on the site was proven against Price, who flatly refused to pay the fine. When a warrant was issued for his arrest, William promptly fled back to Paris and resumed his practice in 1860. He spent another six years there, where he consorted with Proudhon, the anarchist and revolutionary philosopher, and returned to Wales in June, 1866.

Price supported the coal-miners in their 1871 strike, writing to the newspapers against the coal-owners: *'You are the Welsh Pharaohs who think you can suck the life-blood of the colliers forever. You have grown fat and prosperous; you own the big houses; you wear the finest clothes; your children are healthy and happy; yet you do not work. Let me tell you. You have been stealing the balance of low wages which you have been paying them. Take heed, you men whose bodies and souls are bloated by the life-blood of the poor, take heed before it is too late. Remember that the oppression of the Pharaohs of Egypt did not last forever, and neither will the oppression of the blood-sucking Pharaohs of Wales.'* In 1875, Dr William Price made the long journey to Dean Street, Soho, to meet Karl Marx, whom he found to be a *'fascinating personality'*, but he was *'less than impressed'* with Marx's phrase 'historical inevitability' as there was no educated industrial proletariat in Wales which would force revolution.

He did not approve of marriage as it *'reduced the fair sex to the condition of slavery'* and lived openly 'in sin' with his young housekeeper. This precursor of the Hippy Movement had a son when he was eighty-three, and named him *'Iesu Grist'* (Jesus Christ). When Iesu died, aged five months, in 1884, Dr Price cremated him on an open funeral pyre. Price was dressed in flowing druidical robes, and timed the event to take place as the locals were leaving their chapels. The local population attacked him, rescuing the charred remains of the child, and the police arrested Price. The mob then went to find the mother, Price's young housekeeper, Gwenllian, but were deterred by Price's twelve large dogs. (Price did not believe in marriage as *'it turned women into slaves.'*) The doctor was acquitted after a sensational trial in Cardiff, and *cremation was legalised in Britain as a result.* Another infant was born, named *'Iarlles Morgannwg'*, the *'Countess of Glamorgan'* and in one of his many law-suits he called the child as assistant counsel to him. He issued medallions to commemorate his legal victory, and at the age of ninety had another son, again called Iesu Grist. At the age of ninety-three, he died and was cremated in front of twenty thousand spectators at East Carlan Field, Llantrisant. This was the first legalised cremation (1893), and a ton of coal and

Dr. William Price

three tons of wood were used to accomplish the mission. Price had organised the cremation himself, selling tickets to the estimated twenty thousand people that later attended it. Llantrisant's pubs ran dry.

Price, with a long flowing beard and hair past shoulder-length, habitually wore only the national colours of red, white and green. On his head was a red fox-skin pelt, with the front paws on his forehead and the tail hanging down his back. His cloak was white, his waistcoat scarlet, and he wore green trousers - the colours of Wales. He started building a druidic temple, of which the gatehouses are lived in today. One of the two round 'Druidic' towers he built in 1838 as a gatehouse for his projected eight-storey Druidic Palace was recently on the market. He had dreamed of *'a golden age'* when Wales would once again be ruled by Druids. His birthplace, the Green Meadow Inn at Waterloo, near Newport, was in the news in 1996. Discovery Inns wished to demolish it, to put up 13 boxes that pass for living dwellings these days. CADW, the historic monuments society in Wales, washed their hands of the matter, although the local community desperately wanted to save this historic site.

Dr. Price's last dying act was to order and drink a glass of champagne before he moved on to his next destination. Eat your heart out, Hollywood, no-one could make up a life like this. An anti-establishment campaigner for women's rights, socialist, progressive doctor, rebel, Chartist, druid, hippy, vegetarian, consort of Heine, Proudhon and Marx, environmentalist pioneer of cremation who foresaw the dangers of smoking two-hundred years ago.

ROBERT RECORDE 1510 - 1589
MATHEMATICIAN WHO REVOLUTIONISED ALGEBRA AND INVENTED THE = SIGN

Born in 1510, Robert Recorde of Tenby, the son of Thomas Recorde of Tenby and Rose Jones of Machynlleth, went to All Souls College. *His invention of the 'equals' sign (=) revolutionised algebra*, and his mathematical works were translated and read all over Europe. Recorde is commemorated in the great parish church at Tenby*. He died a bankrupt, despite his book going into twenty-six editions in his lifetime. From 1549-1551 Recorde was Comptroller of the Bristol Mint before going to Ireland from 1551-53 and 1556.

A leading mathematician, the writer of the first English language texts on algebra and arithmetic, Recorde invented the equals (=) sign, to *'avoid the tedious repetition of equals to'*. His arithmetic book went into fifty editions and was notable in being innovative in two respects. It was written as a dialogue between a master and pupil to keep it interesting (shades of 'Sophie's World'), and it used the device of pointing fingers (precursing Windows icons !) Recorde studied at Oxford, qualified as a Doctor of Medicine in Cambridge, was a doctor in London and in charge of mines in Ireland, but died in prison because of a lawsuit taken out by the Duke of Pembroke.

Recorde virtually established the English school of mathematics and introduced algebra to England. He was educated at Oxford from 1525-1531 where he gained a BA and became a Fellow of All Souls, and he passed his MD in Cambridge in 1545. He seems to have been practising as a doctor in Oxford from 1533, before his medical degree. In 1547 Recorde published *The Urinal of Physick*, a traditional medical work. From 1545-1547 it appears that Recorde taught mathematics privately in Cambridge and Oxford. However, although a doctor of medicine at the Royal Court, he was more noted for his astronomy and mathematics. Recorde practised medicine in London from 1547-1549.

In 1551 Recorde wrote *Pathwaie to Knowledge*, which some consider to be an abridgement of Euclid's Elements. It is certainly the first English translation, in which he rearranged Euclid's writings to make better sense. This is his only book that is not written in the form of a dialogue between a master and student. 1552 saw the publication of his *The Ground of Artes*, a book for learning arithmetic. (This was dedicated to King Edward VI, his patron.) This was very successful commercially, *teaching the perfect work and practice of Arithmeticke etc.* in Recorde's own words. It discusses arabic numeral operations, counter computation, proportion, fractions and the 'rule of three', etc. Some time after this he wrote *The Gate of Knowledge*, which seems not to have been published and has been lost - it was a treatise upon measurement and the use of the quadrant. He later spoke of a quadrant that he

Robert Recorde

invented (whether for mensuration or for navigation is unknown), which is probably described in this lost book.

In 1556 *The Castle of Knowledge* was published, dealing with the science of construction and the use of the sphere, using Ptolemaic astronomy, and mentioning

Copernicus favourably and dangerously**. (This was dedicated to his patron, Queen Mary, and its Latin version to Cardinal Pole.) In 1557 appeared *The Whetstone of Witte*, his textbook of elemetary algebra. In this he invented the = sign using two parallel line segments, *'bicause noe 2 thynges can be moare equalle'.* The symbol of = took some time to be accepted, with vertical parallel lines being used by some and 'ae' by others until the 1700's. ('ae' was abbreviated from the Latin *aequalis*, meaning equal). *The Whetstone of Wytte* was dedicated to The Muscovy Company, for whom he planned a textbook on navigation, and to whom he was an advisor.

After being physician to King Edward VI and then Queen Mary, which required a swift change of religion, he became Comptroller of the Bristol Mint from 1549-1551. Recorde was then made Surveyor of Mines and Monies in Ireland, based at Wexford, from 1551-53 and in 1556. (He would possibly have begun life as a Catholic, averred to Protestantism under Edward VI, returned to Catholicism under Mary, and then gone back to Protestantism under Elizabeth). As Surveyor in Ireland he was in charge of the silver mines in Wexford, but the lode was not as rich as expected and they failed. For 'mismanagement' of the enterprise, Recorde was thrown into gaol.

His death occurred at the age of 48, at King's Bench Prison in Southwark, where he had been committed for debt, and his will was proved upon June 18th, 1558. A mathematician, merchant, doctor of medicine, navigator, teacher, metallurgist, cartographer, inventor and astronomer, he was shortly replaced as a polymath in Tudor society by Dr John Dee (q.v.), another brilliant mathematician. Dee published an augmentation of Recorde's 'Grounde of Arts', the mathematical textbook which ran to twenty-six editions by 1662 and wrote his own seminal 'Preface to the English edition of Euclid', which has been called a *'landmark in mathematical thought.'*

*The Robert Recorde Memorial at the church reads:

> *In Memory of*
> ROBERT RECORDE
> *The Eminent Mathematician*
> *Who Was Born at Tenby, circa 1510.*
> *To His Genius We Owe the earliest*
> *Important English Treatises on*
> *Algebra, Arithmetic, Astronomy and Geometry;*
> *He Also invented the Sign of*
> *Equality = Now Universally Accepted*
> *By the Civilised World*
> ROBERT RECORDE
> *Was Court Physician to*
> *King Edward IV and Queen Mary*
> *He Died in London*
> *1558*

**Copernicus' ideas were only around 20 years old, and 'heretical' at this time, yet the mention of him in the fourth treatise of T*he Castle of Knowledge* is as follows:

Scholar:

I perceive it well: for as if the earth were always out of the centre of the world, those former absurdities would at all times appear: so if at any time the earth should move out of his place, those inconveniences would then appear.

Master:
    This is truly to be gathered, howbeit, Copernicus, a man of great learning, of much experience, and of wonderful diligence in observation, hath renewed the opinion of Aristarchus Samius, and affirmeth that the earth not only moveth circularly about his own centre, but also may be, yea and is, continually out of the precise centre of the world 38 hundred thousand miles: but because the understanding of that controversy dependeth upon profounder knowledge than in this Introduction may be uttered conveniently, I will let it pass till some other time.

Scholar:
    Nay sir in good faith, I desire not to hear such vain fantasies, so far against common reason, and repugnant to the consent of all the learned multitude of Writers, and therefore let it pass forever, and a day longer.

Master:
    You are too young to be a good judge in so great a matter: it passeth far your learning, and theirs that are also much better learned than you, to improve (disprove) his suppositions by good arguments, and therefore you were best to condemn no thing that you do not well understand: but another time, as I said, I will so declare his supposition, that you will not only wonder to hear it, but also peradventure be as earnest then to credit it as you are now to condemn it. In the mean season, let us proceed forward to our former order..........'

FOOTNOTE:
In 1706, William Jones of Llanfihangel Tre'r Beirdd, Anglesey, was the first person to use the symbol pi to denote the ratio of the circumference of a circle to its diameter.

RHODRI MAWR   820 - 878
RHODRI AP MERFYN FRYCH AP GWRIAD, RHODRI THE GREAT, 'THE GREATEST OF ALL THE KINGS OF WALES'

Possibly because of the lasting Roman influence in Wales, and their much later adoption of Christianity, the Saxons and neighbouring Mercians were regarded as uncultured and aggressive pagans by the Welsh, but the border held against them, albeit with some fluidity. There were also constant Pictish attacks on the coastal areas of Wales. However, the next severe threat to Wales was that of the Norsemen, whose first recorded attack was in 850. Merfyn Frych spent his reign fighting against the Danes and Mercians, and fell at Cetyll against Burchred of Mercia in 844.

    His son Rhodri Mawr unified most of Wales to move it towards statehood, thanks in part to the need to fight this Viking threat. A descendant of Llywarch Hen, the warrior-bard, he had succeeded his father in 844, and it is notable that Wales achieved **national unity** under him, whereas England had to wait for statehood until the coronation of Edgar at Bath in 973. (A columnist named Simon Heffer has recently received national publicity by stating that the Wales has never been a nation. Knowledge of true history is a rare commodity). Rhodri was the only Welsh King to be called 'The Great', and earned thanks from Charlemagne for his victories against the Viking threat, killing the Viking leader Horm, off Anglesey in 856. (Orme's Head at Llandudno may be named after Horm). His great success as a warrior was noted in *The Ulster Chronicle*, and also by Sedulius Scottus, an Irish scholar at the Liege court of the Emperor Charles the Bald. His great victory over the Vikings was acclaimed by Irish and Franks alike. In fact, Alfred and Charlemagne were the only other rulers to be bestowed with the title of 'Great' in this century. Nora Chadwick called Rhodri *'the greatest of all the kings of Wales'*. Rhodri dominated Wales from the castle he built at Dinefwr.

Until his death in battle in 878, he held Wales together, even making an alliance with King Alfred of Wessex against the Norsemen. He had assumed the throne of Gwynedd upon his father's death, taken control of Powys upon the death of his mother's brother Cyngen (on a pilgrimage to Rome) in 872, and ruled Seisyllwg from 872 when he married the sister of its last king. Now leader of nearly all Wales, his inherent hatred of Mercians led him to ally himself with the Danes against a Mercian invasion in 878, and he died in battle against them, protecting Powys from invasion. His son Gwriad fell at his side. His kingship of Powys had automatically led him into intense hostilities with the kingdom of Mercia, as Offa's Dyke proved no real frontier. Rhodri's dominions were divided, with Anarawd becoming King of Gwynedd, Cadell King of Deheubarth, and Merfyn King of Powys. Three years later at the Battle of Conway, the Welsh victory under Anarawd ap Rhodri was known as *'Dial Rhodri'* ('Rhodri's Revenge') - 'God's vengeance for the slaughter of Rhodri'.

The practice of partible inheritance, gavelkind, meant that each of Rhodri's six sons had a part of Wales to control. Unusually for Welsh sons, they seemed to work well together, with the result that Rhodri's grandson, Hwyel Dda ap Cadell ap Rhodri eventually came to rule Wales. The Viking raids carried on until 918, and the rule of Hywel Dda, and restarted on his death in 952, especially focusing upon Welsh monasteries. St David's Cathedral was sacked by them for the sixth time, as late as 1091.

The Chronicle of Ystrad Fflur records the turbulent times of Rhodri Mawr:
816... *the Saxons ravaged Eryri and took Rhufoniog by force*
817   *In this year was the battle of Llan-faes*
818   *Coenwulf ravaged the land of Dyfed*
822   *Deganwy was destroyed by the Saxons and they took the kingdom of*
      Powys into their own control
823   *In this year Brother Nennius compiled his book*
844   *In this year Rhodri ap Merfyn was High King*
848   *In this year was the battle of Ffinant. And the men of Brycheiniog slew*
      Ithel, king of Gwent
849   *In this year the Saxons slew Meurig*
850   *In this year Cynin was killed by the Black Gentiles (Dublin Vikings)*
853   *In this year Mona (Anglesey) was laid waste by the Black Gentiles*
855   *In this year Cyngen of Powys died on pilgrimage; and Rhodri took Powys*
      from the Saxons
864   *Duda laid Glywysing (Glamorgan) waste*
869   *In this year was the battle of Bryn Onen*
872   *In this year Gwgan ap Meurig drowned and Seisyllwg came to Rhodri*
874   *In this year were the battles of Banolau and Ynegydd*

876   In this year Rhodri was in Ireland
877   In this year Rhodri and Gwriad fell to the Saxons

HENRY RICHARD April 3 1812 - August 20 1888
'APOSTOL HEDDIWCH' (THE APOSTLE OF PEACE), 'THE MEMBER FOR WALES'

Born at Prospect House, Tregaron, Henry was the son of Ebeneser Richard, a powerful Calvinistic Methodist minister, whose own father (another Henry) had been a Methodist minister and one of the circulating teachers of Griffith Jones (q.v.) Henry Richard's mother was Mary, the daughter of William Williams of Tregaron. After schooling in Llangeitho, Henry worked as a draper's apprentice in Carmarthen before deciding to enter the ministry. After attending London's Highbury College, he was ordained minister in the Marlborough Congregational chaple in the Old Kend Road, where he remained until retiring from the ministry in 1850.

The Peace Union was founded in 1816 through the hard work of Joseph Tregelles Price, a humanitarian Quaker who tried desperately to save the doomed Dic Penderyn. Its first secretary was Evan Rees of Montgomeryshire, author of *'Sketches of Horrors of War'*. He was followed as secretary by Henry Richard in 1848, and the secretaries for the first hundred years were all Welsh. The pacifist Henry Richard of Tregaron was known as Apostol Heddwch (*'The Apostle of Peace'*) in Wales. After playing a prominent part in a Brussels peace conference, Price became active in the promotion of such conferences in Paris, Frankfurt and elsewhere, and in the overseeing of publications for peace. The Peace Union was the *forerunner of the League of Nations*, which in turn changed into The United Nations. It had been set up, mainly by Nonconformists and Quakers, as being *'principled against all war, upon any pretence'*, its object being to *'print and circulate Tracts and to diffuse information tending to show that War is inconsistent with the spirit of Christianity, and the true interests of mankind; and to point out the means best calculated to maintain permanent and universal peace, upon the basis of Christian principles.'* Its most important staff appointment was that of Henry Richard. With the reformers John Bright and Richard Cobden, he tirelessly carried the ideals of pacifism, peace and reconciliation into every part of England, until his retirement in 1885, aged 73. He was also the editor of the Peace Society's monthly magazine, *Herald of Peace*. Under Henry Richard's guidance, the Union opposed the Boer War (like Lloyd-George, q.v.) The Welsh connection was kept up with the appointment of Richard's successor, William Evans Darby, who held the post until 1915.

A nonconformist radical and a friend of Richard Cobden, Richard travelled widely in Europe, holding peace conferences and encouraging the use of arbitration in international disputes. Becoming involved in politics, in 1865 he withdrew from candidature as Liberal candidate for Cardiganshire. By 1866, Henry had published diaries of his European tours, many pamphlets and *'Letters on the Political and Social Conditions of Wales'*, and in that year married Matilda Farley. Richard was elected MP for Merthyr Tydfil at the age of fifty-six in 1868, and previously in 1847 had repudiated 'The Blue Books' which maligned Welsh education. His first act in The House of Commons was to condemn those landlords who evicted their Welsh tenants for voting Liberal. This protest facilitated the Ballot Act of 1872. He was the first proponent of Welsh Nonconformism in the House of Commons. As an MP, he was passionately interested in Welsh education, land reform, disestablishment of the English church in Wales, and the protection of the Welsh language. His interests led to his nickname as 'The Member for Wales'. He wrote to the English press explaining why the Rebecca Riots were happening in Wales.

In July 1873, apart from his work in upholding Welsh and Nonconformist rights, Henry Richard succeeded in carrying a motion in favour of international arbitration. He was elected Chairman of the Congregational Union of England and Wales in 1877, the first layman to be chosen for this office. He became closely associated with the University of Wales in Aberystwyth, and in 1880 served on the committee studying intermediate and higher education in Wales. Henry Richard died at Treborth, near Bangor, and there is a prominent statue of this political reformer and idealist in Tregaron's main square. Tom Ellis (who will appear in 2002's 'Another 100 Great Welshmen') opined that Richard was the first to represent in Parliament the new national spirit which arose in Wales in the second half of the 19th century.

BARTHOLOMEW ROBERTS   1682 - 1722
THE LAST AND MOST LETHAL PIRATE

Llewelyn Penrose's *'Journal'* was one of the earliest stories of buried treasure, upon which Edgar Allen Poe based his *'Gold Bug'*. We have seen that Wales produced the most famous buccaneer in history, Sir Henry Morgan. It also produced a notable series of pirates, including the greatest and most curious them all, Black Bart, whom 'Newsweek' called the *'last and most lethal pirate'*, also known as *'The Black Pirate'*. Daniel Defoe called his aspect *'black'*, as he had black hair and a dark complexion, and he was simply **the most formidable pirate in history**.

To put piracy into context, the English Navy was a bitterly cruel organisation, and deserters were common. It had to 'press-gang' most of its unfortunate seamen from British ports. Conditions were not as bad in the merchant navy, but there was still a constant flow of dissatisfied seamen men willing to sail under the black (or red) flag of piracy. Bartholomew Roberts wrote of the motives for becoming a pirate: *'In an honest service there is thin rations, low wages, and hard labour; in this, plenty, satiety, pleasure and ease, liberty and power; and who would not balance creditor on this side, when all the hazard that is run for it, at worst, is only a sour look or two at choking (dying) ? No, **a merry life and a short one shall be my motto.**'*

This "Last and Most Lethal Pirate", Black Bart (Barti Ddu), captured an amazing four hundred ships between 1719 and 1722, bringing commerce in North America, the West Indies, West Africa and the whole Atlantic almost to a standstill. Born in 1682 at Little Newcastle near Haverfordwest, Bartholomew Roberts went to sea as boy and became a skilled navigator. We first hear of him as the thirty-seven year old third mate on the Princess galley, picking up slaves from the Gold Coast. He was captured by two pirate ships, captained by another Welshman, Hywel Davis, and given the choice of joining them, which he did, despairing of lack of any promotion because of his class. Black Bart's favourite oath was *'Damnation to him that ever lived to wear a halter!'* He was known as *'pistol-proof'*, as he was expert in ship-handling, crew control, and the tactics of naval warfare.

Within six weeks, Hywel Davis was dead in an ambush by the Portuguese, and Roberts was voted the new captain. Accepting, he said *'If I must be a pirate, it is better to be a commander than a common man'*. He swiftly avenged Davis' death, attacking a Portuguese fleet (although outnumbered forty-two merchant ships to his own ship). Roberts escaped with the richest merchantman in the fleet - £50,000 in the currency of the day - *the most profitable raid in West Indian pirate history.*

He allowed no boys or women on his ships, was a teetotal tea-drinker, and the ship's band played hymns for Sunday services. No drinking or gambling was allowed on board on Sundays. The band also played Black Bart into battle - he dressed in red damasks and velvet from head to toe, with a three-cornered red hat with a huge scarlet plume, armed with cutlasses and pistols. His demeanour and scarlet dress were such that French traders called him Le Joli Rouge - **the origin of the 'Jolly Roger'**. It is also said that *Black Bart's flag was the origin of the skull and crossbones* - a skeleton with an hourglass.

Suffering mutinies, internal fights, and terrible deprivations at times, he was feared by all sea-going vessels. Being annoyed at the persistent attempts of the governors of Barbados and Martinique to imprison and execute him, he designed a personal flag and plate for his cabin door, with ABH (a Barbadian's head) and AMH (a Martinican's head) illustrated on them. He later captured, and hung, the Governor of Martinique in October 1720 from his yardarm.

Roberts' crew was drunk when he was finally ambushed by a special convoy of Royal Navy frigates. It seems that Roberts deliberately sought death. He was tired of trying to control a drunken, womanising rabble. Black Bart could have escaped, but inexplicably ordered his ship to turn to face his pursuers, although the majority of his crew were incapable of standing, let alone fighting the Royal Navy. Captain Ogle was knighted for his singular service in killing *'the great pirate Roberts'*, the only naval man honoured for service against the pirates. Black Bart was not yet forty years old. Ogle himself made a fortune, from illicitly purloining the plundered gold dust he found in Roberts' cabin.

Of the two hundred and fifty four pirates captured, fifteen died en-route to the Gold Coast, and four more in the slave hole there during the trial. Some musicians and 'forced men' were acquitted. *'The House of Lords'*, the hardest and longest-serving members of the crew, had followed Hywel Davis, and regarded themselves as the 'aristocracy' of the pirate profession, giving each other honorary *'lordships'*. They were not contrite at their trial. Seventeen of Robert's crew were committed to prison in London, of whom thirteen died in transit. Of the fifty-two members of Roberts' crew hung on the Gold Coast, a third were from Wales, and a third from the West country. (After an act of betrayal, it seems that Roberts would allow no Irish to serve with him). The oldest to be executed was forty-five, and the youngest just nineteen.

The bodies of the eighteen worst offenders, the members of the famous *'House of Lords'*, were dipped in tar, bound with metal strips and hung in chains from gibbets on three prominent hills overlooking the sea-lanes. The shock of the death of this most famous, brave and dreaded pirate helped end the so-called *"golden age"* of piracy. Much more on Morgan, Davis and Roberts will be found in the author's forthcoming book upon British (Welsh) pirates.

CHARLES ROLLS   1878 - 1910
AVIATION PIONEER AND FOUNDER OF ROLLS-ROYCE

Charles Stewart Rolls, co-founder of Rolls Royce, came from Monmouth, the only town with a fortified gateway on a bridge in Britain. Monmow Bridge is 13th century and once possessed a portcullis and a rampart for sentries. *Only three such stone gated bridges survive in Europe.* King Henry V, of Agincourt glory, who finally ended Glyndŵr's dreams of an independent Wales, was also born here.

Son of Lord Llangatock MP, Charles Rolls had his first car at the age of nineteen, in 1896, when its speed was restricted by the need to have a man walking in front with a warning flag. It thus took him three days to drive home from his studies in Cambridge. From his days at Eton, he was besotted with engineering, and had enrolled for a mechanical engineering degree at Trinity College. At Eton he had bought a massive dynamo and sent it back to the family mansion, so that he could experiment with electric lighting in the house during the school holidays. He was the first undergraduate and the fourth person in Britain to possess a car, a Peugeot. He told friends of his ambition to have a car associated with his name, so that *'in future it might be a household word just as much as Broadway or Steinway in connection with pianos.'* (Unfortunately, the sale of Rolls Royce and Bentley to Germany a hundred years later, leaves Britain with just two indigenous manufacturers, TVR sports cars in Blackpool, and Morgan sports cars in Malvern on the Welsh borders. The Morgan family was originally Welsh). Rolls showed remarkable foresight in his vision for motoring, because at this time the maximum speed limit was four miles an hour, and a man with a warning flag had to walk in front of the car. To travel from London to Cambridge took 11 hours.

Rolls invented a bicycle for four, learned mechanical skills in the railway workshops at Crewe, obtained a third engineer's certificate so he could act as engineer on his father's yacht, and became an accomplished motor racing driver. After leaving Cambridge he opened his own car showroom in London, C.S.Rolls & Co., selling mainly French Panhards.

In 1904, he met Henry Royce for lunch in Manchester's Midland Hotel, and was so impressed by his two-cylinder car that he financed the production of Royce's cars, ordering nineteen to sell in London, wanting to be able *'to recommend and sell the best cars in the world'*. He told a business partner that Royce's car *'beats the Panhard hollow'*. The French Panhard was the leading car of its day. In 1906, Rolls and Royce formed Rolls-Royce Ltd., and their first car, the fabulous 6-cylinder Silver Ghost was available to the gentry. Royce was chief engineer, on a salary of £1250 pa, and Rolls took £750 and 4% of the profits as the technical managing director. Rolls *publicised the cars by racing them*, setting a record between Boulogne and Monte Carlo of 28 hours and 14 minutes in 1906. He earned the dislike of Queen Victoria because she thought cars scared horses.

Living life at the maximum, and looking for fresh challenges, Rolls took up aviation with ballooning, and then moved on to biplanes. Rolls became the first Briton to fly more than half-a-mile, and made the *first non-stop flight to France and back*. However, on July 12, 1910, he achieved a more tragic first - he was the first British aviator to be killed in a plane crash. His Wright biplane broke up in an air display over Bournemouth, and the wreckage was towed away by a Silver Ghost.

Of course, Rolls-Royce is now German-owned, and Rolls' vast family estate at the Hendre, Llangatock (Llangadog), Monmouthshire, is now part of a Japanese-owned golf complex. His grave lies untended, with no note of his achievements, in the family cemetery. His elder brother died in World War One, and the direct family line died out.

BERTRAND RUSSELL 1872 - February 2 1970
THE 3RD EARL RUSSELL, 'THE 20TH CENTURY'S MOST IMPORTANT LIBERAL THINKER, ONE OF TWO OR THREE OF ITS MAJOR PHILOSOPHERS, AND A PROPHET FOR MILLIONS OF THE CREATIVE AND RATIONAL LIFE'*

His grandfather Lord John Russell was the architect of the Great Reform Bill of 1832, which began to open up voting to the middle classes. Born in Trellech, Gwent, an orphan from the age of 3, Bertrand Russell was brought up by his grandmother, who tried to train him in to become Prime Minister like her husband. Educated in virtual isolation, not until he went to Trinity College, Cambridge in 1890 did he mix with his peers. He gained firsts in mathematics and moral sciences. Russell had found to his surprise that he was extremely gifted in philosophy and mathematics, and quickly became a world authority, and an FRS in 1908. Between 1910 and 1913 he jointly authored with Alfred Whitehead the ground-breaking *'Principia Mathematica'*. His work on the foundations of epistemology, logic and mathematics forced English philosophy in a new direction, towards science, despite the reservations of Wittgenstein.

Russell argued for Free Trade in 1903-04, and supported the Women's Suffrage Movement from 1906-1910. For his speaking against the First World War, which he thought would permanently impair European civilisation, he was fined for anti-war activities and dismissed from Trinity College. Two years later, he was imprisoned for five months. He visited Russia in 1920, hoping that the new society would transcend the warlike nature of capitalist society, and returned appalled by what he had seen. He also visited China at this time. In the 1920's and 30's, Russell ran an experimental, pacifist school. He was offered a teaching appointment in City College, New York, but the appointment was rescinded in 1940 because of protests that he was *'morally unfit'* to teach.

Along with George Orwell, he was one of the few Western intellectuals not to sympathise with communist Russia in the 1920's and 1930's. He abandoned his advocacy for peace, in the face of Hitler's

Bertrand Russell

fascist onslaught, and spent the Second World War years in America, where he wrote the *'History of Western Philosophy'*. Returning to Britain in 1944, he now campaigned ceaselessly until the end of his life against nuclear weapons, being the Founding President of the Campaign for Nuclear Disarmament (CND). He was also a passionate opponent of American involvement in Vietnam, and he wished to set up a War Crimes Tribunal to indict the Johnson administration's policy-makers. An inspiration to younger generations who also saw the futility of nuclear aggression, in 1961 he was imprisoned for anti-nuclear protests. Upon appeal, the 89-year-old served one week in the prison hospital. No wonder the British legal system is seen as 'unique' by the inhabitants of these Isles. He spent his last years at his home in North Wales, at Penrhyndeudraeth. He died of influenza, aged 98. When asked what he would say to God if he found himself before Him, Russell answered, *'I should reproach Him for not giving us enough evidence'*.

Despite a tangled personal life, involving four wives and many mistresses, Russell was *'with Kurt Godel, one of the two most important logicians of the 20th century'*, the pioneer of logical positivism, as well as Britain's most important social critic. In 1949 he received the Order of Merit, and in 1950 the Nobel Prize for Literature. The author of over ninety books, beginning with 'German Social Democracy' in 1906, Russell imposed himself upon the fabric of 20th century Britain like no other non-politician. According to Simon Blackburn, *'Russell was the last important public intellectual in Britain. With him, the tradition of Jeremy Bentham and J.S. Mill came to an end.'*

*source - McMaster University website

FOOTNOTES:
1. 'Russell's Paradox', according to the Stanford Encyclopaedia of Philosophy, was discovered in 1901 when he was working on his *'Principles of Mathematics'* : *'Russell's Paradox is the most famous of the logical or set-theoretical paradoxes. The paradox arises within naive set theory by considering the set of all sets that are not members of themselves. Such a set appears to be a member of itself if and only it is not a member of itself, hence the paradox. Some sets, such as the set of all teacups, are not members of themselves. Other sets, such as the set of all non-teacups, are members of themselves. Call the set of all sets that are not members of themselves S. If S is a member of itself, then by definition it must not be a member of itself. Similarly, if S is not a member of itself, then by definition it must be a member of itself. Discovered by Bertrand Russell in 1901, the paradox prompted much work in logic, set theory and the philosophy and foundations of mathematics in the early part of the twentieth century.'* So there.

2. Ray Monk's biography of Russell, *'The Ghost of Madness'*, required him to read Russell's extant output of 60,000 letters, 70 books and 2000 articles. He was asked if Russell and Wittgenstein, *'the Towering Twins of early 20th-century philosophy'* could have fitted into modern academic life. He answered *'Oh, that's easy. There's not a university in Britain now that would put up with a Wittgenstein. And Russell wouldn't have put up with a modern university. Genius is not rewarded in universities at present.'*

WILLIAM SALESBURY c.1520 - c. 1584/99*
TRANSLATOR OF THE NEW TESTAMENT, 'THE MOST LEARNED WELSHMAN OF HIS DAY'

Given the same holy day of September 10th by the Church in Wales as William Morgan, he was born in Llansannan, the second son of Ffwg ap Robert ap Thomas Salbri Hen (Ffowc Salesbury) and Annes ferch Wiliam ap Gruffydd ap Robin of Cochwillan, of Y Plas Isa, Llanrwst, Denbighshire. Salesbury may have been educated at the nearby Maenan Abbey before studying at Oxford, where he seems to have converted to Protestantism.

The Act of Union of 1543 annexed Wales to England, and destroyed the humane system of Welsh laws, also threatening to extirpate the language. Without its language, it is difficult for a nation to survive, so the printing of books in Welsh became a priority for patriotic Welshmen. In 1547, Salesbury published a dictionary to instruct the Welsh to better understand English. He wrote *'And, take this advice from me; unless you save and correct and perfect the language before the extinction of the present generation, it will be too late afterwards.'* This was the second book printed in Welsh**, and in the following year he published a complementary dictionary to help the English understand Welsh. In the same year he published an edition of Gruffydd Hiraethog's Welsh proverbs, *'Oll Synnwr pen Kembero ygyd'*, trying to tell the Welsh people about the traditional wisdom of their nation. In this, Salesbury wrote: *'If you do not wish to be worse than animals...obtain learning in your own language, if you do not wish to be more unnatural than any other nation under the sun, love your language and those who love it. If you do not wish utterly to depart from the faith of Christ...obtain the Holy Scripture in your own tongue as your happy ancestors, the ancient British, had it.'* He also wrote an unpublished book in Welsh on Rhetoric in 1552, and not until 1916 was 'Llysieulyfr' published. This was a 'herbal' translated from Latin and Welsh sources.

At Oxford he had started thinking about translating the Bible into Welsh, wanting to impart learning to the Welsh in their own language, and he appealed to the bishops to preach in Welsh. Salesbury also advocated asking the King's permission to have the Bible translated. In 1551 he published his translation of the lessons which were read in church Communion services, under the title *'Kynniver Llith a Ban'*. However, under Queen Mary's Catholic reign of 1553-58 he had to keep silent, but under Elizabeth in 1561 it was ordained that the lessons should be read in Welsh, after they had been read in English. In 1563 a law was passed commanding that the Bible and the Prayer Book should be translated into Welsh, setting a time period of three years for this completion. It was accepted that the vast majority of the Welsh people understood no English, and a Welsh Bible could help the acceptance of Protestantism thorough the country.

The major reason, however, was that there was anger at the slow progress of the Welsh in taking up the English language. It was thought that, by having Welsh translations placed next to English texts in churches, the congregations would learn English. The opposite happened - why should the Welsh bother with English, when they had their own language, and a church far more ancient than that of England? Salesbury began work with Richard Davies, Bishop of St David's, and was responsible for most of the work involved leading to the publication of the Welsh New Testament in 1567, while Davies contributed most to the Prayer Book published at the same time. Thomas Huet, precentor of St David's, also assisted

Salesbury. It appears that Salesbury and Davies now began a translation of the Bible, but according to Sir John Wynn of Gwydir argued over the translation of one word, and the work stopped. The Welsh Bible had to wait until William Morgan's (q.v.) translation in 1588.

A wonderful scholar, his strong opinions sometimes got the better of his common sense. For instance, in the printed version of the New Testament he ignored nasal mutations; he used a different typeface to show the part of a literary word which differed from its colloquial form; and Salesbury also altered the spelling of some words to make them resemble more closely their Latin origins. However, despite contemporary criticisms, his intentions were to make the Gospels understandable to everyone, rich and poor, and Morgan's Bible owes a great debt to Salesbury's work. His translation *'laid a solid foundation for the translations of the next two centuries, and for modern Welsh, which is able to deal in its own idiom with the most complicated subjects.'*

A master of Greek, Latin, Hebrew and modern languages, he was a *'brilliant representative of Renaissance humanism in Wales. It would be hard to find anybody who has rendered greater service to the Welsh nation than William Salesbury. His great contribution was his translation of the Bible into Welsh, thus laying the foundations of modern Welsh prose'* (- 'The Dictionary of Welsh Biography').

*John Wynn of Gwydir and others have said that he lived almost until the next century, but c.1584 seems a more likely date.

**Sir John Prys of Brecon published a collection of basic religious texts, *'Yn Llyvyr Hwnn'* just a year previously, but Salesbury was *the pioneer of Welsh publishing.*

SIR HENRY MORTON STANLEY January 28 1841 - May 10 1904
JOHN ROWLANDS, THE EXPLORER WHO 'FOUND LIVINGSTONE'

Sir Henry Morton Stanley, of *'Dr Livingstone, I presume'* fame, was born in Denbigh, and one of his claims to fame was killing five Africans with four shots from his elephant rifle when attacked. He had loaded the gun with explosive charges as a precaution. Born in 1841 in a cottage outside Denbigh Castle, he was the illegitimate son of John Rowlands and Elizabeth Parry, and was brought up as John Rowlands in St Asaph's workhouse from the age of 6. He went to sea as a cabin boy in 1859, was befriended by Henry Morton Stanley of New Orleans, and took his benefactor's name. He fought on both sides in the American Civil War, being captured at the terrible battle of Shiloh in 1862 while serving in the Confederate Army. To escape the terrible conditions of the prison camps, he joined the Union Navy but was discharged because of ill health.

In 1867, Stanley joined the 'New York Herald'. As a roving reporter, Stanley accompanied the British punitive expedition led by Napier against king Theodore II of Abyssinia (modern Ethiopia), and was the first to relay the news of the fall of its capital, Magdala. As the Herald's correspondent, he had travelled to Abyssinia, Asia Minor and Spain, and was told by his editor to find the 'missing' missionary and explorer David Livingstone in 1869. The Scot had been seeking the source of the Nile. Stanley left Zanzibar in March 1871, with a force of 2000 men, and found the ailing Livingstone at Ujiji, near Lake Tanganyika on November the 10th of that same year (described in 'How I Found Livingstone'). Stanley himself had been deserted by his bearers, and had been plagued by diseases and warring tribes. The 'Dr Livingstone, I presume' greeting, upon discovering the lost man the uncharted depths of Africa, is one of the very few quotations most people remember. Staying with the doctor, Stanley nursed him back to health. He then travelled with Livingstone until February 1872, while they both explored Lake Tanganyika, but Stanley could not persuade the doctor to return home with him.

Upon news of Livingstone's death, Stanley was sent once again to Africa, becoming the first white man to cross Central Africa from East to West. Stanley's mission this time was to report on the British campaign against the Ashanti in Ghana. Livingstone died in 1873, and the New York Herald and London's Daily Telegraph jointly financed an expedition to continue Livingstone's work in 1874. Stanley followed up Livingstone's researches on the Congo/Zaire and Nile systems, and examined the findings of the other explorers Speke, Burton and Baker. Stanley's further explorations are detailed in 'Through The Dark Continent' and 'In Darkest Africa'. Stanley traced the course of the River Zaire (Congo) to the sea 1874-77, visiting King Mutesa of Buganda, becoming involved in several

skirmishes when circumnavigating Lake Tanganyika, and heading west to the Lualaba, a headstream of the Congo. Navigating both rivers as far as Livingstone Falls, which he named, his party reached the Atlantic in August 1877. He travelled the great Congo for 2000 miles. Half of his 2000 men had died of fever, starvation, murder, dysentery, drowning and in fights with natives. He had to leave 53 men, crippled with leg ulcers and suffering from malnutrition, at the aptly-named Starvation Camp. All three of the Europeans who had accompanied him were also dead.

Returning to London in 1878, Stanley was given a commission under the sponsorship of King Leopold of Belgium in 1879, and he returned to the Congo for another five years. He constructed a road from the lower Congo to Malebo pool, and laid the foundations for the establishment

Henry Morton Stanley

of the Congo Free State (Zaire) By 1884 he had carved out a huge colony in Central Africa for his friend and employer on this mission, King Leopold. Stanley was called by the Congolese 'Bula Matari', 'Breaker of Rocks'.

In yet another expedition, Stanley charted much of the unexplored African interior between 1887 and 1889 when he led an expedition to relieve Emin Pasha (the German explorer Eduard Schnitzer, governor of the Equatorial Province of the Egyptian Sudan). Emin Pasha was surrounded by rebellious Mahdist forces, but refused to return to Egypt. Not until 1889 did Stanley persuade him to return to the coast under Stanley's escort. Stanley found the Mountains of the Moon (the

Ruwenzori Range, mentioned by Ptolemy), and discovered that the Semliki River linked Lake Albert to Lake Edward. Stanley Falls, Stanley Pool and Stanleyville have now been renamed Boyoma Falls, Pool Malebo and Kisangani. These vast lands became known as the British East African Protectorate, but not until 1999 was he awarded the GCB and became Sir H.M. Stanley.

On his return he married Dorothy Tennant, of Cadoxton Lodge, Neath, in 1890. For a short time he was an MP for North Lambeth. Stanley travelled on lecturing tours almost until the end of his life, in America, Germany and Australia. He made one more visit to his beloved Africa in 1897. Stanley had wished to be buried in Westminster Abbey, but the dean refused, and he was interred near his home at Pirbright, Surrey. This poor Welsh urchin ended up a celebrated explorer, author, MP and with the Grand Cross of the Order of the Bath. As with Glyndŵr, Bart Roberts and Llawgoch, this Welshman's life would make a wonderful film.

TALIESIN 6th century
ONE OF THE GREATEST BARDS

Nennius noted this British bard writing of the fighting against King Ida of Northumbria and his sons, and he was a contemporary of Aneirin, who wrote the great 'Y Gododdin'. The references in the Mabinogion show him to have been familiar with Bala and Maeglwn Gwynedd's 6th century court at Deganwy, and an eulogy to Cynan ap Brochfael of Powys may place him as coming from north-east Wales. He then moved towards the court of Urien Rheged, Rheged being the British region of Cumbria and Strathclyde.

Iolo Morganwg believed Taliesin to be the son of St Henwg of Caerleon, who erected the church of Llanhenwg there, and is named as *'one of the three baptismal bards of the Isle of Britain'*. Taliesin may have been educated at Llanfeithyn under Cadog or Tathan, and have died at Bangor Teifi in Cardigan. Another tale is that he is buried at Llangynfelin. The legend of his birth is as follows.

At Llanfair Caereinion, Aranwen, mother of Afagddu, concocted a brew of Science and Inspiration to give to her son to compensate for his ugliness. Gwion Bach was instructed to stir the cauldron for a year and a day, but three drops of the magic potion fell onto his fingers which he licked clean. Being able to foresee the future, Gwion fled in fear. Ceridwen followed him, so he turned himself into a hare, whereupon she changed into a greyhound. He became a fish, and Ceridwen an otter, then he flew as a bird but Ceridwen was a hawk. Despairing, Gwion tried to hide by becoming a grain of wheat, but Ceridwen became a hen and swallowed him. She bore him for nine months and delivered him as a beautiful baby, so could not bring herself to kill him. Thus Ceridwen tied the baby in a leather bag and threw him into the sea.

The legend continues in that King Gwyddno, after losing his lands off the Cardigan coast, took to fishing in the Leri's estuary at Borth (Porth Wyddno). May 1st was traditionally the best day's fishing in the year, so he allowed his son St Elffin to take over his fish-weir for the day. However, there were no fish that day, just a leather bag with a baby inside it. The baby had such a beautiful head that he was named Taliesin (Radiant Brow). Being taken home in Elffin's saddlebags, the boy started singing in regular bardic metres, and grew to be Wales most famous bard. Bedd Taliesin, a 3000 year-old Bronze Age cairn near Llyn Geirionydd above the Conwy Valley, was supposed to mark his grave. It was opened in 1847 in the presence of the Deans of Hereford and Bangor. However, traditionally he is said to have been buried above the estuary where he was found by Elffin. However, this legend seems to date from the 9th century rather than from the 6th, and this Taliesin is chronicled in the Mabinogion.

Taliesin prophesied the death of Maelgwn Gwynedd:
'A wondrous beast shall come up from Morfa Rhianedd,
The Sea Marsh of the Maidens,
To avenge the iniquities of Maelgwn.
Its hair and teeth and its eyes shall all be yellow,
And this beast shall be the end of Maelgwn Gwynedd !'
In 547 Maelgwn died of the Yellow Plague.

He is more famously remembered for his prophecy concerning the future of the British nation:

'Their Lord they shall praise,
Their language they shall keep,
Their land they shall lose –
Except wild Wales'.

The ancient Welsh manuscript *'Llyfr Taliesin'* was transcribed by monks around 1275, and it seems that much of it was originally written by Taliesin, although the contents had been amended over the year by Christian scribes to suit the Church of Rome and remove any pagan influences and references, and add praises to God. His lament for Owain ab Urien seems to show that he had seen battle:

'The great host of England
Sleeps with light in its eyes,
And those who did not flee
Were braver than they were wise.
Owain dealt them doom
As the wolves devour sheep
The bright-harnessed warrior
Gave stallions to the bard.'

Taliesin sang the praises of Urien Rheged ap Cynfarch, the chief leader of the Britons, and some of his lines read:

'I am Taliesin, I sing perfect metre
My original country is the Land of the Summer Stars
I was with my Lord in the highest sphere
When Lucifer fell to the depths of Hell
I have borne a standard before Alexander
I know the names of the stars from north to south
I have been a blue salmon
A dog, a stag, a buck on the mountain
A stock, a spade, an axe in the hand
A stallion, a bull, a roebuck
A grain which grew on the hill

I was reaped and cast in an oven
I have been dead, I have been alive
I am Taliesin.'

His 'Saying of the Wise', *'while conversing with Merlin'*, was *'excessive laughter is customary with the fool'*, and the herb brooklime is known as Llysiau Taliesin.

SAINT TEILO d. 580
ELIDIUS, ELIUD, TEILIAU, TELIAUS, THELIAU, BISHOP OF LLANDAF

Feast Date February 9 (then February 20 Ffair Wyl Deilo at Llandaf and Llandeilo Fawr), November 26, June 11

Patron Saint of horses and apple trees in Brittany

Widely venerated in Wales and Brittany, an influential religious leader who founded the monastery at Llandeilo Fawr in Carmarthenshire. Born near Penally (Eccluis Gunnian), by Tenby, the son of Ensic (Enlleu) and Guenhaf*. His first name was Elios, the Welsh name for Helios, the pagan sun-god. He was descended from Cunedda Wledig and supposed to have accompanied Dewi and Padarn on their trip to Jerusalem, caused by the wars against the Irish invaders. At Jerusalem, the Patriarch was said to have given Teilo a magical bell., which was kept at his shrine at Llandaf with his mitre and ritual comb. On his return to Britain, he went first to Cornwall and became Geraint's confessor, but left to avoid the Yellow Plague in 547. He went to Samson's monastery at Dol, founded in 544. Geoffrey of Monmouth believed that Teilo succeeded Samson as abbot there.

Another source states that Teilo was the son of Enlleu (Usyllt) ap Hydwyn Dwn ap Ceredig ap Cunedda, and Tegfedd ferch Tegid Foel of Penllyn. His sister married Emyr Llydaw (see Ismael). Teilo's half-brother was Afan, bishop of Llanbadarn. He was taught by Dyfrig, and founded the college of Llandaf which was called Bangor Deilo. Teilo was also said to have been taught by Dyfrig and Paulinus. He then went to Ty Gwyn, where he came into contact with David, and followed David to the new monastery at Glyn Rhosyn, the present site of St David's Cathedral. During the Yellow Plague he went and stayed with St Samson in Brittany for seven years and seven months, planting the great orchard that stretched three miles from Dol to Cai. Teilo was said to have helped King Budic (Emyr Llydaw) battle a great serpent there. He located a holy spring at Kerfeuntain, and is associated with the stag in Brittany. When Teilo returned, Cadog asked seven 'fundamental questions' to the seven wise men of his college at Llancarfan. Teilo was asked what was the greatest wisdom in a man. Teilo responded *'to refrain from injuring another when he has the power to do so'*.

In 577 the Angles won the great batle of Deorham near Bath, cutting off the Welsh from their fellows in Dumnonia. The victorious army crossed the Wye to chase the defeated Welsh. Prince Iddon, son of King Ynyr of Gwent, asked Teilo as the family priest to lead his army spiritually. Teilo led the prayers on a hill near the battle site, and when Iddon's troops were victorious he gave Teilo the hill for a church, which he founded at Llantilio Crosseny. The White Castle stands where

Teilo prayed. Early in the 20th century this important church between Monmouth and Abergavenny was still pronounced Llandeilo. Croesenni is the Anglicisation of Croes Ynyr, the Cross of Ynyr. The battle took place along the meadows between the church and Tre Adam, and the large field there is still known as Maes-y-Groes, after the cross which Iddon probably raised for his father after the battle. The present church dates from the 14th century.

Teilo died at Llandeilo Fawr, from whence came the fabulous Chartulary which was later appropriated from Llandaf by Lichfield Cathedral. It is now known as the Book of St Chad. Teilo was supposed to have been the second Bishop of Llandaf, and Euddogwy (Oudoceus) was his nephew. Llandeilo, Penally and Llandaf all claimed his body, which miraculously mutiplied into three. In 1850 his tomb was opened in Llandaf cathedral and his staff and pewter 'crotcher' discovered.

Thirty-seven churches are associated with Teilo in south and mid-Wales. The roofless Llandeilo Abercywyn church, outside Carmarthen, stands where the little river Cywyn joins the Taff . A nearby ancient farm building is known as *'The Pilgrim's Rest'*, and there are mediaeval *'Pilgrims' Graves'* in the facing church of Llanfihangel Abercywyn. They may be the resting places of the Lords of Llanfihangel castle, or the tombs of pilgrims on their way to St David's cathedral.

Llandeilo
(photograph courtesy of WTB)

St Teilo's Church, at Llandeilo Llwydarth near Maenchlochog in the Preseli Mountains, is now totally ruined. Burial stones from the fifth or early sixth century, inscrbed to Andagellus and Coimagnus, sons of Cavetus, have been moved to Maenchlochog Church. A third slab, dedicated to Curcagnus, son of Andagellus, was moved to Cenarth. Two of the stones are in Maenchlochog now, and one in Cenarth. The last entry in the Baptismal Register was in 1897, but the ruins lie in a much larger, defended complex which also enclosed the farms of Prisk (Prysg means wood, or bush) and Temple Druid (formerly called Bwlch y Clawdd, (Gap in the Embankment). A few hundred yards from the church is St Teilo's Well, originally called the Oxen Well, which became a centre of pilgrimage to Teilo in the Middle Ages. In his church at Llandeilo, Carmarthenshire, are two ornately carved stone wheelheads, all that remains of the high crosses that marked his early 'clas'.

Rice Rees gave the following existing churches dedicated to Teilo:

Llandeilo Fawr – 3 chapels at Taliaris, Capel yr Ywen and Llandyfaen in Carmarthenshire;

Brechfa in Carmarthen; Llandeilo Abercywyn in Carmarthen; Capel Bettws in Trelech a'r Bettws; Llanddowror in Carmarthen; Cilrhedin – Capel Ifan; Llandeilo near Maenchlochog in Pembroke; Llandeilo – the chapel of St Hywel in Pembroke; Llandeilo Graban in Radnor; Llandeilo Fran in Brecon; Llandeilo Talybont in Glamorgan; Llandeilo Ferwallt (Bishopston) and Caswel in Glamorgan;

Llandaf Cathedral and Whitchurch in Cardiff; Merthyr Dyfan in Glamorgan; Merthyr Mawr – St Roque's Chapel in Glamorgan; Llanarth in Monmouth; Llandeilo Bertloeu i.e Llantilio Pertholey (Porth-halawg) in Monmouth; Llandeilo Rwnnus in Llanegwad near Talley Abbey; Llwyngraddan near Llanddewi Velfrey; Trefgarn in Pembroke; Penally near Tenby; Manorbier (Maenor Byr); Lanion near Pembroke; Llandeilo Llwydiarth near Cemaes; Brechfa in Brecon; Penclecir in Castle Martin, Pembroke; Talgarth, Brecon: Elfael in Radnor; and Llowes in Radnor

One of Teilo's holy wells, north-east of the church at Llandeilo Llwydarth, now is built into a pump-house to supply water to the neighbouring farm. Even up to this century, it was used to cure tuberculosis, whooping coughs and other chest illnesses. In World War I local people dropped pins into the well, hoping to end the slaughter. The water had to be drunk early in the morning out of part of St Teilo's skull, 'penglog Teilo'. From around 1057 the Mathews family were recognised as the hereditary guardians of Teilo's Llandaf shrine, saving it from vandalism and descration. In recognition of this devotion, in the 15th century they were given his skull, which they brought to Pembroke. In 1658 it was inherited by the Melchiors, owners of Llandeilo farm, and it became the focus for the healing waters of Teilo's holy well. This relic became shiny through constant use over the centuries, and was handed to pilgrims by the senior member of the Melchior family. It was bought back by the Mathews family in 1927 for £27. These hereditary keepers of the ancient relic were 'conned' into selling it in the 1950's by two people posing as museum officials, and Penglog Teilo vanished. It reappeared in 1994 in Hong Kong and has now been installed in its own niche in Teilo's chapel in Llandaf. The well has since been capped to provide water for a nearby house.

St Margaret's Church in Marloes, Pembrokeshire, was originally a Teilo dedication. Cilrhedyn Church on the borders of Pembroke and Carmarthen is also dedicated to Teilo. Teilo's Well by the Bishop's Palace in Llandaf came to be known as the Dairy Well, and in its wall was found the remains of a Celtic cross with knotwork, which has now been removed to the south aisle of the cathdral. If visiting Llandaf Cathedral, one can walk a couple of miles south through parkland, following the river Taf, past Cardiff Castle, to go to the National Museum of Wales. It has a room dedicated to casts of all the Welsh Celtic crosses, and some original stone carvings.

Near Waungron, between Gorseinon and Pontardulais, are the remains of St Teilo's Church, Llandeilo Tal-y-Bont. They are to be moved at some point to the Museum of Welsh Life at St Fagans. Known locally as *'the church in the marsh'*, it lies near the first crossing point of the river Loughor upstream from the old Roman fort of Leucarum (Loughor). Normans built two castles on either side of the river here, for it was an important strategic site for their slow and relentless conquest of south Wales. His church at Talgarth is in an area full of megaliths. Unfortunately Croes Llechan was destroyed, sometime in the late 19th century, but Maen Llwyd on Pen Cader and Ty Isaf dolmen can still be seen. There is also a nearby stone circle, sometimes called Gader Arthur, on Pen Cader in the Black Mountains.

Teilo's churches are mainly clustered in south-west Wales, in eastern Pembrokeshire and western Carmarthenshire. However, he has dedications in Llannarth, Llandeilo Gresynni and Llandeilo Porth Haelog in Monmouthshire, Llandeilo'r Fan in Brecom and Llandeilo Graban in Radnorshire, and two in Gower among his thirty-five or so churches.

Teilo was 'claimed' by Llandaf as a saint because of his glory, and somehow the illuminated missal from Llandeilo Fawr was taken there before 850. However, at some time it was stolen and resurfaced in Lichfield Cathedral as the Book of St Chad – possibly the greatest treasure of Wales, comparable with the Book of Kells and the Lindisfarne Gospels. It may have been taken in the time of Wynsi, Bishop of Lichfield from 974-992, but another authority believes that it was taken in the 16th century. More research is needed here to make a serious claim for its return. The Trinity College exhibition of the Book of Kells and the Book of Durrow in Dublin shows how great a tourist attraction it could be for Wales. Nearly everything else of Welsh heritage has been stripped out or melted down during eight-hundred years of legalised looting. Llandeilo Fawr, like many of the other monasteries in Wales, had its own scriptorium, and in the early Middle Ages, Wales was an area of 'tremendous sanctity'. A monk named Ysgolan in the 13th century was responsible for burning those libraries of Welsh princes which had escaped Irish, Viking and Norman depredations. Not only did the writings show pre-Catholic Christianity and influence, but they could have been 'dangerously' tainted with Pelagianism. More valuable early Welsh books were lost in the Civil War, such as the great library of the Herberts at Raglan Castle. It is little known that the Second Civil War was mainly a Welsh affair.

This Gospel contains the earliest known written Welsh. Llandeilo, as recorded in the Gospel, was a bishopric, and two stone cross-heads attest to its importance. When the cult of Teilo was transferred to Llandaf, Llandeilo became a church within the diocese of St David's. Arglwydd Rhys, The Lord Rhys, founded Talley Abbey in the 12th century and passed on much of Llandeilo's wealth to it. This community of Praemonstratensian canons was based on the French model, and Normanised the Welsh 'clas' pattern of churches in the area. All Llandeilo's records have been destroyed or lost except the Gospel.

The boundary dispute between Llandaf and St David's for the premier bishopric in Wales lasted for a few hundred years, with both claiming Teilo. Teilo was far more associated with David, however, and may have travelled with him to Brittany and Cornwall. In Brittany Teilo is the patron saint of apple trees and horses. Chateauneuf du Faou and Lennon, near Pleyben may be his foundations. Throughout the Middle Ages, oaths were taken on Teilo's tomb. When it was opened in 1736, the remains of his staff and chalice were found. An old Glamorgan proverb is that if no snow falls before Teilo's Day (February 9), then any that falls after will clear quickly from the ground. His 'Saying of the Wise', 'while doing penance' was 'it is not wise to contend with God.'

There were four fairs a year in the churchyard at Llandeilo Fawr, about which the churchwardens were 'reticent in telling their Bishop'. The following notes are from the church's excellent parish magazine 'Y Groesfaen'. 'Archdeacon Tenison tells us about these: "On the fair-days" he reported, "Horses, sheep and lambs, & casks of Ale are brought into the Churchyard and sold there." The main fair was held on St Barnabas' Day (June 11th), and indeed was the only official fair recognised by the manor court, as the court record stated in 1710: "We present no fair or markett should be kept in the church yard except Barnaby faire." It was a fair with a long history, first being mentioned in 1324, when the Black Book of St David's recorded of Llandeilo that "The Lord (of the manor) has a fair once a year, namely, on the feast of St Barnabas the apostle, and it lasts for three days."'

From 'Teulu Teilo', the church magazine of Brechfa (written by Bob Lenny and the Reverend Patrick Thomas), the author notes the following commemorative services:

Sul y Blodau (Palm Sunday) young people carry the cross to Maes-y-Groes Farm, where there is an open air service, before returning to the church for Hot Cross Buns. Sul y Pasg (Easter Sunday) begins with the 8 am service and lighting of the Paschal Candle, then at 11 am the Easter garden is blessed and Easter eggs and butterflies given to the children. On Sul y Drindod (Trinity Sunday) there is a joint Cymanfa Ganu (singing festival) with the parishes of Abergorlech, Caio, Talley, Llansawel and Llanfihangel Rhos-y-Corn. A recent addition is the Gwyl Sant Teilo a'r Afallennau (The Feast of St Teilo and the Apple Trees) on the third Sunday in September, following the Breton custom. Lessons are read in Breton, French, Welsh and English and the church is decorated with apple branches. (This is the type of innovation based upon tradition that the author would like to see spreading across Wales). Y Cyrddau Diolchgarwch am y Cynhaeaf (Harvest Thanksgiving Services) are bilingual, in mid-October.

Apart from the holy wells mentioned, in Carmarthen they were also at Llandeilo Fawr, and near Cydweli, the latter being good for curing rheumatism and sprains and next to Capel Teilo. In Pembroke, Ffynnon Deilo was near Crinow Church, Lampeter Velfrey.

* Although 'Guenhaf' is given as his mother, this may be another name (White, or Holy Summer) for Tegwedd ferch Tegid Foel.

FOOTNOTE:
The above is taken from 'The Book of Welsh Saints' by T.D. Breverton. Further information upon the theft of Teilo's Gospel, and the disinformation given by present and past staff of Lichfield cathedral is given in a wonderful article by Rhodri Pugh in Cambria magazine, Canol Haf 2000. *The Lost Treasures of Wales* should be read by all Welsh people, (preferably after a blood-pressure test) and a group be set up to bring this stolen and priceless Gospel back to Wales. An early medieval Welsh poem mentions *'the book-grabbing monks of Lichfield'*. The greatest expert of early Welsh script, Professor Lindsay Wallace, stated that the book should be called 'The Teilo Gospels', as it was a product of a Welsh, nor Irish or English, scriptorium. Perhaps someone at Wales' toothless National Assembly might take an interest in its return, thereby helping Wales materially for a change. The official guide to this 9th century gospel in Lichfield Cathedral notes that *round the edge a 9th-century Welsh hand has scribbled names' and 'the evidence is strongly against the book being a product of a Welsh scriptorium..... The quality of its (Wales) artistic output was far below that of the Lichfield Gospels.'* This last sentence is particularly stupid - as noted above, Welsh land ownership and grants were noted in the Gospels in the great holy places of the day (when England was mainly barbarian), so invading Normans destroyed all written evidence in Wales when they claimed lands and burned the churches. There is no remaining literature from this time in its original form. So how can the writer compare the so-called 'Lichfield' Gospels with something that has not existed for hundreds of years? What on earth *'artistic output'* is he talking about? The problem is that mendacities in print are usually unthinkingly accepted and believed, the curse of Welsh history since the Venerable Bede supported barbarian attacks upon the most Christian

country in the world. The Stone of Scone was returned to Scotland, the Lindisfarne Gospels will go back north, and Wales needs this lost treasure back, and on display in Cardiff. Lindsay proved that the Gospel could not possibly have been English, and concludes that it is far more likely to be Welsh than Irish. (see *Early Welsh Script* by W.M. Lindsay, published by James Parker, London 1912, St Andrew's University Publications No. X).

DYLAN MARLAIS THOMAS October 27 1914 - November 9 1953
WALES' BEST-KNOWN POET, THE SELF-STYLED 'RIMBAUD OF CWMDONKIN DRIVE'

Dylan Thomas is the Welsh poet in essence, throwing words around like confetti, unlike the more restrained (and Christian) R. S. Thomas. His radio play 'Under Milk Wood', was later filmed in Lower Fishguard with Elizabeth Taylor and Richard Burton. The boathouse near Laugharne Castle, where he wrote much of his work, is open to the public. Buried at Laugharne in a simple grave, many visitors go to Browns Hotel where he used to become famously drunk. He died, allegedly of alcoholic poisoning, on a reading tour of the United States, possibly burnt out as a poet. 1997 evidence points out to malpractice by an American doctor, not treating Dylan for a diabetic coma, as the cause of his death.

Probably strongly influenced by Gerard Manley Hopkins, his writings are emotive, and a link to Wales for anyone who leaves the country to find work. The free-form thought processes, refined by dozens of rewrites, have given us poetry that will last forever. Dylan throws thoughts, ideas and words into a magical blender. His 'Do Not Go Gentle Into That Good Night' was recently voted the second most popular poem written in English - he asked his dying father to *'rage, rage against the dying of the light'*, as *'old age should burn and rave at close of day.'* In his short life before he succumbed in the States, he kick-started Welsh poetry into word-plays never seen before in the English language. I could pick just about any passage from Dylan's prose and poetry and be thrilled with its spine-tingling joie de vivre.............from 'A Child's Christmas in Wales'...............

Dylan Thomas

'Years and years and years ago, when I was a boy, when there were wolves in Wales, and birds the colour of red-flanneled petticoats whisked past the harp-shaped hills.......when we rode the daft and happy hills bareback, it snowed and snowed.'

Or, the first lines from 'Under Milk Wood'...........

'It is spring, moonless night in the small town, starless and bible-black, the cobblestreets silent and the hunched, courters'-and-rabbits' wood limping invisible down to the sloeblack, slow, black, crowblack, fishing-boat bobbing sea.'

Or,

'The force that through the green fuse drives the flower
Drives my green age; that blasts the roots of trees
Is my destroyer.
And am I dumb to tell the crooked rose
My youth is bent by the same wintry fever'.

Or,

'It was my thirtieth year to heaven,
Woke to my hearing from harbour and neighbour wood
And the mussel pooled and the heron
Priested shore'

Or,

'Though they go mad they shall be sane
Though they sink through the sea they shall rise again;
Though lovers be lost love shall not;
And death shall have no dominion.'

Ceri Richards, in his wonderful suite of lithographs dedicated to Dylan Thomas, uses 'Prologue' as his inspiration;

'This day winding down now
At God speeded summer's end
In the torrent salmon sun,
In my seashaken house
On a breakneck of rocks
Tangled with chirrup and fruit,
Froth, flute, fin and quill
At a wood's dancing hoof,
By scummed, starfish sands
With their fishwife cross
Gulls, pipers, cockles and sails,
Out there, crow black, men
Tackled with clouds, who kneel
To the sunset nets,
Geese nearly in heaven, boys
Stabbing, and herons, amd shells
That speak seven seas................'

Dylan's mother, Florence, was from the Llansteffan peninsula, a short ferry-ride from Laugharne. Although she moved to Swansea, many relations stayed in the Llansteffan area, and her sister's farm of Fernhill, near Llangain, is the setting for one of Thomas's most celebrated poems. After meeting Caitlin at Castle House in Laugharne, Dylan married in 1938, and they lived there, in 'Sea View', paying a rent of ten shillings a week. Their first child, Llywelyn, was born in 1939, and Aeronwy in 1942. Richard Hughes allowed Dylan access to a gazebo in the castle grounds where he wrote *'Portrait of the Artist as a Young Dog'*. Dylan habitually wrote in the gazebo from 2-7 each day, after which he would be 'rewarded' by going to Browns Hotel for some beers. In 1948 Hughes gave up the lease on Castle House, and Dylan hoped against hope that he would be able to live there - *'dreamily grinning, hopelessly shaking our heads, then beaming and gabbling together again as we think of the great house at the end of the cherry treed best street in the world, bang next to the Utrillo tower,*

Laugharne Castle, where Dylan wrote his poetry
(photograph courtesy of WTB)

with its wild gardens and owly ruins, the grey estuary, forever linked to me with poems done and to be.' However, it was not to be, and an admirer, Margaret Taylor, bought him the Boathouse overlooking the estuary in 1949. His pattern of work remained the same, rounded off with late night 'stop-ins' at Browns Hotel. When Dylan was touring in America, Caitlin, possibly jealous, embarked upon a series of affairs with local men. After Dylan died, she emigrated to Italy.

His place of birth at 5 Cwmdonkin Road, in Swansea's Uplands district, has been a place of pilgrimage by admirers from all over the world, including Mick Jagger and ex-President Jimmy Carter. (Famously, a less salubrious future President, Bill Clinton, attempted to drive there, but drove to Bristol instead of Wales.) Dylan's best work was accomplished when Dylan was young - he extensively 'quarried' from his schoolboy notebooks, and worked, and reworked lines of poems constantly to achieve the right feeling and flow. In 1927, aged just 13, he had a poem published in *'Boys Own'*, and in 1931 left school to work as a journalist on the South Wales Evening Post in Swansea. In 1933 *'And Death Shall Have No Dominion'* became his first poem to be published in a London magazine, the 'New English Weekly'. In 1933 he visited London for the first time and the following year won a competition which ensured the publication of his first book, *'18 Poems'*. He was now living in London, and in 1936, *'25 Poems'* was printed. In 1937 he made his first radio broadcast and married Caitlin MacNamara (see Augustus John). In 1939, his third book, *'Map of Love'* was published and he appeared in the USA to read his poems. From 1942 he and Caitlin and their two children lived in London, before moving to the Boathouse, Laugharne in 1949, when another boy, Colm, was born. In 1950, 1952 and 1953 he toured America, performing 'Under Milk Wood' for the first time in New York in 1953. On his fourth tour, in 1953, he died.*

Idris Davies, in 1946, wrote of Thomas:

'He saw the sun play ball in Swansea Bay,
He heard the moon crack jokes above the new-mown hay,
And stars and trees and winds to him would sing and say:
Carve words like jewels for a summer's day.'

*Controversy about Thomas's death has arisen. He was supposed to have supped 18 straight whiskies at his favourite bar, the White Horse Tavern in Greenwich Village, and mumbled *'I think that's the record'*. However, there is other evidence that he was a diabetic, and was in an undiagnosed diabetic coma when he was given a lethal dose of morphine by his New York doctor.

EDWARD THOMAS March 3 1878 - April 9 1917
WAR-POET, 'THE POET'S POET'

Philip Edward Thomas was a superb poet, and one of the few Welshmen in recent history to promote Welsh heritage and disdain the English - his book *'Beautiful Wales'*, published in 1905, has been in print ever since. His tragic death in the First World War in 1917, robbed Europe of a major poet. A line of his that always is remembered, from 'Early One Morning', is *The past is the only dead thing that smells sweet.'* Leavis called him *'an original poet of rare quality.'*

Both his parents were Welsh, his father from Tredegar, and Thomas was born in London, spending his school holidays with relatives in South Wales or Swindon. A nature-lover, he had published articles on natural history before he won a history scholarship to Lincoln College, Oxford, in 1897. In 1899, he married Helen Noble, and their first child was born just six months before his finals. Helen's father had encouraged Thomas's writing talent. He was dependent upon his father, who wished Edward to be a civil servant, but Edward never deviated from his intention to become a full-time writer. Upon graduating, Edward precariously supported his family by editing, wiring essays, biographies and reviews, but felt trapped into writing for the sake of relieving poverty, rather than writing what he wanted to. He became depressed by the sheer volume of work he was forced to undertake to survive. His first child was Mervyn, followed by Bronwen in 1904 and Helen Elizabeth Myfanwy on 1910. In virtual slavery to commissioned works, he wrote *'The Woodland Life'* in 1897, followed quickly by *'Oxford'*, *'Beautiful Wales'*, *'Richard Jeffries'*, *'A Literary Pilgrim in England'*, *'Feminine Influence on the Poets'*, *'Borrow'*, *'Swinburne'*, *'Marlborough'* and many others. Despite the support of the great O.M. Edwards, Thomas failed to find a desired teaching or library post in Wales.

In 1914, on the eve of the outbreak of war, Thomas and his family moved to the village of Dymoke in Gloucestershire, around which a small group of Georgian poets - Abercrombie, Drinkwater and Gibson - lived. The great American poet, Robert Frost, had arrived with his family a few months before, and Frost and Thomas formed a legendary friendship. They went for long walks, and Frost urged Thomas to write poetry. Other friends such as W.H Davies (the tramp-poet of Newport) and Walter de la Mare, added their weight of opinion, and Edward wrote his first poem in December 1914. All 143 of his poems were written in an

astonishing creative spell between that date and
January 1917 when he went to France. The poems
that were published in his lifetime were under his
pseudonym Edward Eastaway. It is impossible to
summarise the feeling that Thomas conveyed in his
poems - a placid acceptance of sadness, perhaps.
However, one of his loveliest 'little' poems is
'Snow':

'In the gloom of whiteness,
In the great silence of snow,
A child was sighing
And bitterly saying: "Oh,
They have killed a white bird up there on her nest,
The down is fluttering from her breast!"
And still it fell through that dusky brightness
On the child crying for the bird of snow.'

Edward Thomas

Between August 1914 and July 1915, Thomas
agonised over whether to take his family and rejoin the Frosts in New England, or
to enlist. Finally, in July 1915 he entered the Artists Rifles, followed by Wilfred
Owen just two months later. As a lance-corporal at Hare Hall Camp, Romford,
Essex, Thomas composed 40 poems in the ten months he was stationed there. In
August 1916, he was commissioned in the Royal Garrison Artillery, serving in
Wiltshire before embarking for France in January, 1917. On Easter Monday (April
9), the first day of the Battle of Arras opened with a massive artillery
bombardment. At 7.30 a.m. Thomas was killed by a shell-blast at the Beaurains
Observation Post.

Thomas's poetry linked his Georgian contemporaries to modern poetry, and for
many years he was regarded as *'the poet's poet'* by poets as diverse as W.H. Auden,
Philip Larkin and Derek Walcott. He is now seen as one of the most influential
20th century poets. The wonderful poem 'To Edward Thomas' by Alun Lewis, who
himself died in the Second World War, ends with the verse:

'Divining this, I knew the voice that called you
Was soft and neutral as the sky
Breathing on the grey horizon, stronger
Than night's immediate grasp, the limbs of mercy
Oblivious as the blood; and growing clearer,
More urgent as all else dissolved away,
– Projected books, half-thoughts, the children's birthdays,
And wedding anniversaries as cold
As dates in history —- the dream
Emerging from the fact that folds a dream,
The endless rides of stormy-branched dark
Whose fibres are a thread within the hand—

Till suddenly, at Arras, you possessed that hinted land.'

FREDERICK HALL THOMAS March 5 1886 - July 28 1927
THE WELSH WIZARD, FREDDIE WELSH, LIGHTWEIGHT CHAMPION OF THE WORLD

Frederick Hall Thomas of Pontypridd was easily one of the finest boxers that Europe has produced, and one of his peers, 'Gentleman Jim' Driscoll will appear in a future volume of 'Eminent Britons'. Freddie Thomas was criticised for his 'over-competitiveness', but won the World Lightweight Title in 1914 from Willie Ritchie at Olympia and held it for three years. After 15 rounds, Ritchie knew that he was so far behind on points that he would have to KO Freddie, but the Welshman finished stronger and won the 20-round contest. Freddie 'Welsh' won his title before the multiplicity of titles and weights* that we have today, and remains the only vegetarian ever known to have won a world boxing championship. Standing just 5 feet 7 inches, with a weight that varied between 130 and 140 pounds, he was one of the finest boxing champions of all time. He seemed to be known as 'English' Freddie Thomas as one of the very few foreign boxers in America, but insisted he was Welsh, and to some thereafter was reported as 'English' Freddie 'Welsh'. He was never a great knock-out specialist, as was Jimmy Wilde (q.v.), but had to rely on boxing skills to hold off more powerful opponents. Welsh was the first boxer to win a Lonsdale Belt.

Suffering from tuberculosis as a 16-year-old, Freddie Thomas was lucky to survive his teens, and in his professional career won 77 fights and drew 7. Aged 17, he was working in Pentre iron-foundry, when he decided to emigrate to the glittering shores of the USA. In Philadelphia, the young man was gulping down food at a free lunch counter. When pushed over, he became involved in a brawl with a bar-tender, and defended himself so well that he was offered a job in a nearby boxing booth. He received just two dollars for his first fight there, that afternoon. Turning professional in America, he returned to Britain to fight. In 1910, he fought Jim Driscoll, a featherweight, at the National Sporting Club and beat the lighter man in a display which degenerated into a street-brawl. Driscoll tried to outbox the heavier man, but Welsh used the dubious tricks learned in the boxing-booth. Gentleman Jim appealed to the referee, then eventually lost his temper, hooking Welsh several times in the kidneys and head-butting him, to receive the only disqualification of his career, in the 9th round.

Freddie's first professional fight in America was in Philadelphia, when he knocked out 'Young' Williams in 1905. In 1906 he had 24 fights, mainly in Philadelphia, that most 'Welsh' of all American states, all unbeaten. The majority were 'No Decisions' but the only contests outside Pennsylylvania were when he fought an 20-round draw in Dayton, Ohio, and another 17-round knock-out of Hock Keys at the same venue. Ohio, after Pennsylvania, probably has the greatest concentration of Welsh people in the USA. Finding it difficult to get fights, Freddie Welsh came back to fight in boxing booths in Wales, and on one spectacular night knocked out the lightweight Evan Evans, the welterweight Charlie Weber and the heavyweight Gomer Morgan. He also became Champion of Wales, knocking out Johnnie Owen in the 7th round. 1907 saw another 18 unbeaten appearances, starting the year in London, then boxing in Pontypridd and Merthyr, before returning to fight in Philadelphia and Boston. In 1908, Freddie Welsh lost his first professional contest on points in his 48th professional fight, to Packey McFarland in Milwaukee, Wisconsin. He was unbeaten in his other 9 fights in the same year, drawing later over 25 rounds with McFarland. He also fought the world featherweight champion, the USA's Abe Attell, which was a 'no decision' - i.e. the 'home' boxer was given a draw. He boxed in Philadelpha, Milwaukee (4 fights), Los Angeles (4 fights), and Vernon, California.

With constantly harder matches, as he rose through the ranks of boxers, 1909 was another invincible year, with 8 wins, 3 no decisions and a draw. After a bout in Los Angeles, Freddie boxed 3 times in New Orleans, twice in New York, then in Boston, before crossing the Atlantic again to fight three times in Mountain Ash, Wales, before going to London to beat Johnny Summers for the Lightweight Championship of Britain, over 20 rounds. In 1910, he knocked out Jack Daniels in London, before yet another draw with Packey McFarland over 20 rounds in London, then won twice in Liverpool, before the infamous match with 'Gentleman' Jim Driscoll in Cardiff. There was an inauspicious start to the year in 1911, when he lost his second fight, the British Lightweight Championship going to Matt Wells over 20 rounds in London. Returning to the USA, after a no decision in New York, the Welshman won two 20-round contests in California. In 1912, there were another 12 unbeaten fights, in Winnipeg, Buffalo, Columbus and Liverpool, culminating in

Freddie Welsh

the regaining of his British lightweight championship from Matt Wells over 20 rounds in London. He defended it the same month in London.

There was yet another unbeaten year in 1913, appearing in Aberdare, London, Sheffield, Liverpool and Bridgeport before re-crossing the Atlantic to fight in Winnipeg, Edmonton, Saskatchewan, Vancouver, Montana, New York and Montreal. Apart from his two losses, he was unbeaten by now in his other 96 fights. 1914 was a hard year - his greedy manager booked him *six* fights in January alone. His opponents were Johnny Dundee in New Orleans (no decision - 10 rounds), Frank Whitney in Atlanta (won - 10 rounds), Sam Robideau in Philadelphia (no decision 6 rounds), Mickey Sheridan in Kansas City (won - 10 rounds), Earl Fisher in Cincinnati (no decision - 10 rounds) and just 3 days later Leo Kelly in St Louis (no decision - 8 rounds). After another no decision in St Louis, Freddie Welsh won two contests in Los Angeles and another in New Orleans before arriving in London to gain the Lightweight Championship of the World off Willie Ritchie over 20 rounds at Olympia. Ritchie demanded so much money to fight that Welsh virtually fought for free. News hit the Ritchie camp that the Welshman had injured an eye in training, but Freddie 'conned' the American by wearing a plaster over his undamaged eye. He won by staying out of range and outscoring the champion.

In 1914 he was unbeaten in another 7 contests, in Boston, Buffalo, New York, Milwaukee and Syracuse. 1915 saw another 17 unbeaten matches, and in 1916 Welsh again was invincible in another 20 fights, including two draws against Benny Leonard, and World Title defences against Adolph Wolgast in Denver and Charley White in Colorado Springs. These two years were spent solely in the USA and Canada, with war raging across Europe. Incidentally, Benny Leonard features 5th to Jimmy Wilde's 4th on lists of all-time Boxing 'Greats' on the www.coxscorner website.

In 1917, there were another 5 unbeaten bouts, including one in that most 'Welsh' of all American towns, Scranton, Pennsylvania, before Benny Leonard, on his third attempt, beat Freddy Welsh in New York to take the world-championship. Aged 31, against a man 10 years younger, it was the only time that Fredddie Welsh was 'stopped' in any fight. Benny Leonard, the 'Ghetto Wizard', is usually rated in the 'best 3' lightweights of all time, and stayed as world champion until 1923. In this title fight, stopped in the 9th round, Welsh's American manager had staked the entire purse upon Freddie winning. Not only did Freddie lose his world championship, but he left the ring empty-handed. In the aftermath of the Leonard defeat, Freddie Welsh won a match in Newark in 1920, and then two in Pennsylvania and Calgary in 1921, before losing in Winnipeg, followed by his final bout, a loss in 1922 in Brooklyn. Before these final two fights, aged 35, Frederick Hall Thomas had lost just three times in 160 contests. Before he fought Benny Leonard in the 3rd contest, over 12 years Welsh had only lost twice in 159 fights! The record is as follows:

Year	Contests	Losses	Cumulative
1905	1	-	1-0
1906	25	-	26-0
1907	18	-	44-0
1908	10	1	55-1
1909	11	-	66-1
1910	5	-	71-1
1911	4	1	76-2
1912	8	-	84-2
1913	16	-	100-2
1914	18	-	118-2
1915	17	-	135-2
1916	21	-	156-2
1917	31	1	60-3
1918	-	-	-
1919	-	-	-
1920	-	-	-
1921	3	1	163-4
1922	1	1	164-5

After the Leonard fight, Freddie joined the US Army as a captain, but after the war his business ventures failed, forcing him to fight again. Freddie had opened a gym, managed a few fighters, lectured on physical education and operated a health farm. He died penniless and alone in a dingy New York apartment, aged just 41. Nat Fleischer rated him the 4th best all-time lightweight, and Charley Rose as the 5th.

*There are not only 3 'world' titles at any weight now, there are 18 weights compared to the 8 traditional weights of boxing. Thus 8 'true' world champions have been replaced by 54 squabblers

FOOTNOTE:
On a table in St Fagan's Castle at The Museum of Welsh Life, Cardiff, the author spotted a South Wales newspaper with an advertisement for the Welsh-Driscoll fight in Cardiff, the purse being £2500, and claiming that the bout was due to massive public demand. The 'exhibition' match, at The American Roller Coaster Rink in Westgate Street, Cardiff, was agreed to reluctantly by Driscoll, because a percentage of the proceeds would go to his favourite charity, Nazareth House. Driscoll was the local Cardiff hero, and Freddie Thomas wanted recognition back in his native land. Driscoll was in constant pain from stomach ulcers and had an ear abscess. He bandaged the other ear, so Freddie Welsh would concentrate on it. There was 'bad blood' between the two from the days when Driscoll was working in a boxing booth near Bridgend in 1907. The unknown Freddie Welsh had accepted the barker's offer of £1 if he could 'stay' 6 rounds with Driscoll, and used the rabbit-punching and other techniques that he had learned in America. Freddie Welsh put up his Lightweight title, plus a donation to St Nazareth House, to meet Driscoll, and the match started evenly enough. In the 4th round Driscoll slipped and was helped up by a smiling Welsh. However, by the 5th round Welsh was hurting from the blows of the superior boxer, and his illegal retaliation was disregarded by the female referee. (Referees stayed outside the ring at this time). Driscoll's retaliation turned it into probably the 'dirtiest' British title fight ever staged. The pair elbowed, gouged and butted for another five rounds, until Driscoll headbutted Welsh under the chin so 'outrageously' that the referee Peggy Bettinson entered the ring and awarded the fight to Welsh. There was then a fight between the boxers' seconds.

   Incidentally and strangely, Freddie Thomas has not been honoured as yet in the 'Welsh Sports Hall of Fame' at St Fagans. Boxing historian Herb Goldmann spoke when Welsh was inducted into the International Boxing hall of Fame in 1960: *The Welsh Wizard came to America from England (sic) and won the lightweight title in 1914 and fought legends Johnny Dundee, Battling Nelson, Rocky Kansas and Johnnie Kilbane as well as Benny Leonard, Willie Ritchie and Ad Wolgast. He twice fought a 25-round draw with Packie McFarland... Goldmann talked about these fighters, and their famous fights, as if they happened recently.'

R. S. THOMAS March 29 1913 - September 25 2000
THE POET-PRIEST, 'THE SOLZHENITSYN OF WALES'

Ronald Stuart Thomas was a poet-priest, nominated for the 1996 **Nobel Prize** for Literature. Born in Cardiff in 1913, he studied classics at Bangor University and theology at Llandaff. 'R.S.' became an Anglican priest in 1936, retiring in 1978. Ending his days on the Llyn Peninsula, he was to my mind *the finest poet writing in English*, with no sign of any weakness in his powers to transfix the reader, with visions of bleakness and beauty. He represents the uncompromising conscience of a Wales, under ceaseless alien attack, and tries to work out our difficult relationship with God.

In 1914, his family moved to Holyhead, and he was ordained as a priest in 1936 after graduation from Bangor. He was curate of Chirk and Hanmer from 1936-40, then moved to Manafon and in 1943 began to learn Welsh. After learning Welsh he scoured the country for parishes in which to preach and perfect his knowledge, but always regretted that his linguistic skills in poetry were better in English. He published collections of poems, 'The Stones of the Land' (1946), 'An Acre of Field' (1952) and 'The Minister' (1953) before moving to Eglwysbach outside Aberystwyth in 1954. 'Song of the Year's Turning' won the Heinemann Prize for Poetry in 1955, 'Poetry for Supper' was published in 1958, and with 'The Bread of Truth' in 1963, he was Stratford-upon-Avon's* Poet of the Year. In 1966, Thomas won the Queen's Gold Medal, and in 1967 became vicar of the ancient church of St Hywyn, Aberdaron, overlooking the 'Isle of Saints', Ynys Enlli (Bardsey Island). In 1972, he became vicar of Rhiw with Llanfaelrhys, and published 'What is a Welshman' (1974), 'Laboratories of the Spirit' (1975) and 'The Way of It' (1977). In 1978 R.S. retired from the church, won the Cholmondely Award and published 'Frequencies'. From 1981 to 1986 he published 'Between Here and Now', 'Later Poems', 'Ingrowing Thoughts', 'Destinations', 'Neb' (Nobody) - an autobiography, and 'Experimenting with an Amen.' His worries about the future of Wales were evident in these lines from 'Welsh History'....

'We were a people bred on legends,
Warming our hands at the red past.
The great were ashamed of our loose rags
Clinging stubbornly to the proud tree
Of blood and birth, our lean bellies
And mud houses were a proof
Of our ineptitude for life.

We were a people wasting ourselves
In fruitless battles for our masters,
In lands to which we had no claim,
With men for whom we felt no hatred.

We were a people, and are so yet.
When we have finished quarrelling for crumbs
Under the table, or gnawing the bones
Of a dead culture, we will arise,
Armed, but not in the old way.'

R.S.Thomas incurred the wrath of the police in 1988, when he said of a fire-bombing campaign that it would be better for someone to die as a result of this campaign than for the language to die out. In 1992 and 1995, 'A Mass for Hard Times' (dedicated to his deceased wife) and 'No Truce with the Furies' appeared, and in 1996 he won the Lannan Literary Prize for Lifetime Achievement, the same year as his Nobel nomination. In 1999 he won the Western Mail and Welsh Books Council 'Book of the Century' Award for his collected poems. He had married the artist Mildred Eldridge in 1940, after which she was known as Elsi Thomas, and she died in 1991. He wrote of her:

'...*She is at work*
always, mending the garment of
our marriage, foraging
like a bird for something for us
to eat. If there are thorns
in my life, it is she who
will press her breast to them and
sing.'
And also:
'*We met*
            under a shower
of bird-notes.
            Fifty years passed,
love's moment
            in a world in
servitude to time.
            She was young;
I kissed with my eyes
            Closed and opened
them on her wrinkles.
            "Come", said death,
choosing her as his
            partner for
the last dance. And she,
            who in life
had done everything
            with a bird's grace,
opened her bill now
            for the shedding
of one sigh no
            heavier than a feather.'

His poem 'Reservoirs' sums up his disgust with abandoned communities ('*smashed faces of farms*'), with the alien conifers of the Forestry Commission ('*gardens gone under the scum of forests*'), with tourist '*strangers*' to whom these reservoirs have '*the watercolour's appeal to the mass*'. He had become, over time, a committed Welsh Nationalist. RS displays a scorn for those complicitous in the loss of language, and the turning of Wales into some quaint theme parks for the richer, more sophisticated English. ....

'*Where can I go, then, from the smell*
Of decay, from the putrefying of a dead
Nation ? I have walked the shore
For an hour and seen the English
Scavenging among the remains
Of our culture, covering the sand
Like the tide and, with the roughness
Of the tide, elbowing our language
Into the grave that we have dug for it.'

Ted Hughes has described R. S. Thomas' poetry - it *'pierces the heart'*, and Thomas' indignation at the way history has treated the Welsh demonstrates this in his 'Welsh Landscape'.......

'To live in Wales is to be conscious
At dusk of the spilled blood
That went to the making of the wild sky,
Dyeing the immaculate rivers
In all their courses.
It is to be aware,
Above the noisy tractor
And hum of the machine
Of strife in the strung woods,
Vibrant with the sped arrows.
You cannot live in the present,
At least not in Wales,
There is the language for instance,
The soft consonants
Strange to the ear.
There are cries in the dark at night
As owls answer the moon,
And thick ambush of shadows,
Hushed at the fields' corners.
There is no present in Wales,
And no future;
There is only the past,
Brittle with relics,
Wind-bitten towers and castles
With sham ghosts;
Mouldering quarries and mines;
And an impotent people,
Sick with inbreeding,
Worrying the carcass of an old song.'

(from 'Welsh Landscape', 1955)

R. S. Thomas
(photograph by Bernard Mitchell)

Lord Gowrie, Chairman of the Arts Council of Great Britain, found Thomas's work *'offensively nationalistic'*. The rightful bitterness present in much of his work can be explained in an interview he gave to Nia Griffith, when he was aged 82. *The anger born out of the exile that Thomas has felt in Wales and with an expanding Welsh culture, has, however, calmed in later years. "It was all part of this hyphenated person that I am, thinking myself Welsh, learning the language, but with an English upbringing, always being on the outside. Now, though, I feel completely integrated....Also, my move from the Llyn to Anglesey, where there are less caravans, and less political stirrings has caused me, along with my age, to become less involved....But I still stand for the de-anglicisation of Wales and for the true Welsh identity to re-emerge. I just don't think it's going to happen. My words have been misinterpreted. I've always been a pacifist and never encouraged violence. The language is the one thing we have left, and if that goes, everything goes.'*

'The Guardian' obituary of September 27th 2000, by John Ezard and Geoff Gibbs, reads:

'*The poet RS Thomas was embraced by the admiration of Wales and a wider world when his death was announced yesterday. Thomas, one of the most uncompromising, purest and most sustained lyric voices of his century, died at his virtual hermit's home at Pentrefelin, near Criccieth. He was 87 and had been ill with heart trouble. He was being treated at Ysbyty Gwynedd hospital until two weeks ago. The unchanging themes of his poetry were God and the sparse natural world of the north Wales parishes which he served for 40 years as a Church in Wales priest. He was still railing like a prophet against "the technological smugness, the awful atheism, the political sleaze" of the contemporary world in one of his last interviews late last year. But his views were felt modern enough for a line from one of his poems to be quoted two years ago on the cover of the Manic Street Preachers album "This is My Truth, Tell me Yours". In another poem, he wrote that he hated the Welsh "for your irreverence, your scorn even/of the refinements of art and the mysteries of the church". He accused them of committing their own cultural suicide, as "an impotent people/sick with inbreeding/worrying the carcass of an old song." But in the Principality yesterday he was hailed as a greater poet than Dylan Thomas. For the Welsh language Society, Dafydd Lewis said, "He was probably Wales' most outstanding poet of the 20th century. He was a very good friend of ours. He was quite a character and did not mind supporting unpopular causes if he thought they were correct. Even if you didn't agree with his views, they were interesting and thought-provoking." But the society disagreed with him over his support for the campaign of arson attacks on holiday homes in Wales. Praising those who were fire-bombing English-owned property, Thomas asked in 1998, "What is one death against the death of the whole Welsh nation?"*

Yesterday Rhodri Morgan, first secretary of the Welsh National Assembly, said the country had lost a grand man of letters, a fierce and passionate man who had a unique knowledge of Wales and Welshness. "He leaves behind a rich legacy; a fascinating vision of an idyllic Welsh rural past and spirituality which will be read with admiration for generations." The Plaid Cymru President, Ieuan Wyn Jones, called Thomas one of Wales's greatest literary voices. He had helped put it on the cultural map of the world. "His profound spirituality and unashamed patriotism made his poetry unique and gained him an international audience," Mr Jones said yesterday. "His work will remain with us as a testament to the flowering of Welsh writing in English and the emerging Welsh identity in the latter part of the 20th century." M. Wynn Thomas, a professor at the University of Wales, Swansea, said "He was the Solzhenitysn of Wales because he was such a troubler of the Welsh conscience. He was one of the major English language and European poets of the 20th century." Al Alvarez, the English poetry critic, poet and author who first promoted Thomas's work in the 1950's - along with that of Ted Hughes and Sylvia Plath - said last night: "He was wonderful, very pure, very bitter but the bitterness was beautifully and very sparely rendered. He was completely authoritative, a very, very fine poet, completely off on his own, out of the loop, but a real individual. It's not about being a major or minor poet. It's about getting a work absolutely right by your own standards and he did that wonderfully well". Mr Alvarez said Thomas's work would survive as securely as that of Henry Vaughan, the 17th century metaphysical poet who wrote: "I saw Eternity the other night/like a great ring of pure and endless light".'

*This author is of the absolutely firm opinion that Edward de Vere, Earl of Oxford, was the real Shakespeare, not the illiterate wool-merchant 'Shaksper' of Stratford.

FOOTNOTES:

1.It is indicative of the way that Welsh people think of their greatest heroes – their names invariably get shortened to RS, Dylan, Pantycelyn, Glyndŵr, Bleddyn, Gareth and JPR – that is three poets, a warrior and three rugby players.

2. 'The Daily Telegraph' obituary is as follows: 'R.S. Thomas, Poet, 1913-2000. R.S. Thomas was a fervent defender of Wales and the Welsh language, which made it odd that he should have been one of the best poets writing in English since the second world war.

The style of his verse - spare, harsh, austere (though lit by sudden flares of lyrical splendour) - reflected the appearance of the man. But the economy of the phrasing carries complex meanings and the surface clarity deep resonance.

Ruthlessly unsentimental, he did not hesitate, in his fiercer moods, to depict the hill farmers as vacant, miserly and mean-spirited.

There were no newspapers in his house; still less television. To feed his intellect he read philosophy. Thomas's defence of Wales and the Welsh language became ever more extreme, until in 1990 he called for "non-violent night attacks" on English properties. He could not support Plaid Cymru because it recognised Westminster. "Britain does not exist for me," he explained. "It's an abstraction forced upon the Welsh people."

But he also castigated the Welsh themselves who, "through indifference, lack of backbone, snobbishness and laziness", had chosen to speak English and cast away their inheritance.

He received the Queen's gold medal for poetry in 1964, and the Cheltenham prize in1963. "Prizes are irrelevant" he said.'

SIDNEY GILCHRIST THOMAS April 16 1850 - February 1 1885
THE MAN WHO CREATED THE MODERN STEEL INDUSTRY

Born in Canonbury, London, Thomas had to give up his dreams of studying medicine when his father died in 1867. William Thomas, his father, was from Llanafan, Ceredigion, and had married Melicent Gilchrist of Cardigan before working for the Inland Revenue in London. Forced to leave Dulwich College for lack of finances, Sidney worked for a short while as a teacher in Essex, then took a post as a junior clerk at London's Marlborough Street police court. He held this clerk's job for many years, while devoting most of his evenings and other leisure time to studying science, especially chemistry.

When Bessemer* revolutionised steel-making with his 'process' of using a converter to make bulk steel in 1856, he did not know that it could not be used for iron ores that included phosphorous. He had used pig-iron from Blaenavon, which was phosphorous-free. Phosphorous made steel very brittle, and was present in over 90% of European iron ores, and around 98% of American ore. From 1870, Sidney Gilchrist Thomas engaged in the project of experimentation to solve the problem of de-phospourising the pig-iron. In the other main process used in steel-making, the Siemens-Martin process, the problem of brittle steel also occurred, and steel-foundries across the world were employing the greatest scientists to solve the problem. Towards the end of 1875, Sidney Thomas found a provisional solution, and passed his findings to his cousin, the industrial chemist Percy Gilchrist, then chemist to a large iron-works in Blaenavon. Both men carried out more experiments.

In 1877 the cousins found out how to remove the phosphorous, and Thomas died just seven years later, probably as a result of his continuous experiments with little protection, at the age of thirty-five. In 1878 Thomas sensationally announced to the Iron and Steel Institute of Great Britain his invention, and took out his first patent. On April 4th, 1879, the experiments carried out by Sidney in his home laboratory, and at Blaenafon by Percy, were confirmed in a demonstration in Middlesborough with a 15,000 kg converter. Steel producers from all over the world rushed to London to buy the 'exploiting licence' of the new patent. Just one example is the Luxembourg-German producer Metz & Cie, which obtained its licence on April 20th, just 16 days after the successful trial, and built a new steelworks to take advantage of the process.

The basis of Thomas's invention was replacing the acidic fireclay refractory lining in the Bessemer converter with a basic lining of calcined dolomite. The addition of limestone then allowed the formation of a basic slag which would absorb the phosphorous as it was oxidised from the molten metal. Bessemer converters were adopted across Europe, and the process also used by the open hearth steelmakers. This was the basic process used across the world until the introduction of the Basic Oxygen process, which also relies upon Thomas's invention. Steel production in Britain and worldwide soared, which led to a great increase in the amount of 'slag' left in the converter. Because Thomas's process came to be known as 'basic', adding a chemically basic lining to the converter, it was called 'basic slag'. Thomas experimented upon it, and discovered that it made an excellent soil fertiliser. The phosphate-rich fertiliser is called 'Thomasmehl' (meal of Thomas) in German.

Not until 1879 had Thomas resigned his clerkship, and in extremely poor health pursued health cures overseas in his few remaining years, dying in Paris. He was buried at Passy cemetery, near the Eiffel Tower. His large and accumulating fortune was left on trust to his sister Lilian to be dispersed in charitable causes.

An obelisk in Blaenavon commemorates the cousins for the 'invention (which) pioneered the basic Bessemer or Thomas process'. They invented the new process of steel production on the Forge site in 1878. The process used phosphoric ores, revolutionising steel manufacture by perfecting the 'Bessemer Process'. He sold the patent to a Scot called Andrew Carnegie, who then made multi-millions of dollars in the USA and elsewhere from what is known today as 'The Carnegie Process'.

Sidney Thomas' discovery vastly accelerated industrial expansion in Europe and America. In 1890, Britain was the world's greatest steel producer, but by 1902 this great invention had allowed Carnegie, and Krupp of Essen to propel the USA and Germany into the first two places in steel production. Everyone has heard of the Scot Andrew Carnegie and his philanthropy, but no-one knows the Welshmen. At least Carnegie had the grace to admit that the 'Carnegie Process' was not his – 'These two men, Thomas and Gilchrist of Blaenavon, did more for Britain's greatness than all the kings and queens put together. Moses struck rock and brought forth water. They struck the useless phosphoric ore and transformed it into steel, a far greater miracle.'

Blaenafon Ironworks opened in 1789, operating until 1900 and the remains, the best-preserved in Western Europe, are open to visitors. This historically important site includes a bank of blast furnaces, casting houses, water balance lift and workers' cottages, and is presently in the care of CADW (Welsh Historic Monuments). Blaenafon is so internationally important in its archaeological remains that it has recently become a 'World Heritage Site', to join the ranks of North Wales 'Iron Ring' of castles, Stonehenge, The Pyramids and so on. Built in 1789, the ironworks with three blast furnaces was one of the largest in the world.

*Henry Bessemer was trying to design guns, and needed to know how to manufacture more and better quality iron. The Bessemer Process involves a converter where air is blown through molten cast iron. The violent reaction removed carbon from the iron, making mild steel instead of wrought iron. Non-phosphric ores had to be imported from Sweden or Spain for the process. Most ore contained phosphorous, which stopped the process. Sidney Gilchrist Thomas's invention allowed the manufacture of high-grade steel using ores with phosphorous content, opening up the vast reserves of phosphoric ores to steel production across the world.

FOOTNOTE:
Germany was not a serious rival to Britain in steel production until the 'minette', the phosphoric ores of Lorraine, were made available by the Gilchrist-Thomas process. R.C.K. Ensor stressed that *'the discovery created a gigantic German steel industry which would not have been possible without it; and this, which by 1895 had a larger output than the British, played a very important part in predisposing Germany to aggressive war and enabling her after 1914 to sustain and prolong it.'*

JIMMY WILDE May 15 1892 - March 10 1969
THE MIGHTY ATOM, THE TYLORSTOWN TERROR, THE GHOST WITH THE HAMMER IN HIS HAND, THE HARDEST POUND FOR POUND PUNCHER IN BOXING HISTORY

His name is inexcusably missing from 'The Dictionary of Welsh Biography', as is that of Freddie Welsh. Born at 8 Station Road, Pontygwaith, near Quakers Yard, he fought the best flyweights in the world, when there were just eight weight categories, and just one world title in each. His natural weight was only 6 stone 4 pounds, his maximum fighting weight was 7 stone 4 pounds, and nearly all of his opponents weights around 8 stone. *'He would often weigh in fully clothed, wearing a hat, and carrying weights in his pockets'* (The Western Mail, November 4, 1998).

In 1904, aged just 12, Wilde went to work underground in a colliery. He turned to boxing in his early teens, but promised to give up boxing to his fiancée. However, the miners' strike of 1911 meant that Wilde's young wife (both were 19) acquiesced to his boxing for money. Jimmy knew that he and his new wife had to support his four brothers and sisters, and there was no alternative to starvation. He gate-crashed a boxing booth at Pontypridd, shouting challenges to everyone and making such a commotion that he was allowed into the ring to 'shut him up'. He won five shillings that afternoon, a considerable sum and enough to feed the family for a week, and caught the eye of boxing promoters. Wilde had entered the ring knowing that he had to win. Another source states that Wilde started exhibiting in 1909, and from then to 1914 he appeared in over 500 fights in Jack Scarrott's boxing booth. It is thought that he engaged in at least 700 booth matches up until his retirement. He was sometimes outweighed by up to 60 pounds (27 kg) in boxing matches (e.g. in his 11th fight, against the former middleweight champion, Billy Papke), as from his booth experiences he did not fear heavier men.

Despite the interference of the Great World War, he fought 151 times between 1911 and 1923, winning 132 (101 inside the distance), drawing 2, with 13 no-decisions and only 4 defeats. That is the official record, but Wilde had his own record, including booth and exhibition bouts, of 864 fights from 1910. '*On one day, in a booth in Pontypridd, he knocked over 17 opponents before lunch and, after a cup of tea, demolished another 8 opponents*'. This is possibly the day recorded when he knocked out 20 opponents in 4 hours to earn £40, with no fight lasting more than 30 seconds!

On Boxing Day, 1926, Wilde fought a 'no decision' with Les Williams at Pontypridd, and in the following year beat 29 opponents in Pontypridd, Cardiff and Edinburgh. In 1912 he won another 20 fights, in Tonypandy, Cardiff, Merthyr, Swansea, Pentre, Pontypridd, Sheffield, Liverpool and London. In 1912, 'The Tylorstown Terror' won his first title, the Welsh Flyweight Championship, from George Dando in Cardiff. His invincible 1913 saw another 33 fights, in Tonypandy, Merthyr, Swansea, Cardiff, Hanley, Ferndale, Liverpool, Manchester and Glasgow, where he beat Billy Padden for the 98-pound Championship of Great Britain on New Year's Day. In 1914, he beat Eugene Musson of France for the European Championship. In this year he also conquered Young Joe Symonds, but lost in 17 rounds to the stone heavier Tancy Lee. Wilde had been in bed with influenza the previous days. He won 19 of his 20 fights this year, appearing in Tonypandy, Aberdare, Ashton, Liverpool, Leicester, London, Birkenhead, Sheffield, Manchester and Leeds. This was the first year he fought more fights outside Wales, with only three Welsh appearances.

Wilde was twice rejected as unfit for military service in World War I, before being recruited as a sergeant-instructor on the Army PE staff. Meanwhile, the Scot Tancy Lee had lost his British Championship to Young Symonds, and Wilde regained the title in 1915. Four months later he floored Lee after four rounds, avenging his single luckless defeat.

Jimmy Wilde

In 1915, because of the war, there were only 10 fights, won in London, Liverpool, Sheffield, Dublin, Barrow and Bradford. 1916 saw wins in Swansea, London and Liverpool, before gaining the Flyweight Championship of the World from Joe Symonds in London, followed by two more wins in London. He then defended his world title in Liverpool against Johnny Rosner, and beat Benny Thomas in Cardiff. Upon May 13th he beat Darkey Saunders and Joe Magnus on the same day at

Woolwich. After another win in London, he fought Tancy Lee for the British, European and World titles and won in London, before another two wins in London and Liverpool. He finally beat Young Zulu Kid in London over 11 rounds to retain his World Flyweight Championship. The Americans had just recognised the Flyweight division, and the match was a unification title, making Wilde the first World Flyweight Champion recognised across the world. For good measure he had defended his British Championship by knocking out Johnny Hughes, and also flattened the Canadian champion in 4 rounds in 1916.

With the Great War at its height, there were only 4 fights in 1917, all in London, and Wilde retained his World, European and British championships against George Clarke. 1918 saw just three wins in London and one in Aldershot. In 1919, he beat the revered American Joe Lynch at the heavier Bantamweight level in London, and also won in Liverpool, London (twice) and Milwaukee against Jack Sharkey. 1920 saw an unbeaten tour of North America, winning in St Louis, Milwaukee, Jersey City, Philadelphia, Toledo, Windsor (Ontario, where he again defeated Young Zulu Kid), Camden (New Jersey), Lawrence (Massachusetts), Philadelphia again, and Toronto.

In January 1921, Wilde fought for the World Bantamweight Title. Wilde had been suffering from influenza, and was giving 2 stones away to Pete Herman. Herman had refused to weigh in. After being badly hurt in the 17th round, the referee carried Wilde to his corner and told him *'I'm picking you up, because you don't know when to lie down.'* His only other fight that year was a win, a month later in Wales. For the next two years there were no serious challengers for the world flyweight title, and he had just one winning bout in London in early 1923. Wilde returned to booth fighting to keep in shape, and had no professional matches for two years. However, in June 1923, he was offered the fabulous amount of £23,000 to then fight the Filipino, 'Pancho Villa', 10 years his junior, and like Wilde one of the greatest fighters of all time. Jimmy was floored by a right to the head after the bell ended Round 2, but despite calls from spectators to disqualify the Filipino, the referee did nothing. After that, Wilde was fighting a losing battle. He lost at the New York Polo Ground, being knocked out in the 7th round. Wilde did not recognise his wife until three weeks later. The new champion* burst into tears at the end of the fight, saying *'Me no want to hurt him'*. Gene Tunney, the World Heavyweight Champion, called Wilde *'the greatest fighter I ever saw'*.

Boxing Illustrated, in April 1993, ran an article upon the *'40 hardest punchers, pound for pound in boxing history.'* At numbers 9 and 8 were Jack Dempsey and Joe Louis. 3rd and 2nd were Bob Fitzsimmons and Max Baer. Seventy years after his last fight, Jimmy Wilde was rated number one. The great critics Nat Fleischer and Charlie Rose rated Wilde as the *'all-time number one Flyweight'*, and he was elected in the inaugural class of the International Boxing Hall of Fame in 1990. His other claim to fame is that his is still the longest uninterrupted title reign of any world flyweight champion at 7 years and 4 months. His record reads: Fought 864 times, Lost 3, including 2 of his last 3 fights. 89% of his wins recorded below were by knock-out. His KO wins by round were: in round 1 - 3 knock-outs; round 2 - 17; round 3 - 21; round 4 - 10; round 5 - 9; round 6 - 4; round 7 - 4; round 8 - 11; round 9 - 4; round 10 - 4; round 11 - 6; round 12 - 3, and one KO in each of rounds 13, 14, 15, 17 and 18. Wilde's 18-round knockout was for his 98 pound championship against Billy Padden in 1913. His 101 consecutive fights without a loss is *an all-time boxing record at any weight.* It is fairly easy to make a case for the Welshman being the greatest boxer of all time, yet few have heard of him.

DATE	FIGHTS	WIN	Knock-out	Points	No Decision	DRAW	LOSS
1910	1	*	-	-	1	-	-
1911	29	27	21	6	2	-	-
1912	17	15	11	4	2	-	-
1913	33	29	19	10	4	-	-
1914	20	20	13	7	-	-	-
1915	10	9	9	-	-	-	1
1916	15	15	14	1	-	-	-
1917	2	2	2	-	-	-	-
1918	3	3	3	-	-	-	-
1919	5	4	2	2	1	-	-
1920	10	6	5	1	4	-	-
1921	2	1	-	1	-	-	1
1922	-	-	-	-	-	-	-
1923	2	1	-	1	-	-	1
	149	132	99	33	12	2	3

The Mighty Atom retired to Victoria Park, Cadoxton, Barry, where the author was privileged to carry out a 'bob-a-job' weeding his path, but at the age of 72 he was mugged by some mindless pigs on a deserted platform at Cardiff Railway Station. His mind was never the same after, and he spent the last four years of his life in Whitchurch, Cardiff's hospital for the mentally ill, before dying in a coma in 1969 aged 76. The year before his death, Wilde had been voted the greatest boxer of all time, by the four leading American boxing commentators and writers.

*Pancho Villa of Manila died in 1925 of blood poisoning, aged just 25. Nat Fleischer and Charley Rose both rank Villa as the second best flyweight of all time after Jimmy Wilde.

DAVID WILLIAMS 1738 - June 29 1816
FOUNDER OF THE LITERARY FUND, FRENCH CITIZEN

David Williams, who founded the Royal Literary Fund, was born at Waunwaelod (later called 'The Carpenter's Arms') in Eglwysilan near Caerphilly. His father was William David, from Llwynybarcud, Llanhari, Glamorgan, and he was educated by the influential David Williams (1709-1784), the Dissenting minister of Trinity Chapel, Womanby Street, Cardiff, and of Watford Chapel Caerphilly. In response to the request of his dying father, David Williams became a Dissenting minister himself in 1752. He studied at Carmarthen Academy, and became Independent minister at Frome in 1758, moving on to Exeter in 1761, and Highgate, London from 1769 until 1773. Abandoning the ministry, he now maintained himself on incomes from political pamphlets, teaching and lecturing. He could not survive in London on a cleric's single stipend, so he opened an expensive boarding school in Chelsea in 1774. In this year, he wrote his 'Treatise on Education'. Upon December 9th of 1775, a daughter Emilia was born, but his wife Mary died of childbirth complications just eleven days later. David Williams abandoned the school upon his wife's death, and it did not reopen in 1776.

His writings on liturgy and education had attracted Benjamin Franklin's attention, and he stayed in Williams' house in Chelsea, when Franklin *'took refuge from the political storm.'* in 1776. They formed the '13 Club', a group of Deists for which Williams wrote *'A Liturgy on the Universal Principles of Religion and Morality'*. The work was eulogised by no less than Rousseau, Voltaire and Frederick II.

A friend of many eminent thinkers, in 1777 Williams gave shelter to Benjamin Franklin when he stayed in Wales. Williams advanced Richard Price's (q.v.) philosophy that parliamentarians are trustees of the people, in his *'Letters on Political Liberty'* in 1782. It was a defence of the American colonists, a schedule for revolution and radical reform, and its French translator, Brissot, was imprisoned in the Bastille. However, after the Revolution David Williams, held in high esteem in France, was asked to become an honorary French citizen by the leading French revolutionaries, and to take a seat in their Convention of 1792. He accepted an invitation to criticise and amend the draft of the First Constitution of the French Republic, by the Girondists. He remained in Paris until 1793, and was asked by the French foreign minister, Le Brun, to make overtures for peace with the English government, itself afraid of the revolutionary example being followed.

Williams maintained his income by taking private pupils, delivering courses of public lectures and by writing. He wrote a *History of Monmouthshire* in 1796, and published another 25 books. (His manuscripts are in Cardiff Library and The National Library of Wales.) The British Government asked Williams to visit France after the Treaty of Amiens, to report on public opinion on Napoleon Buonaparte. Williams first proposed a fund for writers in 1773. In 1790, The Literary Fund as established through his efforts to assist needy authors, and David Williams lived at its headquarters at 36 Gerrard Square, Soho, until his death on June 29th, 1816.

WILLIAM WILLIAMS 1717 - January 11 1791
PANTYCELYN, 'WALES' FINEST POET', 'Y PER CANIEDYDD' ('THE SWEET SINGER'), 'THE FIRST ROMANTIC POET IN WALES'

He was born at Cefn-y-Coed, near Llandovery and educated at the Llwyn-Llwyd Academy, near Hay-on-Wye, preparing for a career in medicine, when he heard Howel Harris preach at nearby Talgarth in 1738 and was completely converted. Williams said that *'God's word penetrated his heart'**. He joined the church and was ordained as a deacon in 1740, working as a curate for Theophilus Evans at Llanwrtyd, Llanfihangel and Llanddewi Abergwesyn until 1743. However, for 'nineteen reasons' he was refused ordination by Evans in 1743, and Williams turned towards the Methodist movement, becoming one of its leaders in Wales. The reasons had included refusing to read parts of the service, preaching in unconsecrated places, and *'rambling into several other counties to preach'*. Becoming for a time a school-teacher, Williams was present at the early meeting of Calvinistic Methodists at Watford near Caerphilly in 1743, where George Whitefield was moderator. A resolution was passed that the Rev. Williams *'should leave his curacies and be an assistant to the Rev. Mr Rowland.'*

Marrying Mary Francis of Llansawel in 1748, they went to live in his mother's old home at Pantycelyn, hence his epithet among the many 'William Williams' of his day. In the Rowland-Harris dispute of 1751, Williams sadly decided he had to side with Daniel Rowland, because of Harris's conduct and doctrinal errors, but he wrote a touching reconciliatory letter to Harris saying that the church was in great need of him, and that the church owed him a huge debt for its progress.

The great revival at Llangeitho in 1762 coincided with the end of the dispute, assisted by the collection of Williams' hymns 'The Songs of Those upon the Sea of Glass'. Williams spent most of his life as an itinerant preacher, travelling the length and breadth of Wales. He estimated he covered more than 150,000 miles on horseback to preach, published over 90 books and pamphlets in his lifetime, and wrote over 1000 hymns. As Methodism swept across Wales, his works became hugely popular, and he attracted massive crowds to hear him preach. His hymns were important not only for religion's sake, but a valuable contribution to the nation's literary culture. In his epic poem *'Bywyd a Marwolaeth Theomemphus'*, Williams interpreted the religious experience of the Methodist movement with intense feeling and sensitivity. Apart from his religious poems and prose treatises, he also attempted a history of world religions from 1762 onwards, in *'Pantheologia.'* Some of his books were written to educate the Welsh in their own tongue, and for his own use in teaching them to read.

A successful farmer and businessman, he also had a thriving tea-selling business. He was also successful in selling his own books. When he tired of writing he worked the farm, and was often not in bed until nearly dawn. Interestingly, he always considered himself as an Anglican clergyman, although he spent most of his life in evangelical tours as a Methodist minister. He is buried at Llanfair-ar-y-Bryn, Llandovery. Harris's view of Williams, the hymn-writer, preacher, counsellor, theologian, writer and instructor, was as follows:

'Hell trembles when he comes and souls are daily taken by Brother Williams in the gospel net...He is eminently owned by his Heavenly Master in his service: he is indeed a flaming instrument in his hands: and he is on the stretch day and night.'

William Williams of Pantycelyn was renowned as Wales' finest poet, along with Dafydd ap Gwilym. He was known throughout Wales as 'Pantycelyn', and Cwm Rhondda, his most famous hymn, was originally written in Welsh by Ann Griffiths. It is sung to John Hughes' tune of 'Cwm Rhondda':

'Guide me O Thou Great Jehovah,
Pilgrim through this barren land;
I am weak but Thou art mighty,
Hold me with Thy powerful hand
Bread of Heaven, Bread of Heaven,
Feed me now and evermore,
Feed me now and evermore.'

In his prose works, Williams attempts to classify the emotions and experiences which move the mind and heart of man, but his hymns are more important. We see his importance in literature, with emotions, thoughts and feelings taking expression in them. They are unaffected, in simple language and their pure lyricism began the modern period in Welsh poetry, casting aside the 'strict' metres of the past, much as Wordsworth destroyed the formalism of his times. *'Earlier Welsh poetic tradition was almost unknown to him, and his bare metre, burning sincerity of language, mystical reflection, and spiritual longing were new to Welsh poetry.'*

*His elegy for Harris contains the following (translated) lines:
'This the morning, still remembered,
That I first heard Heaven's sound;
And the summons straight from glory,
By His voice my heart did wound.'*

RICHARD WILSON August 1714 - May 15 1782
THE FOUNDER OF BRITISH LANDSCAPE PAINTING

Son of the Vicar of Penegoes, near Machynlleth, Wilson was educated by his father and showed signs of being an excellent artist. He was supposed to have been born at the Felin Crewi watermill, which is now a private house. His family was one of the old Welsh families of the Arwystli, based around Trefeglwys, Montgomery. He seems to have moved to Mold with his mother when his father died, and shortly after went to London. His uncle, Sir George Wynne, took him to London in 1729 and placed him under the charge of the eminent painter, Thomas Wright. Wilson soon succeeded as a portrait painter, painting the young Prince of Wales and Duke of York, but wished to study Italian painting to complete his education as an artist. He had painted a few landscapes in this period, and one of Westminster Bridge is in Philadelphia. Unfortunately, the only way to make a living as an artist in England was as a portrait painter, and there was great competition with the likes of Reynolds and Gainsborough at this time.

With his own savings, and gifts from friends, Wilson went to Venice in 1750, then Rome in 1751, studying the Old Masters and the natural scenery of Italy. From Rome, he explored the Neapolitan coast, the Alban Hills and Tivoli. Zuccarelli and Vernet advised him to concentrate solely upon landscape painting. Returning to London in 1757, from 1760-68 he was at the peak of his powers, exhibiting *'Niobe'*, *'View of Rome from the Villa Madama'* and other works. In 1768 he was a founder-member of the Royal Academy, and its Librarian from 1776. However, he had incurred the great enmity of the leading portrait painter of the day, Sir Joshuah Reynolds, who alongside other painters conspired against Wilson. The reasons for this are unknown, but it may well be that Wilson championed landscapes over portraits. Joseph Wright of Derby, Constable and Turner acknowledged their debt to Wilson, who himself had been inspired by the works of Claude Lorrain and Claude and Nicolas Poussin.

Wilson was forced into accepting commissions of pawnbrokers, but the quality of his artistic output never faltered. In 1781 Wilson returned to Wales and died at the Colomendy estate near Llanferres outside Mold, being buried in Mold churchyard, next to his mother's grave. The estate was owned by his aunt, Catherine Jones, and the hall now belongs to Liverpool Council. Wilson is now accepted as one of the greatest of European landscape artists, and the pioneer of the genre in Britain. Some of his works may be seen in the National Museum of Wales, and his works are exhibited in most of Europe and America's major public collections. The National Museum of Wales in Cardiff has 14 magnificent paintings, covering the whole range of his output (portraits, British and Italian landscapes, classical scenes), and an important portrait of Wilson by Mengs The Yale Centre for British Art at New Haven, Connecticut, has one of the largest Wilson collections in the world, and Wilton House near Salisbury has nine Wilsons. According to 'The Dictionary of Welsh Biography', '*At his best, he is a master of style; as an interpreter of light he is the successor of Claude and Cuyp, and an inspirer of Constable and Turner. His own inspiration came equally from Italy and Wales, enabling him to express romantic emotion within a classical framework.*'

Richard Wilson

Peter Pindar wrote in the 19th century: '*Wilson has been called the English Claude; but how unjustly, so totally different their style. Claude sometimes painted grand scenes, but without a mind of grandeur; Wilson, on the contrary, could infuse a grandeur into the meanest objects; Claude when he drew on the bank of his own ideas was a mere castrato in the art;.... Wilson on the contrary was a Hercules.*' Constable wrote many kind words about his debt to Wilson, including '*Poor Wilson! Think of his fate. Think of his magnificence*' and '*One of the great men who show the world what exists in nature but which was not known till his time.*' Ruskin said '*with the name of Richard Wilson the history of sincere landscape art founded on a meditative love of nature begins for England*'. Turner went for inspiration to Wilson's birthplace as a young man, and the curator of the Turner Collection in the Tate stated in 1988 '*For the first few years of Turner's career as a painter, Wilson was quite explicitly his hero and his chief model.*'

FRANK LLOYD WRIGHT June 8 1867 - April 9 1959
'*THE GREATEST AMERICAN ARCHITECT OF ALL TIME*'

Frank Lloyd Wright, the leading 20th century architect, along with Le Corbusier, was so proud of his Welsh heritage that he called the Wisconsin home he built for himself, 'Taliesin'*, after the legendary Welsh bard (q.v.). Another home and school, Taliesin West, was built near Phoenix, Arizona in 1938. A controversial and daring architect, his weekend home of Falling Water (near Pittsburgh) is famous world-wide, as was the earthquake-proof Imperial Hotel in Tokyo, and the brilliantly designed Guggenheim Museum of Modern Art in New York. His mother had been born in Llandysul and his Welsh upbringing is described lovingly in his sister's book '*The Valley of the God Almighty Joneses*'** (by Maginel Wright Barney). He used Iolo Morganwg's motto '*Y Gwir yn Erbyn y Byd*', '*The Truth Against the World*' Franks' mother Hannah (Anna) Lloyd Jones was a teacher before she married William Carey Wright, a widower with three children. Frank was the first child of William and Hannah, born in Richland Center, Wisconsin. Growing up, Frank spent his summer months on the farm of James Lloyd Jones in Wisconsin. He wrote in his autobiography: *'I learned to know the ground plan of the region in every line and feature. For me now its elevation is the modelling of the hills, the weaving and fabric that clings to them, the look of it all in tender green or covered in snow or in full glow of summer that bursts into the glorious blaze of autumn. I still feel myself as much a part of it as the birds and bees are, and the red barns.'* He also referred to his immigrant grandfather, Richard Lloyd Jones: *'He was in league with the stones of the field and he taught his children to work hard until the valley blossomed like a garden. **His New Wales.** He planted a small world within the world that is again within other worlds, without end.'*

In 1885, aged 18, Wright's parents divorced, and his preacher-musician father left the family in Madison, Wisconsin. Wright never saw his father again, and had to help support his mother and two sisters. Frank took a part-time job as a draughtsman with Allan Conover, the University of Wisconsin engineering professor, and from 1886 attended the University as a 'special student'. From 1887-89 Frank worked for Chicago architects Adler and Sullivan, and in 1889 married Catherine Lee Tobin. A year later, their first child, Lloyd Lloyd Wright, was born. Wright recognised Louis Sullivan as a great influence, who based his designs on natural themes, saying *'form follows function'*. Wright lated developed this idea further, believing that *'form and function are one.'* By now he was designing all residential buildings for Adler and Sullivan, including his own home in Oak Park, Illinois. 1892 saw the birth of John Lloyd Wright. In 1893, Wright was forced to leave the firm and open his own architectural practice (he was discovered taking on outside commissions), and his first revolutionary masterpiece was the 'Winslow House' in River Forest, Illinois. His *'organic architecture'* idea meant that his buildings tried to form a natural link between mankind and his environment. Notable designs followed, called his *'prairie house'* phase, where homes reflected the long, low horizontal prairie, with low pitched roofs, deep overhangs, and long rows of casement windows emphasising the horizontal theme. Native materials were used, and the wood was always stained, never painted, to show the natural beauty. He was the chief practitioner of the *'Prairie School'* of architecture.

He held his first exhibition in Chicago in 1894, the year in which Catherine Lloyd Wright was born. Another exhibition followed in 1895, with a son David being born, followed by Frances Lloyd Wright in 1898. His commissions were now becoming grander, and by 1900 he was lecturing upon architecture to the American Architectural League. In 1903, Robert Llewellyn Wright was born. In 1905, Frank and Catherine made their first trip to Japan, accompanied by some clients, and he became a serious collector of Japanese prints. In 1909 Wright took his family to Europe for further inspiration, and in 1911 began work on a new studio and home, Taliesin, near Spring Green, Wisconsin. His publications and buildings gained him international acclaim at this time. 1913 saw the architect in Japan securing the commission for the Imperial Hotel, but in 1914 disaster struck. A crazed servant killed a clinet's wife, her two children and four others, and set fire to Taliesin. Wright began to rebuild it, as Taliesin II. 1916 saw the building of the Imperial Hotel, with Wright personally supervising in Tokyo, and in 1918 he visited China. His first honour came in 1919,

Frank
Lloyd Wright

with the citation of *'Kenchiko Ho, Royal Household Japan'*. He constructed other buildings there. In 1922, Catherine and Frank divorced and in 1923 he married Miriam Noel. That same year saw the great Kanto earthquake which demolished much of Tokyo, but the Imperial Hotel survived.

Miraim Noel and Wright separated in 1923, and he met Olga Lazovich (Olgivanna), who gave birth to a daughter, Iovanna in 1925. There was another fire at Taliesin, and Taliesin III was built. 1926 was a bad year, as Taliesin was repossessed by the Bank of Wisconsin for debts incurred by Wright in its rebuilding. He and Olgivanna were also arrested near Minneapolis for violating the Mann Act, a law which prohibited taking women across a state border for immoral purposes. In 1927 he divorced Miriam and the following year married Olgivannaa. Also in 1928, a group of friends and admirers clubbed together to buy Taliesin from the bank and return it to Frank. He received honours from Belgium and Germany, but the great stock-market crash of October 29, 1929, halted all his work for a time. He turned more to lecturing, touring and trained young architects at Taliesin. 1932 saw the publication of his autobiography and *'The Disappearing City'*, influencing several generations of young architects.From now on was a halcyon period for Wright, with honours accruing across the world as his value was recognised. In 1937 he bought 800 acres near Phoenix, Arizona and began construction of Taliesin West, and in 1938 was on the cover of 'Time' magazine. Taliesin West was his *'architectural laboratory'* for the next 20 years, where he experimented with designs and structures, and taught students in winter. 1935's house 'Fallingwater', built on a waterfall in the Pennsylvania countryside, and other designs had brought a new flood of commissions, but World War II again interrupted his work. In 1941, he was made a member of RIBA by King George VI, and in 1951 his exhibition 'Sixty Years of Living Architecture' opened in Florence, before going to Zurich, Paris, Munich, Rotterdam, Mexico, New York and Los Angeles. Although most of his designs had been residential, in 1957, 35 of his 59 new projects were for public buildings. It is remarkable that in 1958, in his 90's, he received another 31 new commissions.

Frank Lloyd Wright spent over 70 years creating designs which revolutionised the art and architecture of the 20th century. Of the 1141 works he designed, from houses to bridges, offices to churches, 532 were built and 409 still stand, many open to the public. Over a third of his buildings are in the USA's National Register of Historic Places or in a National Historic District. He tried to achieve rooms that flowed into each other, moving away from the 19th century 'box-plan' houses. Wright believed that *'A building is not just a place to be. It is a way to be.'* His works show an instinctive understanding of social and human needs, with a superb command of the use of natural, local materials. He also designed furniture fabrics, glass, tableware, and was influential in graphic arts. He described architecture as *'frozen music'*, and an excellent pianist, he experimented with rhythm and composition in his designs. The eminent architect Charles Montooth wrote:

'Frank Lloyd Wright came upon the American scene at precisely the right moment for what his mother had decided he would become - an architect. He was born in a booming, building, expanding nation to which he to bring a philosophical and spiritual message in the form of architecture, just the proper medium for a pragmatic people in a material-oriented society to understand. He was a unique creative force in the world for fine art. It was as if the talents of a Bach, a Beethoven, and a Schoenberg were combined in one person. He can be

compared to Bach, a master of geometry, form and tradition; or Beethoven, a bold innovator breaking with tradition; or Schoenberg, an influential teacher of pupils anxious to follow new paths.'

*Taliesin means 'shining brow', and Frank said *'the hill on which Taliesin now stands as "brow" was one of my favourite places when I was a boy, for pasque flowers grew there in March sun, while snow still streaked the hillsides..... I began to build Taliesin to get my back against the wall and fight for what I saw I had to fight.... Taliesin was the name of a Welsh poet, a druid bard who sang to Wales the glories of fine art. Many legends cling to that beloved revered name in Wales.'* In a later filmed interview in 1953, Lloyd Wright said *'All my people had Welsh names for their places - my sister's place was called Tan-y-Deri (Under-the-Oaks)'.* Taliesin was nominated as a World Heritage Site, as well as being a National Historic landmark. On the estate is still the remarkable 'Tan-y-Deri' building.

**On his maternal side, Wright's grandparents were Richard Jones and Mary (Mallie Thomas). His uncle Thomas Lloyd Jones was a builder, who along with a Welsh stone mason David Timothy helped Wright with his early practical construction experience. Thomas married a Welshwoman Esther Evans. Another uncle was John Jones, a miller who married another Welshwoman, Hannah Reese. John bought the property where Taliesin is situated, which Frank's mother Hannah Lloyd Jones later purchased for him. Wright's aunt Margaret Jones first married Thomas Evans, and on his death married another Thomas Jones. Aunt Mary Jones married Welshman James Phillip. Aunts Nany, Jane and Ellen Jones never married. Uncle Enos Jones married Eleanor Jones, eldest daughter of Thomas Jones, Margaret's second husband. Uncle James Jones seems to have been the only member of the family who married an English/American, Laura Hickox. Thus virtually all of Frank Lloyd Wright's extensive maternal family were Welsh and also married into Welsh families.

APPENDIX 1

From 'An A-Z of Wales and the Welsh' by T.D. Breverton

LANGUAGE

The Welsh word for Wales is Cymru. Y Cymry is the Welsh people, Cymro is a Welshman, and Cymraes a Welshwoman. Cymreig is the adjective for all things Welsh and Cymraeg means the Welsh language. Cymry, fellow-countrymen, gave the relic Celtic population in Cumbria their name. (Cymry derives from the Brittonic 'Combrogi', meaning fellow countrymen). The British being pushed back to the West of England and Wales by successive invaders thus called themselves a Celtic word, 'Cymry' to form a common bond. Romans Latinised Wales as Cambria. Sais, the Welsh for Saxon, has come to mean Englishman, and the English language is 'saesneg'.

'Lloegr', the old Welsh name for England, came to be used in French and British literature as 'Logres', the realm of King Arthur.The Saxons that settled in Britain, pushing the Celtic Britons into the Western peripheries, adopted the collective name of 'Engle' or 'Engisc', which Latin writers termed 'Angli' ('Angles'). These English invader-settlers called the native British 'foreigners', 'wallas', 'wealh', 'wylisc' or 'walsci', and called the Welsh language 'weallas', which became known as Welsh. The name Wales is therefore Saxon. So the Welsh became unwanted strangers in their own land at a very early date. The settling English called the settled Celts alien, a habit that they kept up through the centuries as they conquered other, more exotic lands.

Wales has a common root with 'Walloon' in Belgium, 'Wallachian' in Romania, 'Walachian' in Greece, 'Vlach' in Romania and 'Valais' in Switzerland - foreigners in one's own lands. French-speaking Walloons are known to the Flemish Belgians as 'Waalsch'. In German or High-Dutch, the world welsch means foreign, and to them, the Italians were the 'Welsch' or 'Walsch'. Slavs also call Latins 'Vlachy', 'Wallachs' or 'Wlochy'. In turn, these assorted Vlachs and Wallachians in the Balkans call themselves 'Romani', 'Rumeni' (Romanians) or 'Aromani' (Romans).

The Celtic-British province of 'Cerniw' was suffixed with the same root ('wal'), making 'Cornwall', the Welsh-speaking tip of the West Country. Cornish for Cornwall is 'Kernow'. Welsh settlers pushed from the West of England and Wales in the fifth and sixth centuries to settle the province of 'Cornouaille' in Western Brittany. Perhaps 'Wal' and 'Gaul' were the same word, with Wal being the shortened form of 'Gwal' ? The Celtic root 'gal' means land of the Gauls or Gaels. Wales is 'Pays de Galles' in French, 'country of the Gauls'. Portugal, Galicia (in Spain and Poland), Galloway, Calais, Caledonia, Donegal, and Galatia have the same origins. Whatever the entymology, Welsh is a term meaning foreigner, which is a fairly strong reason to refer to ourselves as Cymry, rather than Welsh.

Taliesin and Aneirin were writing in Welsh around 600, and as John Davies writes in his superb 'History of Wales' – *'This was a bold act for, throughout the territories that had been part of the Western Empire, the Latin of Rome was the sole written medium, and hardly any attempts were made to write Latin's daughter-languages, French, Spanish and Italian, until after 1000.'* Unfortunately, the disappearance of paper from Europe and the expense of parchment means that most surviving Welsh from this period is in the form of marginalia on religious parchments. There was a cell containing Welsh manuscripts at the fort in Tenby around 880, but the only surviving literature consists of later copies.

Welsh is spoken by about 20% of the population as a first language, with around 70% in its heartlands of North and West Wales. Compared to Erse (Irish) and Gaelic (Scots), it is surviving, partially because of the 1967 Welsh language Act, and partially because of S4C, Sianel Pedwar Cymraeg. This Welsh television channel produces twenty-two hours of programmes a week, including the 'soap opera' set in the Valleys, 'Pobol Y Cwm' ('People of the Valley'). BBC's Radio Cymru also broadcasts in Welsh for twelve hours a day, and 'Y Cymro' is a weekly newspaper in the Welsh language.

The Welsh language is one of, if not the, **oldest living language in Europe**, belonging to the Celtic family of languages rather than the Germanic (Dutch, German) or Latin (French, Italian, Spanish) groups. Welsh comes from the Brythonic form of Celtic, which existed in Britain before the coming of the Angles, Saxons and Jutes in the 4th and 5th centuries AD. Brythonic, or P-Celtic, gave us Welsh, Breton and the nearly extinct Cornish language. Goedelic, or Q-Celtic, is the origin of Scottish and Irish Gaelic and the extinct Manx language. (There is no Q in Welsh, and the form mac, of son of, in Scots and Irish Gaelic is replaced by map, or ap, in Welsh.)

Welsh has been used as a written language since 600AD, **300 years before French and German** *were first written, and over 600 years since the first English (semi-recognisable to today's reader)* occurred in Chaucer's Canterbury Tales and the like. What we would recognise as Modern English dates from nearer Shakespeare's time around 1600.

Apart from modern electronics terms, the only significant intruders to the Welsh language were borrowed from the Romans in the years to 500, e.g. 'porth' for door or gateway (porta) and 'ffenestr' for window (fenestra), which demonstrates the antiquity of the language. Around a thousand words were derived from Latin, e.g. 'llyfr' (liber, book), 'pyscod' (piscis, fish), 'eglwys' (ecclesia, church), 'mur' (wall, murus), 'milltir' (mile, mille), 'cyllell' (knife, cultellus), 'melys' (sweet, or honey, mel), 'ceffyl' (horse, caballus), 'perygl' (danger, periculum) and 'pont' (pons, bridge).

There are 28 letters in the Welsh alphabet, with the following consonants being added to the English alphabet :

ch (pronounced as in loch), dd (as the th in then), ff (as in off), ll (as in Loch Lomond, running the ch and L together), and th (as in teeth). The consonants j,k,v,x and z do not exist in Welsh, but k and z appear in Cornish and Breton. The author is unsure why v and k have been lost from the official alphabet over the years. In Tudor times, we could read about the Kymry, and Idwal Voel. All consonants are pronounced 'hard' phonetically. Note that c is always hard, as in cat, never soft as in proceed, and that f is also hard, as in of, not off. Also g is like the g in garden, not George, and h is always pronounced as in hat, not left silent as in honest.

The vowels are a (as in hat), e (as in bet), i (either pronounced as in hit or like the e in me), o (usually as in hot), u (pronounced ee), w (pronounced oo, either as in book, or room), and y (pronounced as the u in understand or as ea as in tea).

It was a Welshman, Sir William Jones, serving as a judge in Calcutta, who *'made the epoch-making discovery that the main languages of Europe are closely related* to the principal languages of India. Jones saw the link between the classical Latin and Greek and ancient Sanskrit. It subsequently turned out that many modern Indian languages formed part of the same family as their counterparts in Europe, namely the Romance, Celtic, Germanic, Baltic and Slavonic groups' ('Europe – A History', by Norman Davies).

THE SURVIVAL OF THE LANGUAGE

The Act of Union with England of 1536 stated that 'No person or persons that use the Welsh speech or language shall have or enjoy any manor, office or fees within the realm of England, Wales or other of the king's dominions upon forfeiting the same offices or fees unless he or they use and exercise the speech or language of English'.

This Act of Henry VIII, son of the Welsh King Henry VII, also stated that English was to be the only language used in the courts of Wales, causing vast areas of land to be taken from monoglot Welshmen by English litigants. This was yet another step by England to rid itself of the oldest and once dominant native language of Britain, following the laws from the Statute of Rhuddlan in 1282 and those passed in the early fifteenth century during and after the Glyndŵr Rising. For a period after 1549, English was the language used in church services, all law and administration, and its mastery was the only method for a Welshman to rise in life. As Gwynfor Evans said, it was the English language that made Englishmen out of the Brythons, Angles, Saxons, Danes and Normans that made up their nation. From 1536 until today it has been used to try and make the Welsh into Englishmen.

In 1585 there was a lawsuit in Whittington, Shrophire, a Welsh-speaking part of England in the diocese of St. Asaph. The Bishop brought a lawsuit against the patron of the living of Whittington, claiming that the nominee, Bagshaw, knew no Welsh. The court eventually declared in the bishop's favour, but did nothing to nullify the appointment.

The turning point in the survival of the Welsh language was the translation of The Bible into Welsh. The preacher William Morgan ministered in Llanrhaeadr-ym-Mochnant, and by 1588 had completed the translation, with three other clergymen working over 25 years. His most able assistant was the brilliant Bishop Richard Davies of Abergwili. One of Morgan's precursors in religious translation, William Salesbury (Salebury, Salusbury), was said to be a former privateer, a profession at which the Welsh have gained some international renown over the centuries. Morgan said that 'Religion, if it is not taught in the mother tongue, will lie hidden and unknown'. The Privy Council decreed that a copy should be placed in every Welsh church. 'Y Beibl' standardised the different types of prose and dialects of the time into the Welsh of today.

The Bible moved the people towards a standardised national language based on the speech of the North and North-west of Wales, but there are still four recognizable dialects: y Wyndodeg (Venedotian) of the north-west; y Bowyseg (Powysian) of north-east and mid-Wales; y Ddyfydeg (Demetian) from the south-west; and Gwenhwyseg (Gwent and Morgannwg) in the southeast. Today's dialects interestingly coincide with today's major and oldest bishoprics, which are based on the old Welsh princedoms, which were themselves founded from the ruling Celtic tribes in the area. Thus the dialects date back two-thousand years. The past is an interesting place !

In 1621, John Davies wrote 'It is a matter of astonishment that a handful of the remaining Britons, in so confined a corner, despite the oppression of the English and the Normans, have for so many centuries kept not only the name or their ancestors but also their own original language to this very day, without any change of importance, and without corruption' (- 'Antiquae Linguae Britannicae').

Building on the Welsh Bible was Griffith Jones (1683-1761), Rector of Llandowror, Carmarthenshire. His circulating schools made Wales the most highly literate country in Europe

By 1757, with a third of the population being able to read, and the main reading being, of course, the family Bible. The emphasis upon the importance of the Bible and reading is another factor in keeping the language alive.

One problem in the survival of Welsh was the appointment of Englishmen to Welsh bishoprics and clericships, with Welsh being excluded from church services, to which Lewis Morris referred in a letter in 1764 'What can you expect from Bishops or any other officers ignorant of a Language which they get their living by, and which they ought to Cultivate, instead of proudly despising. If an Indian acted thus, we would be apt to Call him Barbarous. But a Scot or Saxon is above Correction'. This was written to Evan Evans, a Welsh poet-curate who could not obtain a living in Wales, only a curacy under an absentee English rector.

In 1766, a seventy-year old, ailing English monoglot was given the living of Trefdraeth and Llangwyfan in Anglesey. Only five of the five hundred parishioners spoke any English. In 1768 the churchwardens brought a case of unfitness against him on the grounds that he spoke no Welsh. In 1773 Canterbury decided in their favour, but the English rector kept the job. The argument used by the rector's counsel in court should be read by all Welshmen:

'Wales is a conquered country, it is proper to introduce the English language, and it is the duty of the bishops to endeavour to promote the English, in order to introduce the language........It has always been the policy of the legislature to introduce the English language into Wales........The English language is, by act of parliament, to be used in all courts of judicature in Wales, and an English Bible to be kept in all the churches in Wales that by comparison with that of the Welsh, they may the sooner attain to the knowledge of English'.

In 1799, a traveller to Flintshire noted the education system 'If therefore, in the colloquial intercourse of the scholars, one of them is to be detected in speaking a Welsh word, he is immediately degraded with the "Welsh lump", a large piece of lead fastened to a string, and suspended round the neck of the offender. The mark of ignominy has had the desired effect: all the children of Flintshire speak English very well.' And in 1804, John Evans wrote that 'North Wales is becoming English' and Benjamin Hakin stated 'The language of Radnorshire is almost universally English. In learning to converse with their Saxon neighbours, they have forgotten the use of their vernacular tongue.'

In 1846, an inspection was carried out of the Welsh-speaking Nonconformist schools, by three English barristers and seven Anglican assistants. Their report became known as 'Brad y Llyfrau Gleision' ('The Treason of The Blue Books'), as it called standards deplorable, blaming the Welsh tongue 'the language of slavery'. The language condemned the Welsh to intellectual backwardness, encouraged depraved sexual habits, and had produced 'no Welsh literature worthy of the name'. As well as criticising the dirtiness, laziness, ignorance, superstition, promiscuity and immorality of the Welsh, it lamented the effects of the Nonconformist religion and stated *'The Welsh language is a vast drawback to Wales and a manifold barrier to the moral progress and commercial prosperity of the people. It is not easy to over-estimate its evil effects.'*

English papers then reported that the Welsh were settling down into savage barbarism, with the habits of animals. Chambers Edinburgh Journal of 1849 stated that the use of the Celtic tongue was a 'national discredit.' In 1852, the Inspector of Schools announced that it was *'socially and politically desirable'* that the language be erased. English-only Board Schools were imposed to hasten the decline of Welsh. By 1847, only three out of one thousand six hundred and fifty seven day schools in Wales taught any Welsh. By 1899, Welsh was being examined in only fifteen out of one thousand eight hundred and fifty two elementary schools. The effects were dramatic. It looked as if the language could never recover from this official onslaught. In 1801 Meirionydd (Merioneth) was totally Welsh-speaking, closely followed by Gwynedd. By 1881 just 12% of the population spoke only Welsh. By this year only Anglesey had significant strength in Welsh speakers, where for 40% it was their sole language. The process of Anglicisation had been quickly accelerated by the disgusting 'Welsh Not', which had been hung around the necks of Welsh speakers in many schools for half a century.

The English poet and schools inspector, Matthew Arnold, declared in 1855 that the British regions must become homogeneous....... *'sooner or later the difference of language between Wales and England will probably be effaced'......an event which is (yet again) 'socially and politically desirable'.* In 1865 The Times called the language *'the curse of Wales...............the sooner all Welsh specialities vanish off the face of the earth the better'.* Even as late as November 1996, 'The Times' was still criticising minority languages in a leader article, this time the use of the Irish language, which drew a speedy response from Gerry Adams in its 'letters' column.

The 1847 Report had stated that Welsh was a *'peasant tongue, and anyone caught speaking Welsh were to be severely punished'.* The 'Welsh Not' (see entry), a ban upon the speaking of Welsh in schools, was carried out with some vehemence in yet another attempt to exterminate the language. A wooden placard had to be worn around the neck, passed on to anyone heard speaking Welsh, with the last child at the end of the day being thrashed by the teacher. This piece of wood on a leather strap was called a 'cribban', and Irish children had Gaelic thrashed out of them in a similar manner. In other Welsh schools, a stick was passed on to the same effect. In others, the child was fined half-a-penny, a massive sum for poor parents.

More than any other influence or reason for the writing of 'An A-Z of Wales and the Welsh', was the reminiscence by Owen Edwards (1858-1920) of the 'Welsh Not', also known as the 'Welsh Note'. I have taken Meic Stephens' admirable translation from Edwards' 'Clych Atgof' of 1906. This piece of writing still brings tears to my eyes as I think of the systematic abuse of native children, and the natural cussedness and nobility of people like Owen Edwards who kept the language alive against the wishes of authority......

'The school was in Y Llan (Llanuwchllyn, near Bala), a few miles from where I lived. It belonged to the landowner, as did almost the entire district, and his wife, a tall dignified lady, took a great interest in the education of the locality. When I first went to the school it had a schoolmistress. I was taken to the school-house;

school had already begun and not a child was to be seen in Y Llan. The schoolmistress appeared, a small woman with piercing eyes, her hands folded in front of her. She spoke a little Welsh, the common people's language, with an English accent; her language, obviously, was English, the gentlefolk's language, the language of the parson from Cardiganshire. She could smile only when speaking English. Her face was very sour because she was forced to degrade herself by speaking Welsh; indeed, it was a sourness I always saw in her countenance, except when her thin face wore a smile to meet the generous lady who paid her wages. I did not listen to her words, and I did not like her face; it brought to mind the nose of a she-fox that I saw once, close up, after dark.

"My boy," said my mother, "here is your new teacher. Look at her, take the peak of your cap from your mouth, she is going to teach you everything. Shake hands with her."

She offered me her hand, with a weak smile dying on her face - "Oh, we shall," she said (in Welsh), "we'll teach him everything he needs to know; we'll teach him how to behave."

It was not to learn how to behave that I wanted, but how to make a bridge and build a chapel. A great desire came over me to go home with my mother; but it was with the schoolmistress I had to go. The school's door was opened; I heard a strange din, and I could see the children packed tight on many benches. There were two open spaces on the floor of the school, and I could see two people on their feet, one in each open space. I understood later that they were the assistant master and mistress. The schoolmistress took me to one of them, but I only recall the words "a new boy" from what she said. I could read Welsh quite well by then, and I was put in a class of children who were beginning to read English. The reading book was one of the SPCK's, and I still loathe those letters, on account of the cruelty I suffered while trying to read from that book. The teacher was a pleasant fellow, and he was kind to me, but after the reading-lessons he went back to his other pupils. The word soon went round that someone new, and ridiculous at that, had come to the school. Several of the cruel children had their eye on me - I knew about them all, loud-mouthed children from Y Llan most of them were, and they never amounted to much. The teacher had whispered to me not to speak a word of Welsh; but these naughty boys did all they could to make me raise my voice, and in the end they succeeded. I lost my temper and began to speak my mind to the treacherous busybody who had contrived to torment me. As I began to speak my rich Welsh everyone laughed, and a cord was put around my neck, with a heavy wooden block attached to it. I had no idea what it was, I had seen a similar block on a dog's neck to stop it running after sheep. Perhaps it was to prevent me from running home that the block was hung round my neck ? At last it was mid-day, the time to be released. The school-mistress came in with a cane in her hand. She asked a question, and every servile child pointed a finger at me. Something like a smile came across her face when she saw the block around my neck. She recited some long rhyme at me, not a word of which I could understand, she showed me the cane, but she did not touch me. She pulled off the block and I understood that it was for speaking Welsh that it had been hung around my neck.

That block was around my neck hundreds of times after that. This is how it was done, - when a child was heard uttering a word of Welsh, the teacher was to be told, then the block put around the child's neck; and it was to stay there until he heard someone else speaking Welsh, when it was passed on to the next poor child.

At school's end the one who was wearing it would be caned on his hand. Each day the block, as if by its own weight, from all parts of the school, would come to end up around my neck. Today I take comfort from the fact that I never tried to seek respite from the block by passing it on to another. I knew nothing about the principle of the thing, but my nature rebelled against the damnable way of destroying the foundation of a child's character. To teach a child to spy on a smaller one who was speaking his native language, in order to pass the punishment to him? No, the block never came off my neck and I suffered the cane daily as school drew to its close.'

At the same time the prominent Welsh industrialist, David Davies was saying that Welsh was a second-rate language – *'If you wish to continue to eat barely bread and lie on straw mattresses, then keep on shouting "Bydded i'r Gymraeg fyw am byth" (May the Welsh language live forever, the chorus of the National Anthem). But if you want to eat white bread and roast beef you must learn English!'*

In years to come, older people used to boast of how many times they had been caned for wearing the 'Welsh Not' at the end of the day. The 1870 Education Act made the English school system compulsory in Wales. Many children refused to speak English, so learned nothing at school, for instance Sir Owen M. Edwards, a distinguished educationalist of the early 1900's, who would have remained semi-literate but for the Welsh-speaking Sunday schools. It is difficult to control the Welsh with violence - it arouses the native stubbornness and refusal to co-operate with authority. The proudest time of my own schooldays was never being considered prefect material in a Boys Grammar School run on fear and punishment. This remnant of the English system specialised in systematically knocking the love of learning out most people who passed through it. Children from the 'wrong' end of Barry, Cadoxton, were mainly forced out of the educational system before they reached the VIth form.

In 1871 a number of people led by the Liberal MP, Osborne Morgan, petitioned the Lord Chancellor to appoint just one Welsh-speaking judge, as the majority of Welsh people spoke mainly Welsh, and there were substantial monoglot communities. The Lord Chancellor replied that *'there is a statute of Henry VIII which absolutely requires that legal proceedings in Wales shall be conducted in English, legal proceedings had been in English for 300 years, and, moreover, the Welsh language is dying out..... probably the best thing that can happen for Wales is that the Welsh tongue should follow the Cornish language into the limbo of dead languages.'*

A rallying call, broadcast by Saunders Lewis in 1962 led to the founding in 1963 of 'Cymdeithas yr Iaith Gymraeg', the 'Society for the Welsh Language'. By various methods of civil disobedience, it forced the English Parliament to pass the Welsh Language Act in 1967, *giving equal status to the Welsh language for the first time since 1536.*

As recently as 1965, a Mr. Brewer-Spinks tried to enforce an 'English Only' language rule at his factory at Blaenau Ffestiniog. Three staff resigned, and he only rescinded the rule after a meeting with The Secretary of State for Wales. In 1970, Dafydd Iwan, the Welsh folk singer and nationalist, was imprisoned for refusing to pay a fine for defacing English road signs. Twenty-one Welsh magistrates paid his fine to release him. Later, Gwynfor Evans' intended hunger strike forced the English government to give Wales its own Welsh-language media and help the survival of the language.

Until recently, the Welsh National Rugby Team always called its line-out ball throw-in in Welsh - usually some alpha-numeric code is needed to disguise where the hooker is throwing the ball. The Royal Welsh Fusiliers in the recent Bosnia peace-keeping mission also communicated in Welsh over the radio, thereby preventing interception of messages.

In the more Anglicised parts of Wales, there is still a strong feeling against the use of the language. Recently, I was in the Welsh Arts Council's bookshop, Oriel, in Cardiff, and everyone, including the assistants, were speaking in Welsh. I found the experience quite moving. Upon the same evening, I was quietly sitting in the 'Old Arcade' pub sipping Brains SA, before seeing what Cardiff calls a rugby 'team' being hammered by London's Harlequins. I read a letter in The South Wales Echo (October 9, 1996), from a Mrs Keenan....... *'Although born and educated in Wales, I spent many years in England. It was disconcerting to discover that we are perceived as a backward nation, clinging to an esoteric tongue, and spending our leisure time watching rugby. Are there no local politicians with the courage to influence a referendum on the language issue ? Let's be rid of the signs, the bilingual correspondence and the teaching of this useless language in schools'.*

One of the aims of this book is to try and 'influence' people like Mrs Keenan of St Mellons that the language is vital to our survival as a nation. It is a matter of pride, nationalism, literature, heritage and 'Cymreictod' (belonging). We are not English - we have a different culture - a pacifist, socialist, poetic, literary, cultured Christian history unlike that of any other nation. Kill the language, and everything falls with it. We must keep returning to Santayana, *'without a knowledge of history, we are condemned to repeat the mistakes of the past'* - if Mrs Keenan wants to bring back the Welsh Not, it is her problem - Welsh will always survive.

The percentage of people speaking Welsh has dropped from 54.4% in 1891 to only 18.7% in 1991. According to the 1992 Welsh Office survey, 70% of the Welsh-speaking households they surveyed were childless. The last monoglot Welsh speakers - my maternal grandmother had extremely poor English - seemed to have died out in the mid-twentieth century.

Of the eight new Welsh counties, the largest are Dyfed, Powys and Gwynedd, with 27.8%, 24.4% and 18.6% respectively of the area, making up over 60% of Wales. The percentage of the population who speak Welsh is these areas is high - 61%, 20% and 44%. Dyfed's figure would be nearer the 67% of its Dinefwr, and 59% of its Carmarthen and Ceredigion districts, if it was not for the English settlements, retirement bungalows and holiday weekend homes of South Pembrokeshire, the 'Englishry' south of the Landsker. Gwyneddd is solidly Welsh except for the Aberconwy holiday home area with 36% - many people from the North-West and Midlands of England retire in Conwy's congenial surroundings. However, Gwynedd's Dwyfor was the last district in Britain to abolish Sunday closing of public houses, and has over a 75% Welsh-speaking population. Powys has been under threat since the war with non-Welsh people moving into the old counties of Brecon, Montgomery and Radnorshire. Certain other areas have a high proportion of Welsh speakers, e.g. the Lliw Valley in West Glamorgan with 37% and Glyndŵr in Clwyd with 40% (- Owain Glyndŵr's homeland).

The main danger is the mobility of people in modern times, **especially into the main Welsh-speaking areas.** For instance, in the 1991 Census, only 67% of Gwynedd's population was born in Wales. For Powys it was only 61%, and for

Dyfed 75%. In the non-Welsh 'industrialised' counties of Gwent, Mid-, South-, and West-Glamorgan, the Welsh native birth statistics are much higher, at 82%, 89%, 78% and 87%. This is the main pressure on the language, as more and more people come to this relatively safe, inexpensive and unspoilt area of the United Kingdom to retire. The proportion of Wales' inhabitants aged over 60 has trended as follows:

%	1871	1901	1931	1961	1981	1991
aged over 60	8	7	11	18	21	23

As we have seen with Welsh folk dance, it hung on by a thread in the memory of one old woman. There are now similar fears for the language. According to a 1997 report by 'Cymdeithas yr Iaith Gymraeg', only 21 villages and towns will be able to be classified as Welsh-speaking by 2001. This report takes 75% of Welsh speakers as meaning a Welsh community. Most of such communities will be clustered at the end of the Llyn peninsula beyond Porthmadog, and in Caernarfon and Blaenau Ffestiniog, with Llangefni the only Welsh-speaking community in Anglesey. The report blames English immigration, attracted to rural Wales by house prices which remain low while those in the South-East of England rise rapidly.

Even the strongholds of the Princes of Gwynedd are now threatened, and there is disagreement with the quango known as The Welsh Language Board, which believes that the language is safe, because of the number of new learners in South-East Wales. The report's authors point out that they 'feel very strongly that, if it is to survive, the Welsh language must keep its community base, its foothold as a community language. Otherwise we would go the way of the Irish, with lots of speakers on paper, but which does not exist as a community language except in a very few areas'.......... 'The Welsh language will not survive unless there is an environment where people can communicate through Welsh, can live their lives through Welsh, rather than as individual Welsh speakers'.

The Welsh language has to survive and prosper.

FOOTNOTE:
It is entirely in character with the nature of the people that no swear-words seem to exist in the language. Unlike English, with its rich repertoire of Anglo-Saxon expletives, Welsh has to improvise. I call any stroppy/stupid driver who threatens my survival a 'carrot' from the shelter of my car. The Welsh for carrot is 'moron'. Others mutter 'chick peas'. Chick peas in Welsh is 'ffa cyw'.

APPENDIX II

From 'The Book of Welsh Saints' by Terry Breverton

The Language Problem

In the text has been noted the problems of retirement homes and holiday homes in Wales destroying local language and heritage. Flint adjoins Cheshire and Lancashire, so is a border environment, and has the highest rate of people born outside Wales. Denbigh again has similar problems adjoining the former Welsh territory of Shropshire. However, the third placed Welsh area, Conwy, was formerly a stronghold of the Welsh language. Again, the attractive and massive county of Powys, across mid-Wales, has almost 40% of its people born outside Wales. Fifth is the border county of Monmouth, but worryingly the far West county of Cardigan is in 6th position. In seventh place is the holy island of Anglesey, with Gwynedd a former stronghold of the Welsh language. 8th is another extremity of Wales, Pembroke, and yet another extremity, the Welsh-speaking Gwynedd is 9th. This is not a nationalist, but a cultural problem.

The following analysis is from statistics upon local government in Wales supplied in 'The Wales Yearbook 2000.' It also demonstrates the extent to which the Conservative party is very much a minority force in Wales, with a reasonable showing in only two administrative areas (Monmouth and the Vale of Glamorgan) out of twenty. Its performance in the Vale has been greatly assisted by scandals involving former Labour council leaders in Barri. The Labour Party is losing its grip upon Wales, as the Blair government is seen to be a London-centred continuation of the Thatcher-Major years. The Welsh economy has suffered for decades compared to the rest of Britain, and the controversy which raged over Blair's undemocratic 'placing' of Alan Michael as leader of the National Assembly has also helped swell the feeling of disappointment across the land. The only jobs coming to Wales are 'call-centres', low-paid, high-pressure and unskilled. The greatest warning for Labour is in the constituencies of their former strongholds of Rhondda-Cynon-Taff and Caerffili. These areas have moved massively towards Plaid Cymru, giving the party its first toe-hold in the heavily-populated south-east of Wales.

Non Welsh-born citizens have moved towards the most attractive coastal areas of Wales. The % speaking Welsh is 'people over 3 years old', and is a very imperfect measure which overstates reality. The ability to speak a little 'school-Welsh' and the propensity to use the language in every-day conversation are two very different things. The Welsh Language Board uses this measure, as it reflects that it seems to be an effective body. However, the Welsh Language Society, unlike the former subsidised quango, believes that only where Wales is a 'living' language should be reflected in these tables. The % should be based upon those who use Welsh as their first language in everyday life, in which case the proportions would be miniscule. The danger to the survival of the Welsh language cannot be over-stated. The author is learning Welsh.

	AREA	Lab.	Plaid Cymru seats	Lib. Dem. seats	Ind. + other	Cons seats	Pop.	% speak Welsh	% born in Wales
1	Flint	*42	2	7	17	1	147000	15.7	BC53.0
2	Conwy	19	7	15	13	5	111900	35.8	C53.5
3	Denbigh	14	8	1	22	2	90500	29.6	BC57.3
4	Powys	6	-	7	*59	1	126000	20.4	B60.3
5	Monmouth	18	-	1	4	19	86300	7.1	BC62.1
6	Cardigan	1	13	1	30	-	70700	60.9	C64.2
7	Anglesey	4	9	-	27	-	65400	62.6	C67.7
8	Pembroke	*13	2	3	3	3	113700	20.4	C69.7
9	Gwynedd	12	*44	6	19	-	117500	74.3	C71.8
10	Wrexham	*26	-	7	15	4	125200	16.3	B73.6
11	Vale of Glam.	19	6	-	-	22	121300	9.6	C75.8
12	Cardiff	*50	1	18	1	5	320900	9.0	C79.1
13	Newport	*40	-	-	2	5	139200	8.4	BC81.1
14	Carmarthen	28	14	1	31	-	169000	53.5	C81.8
15	Swansea	*47	2	10	9	4	229,500	14.0	C84.1
16	Torfaen	*39	-	1	3	1	90200	8.3	B85.1
17	Bridgend	*41	2	5	5	1	131400	10.1	C85.2
18	Neath/P.Talb	*40	10	2	11		138800	19.1	C90.4
19	Caerffili	28*	39	3	3	-	169600	7.4	90.4
20	Rhondda	26	*42	2	5	-	240400	9.5	91.1
21	Merthyr	16	4	-	13	-	57000	8.1	92.0
22	Blaenau	34	-	1	8	-	72000	6.4	92.5
=	1232 seats	563	205	92	300	72	2933500		
		46%	17%	7%	24%	6%			

(* = overall majority. C = Coastal constituencies. B = 'Border' constituencies)

Another way of examining these statistics, and their implications for the heritage, and future, of Wales, is to see where people are retiring and unemployed, keeping the same rankings of % born in Wales, as above. It is fairly easy to see that the eight attractive areas ranked 2nd to 9th, from Conwy to Gwynedd, are retirement havens for people from outside Wales. Of these areas, Cardigan, Anglesey and Gwynedd are the traditional heart-lands of the Welsh language. It is equally easy to see why Plaid Cymru has captured Caerffili and Rhondda Cynon Taff after decades of Labour dominance. The four areas of Wales with the highest percentage of the population born in Wales have the worst deprivation statistics in Wales, and thereby the United Kingdom.

	AREA	% ret'd.	% unemp.	Total % ret'd. + unemp.	% in buildings B+D	B+D council tax £	% GCSE A-C	% speak Welsh	% born in Wales
1	Flint	17.3	3.8	21.1	19	592	55.3	15.7	BC53.0
2	Conwy	26.6	5.3	31.8	22	488	60.4	35.8	C53.5
3	Denbigh	23.8	4.2	28.0	20	647	59.12	9.6	BC57.3
4	Powys	21.9	3.4	25.3	17	552	63.0	20.4	B60.3
5	Monmouth	20.0	3.3	23.3	19	485	62.3	7.1	BC62.1
6	Cardigan	21.9	3.8	25.7	22	670	67.7	60.9	C64.2
7	Anglesey	21.3	8.0	29.3	22	534	59.3	62.6	C67.7
8	Pembroke	21.0	6.0	27.0	19	542	59.0	70	C69.7
9	Gwynedd	22.0	5.4	27.4	15	618	60.2	74.3	C71.8
10	Wrexham	18.8	3.8	22.6	16	633	57.6	16.3	B73.6
11	Vale/Glam.	19.2	4.4	23.6	18	532	58.5	9.6	C75.8
12	Cardiff	17.3	4.3	21.6	16	573	57.3	9.0	C79.1
13	Newport	18.7	5.0	23.7	16	531	60.8	8.4	BC81.1
14	Carmarthen	23.1	6.0	29.1	16	666	64.7	53.5	C81.8
15	Swansea	20.5	5.6	26.1	15	596	58.7	14.0	C84.1
16	Torfaen	18.6	4.4	22.8	9	564	55.1	8.3	B85.1
17	Bridgend	19.2	5.2	24.4	16	647	60.2	10.1	C85.2
18	Neath/P.Tlb	21.0	6.5	27.5	12	750	62.7	19.1	C90.4
18	Caerffili	17.6	6.8	24.4	9	633	52.5	7.4	90.4
20	Rhondda	18.2	6.5	24.7	8	686	55.2	9.5	91.1
21	Merthyr	18.6	7.7	26.3	7	712	54.1	8.1	92.0
22	Blaenau	19.5	10.0	29.5	4	640	42.0	6.4	92.5

(* = overall majority. C = Coastal constituencies. B = 'Border' constituencies)

APPENDIX III

The Death and Defeat of Llywelyn ap Gruffudd
Prince of Wales - December 1282

By Anthony Edwards

Llywelyn's pre-eminence as a man of destiny who ruled at a turning-point in Welsh history is beyond dispute. Unfortunately many of the facts of his life are unknown or uncertain and today we must resign ourselves to living with this uncertainty. The year of his birth is not known precisely, some historians believe it was in the early 1220's, and some in the later years of that decade. There is argument over the identity of his mother, either Senana descended from the princes, or Rhuallt daughter of the King of Man. Convincing arguments have been brought forward for both views. The circumstances of his death and burial are disputed and these will be discussed below. Llywelyn's importance in history comes from his intention to unite all the Welsh rulers under one prince, and for his success in this aim over many years. He was not the first ruler to do this and to view his career in perspective the achievements of some of the earlier rulers with this aim should be considered.

Rhodri Mawr ap Merfyn Frych was born some 25 years after the death of Offa, King of Mercia, who had established his rule over all other Anglo-Saxons south of the Humber. (Offa was killed in a battle with the Welsh at Rhuddlan). Unable to conquer the Welsh, he fortified the whole border with a trench still known as Offa's Dyke. This represented the limits of his military power, and there will still large areas of British-speaking (Welsh) population east of the dyke. Over a dozen generations during the slow retreat of the Britons before the Anglo-Saxon tribes, they had been ruled by descendants of Cunedda, the Romano-British ruler of north-west Britain. Rhodri was not in the direct male line of Cunedda but was connected with this line through his paternal grandmother, Ethyllt the daughter of Cynan ap Rhodri Molwynog. Rhodr Mawr ap Merfyn Frych established his rule over the whole of Wales by his military prowess, from his first victory in 855 AD until his death in battle against the Saxons in 877. He set his son Anarawd to found the ruling line of Gwynedd, and his son was Cadell of Deheubarth.

The nest ruler to be recognised as ruler of all Wales was Hywel Dda, the son of Cadell and thus Rhodri's grandson. Though he must have been effective on the field of battle, his great achievement was to establish his dominance by diplomacy and his own learning and knowledge of the law. He was always ready to pay homage to the contemporary kings of England and admit their superior military power, to the son of King Alfred in 918 and to King Athelstan in 926, but retained his undisputed authority in Wales. He minted coins in his own name and created a legal system based on Welsh legal tradition that was accepted throughout Wales. He was fortunate in being the contemporary of English kings who were prepared to accept this.

The next ruler to unite all Wales was of a very different character. Gruffudd ap Llywelyn ap Seisyll rules in the first place Gwynedd and Powys, but from 1055-1063 was recognised as ruler of all Wales. He was a warlike man who made victorious incursions far into England. He was less successful in ruling his conquered lands in a way acceptable to those he had conquered. His centre of government was Rhuddlan on the banks of the Clwyd, and he fortified a hill there which later became the site of a Norman castle. In 1063 he was attacked unexpectedly by Harold, the son of Earl Godwin, who became King of England in 1066. Gruffudd managed to escape from the battle-field, but his subsequent life was that of a fugitive. Harold himself survived for only three more years that ended with the Battle of Hastings where he was defeated by William of Nrmandy, known as the Conqueror.

In the 12th century there were two outstanding figures in Welsh history who, although they did not unite the whole of Wales, did in effect ensure that Wales was left alone to manage its affairs. These were Owain Gwynedd (1100-1170) and a generation or so later Rhys ap Gruffudd (Yr Arglwydd Rhys, 1132-1197). Both had to face initial hostility from the English King Henry II and in both cases the king secured qualified victories, which made him reluctant to face further hostility from Wales. Both paid homage to the English king and were left afterwards to run their own affairs. Owain Gwynedd is buried in Bangor Cathedral, and The Lord Rhys at St David's cathedral. The two rulers had family connections through Madog ap Maredudd, recognised as king over the whole of Powys. Madog's daughter Gwenllian married Yr Arglwydd Rhys, and another daughter Marged married Iorwerth Drwyndwn ap Owain Gwynedd, the father of Llywelyn Fawr.

Llyweln ab Iorwerth, Llywelyn the Great, won an unrivalled position as ruler of Wales (1173-1240). During his early years he had faced rather weak opposition from the English kings. The absentee monarch Richard I (Coeur de Lion) was king from 1199, when his younger brother John became king and ruled until 1216. John had faced opposition from his own subjects owing to his subservience to the papacy, and on his death the nine year-old King Heny III took over and in turn faced revolt from his own nobility. This enabled Llywelyn to establish a situation in Wales where his own military might and gifts as a statesman and administrator combined to strengthen him against any military challenge. He wished to hand on his own hard won supremacy to his son Dafydd. In cultural matters Norman habits and the French language were making steady inroads. Llywelyn had married Joan the illegitimate daughter of King John, and Dafydd was to marry Isabel de Breos from a Norman family. The bard Dafydd Benfras praised Dafydd ap Llywelyn for his fluent Welsh. This would seem to indicate that Welsh was not his only language, perhaps not even his first. Dafydd's inheritance of the realm of his father was not to go unchallenged, but he was winning back his position when he died mysteriously at Aber* in 1246.

King Henry III had received the homage of Dafydd ap Llywelyn shortly after the death of Llywelyn Fawr, but his support of his authority was unreliable. Dafydd had an elder brother Gruffudd, not the son of Joan but of Llywelyn's previous consort Tangwystl. She was the daughter of Llywelyn Goch of Rhoas and of pure Welsh descent, so Gruffudd commanded the support of many of the Welsh chieftains. Henry imprisoned Gruffudd in the Tower of London, no doubt comfortably enough, to be used as a pawn should Dafydd's power become oppressive. Ironically too, as a counter-poise to Dafydd, Henry seems to have offered encouragement to Gruffudd's son Llywelyn, who was about 20 years old when Dafydd died, and who held lordships in Dyffryn Clwyd. Gruffudd fell to his death while trying to escape from the Tower on March 1st, 1244. In the subsequent struggle for power between his four sons, Llywelyn was victorious and proved a formidable challenge to Henry III's authority in Wales.

After the defeat of his brothers at Bryn Derwin in 1255, Llywelyn became increasingly cast as the leader of a united Wales to whom lesser Welsh chieftains could turn for support. It was some 300 years since Rhodri Mawr had first united Wales and the fate of those who aspired to this course should now be considered. The important factor which decided the success or failure of their efforts was the character of the contemporary English kings, and the stability of their rule in England. The Welsh leader had to show his ability to withstand a frontal assault from England, and at the same time permit the Welsh to run their own affairs as they wished. It was not always the weak and ineffective English kings who were prepared to do this. Athelstan and Henry II could not by any means be so described. The Welsh leader in turn had to rule his Welsh subjects in a manner acceptable to them. Gruffudd ap Llywelyn ap Seisyll, the (half-Viking) leader in the years before the Norman Conquest, had been merciless in executing members of his own family who might challenge his position, but in so doing had gradually built up opposition to his rule. The Welsh leader had to acknowledge clearly the superior military might of his English neighbours and assure them than no threat to their authority was to come from Wales. Llywelyn ap Gruffudd after the defeat of his brothers at Bryn Derwin had treated them mercifully. The eldest Owain he imprisoned, and like his father Gruffudd he had to endure many years of comfortable but boring confinement. The younger Dafydd, in his early twenties, he briefly imprisoned but was soon pardoned and given posts of authority under Llywelyn. There was an even younger brother Rhodri, who was too young to be involved in the power struggle at Bryn Derwin but made a name for himself under the protection of the English king, to be used against Llywelyn if the occasion arose. (When the House of Gwynedd was wiped out, it was only a single descendant of this Rhodri, Owain Llawgoch (q.v.) who surfaced a few years later, to be assassinated by the English crown.) Llywelyn's merciful treatment of Dafydd was to prove a fatal weakness to his position at the very end, when the heads of both men were on display, stuck on lances outside the Tower of London.

After the decisive Battle of Bryn Derwin, Llywelyn ap Gruffudd won authority over the whole of Gwynedd west of the Conwy river. In the following year, Price Edward came to view his father's pssessions east of the Conwy. He tried to impose the yoke of total subjection on the inhabitants and had aroused intense resentment. In their distess they appealed to Llywelyn who advanced into the area and quickly gained complete possession. In November 1256 Llywelyn released Dafydd from captivity and made him his trusted administrator in the newly conquered Perfeddwlad. However, Dafydd's loyalty was still doubtful, and when King Henry III was in Chester in 1257 he respnded favourably to the king's probings. In 1263, Dafydd left his brother's service and allied himself to the king of England. In 1274 Dafydd joined Prince Gruffudd ap Gwenwynwyn of Powys, who resented the rising power of Llywelyn, in a plot to murder Llywelyn. Before the plan could be carried out, Llywelyn summoned both Dafydd and Gruffudd to appear before his court and explain their actions. Dafydd fled to England and offered his services to Edward, and Gruffudd fled to Shrewsbury and left Llywelyn to gain possession of all his lands. Dafydd fought with King Edward's army in the crucial assault on Wales in 1276, and won his reward at the Treaty of Aberconwy in 1277, when he was made Lord of Denbigh.

Relations between Llywelyn and Edward now reached a state of relative stability. King Edward had quailed before facing an all-out assault on Snowdonia, and had chosen to come to terms with Llywelyn. Neither wanted to return to a military solution to their differences. Edward had virtually mortgaged his kingdom to fight in Wales, and a war would mean a vast expenditure of money and time that could be better used elsewhere. The terms of the treaty, although harsh for Llywelyn, still allowed him his title the Prince of Wales, his high-born bride (King Edward's cousin), and undisputed rule over Gwynedd west of the Conwy.

It was Dafydd ap Gruffudd, Llywelyn's brother, who destroyed what stability had been achieved between English and Welsh rule. Dafydd owed everythin he possessed to the king, and Edward expected complete loyalty in return. English rule was harsh in Gwynedd, east of the conwy, and still resented. Dafydd hoped to exploit this by putting himself at the head of a rebellion against English rule. On Palm Sunday 1282 he took the castle of Hawarden by assault, and forced Llywelyn to join him or his foes. Dafydd was quite undeterred by the likelihood of the complete destruction of the Welsh race, or by any sense of gratitude either to his brother Llywelyn or King Edward. Such was his part in the downfall of Llywelyn, but it was the lot of some more distant members of his family to play an equally decisive role. These were the Mortimers.

The ancestral Mortimers had come from Normandy with William the Conqueror and had been rewarded with estates at Wigmore in the Welsh Marches, where they had prospered over many years, both fighting the Welsh and in alliance with them against common enemies. The Mortimers had been supporters of John in his rebellion against his brother Richard I, and had been punished for their support when Richard gained the advantage. Later, when John became king after Richard's death, the Mortimers were richly rewarded. Llywelyn ab Iorwerth had been ruler of Wales at that time, and he had married Joan, John's illegitimate daughter. Their daughter Gwladus Ddu married Ralph Mortimer of Wigmore, and to them a son was born, probably about 1231, Roger. Roger was about 15 years-old when Dafydd ap Llywelyn died with no direct heir, and he thus legally had a better claim to Llywelyn's possessions that the other grandsons. During the years of Llywelyn ap Gruffudd's supremacy, Roger Mortimer was not able to do much to further his claim, but he remained a powerful challenge to Llywelyn's power in the Marches. This lifelong rivalry was softened after the Treaty of Aberconwy in 1277, when both Roger and Llywelyn found themselves edged out by the rising influence of the king's favourite, Grufydd ap Gwenwynwyn of Powys.

This led to the signing of a treaty of friendship between Roger and Llywelyn at Radnor in 1281. Roger was careful to emphasise that in no way was the treaty directed against the king. Other points of dispute between the two must have been discussed at this time, although they were not mentioned in the treaty, the most important being Roger's still unsatisfied claim to the inheritance of Llyweln Fawr. It is more than possible that Llywelyn agreed to favour Roger's claims at the expense of his brother Dafydd, who had plotted to kill him and joined King Edward's forces against him in the crucial war of 1276. (Llywelyn at this time had no heirs - his wife Elinor later died giving birth their only child Gwenllian in early 1282. Gwenllian was incarcerated as a nun in the east of England until her death, and the children of Dafydd were likewise never allowed to breed heirs to the line of Gwynedd. The only line extant was that of Rhodri in England, whose son Thomas had luckily sent his own son Owain Llawgoch [q.v.] to France as a boy to save him. Thomas was killed on the orders of the king. Such was the power of the name of the princes of Gwynedd, that Owain Llawgoch, the last in the line, was assassinated). This possibility had also occurred to King Edward, who wished first to secure the undivided loyalty of Edmund Mortimer, Roger's eldest surviving son.

On March 22nd, 1282, when the second Welsh War broke out, Roger was given command of the king's forces in the Middle March. On September 2nd, he was sent £500 'to expedite certain special business of the king in those parts'. Edward hatched a plot to lure Llywelyn to the March where he could be ambushed and killed far from his strongholds in Gwynedd. Roger died on October 16th, 1282. His successor Edmund Mortimer was to feign treason and induce his Welsh subjects to rebel and appeal for help to Llywelyn. The plan was surely most distasteful to Edmund Mortimer. It would offer King Edward an excuse to put Mortimer to death for treason whenever he wished, whether things had gone well or badly. Furthermore it would destroy his credibility with his Welsh tenants, whose trust and loyalty he would require if he were to rule in Gwynedd. In the spring of 1282, Llywelyn received a letter from Gruffydd ab Owain, promising support with his brothers Llywelyn and Iorwerth, also rulers in Elfael**, and from Edmund Mortimer. Llywelyn ap Gruffudd raised an army, leaving his brother Dafydd in charge of Gwynedd, and marched to Builth where he encamped at Llanganten.

It was not difficult to persuade him to leave his army on the evening of December 11th, and come lightly armed with a small escort to meet the Mortimers and the rulers of Elfael, at Gruffydd ab Owain's castle at nearby Aberedw. Llywelyn brought his seal, necessary for signing a treaty, and was accompanied by a high-ranking Cistercian monk from Abbey Cwm Hir to witness it. Llywelyn and his followers were slaughtered at Aberedw, and Gruffydd and his brothers were also put to death, if not on that occasion, then shortly afterwards. The high-ranking Cistercian monk was killed by Roger, Edmund's younger brother, who took possession of his vestments, possibly as a peace offering to his chaplain whom he had imprisoned as the result of a dispute.

The Cistercians of Abbey Cwm Hir would most certainly have come to collect the corpse of their brother from Aberedw, and may have collected Llywelyn's headless body at the same time, and taken both back to their Abbey. Such was the end of Llywelyn's rule in Wales in the face of more formidable enemies than any previous ruler had faced.

Postscriptum:
The Author would like to take this opportunity to give his opinion on some of the uncertainties in Llywelyn's history. They are not based on new evidence, but simply on the balance of probability as it appears to him. They are opinions and no more.

Where was Llywelyn killed? At Gruddydd ab Owain's castle at Aberedw with near certainty.

Where was the corpse buried? I believe the corpse was taken to Abbey Cwm Hir, but with Roger Lestrange's army roaming the area as victors, the monks would have been anxious to get rid of it. When any refugees from Llywelyn's army came to the Abbey requesting food and lodging, the monks may have agreed to provide for them if they took the corpse with them for burial at Aberconwy. When they reached Prysgduon they probably buried most of the remains, perhaps taking a few small clean bones home to Gwynedd.

What was the date of his birth? I suggest 1227 as an approximation. This would make him 19 when his uncle Dafydd ap Llywelyn died, 28 when he defeated his brothers at Bryn Derwin, 40 when he signed the Treaty of Montgomery, 51 when he married Elinor de Montfort and 55 at his death.

Who was his mother - Senana or Rhunallt? I must leave you to decide, your opinion is as good as mine, probably better.

Notes by Terry Breverton upon the above, using other researches by Anthony Edwards:

*Lywelyn used to send letters from his court at 'Aber', or 'Garth Celyn'. Pen-y-Bryn, Abercaseg, an ancient mansion on this site, is known to the locals as (Twr Llywelyn) Llywelyn's Tower, and is the most exciting historical find in Wales in the 20th century. In November, 1282, John Peckham stayed there discussing peace terms with Llywelyn. It has taken tremendous efforts by the owner, Kathryn Gibson, to identify the house with Llywelyn's palace, but the case is clear and evident. A sheaf of ancient letters in Latin were burned by the old lady who owned the house before Mrs Gibson - they were found inserted into a niche in the chapel wall.

**'Quo Warranto, 687' of 1292 seems to have been ignored by historians, and is discussed in Anthony Edwards' 'Massacre at Aberedw'. In the late 19th century, 200 skeletons, mostly male and of military age, were found north-east of Aberedw Church of St Cewydd. St Cewydd's cave nearby is also known as Llywelyn's Cave (where traditionally his body was kept hidden). Aberedw was held by Gruffydd ab Owain, and the surrounding commotes by his brothers Madog, Llywelyn and Iorwerth. This area of Elfael had been part of Llywelyn's lands until the war of 1277, but the family then paid homage to Roger Mortimer, and from November 1282 to Edmund Mortimer. After Llywelyns' death in 1282, Elfael was given to Edmund Mortimer as 'escheat', and all the sons of Owain ap Maredudd dispossessed in December 1282. In legal terms, an 'escheat' is to take the estates of the dead. A Chancery Rolls document of November 24th, 1284, dates the dispossession to December 1282 or shortly after. Llywelyn was murdered upon December 11th. It appears that the Welsh lords of Elfael and their followers may have been executed at the same time. In the words of Anthony Edwards, 'After the defeat of Llywelyn ap Gruffudd in 1282, King Edward carried out a systematic slaughter of the Welsh in many parts of Wales, probably to reduce the Welsh manpower. For instance, the 3000 footsoldiers, the leaderless remnants of Llywelyn's army, were put to death between Llanganten and Builth, and while King Edward was at Rhuddlan very many Welsh, including priests, were put to death, bringing on him the reproof of the archbishop of Canterbury.'

FOOTNOTE:

Anthony Edwards' 'The Massacre on the Fairway' is based upon his booklet 'Marwolaeth Llywelyn ap Gruffudd - Y Gwirionedd', and contends that the surrendered army of Llywelyn, of 3000 footsoldiers and 160 horsemen, was executed in cold blood where Builth golf-course is today. Historians are generally the worse people to investigate such claims - they intensely dislike agreeing with what they have been taught, as it gives them an uncomfortable dissonance in their lives. As Anthony states, 'we can surely agree that those historians who lack the moral courage to face and record the truth deserve nothing but contempt.' Welsh historians in particular are afraid of affecting an anti-English bias, with scant regard to the rewriting of history by conquering nations across the world. If it may help, we are not here discussing the vices of the English, a nation of mainly British genetic stock, especially on its western sides (e.g. Lancashire and Cumbria against Yorkshire and the North-East, the West Midlands against the East Midlands, the South-West against the South-East), but against their foreign rulers. The vices of the Normans, Angevins and Plantagenets - the 'great' heroes like Richard the Lionheart and the Black Prince - are truly appalling. If one favours rule by illiterate French monoglots who delight in slow torture of the innocent and weakest, rather than by literate men of culture who only use war in the last resort as a means of defence, then please keep reading the established text-books which glorify in the exploits of such animals. Llywelyn ap Gruffudd was not fighting the 'English', but a megalomaniac who almost bankrupted his country with wars, who slaughtered defenceless men, women and children indiscriminately, exterminated Jews, who invented the torture of hanging, drawing and torturing for Prince Dafydd, who could only speak the French language, who could not read, who could only write his name, who was a liar and a murderer. Edward I, 'The Hammer of the Scots' failed to conquer Scotland because his finances were drained in Welsh campaigns, particularly by the building of the Iron Ring of castles, including Conwy, Caernarfon and Harlech, which now form a World Heritage Site surrounding Gwynedd. As a youth he had cut off the ear and gouged out the eye of a young nobleman who had not bowed low enough to him. After the defeat of Simon de Montfort (the father of Llywelyn's wife) at Evesham, Edward had him killed, and his head and genitalia cut off and sent to Lady Matilda, the wife of Lord Roger Mortimer at Wigmore. The 16 year-old Edmund and 9 year-old Roger who witnessed this, will have known not to cross him. The 'great' historian S.B. Chrimes calls Edward a great law-giver, 'the most juristically-minded king in 14th century Europe; he was the greatest legislator in England before the 19th century...the defender of legal rights...justice according to law was his business'. Edward had no scholarship and found litigation tedious, preferring torture, an illiterate brute who used the legislation created by equally revolting and rapacious Chancellor, Burnell, for his own ends. Thus, the tone of Anthony Edwards and Terry Breverton is not anti-English, but pro-truth, not pro-Welsh but anti-French king, not pro-power but anti-hagiography.

The death of Llywelyn is a detective story, in deliberately muddied waters. A letter from John Peckham, Archbishop of Canterbury to the King, written a few days after Llywelyn's death, reads: 'Lord, know that those who were at the death of Llywelyn found in the most secret part of his body some small things which we have seen. Among the other things there was a treasonable letter disguised by false names. And that you may be warned, we send a copy of this letter to the Bishop of Bath, and the letter Edmund Mortimer has, with Llywelyn's privy seal, and these things you may have at your pleasure. And this we send to warn you, and not that any one should be troubled for it. And we pray you that no one may suffer death or mutilation in consequence of our information, and that what we send you may be secret. Besides this, Lord, know that Lady Maud Lungespeye prayed us by letter to absolve Llywelyn, that he might be buried in consecrated ground, and we sent word to her that we would do nothing if it could not be proved that he showed signs of true repentance before his death. And Edmund Mortimer said to me that he had heard from his servants who were at the death that he asked for the priest before his death, but without sure certainty we will do nothing. Besides this, Lord, know that the very day that he was killed, a white monk sang mass to him, and my lord Roger Mortimer has the vestments.' In the copy of the letter Peckham sent to the Bishop of Bath, is the amended phrase 'under the false names by certain magnates of the March.' The Bishop of Bath was the King's Chancellor and right-hand man Robert Burnell. The only reason that Roger could have the Cistercian monk's vestments was that he had him killed as a witness to the betrayal meeting. As Edmund Mortimer kept the original letter after Peckham had copied it, probably he was its originator. Peckham appealed that the whole affair be kept secret, and the original letter has vanished.

A 1590 Welsh manuscript records that Llywelyn was killed at Aberedw, where he had come to 'meet a lady', and Lady Maude Langespey's castle of Bronllys was just ten miles away. She was a cousin of the Mortimers, and engaged to John Giffard, whose castle at Builth Llywelyn was going to attack. Maud had been seized by force in 1271, born Giffard several children, and married him in 1282. She was the heiress of Walter Clifford, owned Clifford and Bronllys castles, and possessed castles and land in Carmarthen and Cardigan. Llywelyn's wife had died six months earlier, leaving him with just his daughter Gwenllian. She was a grand-daughter of Llywelyn Fawr and a cousin of Llywelyn, and was possibly seen as a future queen by Llywelyn. Traditionally Llywelyn set out unarmed from Llanganten, leaving his army, with a small party of 18 horsemen and a white monk, to meet the Mortimers, Gruffudd ab Owain (and possibly Lady Maud) at Aberedw. Welsh tradition is that lady Maud had sent Llywelyn a ring as an assurance of safe conduct, and one was unexpectedly found on his body. (In 1447, Harry Grey, lord of Powys castle, murdered Gruffydd Fychan after his wife had sent him a ring as a sign of safe conduct. This was seen by the bards as a repetition of the murder of Llywelyn.)

Roger Lestrange was captain of a crack troop of the King's bodyguards, involved with the capture of Llywelyn. He wrote immediately after Llywelyn's death to Edward that the flower of Llywelun's troops had been put to death in a way which he would not relate by letter, slaughtered in a manner which would be difficult to believe: 'Know Lord, that you good men whom you assigned to me from your entourage fought with Llywelyn ap Gruffudd in the country of Builth on the Friday next after the feast of St Nicholas; so that Llywelyn ap Gruffudd is dead and his men discomfited and all the flower of his troops dead, as the bearer of this letter will tell you; and believe him concerning that which he shall tell you from me.'

There is a tradition that Llywelyn was betrayed by a Welsh churchman. Peckham's series of peace letters to Llywelyn would have been read by Madog ap Cynwrig, Archdeacon of Anglesey, in the absence of Bishop Anian of Bangor. In 1282, Anian joined the King at Rhuddlan. Peckham wrote to his intermediary, the cleric Adda ab Ynyr, a few hours before Llywelyn's ambush, calling him back from Gwynedd. Madog remained in power in Anglesey. At the time of the murder, Peckham was just 20 miles away, at Sugwas-on-Wye, and straight afterwards moved on to Pembridge castle, just 8 miles from the Mortimers' base at Wigmore. At Pembridge he copied the incriminating letter and sent it to the king's chancellor.

At Llanganten, the Peterborough Chronicles tell us that the Welsh army numbered 7000 footsoldiers and 160 horsemen. It records that 3000 of his footsoldiers and all of his horsemen were killed, and Roger Lestrange implies that this was occasioned in a manner which was difficult to believe. There is no record of a single English casualty in any battle. The attack on Llywelyn's army probably occurred upon Saturday 12th, the day after he was murdered. Possibly his head was displayed to his army, which surrendered.

Letter CCCLXI from John Peckham to an unknown recipient again mentions the ignominious death that the Mortimers caused Llywelyn: 'Llywelyn he aforesaid Prince of Wales, moreover having rejected all offers and plans for peace previously described, invaded the land of the lord king of England as an enemy, laying waste, burning it and pillaging; he also drew the men of that land over to his side depriving them of the benefits of the king's peace.

Nevertheless it was the prince who was killed, the first of his own army, in an ignominious death through the family of Lord Edmund de Mortimer; and his whole army was either killed or put to flight in parts of Montgomery after the feast of St Lucy, in other words the 11th of December 1282 AD'.

This is an absolutely critical letter, as there is no addressee, and it seems to be a fragment of a longer document, ending abruptly, and letters are missing between his warning to Adda ap Ynyr on November 11th and this date. In this context, 'ignominious' means 'disgraceful', and probably refers to a sentence of death on a captured and convicted prisoner. The missing parts of the letter may be in the Lambeth Palace archives.

Llywelyn camped near Abey Cwm Hir on 10th December, and seems to have discussed support with neighbouring Welsh lords. According to the Welsh Chronicle, he then gained possession of Buellt up to Llanganten just west of Builth castle. Llywelyn 'sent his men and his steward to receive the homage of the men of Brycheiniog, and the prince was left with but a few men with him.' He left his main force with 17 or 18 men and the Welsh Chronicles say then that he was 'killed in battle' near Builth. The Annals of Chester agree that 'Llywelyn and a few followers were killed in the land of Buellt.' The Peterborough Chronicle states that they were killed around Vespers (dusk), and this was probably effected by the troops of Roger Lestrange, captain of the army of Montgomery, and Roger Mortimer of Chirk. William Rishanger says that Llywelyn came into the land of Buellt with just a handful of knights, and John Giffard and Edmund Mortimer came to the little band 'with nothing arousing the suspicion of the prince, himself or his allies', and the small company met their death 'like lambs', which prompts the question as to whether they were armed. The Welsh Chronicles say that 'Roger Mortimer and Gruffydd ap Gwenwynwyn, and with them the king's host (the army of Montgomery), came upon them without warning; and then Llywelyn and his foremost men were slain on the 11th December.' Thomas Wykes wrote that Llywelyn's band had been tempted from their Snowdonia stronghold by 'a cleric or notary acting as a spy'. In the margin of a contemporary manuscript in the British Library, known as Cotton Nero Ms. D II, folio 182, is a drawing of a man in mail armour kneeling with his hands clasped, awaiting a soldier behind him to strike off his head. This is the fate of the last Prince of Wales.

NOTE ON THE MARCHER LORDS:
Edmund Mortimer's son Roger made himself ruler of the whole of Wales and murdered Edward II, before being executed by Edward III. A later Edmund Mortimer was captured by Glyndŵr (q.v.) and ended up fighting for him against the English crown. For most of their history they replicated the vile actions of the Greys of Ruthin and the de Braose family, the latter family particularly featuring some of the most treacherous villains in British history.

'The Chronicles of the Princes' tell us of Iorwerth ab Owen, a descendant of the princes of Gwent, who controlled the lands around Caerleon. Rhys ap Gruffydd had given King Henry II free passage to cross Wales and invade Ireland in 1171. Henry took Caerleon from Iorwerth and installed a garrison. Iorwerth retook the ancient fort, and told the Normans to follow their king to Ireland. He then burnt the site so that the king would never want it again. In 1172, Henry returned, offering a pardon and the return of Iorwerth's lands. He invited Iorwerth to meet him for a peace treaty, and gave safe conducts for him and his sons. The Welsh leader was well aware of Henry's practice of blinding hostages, and sent just one son Owain, bearing gifts. Owain was killed, so Iorwerth crossed the Wye, attacking Gloucester, burning Hereford, and returned to Caerleon and rebuilt the town. His brother-in-law Seisyllt ap Dynwal captured Abergavenni Castle, and another kinsman Seisyllt ap Rhirid took the king's castle at Crickhowel (Crug Hywel), killing the garrison. In 1175, the Normans attacked suddenly and retook Caerleon from Iorwerth and his surviving son Hywel. However, The Lord Rhys arbitrated, and it was restored to Iorwerth soon after.

In 1175, William de Braose, the Norman Lord of Brecon and Abergavenny, held vast tracts of land which he had conquered in south-east Wales. Seisyllt ap Dynwal, Lord of Upper Gwent, held the manor of Penpergwm and Castle Arnold for de Braose as his feudal overlord. The Norman invited Seisyllt and another seventy local Welsh lords to Abergavenny castle for a feast and to hear a royal declaration. Hidden outside the banqueting hall were soldiers under the command of Ranulph Poer, Sheriff of Hereford. Seated during the feast, the Welsh nobles were massacred by Norman troops. Only Iorwerth ab Owen escaped, snatching a sword and fighting his way out of the castle. The antiquary Camden noted that Abergavenny 'has been oftner stain'd with the infamy of treachery than any other castle in Wales'.

William de Braose then raced to Castle Arnold, seized Sisyllt's wife Gwladys, and murdered Seisyllt's only son, Cadwaladr, before her eyes. Norman law stated that conquest of Welsh territories by any means whatsoever was fair. Iorwerth led his men to Abergavenny, forcing De Braose to flee to his stronghold in Brecon Castle. In 1282, Seisyllt's kinfolk managed to scale the high walls of Abergavenny and took the castle, but unfortunately de Braose was absent. Seisyllt ap Eudaf had told the Constable of the castle that he would attack the castle at a certain angle, in the evening. The Normans waited all night for the attack, and were all asleep at dawn, whereupon the Welsh threw up their scaling ladders in the area that Seisyllt had said, taken the castle and burnt it to the ground.

Ranulph Poer and de Braose marched to Dingestow (Llandingat) near Monmouth to begin building another castle. The Welsh attacked and Poer was killed, and de Braose only just escaped with his life. This battle is known from the descriptions of the capacity of the bowmen of Gwent. Arrows could penetrate a width of four fingers of oak. One arrow passed through a Norman's armour plate on his thigh, through his leg, through more armour and his saddle, killing his horse. Another Norman was pinned through armour plating around his hip, to his saddle. He wheeled his horse, trying to escape, and another arrow pinned him to the saddle through the other hip.

Like his king, the Norman Marcher Lord de Braose was notable for blinding and torturing any Welshman he could lay his hands on. In 1197 he pulled Trahaiarn Fychan through the streets of Brecon behind a horse, until he was flayed alive. Maud de Valerie, his huge wife, also enjoyed seeing prisoners tortured. With the death of The Lord Rhys, de Braose pushed even more into Welsh territories. However, he fell out of King John's favour, and escaped to France in 1204, leaving his wife and eldest son behind. John took them to Corfe Castle and locked them up with just a piece of raw bacon and a sheaf of wheat – this was this Angevin king's favourite form of execution.

As for the Mortimers, the following excerpt is taken from the author's 1911 copy of 'A Short Analysis of Welsh History' by W.J. Griffith:

'Ralph (d.1104), the first of the Mortimers who held land in the middle marches of Wales, served under his kinsman Fitzosbern the Earl of hereford, after whose fall he was a subtenant to the Earl of Shrewsbury. The fall of the latter (1102) gave him more lands.

Hugh Mortimer (d.1184) son or grandson of Ralph, lived during the troublous times of Stephen. In 1148 he blinded Rhys ab Howel, and later added Bridgnorth to his territories. The rise of Owen Gwynedd (q.v.) and Rhys ap Griffith (see Yr Arglwydd Rhys) had a steadying effect on the mad rapacity of the Mortimers, like other border families; while Llywelyn the Great (q.v.) secured their alliance and diverted their energies to aid his own policy.

Roger II (d.1282) succeeded his father as Lord of Wigmore in 1246. Next yearhe added considerably to his estates by marrying Matilda de Braose, daughter of William de Braose, whom Llywelyn hanged in 1230. His attachment to the king's cause brought him into trouble with his powerful kinsman Llywelyn ap Griffith. He lost Gwrtheinion (1256), Builth Castle (1260), Maelienydd (1262); and although the king was successful in 1265, Llywelyn was still powerful enough to defeat Mortimer at Brecon (1266) and to dictate terms to him. During Edward's absence he was regent, and his captain for Shrewsbury 1276. He died in 1282, when the family was entering into the heritage which he had so long coveted.

Roger, his son, participated with Warrenne in the murder of the sons of Griffith ap Madog and took the lordship of Chirk as his share of the spoil.(John de Warrenne, half-brother of Henry II, was entrusted with the care of Griffith's two sons, who they drowned. Warrenne took the lordship of Bromfield and Yale, near Wrexham). It was he that Edward I entrusted with the government of North Wales as the justice of Wales, an office which he performed in a most despotic fashion. The latter's nephew, Roger Mortimer of Wigmore, was soon to become equally powerful in the Marches.The doings of these two assume the importance of national affairs; they figure in the darkest deeds in national history.'

CHALICE

By David Jervis 1996

For the sculptured novelist and bon viveur Martin Amis, as quoted in discussion with A.N.Wilson, The London Evening Standard, 17th July 1991.........this was before he spent over £20,000 upon having his rotten teeth transformed into humanoid ones and left his wife for a younger model.......

"*The South Waleyans are a particularly bitter and deracinated breed*". He began a bad-taste joke about Aberfan causing a "*ripple of pleasure*" through the mining valleys, but he choked it back with a giggle.....Martin does the Welsh voice with an accuracy which reflects real loathing".

The Lordship of Senghenydd
Green on Grey on Black
Betrayed by Norman Englishmen
A Thousand-Year Attack

On the only nation
Which has never
Declared war
On anyone

We were your first and last colony
And a prototype of ethical cleansing
You almost killed our language
Because it was fifteen-hundred years older than yours
With your Welsh Not just out of living memory
You killed our Church at the Synod of Whitby
Taking it away from the people and giving it to Rome
You gave us a higher density of castles and forts
Than anywhere in the world
You killed the old laws of Hywel Dda
Because they looked after the people and accepted women as equal
And instead gave all rights
            in ascending importance
                        to people with property and titles
You tried to kill our countryside with water on villages
Like Trywerin and charge us more than your Middle Saesneg for it
You tried to kill our culture by using our best in your wars
And you stripped out all our minerals.............

In return you gave us nystagmus and insanity;
Emphysema, silicosis, pneumoconiosis - slow death

And fast death.................

    Last century, children under 8 spent hours in the pitch black opening and closing the trapper doors of ventilation tunnels. If over 8, they dragged baskets of coal to the bottom of the shaft.

In 1840, 6-year-old Susan Reece said '*I have been below six or eight months and I don't like it much. I come here at 6 in the morning and leave at 6 at night. When my lamp goes out or I am hungry I go home. I haven't been hurt yet*'. Her mission was to open and close the ventilator at Plymouth Colliery, Merthyr Tydfil.

The boys who, with chains around their waist, pulled trucks of coal through galleries too low for pit-ponies, were called 'carters'. James Davies, an 8-year-old carter, reported that he earned 10 pennies a week, which his father took from him. John Saville, a 7-year-old carter, said that he was always in the dark and only saw daylight on Sundays.

Listen to my inventory of lost human capital:

1825 Cwmllynfell 59 men and children killed in an explosion
1842 The English Parliament under Lord Shaftesbury forbids the employment
     underground of women, girls and boys under 10 years old as miners
     The mine owners opposed the bill and there was little inspection

1844	Dinas Middle, Rhondda,	12 men and boys killed
1849	Lletyshenkin, Aberdare,	52 men and boys killed in an explosion
1849	Merthyr, Dowlais, Rhondda	884 people killed by cholera
1852	Middle Duffryn, Aberdare,	65 men and boys killed in an explosion
1856	Cymmer, Porth	114 killed
		7 of the 114 were UNDER THE AGE of 10,
		7 were 10, and 7 were 11 years old
1867	Ferndale, Rhondda	178 killed
1869	Ferndale, Rhondda, another	60 killed
1877	Tynewydd	5 killed in a flooded pit
1880	Naval Colliery, Rhondda	96 killed in an explosion
1885	Maerdy	81 killed in an explosion

The first "firemen" were covered with water-soaked rags and crawled towards seepages with a naked flame on a long stick to explode the gas

Some survived

Methane	=	Firedamp
Carbon Monoxide	=	Afterdamp
Carbon Dioxide	=	Blackdamp
Hydrogen Sulphide	=	Stinkdamp

In 1889, there were no major disasters
- it was a good year - just 153 deaths in the pits. Among them............

John Evans age 14	killed in a roof fall at Ocean Colliery, Treorchy
Thomas Evans age 16	killed in a roof fall at Seven Sisters, Neath
James Minhan age 13	fell from shaft at Great Western Colliery, Pontypridd
Thomas Jones age 17	rushed by trams at Cwmheol Colliery, Aberdare
Thomas Jones age 17	knocked down by tram at Duffryn Main, Neath
Morgan Harris age 16	run over by a coal wagon at No 9 Pit, Aberdare
James Webber age 17	killed by falling stone at No 1 Pit, Ferndale
Richard Jones age 17	killed in roof fall at Abercanaid Colliery, Merthyr

Thomas Cooper age 15   killed by a roof fall at Albion Colliery, Cilfynydd
Joseph Grey age 17   crushed between tram and coal face Gendros Colliery,
                       Swansea
John Howells age 13   crushed by trams at Penrhlwceibei Colliery
Thomas Davies age 17   head crushed between crossbar and tram at Cwmaman
                       Colliery
Thomas Pocket age 16   killed in roof fall at Brithdir Colliery, Neath
Thomas Evans age 17   killed in roof fall at Dunraven Colliery, Treherbert
Richard Martin age 15 killed in roof fall at Coegnant Colliery, Maesteg
David Jones age 17   crushed by tram at North Tunnel Pit, Dowlais
William Meredith age 15 crushed by pit cage at Maritime Colliery, Pontypridd
Aaron Griffiths age 14 crushed by tram at Clydach Vale Colliery
W.R. Evans age 15   died in roof fall at North Dunraven Colliery, Treherbert
Henry Jones age 14   killed in roof fall at Blaenclydach Colliery, Clydach Vale
Samuel Harris age 14   killed in roof fall at Fforchaman Colliery, Cwmaman
Joseph Jones age 16   killed in roof fall at Ynyshir Colliery
John Barwell age 13   fell into side of tram at Clydach Vale Colliery
Thomas Welsh age 15   killed in roof fall at Nantymelyn Colliery, Aberdare
Walter Martin age 15   killed in roof fall at Albion Colliery, Cilfynydd
Robert Thomas age 17   killed in roof fall at Treaman Pit, Aberdare
David Thomas age 17   killed in roof fall at Old Pit, Gwaun Cae Gurwen
Thomas Evans age 13   run over by trams at Glamorgan Steam Colliery,
                       Llwynypia
David Arscott age 14   run over by tram at Abercanaid Colliery, Merthyr
Ben Rosser age 14   killed by fall of rock at Gadlys New Pit, Aberdare
William Osborne age 14 crushed in engine wheels at Albion Colliery, Cilfynydd

1892 Parc Slip   114 killed - in a gas blast - the school had a half holiday

1893 A Health Report on the Rhondda Valleys stated " *the river contained a large proportion of human excrement, pig sty manure, congealed blood, entrails from slaughterhouses, the rotten carcases of animals, street refuse and a host of other articles - in dry weather the stink becomes unbearable*"

1894 Albion Colliery, Cilfynydd   290 killed of the 300 on the shift - 11 could not be identified. One miner's head had been blown 20 yards from his body. "*All through the darkness the dismal ritual of bringing up the dead continued, illuminated only by the pale fitful glare of the surrounding oil lamps....each arrival of the cage quenched the glimmer of hope that lived in the hearts of those who waited*" A court case was brought against the mine owners and managers but all serious charges were dropped.

There is no compensation
For the dust of our land
Now in our lungs
And in every pore of our bodies
Except our white eyes

A solitary, disfigured, maddened , cripple
Was unlucky to survive

The 1901 explosion
At Universal Colliery, Senghenydd
When 81 miners died

A forewarned accident
But never responsibility
So back to work, it is lads
Serene immutability

For the company,
Lewis Merthyr Consolidated Collieries Ltd.,
All charges were of course dismissed

1901 Morgan Morgans died in a fall at Cymmer Colliery, Porth, which pushed him
onto a pick axe, which went through his head. His son, Dai Morgans, aged 13,
witnessed the accident and was so traumatised that he never worked again

1905 National Colliery, Wattstown, 109 killed and the first disaster at Cambrian
Colliery, Clydach Vale, 31 killed

October 14, 1913,
Let us return to Senghenydd
Same pit, different scale
Cover their faces with their coats
There are plenty more Welsh males

The Universal was known as "fiery" pit, full of hidden methane-filled caverns.
A miner went to the lamp room to light his wick, a roof-fall nearby released
methane into the tunnel, the explosion ignited the coal dust, the fire caused a
massive second explosion that roared up the Lancaster Section of the pit, smashing
through the workings.

The fires could not be put out for a week, during which all but 18 of the survivors
died of carbon monoxide poisoning

The pit cage was blown right out of its shaft
Into the clear blue air

Aged a little over 14 years
Harry Wedlock's first day
As a colliery boy was spent in tears
With cracking timber falling away

Fire and foul air filled his chest
While Sidney Gregory cwtched him best
As he could in the black smoke and dust
2000 feet under the management offices

Upon October 14, 1913, at the Universal Colliery
The dead included:

8 children of 14 years
5 children of 15 years
10 children of 16 years
44 children of 17 to 19 years

And.....................377 other miners

8 bodies were never identified and 12 could not be recovered

Of the 440 dead, 45 men were from Commercial Street, Senghenydd
and 35 from the High Street

Not one street in Senghenydd was spared -

Parc Cottages	1 dead	Coronation Terrace	10 dead
Gelli Terrace	2 dead	Station Terrace	11 dead
School Street	2 dead	Woodland Terrace	12 dead
Windsor Place	2 dead	Graig Terrace	14 dead
Cross Street	2 dead	Parc Terrace	15 dead
Clive Street	3 dead	Grove Terrace	19 dead
Kingsley Place	4 dead	Stanley Street	20 dead
The Huts	6 dead	Cenydd Terrace	22 dead
Alexandra Terrace	8 dead	Caerphilly Road	39 dead
Station Road	8 dead	High Street	40 dead
Brynhyfryd Terrace	8 dead	Commercial Street	44 dead
Phillips Terrace	9 dead		

Some women lost their husbands in 1901 and their sons in 1913

Mrs Benjamin of Abertridwr lost her husband and her sons, aged 16 and 14

At 68 Commercial Street, the widowed Mrs Twining lost each one of her 3 sons,
the youngest aged 14

Richard and Evan Edwards, father and son, of 44 Commercial Street, were found
dead together

Half the village rugby team died -
They changed their strip from black and white
To black

*"For weeks, there was no rugby on Saturday
....only funerals"*

In 12 homes, both father and son died

*"When Edwin John Small died
with his 21 year-old son
it left his 18 year-old daughter Mary
to rear 6 children
the youngest 3 years old"*

A survivor, William Hyatt, recalled
"My father always said
That there was more fuss
If a horse was killed underground
Than if a man was killed..............

Men come cheap
..........................they had to buy horses"

Houses are better than people we know
But that's not the reason the argue
They're all tax exempt for those in the know
We know of a price, not a value

It was 75 years ago today
That the pit boss brought the band to play
But it didn't help him
They've been going in and out of style
But they're guaranteed to raise a pile
The manager was found guilty on 8 charges
So let me introduce to you
The one and only real scapegoat
Of breaches of the 1911 Coal Mines Act
And fined £24..............

Five-pence ha'penny a corpse
In old money to us
2 p to you

There was no compensation
Wrth gwrs

For the company,
Lewis Merthyr Consolidated Collieries Ltd.,
All charges were
Of course
Dismissed

But we appealed, we showed em

And Lewis Merthyr Consolidated Collieries Ltd.
Were fined £10
With costs of £5 and 5 shillings
The copper content of the bodies

There was no compensation

"We slunk to the biblical parlours to stare in shock
At the coke of flesh in the coffin, the ashes of a voice;

There we learned above the lids screwed down before their time
Collects of red rebellion, litanies of violence"

In Senghenydd and Abertridwr
The graves are brambled now
Monuments overgrown
The 14 year-old's place
Into the ground is sewn

Death rolls around this country
A skull with dust in its sockets

   1915 Thomas Williams was killed at Lucy Drift Mine, Abercanaid, leaving a
widow and seven children, five of whom were still at home. No compensation was
paid.

St David's Day, 1927 Marine Colliery, Cwm, Ebbw Vale - 52 dead

Half a mile underground
1934 Gresford
262 colliers dead
And 3 of the rescue brigade
Despite the shotfirer's premonition
About the gas in Dennis Deep Section

"The fireman's reports are all missing
The records of 42 days,
The colliery manager had them destroyed
To cover his evil ways"

Charges ? What charges ?

The dust comes out of the ground
Into our silicotic lungs
To be vomited near to death
Not hootering death
But doubled-up suffering wheezing darkness before our time death

Buckets of death feed the flames
More dust goes on the slag heaps

Fear of tears, insider squealing, new markets, Newmarket and
The Falklands hide the blameless obscenity of pulverised spines

The Great War hid Senghenydd
A slag heap hid the school
Can hate fade like pain ?

Who wants to know ?

Between 1837 and 1934 there were more than 70 disasters in Welsh mines,
And in 11, more than 100 were killed in a single day

Who worries, Lord Bute ?
Fill the boneyards and build mock castles over them

1931 Cilely Colliery, Tonyrefail, John Jones killed. Wife and four children receive
£6 compensation

1937 - from the notebook of Idris Davies, miner and poet - *'I looked at my hand
and saw a piece of white bone shining like snow, and the flesh of the little finger
all limp. The men supported me, and one ran for an ambulance box down the
heading, and there I was fainting away like a little baby girl.'*

Davies understood the sullen slavery of his fellow colliers -
'There are countless tons of rock above his head,
And gases wait in secret corners for a spark;
And his lamp shows dimly in the dust.
His leather belt is warm and moist with sweat,
And he crouches against the hanging coal,
And the pick swings to and fro,
And many beads of salty sweat play about his lips
And trickle down the blackened skin
To the hairy tangle on the chest.
The rats squeak and scamper among the unused props
And the fungus waxes strong.

And Dai pauses and wipes his sticky brow,
And suddenly wonders if his baby
Shall grow up to crawl in the local Hell,
And if tomorrow's ticket will buy enough food for six days,
And for the Sabbath created for pulpits and bowler hats,
When the under-manager cleans a dirty tongue
And walks with the curate's maiden aunt to church ....

Again the pick resumes the swing of toil,
And Dai forgets the world where merchants walk in morning streets,
And where the great sun smiles on pithead and pub and church-steeple.'

1941 Coedely Colliery - Hugh Jones was killed and his mother received £15
compensation, of which the coffin cost £14 14s. She went to the pit with the £15
and waved it at miners, shouting *"Look, boys, get out of this pit as quick as you
can - because this is all your lives are worth"*

1941 Markham Colliery - Leslie James killed, family also receives £15 for the
funeral

1947 Lewis Merthyr Colliery - George Waite killed - wife and five children receive £500 compensation

1947 Lewis Merthyr Colliery - 18 year old Neil Evans suffocated in roof fall. His family receives £200 compensation but the National Coal Board takes away their entitlement to free coal in return

Between 1931 and 1948, of the 23000 men who left mining because of pneomoconiosis, almost 20,000 came out of the South Wales pits.

1950 Maritime Colliery, Pontypridd - John Phillips dies - no compensation for family

1951 Wern Tarw Colliery - two brothers, Aaron and Arthur Stephens were killed in a roof fall - Aaron's widow received £200 compensation, and Arthur's widow £250. The differential was explained by the fact that Arthur had two children.

1957 Bedwas Colliery - Bobby John killed - parents receive £300 compensation

1960 Six Bells Colliery, Abertillery, 45 dead

In 1961 No 7 Pantglas Tip was started, on top of a mountain stream, next to 6 other slag heaps on boggy ground on the side of a hill. Directly underneath it was Pantglas School. There were local protests.

1962 Tower Colliery, 9 dead - Dai Morris was decapitated. The miner with him reminisced *"when the nurse pulled my shirt off, she pulled away half my skin with it"*

Ken Strong died - his wife, Mary was only 32 and never left her home for 15 years until she died in 1977

No 7 Pantglas Tip was getting bigger - the National Coal Board - a nameless, faceless, ignorant bureaucracy, used it to deposit "tailings", tiny particles of coal and ash.

1963 a Merthyr Council official wrote to the National Coal Board " *You are no doubt aware that tips at Merthyr Vale tower above the Pantglas area and if they were to move a very serious situation would accrue"*

When wet, tailings formed a consistency identical to quicksand

1965 Another disaster at Cambrian Colliery, Tonypandy, with 31 dead in the explosion

But we digress, it was only a 'small' disaster - hardly touched the 'Nationals'

Let us instead return to Merthyr Vale and Pantglas

After three inches of rain in the week, men working on No 7 Pantglas Tip arrived at work at 7.30 am.

A 30 foot crater had developed in the centre of the tip. Just after 9 the tip moved.

Within seconds it rolled down the hillside, over 20 sheep, covered some walkers on the canal bank, smashed through 8 terraced houses in Moy Road, and buried the school.

9.15 am
21st October
1966
Just three hours before
The half term holiday was to begin
at
Pantglas Junior School
Aberfan

1 in 2 families bereaved

There were warnings, of course

As always

The Lord helps them now as helps themselves
[Thanks to Lady Thatcher]

They are the rich men, the hollow men, stuffed with air
Whispering no meanings, to show they really care........
Soft-talking, seductive, motionless promises,
They have the answers, the questions and the messages
Made-up, but not so false, for we know what they are:
Powdered faces, 5 houses and a Minister's car.

Aberfan
A round gross of crushed Taffs -
A lovely cemetery with a white arch
For each of the 116 children
And 28 adults
Was built

The deputy headmaster tried to use the blackboard to shelter the children in his class - all 34 were killed

On a tombstone
"Richard Goldsworthy, Aged 11,
Who loved Light, Freedom and Animals"

On another
"The parting was so sudden
One day we will know why

But the saddest part of all
We never said goodbye"

"I'ı Rhai a Garwn ac y
Galarwn o'u colli"..........

Today's your birthday
Happy birthday to you

To ease the pain
But not the hate
Or "The Dust"

"See those rows of white arches ?
Each one's a child.
You can't imagine what it was like.
It was as if someone took the roof off your house,
Filled it up to the top with dust and dirt,
And then put it back on.
They found 6 of the children still standing up around their teacher,
It happened so fast"

What a joke
Sup your brandy, Kingsley
Suck your rusk, Martin - how are the new teeth ?

Intelligentsia, it's funny
It makes your brain go runny

"My supervisor called me out of the mine
And we went to help.
A farmhouse near the school
Had been pushed right through it.
I didn't cry until I saw them
Bring a little baby from the farmhouse,
Suffocated by the dust"

Apart from the baby, the village lost a three year old, 7 seven year olds, 25 eight year olds, 35 nine year olds, 35 ten year olds, 5 eleven year olds, 1 twelve year old, 3 thirteen year olds and 3 fourteen year olds - 116 potential novelists

Let the children sing

" I can still remember the noise,
a tremendous noise, like a thunder
but magniified a thousand times;
it sounded frightening.

Some instinct made me jump from my seat and try to run for the door.

After that,
nothing,
till I came round and found
myself buried up to my waist
in black slurry.

The walls and roof of the classroom
had caved in
and beside me,
under the rubble,
was a little boy I knew,
lying
dead.

Another child's hand was hanging above me,
poking through from the next class where the wall had given way.
I took hold of the hand
and squeezed it.

I still don't know whose hand it was -
a child who was already
very probably dead.

On that day
116 children were killed,
my younger brother Carl, 7,
my sister Marilyn, 10,
among them.

I was eight years old
and spent the months
following the tragedy
in hospital with hip
and leg injuries.

The world mourned for Aberfan,
but the focus was on the children
who had been lost
rather than those who had survived.
Everyone was so busy looking for someone to blame,
we were chucked aside,
forgotten.

It was about 30 years ago,
and nobody thought about
our traumas and nightmares
then.

The attitude was that you should be grateful
that you were alive. For years I never spoke
about what had happened.

At that age I was too embarrassed to talk about how I felt.
I thought I would be laughed at.
All of us were brought up then to bottle up emotions,
to bury what had happened and
get on as best we could.
But I needed to get it out of my system.

At 12, I wrote it all down in a blue school exercise book, every detail of what I
had seen and how I felt at the time and afterwards.
Nobody saw it but my family and one teacher.
After he had read it he did not even speak to me, he seemed so shocked.
My parents were horrified.

It was another 20 years before I took it out and showed it to a woman who was
wrtiting a book about Aberfan. In the meantime, I had tried to forget and I was
shocked at how forcibly it all came back to me. I realised I still had a great deal of
suffering inside me, that I needed to talk and to think about how Aberfan had
affected all of us who were involved. A lot of people had breakdowns, probably
because they were never adequately able to share their grief'.

No individual was to blame
For a tip
Smothering
A school

The Chairman of the NCB
Lord Robens
Claimed that they did not know
That the tip was placed on a stream

What a scream
If you had but the chance
Who bloody cares as long as Income Tax is under 25 pence ?

That seems to be the going rate for discussion -
Of course we'll be forced to leave the country if taxes rise.
{ Thankyou, Messrs Caine, Lloyd-Webber and Collins - be sure you take your
muzak and money with you as you close the door]

"And in the end
The love you take
Is equal to the
Love you make"

It has started

The white arches
are becoming overgrown tombstones
in abandoned graveyards in our memories

'Without a knowledge of history
One is condemned
To repeat the mistakes
Of the past'

Who realizes that ALL wealth
stems from some poor bastard
digging something out of the ground ?

It never ends
every night
in tears
the "nightmare never dies"

Mothers still die of broken hearts
Front rooms are their children's shrines

Miners used bare, bleeding hands to remove tons of slurry off the buried children - in the black slime they were afraid of driving a spade into a child's body
....
" *When the tip collapsed on October 21, 1996, Idris Cole had been at work since 7.30am. He recalls that he and his colleagues were struck by an uncanny silence in the air just befor the calamity. Here, (thirty years later) he reveals for the first time what happened next.*"

"*Suddenly, someone shouted to my workmates that the tip had collapsed and was on the move. The main water pipe carrying water to Cardiff had been crushed with the weight of the tip and torrential rain, until it was like a wafer, causing the tip to slide down the mountain. We rushed to the school, wading through slurry which had gone through the houses over a large area and on down to the river. The whole tip had moved silently, like a volcano spewing lava, but this was horrible black slurry. The scene as we approached the school was horrendous and frightening beyond description - screams and shouts of mothers and fathers, some of them who had just taken their children to school and had stopped for a chat. It was all so terrifyingly unbelievable. In their panic, people were unable to think what to do.*

Their screams have never gone away. My workmates and myself waded on through the slurry and the rubble of the crushed building. I dived down to where I could see some of the children, the ones who had not been completely buried. Some, like rag dolls, were crushed against a radiator. And a teacher with outstretched arms, as if to protect the little ones. I was one of the first people to get right in the middle of it, and I couldn't believe what I was seeing. I recall one distraught father frantically searching for his two children. He was hysterical and kept pushing me away from what I was trying to do. He was out of his mind with anguish and had to be led away and physically restrained.

I think I went mad myself, from what I was seeing. But I just had to get on with using my skills and trying to keep the slurry back. Some part of the roof was still there, but hanging dangerously.

The skills of the building trade enables my mates and myself to jack it up to prevent further falls. We worked late in the night by the light of lamps which were brought in. I have never done so much crying as that day; we all did. The slurry was so deep, at one point I almost got sucked down into it. They had to pull me out and strip off my denims and my shirt, but I just wanted to carry on. Eventually, I collapsed from exhaustion and was carried off. I had double pneumonia and was given an injection which put me to sleep for many, many hours. I didn't know where I was by then; all I remember is seeing the doctor bending over me to give me the injection.

I don't think I have ever felt completely normal since that day. I had experienced may horrors during the war, from the beaches of Dunkirk, to a naval battle on the battleships taking us to Malta where I served for three years. Malta was under siege, continuously being bombed, and on very meagre rations. From there, I went to Minterno and Cassino, where we had to bury many of our comrades who were slaughtered. But nothing can ever erase the memory of that fateful morning at Aberfan and the loss of 116 little children. It was much worse, because it was the children who died. Their laughter would never ring out again in that sad, sad, village. I can never forget it. Let no-one ever forget that terrifying, sad day - or the lesson to be learned."

Most villagers will still not talk about it
Grief is private
And unrewarded
The proud humility
Of non-acceptance

An Appeal Fund raised £1.75 million from the British public.
The National Coal Board asked for £250,000 from it
And accepted £150,000
To meet the costs of clearing the remaining slurry
From the hilltops around the town
(Thank you, Queen George)

The families of the bereaved were offered £500 each
Regardless of how many children
The National Coal Board had killed.
Eventually, the generous NCB
Gave £1500 per family
From the Appeal Money
It had taken

Tiny front rooms in the packed terraces
Are shrines to the dead generation
And the generation of broken-hearted deaths

The mine closed in 1989

The 4236 page enquiry
Banished all tips
From the edges of mining villages

There is no money left
From the Appeal Fund
To restore the Portland Stone Monument
Or maintain the Memorial Gardens
The White Arches
Of the dead children

The Fund built an expensive community centre
With no monies for its upkeep
So the local council took it over

£1500 per family
The Royalties of Murder

As bitter as he's ugly
Just like his scabby daddy
This pox-scarred whelp
Needs some real help
Because he's his mummy's babby

"No Iranian torturer could have elicited a greater variety of winces and flinches"
states Amis fils, being forced to endure the whole of the screening of
"Four Weddings and A Funeral" with one of his fellow illuminated glitterati,
Salman Rushdie.
They cannot leave early because of security reasons.
The great Rushdie explains that
"The world has bad taste. Didn't you know that ?"

Blest are those with choice and no contempt

when you came
in your wars
you called us Walsci
- "foreigners"
in our own lands
- and pushed us to peripheries

you trespass
on our mirrors
of hills and grass

you do not want the history
so you will repeat the mistakes of the past
you do not want our language
so your mongreloid tongue conquered the world

while the Welsh Not was yoked round our
brightest necks

[I have a cunning plan
Said the Ministry Man
Let's cut out the Tongue
Heart, Liver and Lung]

you want our water and you took our coal
and only Japanese arrogance employs our women
.... on a pittance
and temporary call centres
are the great white hope
our new imported peasantry, Thatcher's people, agree with you

our laws date from before windows
        [a word borrowed from the Romans]
our laws were the first to believe women's words
our church was socialist

you believe in fate when you run out of chances

our battle honours are Gresford and Aberfan
yours are Ramillies and Agincourt

we are the red kites of europe
once in the natural centre
then feeding off carrion in the urban sprawl
so pushed out to peripheries
away from the Saesneg and assorted killers
few remain
worrying R.S. Thomas' "dead carcass"
to the lazy ebb and flow of the buzzard's beat of wing

in 2000 years we have never started a war
perhaps it is time
for vibration white fingers to drum on the coffins

Listen to John Evans, a miner aged just 47 and looking into darkness:
'I'm glad I haven't a son......
It must be a heart-breaking business to watch your boy
Grow into manhood and then see him deteriorating
Because there is no work for him to do.......
I've been out of work now for eight years,
And I've only managed to get eleven days work
In all that time.
Work used to shape the whole of my life
And now I've got to face the fact
That this won't be so any more.

I am really glad I live in the Rhondda.
There's real kindness and comradeship here,
And that just about makes life worth living.
The spirit here in this valley helps to soften
Many of the hardships of unemployment.'

Crush our language
Crush our men
Crush our youth
Crush our children
Turn the babies back to dust

Parfait gentil knights
Sir Galahad and Sir Tristram
1982 The Malvinas
43 Welsh Guards
Sitting ducks
In another futile English war
No-one was to blame
Although the captain was implored
To disembark

"After all, it never would have happened if Mark Thatcher had been in the army
instead of secreting millions of pounds in his Swiss bank accounts and why should
multimillionaires fight for their country anyway they are far too valuable of course
and just why should we pay taxes in Britain and what do you think of the claret ,
perhaps a teensy robust ?" warbles the acclaimed novelist, wit and raconteur

Unlike Simon Weston
The name with no face
Or skin

Glory Glory Maggie Thatcher
Glory Glory Maggie Thatcher
Glory Glory Maggie Thatcher
Hide all the cripples away

Only complete heroes sit in the front, please,
You'll upset the voters

"Everywhere there's lots of piggies
Living piggy lives
You can see them out for dinner
With their piggy wives"

The pits have gone
Except for one
The dust is going
The wealth has gone

The slag heaps are going
The breed is still here
Uproot us if you can

Our brightest and best
Are forced to leave
But they always come back

You are in our country
You changed it
We made the money
You spent it
We held together
You used us
Take what's left
And leave us

Never understand

...........................Real ghosts.

Deracinate intrenchant cultures, now !
And place fresh holly on sweet Jesus' brow,
Slit sad sores, suck old pus, and buy
Abetting of such sights, by starving blue bridges of the sky,
Regretting rien for our plight, forgetting in the laxer light,
Shame washed with blood, disputes with death,
The hurdling towards night.

Norman bastards

[Quotes from eyewitnesses, Lennon-McCartney, D.Gwenallt Jones, "The Dead", Santayana, 'Gwalia Deserta' Versse VII by Idris Davies, and The Western Mail article upon Idris Cole upon the thirtieth aniversary of Aberfan. Martin Amis comments upon watching a popular film being worse than castration, rape and murder were in his New Yorker column in January 1996, and also reported in Private Eye, Feb 9, 1996. The remembrances of a survivor were reported in The Sunday Times, 15 September 1996, and Gaynor Madgwick's book of dealing with the horrors of memory is 'Struggling Out of The Darkness', published by Valley and Vale in September 1996. John Evans is quoted in Time To Spare, 1935, by F.Green]

A collection of poems by David Jervis, 'From Paths to Inexperience', will shortly be published by Wales Books (Glyndŵr Publishing).

REVIEWS OF OTHER BOOKS FROM WALES BOOKS
(GLYNDŴR PUBLISHING)

THE BOOK OF WELSH SAINTS - T.D. Breverton ISBN 1-903529-018 £24.99
hardback, 606 pages, illustrated, signed edition limited to 850 copies Glyndŵr
Publishing) (stock remaining 400)

*'The book is a really extraordinary achievement: a compilation of tradition, topography
and literary detective work that can have few rivals. I have enjoyed browsing in it
enormously , and have picked up all sorts of new lines to follow up'* - **Dr Rowan
Williams, The Archbishop of Wales**

Review from 'Cambria', January 2001:
*'Another work from the prolific pen of Terry Breverton who is blazing a trail in
producing bodies of knowledge about Welsh heritage and history. The Book of Welsh
Saints is **an enormous work of research and will provide a welcome and ready book of
reference** to the men and women who in Tad Deiniol's words "created Wales". The
much bandied term "The Dark Ages" may well have meant just that east of the Severn,
but to us this period is the Age of Saints. And there are hundreds of them - over 900 in
fact - monks, scholars, warriors, missionaries. Breverton places Arthur firmly in the
context of Welsh history and shows how the seminal folk legends of European romance
and literature originate in Wales. We see Wales at the very heart and very root of
western Christian civilisation, a pre-eminent position from which it was thrown down
by greedy, rapacious invaders who not only usurped its legacy but traduced its memory
with sickening arrogance and chilling contempt.'*

Review (part) from The Western Mail 17th November 2000
An Age When Saints Could Be Counted in the Hundreds by Phil Davies
*Is there truth in the notion that to build a country anew one has to know something of
the glory of the past? Perhaps this is why children are growing up knowing more about
Alfred the Great, Henry VIII, Agincourt, Nelson and Churchill than figures in Welsh
history. So T.D. Breverton's new offering, The Book of Welsh Saints, is another rallying
call to Wales to rediscover its own history. The English call the fifth and sixth centuries
the Dark Ages when, in fact they were the Age of Saints in Wales, a time of great
civilisation and culture. Part of this sophistication was the swift adoption of
Christianity, soon after the alleged arrival here of Joseph of Arimathea (Jesus'
godfather) in AD63, before anyone else of note in the entire British Isles.
By the middle of the age, Wales could count its saints in the hundreds - the historical
total is more than 900 - and over 100 were linked to Arthwys ap Meurig ap Tewdrig
(Artorius ap Mauricius ap Theoderic), probably **the real King Arthur**.
Some experts argue that Wales, because of the way it embraced and nurtured
Christianity so early on, is owed a debt by the entire world for providing a foothold in
the West. (St Patrick, founder of the Irish Church, was Welsh). The evidence is that
Wales, a place that also has one of the oldest languages in Europe, was accepted by
Rome and the rest of the Continent as the **'cradle of the Western church'**. Breverton
says that this important historical period of early Britain, prior to the Germanic
invasions that led to the creation of England, has been 'wilfully' hidden. "Wales has an
importance, unique in the world, which should be known not only to tourists but to its
people". The author argues that widened knowledge of the 5th and 5th century saints
and their feast weeks can be used in this modern age as one of the tools of tourism.
Breverton also says in the book that past researches had shown him that Wales has a
scarred national psyche because people spent hundreds of years appeasing a more
powerful neighbour.*

Even a Chapel Devoted to Elvis *T.D. Breverton is anxious that people do not think that his latest book is a dry tome for academics only. It actually contains, he says, insightful anecdotes about many areas where the saints lived and died. If a saint is associated with King Arthur it is mentioned and there is also a whole list of historical questions that Breverton claims to answer. One of the most eye-catching is whether - yes, we are serious, Elvis Presley has a Welsh connection.* The Book of Welsh Saints *also claims to answer such questions as: When was the first Harvest festival? What is the link between the first house used in Rome for Christian worship and Wales? Where is the original 'Avalon'? Did Queen Elizabeth I have a baby? When and where is it still legal for an Englishman to kill a Welshman? Mr Breverton, a former businessman and now a university lecturer said the Elvis connection is feasible. It concerns the Preseli Mountains of Wales where there is still an ancient chapel, holy well and Dark Age monastery devoted to St Elvis. All of Elvis' nuclear family also had Christian names only associated with Wales, his parents Vernon and Gladys and his twin Garon ......*

AN A-Z OF WALES AND THE WELSH - T.D. Breverton ISBN 0- 715407-341 £14.99 paperback 296 pages (Christopher Davies Publishing)

Review from 'Cambria', January 2001
'Hwyl and Hiraeth, heritage and history, people and places, myths and imagination all come together in Terry Breverton's comprehensive anthology and compendium of Welshness. He starts by asking the question "What is Wales?" and then goes on to show us. The book is, as Breverton says, a sort of "Hitchhiker's Guide to the Galaxy" that is Wales and declares modestly that his background is more modest than academic. We have just what's needed in this unashamedly proud-to-be-Welsh work. Everything from "Assassination" (Owain Llawgoch) to "Zulu Wars" (Rorke's Drift) is covered with few stones unturned (sadly Tom Ellis, one of the greatest of our political heroes, fails to get a mention). **A massive treasure chest of facts and figures covering thousands of years of history, which no collector of books on Wales can overlook.'**

Review from South Wales Echo, April 14th, 2000, by Penny Taylor (full-page review)
...... (the author) wants the world to know what Wales has to offerÖÖÖÖ alongside the Cool Cymru actors and pop stars, there is a wealth of information on more traditional Welsh culture, history, legend, art, literature and so on. If it takes you more than a song by Catatonia to feel proud of being Welsh, then maybe you should take a peek into a new book by Cardiff lecturer Terry Breverton .'An A-Z of Wales and the Welsh' is the author's personal contribution to his country. And within its covers, alongside rugby, choirs and coal, are entries as diverse as Assassination, Atlantis, Crachach, Bogs, Heroes and Inward Investment......

Review from The New Welsh Review October 2000 , by Peter Stead
Terry Breverton's A-Z is great fun. Until the Welsh Academy publishes its definitive Encyclopaedia this will be an indispensable set of crib notes to be consulted just before American visitors arrive. We have all enjoyed those moments when confused tourists have asked whether Wales has its own currency or whether there are dragons in Snowdonia, just as we have noted their amazement as we claim that nearly everyone who signed the Declaration of Independence was Welsh, and that bourbon, Yale and everything else of quality in North America was our bequest. This book helps in all these respects just as it reminds us when it was that the Celts came and when precisely our language, Christianity, laws, princes, outside-halves and rock bands emerged......

Part Review from The Western Mail, July 15 2000 by Meic Stephens
This is the perfect present for your relatives living abroad or the people you meet on holiday who ask 'Pleess, ver iss Vales?'
The book has been featured on BBC Radio 1, Radio 2, Radio 3, Radio Wales 'The

World Today', Radio World Service, The World (USA), GMTV (two transmissions featuring the author, an Elvis Presley impersonator, the Haverfordwest Male Voice Choir on 5/6/2000), with articles in The Daily Mirror and The Guardian, and interviews on many radio shows including Capital Gold with Dave Lee Travis (6th June), Radio 1, Radio 2 Richard Allinson Show (6th June), BBC Radio Ulster (8th June), Radio 4, Radio Wales (Roy Noble, and Owen Money) and the BBC World Service. The piece about Elvis was even picked up by the Sidney Morning Herald, French television and radio and flashed across the web overnight, including Elvis sites and Reuters, ITN and BBC News online sites. (The A-Z has also been featured in The News of the World, National Enquirer, New York Times, Boston Globe, Japanese newspapers, the Daily Express, Times, Sunday Times, and upon French radio and TV).

THE DRAGON ENTERTAINS - 100 Welsh Stars - Alan Roderick ISBN 1-903529-026 £12.99 paperback, illustrated 230 pages, edition limited to 900 copies (Glyndŵr Publishing) (stock remaining 450)

The Dragon Entertains is a reference book with a difference - a highly readable, informative account of the lives of One Hundred Welsh Stars. Within its pages the reader will find 100 concise mini-biographies, word pictures detailing all the relevant, basic facts of the entertainer's career. For a small country, on the western fringe of Europe, a nation of only 3,000,000 people, Wales' contribution to the world of entertainment is immense. Actors and actresses, playwrights and directors, singers and musicians, composers and comedians - Wales has produced them all. And what other nation of comparable size can boast four Oscar winners?
The first Welsh film star, the Welsh influence on the *James Bond* movies, *Monty Python*, *Dr Who*, *The Goon Show*, the Beatles films and the original Angry Young man can all be found in the pages of Alan Roderick's new book. Stars of Broadway and the West End stage, the Silver Screen, television, radio, the worlds of opera and contemporary rock music - *The Dragon Entertains* has them all. Welsh-speaking and non-Welsh-speaking, North Wales and South Wales - Welsh showbiz life in all its many facets can be found here.
The Dragon Entertains also features stars with Welsh connections and at least one Welsh-born parent including international stars such as Bob Hope, Glenn Ford, Petula Clark and Alan Rickman. Containing forty black and white photographs for the price of one, and a celebration of Welsh talent in all its vibrant variety, stars of the calibre of Richard Burton, Anthony Hopkins, Tom Jones, Shirley Bassey, Catherine Zeta Jones, Jonathan Pryce and many, many more throng its pages. Prepare to be entertained!

THE SECRET VALE OF GLAMORGAN - T.D. Breverton ISBN 1-903529-00X £13.99 paperback, illustrated 230 pages, signed edition limited to 600 copies (Glyndŵr publishing) (stock remaining 180)

In between what may be the oldest university in Europe, and a cradle of early Christianity, Llanilltud Fawr (Llantwit Major), and another shining monastic light from the Dark Ages, the Welsh *Age of Saints*, lies the village of Sain Tathan. From the introduction of this millennium history, we read:
'*We tend to think of where we live as unremarkable, compared to the strangeness of the new. However, the village of St Tathan and the hamlets of Flemingstone, Gileston, Eglwys Brewys and West and East Aberthaw are not only attractive, and set in wonderful countryside, but have a history almost unique in such a small area. We have a river and streams, buzzards, kingfishers and partridge, the Heritage Coast, two*

deserted villages, four mediaeval churches, an important Nonconformist chapel, sixteen listed buildings, three conservation areas, traces of rebellion by the great Welsh heroes Llywelyn Bren and Owain Glyndŵr, Roman remains, the great antiquary Iolo Morganwg who reintroduced the Eisteddfod to Wales, mediaeval wells, four sixth century saints, an astronomer consulted by Sir Isaac Newton, a Rebecca Rioter, the remains of a thriving port, wreckers, ghosts, smugglers, West Indies slave-shiips, hymn-writers, a thatched 14th century pub and no less than four castles. In the 1980's even a Humpback Whale visited......

The book is a new, proactive approach to local history, pleading for changes in attitudes and a lengthening of the heritage Coastline to Cardiff from Gileston. Dring the course of it the author even discovered an unknown medieval chapel on the site where St Tathana traditionally had her 6th century hermitage.

WALES BOOKS AND GLYNDŴR PUBLISHING ARE NON-PROFIT-MAKING ENTERPRISES DEDICATED TO PUBLISHING BOOKS UPON WALES, ITS HERITAGE, CULTURE AND HISTORY. Our (non-subsidised) books are available via the Welsh Books Council and all good Welsh book shops. Our publications all have a real purpose. *The Book of Welsh Saints* is a plea to reinstitute feast-weeks across Wales, the year round, to preserve culture and attract tourism and economic regeneration opportunities, and to place Arthur as a Welsh tourist icon. T.D. Breverton's *An A-Z of Wales and the Welsh* (published by Christopher Davies) is meant to arouse the passive Welsh national psyche and teach the people what they are not told in schools - that British history existed before the Hanovers distorted it. *The Secret Vale of Glamorgan* is an appeal for a crucial reappraisal of Iolo Morganwg and his work, for more local histories across Wales, and to double the length of the Glamorgan Heritage Coast from Gileston to Cardiff. The forthcoming Madoc book will involve DNA testing of surviving Mandan Indians, and the Llawgoch book will involve a search for the French descendants of the last Prince of Gwynedd and Wales, assassinated at Mortagne on the orders of the English crown.

FORTHCOMING TITLES FROM Wales Books (Glyndŵr Publishing)

Summer 2001   100 GREAT WELSHWOMEN - T.D. Breverton
September 2001   THE BOOK OF WELSH PIRATES AND BUCCANEERS - T.D. Breverton
October 2001   FROM PATHS TO INEXPERIENCE - David Jervis
December 2001   DAVID THOMAS - MAN OF STEEL - Peter Williams

2002 OWAIN LLAWGOCH - THE HISTORY OF A LEGEND - Bryn ap Dafydd
2002 MADOC - THE EVIDENCE - Bryn Griffiths
2002 THE QUILT OF DREAMS - Marcella Davies
2002 THE WELSH ALMANAC - T.D. Breverton
2002 ANOTHER 100 GREAT WELSHMEN - T.D. Breverton
2002 WALES AND THE WELSH - THE NEW A-Z -T.D Breverton
2002 THE CAMPAIGNS OF OWAIN GLYNDWR
2002 WELSH ENTREPRENEURS
2002 THE 'LITTLE BOOK' series, starting with Welsh Heroes, Welsh Heroines, Welsh Saints, Welsh Sportsmen, and 'The Little A-Z of Wales and the Welsh'

Printed in Wales for Wales Books (Glyndŵr Publishing), Porth Glyndŵr, Sain Tathan, Bro Morgannwg, CF62 4LW 01446-751693 (tel/fax), email: info@walesbooks.com by J & P Davison, 3 James Place, Trefforest. The walesbooks.com website was created and is maintained by webandit services, Trefforest.